FRONT PAGES THAT SHAPED AUSTRALIA

Stephen Gapps

FRONT PAGES THAT SHAPED AUSTRALIA

100 of the nation's most influential cover stories and newspaper headlines, from 1629 to 2009

PIER 9

Contents

INTRODUCTION 8

1 *Shipwreck, mutiny and massacre*
The wreck of the *Batavia*, 1629 18

2 *The miserablest People*
William Dampier on the Australian bush, 1697 22

3 *Agreeable news*
Reporting the return of Captain James Cook, 1771 26

4 *Progress made in the settlement*
First news of Botany Bay, 1789 30

5 *Journey into the interior*
First sightings of new animals, 1798 35

6 *A troublesome sort of fellow*
Pemulwuy's guerrilla warfare, 1801 39

7 *Information is our only Purpose*
The first issue of the *Sydney Gazette, and New South Wales Advertiser*, 1803 48

8 *The invisible hand of Providence*
The man they couldn't hang, 1803 50

9 *Lay down your arms!*
The Battle of Vinegar Hill, 1804 53

10 *The Rum Rebellion*
Australia's military junta, 1808 56

11 *Tillage and Pasture lands*
Across the Blue Mountains with Surveyor George William Evans, 1814 58

12 *The birth of a free press*
Independent newspapers created in Sydney and Hobart, 1824 62

13 *Equality before the law*
Governor Arthur's message to the Aboriginal people of Van Diemen's Land, 1828 66

14 *European blood has been spilled*
Tasmanian politics and the Black Wars, 1828 68

15 *A colonial afterthought*
The free colony of Western Australia, 1829 72

16 *There was a wild colonial boy*
Bold Jack Donohoe, terror of Sydney Town, 1830 74

17 *Candour, honesty, and honor*
The first issue of *The Sydney Morning Herald*, 1831 80

18 *Getting rid of a governor*
The recall of Ralph Darling, 1831 83

19 *The war in the west*
The death of Yagan, 1833 86

20 *Creating a land rush*
Major Mitchell's *Australia Felix*, 1836 90

21 *An abominable system*
An anti-convict tirade, 1835 93

22 *Celebrating a new bridge*
The opening of the Lansdowne Bridge, 1836 95

23 *Recording a free colony*
South Australia's first newspaper, 1836 98

24 *The chart of advancing civilisation*
Second issue of the *Melbourne Advertiser*, 1838 100

25 *Massacre at Myall Creek*
Attacks on Australian Indigenous people, 1838 **104**

26 *Separation at last!*
Victoria becomes a separate colony, 1850 **108**

27 *Gold fever*
Gold discoveries near Bathurst, 1851 **114**

28 *Evil-disposed persons*
The Eureka Stockade, 1854 **118**

29 *The Continent Crossed*
The Burke and Wills expedition, 1860 **122**

30 *No Chinese*
Race riots at Lambing Flat, 1861 **124**

31 *Triumph of British arms*
Australia and the New Zealand Wars, 1863 **128**

32 *Attempted assassination*
Prince Alfred in Sydney, 1868 **131**

33 *Blackbirding in the Pacific*
The trial of the crew of the *Carl*, 1872 **134**

34 *Desperate encounter*
Ned Kelly's last stand at Glenrowan, 1880 **137**

35 *Idle and depraved*
The emergence of the larrikins, 1881 **148**

36 *Attacked by natives*
Early exploration of New Guinea, 1883 **150**

37 *In aid of empire*
Sending troops to the Sudan Wars, 1885 **154**

38 *Celebrating 100 years*
The centenary of settlement, 1888 **156**

39 *The greatest racehorse of all time*
Carbine wins the Melbourne Cup, 1890 **161**

40 *A disastrous shock*
Bank crashes and depression, 1893 **164**

41 *A cinematographe show*
The first moving pictures, 1896 **166**

42 *Pageants and parades*
Federation celebrations, 1901 **174**

43 *The Great White Fleet*
The US navy visits, 1908 **176**

44 *Splendid conduct and bravery*
Anzac forces in the Dardanelles, 1915 **178**

45 *News from the front*
First World War casualty lists, 1916 **180**

46 *White feathers and yellow streaks*
Conscription referendums, 1916–1917 **182**

47 *Pulled from the monster's jaws*
Coogee Beach shark attack, 1922 **185**

48 *Hooligans take charge*
Melbourne riots during a police strike, 1923 **187**

49 *The hearts of the people*
The US fleet visits in earnest, 1925 **190**

50 *On the north-west frontier*
The Forrest River massacre, 1926 **192**

51 *Smashed and sunk*
Greycliffe ferry disaster, 1927 **196**

52 *Colouring the Truth*
Sonny Clay's jazz band and the White Australia Policy, 1928 **198**

53 *Heroine of the air*
Amy Johnson flies from England to Australia, 1930 **204**

54 *Bradman breaks all records*
Don Bradman in the Ashes, 1930 **207**

55 *The Maltese Voice in Australia*
A foreign-language newspaper, 1930 **209**

56 *Scullin's somersaults*
Bringing down a Labor government, 1931 **211**

57 *The battle of Union Street*
Communists fight police in Newtown, Sydney, 1931 **213**

58 *Fascists open Sydney's bridge*
De Groot and the New Guard, 1932 **216**

59 *A child of the modern world*
Radio sets and new technologies, 1932 **218**

60 *A great shock to all Australians*
The death of Phar Lap, 1932 **220**

61 *The downfall of 'The Big Fella'*
Jack Lang's government dismissed, 1932 **223**

62 *Just not cricket*
The bodyline series, 1932–1933 **225**

63 *Australia's wild west*
Race riots in Kalgoorlie, 1934 **228**

64 *The greatest Anzac gathering*
Commemorating Anzac Day, 1935 **230**

65 *Black Sunday at Bondi*
Mass surf rescues at Bondi Beach, 1938 **232**

66 *Nothing to do with missionaries*
An Indigenous newspaper, 1938 **235**

67 *Black Friday*
Deadly bushfires in Victoria, 1939 **237**

68 *A strong force of Anzacs*
Australians and New Zealanders in the battle for Crete, 1941 **244**

69 *Japanese swarm down*
The fall of Singapore, 1942 **246**

70 *Enemy submarines enter harbour*
Japanese midget subs attack Sydney, 1942 **248**

71 *The great freedom of speech crisis*
Riots over news censorship, 1944 **251**

72 *Inhuman barbarities*
Japanese war atrocities revealed, 1945 **253**

73 *Aftermath of war and genocide*
Jewish refugees arrive in Australia, 1947 **255**

74 *Long rule of the Liberals*
Liberal Party elected, 1949 **258**

75 *Montebello to Maralinga*
Britain tests nuclear weapons in Australia, 1952 **264**

76 *They've struck it!*
Oil found at Exmouth, 1953 **267**

77 *Queen steps ashore*
The royal tour, 1954 269

78 *Russian spy ring in Australia*
The Petrov Affair, 1954 271

79 *Power and multiculturalism*
The Snowy Mountains Hydro-Electric Scheme, 1950s 273

80 *Lithe teenager wins gold*
The Melbourne Olympics, 1956 276

81 *One of the great buildings*
Designs for the Sydney Opera House revealed, 1957 278

82 *A small group of malcontents*
The Bonegilla riots, 1961 281

83 *The big crush*
Riots when the Beatles arrive in Melbourne, 1964 288

84 *Which Johnny goes to war?*
Conscription and the national service lottery, 1964 290

85 *Shocking Melbourne*
The Shrimp in a mini-skirt at the Spring Racing Carnival, 1965 292

86 *Vote Yes for Aborigines*
A referendum to change the Constitution, 1967 294

87 *Whirled out to sea like a leaf*
The death of Prime Minister Harold Holt, 1967 296

88 *Bungers versus batons*
Anti-apartheid demonstrations at rugby matches, 1971 299

89 *Whitlam takes over*
Whitlam Labor government elected, 1972 302

90 *Drunks did it!*
The *Blue Poles* furore, 1973 304

91 *The agony is over*
End of the Vietnam War, 1973 312

92 *It's time for reason*
Dismissal of the Labor government, 1975 314

93 *Destination Darwin*
Refugees and boat people, 1977 317

94 *Died on the job*
The death of Billy Snedden, 1978 320

95 *The dingo has got my baby*
The Azaria Chamberlain case, 1980 322

96 *Yuppie Armageddon*
Financial crash, 1987 325

97 *Our ultimate party*
Bicentennial celebrations, 1988 327

98 *A new beginning*
The Mabo case and land rights for Indigenous Australians, 1992 330

99 *Terrorism strikes home*
The Bali bombing, 2002 332

100 *From bushfire to firestorm*
Black Saturday bushfires, 2009 334

BIBLIOGRAPHY 336

PICTURE CREDITS 340

INDEX 342

Introduction

Our relationship with history is very much shaped by how we receive news. People recall the first landing on the moon as a black-and-white television moment. Others might recall a text message to turn on the television and watch what was happening to the Twin Towers in New York in 2001. Yet for most of modern Australian history, we have learned about cricketing triumphs, election results, natural disasters and other events that have affected our lives by picking up a newspaper.

For the past century or so, newspapers have shouted out history to us in big, bold print and eye-catching graphic images. They have sold history to us as a front page—a historical moment of breaking news. Yet, as this collection shows, newspaper front pages have not always been like this.

In fact, the development of front page news stories was a slow process. Initially, news was found only on the *inside* of a newspaper. In a format that was driven by our first newspaper the *Sydney Gazette*, and because it was a government mouthpiece, the front page was the place for official proclamations, advertisements and public notices.

With the introduction of better graphic and print production techniques from the mid-nineteenth century, newspapers began to include images, and more prominent and varied typefaces that highlighted short summaries of the most important news. Often this was just how the news had arrived at the news desk—as a brief cable or telegram that had to be short, as it cost money for each word sent.

After the population explosion that followed the gold rushes in the Australian colonies from the 1850s, some newspapers were established to cater for the 'working man', and these began to take the shape of tabloid newspapers of the future. They started to put their main stories on the front page. Other papers realised the selling power of images where people could visualise, rather than merely read, the news. Weeklies, such as the *Illustrated Sydney News*, appeared in the 1860s and focused on showing the news to a broader audience, often as artists' impressions of events. The days of photojournalists racing to get 'the shot' were still far off.

By the mid-nineteenth century some papers included a column of news summaries on the side of their front pages. This trend was followed and developed by the tabloid papers, but the more established broadsheets were keen to keep the difference between them obvious and were reluctant to 'splash' news headlines across their front pages.

However, during the early twentieth century most major newspapers gradually brought the news to the front. Nonetheless, *The Sydney Morning Herald* did not use its front page for headlines until as late as 1944. Indeed, several major regional papers did not start to put headline news on their front pages until as late as the 1980s.

Newspaper headlines have had a critical role in defining a national, shared sense of the past.

Newspapers have also been an important archive of history. They are commonly thought of as history-making, as newspapers are often the main arena where historical events are first reported. Newspaper archives are routinely the first port of call for researchers. All our libraries collect and now have copies of newspapers in some format, and many are becoming increasingly available on-line. For all sorts of researchers, from academic historians to family history researchers, newspapers are a critical repository of Australian history. In fact, for the early years of colonial settlement in the country, they are one of the few surviving historical artefacts.

Histories of Australian news stories, media and the press have generally seen the role of the newspaper as an eyewitness to history—providing a snapshot of history in the making. Yet the news has never been merely reported. From the earliest pages of the colony's first newspaper, the *Sydney Gazette*, in 1803, news was very much a controlled affair. It was shaped at first by the colonial government, and then, with the first independent newspapers from the 1820s, the political bent of its publishers and editors (often one and the same in the early days).

Indeed the control of our newspapers has been an important and contested, yet often overlooked, element of Australian history. The independence of early newspapers was seen as vital to the development of democracy and nationhood in nineteenth-century Australia. Editors wrote about despotic tyrannical governors, and even bought about their downfall, and as a result sometimes found themselves in court. In what is a strong Australian tradition, the opposition to the censorship of news was so vehement, even at the height of the Second World War, when there were good arguments for censorship, people rioted in the streets to ensure they would still get independent and uncensored news.

This book is about history viewed through the lens of how events were captured in newspaper headlines. In fact the newspaper's role has been much more that of a historian than an eyewitness. The news that actually makes headlines has been determined by such things as the availability of a printing press, technological developments, such as being able to print photographs, or simply the expense or availability of print and paper. It has also been determined by what editors and journalists have defined as newsworthy.

As the headline or front page has taken such diverse forms over the years, before it achieved the look we know today, so too this book has taken a broad view on exactly what constitutes headlines or front page news. We begin well before there were newspapers in the new colony of New South Wales and look at a few examples of images and publications that might not be traditionally considered newspaper front pages, but that performed the same function in their day.

This book includes some headlines that were not front pages, but were nonetheless critical news stories. Before the expansion of newspapers and the media in the mid-nineteenth century, the first notices of events that shaped Australian history were often documents such as government proclamations, broadsheets or even paintings that depicted news, government orders or historical events.

Indeed much of our history-making news was never recorded. From Aboriginal histories to convict legends of escape routes to China or mythical white colonies in the interior, early news was transmitted via word of mouth.

In the first few years, apart from the odd broadsheet, there was no news as such. However some paintings and other images of important events, such as the 1804 Battle of Vinegar Hill and the 1808 Rum Rebellion served as records of the day and stand-in headlines. So too, printed proclamations, or handbills, spread announcements of events or government orders throughout the early colony.

This book takes a wide view of Australian headlines that includes some well-known and some not so well known stories and news formats. We will never truly know how perhaps the greatest headline in Australian history—the arrival of the First Fleet off the shores of Botany Bay—was received by Indigenous people. The event was obviously transmitted as news across the Sydney region and beyond: several Aboriginal rock carvings of European tall ships could arguably have been included here as early headlines.

This book brings together a collection of significant newspaper lead articles and headline stories from Australian history. It begins with some of the earliest reporting on Australia from the first Europeans to sight Indigenous Australians, and follows the development of the printed news format right up to the present day.

It is a compilation of breaking news—of front pages, graphics and headlines that communicated important events. Of course, that importance changes over time. The close attention paid to the royal tour of 1954 or the importance accorded the building of a sandstone bridge over a creek just south of Sydney in 1836 may seem somewhat exaggerated in today's terms. At the time, however, these were important events that received intense media scrutiny.

This collection of headlines explores how these changes occur—how Australians have placed importance on some historical events rather than others, how journalists have covered some stories and not others. For example, why did the Azaria Chamberlain case hold the attention of a nation for so long?

Sometimes headlines are best remembered for being controversial reports or providing the results of ground-breaking investigative journalism. Even as early as the 1850s, journalists were picking up scoops before they became public, such as the news of Victoria's official assent as a colony, which landed on a journalist's lap before the colonial governments had been informed.

Many of the headlines collected here are from the major dailies of Sydney and Melbourne, but there is also a broad selection from some lesser known publications such as the *Illustrated Sydney News* and from other states—the *West Australian*, Brisbane's *Courier-Mail* and the *Canberra Times* to name a few.

Some papers, such as the *Hobart Town Gazette*, were early alternative forms of political expression. Andrew Bent's tirade against Lieutenant Governor George Arthur in this paper is an excellent example of the power of the press.

Newspapers were also critical in providing information in remote colonies in early modern Australian history. Other papers selected here show the progression of technologies from the handwritten news sheets of the early goldfields, to the first images in newspapers in the late nineteenth century, to full colour wraparound covers.

This book investigates the formation of Australian history through snapshots of momentous events as they appeared in headlines. It also looks at some events that had a huge impact and influence at the time, but were relegated to the margins of Australian history. Importantly, it includes some historical moments that did not make headline news, but that reflect significant historical themes and processes that were to later make the headlines. This collection ultimately provides an excellent context for understanding the formation of modern Australian history and society.

No single book could encompass all of the grand headlines of Australian history. Ultimately, this is just a selection of front page news. I trust it is an interesting one.

In the following selection of front pages, many of the earlier documents reproduced here are transcribed for ease of reading. Some of the early nineteenth century newspapers used arcane language and spelling. Other pages in early newspapers have small typeface in dense typesetting and the full text is difficult to read. In some examples, the quality of printing is poor. From the late nineteenth century however, better printing facilities and larger and bolder fonts appeared and transcriptions are not used in the later sections of this book.

WARNING: This book contains the names and images of Aboriginal and Torres Strait Islander people now deceased.

Before the first newspapers

Until

1802

The earliest news in Australia did not appear in newspapers. Story, song and dance were prominent means of communication among the First Australians. And message sticks, fire smoke and messengers were used to tell different Aboriginal groups news of major events. These methods were very efficient, as there are reports of news rapidly travelling hundreds of kilometres through many different Aboriginal language groups across the country. In 1790 for example, Awabakal people travelled over 150 kilometres from Lake Macquarie near Newcastle to feast on the meat of a whale beached in Sydney Harbour.

WITH THE ARRIVAL OF EUROPEANS FROM 1788, SUCH TRADITIONAL FORMS OF COMMUNICATION WERE USED TO DESCRIBE, MAKE SENSE OF, AND SPREAD THE NEWS OF THE STRANGE, WHITE-SKINNED PEOPLE WHO HAD LANDED IN SYDNEY COVE OR 'WARRANG'. THE GADIGAL CLAN ON THE SOUTHERN SHORES OF SYDNEY HARBOUR AND THE DARUG, DHARAWAL AND GANDANGARA PEOPLES FROM THE WIDER SYDNEY REGION, ALL RECORDED THESE STRANGERS AND THEIR OBJECTS AND ARTEFACTS. THEY DEPICTED THESE STRANGERS IN CARVINGS AND PAINTINGS, AS WELL AS ROCK ENGRAVINGS—WIDESPREAD IN A SYDNEY LANDSCAPE FULL OF SANDSTONE PERFECT FOR THE TASK.

An engraving of a bull near the Cow Pastures south-west of Sydney and another north of Sydney showing a tall ship, remain as testament to the first people in Australia who tried to make sense of the Europeans. Unfortunately such engravings showing views of the invading Europeans are rare, as an estimated 50–90 per cent of Sydney Aborigines died in an outbreak of smallpox in 1789. There were not many people left to continue traditional art forms, and those that were quickly focused on surviving the onslaught brought about by the arrival of the Europeans.

Considering that these invaders came from an increasingly literate eighteenth-century European society, it is perhaps surprising that the communication of news through art and story was, particularly in the early colonial period, important to the British colonisers as well. Although a printing press had been brought out on the First Fleet, it lay idle for years as there was no-one in the colony who could operate it. With such limited opportunities for publishing, reports of significant newsworthy events were often presented cartoon-style in paintings. At first, announcements and reports were made orally to a largely illiterate convict population. Maps and views of the new land, its animals and peoples were the means of communicating news of the exotic lands of the far-off colony of New South Wales to European audiences.

Yet the continent on which this little colony perched precariously had in fact been in the news in Europe well before the First Fleet left Portsmouth, England in 1787. Since the early 1600s the Dutch had regularly bumped into the west coast of what they termed New Holland on their way to their colonies in the Spice Islands of Indonesia. Dutch depictions and descriptions of Indigenous Australians were in effect the first news in Europe of the mysterious Great South Land that many people believed the Australian continent to be part of.

The idea of a great southern continent generated fantastical images and ideas about what the land might hold. But the earliest news reports of Australia that reached Europe were quite disparaging. In 1697 it was described as a land of 'miserable savages' by the buccaneer and explorer William Dampier.

What might be considered the first published headline story of events on Australian soil occurred in 1629. Australia was the remote and deserted backdrop for a Dutch account of the savagery that occurred among the survivors of the shipwreck of the *Batavia*. Murder and massacre quite bizarrely formed the subject of what is perhaps the first written news headlines of events on the Australian continent: the account of the shipwreck, mutiny and massacre of the *Batavia* crew and passengers.

By 1787 when the First Fleet left Portsmouth harbour, with its eleven ships full of convicts en route to Botany Bay, newspapers were well established in Europe. They reported the comings and goings of politicians and parliament, of wars, scandals, shipwrecks, financial markets, real estate and goods for sale. There had been irregular publications of particularly newsworthy items in the late 1500s, but these were really broadsheets or pamphlets. The first true newspapers began in Europe in the 1620s. *The Corant [current] or Weekly Newes from Italy, Germany, Hungaria, Polonia, Bohemia, France and the Low-Countries* was the first newspaper published in English, in 1621.

The date of the appearance of the first true newspaper has been much debated—indeed what constitutes a 'true' newspaper is arguable. In Britain, the appearance of the *London Gazette* in 1666 appears to fit the bill of the first regularly produced printed form of news reporting. Whatever the case, English newspapers of the late 1600s would be familiar to us today as having a form and content not unlike modern news. By the 1700s, the whole array of official news reports, 'world news', local news, sporting news and social events was being produced in competing publications—across a spectrum of what could be called 'respectable' newspapers and tabloids, or popular press. It is fascinating to examine eighteenth-century papers and see so much of the same format of today's newspapers.

The expansion of the newspaper is an excellent reflection of the changes that were occurring in European society during this period. As Europeans bean to colonise distant areas of the globe, news of events in other European countries, as well as in their colonies, was increasingly important—not only to governments, but to what was increasingly being called the 'general public'.

The growth of newspapers not only reflected changing societies: it also in some ways generated them. As news of the world was transmitted via increasingly cheap and mass-produced printed forms, it became more and more important for people to be able to read. At first this readership was largely an expanding middle class: the businessmen who relied on shipping news, or the merchants who needed to know the price of coal. But it increasingly became important to all classes of society. Even the rapidly growing numbers of industrial workers and urban poor during the beginning of the Industrial Revolution found literacy to be a critical key in the possibility of social mobility. During the heady times of what has been called the 'long eighteenth century', being able to read the newspaper was becoming more useful to all levels of society.

Still, most of the British population remained illiterate. Industrial progress had also meant massive urbanisation and the creation of a large class of dispossessed poor. It was these people who were to form the bulk of the British experiment to establish a colony on the far side of the globe—a colony that could reduce the numbers in England's overflowing prisons.

While newspapers were important in Europe, they were not part of early Australians' everyday lives. Far from it. If we were to wander the streets of Sydney Town in the early 1790s we would have seen a people without newspapers. Unlike the London streets that many of these people had come from, there were no daily gatherings at coffee houses to hear the latest news. Few people would have been clustered in the streets reading the latest papers.

Yet in the 1790s, these people were very much concerned with news—news from Britain. When ships arrived, the British newspapers they brought with them were so out of date, after a six-month voyage, that it must have felt like living in a time lag. Indeed, ships travelling back to England were wary of foreign vessels in case war had been declared between Britain and some European power since the last news had arrived in the colony.

The colony's printing press lay idle, since no one knew how to use it, and the new settlement was experiencing more pressing problems than the need to disseminate news. During John Hunter's rule as governor between 1795 and 1800, it was occasionally used to produce handbills or broadsheets that transmitted government orders or regulations, which were critical in a penal colony where 60 per cent of European residents were 'prisoners of the crown'. Others who had been freed from their sentences and given 'tickets of leave' often still lived off the government stores. The colony was like a huge public service department—including the military and government officials, most colonists were in some way employed by the government. With such a situation, for the first few years at least, in a small colony of a few thousand souls, communicating government news via word of mouth worked well enough.

Another means of communication was effective in these early years. With crime, escapes and attempts at rebellion constantly fomenting—and sometimes succeeding—among the settlement's convicts, graphic demonstrations of punishment were also a form of communication. Until the early 1800s, the rotting bodies of executed prisoners were left hanging by the roadside until they were mere chained skeletons swinging in the breeze. These gruesome official statements conveyed one of the most important pieces of news in the early days of the prison colony—the results of crime and rebellion.

This chapter includes interesting examples of headline news preceding the introduction of newspapers in New South Wales. Accounts of the land of New Holland (much later to be called Australia) by explorers such as Captain James Cook and William Dampier were quickly published and avidly read. These accounts appear like journalistic eyewitness reports on events in the first contact between Europeans and Australians.

The colonists' first accounts of the early years establishing an outpost in the southern Pacific Ocean served as extended news reports back in Britain. The observations of military officers such as Captain-Lieutenant Watkin Tench about the land and people at Botany Bay, as the colony was colloquially known, were critical in shaping future British policies—and the British public's imagination of the far-flung penal settlement.

As part of a period of great curiosity about Australia and newly explored Pacific Ocean islands, images and reports on the strange flora and fauna were prominent in accounts of New South Wales. While James Cook's crew on the *Endeavour* in 1770 had encountered the kangaroo, other creatures, such as the wombat, koala and lyrebird, were not sighted until more than ten years after the first settlement in 1788. There was plenty of reporting of strange animals and plants to be done.

One news item that may have been somewhat downplayed in official reports of the colony was the conflict with Aboriginal people that developed not long after the British arrival in 1788. The final story in this chapter is a rare example of the documentation of this conflict with the Indigenous inhabitants of the Sydney area; it also shows just how significant it was for the early colony.

Perhaps if there had been a newspaper operating in the fledgling colony of New South Wales it would have recorded the guerilla warfare of the legendary Sydney Aboriginal warrior Pemulwuy in greater detail. It may have offered later historians a wealth of information on this period of early colonial history that seems lost in the past. How differently might we view this period of history if there had indeed been a nascent press? Yet news, headlines and front pages were not always the preserve of the newspapers.

Shipwreck, mutiny and massacre

The wreck of the *Batavia*, 1629

PERHAPS ONE OF CHINESE ADMIRAL ZHENG HE'S 'TREASURE SHIP' EXPEDITIONS BETWEEN 1405 AND 1433 SAW THE FIRST FOREIGN STEPS ON AUSTRALIAN SHORES. CERTAINLY INDONESIAN FISHERMEN HAD BEEN VISITING THE NORTH COAST FOR MANY YEARS BEFORE THE BRITISH ARRIVED. BUT THE FIRST MAJOR EUROPEAN CONTACT, AND PERHAPS THE FIRST HEADLINE STORY OF EVENTS ON AUSTRALIAN SHORES, WAS CREATED BY THE DUTCH SHIPS TRAVELLING TO AND FROM THE SPICE ISLANDS OF PRESENT-DAY INDONESIA.

The Dutch had been colonising Indonesia, then called Batavia, since 1602 and reports of the western coastline of the southern continent began to return to Europe. In 1606 the ship *Duyfken* had charted the Gulf of Carpentaria, and in 1616 Dirk Hartog (c. 1580–1621), Master of the Dutch East India Company ship *Eendracht*, left an inscribed pewter plate nailed to a tree on an island off the West Australian coast.

In 1629 the ship *Batavia*—loaded with coins and jewels destined for the Dutch colonies—ran aground on the Abrolhos Islands, off present-day Geraldton. The survivors found safety on two low-lying coral islands. Captain Ariaen Jacobsz, Senior Merchant Francisco Pelsaert (c. 1591–1630), and forty-six passengers and crew set sail in two small ship's boats in search of fresh water, and then headed to Indonesia to bring back a ship to rescue the remaining 268 people and collect the precious cargo.

Meanwhile, the ship's junior merchant, Jeronimus Corneliszoon, led a group of mutineers and seized the ship's treasure. With his followers, Corneliszoon began a reign of terror, raping women and massacring anyone who refused his authority. Over the next three months, the mutineers systematically killed almost 100 people.

When Pelsaert returned to the islands several months later in September 1629, he was confronted by armed mutineers stockaded in stone forts. After what must be the first European battle on Australian shores, the mutineers were captured and tried before Pelsaert and a council of his fellow officers. Seven men were found guilty of murder and, in the case of Corneliszoon, heresy as well. Three days later, after having their right hands cut off, they were hanged. Two men who were condemned to death were reprieved and abandoned on the mainland, perhaps surviving with Aboriginal people. Another six mutineers were later hanged in Batavia.

The story was not headline news in Europe—shipwrecks, piracy and mutinies were all too common in remote European colonies. But the images and account in Pelsaert's *Unlucky Voyage of the Ship Batavia*, were the first news of events in Australia.

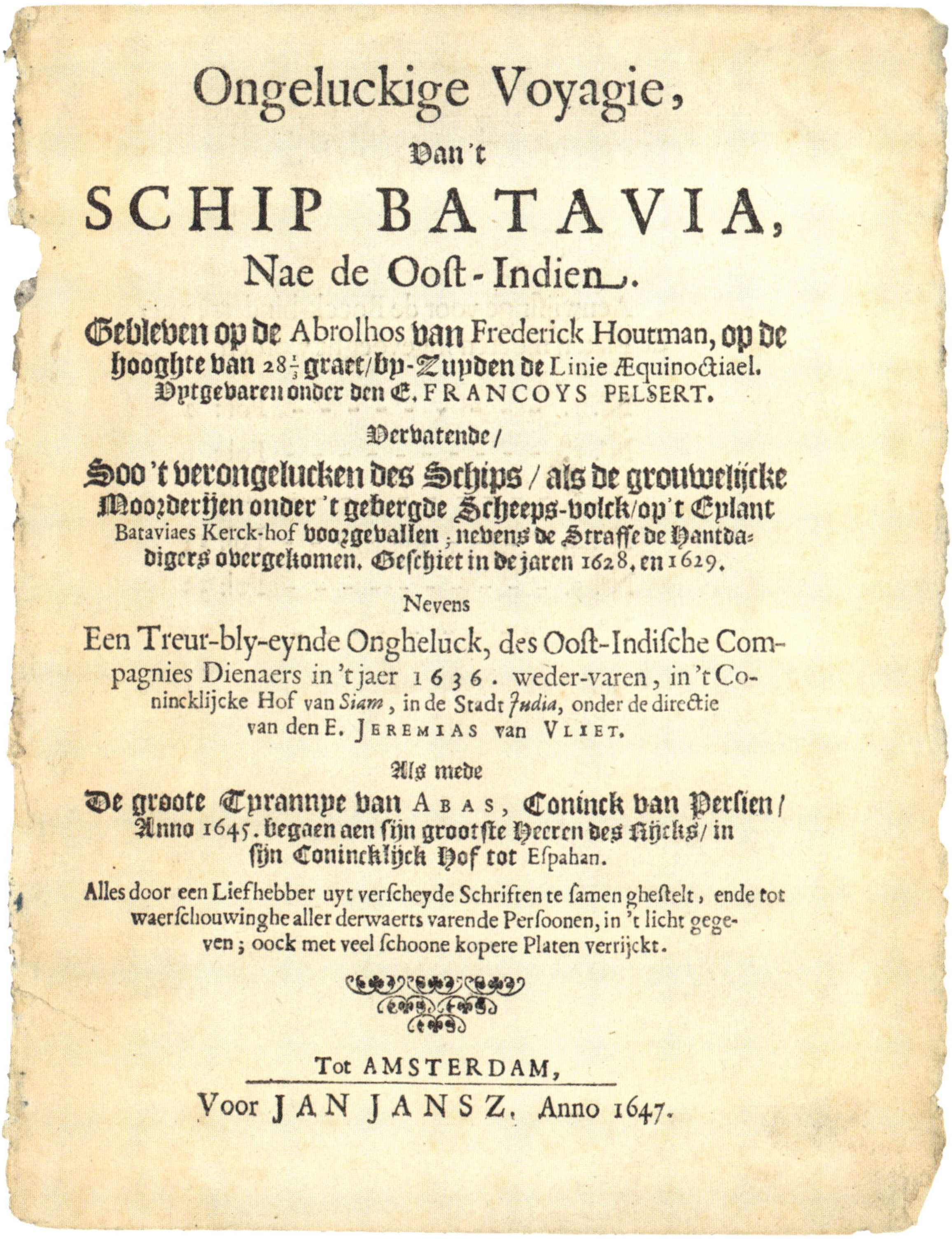

Ongeluckige Voyagie,

Van 't

SCHIP BATAVIA,

Nae de Ooſt-Indien.

Gebleven op de Abrolhos van Frederick Houtman, op de hooghte van 28⅓ graet/ by-Zuyden de Linie Æquinoctiael. Uytgevaren onder den E. FRANCOYS PELSERT.

Vervatende/

Soo 't verongelucken des Schips/ als de grouwelijcke Moorderyen onder 't geberghde Scheeps-volck/op 't Eylant Bataviaes Kerck-hof voorgevallen; nevens de Straffe de Hantdadigers overgekomen. Geschiet in de jaren 1628, en 1629.

Nevens

Een Treur-bly-eynde Ongheluck, des Ooſt-Indiſche Compagnies Dienaers in 't jaer 1636. weder-varen, in 't Conincklijcke Hof van *Siam*, in de Stadt *Judia*, onder de directie van den E. JEREMIAS van VLIET.

Als mede

De groote Tyrannye van ABAS, Coninck van Persien/ Anno 1645. begaen aen ſijn grootſte Heeren des Rijcks/ in ſijn Conincklijck Hof tot Eſpahan.

Alles door een Liefhebber uyt verſcheyde Schriften te ſamen gheſtelt, ende tot waerſchouwinghe aller derwaerts varende Perſoonen, in 't licht gegeven; oock met veel ſchoone kopere Platen verrijckt.

Tot AMSTERDAM,

Voor JAN JANSZ. Anno 1647.

The title page of Francisco Pelsaert's Ongeluckige Voyagie, van't schip Batavia, nae de Oost-Indien, *or* The Unlucky Voyage of the Ship Batavia, *published in Amsterdam in 1647, represents some of the earliest headline news about Australia.*

ABOVE A 1647 *engraving shows the Abrolhos Islands massacre of survivors of the* Batavia *shipwreck.*

BELOW *Gruesome images from Dampier's book about the wreck of the* Batavia *show the mutineers being hanged and tortured.*

Hessel Gerritsz, official cartographer to the Dutch East India Company in the early 1600s, produced this map showing the first recognisable outline of the west coast of Australia. Merchants and explorers working for the company gave him their logs and charts, and he gradually built up better maps of the region.

2 The miserablest People

William Dampier on the Australian bush, 1697

ONE OF THE EARLIEST—AND OFTEN CONSIDERED ONE OF THE WORST—WRITTEN REPORTS ABOUT INDIGENOUS AUSTRALIANS WAS BY THE BUCCANEER AND AUTHOR WILLIAM DAMPIER (1651–1715). HIS ACCOUNT, *A NEW VOYAGE ROUND THE WORLD*, WAS PUBLISHED IN 1697. IN THE 1680S DAMPIER HAD BEEN RAIDING SPANISH POSSESSIONS IN SOUTH AMERICA AND CROSSED INTO THE PACIFIC OCEAN TO RAID THE EAST INDIES. HIS SHIP, THE *CYGNET*, WAS BEACHED FOR REPAIRS ON THE NORTH-WEST COAST OF AUSTRALIA NEAR KING SOUND, AND HERE DAMPIER MADE SOME OF THE EARLIEST DETAILED NOTES ON THE FLORA, FAUNA AND PEOPLE HE FOUND THERE.

The 1697 publication of his journals with their stories of piracy and observations of exotic lands created a deal of interest and led to Dampier's commission by the British Admiralty to explore the east coast of what was then called New Holland. Dampier set out in 1699, and only a leaky ship prevented him from continuing his voyages along towards the eastern Australian coastline, well before Captain James Cook's 1770 voyage.

Dampier's journals and discoveries have been overshadowed in later Australian history by a focus on Cook and the *Endeavour*'s voyage along the eastern coast of the continent. Nonetheless, Dampier's detailed descriptions of Australian flora and fauna has led to him being described as 'Australia's first naturalist'—he was quick to note the prevalence of the great Australian blight, the masses of flies. His extensive travels across the Indian and Pacific oceans also make him one of the greatest nautical explorer–adventurers of his time.

Dampier might be described as the first reporter on Indigenous Australian people. His descriptions of Aboriginal people were written through the lens of a racism that saw Europeans as standing at what they believed was the pinnacle of a hierarchy of societies. The peoples that Europeans were colonising were thought to be inferior. Dampier's words did not provide an inspiring view of the Australian land and its first peoples for future visitors.

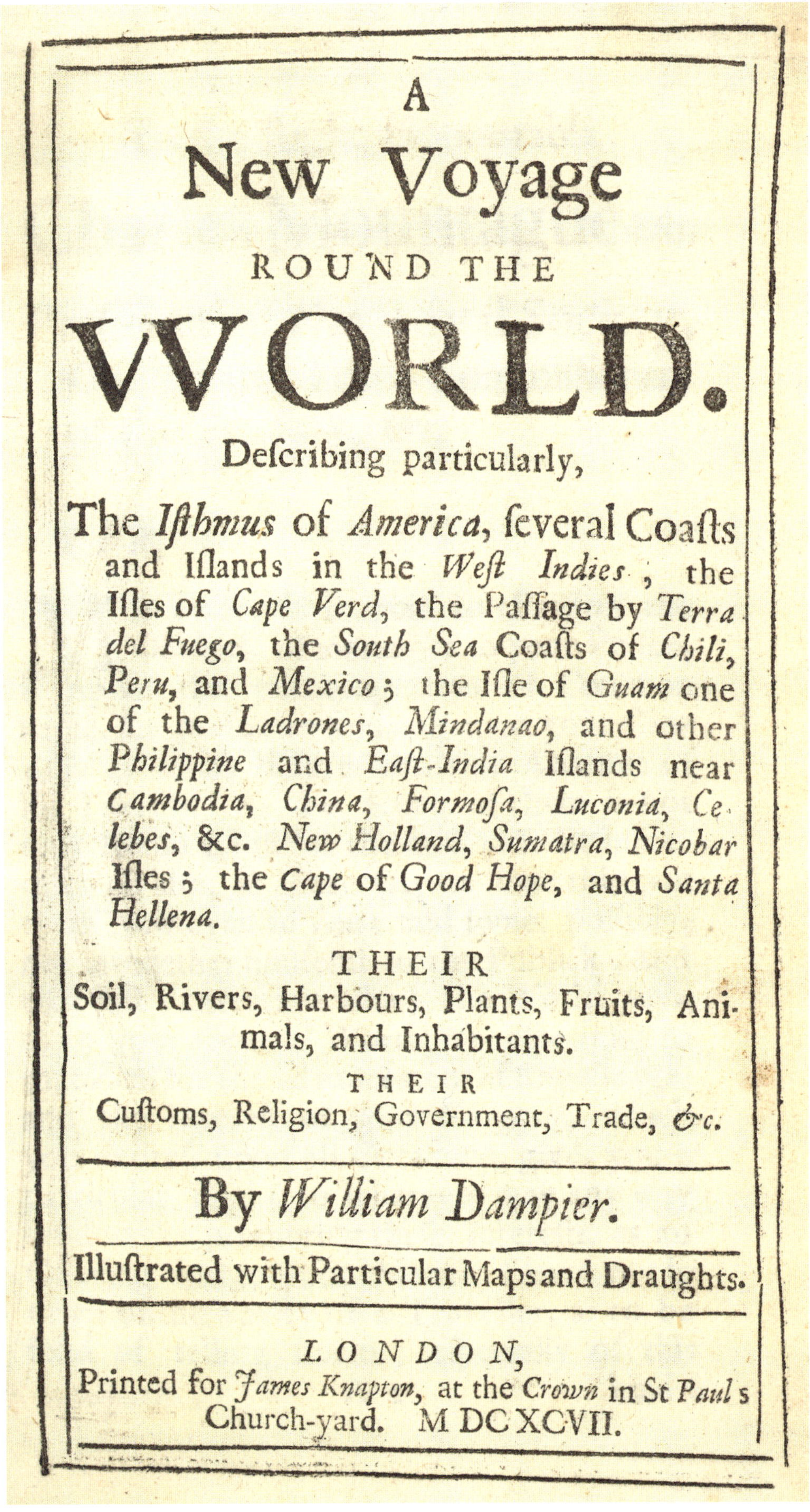

A

New Voyage

ROUND THE

WORLD.

Describing particularly,

The *Isthmus* of *America*, several Coasts and Islands in the *West Indies*, the Isles of *Cape Verd*, the Passage by *Terra del Fuego*, the *South Sea* Coasts of *Chili*, *Peru*, and *Mexico*; the Isle of *Guam* one of the *Ladrones*, *Mindanao*, and other *Philippine* and *East-India* Islands near *Cambodia*, *China*, *Formosa*, *Luconia*, *Celebes*, &c. *New Holland*, *Sumatra*, *Nicobar* Isles; the *Cape* of *Good Hope*, and *Santa Hellena*.

THEIR

Soil, Rivers, Harbours, Plants, Fruits, Animals, and Inhabitants.

THEIR

Customs, Religion, Government, Trade, *&c.*

By *William Dampier*.

Illustrated with Particular Maps and Draughts.

LONDON,

Printed for *James Knapton*, at the *Crown* in St *Paul*'s Church-yard. M DC XCVII.

The title page of the 1699 edition of William Dampier's A New Voyage Round the World. *Page 464 included his description of the local inhabitants as the 'miserablest People in the world'.*

The miserablest People

An. 1688 shy; though the Inhabitants cannot trouble them much, having neither Boats nor Iron.

The Inhabitants of this Country are the miserablest People in the world. The *Hodmadods* of *Monomatapa*, though a nasty People, yet for Wealth are Gentlemen to these; who have no Houses and Skin Garments, Sheep, Poultry, and Fruits of the Earth, Ostrich Eggs, *&c.* as the *Hodmadods* have: and setting aside their humane shape, they differ but little from Brutes. They are tall, strait bodied, and thin, with small long Limbs. They have great Heads, round Foreheads, and great Brows. Their Eye-lids are always half closed, to keep the Flies out of their Eyes: they being so troublesome here, that no fanning will keep them from coming to ones Face; and without the assistance of both hands to keep them off, they will creep into ones Nostrils; and Mouth too, if the Lips are not shut very close. So that from their Infancy being thus annoyed with these Insects, they do never open their Eyes, as other People: and therefore they cannot see far; unless they hold up their Heads, as if they were looking at somewhat over them.

They have great Bottle noses, pretty full lips, and wide mouths. The two fore teeth of their upper Jaw are wanting in all of them, men and women, old and young: whether they draw them out, I know not: Neither have they any Beards. They are long visaged, and of a very unpleasing aspect; having no one graceful feature in their faces. Their Hair is black, short and curl'd, like that of the Negroes: and not long and lank like the common *Indians*. The colour of their skins, both of their faces and the rest of their body, is coal black, like that of the Negroes of *Guinea*.

They have no sort of Cloaths; but a piece of the rind of a Tree ty'd like a Girdle about their wastes, and a handful of long Grass, or 3 or 4

small

ſmall green Boughs, full of Leaves, thruſt under their Girdle, to cover their nakedneſs. *An.* 1688

They have no Houſes, but lye in the open Air, without any covering; the Earth being their Bed, and the Heaven their Canopy. Whether they cohabit one Man to one Woman, or promiſcuouſly, I know not: but they do live in Companies, 20 or 30 Men, Women, and Children together. Their only food is a ſmall ſort of Fiſh, which they get by making Wares of ſtone, acroſs little Coves, or branches of the Sea: every Tide bringing in the ſmall Fiſh, and there leaving them for a prey to theſe people, who conſtantly attend there, to ſearch for them at low water. This ſmall Fry I take to be the top of their Fiſhery: they have no Inſtruments to catch great Fiſh, ſhould they come; and ſuch ſeldom ſtay to be left behind at low water: nor could we catch any Fiſh with our Hooks and Lines all the while we lay there. In other places at low water they ſeek for Cockles, Muſcles, and Periwincles: Of theſe Shell-fiſh there are fewer ſtill; ſo that their chiefeſt dependance is upon what the Sea leaves in their Wares; which, be it much or little, they gather up, and march to the places of their abode. There the old People, that are not able to ſtir abroad, by reaſon of their Age, and the tender Infants, wait their rerurn; and what Providence has beſtowed on them, they preſently broil on the Coals, and eat it in common. Sometimes they get as many Fiſh as makes them a plentiful Banquet; and at other times they ſcarce get every one a taſte: but be it little or much that they get, every one has his part, as well the young and tender, as the old and feeble, who are not able to go abroad, as the ſtrong and luſty. VVhen they have eaten they lye down till the next low water, and then all that are able march out, be it night or day, rain or ſhine, 'tis all one: they muſt attend the Wares,

The miſerableſt People

3 Agreeable news

Reporting the return of Captain James Cook, 1771

PERHAPS THE MOST FAMOUS NEWS OF THE EARLY EXPLORATION OF AUSTRALIA WAS TO APPEAR IN THE PUBLISHED JOURNALS OF CAPTAIN JAMES COOK'S (1728–1779) VOYAGE OF 1770. YET AT THE TIME OF COOK'S RETURN TO ENGLAND, NEWS OF HIS JOURNEY ALONG THE EAST COAST OF THE CONTINENT THE DUTCH HAD NAMED NEW HOLLAND WAS COMPARATIVELY UNREMARKABLE.

On 13 July 1771 the popular and often political *London Evening Post* rather matter of factly—considering Cook and his crew had just circumnavigated the globe and explored several Pacific Islands unknown to Europeans—reported that the *Endeavour* had returned the previous day. The *Post* not only spelled his name 'Cooke', but as with all the news reports of the *Endeavour*'s Pacific voyage, the *Post* was much more interested in the reports on the journey produced by the 'gentleman-scientist' Joseph Banks.

Banks' descriptions of their encounters with strange people, and new animals and plants were indeed fascinating news. However Cook's rather dry account was to become more famous than Banks'. His publisher and editor John Hawkesworth transformed Cook's journal into a popular book and marketed the 'official version' above all others. The publication of Cook's journal was eagerly anticipated and first published in June 1773. It was a sellout and became one of the most popular publications of the eighteenth century.

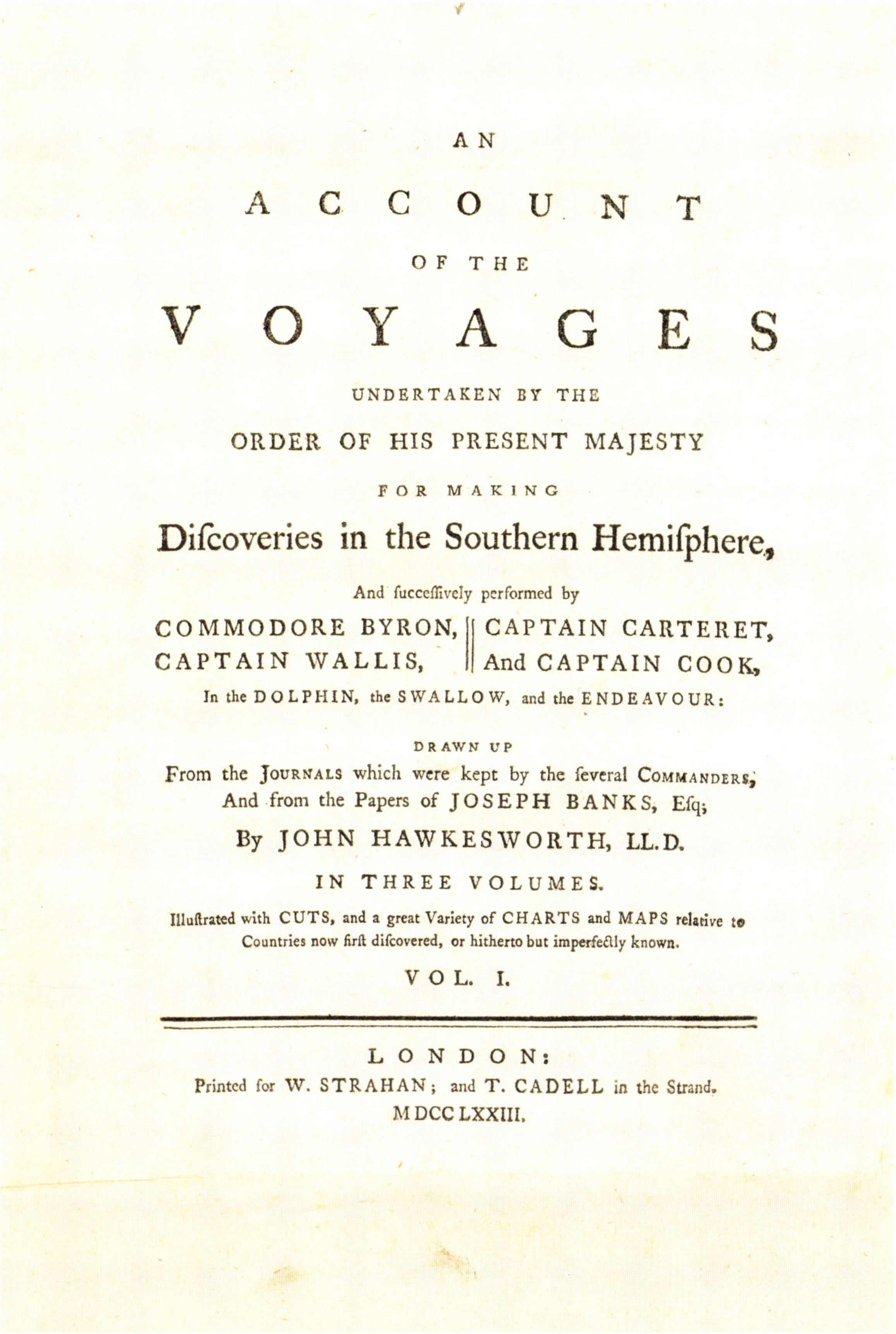
AN

ACCOUNT

OF THE

VOYAGES

UNDERTAKEN BY THE

ORDER OF HIS PRESENT MAJESTY

FOR MAKING

Diſcoveries in the Southern Hemiſphere,

And ſucceſſively performed by

COMMODORE BYRON, | CAPTAIN CARTERET,
CAPTAIN WALLIS, | And CAPTAIN COOK,

In the DOLPHIN, the SWALLOW, and the ENDEAVOUR:

DRAWN UP

From the JOURNALS which were kept by the ſeveral COMMANDERS,
And from the Papers of JOSEPH BANKS, Eſq;

By JOHN HAWKESWORTH, LL.D.

IN THREE VOLUMES.

Illuſtrated with CUTS, and a great Variety of CHARTS and MAPS relative to
Countries now firſt diſcovered, or hitherto but imperfectly known.

VOL. I.

LONDON:
Printed for W. STRAHAN; and T. CADELL in the Strand.
MDCCLXXIII.

Banks and Solander discovered so many new plants at the expedition's first landfall in Australia that Cook changed the name of the bay from Stingray Harbour to Botany Bay.

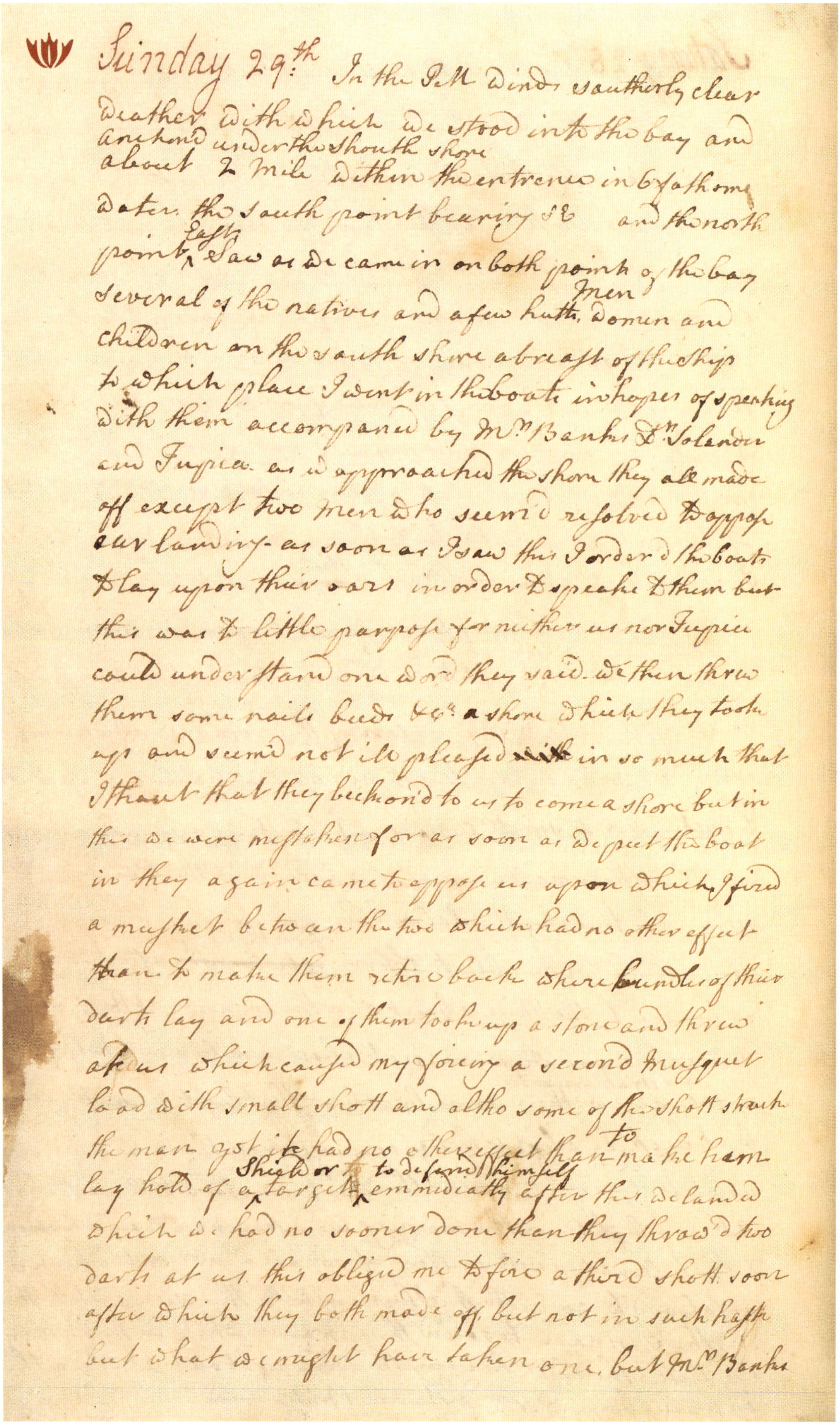

Sunday 29th In the PM winds southerly clear
weather with which we stood into the bay and
anchor'd under the South shore
about 2 Mile within the entrence in 6 fathoms
water, the south point bearing SE and the north
point East, Saw as we came in on both points of the bay
several of the natives and a few hutts, Men women and
children on the south shore abreast of the Ship
to which place I went in the boats in hopes of speaking
with them accompanied by Mr. Banks Dr. Solander
and Tupia. as we approached the shore they all made
off except two men who seem'd resolved to oppose
our landing. as soon as I saw this I order'd the boats
to lay upon their oars in order to speake to them but
this was to little purpose for neither us nor Tupia
could understand one word they said. we then threw
them some nails beeds &ca a shore which they took
up and seem'd not ill pleased with in so much that
I thout that they beckon'd to us to come a shore but in
this we were mistaken for as soon as we put the boat
in they again came to oppose us upon which I fired
a musket between the two which had no other effect
than to make them retire back where bundles of their
darts lay and one of them took up a stone and threw
at us which caused my fireing a second Musquet
load with small shott and altho some of the shott struck
the man yet it had no other effect than to make him
lay hold of a Shield or target to defend himself emmidiately after this we landed
which we had no sooner done than they throw'd two
darts at us. this obliged me to fire a third shott. soon
after which they both made off, but not in such haste
but what we might have taken one, but Mr. Banks

Despite the simplicity of Cook's record of the new continent, it became a best seller in its time.

29 April 1770

Sunday 29th: In the PM winds southerly clear weather with which we stood into the bay and Anchor'd under the South shore about 2 Mile within the entrence in 6 fathoms water, the south point bearing SE and the north point East, Saw as we came in on both points of the bay Several of the natives and afew hutts, Men women and children on the south shore abreast of the Ship to which place I went in the boats in hopes of speaking with them accompaned by Mr Banks Dr Solander and Tupia- as we approached the shore they all made off except two Men who seem'd resolved to oppose our landing- as soon as I saw this I orderd the boats to lay upon their oars in order to speake to them but this was to little purpose for neither us nor Tupia could understand one word they said. We then threw them some nails beeds &C[a] ashore which they took up and seem'd not ill pleased with in so much that I thout that they beckon'd to us to come ashore but in this we were mistaken for as soon as we put the boat in they again came to oppose us upon which I fired a musket between the two which had no other effect than to make them retire back where bundles of their darts lay and one of them took up a stone and threw at us which caused my fireing a second Musquet load with small shott and altho' some of the shott struck the man yet it had no other effect than to make him lay hold of a Shield or target to defend himself emmediatly after this we landed which we had no sooner done than they throw'd two darts at us this obliged me to fire a third shott soon after which they both made off, but not in such haste but what we might have taken one, but Mr Banks [*and Cook's journal continues*] being of opinion that the darts were poisoned made me cautious how I advanced into the woods - We found here a few Small hutts made of the bark of trees in one of which were four or five small children with whome we left some strings of beeds &C[a] a quantity of darts lay about the hutts these we took away with us - three Canoes lay upon the bea[c]h the worst I think I ever saw they were about 10½ or 14 feet long made of one peice of the bark of a tree drawn or tied up at each end and the middle kept open by means of peices of sticks by way of Thwarts —

... - the strings of beeds &C[a] we had left with the children last night were found laying in the hut this morning probably the natives were afraid to take them away - after breakfast we sent some empty casks ashore and a party of men to cut wood and I went my self in the Pinnace to sound and explore the Bay - in the doing of which I saw severl of the natives but they all fled at my approach - I landed in two places one of which the people had but just left as there were small fires and fresh muscles broiling upon them - here likewise lay vast heaps of the largest oyster shells I ever saw. I likewise saw of the oysters themselves as I rowed over ths shoals but being highwater I could not get any having nothing we me to take them up —

4 Progress made in the settlement

First news of Botany Bay, 1789

THE FLEET OF ELEVEN NAVAL, TRANSPORT AND STORE SHIPS THAT HAD MADE UP THE EXPEDITION TO ESTABLISH A BRITISH PENAL COLONY AT BOTANY BAY ON THE EAST COAST OF NEW HOLLAND BEGAN TO LEAVE THE NEW SETTLEMENT SOON AFTER THEY LANDED THEIR CARGOES OF CONVICTS, SUPPLIES, SETTLERS AND GOVERNMENT OFFICIALS. IT WAS IMPORTANT THAT NEWS OF THE FLEET'S SAFE ARRIVAL WAS RETURNED TO ENGLAND, AND THAT THE REQUEST FOR FURTHER SUPPLY SHIPS WAS MET: NEW HOLLAND DID NOT APPEAR TO BE AS 'AGREEABLE' AS IT HAD BEEN DESCRIBED BY JAMES COOK AND JOSEPH BANKS.

The *Alexander, Borrowdale, Friendship* and *Prince of Wales* left the new settlement on 14 July. The last vessels to leave, the store ships *Fishburn* and *Golden Grove*, departed on 19 November 1788. The fledgling colony of New South Wales was left remarkably isolated.

News travelled with the returning ships. In addition to many private letters, including a long and detailed letter from Surgeon James Callam of the *Sirius* to his brother in London, they carried detailed reports and government dispatches from the newly created governor, Captain Arthur Phillip (1738–1814).

The ships also carried a manuscript by one of the officers of the Marines that accompanied the voyage, Captain-Lieutenant Watkin Tench (1759–1833). His *Narrative* of the expedition described the colony's 'Productions' and 'Inhabitants' as well as the initial 'progress' of settlement. Tench wrote for an audience that was fascinated by the strange colony that had been established to command the southern Pacific Ocean, yet to be built by the labour of thieves and criminals.

His *Narrative* was quickly printed in London in 1789, as it seems Tench had astutely made advance arrangements for its publication. His descriptions, particularly of Aboriginal people and the efforts to establish agriculture in the colony, were in effect one of the most important early journalistic news reports about the colony of New South Wales.

(132)

C H A P. XVI.

The Progreſs made in the Settlement; and the Situation of Affairs at the Time of the Ship, which conveys this Account, ſailing for England.

FOR the purpoſe of expediting the public work, the male convicts have been divided into gangs, over each of which a perſon, ſelected from among themſelves, is placed. It is to be regretted that Government did not take this matter into conſideration before we left England, and appoint proper perſons with reaſonable ſalaries to execute the office of overſeers; as the conſequence of our preſent imperfect plan is ſuch, as to defeat in a great meaſure the purpoſes for which the priſoners were ſent out. The female convicts have hitherto lived in a ſtate of total idleneſs; except a few who are kept to work in making pegs for tiles, and picking up ſhells for burning into lime. For the laſt time

(133)

time I repeat, that the behaviour of all claſſes of theſe people ſince our arrival in the ſettlement has been better than could, I think, have been expected from them.

Temporary wooden ſtorehouſes covered with thatch or ſhingles, in which the cargoes of all the ſhips have been lodged, are completed; and an hoſpital is erected. Barracks for the military are conſiderably advanced; and little huts to ſerve, until ſomething more permanent can be finiſhed, have been raiſed on all ſides. Notwithſtanding this the encampments of the marines and convicts are ſtill kept up; and to ſecure their owners from the coldneſs of the nights, are covered in with buſhes, and thatched over.

The plan of a town I have already ſaid is marked out. And as free-ſtone of an excellent quality abounds, one requiſite towards the completion of it is attained. Only two houſes of ſtone are yet begun, which are intended for the Governor and Lieutenant Governor. One of the greateſt impediments we meet with, is a want of limeſtone, of which

Watkin Tench, officer of the Marines, wrote his book, A Narrative of the Expedition to Botany Bay; with an Account of New South Wales, Its Productions, Inhabitants, &c., *in the earliest days of the colony, and it was published in London in 1789. Tench was a keen explorer and an enthusiastic observer of life in and around Sydney.*

Progress made in the settlement

POSTSCRIPT continued.

EXPEDITION *to* BOTANY-BAY.

The two ſhips of war, named the Sirius and Supply, with the tranſports, under the command of Commodore Phillips, have made good their voyage to Botany Bay: Of this important arrival intelligence has been brought by the Prince of Wales, Moore, one of the tranſports which carried out the convicts. The Prince of Wales buried only one convict. The diſpatches for Government are not yet arrived, as the Borrowdale tranſport, by which Commodore Phillips ſent them, as well as a third tranſport in company, have not reached England.

On the arrival of this ſquadron at Botany Bay, the deſtined ſpot was found not to have water ſufficient for the ſupply of the new ſettlement: A council was in conſequence held, and the ſhips weighing anchor ſtood away for Jackſon's Bay, where Nature's gifts appeared equal to all their wiſhes: The verdure ſtrong and rich, and the ſprings of the beſt water: The face of the country too poſſeſſing great variety, and well clothed with wood.

The moment Commodore Phillips had made good the landing of the Marines, and ſome lines of limitation were marked out, the convicts were put on ſhore; and the artizans among them, with thoſe belonging to the ſhips, proceeded to cut down wood to form their habitations. This taſk continued for ſome time during the hours of day, and in the evening the workmen and others returned on board the ſhipping, leaving only the Marines, and a detachment of the ſeamen, to guard the works as they advanced towards completion. The natives, when they diſcovered the preparations on foot, and that their viſitors were likely to become ſtationary, appeared ſo diſſatisfied, that ſeveral pieces of ordnance were mounted on the lines to awe them; they however kept at a diſtance, and though they did not provoke a fire, they declined all communion.

Of the convicts and others, from the departure of the ſquadron from Portſmouth, to the time the ſhip which brings the advice left Jackſon's Bay, only 40 appear to have died; and to compenſate for this loſs, 42 infants were born.

Three of the convicts were induced to try their fortunes among the natives, where they hoped to have a favourable reception: two of theſe were in this expedition killed and eaten; and the third, after ſubſiſting on roots for ſome time in the woods, returned, almoſt periſhed through hunger. This operated to deter further adventures of a like nature.

The cattle fared very unpropitiouſly; ſome of the cows died during their paſſage; and others, after their landing, ſtrayed ſo far into the woods, as to be irrecoverably loſt. The ſheep did not thrive; the herbage did not afford the nutriment of their native paſture, and no ſtock, it is feared, will ever be reared from them. The pigs were in a ſtate of better proſperity; and moſt of the poultry promiſe to be beneficial.

When the Prince of Wales tranſport quitted Jackſon's Bay, which was on the 15th of July laſt, a very fine crop of grain was preſented to the eye. This occupied 12 acres of ground, all that could poſſibly be cultivated before the ſeaſon was too far gone for a crop of greater extent.

The fiſh immediately on the Coaſt are found to be very indifferent. The natives live chiefly on teſtaceous fiſh, and the ſmall quadruped which Cooke deſcribes; the hind legs of which are much longer than the fore ones. The ſkins of ſeveral of theſe animals have been ſtuffed and brought to England. An attempt was made to bring ſome of them alive, but failed.

The Prince of Wales is ſaid to have continued her courſe through the South Sea after ſhe left New Holland, and paſſed through the Streights of Magellan. She parted company with the Borrowdale on the 15th of Auguſt laſt, but fell in with her at Rio Janeiro; they ſailed from that place together, but loſt company again on the 24th of December laſt. Capt. Maſon, the Maſter of the Prince of Wales, died on his paſſage home, and Mr. Moore, the Mate, ſucceeded to the command. Four of her ſeamen alſo died.

Capt. Phillips, the Governor of the ſettlement, and Major Roſs, the Deputy Governor, together with Capt. Hunter, Lieut. Ball of the Supply tender, and Lieut. Long of the marines, were all well when the tranſport abovenamed ſailed for England.

The Iriſh penſion bill, which was carried up to the Lords of that kingdom on the 19th inſt. was propoſed to be read a ſecond time on the Monday following; but it was propoſed by thoſe who wiſhed well to Adminiſtration, that it ſhould be read a ſecond time on the Monday ſe'nnight. This motion was carried by 38 to 36; a majority of only two for Government.

Yeſterday was held at the London Tavern, the Anniverſary Meeting of the Society for promoting the Britiſh Fiſheries, for electing the Governor, Deputy Governor, and Directors during the year enſuing, when Mr. Dempſter gave a very particular and intereſting account of the meaſures purſued by the Directors for attaining the laudable ends of their aſſociation, which are principally directed to the promotion of induſtry, and increaſing the reſources for manning the navy of Great Britain, by extending the Fiſheries.

Yeſterday Dr. Stranger, of Soho-ſquare, was elected Greſham Profeſſor of Phyſic, by the Grand Committee for Greſham Affairs of the Mercers' Company.

Tueſday a Meeting of the Freeholders of Middleſex was held at the Mermaid in Hackney, for the purpoſe of conſidering on a congratulatory Addreſs to his Majeſty. The Meeting was reſpectable, though not numerous; about 150 perſons being preſent. A Committee was immediately appointed to draw up an Addreſs, which being accordingly produced, read, and unanimouſly agreed to, a converſation took place on the mode of preſenting it; when it was ſettled, that it ſhould be by the Sheriffs preſented to the Secretary of State, and by him to his Majeſty. It was then unanimouſly agreed, that the Sheriffs only ſhould ſign the Addreſs.

Mr. Byng propoſed, that the Sheriffs ſhould be requeſted to call a meeting of the freeholders on an early day, in order to conſider of a petition to Parliament for the repeal of the county election act. Mr. Skinner wiſhed to know the opinions of the two members. Mr. Mainwaring aſſured the gentlemen that he held it to be an oppreſſive and incomprehenſible act; and that, unleſs he was directed by his conſtituents to ſupport it, he ſhould vote for its total repeal. He thought that it would be impoſſible for the Sheriffs to call a meeting, and have the petition preſented in time. Mr. Wilkes ſpoke to the ſame effect; and concluded by ſaying, that unleſs he was by his conſtituents otherwiſe directed, he ſhould vote for a repeal of the bill.

Tueſday at Guildhall the following Numbers were drawn prizes of above 18l. viz. No. 42,433, a prize of 25,000l. No. 25,617, a prize of 5000l. No. 16,068, a prize of 1000l. and No. 25,816, a prize of 100l.

Yeſterday at Guildhall the following numbers were drawn prizes of above 18l. viz. No. 46,676, a prize of 10,000l. No. 33,242, a prize of 1000l. and No. 7609, 15,273, 47,082, and 47,881, prizes of 100l. each.

At the Aſſizes at Maidſtone, for the county of Kent, 16 priſoners received ſentence of death, four of whom are left for execution, viz. Edward James and Henry Alexander, for entering the dwelling-houſe of James Hodges and Sarah Hodges in Maidſtone, and robbing them of one guinea in gold, 19s. in ſilver, and 2s. in copper; John Smith, for robbing George Sharpe on the highway in Dartford of a ſilver watch; and Joſeph Paſſmore, for wilfully and maliciouſly ſetting fire to the dwelling-houſe of W. Mainwaring, a baker, in St. Nicholas, Deptford.

The trial of Paſſmore commenced at nine in the morning, and laſted three hours; and by the evidence it appeared, that the priſoner was by trade a bricklayer, and had reſided in a houſe at the Stowage in Deptford, which was the property of an infant, whoſe mother the priſoner had married, and thereby got into poſſeſſion. That he quitted Deptford, and ſet up a pork ſhop near the Seven Dials in Weſtminſter, and in December laſt let the houſe in the Stowage to a labourer in the King's yard at Deptford, who was to have poſſeſſion on the 6th day of February 1789; that the tenant accordingly moved part of his goods thither on that day, and preſſed to have the key, but could only obtain a promiſe of it on the next day from the priſoner; that the tenant in the courſe of that day ſaw a parcel of ſhavings laid in a cloſet under the ſtairs, and that dry wood had been laid upon thoſe ſhavings by the priſoner, and ſaw a pitch-kettle in the kitchen, which he carried and left in the waſh houſe, and about ſix in the evening he and the priſoner left the houſe, and the priſoner locked the door and kept the key. That the priſoner had been that day very importunate with Mrs. Rehm, the baker's wife, (who lived next door to the priſoner's houſe) to know what hour her huſband got up to bake; and at ſeven in the evening he came to her houſe, and again enquired with ſeeming earneſtneſs when her huſband would get up to work; and then lighted a very large candle, which he carried into his uninhabited houſe. That ſome ſhipwrights being accidentally near the ſpot about the hour of two the next morning, and ſeeing a ſmoke iſſue from a houſe which nobody dwelt in, they without heſitation broke open the door, and then ſaw it was on fire in the cloſet under the ſtairs, and other places, and that the pitch-kettle (which the tenant had ſo carried into the waſh-houſe) was then on the kitchen-floor, and in flames. That the houſe had been long inſured at the Sun Fire Office for 60l. only, but the priſoner had very lately inſured it for 200l. And that the priſoner had taken the lead from off the gutters, and diſpoſed of it. The ſhipwrights ſpread the alarm, and fortunately preſerved the neighbours from periſhing by the flames, which conſumed the houſe where the fire began, and the baker's, and Mr. Mainwaring's a ſhipwright, who were the priſoner's right and left hand neighbours.

Bank Stock, ſhut	Ditto Ann. ſhut
3 per Ct Red. ſhut	Do. Bonds. 76s.
3 per Ct. Conſ. 74 ¼ a ⅜	South Sea Stock, —
Ditto 1726, —	Old Ann. —
4 per Ct. Conſ. ſhut	New ditto, —
5 per Cent. 113 ⅝ a ¾	3 per Cent. 1751, —
Bank Long Ann. ſhut	New Navy, —
Do. Short, 1777, ſhut	Lot. Tick. —
Ditto 1778, 1779, ſhut	Excheq. Bills, —
India Stock, ſhut	

In a few Days will be publiſhed.

MARY QUEEN of SCOTS. A Tragedy.
By the Hon. JOHN ST JOHN.
As performing with univerſal Applauſe at the Theatre Royal, Drury-lane.
Printed for J. Debrett, oppoſite Burlington-houſe, in Piccadilly.

LONDON. Sold by J. WILKIE, No. 71, the *Bible*, in *St. Paul's Church-yard*; where Advertiſements, and Letters to the Authors are taken in: And where all Perſons, who chuſe to be regularly ſerved with this Paper, are deſired to apply.

The London Chronicle *of Thursday, 26 March 1789 reported the news from the colony as a Postscript extending over several pages and continuing the story begun in the previous issue.*

Farther Particulars of the BOTANY BAY EXPEDITION, *supplementary to the Account given in our last.*

EARLY yesterday morning Lieut. Maxwell, of the marines, arrived at the Admiralty with difpatches for Government: thefe are not very copious, as the principal pacquet is now on its way in the Alexander tranfport. From the accounts brought by the Prince of Wales and Borrowdale we are enabled to lay the following particulars before our Readers:

Commodore Phillips having made the Cape of Good Hope, with the fhips of war, tranfports, and victuallers, ufed the moft unremitting diligence to fupply the fquadron with provifions and water, live ftock for the fhips ufe; and cattle, fheep, and hogs, for the benefit of the intended colony. To thefe we may reckon a large quantity of poultry, in addition to fome which was carried from England.

On the 16th of November 1787 the fignal was given, and the fquadron got under way, and continued their courfe for a time with favourable winds for New Holland; fome fhort tempefts interrupting their courfe, Commodore Phillips removed to the Supply, and propofed going a-head to prepare a reception for the reft of the fleet at the place of deftination: three tranfports, the Friendfhip, Alexander, and Scarborough, failed in company; but retarded the Commodore's courfe fo much, that he did not come in fight of land till the 14th of January 1788. Three days after, he made Botany Bay, and on the 18th of January landed with Lieut. Shortland, Agent for tranfports, and Lieut. King. The natives, who had in fmall bodies witneffed their approach, appeared in great confternation on feeing thefe officers on their territory, and, after fetting up a yell, fled to the woods. They returned foon after more compofed, and, from the figns made by Captain Phillips, were prevailed on to receive fome prefents of beads, necklaces, and other trifles; but they were depofited on the ground, and the Captain withdrawn to a diftance before they would venture to take them. After this, they appeared fo friendly as to conduct, by figns, the officers to a rivulet, where they found fome excellent water, though not in a very abundant fupply. In the evening, the Commodore with his party returned on board; and the next day the three tranfports, which he had outfailed, came to an anchor; on which the Commodore went again on fhore, principally to cut grafs for the ufe of the cattle and fheep, the hay on board being nearly all exhaufted. On the dawn of the day following, the Sirius, Capt. Hunter, with the remainder of the tranfports under his convoy, appeared in fight, and three hours after brought to, and anchored in the bay.

Captain Hunter immediately waited on the Commodore; and thefe gentlemen, with a fmall party of officers and men, went on fhore again towards the South Coaft of Botany Bay, the former vifits having been made to the North of the Bay. Here, as in moft of the early interviews with the natives, Commodore Phillips ufually laid his mufquet on the ground, and advancing before it, held out prefents. A green bough held aloft, or their lances thrown down, were like figns of amity in them. It was a practice with the feamen in thefe intercourfes to drefs up the inhabitants with fhreds of cloth, and tags of coloured paper; and when they furveyed each other, they would burft in loud laughter, and run hollowing to the woods. The marines one day forming before them, they appeared to like the fife, but fled at the found of the drum, and never more would venture near it.

The appearance of this part of the country was not, on examination, fo favourable as was hoped, and in confequence the Commodore, with a party and two boats, fkirted along the coaft for about 12 or 14 miles; and having landed in Sydney's Cove, within the points of Port Jackfon, found the afpect of the country fo promifing, as to induce the Commodore, after a council with his officers, to fix the fettlement here. Accordingly, on the 23d, the whole fquadron weighed anchor, and brought to in good moorings at the entrance of the Cove. The ground being marked out, as we have already noticed, a portable dwelling-houfe for the Commodore, and an hofpital, both of which had been conftructed in England, together with the officers marquees, and tents for the artificers, were fixed out of hand; and ftorehoufes and habitations were planned out, and proceeded on.

On the convicts being landed, Mr. Phillips affumed his office of Governor, and caufed the commiffion given him by the King to exercife fuch authority, to be read; and alfo the abridgment of the code of laws by which he was to govern. By this the fettlers were informed, that four Courts would occafionally be held, as the nature of the offence required: namely, a Civil Court, a Criminal Court, a Military Court, and an Admiralty Court.

The fettlers were then told, that nothing could draw thefe laws into exercife, but their own demerits; and as it was then in their power to atone to their country for all the wrongs done at home, no other admonitions than thofe which their own confciences would dictate, it was hoped, would be neceffary to effect their happinefs and profperity in their new country.

But fuch is the inveteracy of vice, that neither lenient meafures nor fevere whipping operated to prevent theft: rigorous meafures were therefore adopted, and after a formal trial in the Criminal Court, two men were hung in one day, and foon after two others fuffered in a like way.

The Governor, befides the above fettlement, formed a colony on Norfolk Ifland, confifting of Lieutenant King, two petty officers, nine men, and fix women, with fix months provifions. In their paffage to this ifland, Lieutenant Ball, of the Supply, difcovered a new ifland, which he named Lord Howe's Ifland.

It is here neceffary to obferve, that while the fquadron were under way from Botany Bay to Jackfon's Port, two ftrange fail appeared, with their hulls juft in view; and foon after Governor Phillips had landed in Sydney's Cove, he was waited upon by a party bearing a French flag. Thefe fhips proved to be two French frigates, which failed from Europe in Auguft 1785, under the command of Monf. La Perieux, on a voyage of difcoveries to the South Seas. They were in fome diftrefs for ftores and provifions, but the Governor could not contribute much to their relief. However, they remained five weeks in Botany Bay, and during that time vifits were continually reciprocally made, as the diftance from that place to Sydney's Cove was but ten miles acrofs the land.

The convicts, during this interval, were employed in cutting wood for fences, and to collect provender for the cattle and fheep, as the foil produced very indifferent pafture, although it was the middle of the New Hollander's fummer. An averfion to labour, however, induced fome of the new fettlers to project an efcape for Europe on board the French fhips; thefe efforts were, however, in a meafure fruftrated; the officers of the French fhips would not hearken to any propofals except thofe made by the fair; for it was difcovered two days after Monf. La Perieux had failed, that two women were miffing. We muft not omit faying, that Monf. Perieux loft two boats crews in a ftorm, and that he related he had 14 of his people murdered at Navigator's Ifland.

We will now fpeak of the country and its inhabitants: of the latter of which, Capt. Cooke has faid nothing.

The INHABITANTS.

The men and women go without the leaft apparel or fence againft the weather. The men are upright, but not gracefully made: the women ftoop very much, and in their gait are particularly awkward. This arifes, both in the women and men, from a practice of ftanding on one leg, with the foot of the other limb refting on the joint of the knee, and in this pofture they ftand for a long time, and then change the limbs, as if for relief. Their colour is of a dingy copper. Their features are broad and ill formed; the nofe is broad and flat; their lips wide and thick, and their eyes circular and large. From a practice they have of rubbing themfelves with fifh oil, they fmell fo loathfome that they cannot be approached but with difguft. The men have bufhy beards, and the hair on their heads is furzy and ftuck full of fifh teeth and bits of fhells, which are faftened with gum, and this is the only ornament they affume, except another ftill more prepofterous, namely, a bone faftened in the cartilage of the nofe; but this is worn only by a few of the diftinguifhed, as thofe who had them were pointed out to Mr. Phillips with looks of fignificance. Some had alfo a belt of coloured clay fmeared on them; and women out of number were obferved with two joints cut from off the little finger, apparently a mark either of honour or difgrace. They appear, however, from their unreafoning manners, to have few ideas of order among themfelves; and if they have notions of worfhip, they are more than could be afcertained. They feem, however, to regard a black bird of the raven kind with particular veneration; for on one of the gentlemen pointing his fuzee at a bird of this fort, one of the natives ran and threw himfelf in the way of the piece, although he was aware it would have killed him had it gone off.

Their huts are formed of boughs and covered with bufhes. Their canoes are made of bark. Their weapons confift of a long fpear of hard wood, which they jirk with fuch fkill, as fometimes to kill a bird; they have a fhield made of the bark of a tree, which can hardly be penetrated. They have a lance alfo, with which they ftrike fifh, and feldom fail to kill.—Their tackle confifts of a hook made of fhell, and a line formed of bark, beat into thread; and their wants being few, thefe are all the inftruments they have occafion for, except an adze made of ftone, with which they cut wood.

Fifh is their principal food, and this, as well as flefh, they eat fcarce warm through; although they fit round a fire at all times at their meals. They do not appear to have any difpofition to fteal, but certainly were diffatisfied on finding their vifitors likely to abide among them.

In our laft we did not accurately ftate one fact; they killed three of our men in the woods, two of whom were gathering bufhes for thatching; but they did not eat them, as their bodies were reftored and buried.—After this hoftility, they became very fhy, and did not for fome time approach the colony.

ANIMALS.

The Kanguroo is the quadruped alluded to in our laft; it is as large as a fheep; the head, neck, and fhoulders, are very fmall in proportion to the other parts of the body; the tail is long, but thick near the rump, and tapering towards the end; the fore legs in general meafure only eight inches in length, and the hind legs twenty-two; the progrefs is by fucceffive leaps or hops of a confiderable length, in an erect pofture; the fore-legs are kept bent clofe to the breaft, and feem to be of ufe only for digging; the fkin is covered with fhort fur of a dark moufe or grey colour, excepting the head and ears, which bear a flight refemblance to thofe of the hare. One of thefe animals, of uncommon magnitude, is on board the Prince

Progress made in the settlement

EXPEDITION *to* BOTANY-BAY

The two ships of war, named the Sirius and Supply, with the transports, under the command of Commodore Phillips, have made good their voyage to Botany Bay: Of this important arrival, intelligence has been brought by the Prince of Wales, Moore, one of the transports which carried out the convicts. The Prince of Wales buried only one convict. The dispatches for the Government are not yet arrived, as the Borrowdale transport, by which Commodore Phillips sent them, as well as a third transport in company, have not reached England.

On the arrival of this squadron at Botany Bay, the destined spot was found not to have water sufficient for the supply of the new settlement: A council was in consequence held, and the ships weighing anchor stood away for Jackson's Bay, where Nature's gifts appeared equal to all their wishes: The verdure strong and rich, and the springs of the best water: The face of the country too possessing great variety, and well clothed with wood.

The moment Commodore Phillips had made good the landing of the Marines, and some lines of limitation were marked out, the convicts were put on shore; and the aritzans among them, with those belonging to ships, proceeded to cut down wood to form their habitations. This task continued for some time during the hours of the day, and in the evening the workmen and others returned on board the shipping, leaving only the Marines, and a detachment of the seamen, to guard the works as they advanced towards completion. The natives, when they discovered the preparations on foot, and that their visitors were likely to become stationary, appeared so dissatisfied, that several pieces of ordnance were mounted on the lines to awe them; they however kept at a distance, and though they did not provoke a fire, they declined all communion.

Of the convicts and others, from the departure of the squadron from Portsmouth, to the time the ship which brings the advice left Jackson's Bay, only 40 appear to have died; and to compensate for this loss, 42 infants were born.

Three of the convicts were induced to try their fortunes among the natives, where they hoped to have a favourable reception: two of these were in this expedition killed and eaten; and the third, after subsisting on roots for some time in the woods, returned almost perished through hunger. This operated to deter further adventure of the like nature.

The cattle fared very unpropitiously; some of the cows died during their passage; and others, after their landing, strayed so far into the woods, as to be irrecoverably lost. The sheep did not thrive; the herbage did not afford the nutriment of their native pasture, and no stock, it is feared, will ever be reared from them. The pigs were in a state of better prosperity; and most of the poultry promise to be beneficial.

When the Prince of Wales transport quitted Jackson's Bay, which was on the 15th of July last, a very fine crop of grain was presented to the eye. This occupied 12 acres of ground, all that could possibly be cultivated before the season was too far gone for a crop of greater extent.

Journey into the interior 5

First sightings of new animals, 1798

FOR THE BRITISH COLONISERS AUSTRALIA WAS FULL OF NEW PLANTS AND ANIMALS, SUCH AS THE DUCK-BILLED PLATYPUS. AS PEOPLE EXPLORED DEEPER INTO THE BUSHLANDS OCCUPIED BY THE SYDNEY REGION'S INDIGENOUS AUSTRALIANS, NEWS OF THE DISCOVERIES OF ANIMALS RETURNED REGULARLY AND SPECIMENS WERE OFTEN SOUGHT TO SEND BACK TO ENGLAND.

Misunderstandings with local Aboriginal people were common. As Cook had returned to England with some northern Queensland words for various animals, the early colonists in Sydney used these to try to communicate with the Darug and other Sydney people. However the locals thought the word *kangaroo*—in the Darug language *patagorang*—was a European word for animal.

It wasn't until several years after 1788 that Aboriginal people told the colonists that some of their missing 'kangaroos' were a few miles south-west of Sydney. When the Europeans discovered that these kangaroos were a herd of wild cattle that had escaped in 1788, they realised their error and that not all Aborginal people spoke one language.

So, too, many Sydney Aboriginal words were then used by the early colonists to describe the new plants and animals that were found in other areas of the country. *Dingo*, *koala* and *wombat*, to name just a few, are Darug words for these animals.

Europeans did not see their first koala, wombat and lyrebird until 1798. In January of that year, a party of soldiers, convicts and Governor John Hunter's servant John Price were guided south from Sydney by one of the few escaped convicts who had returned alive from living in the bush for years, John Wilson. Wilson led them across the Nepean River and into the Razorback Range to prove to the colony once and for all that there was no settlement of free-living escaped convicts in the interior. Although John Wilson had lived with the Aborigines for several years and had encountered them before, Price was the first European to record in his personal journal a sighting of the *whom-batt* (wombat), *cullawine* (koala) and the lyrebird.

John Wilson was to lead another party to the south-west—in fact to just north of present-day Goulburn, though he was never given any credit for crossing the ring of mountains around Sydney. Wilson, apparently having taken on the Aboriginal name of Bun-bo-e, returned to live in Aboriginal society until around 1800 when he was fatally speared in a reprisal for abducting an Aboriginal woman.

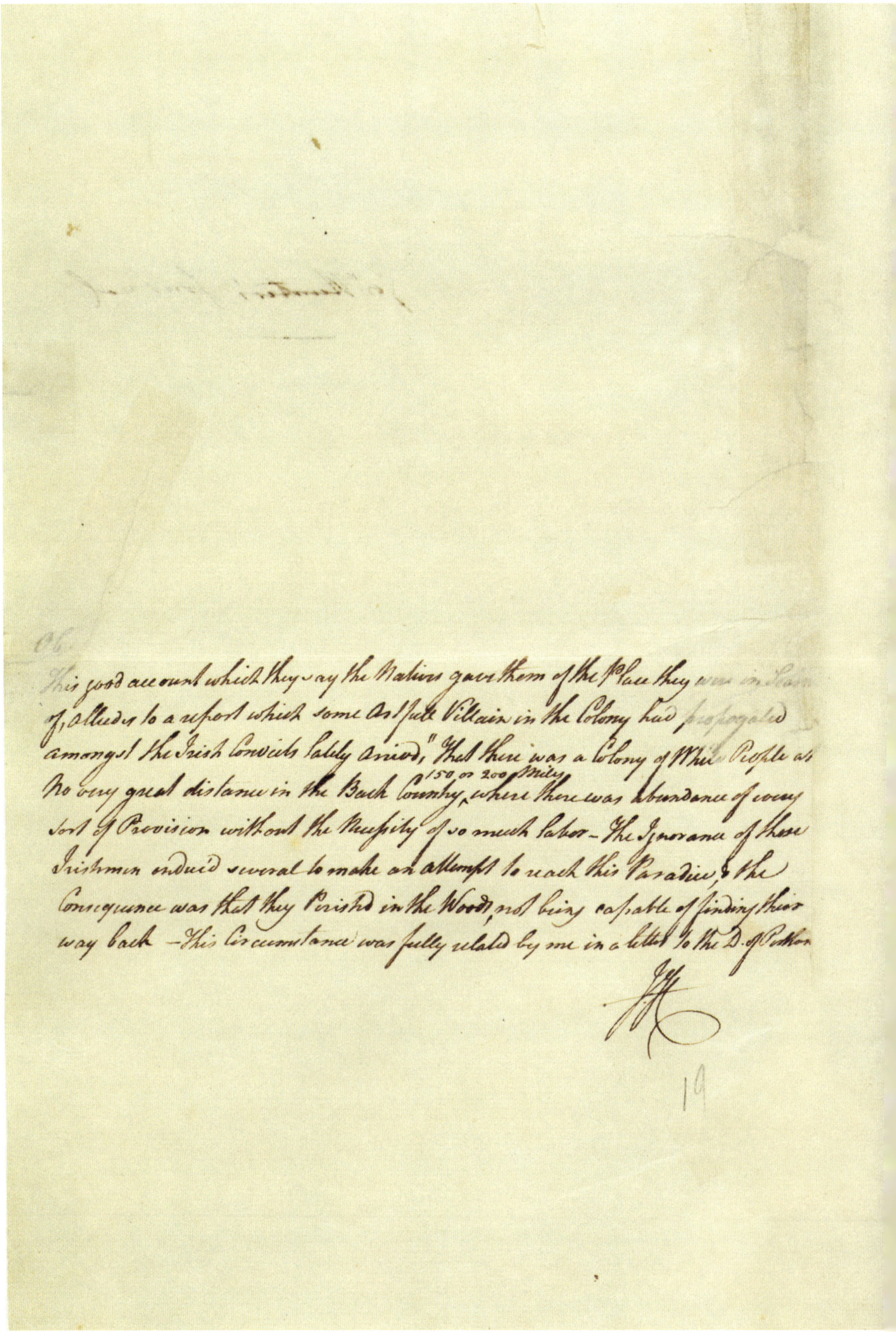
This good account which they say the Natives gave them of the Place they were in Search of, alludes to a report which some Artfull Villain in the Colony had propagated amongst the Irish Convicts lately arrived, "that there was a Colony of White People at No very great distance in the Back Country 150 or 200 Miles, where there was abundance of every sort of Provision without the Necessity of so much labor — The Ignorance of these Irishmen induced several to make an attempt to reach this Paradise, & the Consequence was that they Perished in the Woods, not being capable of finding their way back — This Circumstance was fully related by me in a letter to the D. of Portland

JH

19

This letter of 21 August 1801 from Governor John Hunter accompanied the copy of John Price's journal (opposite) that he presented to Joseph Banks, who retained a life-long interest in the colony he had had been so keen to see established.

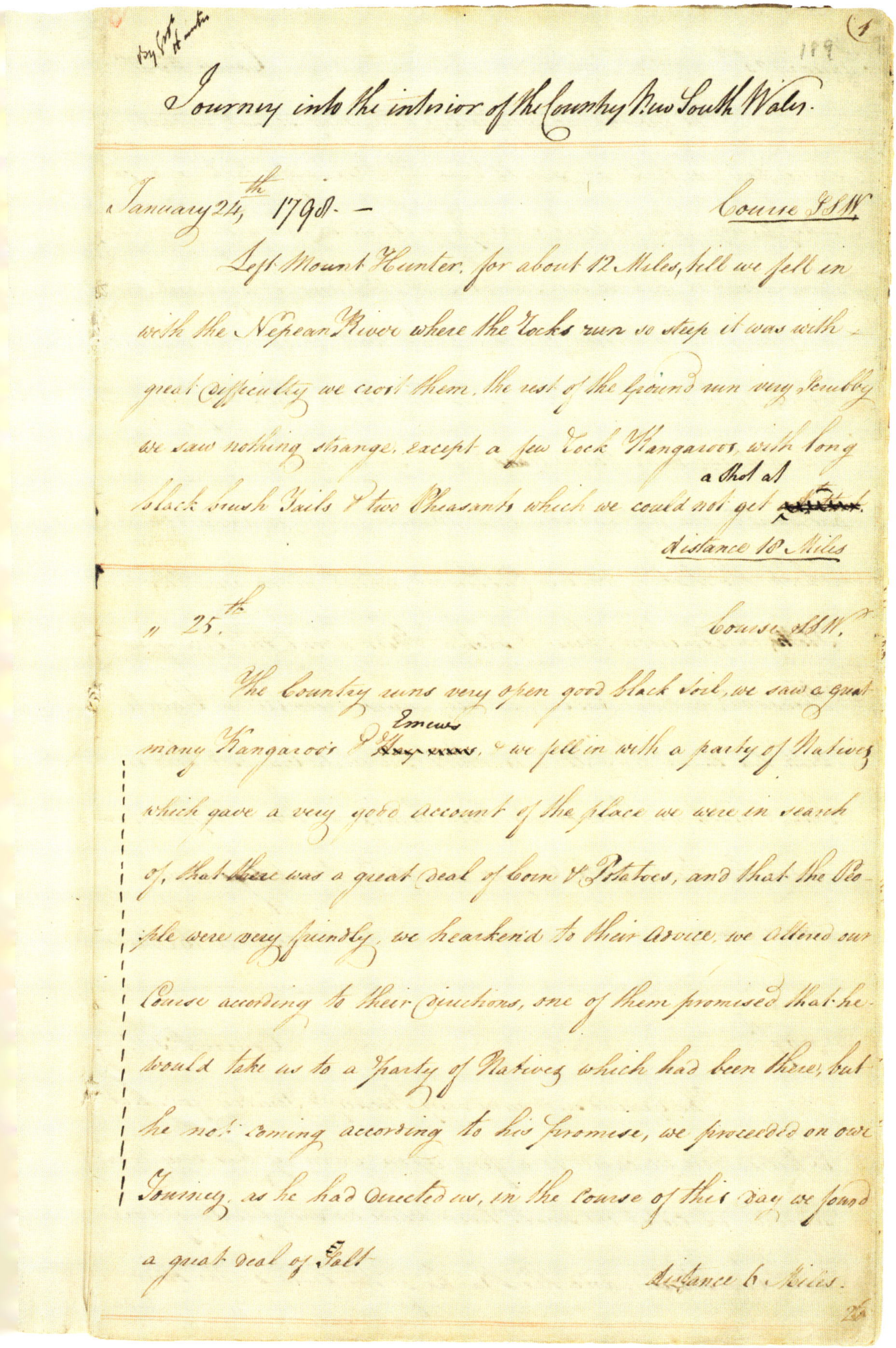
By Capt Hunter

1

179

Journey into the interior of the Country New South Wales.

January 24th 1798 — Course SSW.

Left Mount Hunter, for about 12 Miles, till we fell in with the Nepean River where the rocks run so steep it was with great difficulty we crost them, the rest of the Ground run very Scrubby we saw nothing strange, except a few rock Kangaroos, with long black bush Tails & two Pheasants which we could not get a shot at ~~[illegible]~~

distance 18 Miles

" 25th Course SSW.

The Country runs very open good black Soil, we saw a great many Kangaroo's & ~~[illegible]~~ Emews, & we fell in with a party of Natives which gave a very good account of the place we were in search of, that ~~there~~ was a great deal of Corn & Potatoes, and that the People were very friendly, we hearken'd to their Advice, we Altered our Course according to their directions, one of them promised that he would take us to a party of Natives which had been there, but he not coming according to his promise, we proceeded on our Journey, as he had directed us, in the course of this day we found a great deal of Salt

distance 6 Miles.

26

Governor John Hunter's servant John Price, who had accompanied the 1798 expedition into the interior of the continent south of Sydney, described the journey in his journal. Price recorded the first European sighting of a lyrebird, wombat and koala on 26 January—ten years after European settlement.

Letter of 21 August 1801 from Governor John Hunter

This good account which they say the Natives gave them of the Place they were in [illegible] of, alludes to a report which some Artful Villain in the Colony had propagated amongst the Irish Convicts lately arrived, "That there was a Colony of White People at no very great distance in the Back Country 150 or 200 Miles where there was abundance of every sort of Provision without the Necessity of so much labor—The Ignorance of these Irishmen induced several to make an attempt to reach this Paradise, & the Consequence was that they lived in the Woods, not being capable of finding their way back—This circumstance was fully related by me in a letter to the D. of P[illegible]

JH

By Govr Hunter Journey into the interior of the Country New South Wales.

January 24th, 1798.— Course SSW
Left Mount Hunter, for about 12 Miles, till we fell in with the Nepean River where the Rocks run so steep it was with great difficulty we crost them. The rest of the Ground run very Scrubby we saw nothing strange except a few Rock Kangaroos with long black brush Tails & two Pheasants which we could not get a shot at.

distance 18 Miles

[January] 25th, Course SSW.
The Country runs very open good black soil, we saw a great many Kangaroos & Emews & we fell in with a party of Natives, which gave a very good account of the place we were in search of, that there was a good deal of Corn & Potatoes, and that the People are very friendly, we hearken'd to their advice. we altered our Course according to their directions, one of them promised that he would take us to a party of Natives, which had been there, but he not coming according to his promise, we proceeded on our Journey, as he had directed us, in the course of this way we found a great deal of [salt ?].

distance 6 Miles.

A troublesome sort of fellow 6

Pemulwuy's guerrilla warfare, 1801

BEFORE THE FIRST NEWSPAPER WAS PRODUCED DURING 1803, GOVERNMENT AND GENERAL ORDERS—PRINTED AS HANDBILLS OR READ TO MUSTERS OF CONVICTS AND SOLDIERS—WERE IMPORTANT COMMUNICATIONS ISSUED BY EARLY COLONIAL GOVERNORS. ACTING AS THE FIRST NEWS BULLETINS, THEY INFORMED THE PEOPLE OF SYDNEY ABOUT OFFICIAL APPOINTMENTS AND NEW PUNISHMENTS. GOVERNMENT ORDERS WERE CONCERNED WITH PROHIBITING ACTIVITIES, BUT SOMETIMES OFFERED REWARDS.

Many people believe Australian history has been a relatively peaceful affair, but the frequency of government proclamations of martial law in the early colonial period is significant. Martial law was declared when there were problems with bushrangers and Irish insurgents, and because of conflicts with Australian Indigenous people across the country. In the early 1800s Governor Philip Gidley King (1758–1808) declared martial law against Sydney Aborigines.

By the mid-1790s the Bidjigal leader Pemulwuy had brought together a force of Sydney Aboriginal warriors that regularly attacked the British settlers. Although some conflicts escalated into open warfare, such as at the battles of Toongabbie and Parramatta, in 1797, this was mostly a guerilla war, where warriors raided settlers' farms and hurt the fledgling colony where it was most desperate—its food supplies.

Pemulwuy escaped capture and survived musket-ball wounds, so he was believed to be invincible. Escaped convicts also joined Pemulwuy's forces. By 1801 the number of settlers killed by Pemulwuy's forces was rising, and King had had enough of this 'troublesome sort of fellow' and his warriors. Although King knew the warriors were losing their traditional food supplies and many of the 'depredations' were in retaliation for European crimes, in May 1801 he issued his Government Order that Aboriginal people near 'Parramatta, Georges River and Prospect Hill' were to be 'driven back from the settlers' habitations by firing at them'—allowing settlers to shoot on sight any Aboriginal people who approached their farms.

In November that year he issued a proclamation offering freedom for convicts or 20 gallons of rum for free settlers for bringing in 'Pemulwoy' and two 'delinquent' convicts. Pemulwuy was eventually killed in June 1802, temporarily ending a long period of warfare in the Sydney region. Settler George Suttor recounted in his diary that 'His head was cut off, which was, I believe, sent to England.' Governor King wrote to Sir Joseph Banks that although he regarded Pemulwuy as a terrible nuisance to the colony, he was nonetheless 'a brave and independent character'.

[39]

MAY, 1ſt. A. D. 1801.

Simon Luddit is appointed Superintendant in the room of Thomas Collier, diſcharged for diſobedience of Orders, and other improper conduct.

The delivery of Certificates to thoſe whoſe terms of Tranſportation are expired, is poſtponed to the laſt Friday in June.

From the wanton manner in which a large body of Natives reſident about Parramatta, George's River, and Proſpect Hill, have attacked and killed ſome of Government ſheep, and their violent threat of murdering all the white men they meet, which they have put into execution, by murdering Daniel Conroy, ſtock keeper, in a moſt ſavage and inhuman manner, and ſeverely wounding Smith, a Settler; and as it is impoſſible to foreſee to what extent their preſent hoſtile menaces may be carried, both with reſpect to the defenceleſs Settlers and the Stock, the Governor has directed that this as well as all other bodies of Natives in the above Diſtrict, be driven back from the Settlers' habitations, by firing at them: but this Order does not extend to the Natives in any other diſtrict, nor is any Native to be moleſted in any part of the Harbour at Sydney, or on the road leading to Parramatta.

Two Convicts going in a Boat on board the American that arrived Yeſterday, in diſobedience of the General Order of the 1ſt of October laſt, forbidding any perſon whatever, to have any communication with Veſſels arriving here, until the admiſſion Flag is hoiſted, are ſentenced to Three Months impriſonment in the Goal Gang, and their Boat confiſcated.

Governor King's order of 1 May 1801 permitted settlers to fire at Pemulwuy's warriors to drive them away from settlements. In November of that year he offered a reward for Pemulwuy's death or capture. The series of various government 'standing orders' issued between 1791 to 1802 were bound and published in a book by the government printer George Howe, just before he issued the first newspaper in 1803. This, the New South Wales general standing orders: selected from the general orders issued by former governors, from the 16th of February, 1791 to the 6th of September, 1800: also, General orders issued by Governor King from the 28th of September, 1800 to the 30th of September, 1802, *was the first book published in Australia.*

GOVERNMENT AND GENERAL ORDER

May, 1st A.D. 1801.

Simon Luddit is appointed Superintendant in the room of Thomas Collier, discharged for disobedience of Orders, and other improper conduct.

The delivery of Certificates to those whose terms of Transportation are expired, is postponed to the last Friday in June.

From the wanton manner in which a large body of Natives, resident about Parramatta, George's River, and Prospect Hill, have attacked and killed some of Government sheep, and their violent threat of murdering all the white men they meet, which they put into execution, by murdering Daniel Conroy, stock keeper, in a most savage and inhuman manner, and severely wounding Smith, a Settler; and as it is impossible to foresee to what extent their present hostile menaces may be carried, both with respect of the defenceless Settlers and the Stock, the Governor has directed that this as well as all other bodies of Natives in the above District, to be driven back from the Settlers' habitations, by firing at them: but this Order does not extend to the Natives in any other district, nor is any Native to be molested in any part of the Harbour, at Sydney, or on the road leading to Parramatta.

Two Convicts going in a Boat on board the American that arrived Yesterday, in disobedience of the General Order of the 1st October last, forbidding any person whatever, to have any communication with Vessels arriving here, until the admission Flag is hoisted, are sentenced to Three Months imprisonment in the Gaol Gang, and their Boat confiscated.

Philip Gidley King.

The only known image of Pemulwuy, captioned 'Pimbloy: Native of New Holland in a canoe of that country', appeared in James Grant's account of the voyage of the Lady Nelson.

The first newspapers

1803–

–1830

By 1802 the fledgling colony of New South Wales had survived famine, floods and Aboriginal resistance around Sydney. But it still wasn't really an established European settlement. The British outpost on the far side of the Pacific showed few real signs of civilisation. European progress and prosperity in the eighteenth century was largely measured in terms of bricks and mortar, but Sydney Town was reportedly very much a picturesque, though still motley, collection of mostly wooden buildings. There were no grand sandstone buildings or great towering fortresses—none of the outward signs of civilisation that Europeans expected to see if they arrived in Sydney Harbour in 1802.

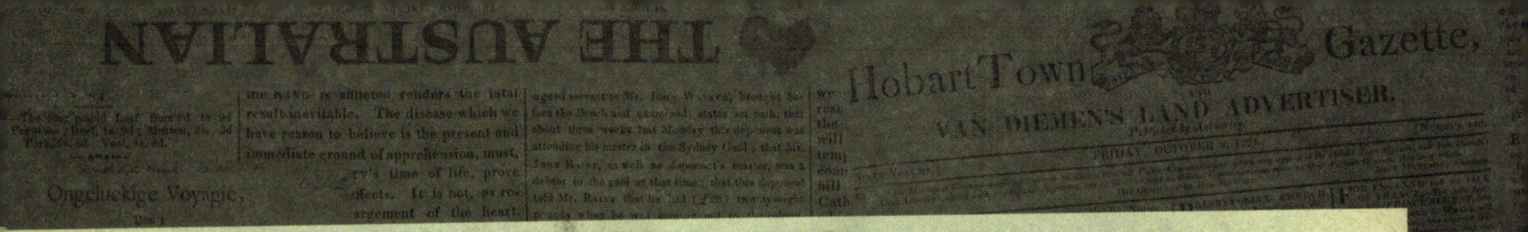

SYDNEY TOWN IN THE EARLY 1800S WAS A PLACE IN CONFLICT WITH ITSELF. IT WAS A TIME OF GOVERNMENT EFFORTS TO INCREASE CONTROL OVER ITS CONVICTS AND EX-CONVICTS, LARGELY IN FEAR OF INSURRECTION BY IRISH POLITICAL PRISONERS AND CONSTANT ESCAPE ATTEMPTS. THE PERIOD OF USING THE AUSTRALIAN BUSH AND THE PACIFIC OCEAN AS EFFECTIVE PRISON WALLS WAS COMING TO AN END. NOW EACH ARRIVAL OF NEW PRISONERS BROUGHT A LOAD OF POTENTIALLY REBELLIOUS IRISHMEN, WHO HAD OFTEN BEEN SENTENCED TO TRANSPORTATION TO THE COLONIES FOR THEIR ROLE IN THE FAILED IRISH UPRISING OF 1798.

At the same time, the authority of the colonial government was being steadily undermined by the officers of the New South Wales Corps. The Corps had been sent to the colony after 1789 to replace the Marines who had accompanied the First Fleet. Brought up in a military tradition of bounty and prize money to supplement their meagre army pay, they sought their due returns in trading monopolies and land grants. Added to this was a small but growing number of free settlers, as well as increasing numbers of ex-convicts who were starting to demand the same rights as the free settlers. These competing interests contributed to turmoil brewing below the surface in Sydney Town.

Into this heady mix of politics, business and colonial authority arrived the first newspaper to be printed in the colony. The printing press that had been sent to the colony with the First Fleet had remained idle, with no-one being able to use it, other than to make one-page handbills. That was until the arrival of convict George Howe in 1800. Howe had some experience with printing presses, and he quickly became responsible for publication of the colony's first newspaper, grandly named *The Sydney Gazette, and New South Wales Advertiser*.

The Sydney Gazette, as it became known, was a functional publication. This newspaper, first and foremost, simply provided a broader distribution of government news as well as official proclamations. It also became the place for a growing number of public notices and ads of goods for sale.

However, it was still a newspaper, as Howe ensured that general news items were included—such as the story of the convict who was reprieved from the death sentence after he survived being hanged by the neck three times. Indeed the *Gazette* quickly became an increasingly important place for

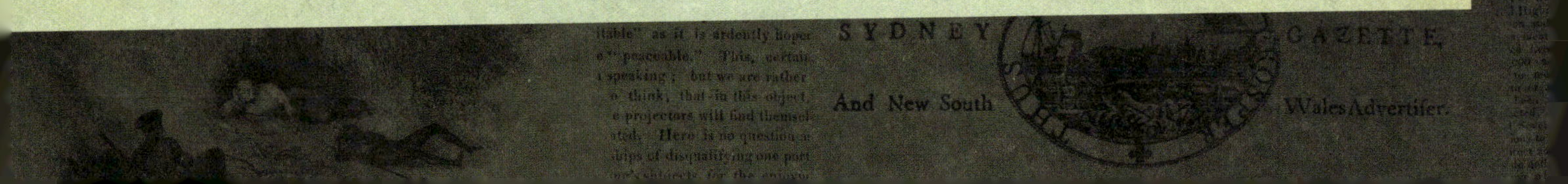

local news items. Only a year after it began, Howe had to report on the tumultuous events of an Irish-led convict rebellion in the colony.

Governor King's long-held fears of an uprising came to reality in March 1804 when around 300 convicts, led by Irish political prisoners, escaped from the government farm at Castle Hill in western Sydney. This, perhaps the most famous of all Australian convict escape attempts, culminated in the Battle of Vinegar Hill. After a night of convicts rioting and stealing weapons, the New South Wales Corps and militia troops swiftly put paid to the rebels' hopes of capturing a ship and escaping the colony.

The Sydney Gazette was still the sole newspaper in the colony at the time of another uprising against the governor in 1808. The Rum Rebellion, as it became known, occurred on 26 January, anniversary of the arrival of the First Fleet and now celebrated as Australia Day. It brought to an end the rule of the unpopular Governor William Bligh and introduced a brief period of military rule in the colony. Perhaps not surprisingly, *The Sydney Gazette* was remarkably quiet during this period, ostensibly because of a lack of paper.

The arrival of Governor Lachlan Macquarie in 1810 saw a period of relative growth and stability in New South Wales. But even with steady population growth in the colony during this period, *The Sydney Gazette* remained the sole newspaper until 1824, continuing to perform its main task of communicating essential government information.

By the 1820s, however, outlets for alternative political voices to the government were beginning to appear. The European population had grown to more than 36,000 by 1828. Nearly a quarter of these people had been born in the colony. During the 1820s the free settlers and freed convicts began to outnumber the convict population and arguments for a non–government run uncensored press increased accordingly.

The development of a free press in Australia reflects the unique circumstances of the Australian colonies. The problem of how to manage the growing demands of business, alongside calls for democracy and political freedoms in a government-run penal colony had plagued successive governors. The drive for such freedoms was generally accompanied by public criticism of the colonial government and the governor. Some governors, notably William Bligh in 1808, could not find it in themselves to appease such threats to the authority of the Crown and when confronted by dissent chose to assert their own authority. So too, in the 1820s Governor Ralph Darling was labelled a tyrant as he struggled to keep government control.

Much of the public political battle during this period became focused on the independence of the nascent Australian press. Efforts to effectively censor the press through a government licence system in fact hastened the development of a free press. The first independent newspaper, *The Australian*, was published in Sydney by William Charles Wentworth in 1824. Andrew Bent's *Hobart Town Gazette* followed soon after. Along with *The Sydney Gazette*, a choice of three colonial newspapers may not seem a wide selection, but to have any variety of political views in newspapers was a significant transformation in what was still effectively a penal colony.

During this period, an older form of news medium was used in some attempts to communicate with the Aboriginal people being dispossessed of their land with expanding settlement. A written proclamation in a newspaper would not be read by Aboriginal people outside European society, so in 1830, Tasmania's Governor Arthur used pictures, rather than words. The pictogram supposedly explained that British justice would be meted out equally to both the Aboriginal people and colonisers—all were subjects of the British Crown. During a time of particularly violent and bloody conflict in Tasmania, the colonial authorities resorted to setting up posters of the cartoon on trees in the bush. Ironically, at the same time these posters were being erected, the independent newspapers of the Tasmanian free press were calling for either the 'removal' or the 'extermination' of 'all the blacks'.

The final series of headline news events in this chapter concerns a different and at times also quite serious threat to the expansion of the early Australian colonies. The 1820s and 1830s were a dangerous time for travellers due to the ever-present threat of bushrangers. Most people went about their business armed.

In earlier times, when the colony was desperate for their labour and industry, convicts had been given relatively more freedom and more incentive to reduce their sentences and take up land grants. As the 'native born' population expanded and there was less need for 'government labour', convicts became more confined to prisons, work gangs and the use of chains and irons. Up to the 1810s convicts were free to wear their own clothes or wear government 'slops'. There was no real convict uniform. However during Governor Macquarie's reign, the first 'parti-coloured' uniforms of black and yellow wool were created so that people would be able to easily distinguish the more hardened criminals.

As this more repressive prison regime developed during the 1820s, there was a consequential rise in bushranging—and it was usually a more desperate character who took up bushranging at this time. Escape from imprisonment at such places as Port Arthur in Tasmania meant that death was often preferred to capture.

One such bushranger, who seemed to have a particularly suicidal bent, was Bold Jack Donohoe, the model of the infamous figure celebrated in 'The Wild Colonial Boy'. Donohoe held Sydney in a reign of terror from 1829 to 1830, seemingly unable to be captured and yet able to rob people with impunity. His reign of terror was short-lived, ending in a deadly gunfight with police and soldiers at Bringelly in south-western Sydney.

Bold Jack Donohue's death in 1830 marked a turning point for the colony, as policing methods were finally coming of age. Rather than relying on the often-unreliable ex-convicts issued with a cutlass and musket, a uniformed mounted police force was born—just in time for the huge expansion of European settlement during the age of squatting.

The headline news stories in this chapter show the development of newspapers from a single government gazette in the early years of the century to a competitive free press in the 1830s. They reflect the early struggles by free settlers and freed convicts to deal with politics and government in a penal colony—a legacy that was to underpin Australians' understanding of their social and political roles for many years to come.

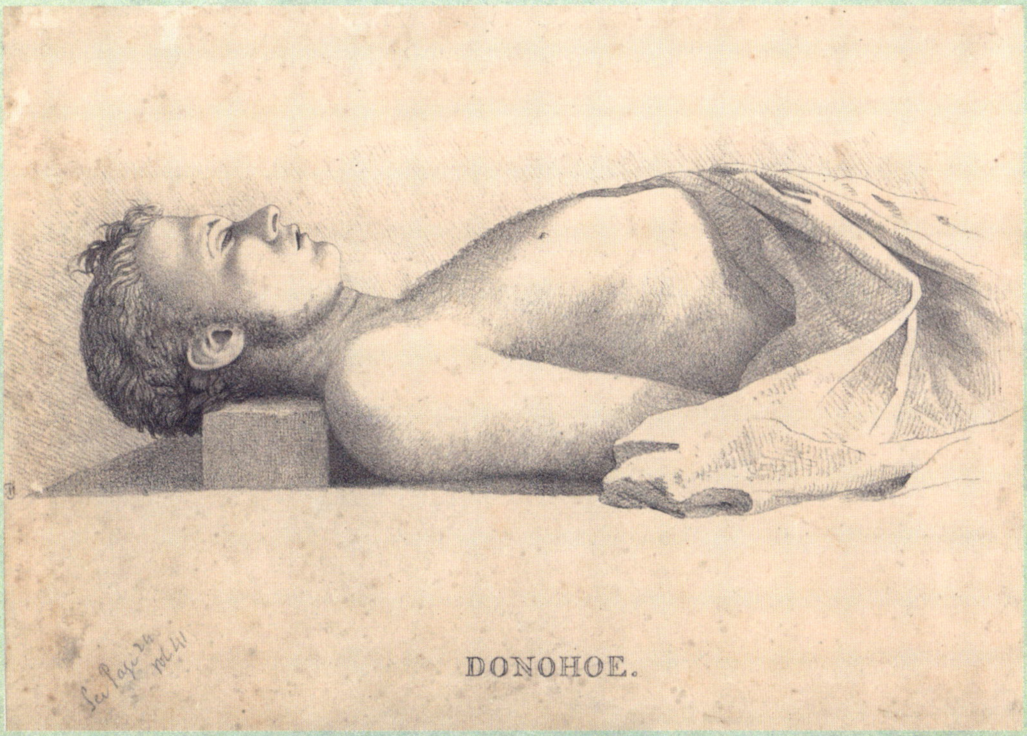

In a colony plagued with bushrangers and with a public clamouring for proof of a notorious criminal's death, published images like this one were to become a common sight in newspapers in nineteenth-century Australia. While Donohue's body lay in the morgue, Surveyor General Sir Thomas Mitchell (1792–1855) sketched a portrait of the dead bushranger, which was published as a lithograph print.

7 *Information is our only Purpose*

The first issue of *The Sydney Gazette, and New South Wales Advertiser*, 1803

GEORGE HOWE (1769–1821) WAS BORN IN THE BRITISH COLONY OF THE WEST INDIES, WHERE HIS FATHER WAS EMPLOYED BY THE GOVERNMENT PRESS. GEORGE WAS APPRENTICED TO THE PRINTING TRADE BEFORE HE MOVED TO LONDON IN THE 1790S AND WORKED AS A TYPESETTER ON *THE TIMES* NEWSPAPER.

Young George must have fallen on hard times in London, because in 1799 he was caught shoplifting and sentenced to death. His punishment was commuted to transportation to New South Wales, where his more fortunate life as an editor and then book publisher began. When he died in 1821 he left an estate of 4000 pounds, though for many years he relied on the income from other enterprises to survive.

Howe appears to have received some support from the future colonial secretary, Alexander Macleay, and shortly after Howe arrived in the colony in 1800 he was offered the position of government printer. In 1802 he issued the first book printed in Australia, *New South Wales General Standing Orders*, which compiled all the Government and General Orders issued between 1791 and 1802.

Howe was also the first editor of an Australian newspaper (and at first, reporter, typesetter, printer and deliverer). As a government employee and in a time of growing politics and factionalism in the colony, he quite understandably took an uncompromising line, writing that the *Gazette* was to 'open no channel to political discussion or personal misadversion; information is our only purpose'.

The rather plain and practical first issue of *The Sydney Gazette, and New South Wales Advertiser* belies its significance in the colony of New South Wales at the time. It was published once a week and despite being sold for the not inconsiderable sum of sixpence a copy (about one Australian dollar in today's terms) it quickly became an important form of communicating news. Howe also offered readers not just government orders and proclamations, but notices of births, deaths and marriages, shipping news, 'news from abroad', as well as major local events. The history of newspapers in Australia had begun, although headline news on the front page of the paper was still a long way off.

THE

SYDNEY GAZETTE, And New South Wales Advertiſer.

PUBLISHED BY AUTHORITY.

Vol. I. SATURDAY, MARCH 5, 1803. Number 1.

It is hereby ordered, that all Advertiſements, Orders, &c. which appear under the Official Signature of the Secretary of this Colony, or of any other Officer of Government, properly authoriſed to publiſh them in the SYDNEY GAZETTE, AND NEW SOUTH WALES ADVERTISER, are meant, and muſt be deemed to convey official and ſufficient Notifications, in the ſame Manner as if they were particularly ſpecified to any ONE Individual, or Others, to whom ſuch may have a Reference.

By Command of His Excellency the Governor and Commander in Chief, WILLIAM NEATE CHAPMAN, Secretary.

Sydney, March 5th, 1803.

General Orders.

REPEATED Complaints having been made of the great loſſes ſuſtained by the Settlers at Hawkeſbury, from the vexatious conduct of the Boatmen by whom they ſend their Grain to Sydney, the following Regulations are to be obſerved.

Every perſon ſending grain from the Hawkeſbury to Sydney in an open boat, or a boat that is not truſt-worthy, the Magiſtrates are directed to take no notice thereof.

If on proof it appears that the Maſter of a Boat receives more grain than the veſſel ought to take with ſafety, the Maſter ſhall make good any quantity he may throw overboard, or otherwiſe damage, loſe the freight of that part, and, on conviction before two Magiſtrates, forfeit 5l. to the Orphan Fund.

If it ſhall appear to the Magiſtrates that grain coming round to Sydney has been wetted, that it might weigh heavier or meaſure more than the quantity put on board, the Maſter will, on conviction, forfeit 5l. to the Orphan Fund.

The Commanding Officer of the New South Wales Corps will direct the Corporal of the Guard on board the Caſtle of Good Hope to read the General Orders that are marked off in the Extracts he is furniſhed with, to the Corporal, and the Party that relieves him; the ſaid Orders are alſo to be read to the Guard on board the Supply Hulk.

By Command of His Excellency W. N. CHAPMAN, Sec.
Government Houſe, Feb. 21, 1803.

THE Receiving Granaries at Parramatta and Hawkeſbury, being filled with Wheat which is ſpoiling, no more can be taken in at thoſe places until further Orders, except in payment for Government Debts, and the Whalers Inveſtments lodged in the Public Stores.

Wheat will continue to be received into the Stores at Sydney, until further Orders.

Wheat will be iſſued to the Civil, Military, &c. until further Orders; except to the detachments and labouring people at Caſtle-Hill, Seven-Hills, and other Out Poſts, who will receive Flour, as they have not the convenience of Mills.

By Command, &c. W. N. CHAPMAN, Sec
Government Houſe, Feb. 24, 1803.

THE GOVERNOR having permitted Mr. Robert Campbell to land 4000 Gallons of Spirits for the domeſtic uſe of the Inhabitants, from the Caſtle of Good Hope, it will be divided in the following proportion, viz.

For the Officers on the Civil Eſtabliſhment, (including Superintendants and Storekeepers), 1000 Gallons;

For Naval and Military Commiſſioned Officers, 1000 Gallons;

For the Licenſed People, 1000 Gallons;

To be diſtributed to ſuch Perſons as the GOVERNOR may think proper to grant Permits to, 1000 Gallons.

The above to include the Civil and Military Officers at Norfolk Iſland.

By Command, &c. W. N. CHAPMAN, Sec.
Government Houſe, March 4, 1803.

ADDRESS.

Innumerable as the Obſtacles were which threatened to oppoſe our Undertaking, yet we are happy to affirm that they were not inſurmountable, however difficult the taſk before us.

The utility of a PAPER in the COLONY, as it muſt open a ſource of ſolid information, will, we hope, be univerſally felt and acknowledged. We have courted the aſſiſtance of the INGENIOUS and INTELLIGENT:---We open no channel to Political Diſcuſſion, or Perſonal Animadverſion:---Information is our only Purpoſe; that accompliſhed, we ſhall conſider that we have done our duty in an exertion to merit the Approbation of the PUBLIC, and to ſecure a liberal Patronage to the SYDNEY GAZETTE.

The first issue of the first newspaper, The Sydney Gazette, and New South Wales Advertiser, *marked an important step in the process of communication for the early colony.*

Information is our only Purpose

8 The invisible hand of Providence

The man they couldn't hang, 1803

THE EARLY ISSUES OF *THE SYDNEY GAZETTE, AND NEW SOUTH WALES ADVERTISER* ARE SOMETHING OF A BRIDGE BETWEEN THE EIGHTEENTH AND NINETEENTH CENTURIES. THE FORMAL AND COMPLICATED LANGUAGE USED IN THE COLONY'S FIRST NEWSPAPER REPRESENT THE CONSERVATISM EXPECTED OF BRITISH GOVERNMENTS AT THE TIME.

In the first years of the publication of the *Gazette*, George Howe worked as a reporter of events in the colony as well as editor, and along with an assistant, completed most of the other jobs involved in producing a weekly newspaper. Howe covered many stories, usually in a very matter-of-fact manner. One of the most interesting of his reports was about a man who cheated death by hanging.

This most unusual news story also reflects the broad range of people in the colony who were not of typically 'English' origin. Convicts included 'Black Ceaser' from the West Indies, French-Canadians, French migrants escaping revolution and Irish political prisoners to name just a few.

Joseph Samuells was involved with several other convicts in stealing from the home of a Mary Breeze in Back Row (now Phillip Street) Sydney Town. Evidence given by the convicted men was contradictory, but it seems at least one of them was stopped by a Sydney constable, Joseph Luker, who was then battered to death—the first recorded murder of a police officer in the country. Samuells was found guilty, even though heavy suspicion lay upon his accomplice Simmonds.

Yet when Samuells was dropped from the back of a cart with a rope around his neck, the rope broke. The second attempt saw the rope unravel, and Samuells—nearly, but not quite, dead—gradually fell to the ground. Finally, a third rope was found, but it broke too.

This was enough for onlookers—convicts, soldiers and government officials—to suggest that God was intervening here and an urgent appeal was sent to the governor seeking a reprieve. Samuells lived, and George Howe ended his report on the matter by wishing him well, with the sentiment, 'May the grateful remembrance of these events direct his future courses.' Unfortunately, little is known of what subsequently happened to the fortunate Samuells.

EXAMINATIONS

Before the Lieutenant-Governor and Magistrates.

SATURDAY, SEPT. 24.

William Garaty, on a charge of ſtealing ſundry articles of property belonging to T. Brown, from the houſe of John Graham at Parramatta, was ordered to labour for the Crown one year.

Catharine M'Laughlane, for receiving certain articles, the property of different perſons, knowing them to have been ſtolen, was ſentenced to receive corporal puniſhment at the cart's tail.

Edward Wills, for having incautiouſly purchaſed ſeven ounces of ſilver from a perſon who ſince confeſſed the ſame to be ſtolen, was ordered to pay a fine of Five Pounds to the Orphan Fund.

MARGARET FOGGERTY petitioned that the Court would order Richard Chears, with whom ſhe had lived ſeveral years, to allow a maintainance to her child, and make a proper compenſation for a houſe that he had ſold, her propetty, without her conſent: He was ordered to provide another houſe for the complainant, of equal value, to that diſpoſed of, and to allow a ſufficient maintainance to the child.

SYDNEY.

At half paſt nine on Monday morning, the New South WALES Corps got under Arms, and proceeded to the place of execution, to which Joſeph Samuels and James Hardwicke were brought, in purſuance of the ſentence paſſed upon them on the preceeding Friday.

Both priſoners conducted themſelves with becoming decency; and when the Reverend Mr. MARSDEN had performed the duties of his function, and quitted Hardwicke, he turned to Samuels (who being a Jew, was prepared by a perſon of his own profeſſion) and queſtioning him on the ſubject of the murder of Luker, he ſolemnly declared, that during the interval of his confinement in the cell with Iſacc Simmonds, nicknamed Hikey Bull, they in the Hebrew tongue exchanged an oath, by which they bound themſelves to ſecrecy and ſilence in whatever they might then diſcloſe.

Conjured by that GOD before whom he was ſhortly to appear, not to advance any thing in his latter moments that would endanger his ſalvation, he now repeated with an air of firmneſs what he had before declared; and appearing deeply impreſt with a becoming ſenſe of his approaching end, appealed to Heaven to bear him teſtimony, that Simmonds had, under the influence of the oath by which they were reciprocally bound, acknowledged to him that Luker had accidentally ſurpriſed him with the deſk belonging to Mary Breeze; and that he, in conſequence thereof, had "knocked him down, and given him a topper for luck!" adding at the ſame time, that if he had not been kept in the dark with reſpect to the concealment of the money that had been taken out of it, that cataſtrophe never would have happened; but as it was, that he would hang 500 Chriſtians to ſave himſelf.

Simmonds, who was purpoſely brought from George's Head to witneſs the awful end of the unhappy culprit, heard what he advanced, and repeatedly endeavoured to check the declaration, which was delivered with mildneſs and compoſure, and which, as it appeared wholly untinctured with acrimony, gained credit among the ſpectators, in whoſe breaſts a ſentiment of abhorrence was univerſally awakened.

Odium and ſuſpicion were attached to Simmonds from the very day on which the dreadful crime was perpetrated, and every eye was fixed in doubt upon his countenance when he aſſiduouſly aſſiſted to lower the mangled corpſe into the grave: Although from the want of that full and ſufficient evidence which the Law requires he had eſcaped Condemnation, yet he had been arraigned at the arbitrary tribunal of Public Opinion, and moſt of the ſpectators had pronounced judgement againſt him in their hearts. It is not to be wondered then that a teſtimony like the preſent, proceeding from the lips of a dying man, whoſe only probable concern it was to eaſe his burthened conſcience in the hour of death, ſhould at once remove all doubt, if ſuch remained, and the feelings of the multitude burſt forth into invective.

At about ten the Criminals reaſcended the cart; and when about to be launched into eternity, a Reprieve for James Hardwicke was received and announced by the Provoſt Marſhal.

Samuels devoted the laſt awful minute allowed him to the moſt earneſt and fervent prayer; at length the ſignal was given, and the cart drove from under him; but by the concuſſion the ſuſpending cord was ſeparated about the center, and the culprit fell to the ground, on which he remained motionleſs, with his face downwards. The cart returned, and the criminal was ſupported on each ſide until another rope was applied in lieu of the former: he was again launched off, but the line unrove, and continued to ſlip until the legs of the ſufferer trailed along the ground, the body being only half ſuſpended. All that beheld were moved at his protracted ſufferings; nor did ſome heſitate to declare, that the inviſible hand of Providence was at work in the behalf of him who had revealed the circumſtances above related. To every appearance lifeleſs, the body was now raiſed, and ſupported on men's ſhoulders, while the executioner prepared anew the work of death. The body was gently lowered, but when left alone, again fell proſtrate to the earth, this rope having alſo ſnapped ſhort, cloſe to the neck.

Compaſſion could no longer bear reſtraint; winged with humanity, the Provoſt Marſhal ſped to HIS EXCELLENCY'S preſence, in which the ſucceſs of his miſſion overcame him; A Reprieve was announced---and if Mercy be a fault, it is the deareſt attribute of GOD, and ſurely in Heaven it may find extenuation!

Samuells, when the Provoſt Marſhal arrived with the tidings which diffuſed gladneſs throughout every heart, was incapable of participating in the general ſatisfaction. By what he had endured his reaſonable faculties were totally impaired; and when his nerves recovered ſomewhat from their feebleneſs, he uttered many incoherences, and was alone ignorant of what had paſt. Surgical aſſiſtance has ſince reſtored him; AND MAY THE GRATEFUL REMEMBRANCE OF THESE EVENTS DIRECT HIS FUTURE COURSES!

One of the ropes which ſever'd at the place of execution on Monday underwent an experiment the ſame day, from which it would appear that it had critically been defective in that particular part alone in which it failed. One of the ends being faſtened to a beam, ſeven weights were ſupported by it, each weighing 56lbs; one of the ſtrands was cut acroſs, and afterwards a ſecond; but the ſingle ſtrand that remained was found ſufficient to ſupport the whole weight depending on it.

The CATO'S large boat, purchaſed by Mr. Lord for the ſum of 60l. has undergone a conſiderable alteration. She has been raiſed upon upwards of four feet, and will be decked and ſloop rigged: her burthen is eſtimated to be from 35 to 40 tons; and in point of appearance promiſes to rank with the foremoſt of her ſize.

A Kangaroo of a ſpecies perfectly diſtinct from any hitherto taken was lately killed by Richard Palmer of the Brickfields, about a diſtance of 30 miles North of Richmond Hill. The animal, which the natives declared to be a very young one, weighed upwards of 80lbs. the Fore quarters differing little from the hind, but both are very different from thoſe of any other ſpecies. The fleſh he reports to be much finer than that of others, the ſkin differing in colour, being nearly black. Some of theſe NEW-DISCOVERED creatures, if his account be accurate, may without exaggeration be eſtimated to weigh upwards of 200lbs.

Another of the Natives died on Saturday the 24th inſtant, in conſequence of two wounds in the body from jagged ſpears, which he received in a puniſhment, as being related to the man by whoſe hand one of another family was accidentally ſlain; nor is this rancour to ſubſide but with the extirpation of all the relatives of the aggreſſor, to whom the other was but a diſtant kinſman. Ten ſpears were thrown at him, five at a time, one of which at each flight pierced his body. Mr. Jamiſon rendered every ſurgical aſſiſtance the poor creature was capable of receiving, but he expired ſhortly after they were extracted. By an unconquerable attachment to theſe barbarous uſages, and an utter diſlike to civilized cuſtoms, this ſavage race of men are principally intent on the work of depopulation, which has not, ſince the fate of Pemulwoy, extended beyond their own wild haunts.

The Sydney Gazette, and New South Wales Advertiser of 25 August 1803 recorded on page 2 the remarkable story of the man saved from the gallows.

Sydney

...

Samuells devoted the last awful minute allowed him to the most earnest and fervent prayer; at length the signal was given, and the cart drove from under him; but by the concussion the suspending cord was separated about the center, and the culprit fell to the ground, on which he remained motionless, with his face downwards. The cart returned, and the criminal was supported on each side until another rope was applied in lieu of the former: he was again launched off, but the line unrove, and continued to flip until the legs of the sufferer trailed along the ground, the body being only half suspended. All that beheld were also moved at his protracted sufferings; nor did some hesitate to declare, that the invisible hand of Providence was at work in the behalf of him who had revealed the circumstances above related. To every appearance lifeless, the body was now raised, and supported on men's shoulders, while the executioner prepared anew the work of death. The body was gently lowered, but when left alone, again fell prostrate to the earth, this rope having also snapped short, close to the neck.

Compassion could no longer bear restraint; winged with humanity, the Provost Marshalled to His EXCELLENCY'S preference, in which the success of his mission overcame him; A Reprieve was unannounced—and if Mercy be a fault, it is the dearest attribute of GOD, and surely in Heaven it may find extenuation!

Samuells, when the Provost Marshal arrived with the tidings which diffused gladness throughout every heart, was incapable of participating in the general satisfaction. By what he had endured his reasonable faculties were totally impaired; and when his nerves recovered some what from their feebleness, he uttered many incoherences, and was alone ignorant of what had past. Surgical assistance has since restored him; And MAY THE GRATEFUL REMEMBRANCE OF THESE EVENTS DIRECT HIS FUTURE COURSES.

One of the ropes which severe'd at the place of execution on Monday underwent an experiment the same day, from which it would appear that it had critically been defective in that particular part alone in which it failed. One of the ends being fastened to a beam, seven weights were supported by it, each weighing 56lbs; one of the strands was cut across, and afterwards a second; but the single strand that remained was found sufficient to support the whole weight depending on it.

Lay down your arms! 9

The Battle of Vinegar Hill, 1804

THE COLONIAL GOVERNMENT WAS CONCERNED ABOUT THE NUMBER OF CONVICTS ATTEMPTING TO ESCAPE TO SUPPOSED COLONIES OF FREE EUROPEANS IN THE INTERIOR, OR TRYING TO WALK OVERLAND TO CHINA. BUT IT WAS THE NUMBER OF IRISH POLITICAL REBELS BEING SENT TO THE COLONY AND THE POSSIBILITY OF AN IRISH UPRISING THAT BECAME TRULY WORRYING. BY 1800 A QUARTER OF THE CONVICT POPULATION WAS IRISH.

On the night of Sunday, 4 March 1804 about 300 Irish prisoners, many of whom had been transported to New South Wales after the failed 1798 Irish uprising against the British, at the Castle Hill government farm led a mass breakout.

The convicts destroyed their barracks, took up arms, began raiding the surrounding countryside, and collected more weapons from outlying farms. They turned back from marching on Parramatta when a pre-arranged signal of another uprising there failed to materialise, and headed along what is now the Old Windsor Road. Soldiers of the New South Wales Corps, under Major George Johnston (1764–1823), caught up with them the next day, near Rouse Hill in western Sydney.

After a short engagement, twenty-five soldiers and around fifty militia under Johnston and Quartermaster Thomas Laycock (1756–1809) routed the convict mob. Twenty convicts were killed; many more were wounded; and the rest were pursued and recaptured. Governor Philip Gidley King's (1758–1808) retribution was swift. Of the two main rebel leaders, William Johnson and Phillip Cunningham, Cunningham was summarily hanged straight after the battle at nearby Windsor. Before the end of March 1804, another seven accused ringleaders had been executed. William Johnson's body was left hanging in chains for several years beside the Parramatta Road as a hideous warning. Most of the rebels were sent back to their places of work. Another seven ringleaders received two hundred or five hundred lashes and, with twenty others, were exiled to the new coal-mining colony at Coal River (now Newcastle).

It is not clear whether the breakout was designed to overthrow the colony, or to capture ships and sail back to Ireland. If the convict rebels had defeated the soldiers and militia at Vinegar Hill, a widespread convict uprising may well have ensued.

The Sydney Gazette of 11 March 1804 published the government orders congratulating the military forces, as well as Governor Philip King's proclamation of martial law in the 'Rebellious districts' of western Sydney. However, few details of the uprising and battle were published.

Now Rebel Dog
oh Innes
We are all ruin'd

This depiction of the Battle of Vinegar Hill is an intricate hand-painted miniature by an unknown artist. It was probably commissioned by the officers of the New South Wales Corps for the commander at the time, Colonel Paterson (1755–1810). The specific detail suggests it is an accurate portrayal by an artist who was intimate with the events and participants. It includes several different moments of the battle in the one image in a style reminiscent of eighteenth-century British political cartoons.

10 The Rum Rebellion

Australia's military junta, 1808

ON 26 JANUARY 1808—TWENTY YEARS TO THE DAY SINCE ARTHUR PHILLIP AND THE OFFICERS OF THE FIRST FLEET HAD RAISED A FLAG TO MARK THE FOUNDING OF NEW SOUTH WALES—A MILITARY COUP STUNNED THE COLONY. MAJOR GEORGE JOHNSTON SENT HIS SOLDIERS INTO GOVERNMENT HOUSE TO ARREST GOVERNOR WILLIAM BLIGH (1754–1817).

Bligh was found hiding from the soldiers in a small room in Government House, but whether he was hiding under a bed, as shown in this painting has been debated. The first printed version of news of the governor's arrest presented him as cowardly—an effective propaganda coup, as Bligh was well known not to be a coward.

Bligh was determined to stamp the governor's authority on a system of trade, labour distribution and land grants that was largely controlled by the officers and ex-officers of the entrenched military garrison, the New South Wales Corps. A small number of entrepreneurs, headed by the vocal government critic John Macarthur (1767–1834), believed the colonial government restricted private enterprise. Whenever Bligh asserted colonial law in a series of ostensibly trivial cases, his opponents argued he was restricting liberty and ruling the colony like a tyrant.

This tense situation gave Major Johnston, acting commander of the Sydney troops, the excuse to claim that the military had to remove the governor to ensure that there would not be a popular 'insurrection and massacre'. But this was never really likely, as most people were apathetic, or convicts or freed convicts who in fact supported Bligh's efforts to rein in the colony's elite. With Bligh under arrest, Johnston was installed as lieutenant governor.

After the rebellion, the mutineers had a deal of work to do in convincing people that Bligh was a tyrant and that military rule was for the good of the colony—however illegal it was. Part of this work began the very night of the rebellion. With no press to call on, some of the mutineers managed to have a picture of Governor Bligh's arrest drawn up, and then put on 'illuminated display' for public view at the house of one of the few more fervent anti-Bligh men who were not commissioned officers, Sergeant Major Thomas Whittle. *The Sydney Gazette, and New South Wales Advertiser*, which had not been published since August 1807, did not reappear in print until 15 May 1808.

Later historians came up with the name of the Rum Rebellion because of the widespread use at this time of rum as a form of currency in the cash-strapped fledgling economy, but the conflict was really about a clash between colonial authority and private enterprise.

Publication of The Sydney Gazette, and New South Wales Advertiser *had been suspended for months, so for some time in 1808 the colony was once more dependent on word of mouth for communication of news and events. The creation of this cartoon of Bligh's arrest allowed the military to present Governor Bligh as cowardly.*

II *Tillage and Pasture lands*

Across the Blue Mountains with Surveyor George William Evans, 1814

IT SEEMS STRANGE THAT THE BRITISH IN SYDNEY COULD NOT FIND A WAY ACROSS THE BLUE MOUNTAINS FOR THE FIRST TWENTY-FIVE YEARS OF SETTLEMENT. EUROPEANS HAD FOLLOWED ABORIGINAL PATHWAYS ACROSS THE CUMBERLAND PLAINS—MARKED TODAY BY ROUTES SUCH AS PARRAMATTTA ROAD, COWPASTURES ROAD AND BOTANY ROAD—BUT THEY FAILED TO FOLLOW DARUG AND GANDANGARA PATHWAYS ACROSS THE MOUNTAINS.

Some Europeans, such as the ex-convict and bushman John Wilson, who had guided the 1798 party of exploration ordered by Governor John Hunter through the southern mountains and had lived with Aboriginal people, had indeed travelled beyond the ranges of hills and mountains that surrounded Sydney. So too Aboriginal people had told the colonists that it could be done. However, it required the official testimony of gentlemen such as William Charles Wentworth (1790–1872), Gregory Blaxland (1778–1853) and William Lawson (1774–1850) for absolute proof that there was a way across the mountains.

Not long after these three explorers returned to Sydney in June 1813, with confirmation of plains and grasslands in the distant west, Governor Lachlan Macquarie (1762–1824) eagerly promoted a survey of the area. The lack of food in the colony, resulting from drought in 1812, was one reason for Macquarie to order the survey and settling of these plains so crops and stock could be raised for the small but growing colony.

The crossing of the mountains by Blaxland, Wentworth and Lawson was not extensively reported in *The Sydney Gazette, and New South Wales Advertiser*. They had turned back after viewing the edge of the mountains in the distance and didn't have much news of the land beyond. It was surveyor George William Evans' (1780–1852) journal of his expedition to the area of present-day Bathurst that made a good story. Evans described the soil and even the large and plentiful fish to be had in the rivers west of the mountains.

Evans' journey was followed by the construction of the convict-built road across the mountains in 1815, under the supervision of the Hawkesbury Magistrate and landowner William Cox (1764–1837). The road opened the Bathurst Plains to settlers who found Evans's early exploration and depiction of the 'Pasture lands' to be true, and began to move well beyond the official 'limits of settlement'.

OPPOSITE Surveyor Evans' grand description of the Bathurst Plains was important news in 1814 and deemed worthy of a special government notice summarising his journey, and publication on page 1 of The Sydney Gazette, and New South Wales Advertiser.

The Sydney Gazette, and NEW SOUTH WALES ADVERTISER:

PUBLISHED BY AUTHORITY.

VOLUME THE TWELFTH.] SATURDAY, FEBRUARY 12, 1814. [NUMBER 529.

HIS EXCELLENCY the GOVERNOR and COMMANDER in CHIEF has thought proper to direct, that all Public Communications which may appear in the SYDNEY GAZETTE, and NEW SOUTH WALES ADVERTISER, signed with any Official Signature, are to be considered as Official Communications made to those Persons to whom they may relate.

BY COMMAND OF HIS EXCELLENCY, JOHN THOMAS CAMPBELL, *Secretary.*

GENERAL AFTER ORDERS.

Head Quarters, Sydney, Friday, 11th February, 1814.

LIEUTENANT COLONEL GEORGE MOLLE, commanding His Majesty's 46th Regiment, having arrived in the Harbour this Afternoon from England, on board the Ship Windham Transport, and being appointed LIEUTENANT GOVERNOR of this Territory, he is to be saluted with thirteen Guns from Dawes's Battery, on his Landing at Sydney.

Lieutenant Governor MOLLE is to be received by all Guards and Sentinels in this Territory with the usual Compliments due to his Rank, namely, those of a Brigadier General.

By Command of His Excellency
The Governor, and Commander of the Forces,
H. C. ANTILL, *Major of Brigade.*

GOVERNMENT AND GENERAL ORDERS.

Head Quarters, Sydney, Saturday, 12th February, 1814.

THE Right Honorable Earl BATHURST, HIS MAJESTY'S Principal Secretary of State for the Colonies, having signified to HIS EXCELLENCY the GOVERNOR, in his last Dispatch, that he had appointed JOHN PIPER, Esq. to be Naval Officer and Collector of the Duties at Port Jackson; and Mr. PIPER having recently arrived in the Colony on board the Ship General Hewett, he is directed to assume the Duties of his Office on Wednesday, the 16th Instant, when Captain GLENHOLME, the present Acting Naval Officer, will be pleased to deliver over Charge of the Office to his Successor.

On this Occasion the GOVERNOR requests *Captain* Glenholme will accept of his best thanks for his zealous, active, and faithful Discharge of his Duty as Acting Naval Officer, for nearly four Years he has now held this Appointment.

By Command of His Excellency
The Governor,
J. T. CAMPBELL, *Secretary.*

GOVERNMENT ORDER.

Government House, Sydney, 12th FEBRUARY, 1814.

IT having been long deemed an Object of great Importance by HIS EXCELLENCY the GOVERNOR to ascertain what Resources this Colony might possess in the Interior, beyond its present known and circumscribed Limits, with a View to meet the necessary Demands of its rapidly encreasing Population; and the great Importance of the Discovery of new Tracts of good Soil being much enhanced by the Consideration of the long continued Droughts of the present Season, so injurious in their Effects to every Class of the Community in the Colony, HIS EXCELLENCY was pleased some Time since to equip a Party of Men, under the Direction of Mr. GEORGE WILLIAM EVANS, one of the Assistant Land Surveyors (in whose Zeal and Abilities for such an Undertaking he had well founded Reason to confide), and to furnish him with written Instructions for his Guidance in endeavouring to discover a Passage over the Blue Mountains, and ascertaining the Quality and general Properties of the Soil he should meet with to the Westward of them.

This Object having been happily effected, and Mr. Evans returned with his entire Party all in good Health, the GOVERNOR is pleased to direct, that the following Summary of his Tour of Discovery, extracted from his own Journal, shall be published for general Information.

Mr. Evans, attended by five Men, selected for their general Knowledge of the Country, and habituated to such Difficulties as might be expected to occur, was supplied with Horses, Arms, and Ammunition, and a plentiful Store of Provisions for a two Months Tour. His instructions were, that he should commence the Ascent of the Blue Mountains, from the Extremity of the present known Country at Emu Island, distant about thirty-six Miles from Sydney, and thence proceed in as nearly a west direction as the nature of the Country he had to explore would admit, and to continue his Journey as far as his Means would enable him.

On Saturday, the 20th of November last, the Party proceeded from Emu Island, and on the 5th Day, having then effected their Passage over the Mountains, arrived at the Commencement of a Valley on the western Side of them, having passed over several Tracts of tolerably good Soil, but also over much rugged and very difficult Mountain; proceeding through this Valley, which Mr. Evans describes as beautiful and fertile, with a rapid Stream running through it, he arrived at the Termination of the Tour lately made by Messrs. G. Blaxland, W. C. Wentworth, and Lieutenant Lawson. Continuing in the western Direction prescribed in his Instructions for the Course of 21 Days from this Station, Mr. Evans then found it necessary to return, and on the 8th of January he arrived back at Emu Island, after an Excursion of seven complete Weeks. During the Course of this Tour, Mr. Evans passed over several Plains of great Extent, interspersed with Hills and Vallies abounding in the richest Soil, and with various Streams of Water and Chains of Ponds. The Country he traversed measured 98½ Miles beyond the Termination of Messrs. Blaxland, Wentworth, and Lawson's Tour, and not less than 150 from Emu Island. The greater Part of these Plains are described as being nearly free of Timber and Brush wood, and in Capacity equal (in Mr. Evans's Opinion) to every Demand which this Colony may have for an Extension of Tillage and Pasture Lands for a Century to come. The Stream already mentioned continues its Course in a westerly Direction, and for several Miles passing through the Vallies, with many and great Accessions of other Streams, becomes a capacious and beautiful River, abounding in Fish of very large Size and fine Flavour, many of which weighed not less than 15lbs. This River is supposed to empty itself into the Ocean on the western Side of New South Wales, at a Distance of from 2 to 300 Miles from the Termination of the Tour.—From the Summits of some very high Hills, Mr. Evans saw a vast Extent of flat Country laying in a westerly Direction, which appeared to be bounded at a Distance of about 40 Miles by other Hills. The general Description of these heretofore unexplored Regions, given by Mr. Evans, is, that they very far surpass in Beauty and Fertility of Soil any he has seen in New South Wales or Van Diemen's Land.

In Consideration of the Importance of these Discoveries, and calculating upon the Effect they may have on the future Prosperity of this Colony, HIS EXCELLENCY the GOVERNOR is pleased to announce his Intention of presenting Mr. Evans with a Grant of 1000 Acres of Land in Van Diemen's Land, where he is to be stationed as Deputy Surveyor; and further, to make him a pecuniary Reward from the Colonial Funds, in Acknowledgment of his diligent and active Services on this Occasion.

HIS EXCELLENCY also means to make a pecuniary Reward to the two Free Men who accompanied Mr. Evans, and a Grant of Land to each of them. To the three Convicts who also assisted in this Excursion, the GOVERNOR means to grant Conditional Pardons, and a small Portion of Land to each of them, these Men having performed the Services required of them entirely to the Satisfaction of Mr. Evans.

The GOVERNOR is happy to embrace this Opportunity of conveying His Acknowledgments to Gregory Blaxland and William Charles Wentworth, Esquires, and Lieutenant William Lawson, of the Royal Veteran Company, for their enterprizing and arduous Exertions on the Tour of Discovery which they voluntarily performed in the Month of May last, when they effected a Passage over the Blue Mountains, and proceeded to the Extremity of the first Valley particularly alluded to in Mr. Evans's Tour, and being the first Europeans who had accomplished the Passage over the Blue Mountains. The GOVERNOR, desirous to confer on these Gentlemen substantial Marks of his Sense of their meritorious Exertions on this Occasion, means to present each of them with a Grant of 1000 Acres of Land in this newly discovered Country.

By Command of His Excellency
The Governor,
J. T. CAMPBELL, *Secretary.*

GOVERNMENT PUBLIC NOTICE.

Secretary's Office, Sydney, 5th February, 1814.

HIS EXCELLENCY the GOVERNOR having found that very considerable Inconvenience and Difficulty are likely to arise (especially to Foreign Merchants resorting to this Colony), from the enforcing that Part of the Proclamation issued on the 1st of July, 1813, which prescribes the Term of Consolidation of the Government Colonial Silver Specie since issued, to the Period of Two Years from the Date of said Issue; and being anxious to remove all Difficulties in the Way of fair open Commerce, is hereby pleased to order and direct, that this Part of the said Proclamation shall be, and it is hereby from the present Date cancelled and rescinded.—Foreign Merchants and all other Persons are therefore to take Notice, that the Deputy Commissary General has received His Excellency's Instructions to consolidate Quarterly, by Bills on the Lords Commissioners of His Majesty's Treasury, all Sums of the said Government Colonial Silver Specie, not under the Amount of One Hundred Pounds Sterling, which shall be presented to him for that Purpose.—The Periods of Consolidation will be publicly notified in the Sydney Gazette, by the Deputy Commissary General.

By Command of His Excellency
The Governor,
J. T. CAMPBELL, *Secretary.*

GOVERNMENT AND GENERAL ORDERS.

Secretary's Office, Sydney, Saturday, 5th February, 1814.

THE GOVERNOR has observed, with great Regret, the Reluctance of the Settlers in general throughout this Colony, in coming forward to supply His Majesty's Stores with Grain in the present alarming Season of Scarcity, and that instead of manifesting a due Sense of Gratitude for the repeated Favors and Indulgencies they have received from Government, they seem determined to take every Advantage of its Necessities, by withholding their Tenders to as late a Period as possible, to give them an Opportunity of exacting a most exorbitant Price for their Grain, knowing that it must be submitted to from the Necessities of the Times.

The Conduct of those Persons who stand considerably indebted to the Crown for Cattle issued to them from the Government Herds, as well as for various Articles which have been furnished them on Credit from the King's Stores, is still more inexcusable and reprehensible, in their not coming forward with their Grain at such a Crisis.—Such Persons can no longer expect any Lenity or Forbearance; and the GOVERNOR will accordingly direct, that they shall be sued for their respective Debts at the next Court of Civil Jurisdiction.—Settlers of a different Description, and especially those who are in opulent Circumstances, principally owing to the Assistance they have derived from the Bounty of Government in originally granting them Lands, Stock, Provisions, and Government Men to cultivate their Grounds, ought to have been the first to come forward at such a Season to supply Government with such Grain as they could conveniently spare at a reasonable and moderate Price.—The GOVERNOR, however, laments to find he has been disappointed in almost every Instance, and therefore conceives it a Duty he owes to the Crown, and to the Trust reposed in him by His Majesty, to signify to the Settlers of this Colony in this public Manner, that unless he shall find in their future Conduct more promptitude in coming forward to supply His Majesty's Stores with Grain, on reasonable Terms, and discharging the Debts they have incurred to the Crown, he shall be under the painful Necessity of resorting and entirely trusting to Foreign Markets for supplying the King's Stores with Wheat, and such other Grain as may be required; which it may not be amiss to remind them can be done at half the Price now paid for that purchased in this Colony. The GOVERNOR, however, will very reluctantly resort to this expedient, and only in the Event of the Settlers manifesting the same Disposition at the ensuing Harvest they have shewn on the present Occasion. The GOVERNOR therefore trusts this Communication of his Sentiments will have its due Effect on their Minds, and that they will see the Necessity of observing a more fair and becoming Line of Conduct in future. He also strongly recommends to the lower Class of Settlers to adopt Habits of Industry, and sedulous Attention to the Cultivation of their Farms, so as to provide a sufficient Quantity of Grain, not only for the Consumption of their own Families, but to enable them to supply the Government with this Article at a reasonable Rate.

Whilst the GOVERNOR has thus had Occasion to animadvert on the Reluctance of the Settlers in general to furnish their Grain to Government, he is desirous thus publicly to make his Acknowledgments to one individual Settler; namely, Thomas Gilberthorpe, in the District of Pitt Town.—This Person was the first to come forward in the present Season of Scarcity with the lowest and most reasonable Tender to supply Government with all the Wheat and Maize he could spare, and was the only Settler in the Colony who last Year delivered into the Store the complete Quantity he had tendered at the stipulated Rate, although Grain had advanced in Price considerably after he had sent in his original Tender.—Such an Instance of fair and upright Conduct is entitled to the GOVERNOR's present Commendation and Acknowledgment, with an Assurance that his meritorious Conduct on both the Occasions alluded to shall not pass unrewarded.

The GOVERNOR directs the foregoing General Order to be read on Sunday the 13th, and Sunday the 20th Instant, by the Chaplains in the several Churches of the Colony.

By Command of His Excellency
The Governor,
J. T. CAMPBELL, *Secretary.*

DEPUTY COMMISSARY GENERAL'S OFFICE,
SYDNEY, 22d JANUARY, 1814.

DEPUTY COMMISSARY GENERAL ALLAN hereby gives Notice, that he is ready to receive Tenders, and treat for the Supply of His Majesty's Stores with Wheat and Maize.

Such Persons as may be desirous of supplying any Quantities, are requested to send in sealed Tenders to this Office, specifying the Quantity and Price (in Words at Length) at which they will supply the same.

The Period for receiving these Tenders is extended to the 10th of February next, in lieu of the Day last advertised for laying the same before HIS EXCELLENCY the GOVERNOR; and Notice will be given thereafter to such Persons whose Tenders may be accepted.

By Command of His Excellency
The Governor and Commander in Chief,
D. ALLAN, *Deputy Commissary General.*

NOTICE.—A General Meeting of the Magistrates of this Territory will be holden at the Judge Advocate's Office, Sydney, on Wednesday, the 16th Day of February Instant, at Eleven o'Clock in the Forenoon, for the Purpose of taking into Consideration the present Deficiency of Wheat and other Grain, and also such Measures as may be most applicable to the State of the Colony in this respect. ELLIS BENT, *Judge Advocate.*

PUBLIC NOTICE.

THE under-mentioned Prisoners having absented themselves from their respective Employments, all Constables and others are hereby strictly required to use their utmost Exertions in apprehending, and lodging them in safe Custody.

William Skinner Dodge, from the Dock Yard.
James Leach, from the Town Gang.
Stephen Waters, Servant to Mr. R. Lowe.
William Barnes, from the Carpenter's Gang.
James Groom, from the Carpenter's Gang.
Nicholas Kearns John Mahon, and *Luke Calverwell*, from the Boat's Crew.
John Brennan, Bullock Driver.
Robert Smith, from the Gaol Gang.
John Frances, from Sydney.
Patrick Bayland, Captain Glenholme's Servant;
Patrick Fitzsimmonds, from the Bricklayers' Gang;
John Reardon, *Isaac Nowland*, *John Armstrong*, and *Robert Simpson*, from the Stone Mason's Gang.
John Neale, Servant to James Mann, Portland Head;
Robert Dawson, Servant to Mr. Mathew.
Thomas Gilham, Servant to Mr. Bradey, Pitt Town.
Redmond Castillo, ditto to Mr. Purcell;
Edward M'Hugh, from Lane Cove;
James Cummings, Servant to Mr Fitz.
From the Factory at Parramatta:—*Sarah Longhurst*, *Sarah Coates*, *Ann Alar*, *Mary Irwin*, and *Catherine Flynn*.
From Newcastle:—*James Batters*, *Eliza Lawler*, *Dan. Thurston*, *George Watts*, and *P. Hogan*.

N. B.—Some of the above Runaways are supposed to have obtained false Certificates.

Any Person or Persons harbouring, concealing, or maintaining any of the said Absentees, will be prosecuted for the Offence.

I. NICHOLS, *Principal Superintendent.*

SYDNEY, 5th Feb. 1814.

AS Agent and Trustee for the Property of Persons dying Intestate in this Colony, I hereby Caution all Persons from interfering with the Property of the late Dennis Brodier, a Government Man on the Estate of the late Doctor Jamieson, who died intestate a few days ago, in consequence of a Stroke of Lightning.—In the mean time [illegible] Charles Throsby, of Glenfield, is authorised to secure and take charge of all the Effects of the [illegible] ceased.

J. T. CAMP[illegible]

NOTICE.—Any Person willing to Contract for the making and burning two Kilns of Bric[illegible]; of from 40 to 50,000 each, on the Lands of Shancomore and Ballymacammon, in the District of Bringelly, will be treated with on Application to the Undersigned. J. T. CAMPBELL.

Sydney, 12th Feb. 1814.

ADVERTISEMENT.

IN Consequence of numerous Applications having been made for Copies of the BIRTH DAY ODES which have been presented to HIS EXCELLENCY the GOVERNOR, and recited at the Levees held on the Festivals of the Anniversaries of OUR GRACIOUS KING, and his Illustrious CONSORT, during the Administration of this Colony by GOVERNOR MACQUARIE, the Author is induced to announce his intention of comprising and publishing the whole Series complete, in one Volume, small 8vo. in boards, dedicated, by Permission, to HIS EXCELLENCY the GOVERNOR, and Printed in a superior Style on the best wove Paper, price 10s. Sterling each; which will be little more than sufficient to defray the Expences of Printing, Stationary, Binding, &c.—And as it is the Author's intention to print no more than will be subscribed for, such Ladies, Gentlemen, and Others as may be desirous of possessing themselves of a Work which in point of Composition and Printing, will, it is presumed, in some degree shew the Encouragement which has tended to the Advancement of Arts and Science in this rising Colony, are respectfully requested to enter their Names with the Printer, Mr. Howe, specifying the Number of Copies they wish to be furnished with; and Care will be taken that they shall be delivered in the Order subscribed for.—The Work will be put to Press as soon as the Number requisite for defraying the Expences shall be ascertained; and will be ready for Delivery to the Subscribers within Two Months from that Time: Half the Subscription Money to be paid at the Time of Subscribing.

☞ A List of the Subscribers will be printed.

GOVERNMENT ORDER
Government House, Sydney, 12th February, 1814

It having been long deemed an Object of great Importance by HIS EXCELLENCY THE GOVERNOR to ascertain what Resources this Colony might possess in the Interior, beyond its present known and circumscribed Limits, with a View to meet the necessary Demands of its rapidly encreasing Population; and the great Importance of the Discovery of new Tracts of good Soil being much enhanced by the Consideration of the long continued *Droughts* of the present Season, so injurious in their Effects to every Class of the Community in the Colony, HIS EXCELLENCY was pleased some Time since to equip a Party of Men, under the direction of Mr. GEORGE WILLIAM EVANS, one of the Assistant Land Surveyors (in whose Zeal and Abilities for such an Undertaking he had well founded Reason to confide), and to furnish him with written Instructions for his Guidance in endeavouring to discover a Passage over the Blue Mountains, and ascertaining the Quality and general Properties of the Soil he should meet with to the Westward of them.

The Object having been happily effected, and Mr. Evans returned with his entire Party all in good Health, the GOVERNOR is pleased to direct, that the following Summary of his Tour of Discovery, extracted from his own Journal, shall be published for general Information.

Mr. Evans, attended by five Men, selected for their general Knowledge of the Country, and habituated to such Difficulties as might be expected to occur, was supplied with Horses, Arms, and Ammunition, and a plentiful Store of Provisions for a two Months Tour. His instructions were, that he commence the Ascent of the Blue Mountains from the Extremity of the present known Country at Emu Island, distant about thirty-six miles from Sydney, and thence proceed in a nearly west direction as the nature of the Country he had to explore would admit, and to continue his Journey as far as his Means would enable him.

On Saturday, the 20th of November last, the party proceeded from Emu Island, and on the 5th Day, having then effected their Passage over the Mountains, arrived at the Commencement of a Valley on the western Side of them, having passed over several tracts of tolerably good Soil, but also over much rugged and very difficult Mountain; proceeding through this Valley, which Mr. Evans describes as beautiful and fertile, with a rapid Stream running through it, he arrived at the Termination of the Tour lately made by Messrs G. Blaxland, W. C. Wentworth, and Lieutenant Lawson. Commencing in the western Direction prescribed in his Instructions for the course of 21 Days from this Station, Mr Evans then found it necessary to return, and on the 8th of January he arrived back at Emu Island, after an Excursion of seven complete Weeks. During the Course of this Tour, Mr. Evans passed over several Plains of great Extent, interspersed with Hills and Vallies abounding in the richest Soil, and with various Streams of Water and Chains of Ponds. The Country he traversed measured 98½ Miles beyond the Termination of Messrs. Blaxland, Wentworth, and Lawson's

Tour, and not less than 150 from Emu Island. The greater Part of these Plains are described as being nearly free of Timber and Brush wood, and in Capacity equal (in Mr Evans' Opinion) to every Demand which this Colony may have for an Extension of Tillage and Pasture Lands for a Century to come. The Stream already mentioned continues its Course in a westerly Direction, and for several Miles passing through the Vallies, with many and great Accessions of other Streams, becomes a capacious and beautiful River, abounding in Fish of very large Size and fine Flavour, many of which weighed not less than 15lbs. This River is supposed to empty itself into the Ocean on the western Side of New South Wales, at a Distance of from 2 to 300 Miles from the Termination of the Tour.—From the Summits of some very high Hills, Mr. Evans saw a vast Extent of flat Country laying in a westerly Direction, which appeared to be bounded at a Distance of about 40 Miles by other Hills. The general Description of these heretofore unexplored Regions, given by Mr. Evans, is, that they very far surpass in Beauty and Fertility of Soil any he has seen in New South Wales or Van Diemen's Land.

In Consideration of the Importance of these Discoveries, and calculating upon the Effect they may have on the future Prosperity of this Colony, His Excellency the Governor is pleased to announce his Intention of presenting Mr. Evans with a Grant of 1000 Acres of Land in Van Diemen's Land, where he is to be stationed as Deputy Surveyor; and further, to make him a pecuniary Reward from the Colonial Funds, in Acknowledgment of his diligent and active Services on this occasion.

His Excellency also means to make a pecuniary Reward to the two Free Men who accompanied Mr. Evans, and a Grant of Land to each of them. To the three Convicts who also assisted in this Excursion, the Governor means to grant Conditional Pardons, and a small Portion of Land to each of them, these Men having performed the Services required of them entirely to the Satisfaction of Mr. Evans.

The Governor is happy to embrace this Opportunity of conveying his Acknowledgments to Gregory Blaxland and William Charles Wentworth, Esquires, and Lieutenant William Lawson, of the Royal Veteran Company, for their enterprizing and arduous Exertions on the Tour of Discovery which they voluntarily performed in the Month of May last, when they effected a Passage over the Blue Mountains, and proceeded to the Extremity of the first Valley particularly alluded to in Mr. Evans's Tour, and being the first Europeans who had accomplished the Passage over the Blue Mountains. The Governor, is desirous to confer on these Gentlemen substantial Marks of his Sense of their meritorious Exertions on this Occasion, means to present each of them with a Grant of 1000 Acres of Land in this newly discovered Country.

By Command of His Excellency
The Governor,
J.T. Campbell, *Secretary.*

12 *The birth of a free press*

Independent newspapers created in Sydney and Hobart, 1824

BY THE 1820S COLONIAL SOCIETY WAS TRANSFORMING NEW SOUTH WALES FROM A FAR-FLUNG BRITISH PRISON INTO A SETTLER SOCIETY. THE GROWING NUMBERS OF CHILDREN BORN TO CONVICT PARENTS AND INCREASING NUMBERS OF FREE SETTLERS, CREATED A STRUGGLE AROUND THE ROLE OF GOVERNMENT IN THE COLONY.

The development of a free press was a critical element in the debate. Under Governor Lachlan Macquarie's administration (1810–1821), political satire had appeared in the pages of *The Sydney Gazette*. William Charles Wentworth's early political efforts and his development of *The Australian* newspaper from 1824 are well known.

But well before Wentworth printed the first issues of his newspaper in Sydney, editor and newspaper owner Andrew Bent (1790–1851) had been producing some short-lived newspapers in the colony of Van Diemen's Land (Tasmania) since 1814. By 1824, with the arrival of a new and energetic lieutenant governor, George Arthur (1784–1854), the battle between the colonial government and the rights of an independent press were being hotly waged in the south.

When Lieutenant Governor Arthur asserted that Bent's *Hobart Town Gazette and Van Diemen's Land Advertiser* was to refrain from all criticism of the government, Bent appealed to Governor Thomas Brisbane (1773–1860) in Sydney, who had just allowed Wentworth and his associate Dr Robert Wardell (1793–1834) to publish *The Australian* newspaper without government supervision. Brisbane confirmed that Bent could do the same.

When he then launched a tirade against Lieutenant Governor Arthur, calling him a 'Gibeonite [slave] of tyranny', Bent was prosecuted for libel, fined 500 pounds and sentenced to prison. Bent boldly printed a new paper—the *Colonial Times and Tasmanian Advertiser*—in competition with a government-issued paper of exactly the same name. Bent was implacable in his quest for an independent press and spent the next ten years establishing and re-establishing newspapers, and falling foul of the law and libel suits. Finally, in 1839, he left Hobart for Sydney, where he established another weekly paper, *Bent's News and New South Wales Advertiser*. He soon sold the paper and it became the *Australasian Chronicle*.

The struggles to establish newspapers that were not subject to colonial government control or censorship in the 1820s and 1830s reflected an intense period of politics between the 'exclusivists'—colonial elites who wanted power sharing with the government—and the 'emancipists'—free settlers and ex-convicts who increasingly called for a form of parliamentary democracy in the colonies.

Hobart Town Gazette,

AND

VAN DIEMEN'S LAND ADVERTISER.

Published by Authority.

NINTH VOLUME.] FRIDAY, OCTOBER 8, 1824. [NUMBER 440.

His Honor the Lieutenant Governor has thought proper to direct, that all Public Communications, which may appear in the Hobart Town Gazette, and Van Diemen's Land Advertiser, signed with any Official Signature, are to be considered as Official Communications made to those Persons to whom they may relate.

(BY COMMAND OF HIS HONOR) JOHN MONTAGU, *Secretary.*

Government & General Orders.

Government House, Hobart Town, October 7th, 1824.

HIS HONOR the LIEUTENANT GOVERNOR, with a View of preventing much unnecessary Correspondence, desires to notify, that he will not feel justified in extending the Grant or Location of Land to any Settler, until he is perfectly satisfied with the Improvements which have been made on the Land already possessed.

The Settler's Claim for an Extension of the Area of his Property, is the Outlay of Capital in the Erection of Buildings and general Improvement of his Land.

Where the Land is arable, the Claims will be considered according to the Quantity which has been cleared and brought into Cultivation; where it is Pastureable according to the Quantity which has been cleared and put into artificial Grass.—This, and not merely the Augmentation of Herds and Flocks, which, roving as they do in vast Numbers through the Country, are Destructive in their Progress and annually deteriorating in their Quality, must be understood as the Criterion by which Claims to additional Land will be considered.

Experience must convince the Agriculturists of Van Diemen's Land, that they are sure of obtaining a fair remunerating Price for any Land they may bring into Cultivation and Improvement, provided, through Economy and Prudence, they are not compelled to dispose of their Produce at an unseasonable Period.

By Command of His Honor
The Lieutenant Governor,
JOHN MONTAGU, *Secretary.*

Government & General Orders.

Government House, Hobart Town, October 7th, 1824.

ALL Boats, the Property of Private Individuals, are prohibited from visiting the Government Sawing Establishments at North West and Birch's Bay, without the Authority of HIS HONOR the LIENTENANT GOVERNOR.

By Command of His Honor
The Lieutenant Governor,
JOHN MONTAGU, *Secretary.*

Government & General Orders.

Government House, Hobart Town, October 7th, 1824.

JOHN M'DONALD, holding a Ticket of Leave, is appointed a Constable of Hobart Town, in Place of WILLIAM MYLES, allowed to resign.

ROBERT DOBSON, holding a Ticket of Leave, is appointed a Constable of Hobart Town, in Place of WILLIAM CLARK.

By Command of His Honor
The Lieutenant Governor,
JOHN MONTAGU, *Secretary.*

Government & General Orders.

Government House, Hobart Town, October 7th, 1824.

MR. JOHN PHILIP DEANE, having entered into the usual Bonds for the Performance of the Duties of an Auctioneer and Vendue Master for the County of Buckinghamshire, has received a License accordingly.

By Command of His Honor
The Lieutenant Governor,
JOHN MONTAGU, *Secretary.*

Government Public Notice.

THE under-mentioned Persons have obtained Certificates during the last Week:—

Thomas Dawkins .. Caledonia
John Sutton .... Surry
John Cothay ...... Lady Castlereagh
James Ingram ...... Ditto
William Betteridge .. Caledonia
James Hyland ...... Earl St. Vincent
Mary Usher or Murtagh .... Elizabeth.

JOHN MONTAGU, *Secretary.*
Secretary's Office, Oct. 7, 1824.

Commissariat Office, Sept. 16th, 1824.

FRESH MEAT.—The under-mentioned Tenders are accepted of, and will be received as stated:—

HOBART TOWN.

			lbs.	
October	15	Champion & Co.	10,000	at 4d.
	15	Ditto	10,000	4d.
	22	James Triffitt	12,000	4½d.
	39	Samuel Hood	10,000	4½d.
Nov.—	5	Ditto	10,000	4½d.
	12	Ditto	10,000	4½d.
	19	Champion & Co.	10,000	4d.
	26	T. Stanfield	12,000	4½d.
Dec.—	3	David Reynolds	5,000	4½d.
		Samuel Hood	7,000	4d.
	10	Ditto	11,000	4d.
	17	Ditto	11,000	4d.
	24	Ditto	11,000	4d.

LAUNCESTON.
At 4d. per lb.

October	15	James Cox	2500
	22	Ditto	3000
	29	Ditto	2500
Nov.—	5	Ditto	3000
	12	Thomas Archer	3000
	19	Ditto	3000
	26	Ditto	2500
Dec.—	3	Ditto	2500
	10	Ditto	2500
	17	Ditto	2500
	24	Richard Dry	3000

GEORGE TOWN.
At 4½d. per lb.
David Gibson .. 15,000 lbs. as required.

SOUTH ESK PUNT.
At 4d. per lb.
A. Barclay 2925, J. Hortel 2935 — 450 lbs. Weekly.

Michael Lackey to Supply the Road Parties on the Port Dalrymple Road at 4½d. per lb.—Silas Gatehouse to Supply the Party at the Coal River at 5d. per lb.

A. MOODIE, *A. C. G.*

Commissariat Office, August 18, 1824.

FORAGE.—Persons having Hay, Straw, or any Description of Forage to dispose of, are requested to transmit Tenders of the same, deliverable at the Lumber Yard, to this Office—Required also, a few Hundred Bushels of Barley. A. MOODIE, *A. C. G.*

Contract for Building a Church.

PERSONS, willing to Contract for the Erection of a New Church, at Launceston, are requested to transmit Tenders for the same before the 24th of October to this Office, or to the Office of the Inspector of Works at Launceston, where the Plans and Specification may be seen.—All Materials to be found by Government.

DAVID LAMBE, *Colonial Architect.*

☞ *The Colonial Architect's Office will in future be attached to the Secretary's Office.*

Colonial Architect's Office, Hobart Town, Sep. 24, 1824.

POST OFFICE.—A Mail for England, India, and the Cape of Good Hope, will be forwarded by the Prince Regent, Captain Wales, expected to leave this Port for the Mauritius, on the 17th Instant.

J. T. COLLICOTT, *Postmaster.*

PRESBYTERIAN CHURCH.—Additional Subscriptions, viz.

	£	s.	d.
Amount Collected at the opening of the Church	£40	0	0
Mr. John Fawkner (2d Sub.)	5	0	0
Mrs. White ditto	3	3	0
T. G. Gregson, Esq. ditto	2	0	0
Mr. Charles Robertson	2	2	0
Mr. John Thomas	1	10	0
Mr. Sinclair Williamson	1	0	0
Mr. William Charlson	1	0	0
Mr. John Elliott	1	0	0
Miss Elliott	1	0	0
	57	15	0
Amount formerly Advertised	864	14	6
Total	£922	9	6

Of which Amount, Subscriptions *here* and at *Sydney* amounting to about £300 remain unpaid.—As the Managers are anxious to liquidate the Debt incurred in erecting the Church, they respectfully request of the Subscribers in both Colonies to pay their respective Subscriptions without delay.—From the length of time that has elapsed since these Subscriptions were received, it is feared they have escaped the Memories of many; it is therefore proposed to advertise those remaining *unpaid* on the 1st of *November* next, which, the Managers trust, will be but few.

Melville-street Chapel.

PERSONS desirous of Contracting with the Trustees of this Place of Worship to put on the Roof and lay the Flooring Joists, are requested to send Tenders, on or before Thursday, the 14th of October, addressed to the undersigned, of whom may be obtained the Plan and Specification, with other Particulars.—The Trustees will not consider themselves bound to accept the lowest Tenders. *By Order of the Trustees,* ESH LOVELL, *Steward, Bathurst-street.*

MR. E. H. THOMAS will immediately remove to his New Residence, adjoining that of the Rev. R. Mansfield, in Brisbane-street.—Albion House is consequently to be Let.

NOTICE.—In Consequence of the Death of JOHN WYLD, Esq. late Agent for the Australian Company in Hobart Town, Mr. WARREN, (the surviving Agent of the Company in these Colonies) requests that all Claims whatever against the Company, and against Mr. WYLD, personally, may be immediately presented at the Australian Company's Stores.

TEAS.—The AUSTRALIAN COMPANY are just landing from the Prince Regent, a Parcel of very superior Hyson-skin Teas, to which the Agent of the Company begs to call the Attention of the Public.

SOUCHONG TEAS in Chests and Half-chests, on SALE, at Messrs. KEMP & Co's. in Macquarie-street, for which Wheat, Cash, or approved Bills will be taken in Payment.

JUST arrived, per the ship Prince Regent, prime CEDAR in Plank, from 1 to 10 Inches thick, which may be had of Mr. E. LOVELL, Bathurst-street, at a very reduced Price, for Cash or approved Bills.

☞ To be Let, a neat small House, (at a very low Rent to a respectable Tenant), situate in Bathurst-street, commanding a fine view of the Town and Harbour.

FOR ENGLAND and the ISLE OF FRANCE.—The fine fast-sailing Ship *PRINCE REGENT*, 540 Tons Burthen, Captain A. WALES, will sail on the 17th Inst.; has superior Accommodation for Passengers, and can take a few Goods.—Being chartered her Detention at the Mauritius will not be more than 30 Days.—For Particulars apply to Mr. WILLIAM MILLIKIN, at Stodart's Hotel.

FOR ENGLAND *via* Rio de Janeiro, the fine fast-sailing Ship *ARDENT*, H. CLEMENTS, R. N. Commander.—Will return from Sydney positively in the beginning of the ensuing Month, having a considerable Portion of her Cargo engaged; her stay at this Port will be very limited.—For Passage and a few Tons of Freight apply to the Agents, BETHUNE & GRANT.

FOR ENGLAND DIRECT.—The fine Ship *PRINCE REGENT*, Lieut. W. B. LAMB, R. N. Commander, now loading at Sydney, direct for England; has superior Accommodation for Passengers.—For Freight or Passage apply to the Commander on board; or to Messrs. ICELY & HINDSON, Sydney; or to F. CHAMPION & Co.

MR. J. C. UNDERWOOD has on SALE, Two very handsome London-made Gigs;—Sherry, Maderia, Champaign, Claret, Liquers, and Jamaica Rum; Porter in bottle and cask; Isle of France Sugar, Cheese, Wool Packs, and Slops.—Also, 250 prime Ewes and 50 Wethers.

ORANGES and BRANDY FRUITS. Just landed, and now on SALE, at Mr. RALSTON'S, Goulburn-street, a choice Lot of Oranges, from one of the best Orchards in New South Wales; also, a variety of French preserved Brandy Fruits in Bottles.—As the demand for the above is likely to be rapid, Families wishing a supply would do well to apply early.

TO LET, those eligible PREMISES, situated at the corner of Argyle and Bathurst-streets, consisting of a convenient Dwelling-house and substantial Brick Store, with a distinct Entrance, having a large Yard attached thereto.—The dwelling-house has a separate Yard, containing a three-stall Stable, and other Out-offices.—Apply to F. CHAMPION and Co.

FOR SALE by Private Contract, from One to Two Hundred choice EWES, with or without Lambs; ten excellent docile Cows, of the improved English breed, in calf or with calves by their sides; a Brood Mare, with a fine Foal by her side; a beautiful Bay Entire Horse, rising seven years old, has good action as a saddle horse, is quite docile, and free of vice, and is a most excellent gig horse; also, a handsome dark brown Gelding, rising four years old, is good in all his paces.—Likewise, six young well-trained Working Bullocks, with a strong double-tired Cart, nearly new, capable of carrying a ton and half.—The above Property will be sold on very moderate terms; and the Proprietor flatters himself that any Gentleman wishing to stock his Estate may travel Van Diemen's Land over and not be better suited.—Application to be made to Mr. JOHN EARLE, at Compton Ferry.

Andrew Bent published his Hobart newspapers under several titles, using this version 1821–1825. After he was sentenced to a fine and imprisonment for libel in 1825, the government took the title Hobart Town Gazette *to publish its notices, so Bent renamed his paper the* Colonial Times and Tasmanian Advertiser *on 19 August 1825.*

Hobart Town Gazette.

FRIDAY, OCTOBER 8.

Sitting Magistrate—E. F. Bromley, Esq.

☞ *Assize of Bread, the Loaf of 2lbs.* 6½d.

SHIP NEWS.—Arrived on Monday morning last from Port Jackson, after a tedious passage of 18 days, the barque Prince Regent, of 540 tons, Captain Wales, having on board the following passengers, viz. Doctor T. B. Wilson, R. N., Geo. Wm. Evans, Esq. Surveyor General of Van Diemen's Land, Major Bates, of the Royal Artillery, Major Mac. Intosh, Alexander Warren, Esq., Evan Henry Thomas, Esq., William Milliken, Esq. Mr. William Bedford, son of the Rev. Mr. Bedford, Chaplain to this Settlement, E. Abel, Esq. Captain Laughton, late Commander of the ship Alfred, and now part owner of the brig Governor Phillips, John Johnson, Esq. James Wood, Esq. Mr. John Hames, Mr. Philip Mills, Mr. Robert Ralston, and several others.—The Prince Regent brought down also a Detachment of the 3d Regiment (Buffs), with their wives and families; likewise, several free women, to join their husbands in this Colony, with three hundred chests of tea, a quantity of cedar, and 15 horses for Government.

Sailed on Sunday evening last, the Australian Company's ship *Portland,* Captain Snell, R. N.; having on board a few of the Passengers who arrived by that vessel from Scotland.

The barque Prince Regent will, we understand, proceed with all possible expedition to England, *via* the Mauritius, where she will take in a cargo of sugar for the London market.

The extremely precarious mode by which, from necessity, our intercourse with New South Wales is at present conducted, justifies complaint; but will, we hope, be speedily superseded by a regular and faithful Packet, as we are fully authorised to state, that if adequate patronage be afforded, the fine brig Governor Phillips may in future be employed as a regular conveyance between the Colonies.

Several Gentlemen having applied to us for copies of " An Act to provide, " until the first day of July, 1827, and " until the end of the next Session of " Parliament, for the better Adminis- " tration of Justice in New South Wales " and Van Diemen's Land, and for the " more effectual Government thereof; " and for other purposes relating there- " to,"—we shall re-print it as soon as possible; but as no more copies will be struck off than may be subscribed for, we request to be immediately furnished with the names of applicants.

By the lamented demise of Mr. Wyld, to whose exemplary worth an appropriate tribute is recorded in another column of this Paper, the only surviving Agent to the Australian Company in New South Wales and Van Diemen's Land is, Alex. Warren, Esq.

We are really glad that the Sydney Court of Requests commenced its much needed functions on the 2d ult.; and we anticipate with earnestness, the protection to industry and honesty, which will, in a short time, result from a similar Tribunal in Hobart Town.

Many a thousand oranges, shipped in the Prince Regent, by some for sale, and by others as intended presents for friends here, were utterly spoiled during the passage. One Gentleman (Captain Laughton), who speculated in this fruit, is thereby a loser of more than £70.

Mr. J. P. Deane, Proprietor of the Waterloo Stores, has obtained a license to act as an Autioneer and Appraiser.—There are now seven auctioneers in the Island.

A full, accurate, and impartial report of the recent investigation, relative to George Richardson and Doctor Scott, will appear in our next number.

The schooner *Governor Brisbane* (now belonging to the house of Kemp & Co.) has returned from Port Dalrymple, and will shortly sail on a sealing voyage.

BIRTH.—On the 24th of August, at Government House, Parramatta, the Lady of HIS EXCELLENCY MAJOR-GENERAL SIR THOMAS BRISBANE, K. C. B., of a SON and HEIR.

THE HOBART TOWN GAZETTE, and VAN DIEMEN'S LAND ADVERTISER.

Equally pusillanimous, equally reprehensible, are the assumption of a false claim, and the abandonment of a just one! With decision, therefore, we have chosen to resist what was jurisprudentially esteemed as a most " unwarranted invasion" of our right to the sole Proprietorship of this Gazette; and, thanks most profoundly permanent to that hallowed spirit of British Justice, which animates SIR THOMAS BRISBANE, our resistance has been consecrated by a perfect triumph. We knew, yes! well we knew, by confident, serene, and cloudless anticipation, that our legally indefeasible title would be confirmed and held intangible at Head Quarters. We were sure that the dignified Representative of England's all-liberal and erudite SOVEREIGN, (may God for ever bless him!) would scorn to sully his name or his nation by *illegally* scathing the literary edifice composed and cemented by a Patriot's industry. We said, in the fervour of our exultation,—Surely HIS EXCELLENCY is a Christian, a Man of Honour, and a Gentleman. Surely he is a Partizan of his Country's Law, surely he is *Amicus humani generis,* and an advocate of bliss-diffusing Liberty. Surely he will not bereave us of an instrument which we created for the public weal, and never have brandished as a public scourge. Surely he is *just and firm,* and therefore *we must be secure* under the venerated and invulnerable wing of his protection. All this we thought—all this we said; and the result of Mr. THOMAS's embassy demonstrates that our best preconceptions of that great and good man, the Commander in Chief, were fully merited.

At present, however, we shall only add the following explanatory paragraph, which, having appeared in the *Sydney Gazette,* by express and supreme Colonial Authority, will " speak volumes" to the prejudiced, and invest our tremulous adherents with a pleasing confidence, that *even yet* the sling of an outraged " *weak* one," when brandished against the Gideonite of tyranny, must be *Laus deo,* irresistible:—

" The Art of Typography, when well employed, is in our estimation so mighty and benignant, that all, who would oppose its judicious operations, must surely be, as we are bold to call them—foes, rank foes, of every talent which adorns, and of every virtue that enobles mankind! Our inducement to offer the above remark, has been furnished by certain occurrences, of recent date and high importance, in relation to " *The Hobart Town Gazette,*" for which *little Struggler* in the cause of the Community who patronize it, we have often denoted our esteem; and, to which, in a great degree, we attribute the improvement of their prospects. It appears, as we are credibly informed, that Mr. ANDREW BENT, Government Printer at Hobart Town, instituted the Hobart Town Gazette at his own expense, and has ever since so conducted it—feeling it to be, as of course it is, both by law and in equity, his own personal property!—It further appears that some efforts were rumoured as in progress to bereave him of the same; and, in consequence, he very properly despatched his newly appointed Editor, on a respectful embassy to Head Quarters, with such documents as could clearly establish his said Proprietorship. And lastly, it appears, as with feelings of pride and satisfaction we inform the Public, that HIS EXCELLENCY was pleased to consider Mr. BENT's claim to publish his said Paper, on his own account, completely indisputable. " It was true," as the liberal and enlightened Representative of Our Gracious Monarch said, ' Lieutenant Governor ARTHUR *might* chuse another vehicle for the dissemination of Official Orders, &c.'—But, that the Journal itself was private property had been alledged on oaths the most sacred! and we are therefore justified in stating, that *on oath alone can it, if ever it can,* fairly be brought within the pale of question."

Some few weeks since an eclipse at Sydney was predicted by " the genius of Australia;" and we therefore opine its occurrence to have veiled " the Thalia" when she silently decamped for Columbia.

Insurrection in Demarara.—With the lamentable circumstances which have recently transpired at Demarara, our Readers are in general acquainted. Mr. Smith, a Missionary, was tried by a Court Martial, and condemned to die for the alledged crime of inciting the slaves to insurrection; but the Governor, feeling the delicacy and importance of the case, thought proper to suspend his fate until His Majesty's pleasure should be known thereon.—And so little did the King in Council coincide with the Court Martial in believing Mr. Smith to have been guilty, that His Majesty decidedly reversed their verdict. It is deplorable to relate, that on the very day on which the Royal acquittal was received by the Governor, Mr. Smith expired from the effects of grief and long imprisonment. Mr. Smith was *not,* as has been rumoured, a *Wesleyan* Missionary; and we are happy to state, on the best authority, that of the Wesleyan Society in that Colony, consisting of twelve hundred and sixteen members, chiefly slaves, only *two* persons had been apprehended on suspicion, and even they were afterwards liberated upon full conviction of their entire innocence!

Sydney Disinterestedness.—Suppose an oyster to cut capers for an Alderman's boiled leg of mutton; suppose an Alderney cow to teach Greek, Hebrew, and Latin, in six lessons; suppose a black swan, when stuffed in a museum, to chaunt *Te Deum* more delightfully than Madame Catalina; suppose, in fine, the reconciliation with nature of all that is monstrous, before O! Tasmanian farmers, you suppose, that the Sydney merchants buy your wheat from disinterested motives. It is an axiom, that commercial sympathies are and must be calculative. It is an undoubted fact, that a desire of gain is the sole inducement to all traffic; and we, therefore, without considering those men in any degree beneath or worse than their neighbours, are compelled to brand all their dealings with us as at least interested, if not mercenary.

DIED—On Sunday, the 9th of August, on board the Phœnix, Captain White, while on his passage from this Port to Sydney, JOHN WYLD, Esq. Agent for the Australian Company in this Colony.—The death of this amiable young Gentleman, although anticipated, too surely by his friends here, from the very weakened state in which he left Hobart Town on the Friday preceding his demise, will, notwithstanding, be felt by his numerous friends as a sudden bereavement of no ordinary kind, and by the whole Colony as a public loss.—There is a something in our nature too, which, in despite of the soul-hardening effects of our mere worldly and every-day employments, makes us pause—and consider—when we hear of the young and promising members of our little community thus cut off, at once, and for ever, from us! We cannot calmly and placidly think of that eye " once expressively beaming" being closed in sorrow—far from kindred and from home—without receiving impressions highly favourable to virtue.

Mr. Wyld's relations have the consolation of knowing that, although the wild wave received his body, and no band of sorrowing friends was enabled to follow his remains to the grave—yet, by all the virtuous in this part of the world, his memory shall continue to be fondly cherished!

SIC TRANSIT GLORIA MUNDI!

Verite sans peur.

The learned biographer of Shenstone has told us that, where there is emulation there will be vanity; and where there is vanity there will be folly! We have been taught that " every man ought to endeavour at eminence not by pulling others down, but by raising himself, and enjoy the pleasure of his own superiority, whether imaginary or real, without interrupting others in the same felicity!—Cherishing these sentiments, we proceed to report some eccentric events, most importantly connected with the Sydney Bar.

An intelligent majority of our Readers are aware, that Mr. W. C. WENTWORTH and Mr. R. WARDELL recently came from England in the ship Alfred, and that, after resisting an established custom attached to our local Government, they proceeded with all the *awe-inspiring* costume of junior Barristers to Australia. Since their important arrival there, they certainly have been industrious, and performed *multum in parvo:* for in two days they have wantonly created more justifiable opponents, than in twice that number of years either will or can be pacified. It seems, on reference to the Sydney Gazette, that these Gentlemen on the 10th ultimo were sworn, in the Supreme Court, not only as Barristers, but likewise " to act in the characters of Proctors, Attornies, and Solicitors." This fact is relatively curious, and we beg particular attention to it. Immediately they were admitted, instead of congratulating themselves on the honourable intimacy they might form with the eminent, and long established professional Advocates then present, they shook their " war denouncing" wigs, and Mr. Wardell moved that the Gentlemen at present practising as Solicitors and acting as Barristers be compelled to retire from the Bar, and " yield to the Barristers the two-fold privilege" of exercising their ordinary functions, and of practising as Proctors, Solicitors, and Attornies! He said, that his motion was founded on the 10th section of the new Judicial Charter, which he admirably mystified while professing a desire to elucidate it. He urged the " undeniable defectiveness" of that clause, and concluded by enforcing, with more superciliousness than we thought became him, the " duty" that should cause the Attornies to retire from his momentous and elevated rank which not being legally their own, they must have illegally usurped.—Mr. Wentworth repeated these observations, and what? seconded the motion?—no, but with much original whimsicality repeated it verbatim! The consequences were, that a Rule issued for the Attornies to shew cause why they should not (as we understand) be turned from the Bar to make room for Messrs. Wentworth and Wardell; that the Attornies did on the 7th ultimo shew the required cause with a very respectable display of temperance, wit, lore, and reasoning; and that, after a truly able Address from His Honor CHIEF JUSTICE FORBES, the *Rule* was *discharged.*—Now, though not at all doubting the propriety of assimilating our Colonial Courts to the Courts at home, which are, as they ought to be every where confessed, unrivalled in their purity and usefulness, we cannot discharge our duty without an expression of regret, combined with equivalent portions of disgust and anger that Messrs. W. and W. had not made a delicate and private overture to the Solicitors, before they determined to publicly attack them with pompous scorn and puerile petulence—before they talked of immense or immeasurable distances between mechanical Solicitors, and intellectual Gentlemen of the Long Robe—before in fact they forgot that the " tap" of an Attorney had been welcomed with even half-a-guinea motion paper at more than one briefless wig-wearer's chamber!—Had these punctilious young aspirants for LEGAL notoriety behaved as a Romilly and an Erskine would have done—had they addressed the Solicitors in words to the following effect:

Gentlemen,—Acknowledging your considerable claims to public and professional gratitude, aware of the powers with which the New Charter has furnished you, and at the same time anxiously desirous of preserving here the mutually serviceable distinctions between Solicitors and Counsel, which are observed in the parent country, we take leave, respectfully, to suggest, that you, Gentlemen, shall confine your valuable exertions to the department in which you were educated, and that we, in becoming reciprocity of concession, shall not perform any services except those which excluding the New Charter from consideration, would peculiarly become us.

Inviting your prompt reply, we have the honour to subscribe ourselves,

Your faithful servants, * * *

—Had an address, we repeat, embodying sentiments like these, been sent, we are nearly certain it would have been read with approval, and satisfactorily answered.—But now the Bar is divided against its

Andrew Bent's brave public stance against Governor George Arthur's restriction of the only press in Tasmania in the 1820s was upheld by Governor Brisbane. Bent then published a famous attack on the governor, judiciously quoting from The Sydney Gazette *(see opposite).*

THE HOBART TOWN GAZETTE, and VAN DIEMEN'S LAND ADVERTISER

Equally pusillanimous, equally reprehensible, are the assumption of a false claim, and the abandonment of a just one! With decision, therefore, we have chosen to resist what was jurisprudentially esteemed as a most "unwarranted invasion" of our right to the sole Proprietorship of this Gazette; and, thanks most profoundly permanent to that hallowed spirit of British Justice, which animates SIR THOMAS BRISBANE, our resistance has been consecrated by a perfect triumph. We knew, yes! well we knew, by confident, serene, and cloudless anticipation, that our legally indefensible title would be confirmed and held intangible at Head Quarters. We were sure that the dignified Representative of England's all-liberal and erudite SOVEREIGN, (may God for ever bless him!) would scorn to sully his name or his nation by *illegally* scathing the literary edifice composed and cemented by a Patriot's industry. We said, in the fervour of our exultation,—Surely HIS EXCELLENCY is a Christian, a Man of Honour, and a Gentleman. Surely he is a Partizan of his Country's Law, surely he is *Amicus humani generis*, and an advocate of bliss-diffusing Liberty. Surely he will not be bereave us of an instrument which we created for the public weal, and never have brandished as a public scourge. Surely he is *just and firm*, and therefore *we must be secure* under the venerated and invulnerable wing of his protection. All this we thought—all this we said; and the result of Mr. THOMAS's embassy demonstrates that our best preconceptions of that great and good man, the Commander in Chief, were fully merited.

... we shall only add the following explanatory paragraph, which, having appeared in the *Sydney Gazette*, by express and supreme Colonial Authority, will "speak volumes" to the prejudiced, and invest our tremulous adherents with a pleasing confidence, that *even yet* the sling of an outraged "*weak* one," when brandished against the Gideonite of tyranny, must be *Laus deo*, irresistible: ...

"... It appears, as we are credibly informed, that Mr. ANDREW BENT, Government Printer at Hobart Town, instituted the Hobart Town Gazette at his own expense, and has ever since so conducted it—feeling it to be, as of course it is, both by law and in equity, his own personal property!—It further appears that some efforts were rumoured as in progress to bereave him of the same; and, in consequence, he very properly despatched his newly appointed Editor, on a respectful embassy to Head Quarters, with such documents as could clearly establish his said Proprietorship. And lastly, it appears, as with feelings of pride and satisfaction we inform the Public, that HIS EXCELLENCY was pleased to consider Mr. BENT's claim to publish his said Paper, on his own account, completely indisputable. "It was true," as the liberal and enlightened Representative of Our Gracious Monarch said, 'Lieutenant Governor ARTHUR *might* chuse another vehicle for the dissemination of Official Orders, &c.'—But, that the Journal itself was private property had been alledged on oaths the most sacred! and we are therefore justified in stating, that *on oath alone can it, if ever it can*, fairly be brought within the pale of question."

13 *Equality before the law*

Governor Arthur's message to the Aboriginal people of Van Diemen's Land, 1828

ALTHOUGH TASMANIA—CALLED VAN DIEMEN'S LAND UNTIL 1856—HAD BEEN SETTLED BY EUROPEANS IN 1803, SERIOUS CONFLICT WITH ITS INDIGENOUS PEOPLE DID NOT BEGIN UNTIL THE 1820S. AS SETTLEMENT EXPANDED, COMPETITION FOR RESOURCES BECAME MORE INTENSE, AND WHEN REPRISAL ATTACKS ON EUROPEANS PEAKED IN 1828, THE GOVERNOR PROCLAIMED MARTIAL LAW AND BANNED ABORIGINES FROM ENTERING SETTLED AREAS.

Arthur's proclamation described how the 'Black or Aboriginal Natives of this Island' were perpetrating 'most cruel and sanguinary acts of violence and outrage; evincing an evident disposition systematically to kill and destroy the white inhabitants indiscriminately whenever an opportunity of doing so is presented'.

To underscore this proclamation to Indigenous people, in 1830 a poster explaining that Europeans and Aborigines were equal before the law was designed by Surveyor General George Frankland (1800–1838). Copies of the poster were painted on wooden boards and nailed to trees in the bush in the belief Aboriginal people would find them, and understand their pictorial language. The series of cartoons or pictograms attempted to communicate the possibilities of peaceful co-existence—albeit on European terms—as well as the idea that under European law, crimes by Aboriginal people and settlers would be punished equally. In practice, this was generally not the case, as crimes committed against Aboriginal people in the bush were rarely reported.

The posters are unique in Australian history in their attempt to communicate across the warring colonial frontier. They were ultimately unsuccessful. Not long after the posters were placed in the bush the infamous 'black line' was formed. In October 1830 the colonial authorities created a chain of armed search parties of all available military, police and settlers, which swept across Tasmania in a desperate bid to capture or kill all Aboriginal people on the island. As the visiting naturalist Charles Darwin (1809–1882) recounted in 1839, the black line was 'similar to that of the great hunting-matches in India: a line reaching across the island was formed, with the intention of driving the natives into a cul-de-sac on Tasman's peninsula'.

Ultimately, it was seen as a costly fiasco: of the estimated population of 500, only two Aborigines were captured and three killed. By the early 1830s such intense concentration by the Europeans on the surviving Aboriginal people saw the end of a period of resistance known as the Black Wars, and for Tasmanian Indigenous people, the beginning of a period of forced removal to islands off the coast.

The poster depicts four scenes: peaceful intermingling of white settlers and Aborigines; an Aboriginal group shaking hands with Governor Arthur; an Aboriginal man spearing a white settler and being hanged by the military; a settler shooting an Aboriginal man and being hanged by the military.

14 European blood has been spilled

Tasmanian politics and the Black Wars, 1828

NEWSPAPER OWNER ANDREW BENT MAY HAVE BEEN A CHAMPION OF FREE SPEECH IN EARLY COLONIAL TASMANIA, BUT HE WAS NO CHAMPION OF THE CAUSE OF ABORIGINAL PEOPLE ON THE ISLAND. AFTER A PERIOD OF ESCALATING WARFARE FROM 1826 TO 1828, WHEN, AS BENT DESCRIBED IT, 'MORE EUROPEAN BLOOD HAS BEEN SPILLED, WITHIN THE LAST TWO YEARS, THAN THERE WAS BY ALL THE BUSH-RANGERS WHO WERE EVER OUT FROM THE FORMATION OF THE COLONY!!!', THE PREVIOUS 'HUMANITY AND COMPASSION' OF THE COLONIAL GOVERNMENT DISINTEGRATED.

Bent's tirade against the Tasmanian Aborigines may have been partly fuelled by the opportunity to attack his nemesis, Governor George Arthur (1784–1854), but it is also an important example of the racism that drove the treatment of Australian Aboriginal people over the next hundred years.

In this early example of a sensational editorial, Bent suggested that the only way to stop the 'devastation and alarm' caused by the Tasmanian Aborigines was to 'remove' them, to 'King's, or some of the other Islands in the Straits' where 'some hope might be entertained of civilizing them'.

Government policies followed suggestions from Bent and others, and the removal of Aboriginal people to Flinders Island in Bass Strait began in earnest from 1831.

A philanthropic free settler, George August Robinson (1791–1866), was made Protector of Aborigines by the colonial government and, guided by Trugernanner (Truganini) (1812?–1876) in a series of remarkable journeys around the island, visited all the Aboriginal groups and convinced many to come with him to a place where they could live unmolested by the settlers, and be well fed and clothed.

By 1835 the Aboriginal population, estimated to have been around 4000 before the arrival of the Europeans, numbered less than 150, half of whom were living on Flinders Island. Introduced diseases, such as smallpox, rapidly reduced the number of survivors. By 1869, Trugernanner, who was reported as the 'last full-blooded' Tasmanian Aborigine, presciently remarked to a missionary, 'I know that when I die the Museum wants my body'. After her death in 1876, Trugernanner's skeleton was studied by scientists and then placed in the Tasmanian Museum, where it was on public display from 1904 to 1947.

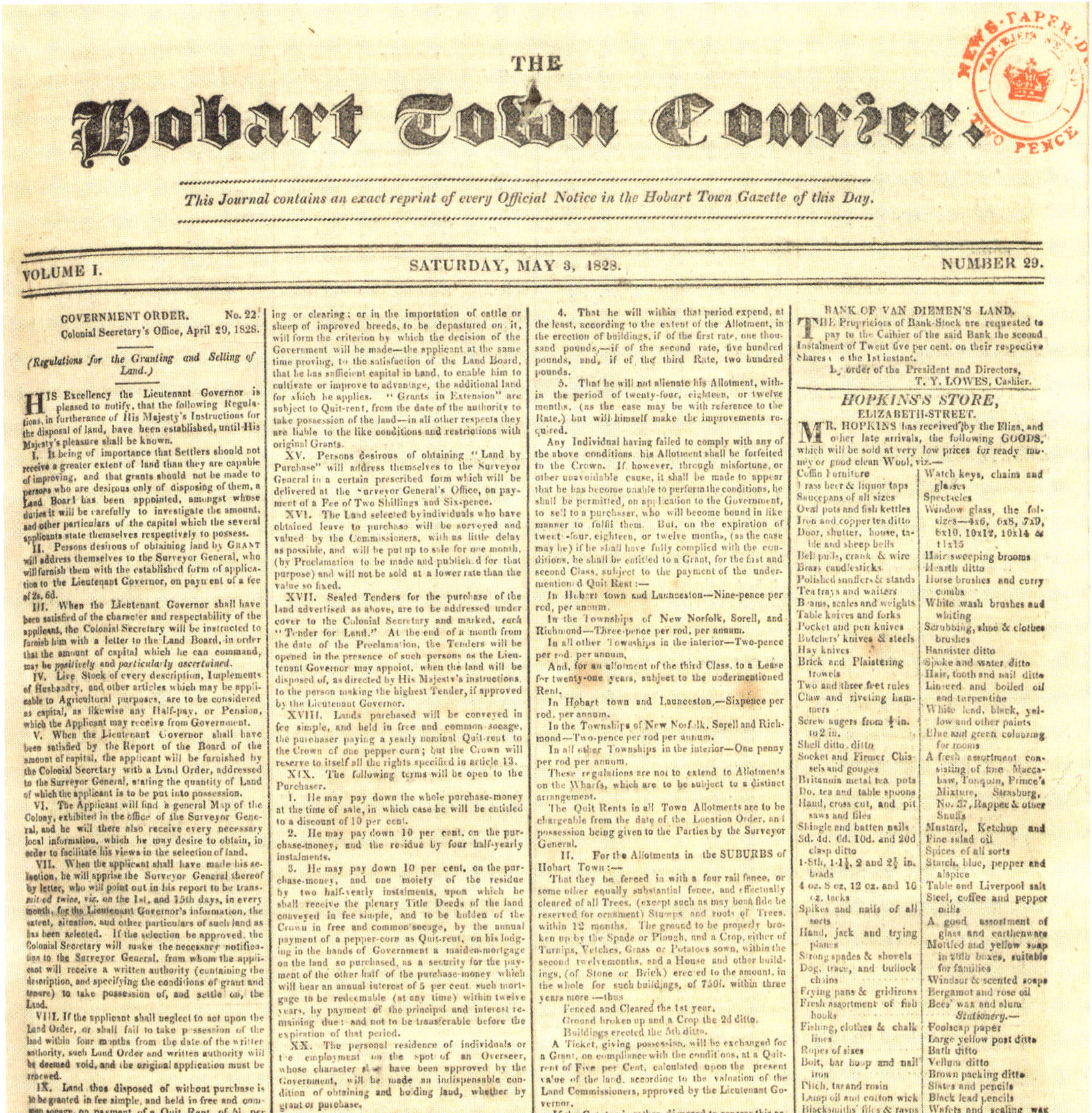

THE

Hobart Town Courier.

This Journal contains an exact reprint of every Official Notice in the Hobart Town Gazette of this Day.

VOLUME I. SATURDAY, MAY 3, 1828. NUMBER 29.

GOVERNMENT ORDER. No. 22.
Colonial Secretary's Office, April 29, 1828.

(Regulations for the Granting and Selling of Land.)

HIS Excellency the Lieutenant Governor is pleased to notify, that the following Regulations, in furtherance of His Majesty's Instructions for the disposal of land, have been established, until His Majesty's pleasure shall be known.

I. It being of importance that Settlers should not receive a greater extent of land than they are capable of improving, and that grants should not be made to persons who are desirous only of disposing of them, a Land Board has been appointed, amongst whose duties it will be carefully to investigate the amount, and other particulars of the capital which the several applicants state themselves respectively to possess.

II. Persons desirous of obtaining land by GRANT will address themselves to the Surveyor General, who will furnish them with the established form of application to the Lieutenant Governor, on payment of a fee of 2s. 6d.

III. When the Lieutenant Governor shall have been satisfied of the character and respectability of the applicant, the Colonial Secretary will be instructed to furnish him with a letter to the Land Board, in order that the amount of capital which he can command, may be *positively* and *particularly ascertained*.

IV. Live Stock of every description, Implements of Husbandry, and other articles which may be applicable to Agricultural purposes, are to be considered as capital, as likewise any Half-pay, or Pension, which the Applicant may receive from Government.

V. When the Lieutenant Governor shall have been satisfied by the Report of the Board of the amount of capital, the applicant will be furnished by the Colonial Secretary with a Land Order, addressed to the Surveyor General, stating the quantity of Land of which the applicant is to be put into possession.

VI. The Applicant will find a general Map of the Colony, exhibited in the office of the Surveyor General, and he will there also receive every necessary local information, which he may desire to obtain, in order to facilitate his views in the selection of land.

VII. When the applicant shall have made his selection, he will apprise the Surveyor General thereof by letter, who will point out in his report to be transmitted *twice, viz.* on the 1st, and 15th days, in every month, for the Lieutenant Governor's information, the extent, situation, and other particulars of such land as has been selected. If the selection be approved, the Colonial Secretary will make the necessary notification to the Surveyor General, from whom the applicant will receive a written authority (containing the description, and specifying the conditions of grant and tenure) to take possession of, and settle on, the Land.

VIII. If the applicant shall neglect to act upon the Land Order, or shall fail to take possession of the land within four months from the date of the written authority, such Land Order and written authority will be deemed void, and the original application must be renewed.

IX. Land thus disposed of without purchase is to be granted in fee simple, and held in free and common socage, on payment of a Quit Rent of 5l. per cent. per annum, upon the value of the Land, as estimated in the survey, by the Land Commissioners, and approved by the Lieutenant Governor.

X. The Quit-rent is not to become payable until the end of seven years after the Grantee shall have been authorized to settle on the land, and is to be redeemable, at the option of the Grantee, at twenty years' purchase: the power of such redemption commencing at the time when such Quit-rent first becomes payable.

XI. Although the ordinary period for issuing the Grant will be at the expiration of seven years, yet, whenever satisfactory proof shall be brought forward, after one year from the entry into possession and actual occupation, that the Grantee has expended in the improvement of the land, a sum equal to its value, as that value was estimated by the Commissioners, at the period of his being put into possession, the Settler in such case shall have an immediate right to receive his Title Deeds to the Grant, without being obliged to await the expiration of the term of seven years; but if he fail, within that period, to expend, in improvements on the land, a sum equal to its estimated value, as aforesaid, possession of the land will be resumed by the Crown.

XII. Lands to be granted in square miles, in the proportion of one square mile, or 640 acres for every £500 sterling of capital, which the applicant can immediately command, to the extent of four square miles, or 2560 acres, which is the largest Grant that will be made to any fresh Settler without purchase, as the smallest is 320 acres.

XIII. The Crown reserves to itself the right of making and constructing such roads and bridges as may be necessary for Public purposes, on lands to be granted as above, and also to mines of gold and silver, and to such quantities of indigenous timber, stone and other materials, as may be required for making and keeping the said roads and bridges in repair, or for constructing other Public works or buildings, or of compelling the Proprietor, after a certain period, to construct roads through his own property, or to contribute either by money-payments, or by work performed, towards an object so desirable.

XIV. Persons desirous of obtaining "Grants in Extension" will make application in a certain prescribed form, which will be delivered at the Surveyor General's Office, on payment of a Fee of 2s. 6d. The best claim for this indulgence will be founded on bona fide residence as a Settler, on the original Grant, but whether the Settler be resident on the land or not, actual outlay of capital in the improvement of it, either by buildings, enclosures, draining or clearing; or in the importation of cattle or sheep of improved breeds, to be depastured on it, will form the criterion by which the decision of the Government will be made—the applicant at the same time proving, to the satisfaction of the Land Board, that he has sufficient capital in hand, to enable him to cultivate or improve to advantage, the additional land for which he applies. "Grants in Extension" are subject to Quit-rent, from the date of the authority to take possession of the land—in all other respects they are liable to the like conditions and restrictions with original Grants.

XV. Persons desirous of obtaining "Land by Purchase" will address themselves to the Surveyor General in a certain prescribed form which will be delivered at the Surveyor General's Office, on payment of a Fee of Two Shillings and Six-pence.

XVI. The Land selected by individuals who have obtained leave to purchase will be surveyed and valued by the Commissioners, with as little delay as possible, and will be put up to sale for one month, (by Proclamation to be made and published for that purpose) and will not be sold at a lower rate than the value so fixed.

XVII. Sealed Tenders for the purchase of the land advertised as above, are to be addressed under cover to the Colonial Secretary and marked, *each* "Tender for Land." At the end of a month from the date of the Proclamation, the Tenders will be opened in the presence of such persons as the Lieutenant Governor may appoint, when the land will be disposed of, as directed by His Majesty's instructions, to the person making the highest Tender, if approved by the Lieutenant Governor.

XVIII. Lands purchased will be conveyed in fee simple, and held in free and common socage, the purchaser paying a yearly nominal Quit-rent to the Crown of one pepper corn; but the Crown will reserve to itself all the rights specified in article 13.

XIX. The following terms will be open to the Purchaser.

1. He may pay down the whole purchase-money at the time of sale, in which case he will be entitled to a discount of 10 per cent.

2. He may pay down 10 per cent. on the purchase-money, and the residue by four half-yearly instalments.

3. He may pay down 10 per cent. on the purchase-money, and one moiety of the residue by two half-yearly instalments, upon which he shall receive the plenary Title Deeds of the land conveyed in fee simple, and to be holden of the Crown in free and common socage, by the annual payment of a pepper-corn as Quit-rent, on his lodging in the hands of Government a maiden-mortgage on the land so purchased, as a security for the payment of the other half of the purchase-money which will bear an annual interest of 5 per cent. such mortgage to be redeemable (at any time) within twelve years, by payment of the principal and interest remaining due: and not to be transferable before the expiration of that period.

XX. The personal residence of individuals or the employment on the spot of an Overseer, whose character shall have been approved by the Government, will be made an indispensable condition of obtaining and holding land, whether by grant or purchase.

By Command of
The Lieutenant Governor,
J. BURNETT.

GOVERNMENT ORDER, No. 26.
Colonial Secretary's Office, April 30, 1828.

THE Lieutenant Governor is pleased to direct that the following Conditions shall be in force on the location of Building Allotments in the Towns and in the Suburbs.

I. IN THE TOWNS.

1. The Allotments will be divided into three Classes or Rates.

2. The Class or Rate of an Allotment, when applied for by any individual, shall be named by the Government through the Surveyor General.

3. Allotments of the first Class shall consist of one Acre of Land and upwards, but not exceeding three Acres.—Allotments of the Second Class, half an Acre and upwards, not exceeding one Acre; and Allotments of the third Class a quarter of an Acre and upwards, not exceeding half an Acre.

4. The extent of the Allotment in either of these three cases to depend upon the remoteness of the situation from the centre of the Town, and the outlay of Capital which the Grantee pledges himself to expend.

5. That on an Allotment of the first Class, a house shall be built of a frontage extending not less than forty-five feet:—On an Allotment of the second Class, a house with a frontage of at least thirty-five feet:—And on an Allotment of the third Class, a house with a frontage of at least fifteen feet.

On granting permission to any individual to occupy an Allotment, he will be required to enter into a written Obligation to perform the following Conditions.

1. That he will make a footpath of nine feet wide on the side or sides of his Allotment next any Street or Public way, and inclose such Allotment with a good fence within six months from the date of the Obligation.

2. That he will commence the erection of a house of brick or stone, of the proper dimensions, according to the Class of the Allotment, within six months after the Location Order is given, keeping the line of the front at a distance of not less than twelve feet from the street.

3. That he will complete the erection of the house, as far as regards the outward appearance, if of the first Rate, within two years,—if of the second Rate, within eighteen months,—and if of the third Rate, within twelve months.

4. That he will within that period expend, at the least, according to the extent of the Allotment, in the erection of buildings, if of the first rate, one thousand pounds,—if of the second rate, five hundred pounds, and, if of the third Rate, two hundred pounds.

5. That he will not alienate his Allotment, within the period of twenty-four, eighteen, or twelve months, (as the case may be with reference to the Rate,) but will himself make the improvements required.

Any Individual having failed to comply with any of the above conditions, his Allotment shall be forfeited to the Crown. If, however, through misfortune, or other unavoidable cause, it shall be made to appear that he has become unable to perform the conditions, he shall be permitted, on application to the Government, to sell to a purchaser, who will become bound in like manner to fulfil them. But, on the expiration of twenty-four, eighteen, or twelve months, (as the case may be) if he shall have fully complied with the conditions, he shall be entitled to a Grant, for the first and second Class, subject to the payment of the undermentioned Quit Rent:—

In Hobart town and Launceston—Nine-pence per rod, per annum.

In the Townships of New Norfolk, Sorell, and Richmond—Three-pence per rod, per annum.

In all other Townships in the interior—Two-pence per rod, per annum,

And, for an allotment of the third Class, to a Lease for twenty-one years, subject to the undermentioned Rent.

In Hobart town and Launceston,—Sixpence per rod, per annum.

In the Townships of New Norfolk, Sorell and Richmond—Two-pence per rod per annum.

In all other Townships in the interior—One penny per rod per annum.

These regulations are not to extend to Allotments on the Wharfs, which are to be subject to a distinct arrangement.

The Quit Rents in all Town Allotments are to be chargeable from the date of the Location Order, and possession being given to the Parties by the Surveyor General.

II. For the Allotments in the SUBURBS of Hobart Town:—

That they be fenced in with a four rail fence, or some other equally substantial fence, and effectually cleared of all Trees, (except such as may bona fide be reserved for ornament) Stumps and roots of Trees, within 12 months. The ground to be properly broken up by the Spade or Plough, and a Crop, either of Turnips, Vetches, Grass or Potatoes sown, within the second twelvemonths, and a House and other buildings, (of Stone or Brick) erected to the amount, in the whole for such buildings, of 750l. within three years more—thus

Fenced and Cleared the 1st year.
Ground broken up and a Crop the 2d ditto.
Buildings erected the 5th ditto.

A Ticket, giving possession, will be exchanged for a Grant, on compliance with the conditions, at a Quit-rent of Five per Cent, calculated upon the present value of the land, according to the valuation of the Land Commissioners, approved by the Lieutenant Governor.

If the Grantee is rather disposed to reverse this arrangement, and commence with the erection of the House, it is optional with him to do so; and, a Grant will be issued as soon as the House is completed.

The largest Allotment not exceeding Ten Acres, and to be decreased according to its vicinity to the Town.

By command of His Excellency,
J. BURNETT.

GOVERNMENT ORDER. No. 25.
Colonial Secretary's Office, April 30, 1828.

THE Government Order of the 18th August, 1821, appearing to be much disregarded, and many Settlers having lately been in the practice of returning their Servants to the Public Works, on the plea of misconduct, or of being useless, without bringing any complaint against them before a Magistrate, in direct violation of the above order, the Lieutenant Governor finds it necessary again to notify, that no Convict Servant can be discharged, except under an order of a Magistrate, or by the special permission of His Excellency, and that none can be considered useless, but such as have been proved to the satisfaction of a Magistrate to be, from physical causes, incapable of bodily labour, which can alone justify their removal. To this Regulation strict conformity is required by all who receive Convict Servants from Government, and any person who may take upon himself to return his Assigned Servant to the Public Works without the proper authority, will be entirely excluded from the benefit of receiving Convicts in future.

By Command of
His Excellency,
J. BURNETT.

GOVERNMENT ORDER, No. 23.
Colonial Secretary's Office, April 29, 1828.

THE Lieutenant Governor has been pleased to appoint Edward Dumaresq, Esq. to act as Collector of the Internal Revenue.

By command of His Excellency,
J. BURNETT.

SUPERIOR WINES.

NOW landing from the Eliza superior Port and Sherry Wines, in six and three dozen cases, the quality of which can be strongly recommended, being laid in from one of the first houses in the city of London. Apply to

H. W. MASON,
Wine and Spirit Merchant.
Macquarie street, April 16, 1828.

BANK OF VAN DIEMEN'S LAND.

THE Proprietors of Bank-Stock are requested to pay to the Cashier of the said Bank the second Instalment of Twent five per cent. on their respective Shares (e the 1st instant.

By order of the President and Directors,
T. Y. LOWES, Cashier.

HOPKINS'S STORE,
ELIZABETH-STREET.

MR. HOPKINS has received by the Eliza, and other late arrivals, the following GOODS, which will be sold at very low prices for ready money or good clean Wool, viz.—

Coffin Furniture
Brass beer & liquor taps
Saucepans of all sizes
Oval pots and fish kettles
Iron and copper tea ditto
Door, shutter, house, table and sheep bells
Bell pulls, crank & wire
Brass candlesticks
Polished snuffers & stands
Tea trays and waiters
Beams, scales and weights
Table knives and forks
Pocket and pen knives
Butchers' knives & steels
Hay knives
Brick and Plaistering trowels
Two and three feet rules
Claw and riveting hammers
Screw augers from ½ in. to 2 in.
Shell ditto. ditto
Socket and Firmer Chissels and gouges
Britannia metal tea pots
Do. tea and table spoons
Hand, cross cut, and pit saws and files
Shingle and batten nails
3d. 4d. 6d. 10d. and 20d clasp ditto
1-8th, 1-1¼, 2 and 2½ in. brads
4 oz. 8 oz. 12 oz. and 16 oz. tacks
Spikes and nails of all sorts
Hand, jack and trying planes
Strong spades & shovels
Dog, trace, and bullock chains
Frying pans & gridirons
Fresh assortment of fish hooks
Fishing, clothes & chalk lines
Ropes of sizes
Bolt, bar hoop and nail iron
Pitch, tar and rosin
Lamp oil and cotton wick
Blacksmiths' files & rasps
Tue irons and plough mouldings
Hook and eye hinges of sizes
Butt and T ditto ditto
Door, cupboard and till locks
Curtain pins
Lamp black and shoe blacking
Shoe hemp, flax and good bristles

Watch keys, chains and glasses
Spectacles
Window glass, the following sizes—4x6, 6x8, 7x9, 8x10, 10x12, 10x14 & 11x15
Hair sweeping brooms
Hearth ditto
Horse brushes and curry combs
White wash brushes and whiting
Scrubbing, shoe & clothes brushes
Bannister ditto
Spoke and water ditto
Hair, tooth and nail ditto
Linseed and boiled oil and turpentine
White lead, black, yellow and other paints
Blue and green colouring for rooms
A fresh assortment consisting of fine Maccabaw, Tonquin, Prince's Mixture, Strasburg, No. 37, Rappee & other Snuffs
Mustard, Ketchup and Fine salad oil
Spices of all sorts
Starch, blue, pepper and alspice
Table and Liverpool salt
Steel, coffee and pepper mills
A good assortment of glass and earthenware
Mottled and yellow soap in 28lb boxes, suitable for families
Windsor & scented soaps
Bergamot and rose oil
Bees' wax and alum

Stationery.—

Foolscap paper
Large yellow post ditto
Bath ditto
Vellum ditto
Brown packing ditto
Slates and pencils
Black lead pencils
Wafers and sealing wax
Wafer stamps

Shot of all sizes from No. 1 to No. 8
Buck and Swan ditto
Fine gunpowder
Brussels carpeting and hearth rugs and various other articles too numerous to mention.
An assortment of door knockers.

N. B. Wanted about 1000 Kangaroo Skins, for which a liberal price will be given.

INVALUABLE PREMISES FOR SALE.

MR. DUNN wishing to retire from his present business, offers for sale the Veranda Stores, occupied by himself; the stock on hand may either be taken or not, the average returns of the business, for these last five years, have been nearly twelve thousand pounds per annum. The house consists of nine apartments and most excellent cellarage underneath, a good garden and plenty of building ground, the store is nearly forty feet in length.

The situation and premises are so well known, that any remarks would be useless, such an opportunity may never occur again.

Time will be given on a part of the purchase money.

Apply to Mr. Dunn on the premises.

AUSTIN'S FERRY.

THE Undersigned, the Proprietor of the above Ferry, at Roseneath, returns his sincere thanks to the public for the liberal support they have afforded him for so many years, during which he has conducted the said Ferry, and begs to inform them that he has now Let the Roseneath Ferry, on the Hobart town side of the river, (having no connection with the other side) to Mr. Charles Medgyett Goodridge, late of the Cove point Ferry. Mr. Goodridge's attention to the safety and accommodation of the public is already too well known to require any comment by the undersigned, otherwise than his soliciting a continuance of patronage and preference to the Ferry at Roseneath, which he feels thoroughly convinced Mr. Goodridge's mertis, and will make it his study to preserve, having superior advantages to conduct such an Establishment. The punts are large, safe, and most superior, the accommodations great, and the circumstance of Mr. Goodridge having been brought up a mariner must be an additional qualification.

JAMES AUSTIN.

The disposal of land through grants, like those announced here for 1828, contributed to the growing tension between settlers and Indigenous Australians in Van Diemen's Land.

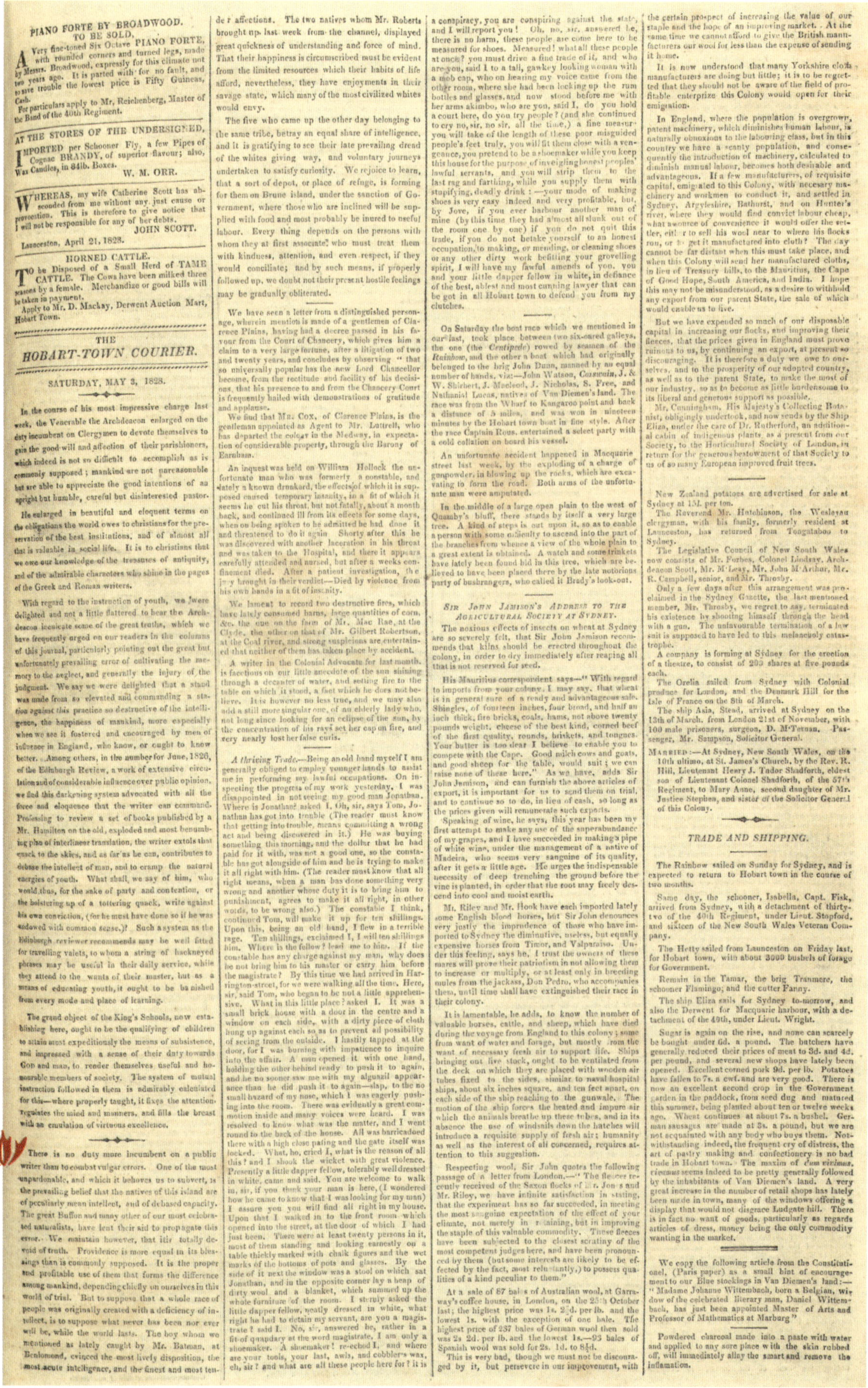

PIANO FORTE BY BROADWOOD.
TO BE SOLD,

A Very fine-toned Six Octave PIANO FORTE, with rounded corners and turned legs, made by Messrs. Broadwood, expressly for this climate not two years ago. It is parted with for no fault, and to save trouble the lowest price is Fifty Guineas, Cash.

For particulars apply to Mr. Reichenberg, Master of the Band of the 40th Regiment.

AT THE STORES OF THE UNDERSIGNED,

IMPORTED per Schooner Fly, a few Pipes of Cognac BRANDY, of superior flavour; also, Wax Candles, in 84lb. Boxes.

W. M. ORR.

WHEREAS, my wife Catherine Scott has absconded from me without any just cause or provocation. This is therefore to give notice that I will not be responsible for any of her debts.

JOHN SCOTT.

Launceston, April 21, 1828.

HORNED CATTLE.

TO be Disposed of a Small Herd of TAME CATTLE. The Cows have been milked three seasons by a female. Merchandize or good bills will be taken in payment.

Apply to Mr. D. Mackay, Derwent Auction Mart, Hobart Town.

THE
HOBART-TOWN COURIER.

SATURDAY, MAY 3, 1828.

In the course of his most impressive charge last week, the Venerable the Archdeacon enlarged on the duty incumbent on Clergymen to devote themselves to gain the good-will and affection of their parishioners, which indeed is not so difficult to accomplish as is commonly supposed; mankind are not unreasonable but are able to appreciate the good intentions of an upright but humble, careful but disinterested pastor.

He enlarged in beautiful and eloquent terms on the obligations the world owes to christians for the preservation of the best institutions, and of almost all that is valuable in social life. It is to christians that we owe our knowledge of the treasures of antiquity, and of the admirable characters who shine in the pages of the Greek and Roman writers.

With regard to the instruction of youth, we were delighted and not a little flattered to hear the Archdeacon inculcate some of the great truths, which we have frequently urged on our readers in the columns of this journal, particularly pointing out the great but unfortunately prevailing error of cultivating the memory to the neglect, and generally the injury of the judgment. We say we were delighted that a stand was made from so elevated and commanding a station against this practice so destructive of the intelligence, the happiness of mankind, more especially when we see it fostered and encouraged by men of influence in England, who know, or ought to know better. Among others, in the number for June, 1826, of the Edinburgh Review, a work of extensive circulation and of considerable influence over public opinion, we find this darkening system advocated with all the force and eloquence that the writer can command. Professing to review a set of books published by a Mr. Hamilton on the old, exploded and most benumbing plan of interlinear translation, the writer extols that quack to the skies, and as far as he can, contributes to debase the intellect of man, and to cramp the natural energies of youth. What shall we say of him, who would thus, for the sake of party and contention, or the bolstering up of a tottering quack, write against his own conviction, (for he must have done so if he was endowed with common sense.)? Such a system as the Edinburgh reviewer recommends may be well fitted for travelling valets, to whom a string of hackneyed phrases may be useful in their daily service, while they attend to the wants of their master, but as a means of educating youth, it ought to be banished from every mode and place of learning.

The grand object of the King's Schools, now establishing here, ought to be the qualifying of children to attain most expeditiously the means of subsistence, and impressed with a sense of their duty towards GOD and man, to render themselves useful and honourable members of society. The system of mutual instruction followed in them is admirably calculated for this—where properly taught, it fixes the attention, regulates the mind and manners, and fills the breast with an emulation of virtuous excellence.

There is no duty more incumbent on a public writer than to combat vulgar errors. One of the most unpardonable, and which it behoves us to subvert, is the prevailing belief that the natives of this island are of peculiarly mean intellect, and of debased capacity. The great Buffon and many other of our most celebrated naturalists, have lent their aid to propagate this error. We maintain however, that it is totally devoid of truth. Providence is more equal in its blessings than is commonly supposed. It is the proper and profitable use of them that forms the difference among mankind, depending chiefly on ourselves in this world of trial. But to suppose that a whole race of people was originally created with a deficiency of intellect, is to suppose what never has been nor ever will be, while the world lasts. The boy whom we mentioned as lately caught by Mr. Batman, at Benlomond, evinced the most lively disposition, the most acute intelligence, and the finest and most tender affections. The two natives whom Mr. Roberts brought up last week from the channel, displayed great quickness of understanding and force of mind. That their happiness is circumscribed must be evident from the limited resources which their habits of life afford, nevertheless, they have enjoyments in their savage state, which many of the most civilized whites would envy.

The five who came up the other day belonging to the same tribe, betray an equal share of intelligence, and it is gratifying to see their late prevailing dread of the whites giving way, and voluntary journeys undertaken to satisfy curiosity. We rejoice to learn, that a sort of depot, or place of refuge, is forming for them on Brune island, under the sanction of Government, where those who are inclined will be supplied with food and most probably be inured to useful labour. Every thing depends on the persons with whom they at first associate, who must treat them with kindness, attention, and even respect, if they would conciliate; and by such means, if properly followed up, we doubt not their present hostile feelings may be gradually obliterated.

We have seen a letter from a distinguished personage, wherein mention is made of a gentlemen of Clarence Plains, having had a decree passed in his favour from the Court of Chancery, which gives him a claim to a very large fortune, after a litigation of two and twenty years, and concludes by observing "that so universally popular has the new Lord Chancellor become, from the rectitude and facility of his decisions, that his presence to and from the Chancery Court is frequently hailed with demonstrations of gratitude and applause."

We find that MR. COX, of Clarence Plains, is the gentleman appointed as Agent to Mr. Luttrell, who has departed the colony in the Medway, in expectation of considerable property, through the Barony of Earnham.

An inquest was held on William Hollock the unfortunate man who was formerly a constable, and lately a known drunkard, the effects of which it is supposed caused temporary insanity, in a fit of which it seems he cut his throat, but not fatally, about a month back, and continued ill from its effects for some days, when on being spoken to he admitted he had done it and threatened to do it again. Shorty after this he was discovered with another laceration in his throat and was taken to the Hospital, and there it appears carefully attended and nursed, but after a weeks confinement died. After a patient investigation, the jury brought in their verdict—Died by violence from his own hands in a fit of insanity.

We lament to record two destructive fires, which have lately consumed barns, large quantities of corn, &c. the one on the farm of Mr. Mac Rae, at the Clyde, the other on that of Mr. Gilbert Robertson, at the Coal river, and strong suspicions are entertained that neither of them has taken place by accident.

A writer in the Colonial Advocate for last month, is facetious on our little anecdote of the sun shining through a decanter of water, and setting fire to the table on which it stood, a fact which he does not believe. It is however no less true, and we may also add a still more singular one, of an elderly lady who, not long since looking for an eclipse of the sun, by the concentration of his rays set her cap on fire, and very nearly lost her false curls.

A thriving Trade.—Being an old hand myself I am generally obliged to employ younger hands to assist me in performing my lawful occupations. On inspecting the progress of my work yesterday, I was disappointed in not seeing my good man Jonathan. Where is Jonathan? asked I. Oh, sir, says Tom, Jonathan has got into trouble (The reader must know that getting into trouble, means committing a wrong act and being discovered in it.) He was buying something this morning, and the dollar that he had paid for it with, was not a good one, so the constable has got alongside of him and he is trying to make it all right with him. (The reader must know that all right means, when a man has done something very wrong and another whose duty it is to bring him to punishment, agrees to make it all right, in other words, to be wrong also.) The constable I think, continued Tom, will make it up for ten shillings. Upon this, being an old hand, I flew in a terrible rage. Ten shillings, exclaimed I, I will ten shillings him. Where is the fellow? lead me to him. If the constable has any charge against my man, why does he not bring him to his master or carry him before the magistrate? By this time we had arrived in Harrington-street, for we were walking all the time. Here, sir, said Tom, who began to be not a little apprehensive. What in this little place? asked I. It was a small brick house with a door in the centre and a window on each side, with a dirty piece of cloth hung up against each so as to prevent all possibility of seeing from the outside. I hastily tapped at the door, for I was burning with impatience to inquire into the affair. A man opened it with one hand, holding the other behind ready to push it to again, and he no sooner saw me with my alguazil appearance than he did push it to again—slap, to the no small hazard of my nose, which I was eagerly pushing into the room. There was evidently a great commotion inside and many voices were heard. I was resolved to know what was the matter, and I went round to the back of the house. All was barricadoed there with a high close paling and the gate itself was locked. What, ho, cried I, what is the reason of all this? and I shook the wicket with great violence. Presently a little dapper fellow, tolerably well dressed in white, came and said. You are welcome to walk in, sir, if you think your man is here, (I wondered how he came to know that I was looking for my man) I assure you you will find all right in my house. Upon that I walked in to the front room which opened into the street, at the door of which I had just been. There were at least twenty persons in it, most of them standing and looking earnestly on a table thickly marked with chalk figures and the wet marks of the bottoms of pots and glasses. By the side of it next the window was a stool on which sat Jonathan, and in the opposite corner lay a heap of dirty wool and a blanket, which summed up the whole furniture of the room. I sternly asked the little dapper fellow, neatly dressed in white, what right he had to detain my servant, are you a magistrate? said I. No, sir, answered he, rather in a fit of quandary at the word magistrate, I am only a shoemaker. A shoemaker! re-echod I, and where are your tools, your last, awls, and cobbler's wax, eh, sir? and what are all these people here for? it is a conspiracy, you are conspiring against the state, and I will report you! Oh, no, sir, answered he, there is no harm, these people are come here to be measured for shoes. Measured! what all these people at once? you must drive a fine trade of it, and who are you, said I to a tall, gawkey looking woman with a mob cap, who on hearing my voice came from the other room, where she had been locking up the rum bottles and glasses, and now stood before me with her arms akimbo, who are you, said I, do you hold a court here, do you try people? (and she continued to cry no, sir, no sir, all the time,) a fine measure you will take of the length of these poor misguided people's feet truly, you will fit them close with a vengeance, you pretend to be a shoemaker while you keep this house for the purpose of inveigling honest peoples' lawful servants, and you will strip them to the last rag and farthing, while you supply them with stupifying, deadly drink: —your mode of making shoes is very easy indeed and very profitable, but, by Jove, if you ever harbour another man of mine (by this time they had almost all slunk out of the room one by one) if you do not quit this trade, if you do not betake yourself to an honest occupation, to making, or mending, or cleaning shoes or any other dirty work befitting your grovelling spirit, I will have my fawful amends of you, you and your little dapper fellow in white, in defiance of the best, ablest and most cunning lawyer that can be got in all Hobart town to defend you from my clutches.

On Saturday the boat race which we mentioned in our last, took place between two six-oared galleys, the one (the *Centipede*) rowed by seamen of the *Rainbow*, and the other a boat which had originally belonged to the brig John Dunn, manned by an equal number of hands, viz:—John Watson, *Coxswain*, J. & W. Shirbert, J. Macleod, J. Nicholas, S. Free, and Nathanial Lucas, natives of Van Diemen's land. The race was from the Wharf to Kangaroo point and back a distance of 5 miles, and was won in nineteen minutes by the Hobart town boat in fine style. After the race Captain Rous, entertained a select party with a cold collation on board his vessel.

An unfortunate accident happened in Macquarie street last week, by the exploding of a charge of gunpowder, in blowing up the rocks, which are excavating to form the road. Both arms of the unfortunate man were amputated.

In the middle of a large open plain to the west of Quamby's bluff, there stands by itself a very large tree. A kind of steps is cut upon it, so as to enable a person with some difficulty to ascend into the part of the branches from whence a view of the whole plain to a great extent is obtained. A watch and some trinkets have lately been found hid in this tree, which are believed to have been placed there by the late notorious party of bushrangers, who called it Brady's look-out.

SIR JOHN JAMISON'S ADDRESS TO THE AGRICULTURAL SOCIETY AT SYDNEY.

The noxious effects of insects on wheat at Sydney are so severely felt, that Sir John Jamison recommends that kilns should be erected throughout the colony, in order to dry immediately after reaping all that is not reserved for seed.

His Mauritius correspondent says—"With regard to imports from your colony, I may say, that wheat is in general sure of a ready and advantageous sale. Shingles, of fourteen inches, four broad, and half an inch thick, fire bricks, coals, hams, not above twenty pounds weight, cheese of the best kind, corned beef of the first quality, rounds, briskets, and tongues. Your butter is too dear I believe to enable you to compete with the Cape. Good milch cows and goats, and good sheep for the table, would suit; we can raise none of these here." As we have, adds Sir John Jamison, and can furnish the above articles of export, it is important for us to send them on trial, and to continue so to do, in lieu of cash, so long as the prices given will remunerate such exports.

Speaking of wine, he says, this year has been my first attempt to make any use of the superabundance of my grapes, and I have succeeded in making a pipe of white wine, under the management of a native of Madeira, who seems very sanguine of its quality, after it gets a little age. He urges the indispensable necessity of deep trenching the ground before the vine is planted, in order that the root may freely descend into cool and moist earth.

Mr. Riley and Mr. Hook have each imported lately some English blood horses, but Sir John denounces very justly the imprudence of those who have imported to Sydney the diminutive, useless, but equally expensive horses from Timor, and Valparaiso. Under this feeling, says he, I trust the owners of these mares will prove their patriotism in not allowing them to increase or multiply, or at least only in breeding mules from the jackass, Don Pedro, who accompanies them, until time shall have extinguished their race in their colony.

It is lamentable, he adds, to know the number of valuable horses, cattle, and sheep, which have died during the voyage from England to this colony; some from want of water and forage, but mostly from the want of necessary fresh air to support life. Ships bringing out live stock, ought to be ventilated from the deck on which they are placed with wooden air tubes fixed to the sides, similar to naval hospital ships, about six inches square, and ten feet apart, on each side of the ship reaching to the gunwale. The motion of the ship forces the heated and impure air which the animals breathe up these tubes, and in its absence the use of windsails down the hatches will introduce a requisite supply of fresh air; humanity as well as the interest of all concerned, requires attention to this suggestion.

Respecting wool, Sir John quotes the following passage of a letter from London.—"The fleeces recently received of the Saxon flocks of Mr. Jones and Mr. Riley, we have infinite satisfaction in stating, that the experiment has so far succeeded, in meeting the most sanguine expectation of the effect of your climate, not merely in retaining, but in improving the staple of this valuable commodity. These fleeces have been subjected to the closest scrutiny of the most competent judges here, and have been pronounced by them (but some interests are likely to be effected by the fact, most reluctantly,) to possess qualities of a kind peculiar to them."

At a sale of 87 bales of Australian wool, at Garraway's coffee house, in London, on the 25th October last; the highest price was 1s. 2½d. per lb. and the lowest 1s. with the exception of one bale. The highest price of 237 bales of German wool then sold was 2s 2d. per lb. and the lowest 1s.—93 bales of Spanish wool was sold for 2s. 1d. to 8½d.

This is very bad, though we must not be discouraged by it, but persevere in our improvement, with the certain prospect of increasing the value of our staple and the hope of an improving market. At the same time we cannot afford to give the British manufacturers our wool for less than the expense of sending it home.

It is now understood that many Yorkshire cloth manufacturers are doing but little; it is to be regretted that they should not be aware of the field of profitable enterprize this Colony would open for their emigration.

In England, where the population is overgrown, patent machinery, which diminishes human labour, is naturally obnoxious to the labouring class, but in this country we have a scanty population, and consequently the introduction of machinery, calculated to diminish manual labour, becomes both desirable and advantageous. If a few manufacturers, of requisite capital, emigrated to this Colony, with necesary machinery and workmen to conduct it, and settled in Sydney, Argyleshire, Bathurst, and on Hunter's river, where they would find convict labour cheap, what a source of convenience it would offer the settler, either to sell his wool near to where his flocks run, or to get it manufactured into cloth? The day cannot be far distant when this must take place, and when this Colony will send her manufactured cloths, in lieu of Treasury bills, to the Mauritius, the Cape of Good Hope, South America, and India. I hope this may not be misunderstood, as a desire to withhold any export from our parent State, the sale of which would enable us to live.

But we have expended so much of our disposable capital in increasing our flocks, and improving their fleeces, that the prices given in England must prove ruinous to us, by continuing an export, at present so discouraging. It is therefore a duty we owe to ourselves, and to the prosperity of our adopted country, as well as to the parent State, to make the most of our industry, so as to become as little burdensome to its liberal and generous support as possible.

Mr. Cunningham, His Majesty's Collecting Botanist, obligingly undertook, and now sends by the Ship Eliza, under the care of Dr. Rutherford, an additional cabin of indigenous plants, as a present from our Society, to the Horticultural Society of London, in return for the generous bestowment of that Society to us of so many European improved fruit trees.

New Zealand potatoes are advertised for sale at Sydney at 15*l.* per ton.

The Reverend Mr. Hutchinson, the Wesleyan clergyman, with his family, formerly resident at Launceston, has returned from Tongataboo to Sydney.

The Legislative Council of New South Wales now consists of Mr. Forbes, Colonel Lindsay, Archdeacon Scott, Mr. M'Leay, Mr. John M'Arthur, Mr. R. Campbell, senior, and Mr. Throsby.

Only a few days after this arrangement was proclaimed in the Sydney Gazette, the last mentioned member, Mr. Throsby, we regret to say, terminated his existence by shooting himself through the head with a gun. The unfavourable termination of a law suit is supposed to have led to this melancholy catastrophe.

A company is forming at Sydney for the erection of a theatre, to consist of 200 shares at five pounds each.

The Orelia sailed from Sydney with Colonial produce for London, and the Denmark Hill for the Isle of France on the 8th of March.

The ship Asia, Stead, arrived at Sydney on the 13th of March, from London 21st of November, with 100 male prisoners, surgeon, D. M'Tetnan. Passenger, Mr. Sampson, Solicitor General.

MARRIED:—At Sydney, New South Wales, on the 10th ultimo, at St. James's Church, by the Rev. R. Hill, Lieutenant Henry J. Tudor Shadforth, eldest son of Lieutenant Colonel Shadforth, of the 57th Regiment, to Mary Anne, second daughter of Mr. Justice Stephen, and sister of the Solicitor General of this Colony.

TRADE AND SHIPPING.

The Rainbow sailed on Sunday for Sydney, and is expected to return to Hobart town in the course of two months.

Same day, the schooner, Isabella, Capt. Fisk, arrived from Sydney, with a detachment of thirty-two of the 40th Regiment, under Lieut. Stopford, and sixteen of the New South Wales Veteran Company.

The Hetty sailed from Launceston on Friday last, for Hobart town, with about 3000 bushels of forage for Government.

Remain in the Tamar, the brig Tranmere, the schooner Flamingo, and the cutter Fanny.

The ship Eliza sails for Sydney to-morrow, and also the Derwent for Macquarie harbour, with a detachment of the 40th, under Lieut. Wright.

Sugar is again on the rise, and none can scarcely be bought under 6d. a pound. The butchers have generally reduced their prices of meat to 3d. and 4d. per pound, and several new shops have lately been opened. Excellent corned pork 9d. per lb. Potatoes have fallen to 7s. a cwt. and are very good. There is now an excellent second crop in the Government garden in the paddock, from seed dug and matured this summer, being planted about ten or twelve weeks ago. Wheat continues at about 7s. a bushel. German sausages are made at 3s. a pound, but we are not acquainted with any body who buys them. Notwithstanding indeed, the frequent cry of distress, the art of pastry making and confectionery is no bad trade in Hobart town. The maxim of *dum vivimus, vivamus* seems indeed to be pretty generally followed by the inhabitants of Van Diemen's land. A very great increase in the number of retail shops has lately been made in town, many of the windows offering a display that would not disgrace Ludgate hill. There is in fact no want of goods, particularly as regards articles of dress, money being the only commodity wanting in the market.

We copy the following article from the Constitutionel, (Paris paper) as a small hint of encouragement to our Blue stockings in Van Diemen's land:—"Madame Johanne Wittembach, born a Belgian, widow of the celebrated literary man, Daniel Wittembach, has just been appointed Master of Arts and Professor of Mathematics at Marburg"

Powdered charcoal made into a paste with water and applied to any sore place with the skin rubbed off, will immediately allay the smart and remove the inflamation.

Despite much aggressive racism, some European attitudes to Aboriginal people in Tasmania were compassionate, though patronising. James Ross' editorial of 3 May 1828 highlights this, and shows no understanding of how removing Aboriginal people to places of 'refuge' would ultimately play out.

THE HOBART-TOWN COURIER.

SATURDAY, MAY 3, 1828

...

There is no duty more incumbent on a public writer than to combat vulgar errors. One of the most unpardonable, and which it behoves us to subvert, is the prevailing belief that the natives of this island are of peculiarly mean intellect, and of debased capacity. The great Buffon and many other of our most celebrated naturalists, have lent their aid to propagate this error. We maintain however, that it is totally devoid of truth. Providence is more equal in its blessings than is commonly supposed. It is the proper and profitable use of them that forms the difference among mankind, depending chiefly on ourselves in this world of trial. But to suppose that a whole race of people was originally created with a deficiency of intellect, is to suppose what never has been nor ever will be, while the world lasts. The boy whom we mentioned as lately caught by Mr. Batman, at Benlomond, evinced the most lively disposition, the most acute intelligence, and the finest and most tender affections. The two natives whom Mr. Roberts brought up last week from the channel, displayed great quickness of understanding and force of mind. That their happiness is circumscribed must be evident from the limited resources which their habits of life afford, nevertheless, they have enjoyments in their savage state, which many of the most civilized whites would envy.

The five who came up the other day belonging to the same tribe, betray an equal share of intelligence, and it is gratifying to see their late prevailing dread of the whites giving way, and voluntary journeys undertaken to satisfy curiosity. We rejoice to learn, that a sort of depot, or place of refuge, is forming for them on Brune island, under the sanction of Government, where those who are inclined will be supplied with food and most probably be inured to useful labour. Every thing depends on the persons with whom they at first associate, who must treat them with kindness, attention, and even respect, if they would conciliate; and by such means, if properly followed up, we doubt not their present hostile feelings may be gradually obliterated.

15 A colonial afterthought

The free colony of Western Australia, 1829

WHEN CAPTAIN JAMES COOK, AND THEN GOVERNOR ARTHUR PHILLIP, MADE THE FIRST DECLARATIONS OF POSSESSION OF THE LANDS OF NEW HOLLAND, THEY CLAIMED FOR THE BRITISH CROWN ONLY THE LAND EXTENDING TO LONGITUDE 129 DEGREES EAST, THE PRESENT-DAY BORDER OF WESTERN AUSTRALIA. THE WEST WAS IGNORED FOR THE NEXT FORTY YEARS.

The few European visitors to the western coastline in the early 1800s did not find any good agricultural land, and so no European colonial power bothered to claim the area. This oversight was rectified in 1829, when the first settlement at Perth was established.

In 1827 Captain James Stirling (1791–1865) had been sent to investigate the continent's western coast near the Swan River and, on his return to England, pushed the idea of establishing a free settlement there—one without convicts.

Rumours of French interest in establishing their own penal colony in this huge uncolonised area in the western part of the continent, seem to have given officials in London a new awareness of the failure to proclaim it as part of the British colonies in Australia. The British Colonial Office agreed with Stirling that a colony should be established in the west of the continent, and it issued official orders proclaiming him lieutenant governor on arrival.

In 1829 Stirling took three ship loads of settlers from Britain to establish what became the Swan River Colony, near the present-day city of Perth. Despite Stirling's over-estimation of potential farmland in the area, the colony just managed to survive until 1832, when he belatedly received his commission to govern the entire colony of Western Australia.

The establishment of a free settlement without convicts was significant in the nascent politics of Australian nationalism. However the cheap labour force that the convict system offered—an alternative to the use of slavery that other colonial powers had followed—was critical for the establishment of most of the British colonies in Australia. Even the 'free' settlement of Western Australia found it difficult without them, and convicts were first transported to the new colony in 1850, several years after the other colonies no longer received convicts.

OPPOSITE
The Sydney Gazette *of 1 September 1829 recorded the passing of the British parliamentary bill organising the government of a colony in Western Australia. The news trailed the arrival of Stirling and his ships, in April-May of that year, by several months.*

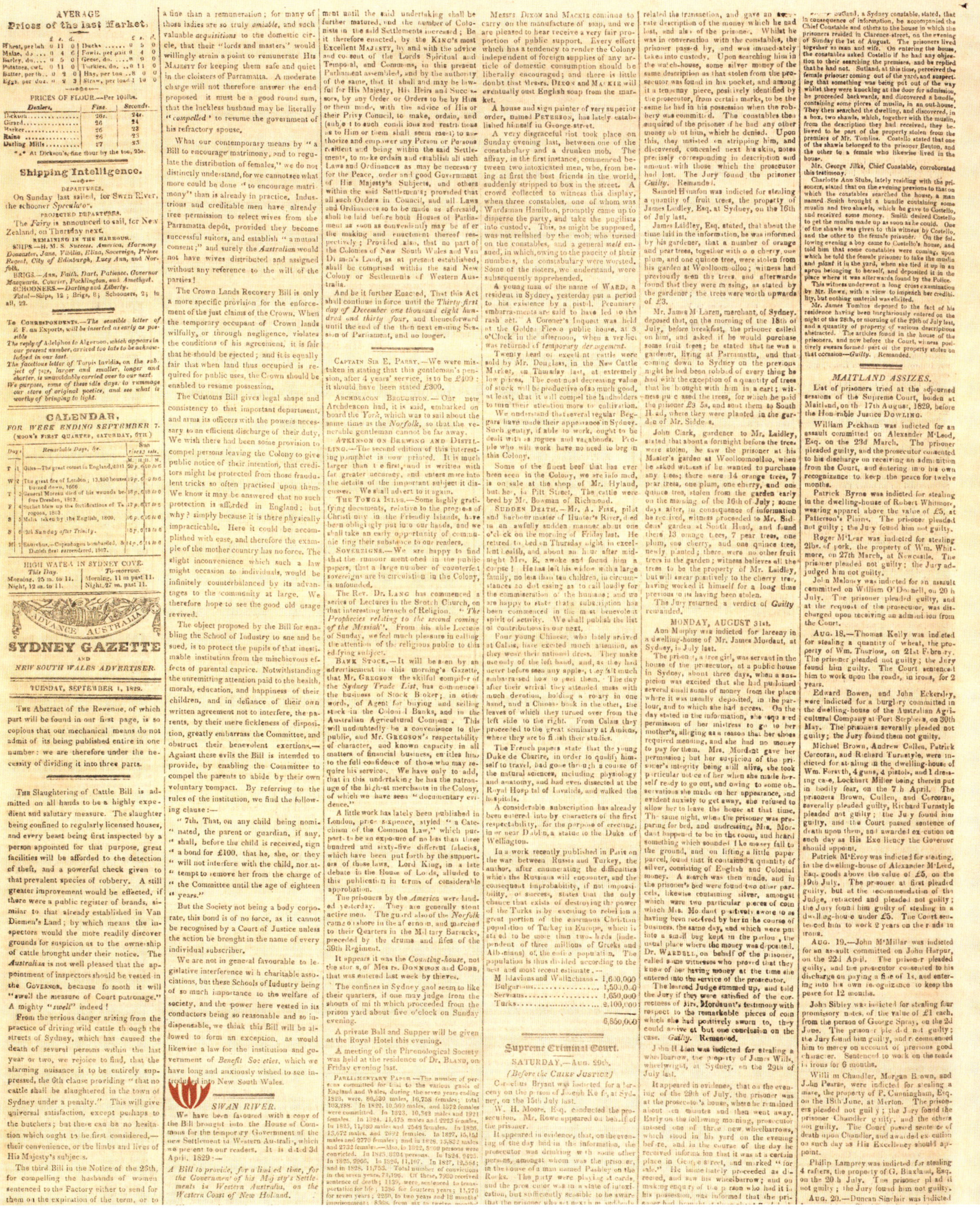

SYDNEY GAZETTE AND NEW SOUTH WALES ADVERTISER.

TUESDAY, SEPTEMBER 1, 1829.

SWAN RIVER.

We have been favoured with a copy of the Bill brought into the House of Commons for the temporary Government of the new Settlement in Western Australia, which we present to our readers. It is dated 3d April, 1829:—

A Bill to provide, for a limited time, for the Government of his Majesty's Settlements in Western Australia, on the Western Coast of New Holland.

Transcription

16 *There was a wild colonial boy*

Bold Jack Donohoe, terror of Sydney Town, 1830

FROM THE FIRST DAYS AFTER LANDING AT SYDNEY COVE, CONVICTS HAD TAKEN TO THE BUSH. MANY TRIED TO ESCAPE OVERLAND OR BY CAPTURED SHIP TO BATAVIA OR CHINA—THOUGH MOST ENDED UP EITHER DYING IN THE BUSH OR EVENTUALLY COMING BACK TO THE SETTLEMENTS, TO FACE PUNISHMENT. A FEW MANAGED TO LIVE WITH ABORIGINAL PEOPLE OR ADOPT ABORIGINAL BUSH SKILLS AND SURVIVE ON THE OUTSKIRTS OF SYDNEY, OCCASIONALLY PLUNDERING OUTLYING SETTLEMENTS. LABELLED 'BUSH RANGERS' BY COLONIAL AUTHORITIES, THEY BECAME A PROBLEM FOR THE NEXT HUNDRED YEARS, AND PART OF AUSTRALIAN FOLKLORE.

Jack Donohoe (1806?–1830) was an Irish convict who arrived in Sydney in 1825. In 1827, with two other convicts, Kilroy and Smith, he robbed a bullock dray on the Sydney to Windsor road. The three were captured and sentenced to be hanged, but Donohoe miraculously escaped from his irons and, over the next two-and-a-half years, became the most celebrated bushranger in the colony.

In mid-1828, Donohoe joined a large gang who were crossing the Blue Mountains in search of a rumoured 'free colony' of escaped convicts. They were closely followed by police constables and Aboriginal guides or 'trackers', who since the 1790s had become an important arm of the early police force. The party met the bushrangers north-west of Bathurst but, after a shoot-out that carried on overnight, a wounded Donohoe escaped once more and fell to plundering the outskirts of Sydney. Operating with a small gang of just two or three, Donohoe quickly became famous for targeting the rich.

In 1830, soldiers were seconded to the police force to help capture Donohoe and eventually, in the late afternoon of 1 September 1830, a detachment found the gang in the Bringelly scrub south-west of Sydney. Donohoe was reported to have used 'the most insulting and indecent epithets' towards the police before he was killed by a double shot fired by Trooper Michael Muggleston.

The announcement of Donohoe's death in *The Sydney Gazette* of 4 September would no doubt have brought great relief to many travellers and people living in the outlying settlements of Sydney. Although Donohoe was an outlaw, he had become a widely admired hero among the convicts and many of the poorer settlers and ex-convicts. Clay pipes were decorated with his likeness and songs were composed about him—he appears to have been the inspiration for the legendary 'Wild Colonial Boy'.

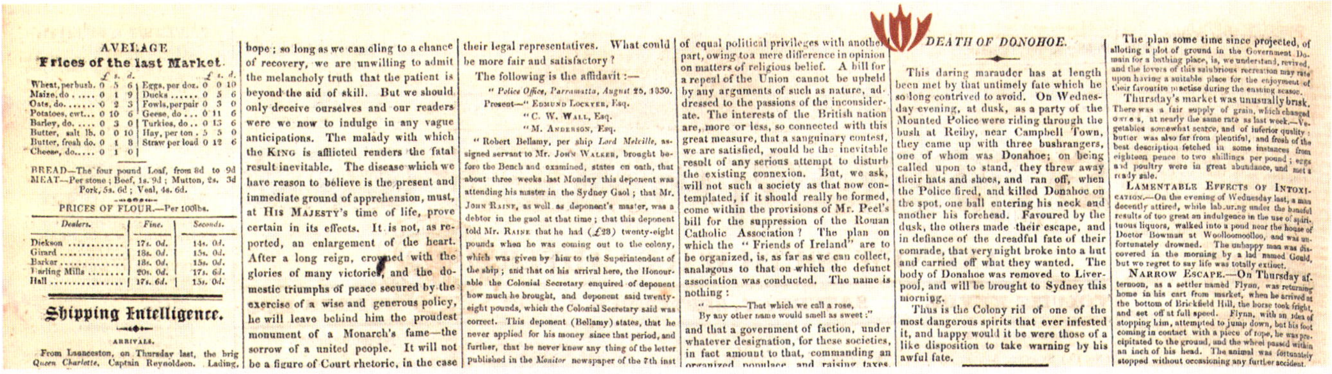

DEATH OF DONOHOE.

This daring marauder has at length been met by that untimely fate which he so long contrived to avoid. On Wednesday evening, at dusk, as a party of the Mounted Police were riding through the bush at Reiby, near Campbell Town, they came up with three bushrangers, one of whom was Donahoe; on being called upon to stand, they threw away their hats and shoes, and ran off, when the Police fired, and killed Donahoe on the spot, one ball entering his neck and another his forehead. Favoured by the dusk, the others made their escape, and in defiance of the dreadful fate of their comrade, that very night broke into a hut and carried off what they wanted. The body of Donahoe was removed to Liverpool, and will be brought to Sydney this morning.

Thus is the Colony rid of one of the most dangerous spirits that ever infested it, and happy would it be were those of a like disposition to take warning by his awful fate.

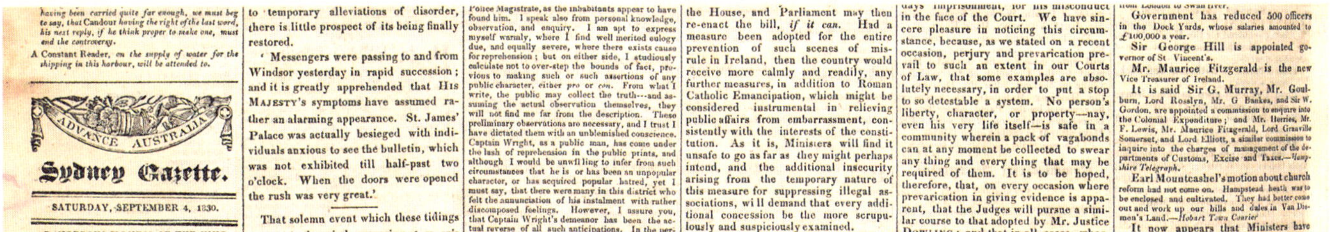

Donohoe's death was important news. The Sydney Gazette *report of his last stand and the escape of the members of his small gang, shoeless and hatless, was written in the thrilling tones of an adventure story—though it ends on a moral note.*

Sheep, squatters and massacres

1831–

-1850

The 1830s and 1840s were a significant turning point for the Australian colonies. While settlers continued to move overland from Sydney into Wiradjuri and other Aboriginal lands in western New South Wales, new settlements and penal outposts at Port Phillip (Melbourne), Swan River (Perth), Moreton Bay (Brisbane) and other smaller sites on the east coast, such as Port Macquarie, were established. The colony's first major export industry—whaling—was to be rapidly overtaken.

WHILE MOST SETTLEMENT STILL CLUNG TO THE MORE FERTILE COASTLINES, THE AGE OF SQUATTING HAD BEGUN. WITH BOOMING POPULATIONS AND INDUSTRIALISATION IN EUROPE, THE DEMAND FOR WOOL INCREASED AND ITS PRODUCTION HAD BECOME AN INCREASINGLY LUCRATIVE BUSINESS IN THE COLONY. THOSE WITH A LITTLE CAPITAL TO INVEST BEGAN TO TAKE SHEEP AND CATTLE INTO AN INTERIOR THAT EXPLORERS DESCRIBED AS GREAT EXPANSES OF GRASSLANDS THINLY POPULATED BY ABORIGINAL PEOPLE. THE GROWTH OF ARGUABLY AUSTRALIA'S GREATEST, AND DEFINITELY MOST ROMANTICISED, INDUSTRY HAD BEGUN.

During the 1820s enterprising gentlemen and government surveyors began to explore the hinterlands of New South Wales and Victoria. Some, such as Surveyor-General Thomas Mitchell, brought back glowing reports of great river systems with well-watered country—perfect for grazing sheep and cattle. Mitchell's vivid descriptions of the grasslands of what he termed *Australia Felix* were published in 1838, and word spread quickly among settlers who could readily see the advantages of taking up large tracts of land for relatively little cost. Apart from government officials ensuring that squatters travelled well supplied with firearms, they gave little thought to the traditional owners of these lands.

Squatting was based on settlers intent on establishing sheep or cattle stations by marking out large areas of land outside the official government boundaries. The squatters took their flocks and herds beyond the official limits of settlement and quite illegally took up runs in the hope of later having them turned into leasehold when settlement finally caught up with them 'beyond the frontier'.

Setting up a squatting run usually required some capital. The growing numbers of locally born men and women as well as ex-convicts found a new avenue to wealth—and social acceptability—and they often financed expeditions to look for new squatting runs. Many, such as Sydney-born William Charles Wentworth, turned a nice profit by setting up a pastoral run, getting it ratified as leasehold, and then selling a working pastoral station lease to a prospective pastoralist. Some squatters tried to claim huge runs, sometimes more than 200,000 hectares in extent, and government officials were soon kept busy trying to sort out these often overlapping and hotly contested land grabs.

Squatting brought with it a new version of the old political squabbles between the government and the colonial entrepreneurs. Yet it was also a critical period in the colonisation of the country. It was a time that laid out the shape of future settlement across the vast interior and established an industry that was to be the backbone of the nation for many years. Beyond the frontier, pastoralism became the most important point of contact between the expanding European population and the many Aboriginal nations that had not yet been impacted by colonialism.

The squatters were often willing employers of Aboriginal workers, who knew the land and were skilful stock workers. Early pastoralism also suited Aboriginal people, as it meant they could obtain employment and remain on their traditional lands. But when the squatters began to fence their runs and control access to rivers and waterways—the lifeblood of the drier inland areas in particular—significant conflict began.

Many Europeans believed they were above the law in dealing with Aboriginal people, whom they saw as a hindrance to European exploitation of the land. In what became a tragic and all too common occurrence, squatters and settlers whose sheep or cattle were speared by Aboriginal people sometimes took revenge by descending on Aboriginal campsites and killing all the inhabitants.

However, not all Europeans, and certainly not the colonial authorities attempting to dispense British justice, turned a blind eye to these massacres. During 1838 several Europeans were bought to trial and faced corporal punishment for a massacre at Myall Creek in northern New South Wales. Momentarily at least, political debates about the rights of Aboriginal people filled the newspapers. In 1838, *The Sydney Morning Herald* editorial supported the accused murderers of Myall Creek and described Aborigines on the frontier as 'pests'.

Away from the frontier in the more settled areas of the colonies, the communication of news itself became an increasingly central issue in colonial politics. Different newspapers took particular editorial lines and showed allegiances to varying political voices. Some newspapers asserted they objectively reported news, while others unashamedly espoused politics. In 1831 *The Australian* newspaper rejoiced at news of the recall of Governor Darling and the instalment of Governor Brisbane.

The early Australian newspapers were modelled on the format of *The Sydney Gazette*. There was still no concept of a front page that contained the important news headlines of the day, and Public Notices rather than headlines filled front pages during the 1840s. While some papers developed sensationalist editorial styles, none published headline stories on their front pages. Bold front pages that led with the most important story of the day were still yet to appear.

17 *Candour, honesty, and honor*

The first issue of *The Sydney Morning Herald*, 1831

THE FIRST ISSUE OF THE LONG-RUNNING *SYDNEY MORNING HERALD*—INITIALLY PUBLISHED AS THE *SYDNEY HERALD*—CAME OFF THE PRESSES AT REDMAN'S COURT NEAR GEORGE STREET IN SYDNEY ON MONDAY, 18 APRIL 1831. THE NEW INDEPENDENT PAPER WAS PRODUCED BY THREE FORMER *SYDNEY GAZETTE* PRINTERS AND WRITERS, ALFRED WARD STEPHENS (1804–1852), FREDERICK STOKES (1805–?) AND WILLIAM MCGARVIE (1810–1841).

The *Herald's* editorial policy—laid out in a bold statement of principles in this first issue—was important news. The first issue is also significant because it was the beginning of a newspaper that was to dominate the Australian news scene for much of the nineteenth century, and it is the only one of the early newspapers to be published continuously until the present day.

Considering the importance of newspapers in political debates in the colony at the time, *The Sydney Herald* was a pointed attempt to insert an 'impartial' communication into the growing mix of often decidedly partial papers. *The Sydney Gazette* had remained conservative. *The Australian* and *The Sydney Monitor* had both been established in the 1820s and were considered to support liberal views. The *Herald* struck a chord with the growing middle classes of Sydney. From an initial 750 copies in 1831, it expanded to become a daily newspaper in 1840, and the most significant paper in the colony.

There were also several attempts to produce newspapers for broader audiences than the one the *Herald* catered for. Some wonderfully named but short-lived papers during the 1840s include the *John Bull, Dispatch, Bee, Star* and *Working Man's Guardian, Sydney Weekly,* the *Citizen* and the *People's Advocate.* However newspapers were still relatively expensive to produce and were seen as something for the educated classes. In the 1830s they did not generally appeal to 'citizens' and 'working men'.

In its editorial pursuit of the virtues of 'candour, honesty, and honor', the *Herald* was to develop a reputation for conservatism, particularly after it was purchased in 1841 by a printer and journalist who had arrived penniless in the colony in 1838, John Fairfax (1804–1877). Fairfax developed a strong editorial line of supporting 'the established order' that was continued with the Fairfax family–dominated company for another 137 years.

While other papers gradually moved news to their front pages from the 1850s, the *Herald* did not follow suit until 1944!

THE SYDNEY HERALD.

"In moderation placing all my glory,
While Tories call me Whig—and Whigs a Tory."—POPE.

TERMS OF SUBSCRIPTION, *Sydney, per quarter 5s.—Single Numbers 7d. Country, (postage included) 6s 3d p. quarter.* VOLUME I. MONDAY, APRIL 18, 1831. NUMBER I. TERMS OF ADVERTISEMENTS. *For Eight Lines and under, 2s 6d, and 1d each for every Line above Eight.*

Public Notice.

Colonial Secretary's Office, Sydney, April 4, 1831.

THE undermentioned Prisoners of the Crown have obtained Tickets of Leave since the last day of publication, viz:—

Government Notice.

HIS Excellency the Governor has been pleased to approve of the appointment of Mr. Charles Cowper, to be Clerk to the Commissioners for managing the affairs of the Church and School Estates.

Government Notice.

HIS Excellency the Governor directs it to be notified, that the following Rules and Regulations, for the conduct of business in the Supreme Court, which have been prepared by His Honor the Chief Justice, have been transmitted to England for His Majesty's confirmation and allowance, as required by the Order of the King in Council, dated the 12th day of October, 1824.

I, Francis Forbes, Esquire, Chief Justice of the Supreme Court of New South Wales, do hereby certify, that the several Rules and Regulations, hereunto annexed ...

Government Notice.

Colonial Secretary's Office, Sydney, April 12, 1831.

A BRICK BARREL DRAIN being required from the rear of the Military Barracks to Darling Harbour, persons disposed to contract for Building the same, are requested to transmit Tenders to this Office, by Twelve o'Clock on Monday the Second of May next, sealed and endorsed "Tender for Drain."

For LIVERPOOL Direct,

THE Fine A. 1 Brig EARL OF LIVERPOOL ...

Penrith, on the Nepean.

THE LEASE of a capital FARM of FORTY ACRES ...

For Sale by Auction,

BY MR. SAMUEL LYONS.

A THIRTY ACRE FARM,

FOUR SECTIONS OF A FARM,

A SECTION, (640) ACRES

For Sale by Auction,

BY MR. SAMUEL LYONS,

A NEAT COTTAGE

ALLOTMENT OF GROUND,

Splendid Views of Scotland and Calcutta.

Government Notice.

HIS Excellency the Governor has been pleased to approve of the following alterations in the Police of the Colony, namely:—

AN APPRENTICE WANTED to the PRINTING BUSINESS. Apply at the Office of this Paper.

CHEAP PRINTING.

IN DRAWING THE ATTENTION of their Friends, and the Public in general, to the following List of Prices,

STEPHENS, STOKES, & M'GARVIE

Redman's-court, George-street, Sydney.

Reproduced here is the front page of the first edition of The Sydney Morning Herald. *The final paragraph of the editorial, reproduced on the following page, is an eloquent expression of the principles of impartiality that many have argued the Herald has not held since it was first labelled 'the Granny' for espousing conservative views in the 1850s.*

Candour, honesty, and honor

For Sale by Auction.

The Sydney Estates of the late John Thomas Campbell, Esq., Member of Council, &c. &c. &c.

TWO MANSIONS, AND A COTTAGE WITH THREE STREET FRONTAGES.

BY MR. BODENHAM.

On the premises, at the corner of Macquarie, Hunter, and Philip streets, on Friday, the 13th of May, at 12 o'clock precisely.

MR. BODENHAM has the honor to notify, that in pursuance of instructions received by Mr. Manning, from the heir at law, of the late John Thomas Campbell, Esq. Member of the Legislative Council, he will bring to the hammer the

out reserve.

Terms of Payment—A deposit of 15 per cent. cash, and approved endorsed bills, at 3, 6, 9 and 12 months, will be taken for the residue, with security upon the property sold.

Purchasers to pay their own conveyances.

The title deeds may be seen at the Office of Mr. Norton, and the ground plan at the Estate, Land Agency, and Surveying Office of Mr. Bodenham.

MESSRS. LAMB, BUCHANAN, and Co., have on Sale at their New Stores in Castlereagh street, the undermentioned GOODS, viz.—

Anchors and Chain Cables
Blacking
Canvass
Carpeting, Venetian, Brussels, and Kidderminster
Corks
Cotton Goods, white
Coopers' Adzes and Axes
Crow Bars
Dairy Ware, assorted
Dennetts and Stanhopes, London built
Farriers' Tools
Flints
Fruits, in three dozen cases
Glass Ware of various kinds
do. Window, of sizes
Gloves
Glue
Guns, Rifle and Fowling
Harness, Gig and Cart
Horse Hair and Satin Seating
Jams and Jellies, in one dozen cases
Ink and Ink Powders, black and red
Iron, square, round, flat and hoop
Lamps, table
Lead Pipes
Medicines, an invoice
Nails and Rivets, assorted
Oil, Linseed, in jars and casks
Paint, of all colours
Paintings, by celebrated masters
Paper and Parchment
Pewter Ware, of different kinds
Plaid, of various patterns
Plated Ware, an elegant assortment
Bennets, Irish velves
Roman Cement
Rotten Stone
Rosin, pale and dark
Rugs
Sickles and Sheep Shears
Shot Belts and Powder Flasks
Spades
Stationery
Tin, Grain
Turpentine
Walnuts
Whale Line and Whaling Gear.
WINES AND LIQUORS,
Champagne, Sparkling Burgundy, Claret, Madeira — In Bottles
Port, in cask or bottle
Taylor's Porter
Charrington's and Ashby's Ale
Rum, Brandy — By the cask or five gallons

Sydney, 16th April, 1831.

NOTICE TO CORRESPONDENTS.

Joseph's Farewell.—The Emigrant.—Oh! Glorious sight to me.—The Convict's Dirge.—The Two Dogs.—The Smile and the Tear.—Ode to Despair, &c., shall appear.

We thank the Gentleman who sent us the French Work on the Vine, it shall be translated.

Servant of All Work.—Soho.—Retired Prig.—Raw Head.—Barney, and others, are cleverly done, and will appear.

Ortho—and Hetero—Doxy, though a true bill, is an unseemly doxy.

Colin Clout's extremely pungent Dialogue with the Land Board is withheld, "*Nous verrons.*"

If Colonus would oblige us with the loan of the work to which he alludes, we will gladly follow his advice.

The Essays on the India Question.—The Vine Husbandry.—Colonial Machinery, and the Extracts from the Canadian Paper on the Dollar System, will meet ready insertion.

Trunnion, on the Sir George Murray.—Pounder, on the Impounding Act.—Typo, on Printing by Contract, &c., are under consideration.

The Sydney Herald.

MONDAY, APRIL 18th, 1831.

"Sworn to no Master, of no Sect am I."

PUBLIC Opinion is so much guided, in the present age, by the Press, that every new attempt to increase its range, must be interesting to the community. It is expected, too, that when an Editor "Makes his first attempt on any stage," he shall conform to custom, and set forth the general bearing of his sentiments, and his claims for support. We shall state our claims to attention in a few words, and trust to our future efforts to please and instruct, for a continuance of patronage.

Editors, it must be acknowledged, are not, in all cases, guided by motives that will bear scrutiny. Armed with an engine of the most comprehensive powers, and wielding, with dexterity, the Editorial *We*, which gives the force of num-

soporific draughts to their drowsy customers. A man of the first class is all fire; touch Magna Charta, and he is in flames; talk of taxes, and he buttons his pockets, seizes his cudgel, arms his pistols to the teeth with broken letter or unsorted *pie*, and threatens destruction to all who pronounce upon the excellence, or the policy of the measure. Speak of war, and he foams—of the Censor, and he raves—of libels and *ex officios*, and he vows and swears with the bitterness of Bedlam. If wholesome restraint be anticipated, he brandishes his shears and his quill with a giant's strength, forgetful that it is tyrannous to use it like a giant. Public men have not the benefit of honest intentions. The Church is denied her benefit of clergy. The scarlet coat of the hoary veteran is dyed black, and the gilded spontoon is ignominiously broken. The gracious dispenser of the loaves and fishes is reprobated, because his fishes are minnows, and his loaves are unpalatable crusts. Prose and Poetry are called in to ridicule and insult the best and the most upright of men; and the Muses, (most questionable characters in all ages) lend their aid for the ignoble purpose. Some men have most incompetent notions of freedom.—Addison says, in Cato,

"———— what is life,
'Tis not to walk about, and breathe fresh air,
And look upon the sun—'Tis to be Free!"

Freedom of this character is not hostile to legal restraint; but that to which allusion has been made, stipulates for perfect freedom on that side, only, upon which the actors dub themselves Patriots, and who, as the Poet says, "Kindle a flame in putting out a spark."

The other plan of Editorial management to which we have referred, is equally indefensible. The voice of opposition, the breath of reprehension, or the symptoms of control, are not permitted in any given case. The flattery is pleasing, while the act is condemned. Fair discussion is ostensibly courted, but "Eat your pudding, slave, and hold your tongue," is still, as in the days of Prior, the rule of most men's practice. Bread is stuffed into the mouth to the distension of both cheeks. The pockets are held out with both hands, like the lank and consumptive purse of the needy Charlatan.—But these men serve ungrateful masters, whether the many or the few. Perpetual opposition becomes habitual malice; and unsparing adulation, sinks into slavish subserviency. A man in power cannot but act for the benefit of the community in some cases; and it is not wonderful, that an Editor, "At the full of the moon," should fall into error. No man should arrogate to himself the office of Political Dictator. The Press is a most unmerciful agent; and, except for the mechanical facilities it supplies, many who wield it, would have applied their talents to other pur-

poses, and states would be left to stand or fall by themselves—It sets risibility at defiance, when we see ignorance, presumption, or profession, assume the place of knowledge. The laughter-loving goddess holds both her sides—not from mirth, but from disgust.

But there is another class of Editors to whom we are desirous of assimilating our practice. Whilst we are bound to respect

ture, and Commerce, is a better bill of fare, than weekly *Sour-krout*, the *Crambe Recocta*, and *Caput Mortuum* over and over of private grievances, which we may regret, though we cannot remedy. We shall consider the high road of political life, like the patent way over the high seas, that surround our adopted country; where men may anchor or sail, furl or unfurl their canvass, trim and repair their barks, may enjoy the pure sky and gentle breeze, the calm or the gale, as profit, or pleasure, or caprice, may dictate—each consulting the general welfare, whilst he promotes his own; and all sailing, as well as ourselves, under the broad banner of British freedom, protection and law, which no one shall be permitted to attack with impunity, or insult without redress.

Having stated the general principles on which we propose to act, in our management of the "*Sydney Herald,*" we shall proceed to state the subjects to which our attention shall be more exclusively directed. The Colony of New South Wales, and its best interests, as a dependency of the Crown, shall be the primary object of our consideration. Van Diemen's Land, the Islands in the South Seas and Pacific, and the commercial and social relations of Australasia in general, shall next arrest our attention. English and Foreign news, bearing upon these subjects, shall be gleaned with care, and all facts and notices of improvements, shall meet with our zealous co-operation. The well-being of the merchant, manufacturer, farmer, and local and civil functionary, shall be the guide of our proceedings, convinced, that on their welfare depends the prosperity of the community.

On the other hand, the interests of literature, and of those connected with its advancement shall not be neglected. Education is a point to which our attention shall be turned with unwearied anxiety. There is, it must be acknowledged, a deficiency in this respect in the Colony—Whether this arises from poverty, or neglect, or insufficiency of means, or want of facilities, we shall not enquire. His Majesty's bounty has, in this respect, been greatly undervalued, and the utility of existing Institutions greatly overrated. We trust an unexceptionable system will be adopted by the Home Government, on the recommendation of His Excellency the Governor, by which the blessings of Education will be communicated to all parties, without test or disqualifying obligation. A system of exclusion gives a character of selfishness to the persons who carry it into effect, to which they are strangers in principle, and to which, in other cases, they would be decidedly hostile. But as the cottage is the last to quit ancient usages, and the Court to adopt

innovations, there are two powerful principles that must be overcome, or modified, before the light of knowledge can beam over the land of our adoption.

To the youth of the Colony in particular, we shall devote much of our attention. They are a generous race, the staple of the Colony, possessing a superior knowledge of the country, and of the capabilities of their native soil. It gives us sincere pleasure to know, that by the fostering care of His Excellency the Go-

partiality. When these bear upon the privileges of the community, extended Reports shall be furnished; in general we shall content ourselves with a brief summary of the leading features of each case, and shall give, on all disputed points the opinions of our Judges, or the law of the case when it can be ascertained.

We have thus stated, at some length, our sentiments on topics of vital importance to the Colony. Our Editorial management shall be conducted upon principles of candour, honesty, and honor.—Respect and deference shall be paid to all classes. Freedom of thinking and speaking shall be conceded, and demanded. We have no wish to mislead; no interests to gratify by unsparing abuse, or indiscriminate approbation. We shall regret opposition, when we could wish to concur, and bestow the meed of praise. We shall dissent with respect, and reason with a desire, not to gain a point, but to establish a principle. By these sentiments we shall be guided, and, whether friends or foes, by these we shall judge others; we have a right, therefore, to expect that by these we shall be judged.

Change of Ministry.

On Tuesday last, the *Earl of Liverpool* arrived with female prisoners, bringing news to the 4th December. We have been favoured with the perusal of some of the latest papers, from which it appears that a revolution of sentiment and principle has taken place in the British Ministry, as effectual as that in France, without its violence and bloodshed. The Ministry of the Duke of Wellington is at an end. Earl Grey, long the ostensible head of the Whigs, has taken his place. The nation was prepared for a change, though the Premier seems to have been the last to adopt the opinion. The late Elections had been decidedly popular; and that coquetting with the leading Whigs, which has been going on even since the accession of Mr. Canning, had given them an influence in the public voice, and Ministerial operations, that has been highly favorable to the interests of the community. In 1807 Earl Grey refused to retain, and since to accept office, unless the hand of the reformer were permitted to probe the wounds of the political body to the quick. The Catholic Bill removed one of those festering places, that "Skin and film, yet ulcerate within," and he has now taken place with a solemn pledge to use his influence to procure, first, a correction of the abuses affecting the Representation in Parliament; second, an unsparing retrenchment of all, but the most unavoidable expenses; and third, a complete system of non-interference on all questions of foreign policy, now disturbing the Continent of Europe, so far as the national honor will permit. His subordinate agents have spent their lives in advocating these points, and we trust they will continue in office, to establish their pretensions, and to prove that political honesty is not extinct, but that principle with power, is of the same character as profession without it. Mr. Brougham had a motion for Reform, which was postponed on the night of the resignation; and the Ministry have already submitted to a reduction of 23 per cent. in their salaries, and mean to appropriate a great part of the Civil List to public purposes.

Having given the King's Speech, an Extract from a Letter written by a member of the Corporation of the City of London, and a list of the new Ministry, in another column of this Paper, we are spared the necessity of lengthened detail. On the 2nd of November, the King delivered his first speech, to his first Parliament, which, to say the least of it, bears more the appearance of a pedantic, argumentative speech of James I. than those we have seen for many years. It seems not to have given satisfaction. The violent declarations of the Duke of Wellington; the disturbances in Kent, and the South of England; the continuance of dissatisfaction in Ireland; the difficulties attending the foreign policy of the country; and the desire manifested for a reduction of taxation, seem to have had much influence on the House of Commons. This was evinced in the impossibility experienced by the Minister to manage the unruly members, who are, in general, more obsequious than at other times, in the first year of their course. On the

Transcription

We have thus stated, at some length, our sentiments on topics of vital importance to the Colony. Our Editorial management shall be conducted upon principles of candour, honesty, and honor.—Respect and deference shall be paid to all classes. Freedom of thinking and speaking shall be conceded, and demanded. We have no wish to mislead; no interests to gratify by unsparing abuse, or indiscriminate approbation. We shall regret opposition, when we could wish to concur, and bestow the meed of praise. We shall dissent with respect, and reason with a desire, not to gain a point, but to establish a principle. By these sentiments we shall be guided, and, whether friends or foes, by these we shall judge others; we have a right, therefore, to expect that by these we shall be judged.

Getting rid of a governor 18

The recall of Ralph Darling, 1831

FROM 1803 TO 1824 *THE SYDNEY GAZETTE* WAS SYDNEY'S ONLY NEWSPAPER. BUT NATIVE-BORN AND FREE-SETTLER LANDOWNERS AND ENTREPRENEURS—KEPT OUT OF COLONIAL POLICY MAKING, BUT VERY MUCH AFFECTED BY IT—WERE CLAMOURING FOR A SAY IN RUNNING THE COLONY. A MEANS OF VOICING THEIR FEELINGS WAS BECOMING INCREASINGLY IMPORTANT, SO TWO INDEPENDENT NEWSPAPERS WERE ESTABLISHED AND TOOK ON THE GOVERNMENT AND THE NEW GOVERNOR, RALPH DARLING (1772–1858).

One of the most vocal among those demanding a greater say in how the colony was run was William Charles Wentworth, a wealthy landowner and barrister, and son of the ex-highwayman and assistant surgeon D'arcy Wentworth. He reflected the growing desire when he wrote in his 1824 *Statistical Account of the British Settlements in Australasia* that 'an independent paper ... which may serve to point out the rising interests of the colonists, and become the organ of their grievances and rights, their wishes and wants, is highly necessary'. Wentworth established *The Australian* in October 1824 to satisfy this need, and he invited London barrister Dr Robert Wardell (1793–1834) to join him as the newspaper's first editor. When Darling took office in 1825, the governor's heavy-handed approach to land grants was soon criticised in *The Australian* as a sign of his despotism.

By 1826 *The Sydney Monitor*, under the editorship of the renowned charity worker Edward Smith Hall (1786–1860), had appeared, and it joined the attack on the governor—though with more emphasis on the plight of the poor in the colony. After the trial of a soldier in which Darling had personally intervened, the newspapers seized on the incident and stirred public opinion against Darling's administration. Despite Darling's attempts to censor the newspapers' criticism of the government by imposing licence and stamp-duty fees (which failed when challenged in court), it was the papers' criticisms that were largely responsible for his recall in 1831.

The success of Wardell's and Hall's portraits of Darling as a tyrant was confirmed when large crowds publicly rejoiced at his departure and burned his effigy. Wentworth put on a 'splendid fete' in the grounds of his Vaucluse estate on Sydney Harbour. Whether it was Darling's downfall or the roasted bullock and grog that had been laid on, thousands of people turned up for the farewell party. It was momentous news that a governor could be recalled largely through the power of a free press.

Getting rid of a governor

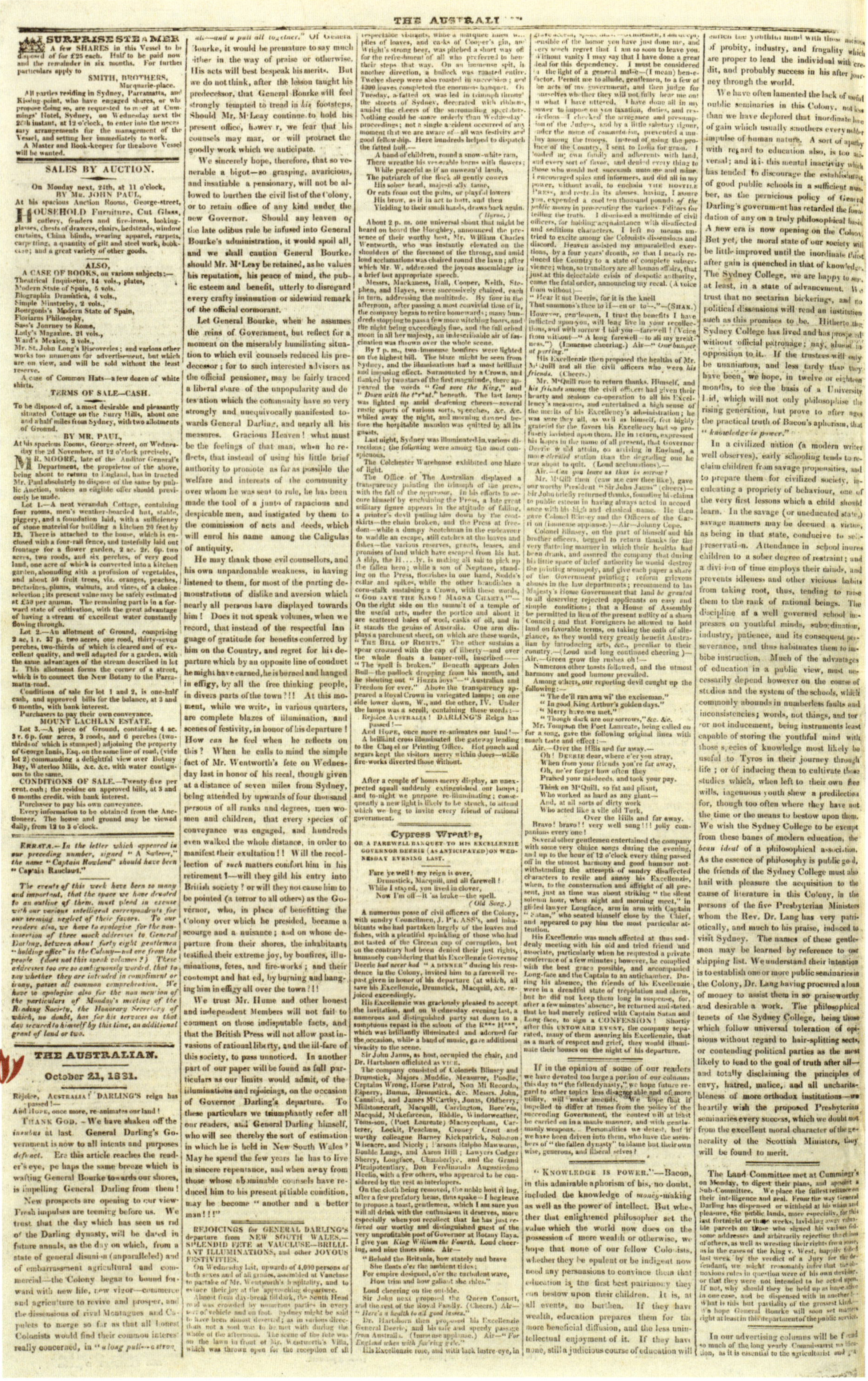

THE AUSTRALIAN.

October 21, 1831.

Rejoice, Australia! DARLING'S reign has passed!—
And Hope, once more, re-animates our land!

Thank God.—We have shaken off the *incubus* at last. General Darling's Government is now to all intents and purposes *defunct*. Ere this article reaches the reader's eye, perhaps the same breeze which is wafting General Bourke towards our shores, is impelling General Darling from them!

New prospects are opening to our view. Fresh impulses are teeming before us. We trust that the day which has seen us rid of the Darling dynasty, will be dated in future annals, as the day on which, from a state of general disunion (unparalleled) and of embarrassment agricultural and commercial—the Colony began to bound forward with new life, new vigor—commerce and agriculture to revive and prosper, and the dissensions of rival Montagues and Capulets to merge so far as that all honest Colonists would find their common interest really concerned, in "*a long pull—a strong pull—and a pull all together.*" Of General Bourke, it would be premature to say much either in the way of praise or otherwise. His acts will best bespeak his merits. But we do not think, after the lesson taught his predecessor, that General Bourke will feel strongly tempted to tread in *his* footsteps. Should Mr. M'Leay continue to hold his present office, however, we fear that his counsels may mar, or will protract the goodly work which we anticipate.

We sincerely hope, therefore, that so venerable a bigot—so grasping, avaricious, and insatiable a pensionary, will not be allowed to burthen the civil list of the Colony, or to retain office of any kind under the new Governor. Should any leaven of the late odibus rule be infused into General Bourke's administration, it would spoil all, and we shall caution General Bourke, should Mr. M'Leay be retained, as he values his reputation, his peace of mind, the public esteem and benefit, utterly to disregard every crafty insinuation or sidewind remark of the official cormorant.

Let General Bourke, when he assumes the reins of Government, but reflect for a moment on the miserably humiliating situation to which evil counsels reduced his predecessor; for to such interested advisers as the official pensioner, may be fairly traced a liberal share of the unpopularity and detestation which the community have so very strongly and unequivocally manifested towards General Darling, and nearly all his measures. Gracious Heaven! what must be the feelings of that man, when he reflects, that instead of using his little brief authority to promote as far as possible the welfare and interests of the community over whom he was sent to rule, he has been made the tool of a junto of rapacious and despicable men, and instigated by them to the commission of acts and deeds, which will enrol his name among the Caligulas of antiquity.

He may thank those evil counsellors, and his own unpardonable weakness, in having listened to them, for most of the parting demonstrations of dislike and aversion which nearly all persons have displayed towards him! Does it not speak volumes, when we record, that instead of the respectful language of gratitude for benefits conferred by him on the Country, and regret for his departure which by an opposite line of conduct he might have earned, he is burned and hanged in effigy, by all the free thinking people, in divers parts of the town?!! At this moment, while we write, in various quarters, are complete blazes of illumination, and scenes of festivity, in honor of his departure! How *can* he feel when he reflects on this? When he calls to mind the simple fact of Mr. Wentworth's fete on Wednesday last in honor of his recal, though given at a distance of seven miles from Sydney, being attended by upwards of four thousand persons of all ranks and degrees, men women and children, that every species of conveyance was engaged, and hundreds even walked the whole distance, in order to manifest their exultation!! Will the recollection of *such* matters comfort him in his retirement?—will they gild his entry into British society? or will they not cause him to be pointed (a terror to all others) as the Governor, who, in place of benefitting the Colony over which he presided, became a scourge and a nuisance; and on whose departure from their shores, the inhabitants testified their extreme joy, by bonfires, illuminations, fetes, and fire-works; and their contempt and hatred, by burning and hanging him in effigy all over the town?!!

We trust Mr. Hume and other honest and independent Members will not fail to comment on those indisputable facts, and that the British Press will not allow past invasions of rational liberty, and the ill-fare of this society, to pass unnoticed. In another part of our paper will be found as full particulars as our limits would admit, of the illuminations and rejoicings, on the occasion of Governor Darling's departure. To these particulars we triumphantly refer all our readers, and General Darling himself, who will see thereby the sort of estimation in which he is held in New South Wales? May he spend the few years he has to live in sincere repentance, and when away from those whose abominable counsels have reduced him to his present pitiable condition, may he become "another and a better man!!!"

In The Australian *of 21 October 1831, editor Robert Wardell doesn't hold back his opinion in his scathing comments on the announcement of the departure of Governor Ralph Darling.*

THE AUSTRALIAN.

October 21, 1831.

Rejoice, Australia! DARLING'S reign has passed!—
And HOPE, once more, re-animates our land!

THANK GOD. – We have shaken off the *incubus* at last. General Darling's Government is now to all intents and purposes *defunct*. Ere this article reaches the reader's eye, perhaps the same breeze which is wafting General Bourke towards our shores, is impelling General Darling from them! …

Of General Bourke, it would be premature to say much either in the way of praise or otherwise. His acts will best bespeak his merits. But we do not think, after the lesson taught his predecessor, that General Bourke will feel strongly tempted to tread in *his* footsteps …

Let General Bourke, when he assumes the reins of Government, but reflect for a moment on the miserably humiliating situation to which evil counsels reduced his predecessor; for to such interested advisers as the official pensioner, may be fairly traced a liberal share of the unpopularity and detestation which the community have so very strongly and unequivocally manifested towards General Darling, and nearly all his measures. Gracious Heaven! what must be the feelings of that man, when he reflects, that instead of using his little brief authority to promote as far as possible the welfare and interests of the community over whom he was sent to rule, he has been made the tool of a junto of rapacious an despicable men …

He may thank those evil counsellors, and his own unpardonable weakness, in having listened to them, for most of the parting demonstrations of dislike and aversion which nearly all persons have displayed towards him! Does it not speak volumes, when we record, that instead of the respectful language of gratitude for benefits conferred by him on the Country, and regret for his departure which by an opposite line of conduct he might have earned, he is burned and hanged in effigy, by all the free thinking people, in divers parts of the town?!! At this moment, while we write, in various quarters, are complete blazes of illumination, and scenes of festivity, in honor of his departure! How *can* he feel when he reflects on this? When he calls to mind the simple fact of Mr. Wentworth's fete on Wednesday last in honor of his recal, through given at a distance of seven miles from Sydney, being attended by upwards of four thousand persons of all ranks and degrees, men women and children, that every species of conveyance was engaged, and hundreds even walked the whole distance, in order to manifest their exultation!! Will the recollection of *such* matters comfort him in his retirement!—will they gild his entry into British society? or will they not cause him to be pointed (a terror to all others) as the Governor, who, in place of benefiting the Colony over which he presided, became a scourge and a nuisance; …

... In another part of our paper will be found as full particulars as our limits would admit, of the illuminations and rejoicings, on the occasion of Governor Darling's departure. To these particulars we triumphantly refer all our readers, and General Darling himself, who will see thereby the sort of estimation in which he is held in New South Wales? May he spend the few years he has to live in sincere repentance, and when away from those whose abominable counsels have reduced him to his present pitiable condition, may he become "another and better man!!!"

19 The war in the west

The death of Yagan, 1833

WHETHER AUSTRALIAN INDIGENOUS WARRIORS WHO RAIDED FARMS OR KILLED EUROPEANS IN RETRIBUTION SLAYINGS WERE RESISTANCE FIGHTERS OR, AS THE GOVERNMENT TERMED THEM, OUTLAWS, THE TACTIC OF OFFERING A REWARD FOR LEADING ABORIGINAL WARRIORS—DEAD OR ALIVE—WAS VERY EFFECTIVE ON THE AUSTRALIAN FRONTIER.

Like Pemulwuy in Sydney, a warrior named Yagan had become the focus of resistance to colonial invasion and settlement around the newly established colony of Swan River in Western Australia. Yagan was an imposing and respected leader of the Whadjuk people of the Noongar language group. After settlement increased along the Swan River, the Noongars began to take the settlers' crops and spear their cattle. They also stole flour and other food supplies from a colony still dependent on external provisions. Their firestick farming—burning the countryside to manage plant growth and hunting areas—threatened settlers' crops and houses.

Settlers began to attack Aboriginal people they saw taking their crops, and a series of retribution killings occurred after one of Yagan's family was killed. Yagan was declared an outlaw and in 1832 he was captured. In an amazing intercession on his behalf, settler Robert Lyon argued that Yagan was not a criminal but a prisoner of war and was entitled to be treated as such. A decision was made to exile Yagan, under the supervision of Lyon, to an island off the coast.

Lyon's plan to civilise and Christianise Yagan failed, and he escaped. After a period of being accepted back in the colony, Yagan and his warriors again commenced raids on settlers' crops and farms. Yagan was both admired and feared by the colonists, but in 1832, the government set a reward of 30 pounds for Yagan's capture, dead or alive.

In July 1833 on the Swan River near Guildford, Yagan was shot in cold blood by two teenage boys, out for the reward. Even *The Perth Gazette* described the death of Yagan as a 'wild and treacherous act' and that it was 'revolting to hear this lauded as a meritorious deed'.

News of Yagan's death was significant for the struggling Swan River colony. Not only was an important resistance leader killed, but also a respected, brave warrior. Like Pemulwuy, Yagan's head was also cut off and sent to England as a 'specimen of curiosity'.

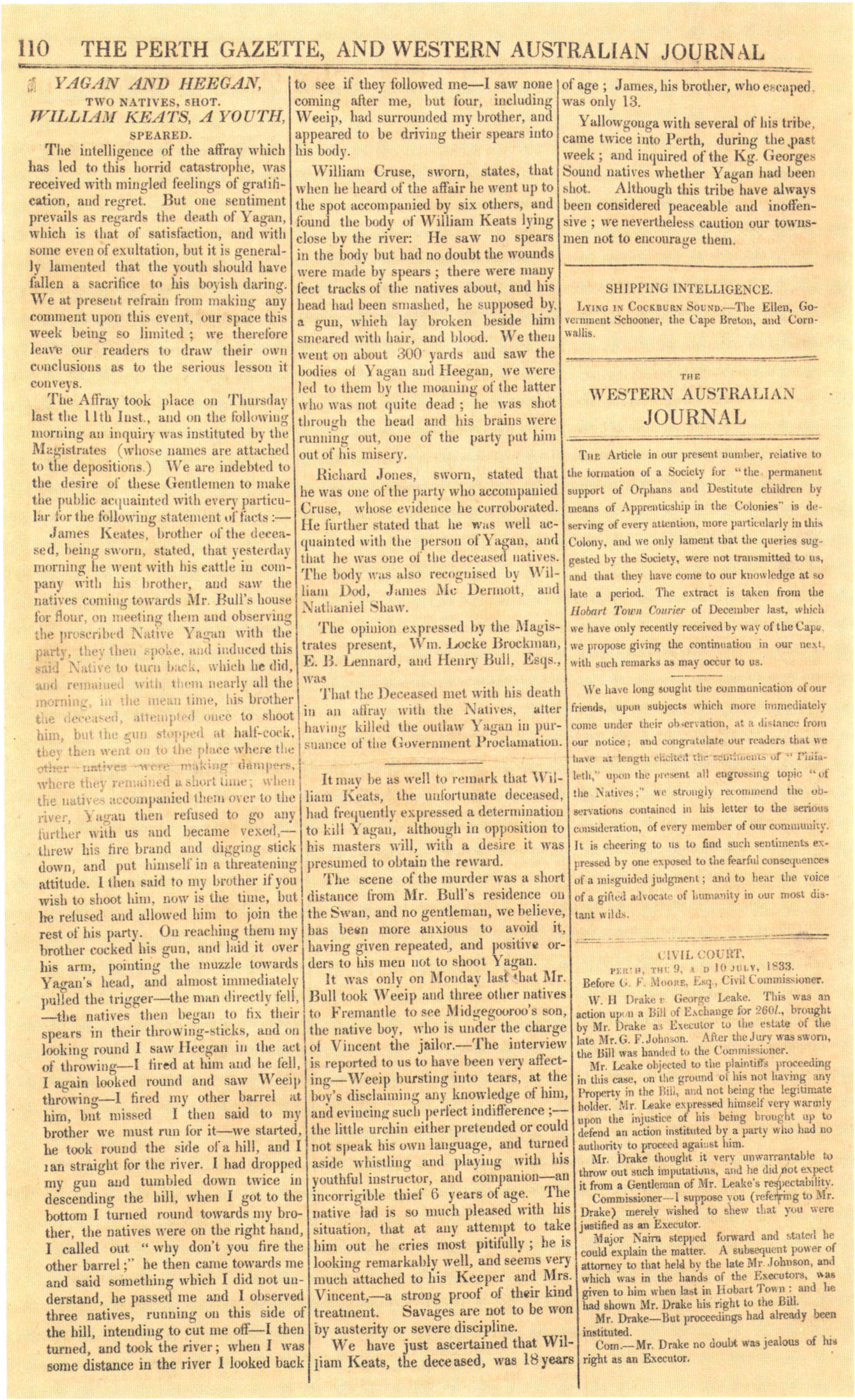

110 THE PERTH GAZETTE, AND WESTERN AUSTRALIAN JOURNAL

YAGAN AND HEEGAN,
TWO NATIVES, SHOT.
WILLIAM KEATS, A YOUTH,
SPEARED.

The intelligence of the affray which has led to this horrid catastrophe, was received with mingled feelings of gratification, and regret. But one sentiment prevails as regards the death of Yagan, which is that of satisfaction, and with some even of exultation, but it is generally lamented that the youth should have fallen a sacrifice to his boyish daring. We at present refrain from making any comment upon this event, our space this week being so limited; we therefore leave our readers to draw their own conclusions as to the serious lesson it conveys.

The Affray took place on Thursday last the 11th Inst., and on the following morning an inquiry was instituted by the Magistrates (whose names are attached to the depositions.) We are indebted to the desire of these Gentlemen to make the public acquainted with every particular for the following statement of facts:—

James Keates, brother of the deceased, being sworn, stated, that yesterday morning he went with his cattle in company with his brother, and saw the natives coming towards Mr. Bull's house for flour, on meeting them and observing the proscribed Native Yagan with the party, they then spoke, and induced this said Native to turn back, which he did, and remained with them nearly all the morning, in the mean time, his brother the deceased, attempted once to shoot him, but the gun stopped at half-cock, they then went on to the place where the other natives were making dampers, where they remained a short time; when the natives accompanied them over to the river, Yagan then refused to go any further with us and became vexed,—threw his fire brand and digging stick down, and put himself in a threatening attitude. I then said to my brother if you wish to shoot him, now is the time, but he refused and allowed him to join the rest of his party. On reaching them my brother cocked his gun, and laid it over his arm, pointing the muzzle towards Yagan's head, and almost immediately pulled the trigger—the man directly fell,—the natives then began to fix their spears in their throwing-sticks, and on looking round I saw Heegan in the act of throwing—I fired at him and he fell, I again looked round and saw Weeip throwing—I fired my other barrel at him, but missed I then said to my brother we must run for it—we started, he took round the side of a hill, and I ran straight for the river. I had dropped my gun and tumbled down twice in descending the hill, when I got to the bottom I turned round towards my brother, the natives were on the right hand, I called out "why don't you fire the other barrel;" he then came towards me and said something which I did not understand, he passed me and I observed three natives, running on this side of the hill, intending to cut me off—I then turned, and took the river; when I was some distance in the river I looked back to see if they followed me—I saw none coming after me, but four, including Weeip, had surrounded my brother, and appeared to be driving their spears into his body.

William Cruse, sworn, states, that when he heard of the affair he went up to the spot accompanied by six others, and found the body of William Keats lying close by the river: He saw no spears in the body but had no doubt the wounds were made by spears; there were many feet tracks of the natives about, and his head had been smashed, he supposed by, a gun, which lay broken beside him smeared with hair, and blood. We then went on about 300 yards and saw the bodies of Yagan and Heegan, we were led to them by the moaning of the latter who was not quite dead; he was shot through the head and his brains were running out, one of the party put him out of his misery.

Richard Jones, sworn, stated that he was one of the party who accompanied Cruse, whose evidence he corroborated. He further stated that he was well acquainted with the person of Yagan, and that he was one of the deceased natives. The body was also recognised by William Dod, James Mc Dermott, and Nathaniel Shaw.

The opinion expressed by the Magistrates present, Wm. Locke Brockman, E. B. Lennard, and Henry Bull, Esqs., was

That the Deceased met with his death in an affray with the Natives, after having killed the outlaw Yagan in pursuance of the Government Proclamation.

It may be as well to remark that William Keats, the unfortunate deceased, had frequently expressed a determination to kill Yagan, although in opposition to his masters will, with a desire it was presumed to obtain the reward.

The scene of the murder was a short distance from Mr. Bull's residence on the Swan, and no gentleman, we believe, has been more anxious to avoid it, having given repeated, and positive orders to his men not to shoot Yagan.

It was only on Monday last that Mr. Bull took Weeip and three other natives to Fremantle to see Midgegooroo's son, the native boy, who is under the charge of Vincent the jailor.—The interview is reported to us to have been very affecting—Weeip bursting into tears, at the boy's disclaiming any knowledge of him, and evincing such perfect indifference;—the little urchin either pretended or could not speak his own language, and turned aside whistling and playing with his youthful instructor, and companion—an incorrigible thief 6 years of age. The native lad is so much pleased with his situation, that at any attempt to take him out he cries most pitifully; he is looking remarkably well, and seems very much attached to his Keeper and Mrs. Vincent,—a strong proof of their kind treatment. Savages are not to be won by austerity or severe discipline.

We have just ascertained that William Keats, the deceased, was 18 years of age; James, his brother, who escaped, was only 13.

Yallowgonga with several of his tribe, came twice into Perth, during the past week; and inquired of the Kg. Georges Sound natives whether Yagan had been shot. Although this tribe have always been considered peaceable and inoffensive; we nevertheless caution our townsmen not to encourage them.

SHIPPING INTELLIGENCE.

LYING IN COCKBURN SOUND.—The Ellen, Government Schooner, the Cape Breton, and Cornwallis.

THE
WESTERN AUSTRALIAN
JOURNAL

THE Article in our present number, relative to the formation of a Society for "the permanent support of Orphans and Destitute children by means of Apprenticeship in the Colonies" is deserving of every attention, more particularly in this Colony, and we only lament that the queries suggested by the Society, were not transmitted to us, and that they have come to our knowledge at so late a period. The extract is taken from the *Hobart Town Courier* of December last, which we have only recently received by way of the Cape, we propose giving the continuation in our next, with such remarks as may occur to us.

We have long sought the communication of our friends, upon subjects which more immediately come under their observation, at a distance from our notice; and congratulate our readers that we have at length elicited the sentiments of "Philaleth," upon the present all engrossing topic "of the Natives;" we strongly recommend the observations contained in his letter to the serious consideration, of every member of our community. It is cheering to us to find such sentiments expressed by one exposed to the fearful consequences of a misguided judgment; and to hear the voice of a gifted advocate of humanity in our most distant wilds.

CIVIL COURT.
PERTH, THE 9, AND 10 JULY, 1833.
Before G. F. MOORE, Esq., Civil Commissioner.

W. H Drake *v.* George Leake. This was an action upon a Bill of Exchange for 260*l*., brought by Mr. Drake as Executor to the estate of the late Mr. G. F. Johnson. After the Jury was sworn, the Bill was handed to the Commissioner.

Mr. Leake objected to the plaintiffs proceeding in this case, on the ground of his not having any Property in the Bill, and not being the legitimate holder. Mr. Leake expressed himself very warmly upon the injustice of his being brought up to defend an action instituted by a party who had no authority to proceed against him.

Mr. Drake thought it very unwarrantable to throw out such imputations, and he did not expect it from a Gentleman of Mr. Leake's respectability.

Commissioner—I suppose you (referring to Mr. Drake) merely wished to shew that you were justified as an Executor.

Major Nairn stepped forward and stated he could explain the matter. A subsequent power of attorney to that held by the late Mr. Johnson, and which was in the hands of the Executors, was given to him when last in Hobart Town: and he had shown Mr. Drake his right to the Bill.

Mr. Drake—But proceedings had already been instituted.

Com.—Mr. Drake no doubt was jealous of his right as an Executor.

Unlike the long wait for a newspaper in early Sydney, Western Australia's Perth Gazette, and Western Australian Journal *was established only four years after the founding of the Swan River colony in Western Australia in 1829. The first edition of the weekly paper appeared on 5 January 1833.*

YAGAN AND HEEGAN, TWO NATIVES, SHOT. *WILLIAM KEATS, A YOUTH,* SPEARED.

The intelligence of the affray which has led to this horrid catastrophe, was received with mingled feelings of gratification, and regret. But one sentiment prevails as regards the death of Yagan, which is that of satisfaction, and with some even of exultation, but it is generally lamented that the youth should have fallen a sacrifice to his boyish daring. We at present refrain from making any comment upon this event, our space this week being so limited; we therefore leave our readers to draw their own conclusions as to the serious lesson it conveys.

The Affray took place on Thursday last the 11th Inst., and on the following morning an inquiry was instituted by the Magistrates (whose names are attached to the depositions.) We are indebted to the desire of these Gentlemen to make the public acquainted with every particular for the following statement of facts:—

James Keates, brother of the deceased, being sworn, stated, that yesterday morning he went with his cattle in company with his brother, and saw the natives coming towrards Mr. Bull's house for flour, on meeting them and observing the proscribed Native Yagan with the party, they then spoke, and induced this said Native to turn back, which he did, and remained with them nearly all the morning, in the mean time, his brother the deceased, attempted once to shoot him, but the gun stopped at half-cock, they then went on to the place where the other natives were making dampers, where they remained a short time; when the natives accompanied them over to the river, Yagan then refused to go any further with us and became vexed,—threw his fire brand and digging stick down, and put himself in a threatening attitude. I then said to my brother if you wish to shoot him, now is the time, but he refused and allowed him to join the rest of his party. On reaching them my brother cocked his gun, and laid it over his arm, pointing the muzzle towards Yagan's head, and almost immediately pulled the trigger—the man directly fell,—the natives then began to fix their spears in their throwing-sticks, and on looking round I saw Heegan in the act of throwing—I fired at him and he fell, I again looked round and saw Weeip throwing—I fired my other barrel at him, but missed. I then said to my brother we must run for it—we started, he took round the side of a hill, and I ran straight for the river. I had dropped my gun and tumbled down twice in descending the hill, when I got to the bottom I turned round towards my brother, the natives were on the right hand, I called out "why don't you fire the other barrel;" he then came towards me and said something which I did not understand, he passed me and I observed three natives, running on this side of the hill, intending to cut me off—I then turned, and took the river; when I was some distance in the river I looked back to see if they followed me—I saw none coming after me, but four, including Weeip, had surrounded my brother, and appeared to be driving their spears into his body.

William Cruse, sworn, states, that when he heard of the affair he went up to the spot accompanied by six others, and found the body of William Keats lying close by the river: He saw no spears in the body but had no doubt the wounds were made by spears; there were many feet tracks of the natives about, and his head had been smashed, he supposed by a gun, which lay broken beside him smeared with hair, and blood. We then went on about 300 yards and saw the bodies of Yagan and Heegan, we were led to them by the moaning of the latter who was not quite dead; he was shot through the head and his brains were running out, one of the party put him out of his misery.

Richard Jones, sworn, stated that he was one of the party who accompanied Cruse, whose evidence he corroborated. He further stated that he was well acquainted with the person of Yagan, and that he was one of the deceased natives. The body was also recognised by William Dod, James Mc Dermott, and Nathaniel Shaw.

The opinion expressed by the Magistrates present, Wm. Locke Brockman, E. B. Lennard, and Henry Bull, Esqs., was

That the Deceased met with his death in an affray with the Natives, after having killed the outlaw Yagan in pursuance of the Government Proclamation.

It may be as well to remark that William Keats, the unfortunate deceased, had frequently expressed a determination to kill Yagan, although in opposition to his masters will, with a desire it was presumed to obtain the reward.

The scene of the murder was a short distance from Mr. Bull's residence on the Swan, and no gentleman, we believe, has been more anxious to avoid it, having given repeated, and positive orders to his men not to shoot Yagan.

It was only on Monday last that Mr. Bull took Weeip and three other natives to Fremantle to see Midgegooroo's son, the native boy, who is under the charge of Vincent the jailor.—The interview is reported to us to have been very affecting—Weeip bursting into tears, at the boy's disclaiming any knowledge of him, and evincing such perfect indifference;—the little urchin either pretended or could not speak his own language, and turned aside whistling and playing with his youthful instructor, and companion—an incorrigible thief 6 years of age. The native lad is so much pleased with his situation, that at any attempt to take him out he cries most pitifully; he is looking remarkably well, and seems very much attached to his Keeper and Mrs. Vincent,—a strong proof of their kind treatment. Savages are not to be won by austerity or severe discipline.

We have just ascertained that William Keats, the deceased, was 18 years of age; James, his brother, who escaped, was only 13.

Yallowgonga with several of his tribe, came twice into Perth, during the past week; and inquired of the Kg. Georges Sound natives whether Yagan had been shot. Although this tribe have always been considered peaceable and inoffensive; we nevertheless caution our townsmen not to encourage them.

20 Creating a land rush

Major Mitchell's *Australia Felix*, 1836

IN THE 1830S THE SURVEYOR-GENERAL OF NEW SOUTH WALES, MAJOR THOMAS MITCHELL (1792–1855), LED SEVERAL OFFICIAL EXPEDITIONS TO MAP, SURVEY AND REPORT ON THE LANDS IN THE INTERIOR OF THE COLONY. HIS JOURNALS, *THREE EXPEDITIONS INTO THE INTERIOR OF EASTERN AUSTRALIA*, PROVIDED A DETAILED ACCOUNT OF INLAND NEW SOUTH WALES AND VICTORIAN ABORIGINAL PEOPLE, AND THE GEOLOGY, GEOGRAPHY, FLORA AND FAUNA OF THEIR LANDS AT THE TIME. BUT IT WAS HIS DESCRIPTIONS OF OPEN FORESTS AND EXTENSIVE GRASSLANDS THAT CAUSED A STIR IN THE COLONY.

Mitchell used the Latin phrase *Australia Felix*, or 'blessed Australia', to describe the recently explored regions of central and western Victoria. His depictions of this 'fine country for colonisation' created what has been called a land rush: *Australia Felix* was great marketing material for Mitchell's book and it generated a new surge of squatting on Aboriginal lands.

During the 1820s and 1830s squatters had taken up lands in the western plains of New South Wales, but few had ventured into the drier interior. Mitchell's third expedition aimed to better understand the inland river system of the continent—a vexing problem at the time, which many, such as explorer Charles Sturt (1795–1869) quite hopefully thought led to an inland sea.

In 1836 Mitchell followed the Murrumbidgee and Murray rivers that Sturt had explored between 1828 and 1830. After several confrontations with Aboriginal warriors along the Darling River, he trekked inland to the south-east towards more promising country along the Murray River. With the aid of Aboriginal guides—including a woman called Turandurey and her young child Balland, whom Mitchell found indispensable to the party's success—they travelled through what was to become Victoria at a time when all the rivers and lakes were full. To Mitchell, the landscape was most enchanting, and his journal accounts enthusiastically describe 'luxuriant grasslands', 'lofty trees' and 'fine running streams'. After being surprised to find a small isolated settlement, founded by the Henty brothers several years before, at Portland on the Victorian coast, Mitchell returned to Sydney in November 1836.

The rapid occupation of *Australia Felix* followed. Settlers arrived from Tasmania and soon others followed Mitchell's tracks south from Sydney. A land rush by settlers willing to illegally 'squat' upon Aboriginal lands far beyond the frontiers of settlement, as well as the attendant period of frontier conflict, had begun.

THREE EXPEDITIONS

INTO THE INTERIOR OF

EASTERN AUSTRALIA;

WITH DESCRIPTIONS OF THE RECENTLY EXPLORED REGION OF

AUSTRALIA FELIX,

AND OF THE PRESENT COLONY OF

NEW SOUTH WALES:

BY

MAJOR T. L. MITCHELL, F.G.S. & M.R.G.S.

SURVEYOR-GENERAL.

SECOND EDITION, CAREFULLY REVISED.

IN TWO VOLUMES.

VOL I.

LONDON:

T. & W. BOONE, NEW BOND STREET.

MDCCCXXXIX.

Although word of mouth and news reports of the fine grazing lands had sent squatters into Australia Felix *well before the 1838 publication of Mitchell's journals in London, the detailed descriptions of rich, green and fertile lands inspired many Europeans to venture into the dangers of inland Australia.*

Portrait by William Hetzer of Sir Thomas Mitchell, surveyor and explorer of south-eastern Australia

An abominable system 21

An anti-convict tirade, 1835

HENRY MELVILLE (1799–1873) HAS BEEN DESCRIBED AS ONE OF THE PRESS MARTYRS OF COLONIAL TASMANIA. LIKE ANDREW BENT, HE SPENT TIME IN PRISON FOR HIS EDITORIALS IN THE *COLONIAL TIMES*, WHICH HE HAD TAKEN OVER FROM BENT IN 1830. HE CRITICISED VAN DIEMEN'S LAND AND ITS AUTHORITIES, AND DESCRIBED THE COLONY AS A GAOL FULL OF CONVICTS, CONTROLLED BY CORRUPT EX-CONVICTS. HE DESPISED THE CONVICT TRANSPORTATION SYSTEM AND CALLED FOR ITS ABOLITION.

The growing anti-transportation movement had much fodder to draw on in the harsh penal society of Van Diemen's Land. And the supposedly tyrannical and despotic rule of Governor George Arthur (1784–1854) added fuel to the fires of free settlers and emancipists. Melville saw the freedom of the press as critical to civil society in the colonies. His editorials were headed with this quotation, appearing just below the masthead: 'Let it be impressed upon your minds—let it be instilled into your children—that the Liberty of the Press is the Palladium of all, your Civil, Political, and Religious Rights. *JUNIUS*.'

Unfortunately for Melville and Gilbert Robertson (1794–1851), the editor of another Hobart newspaper, the *True Colonist*, their questioning of the sentencing of prisoners—in one case the death penalty for stealing a cow—led to their own imprisonment. But incarceration, even in the same cell as the condemned cannibal Matthew Pearce—who had eaten the flesh of his fellow escaped convicts in the Tasmanian wilderness—could not stop Melville from his campaign against the governor. While in prison, he wrote the pamphlet *The Administration of the Government by Colonel George Arthur*.

Melville believed that one of the most pressing problems for the colony was the 'abominable system' of 'appointing felons of the worst description to be constables, and preservers of the lives, properties, and morals of the free population'. He felt that in Tasmania these convict constables were not only 'harassing and tyrannizing over the free', but were also being protected by the authorities. One case he reported highlighted the widespread corrupt system of protection and bribery in the public houses of Hobart.

While not a headline news event at the time, an 1835 editorial by Melville commenting on the case of Mr Robert Bryan shows all the contempt for the convict system that was to lead to the end of transportation to the eastern colonies from 1840. Australian colonial society was being reshaped from its penal colony origins.

348 COLONIAL TIMES.

QUESTIONS TO THE GOVERNMENT PRINTER.

1.—Do you not now possess the whole of the printing, Colonial and Convict, of the Government; and did not the Commissariat advertise for tenders for the Convict printing some time since? Did you send in a tender for such printing, and, if you did, was not your offer refused, and that of another person chosen? How, then, is it you possess such printing, and how is it the Commissariat accounts are adjusted, seeing that the accepted contractor is not paid for the work performed?

2.—Does not the Colonial Government give you a salary of £260 per annum as Government Printer, for which you are to furnish four pages of a *Gazette*, which is the property of the Government?

3.—Does not the Government furnish paper

(a personal enemy of Mr. Bryan) to forward to the Local Government, representations supposed to be prejudicial to Mr. Bryan's character, who was at the time in Hobart Town. The latter, feeling indignant at the conduct of the Magistrate towards him, tendered his own resignation as a Magistrate**** At this period the Council was formed virtually of the Lieutenant Governor, the Chief Justice, and the Colonial Secretary. After no doubt mature consideration on part of the Government, it was thought adviseable that the most marked displeasure of the Government should be shewn towards Mr. Bryan, and forthwith an order was issued to remove the whole of that gentleman's assigned servants—this order was immediately carried into effect! Such a sudden blow as this, few men in the Colony could sustain without ruin! At the time this order was issued, Mr. Bryan was gathering in his har-

time, and the officers returning the warrant not satisfied, further nonstrous process, it is believed is in contemplation. It is the wish of the friends of the Colony, that Mr. Bryan's case may be heard and examined—if the conduct of Mr. Bryan has been such; if he has offended against the laws of his country, justice should be administered; if he has not offended, but has been an injured man, no reparation that can be given in a pecuniary point of view, can compensate him for the odium, the stigma cast upon him by his enemies."

After the above extract, it is only necessary to observe that the nephew of Mr. W. Bryan has been accused of the crime of cattle stealing, and found guilty. Without further observations, let us at once refer to the proceedings on the trial, the

and himself of being cattle stealers? Readers, answer for yourselves. But, to proceed with the trial, there were four witnesses for the prosecution:—one free man—one ticket-of-leave—and two felons without indulgences. In referring to the evidence, it will be found that Boswood* (one of the felon police) holding a ticket-of-leave, and two felons without indulgence, thought it would answer their purpose if they could get up a case against Mr. Bryan; for this purpose, these British convicts perambulated the bush, (prison discipline), and at last agreed to make up a case against him. In reading over the evidence carefully, the question which naturally occurs is this:—Did not the three convicts themselves kill the animal,

Transcription

Mr. Bryan's Prosecution.

The late trial of Mr. Robert Bryan at Launceston, is of the most vital importance to the Colonists; and we therefore intend to trespass largely on the attention of the British and Colonial readers, more especially on the former, in order to demonstrate in what manner the administration of the Government is conducted under Colonel George Arthur.

expose himself?

7.—What was a certain Major not long since tried for, and for what offence was it Mr. Paine received a sentence of seven years transportation? Was not the latter for his appropriating Government wood, valued at a few pence, to his own use and benefit?

8.—Supposing, then, that you dispose of the Government paper and Government printing for your own use and benefit, can you name why a difference should be made between the man who appropriates Government wood to his own use, and the man who appropriates Government printed paper to his own use and benefit?

The only notice taken of the above, appears in the *Courier* of the 9th inst. Dr. Ross, the Government Printer and Editor of that Journal, thus accusing himself of crime we would not dare insinuate. Speaking of the last *Colonial Times*, and its articles, (in alluding to one in particular) he says—

"*The main subject of which is, charging the Government Printer of this place with felony!*" —*Courier, Oct. 9th.*

After this, we ask where are the Crown Law Officers? If such a charge has been made, *why do not those gentlemen do their duty!*

HOBART TOWN:
NOVEMBER 3, 1835.

Let it be impressed upon your minds—let it be instilled into your children—that the Liberty of the Press is the Palladium of all your Civil, Political, and Religious Rights. JUNIUS.

Mr. Bryan's Prosecution.

The late trial of Mr. Robert Bryan at Launceston, is of the most vital importance to the Colonists; and we therefore intend to trespass largely on the attention of the British and Colonial readers, more especially on the former, in order to demonstrate in what manner the administration of the Government is conducted under Colonel George Arthur.

As it is necessary to explain to the reader the origin of the difference between Mr. William Bryan and the Local Government, we cannot do better than offer an extract from a work which is in a state of publication, entitled "The Administration of the Government of Van Diemen's Land by Colonel George Arthur."* It will fully explain that which is necessary for the reader to be made acquainted with:—

"Mr. William Bryan, an Irish gentleman, well connected, and possessing considerable property, arrived in the Colony, in the year 1824. He became a settler on the other side of the island, and was appointed to the magistracy. In the month of November, 1833, a secret examination took place in the Police Office, Launceston, when something transpired, which induced the Police Magistrate

* This work will be published in the Van Diemen's Land Almanack, in Hobart Town, and also by Messrs. Smith and Elder, London.

fellow Magistrate, Mr. Bryan, then absent in Hobart Town. Mr. Lyttleton said something to this effect, that "it was not the man Arnold, but his master, who ought to have appeared that day in the Court House." This expression was immediatety conveyed to Mr. Bryan, who lost not a moment in returning to Launceston, and demanding an explanation. For this purpose, he requested a friend of his, Mr. Lewis, to wait upon the Police Magistrate, to request the explanation, or as Mr. Lyttleton himself afterwards swore, in the Supreme Court, that Mr. Lewis waited upon him to "appoint a time and place to meet Mr. Bryan, to give the satisfaction due from one gentleman to another." For this offence, the friend of Mr. Bryan, was prosecuted, and by a military jury found guilty of endeavouring to incite the Police Magistrate to commit a breach of the peace; and the extraordinary sentence of eighteen months' imprisonment, and a fine of one hundred and fifty pounds, was passed upon him by His Honor, the Puisne Judge, Montagu. It is scarcely necessary to advert to the extraordinary proceeding of the Court during this trial; Mr. Lewis considered that he had been prevented from making his defence, in a manner suitable to the exigency of his case*** At the period at which this trial took place, Mr. Bryan had appealed to the laws of his country, for redress. Shut out from obtaining justice from the Executive Government, he appealed to the Supreme Court. He brought civil actions against the Launceston Police Magistrate, and also against the nominal agents, who had deprived him of his assigned servants. The British Parliament had, long previous to this period, (if the English papers can be believed), considered that Trial by Jury existed in Van Diemen's Land, the same as in England, but such *was* and is *not* the case. The Counsel for Mr. Bryan moved the Court for Trial by civil Jury, in every issue between the Government and his client; but their honors the Judges both decided that Mr. Bryan should not have such Juries. It must be borne in mind, the awkward situation in which his Honor the Chief Justice was placed on this occasion. As member of the Executive Council, he had already decided against Mr. Bryan, and had approved of the Government punishing that gentleman, by depriving him of his assigned servants—as Judge therefore, did he sit upon the bench, to decide a question, upon which he had already come to a decision. The very man to whom Mr. Bryan appealed for the impartial administration of justice, that very Executive Councillor had, in accordance with his oath as such, faithfully and conscientiously advised the Government to do that very deed, which compelled Mr. Bryan to have recourse to the laws of his country for redress. Finding the Executive Government would not investigate the case; that satisfaction, through the medium of the laws of the Colony, was denied him—by means of compelling him to have his case decided by men under Government influence—he ordered his Counsel to throw up his briefs, and has since proceeded to the Imperial Parliament, to seek that reparation of character, which he could not legally, or otherwise, obtain in Van Diemen's Land. Mr. Bryan is yet proceeding before the Imperial Parliament, with his case; but even here, the persecution of his enemies has not stopped. These men, have, when absent, dared to accuse him of the worst of crimes; a felon, a convict of Great Britain, without any indulgence whatever, has made a deposition on oath, that Mr. Bryan is *a cattle stealer*, and a warrant has been issued against this gentleman, whom every body in the Colony well knew to be in England at the

—this is a gentleman generally understood to be waiting for a Government situation; the second called was Lieutenant Skardon, also a Justice of the Peace, a relation of Colonel Arthur's relatives, and, of course, a Government man; the third was Lieutenant Dutton, an independent Colonist The Solicitor General here stopped the clerk—asked him where he got the list of the Jury from, and, being told from the Sheriff (of course in the usual manner of returning Juries) said—"*Never mind—call the Jury afresh from the precept as they are nominated;*" he should have added—*as they are selected by the Governor.* The Clerk of the Court did as he was ordered, and the Jury were called as nominated by the Lieutenant Governor! We refer our readers to the protest* entered against Major Wellman, and his answer that he had *no son holding a Government situation!* But what a miserable quibble was this? Mr. Bryan's was a life and death case, and, in his confusion, he forgot to make use of the word "*son-in-law,*" instead of *son!* Is not Major Wellman father-in-law of Mr. Mason, the Police Magistrate of New Norfolk, which individual has been accused of perjury before the Executive Government by another Magistrate of the Colony! and, is the charge refuted—is there not a civil action very *slowly* proceeding against the accuser for libel? We repeat, what a miserable quibble! The Chief Justice decided there was no ground of challenge—remember, reader, this is the same Judge that recommended the first proceedings against Mr. William Bryan in the Executive Council! And now a word or two respecting the Jury Question.

Colonel Arthur it is said has long since had orders to give the Colonists Trial by Jury as it obtains in New South Wales; but he has refused to obey the orders, although the Colonists have over and over again besought him to grant the boon the British Government has thought proper to give. In New South Wales, a convict is better off than a suspected free man in Van Diemen's Land. The British convicted, suspected of crime in New South Wales, is asked, before trial, whether he will have a Military or a Civil Jury—he has his choice—he can challenge any one—nay, every man on the Jury; but, in Van Diemen's Land, the free British subject *has no choice!* The Sheriff, in the above case, was not allowed to nominate the Jury in the ordinary manner—it must be done by Colonel Arthur; and the challenge of interest was not sufficient to disqualify a juror—is this a fair way to try British subjects? Did, or did not most of the seven Government officers dine with His Excellency the day previous to the trial—and is it, or is it not advisable to blacken Mr. William Bryan's character before the British Parliament, by accusing his nephew

* This prosecution was in every sense of the word "*a prosecution of the Government,*" how got up none but those concerned can tell. Mr. Field, we believe, never complained of the loss of the beast, nor can we find out in what manner the proceedings originated.

there were other hides, and that Mr. Bryan did not seem to be surprised at the finding of the one branded W F. The evidence of Mr. Bonney proves what occurred, no doubt, after all the arrangements were duly made the night previously by the convicts; but, before we leave Mr. Bonny, let us ask whether he never expressed himself, that the charges against Mr. Bryan were disgraceful—that the case was "*a got up case,*" and that he was sorry he had any thing to do with the affair? As to Mr. Field's evidence, the owner of the killed cow, he proves absolutely nothing—he could not say that he ever saw the cow alive; but, that *it must be his cow, because it had his brand!!!*

Here, then, is the case got up!! Three felons swear to certain pretended facts, and two free witnesses prove no guilt on the part of the prisoners. As to Fogerty, his name is scarcely referred to during the trial; but, yet his presence was, no doubt, necessary in the dock. Now, let us call to mind that which the Attorney General has so often repeated, viz.—that he could, if he so chose, get up a case, and convict any man in the Colony, of any crime of which he might choose to accuse him;† and, what has the Judge on the bench often said?—that half-a-crown would purchase oaths in abundance! Let us, then, look at the convict witnesses—the ticket-of-leave man first; what is to be his reward on this occasion? Is it to be the same as that which Lamph received for the Ross burglary?—but, we will come to that in a minute!! Who is the man Gough, is he not a British convict, without indulgence—a man, whose character was so infamous, that he was dismissed as being unworthy of the office of a felon constable? And, the man Scandlebury, pray, what is he? A British convict, whose conduct has been so infamous in the Colony, that he has been again transported to the penal settlement of Port Arthur, from which place he was taken to be made a constable, to watch over the properties and get up cases against His Majesty's free British subjects in this Settlement—this is a specimen of prison discipline! "*I am,*" *said this felon,* "*a prisoner—my sentence was seven years; my sentence has been extended three years. I was at Port Arthur till last May twelve months, since which I have been a constable. I was tried for absconding, and am either dismissed or suspended.*" Pray, what reward will be given these splendid specimens of the Van Diemen's Land constabulary? Will these two felons receive their tickets for the deed done—or, will they receive their pardon, like Lamph? And now a word or two on perjury and the Lamph and Bolter case! We cannot do better than extract a portion of an article on the felon

* We can obtain the affidavit of an individual that can be credited, who has heard this man express himself that "he would hang his father to get his free pardon."

† It is commonly reported that the Attorney General has expressed his determination of putting Mr. William Bryan on his trial, and have him convicted of cattle stealing, as soon as he returns to this Colony. We really *cannot* believe this!

Henry Melville used his newspaper the Colonial Times *to fight the employment of ex-convicts and the convict transportation system, as well as the perceived shortcomings of Governor George Arthur, as this comment from the issue of 3 November 1835 shows.*

Celebrating a new bridge 22

The opening of the Lansdowne Bridge, 1836

PAGEANTS AND PARADES WERE REGULAR AND WELL-ATTENDED EVENTS IN A NINETEENTH-CENTURY AUSTRALIA THAT WAS INTERESTED IN MARKING PROGRESS FROM ITS ORIGINS AS A PENAL OUTPOST TO A COLONY, AND, LATER, A NATION. CEREMONIES OFTEN INVOLVED FLOATS WITH SYMBOLS OF WEALTH AND PROSPERITY, OR CARTS FULL OF LOCAL PRODUCE. STONE CONSTRUCTIONS WERE ALSO REGARDED AS MARKERS OF 'CIVILISATION' IN THE EARLY COLONY.

The 1836 opening of the Lansdowne Bridge combined all of these things and did so on an auspicious day—26 January. The arrival of the First Fleet had been celebrated on this day with growing pomp and ceremony since the earliest anniversaries had seen a handful of military officers toasting the king and the colony. The day was continued to be celebrated until it finally became more important to European Australians than Captain Cook's stay at Botany Bay in May 1770 (though Cook took pride of place in many parades, right up until the bicentenary celebrations of 1988).

The opening of the Lansdowne Bridge was not a particularly important event, but it was treated with great ceremony. The bridge over Prospect Creek near Liverpool was to greatly improve transport and travel to the expanding south-western squatting and grazing districts. Governor Richard Bourke (1777–1855), who called the bridge 'a work of more than ordinary importance', hosted a ball at Government House in Parramatta for the 'gentry of the neighbourhood' . He quoted *The Sydney Gazette* of 28 January 1836 when reporting on the procession—named the 'Great Exhibition' at the time—to Robert William Hay, the undersecretary of the Colonial Office:

> *First a small herd of fat oxen crossed the bridge; some fine horses of Colonial breed came next; sheep ... a dray laden with wool ... cases of preserved ham borne on trucks ... a dray laden with tanned oxhides ... a flock of fine Angora goats ... home-made wine ... a display of fruits, the grape, the orange, the peach, ... in short every fruit and flower cultivated in England.*

The exuberance at the bridge opening was not misplaced: the bridge still carries traffic across the often swollen waters of Prospect Creek. The fine stonework of the bridge, built under the supervision of engineer David Lennox (1788–1873), showed the colony that it too could have solid British foundations and that with such parades and bridges, its future 'greatness and prosperity' seemed ensured.

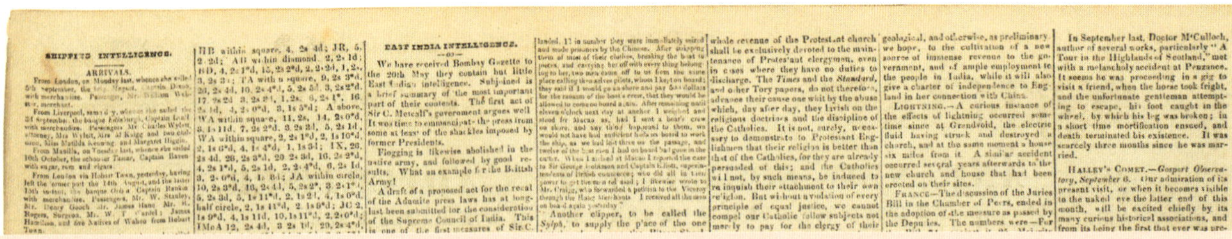

Transcription

THE LANSDOWNE BRIDGE.

This handsome and substantial structure, for the erection of which New South Wales is indebted to Sir Richard Bourke, we are happy to inform our readers is now completed, and will be opened in due form by his Excellency on the 26th instant, a most appropriate day, it being the 48th Anniversary of the foundation of the Colony. This bridge measures 190 feet in length, and 30 feet in breadth. It consists of one arch of 110 feet span; and the height from low water mark is 30 feet. The first stone it will be in the recollection of many of our readers, was laid on the 1st Jan. 1834. The bridge was designed by Mr. David Lennox, Superintendent of Bridges, and under his direction erected by convict labour, at an expense ... of little more than £1000.

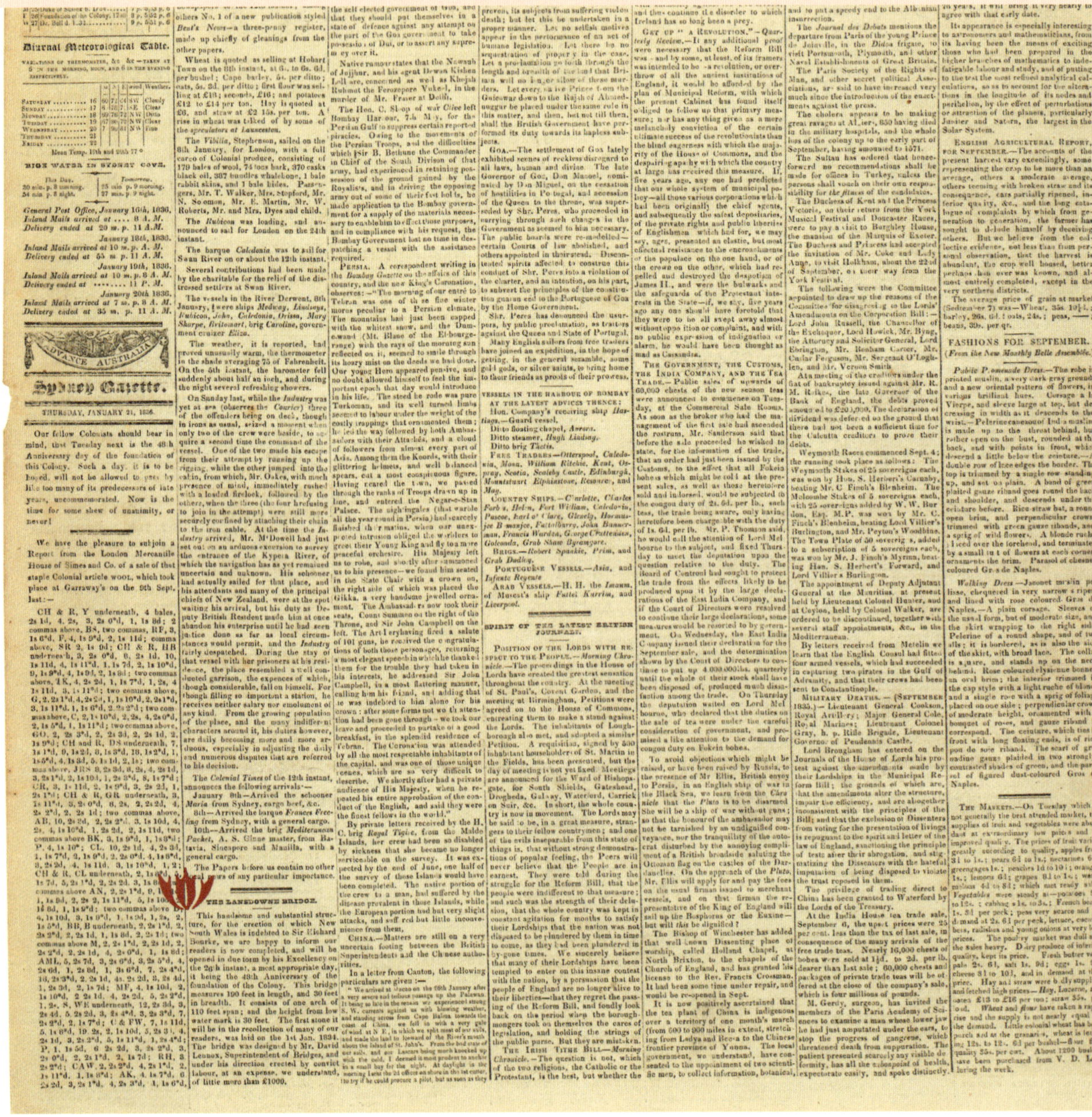

The Sydney Gazette, *in reporting the opening of the Lansdowne Bridge near Liverpool, west of Sydney, described in detail the procession that crossed the bridge, which included a 'cart conveying two Emus.'*

The Lansdowne Bridge is still in use today, though the surrounds bear little resemblance to the picturesque scene shown in this 1836 watercolour by Sydney artist Conrad Martens (1801–1878). The bridge was convict-built, using local sandstone punted along the creek from a quarry downstream. The bridge could not be used for some time after the grand opening, as its toll-booth had not been completed, but the cost of construction was soon recouped once the tolls could be collected.

23 *Recording a free colony*

South Australia's first newspaper, 1836

THE *SOUTH AUSTRALIAN GAZETTE AND COLONIAL REGISTER* HAS UNIQUE ORIGINS AND AN ODD PLACE IN A HISTORY OF HEADLINE NEWS IN AUSTRALIA. IT WAS FIRST PRODUCED IN ENGLAND SIX MONTHS BEFORE THE COLONY OF SOUTH AUSTRALIA WAS ESTABLISHED, AND BROUGHT OUT IN THE SHIPS BEARING THE COLONISTS. VOLUME ONE, NUMBER ONE WAS DATED SATURDAY 18 JUNE 1836 AND PRINTED IN ANTICIPATION OF WHEN THE COLONY WOULD BE FOUNDED. THE SECOND ISSUE DID NOT APPEAR UNTIL THE PRESS WAS OPERATIONAL IN THE NEWLY ESTABLISHED SETTLEMENT OF ADELAIDE—NEARLY TWELVE MONTHS LATER, ON 3 JUNE 1837.

The *Register*, as it became known, was founded in London by newspaper editor George Stevenson (1799–1856) and bookseller Robert Thomas (1781–1860) shortly before they sailed for the new colony, which had been promoted since 1829 as a new way of colonising Australia. The settlement was to be established without the use of convict labour and through the distribution of free land grants to settlers.

The colony of South Australia—proclaimed by an act of the British Parliament in 1834—was to be established at 'no cost' to the Mother Country. By the 1830s, the anti-slavery and prison reform movements were an increasingly vocal element in British public opinion and they influenced the idea of how the colony of South Australia was to be run. One of the platforms of this bold venture was—unlike the other colonies—an officially recognised toleration of 'all religions'.

The first issue of the *Register*, however, shows that there was already tension between the entrepreneurial scheme and the government establishment. The *Register* lays out the rules and regulations of the new colony, while promoting the interests of the South Australian Company, which had been established by businessmen under the auspices of the colonial government in order to manage the sale of land. The editors even identified the *Gazette* part of the newspaper as the official government section, and the *Register* as a separate, non-official, section devoted to the 'principles of colonization' and the 'general news of the place'.

The success of the establishment of this planned and 'free' colony has been much debated since the day the first four shiploads of settlers landed near Adelaide. In a rather inglorious start to the venture, they set up their first camp on Kangaroo Island—which already had a very rough and ready unofficial colony of whalers and sealers who had been living with the Indigenous people. The new settlers quickly transferred their tents and huts to the mainland.

South Australian Gazette and Colonial Register.

Vol. I.—No. 1. SATURDAY, JUNE 18, 1836. Price { 6*d*. Unstamped. 9*d*. Stamped.

The South Australian Gazette.

CONTRACTS FOR PROVISIONS.

HIS MAJESTY'S COLONIZATION COMMISSIONERS for SOUTH AUSTRALIA hereby give notice, that they require immediately a considerable Supply of BEEF, PORK, BREAD, FLOUR, OATMEAL, and PEASE, for the use of the Colony.—Particulars and Forms of Tender may be had at the Office of the Commission, No. 6, Adelphi Terrace, on TUESDAY next the 21st instant.

By order of the Board,
ROWLAND HILL, Secretary.

June 18th, 1836.

NOTICE TO EMIGRANTS.

THE LABOURING EMIGRANTS for SOUTH AUSTRALIA who have been allowed a FREE PASSAGE on board HIS MAJESTY'S SHIP BUFFALO, are hereby informed that they will be received on board that Ship at Portsmouth any day from the 20th to the 25th instant.—The BUFFALO sails on TUESDAY the 28th instant.

ADVERTISEMENTS.

SOUTH AUSTRALIAN COMPANY,
19, Bishopsgate-street Within.

The Establishment of the "COMPANY'S BANK" in South Australia having been approved of by all the Proprietary, it is recommended to the particular attention of Emigrants as a most important medium of facilitating their commercial operations.

A supply of Gold, Silver, Copper, and Bank Notes was forwarded to the Colony some months ago by separate ships, and all necessary arrangements made for carrying on Banking operations upon as extensive a scale as the demands of the Colony may require.

The Board of Directors give Notice that they are ready to RECEIVE DEPOSITS of Money in London from persons intending to emigrate or remit to the new Colony, for which they will grant letters of credit or drafts, at thirty days' sight, on their colonial manager in South Australia, or their promissory notes payable in London.

A limited number of Shares of £25 each, are issued at a premium of £1 per share, on which an instalment of £2. 10*s*. per share will be payable on or before the 1st of July, 1836, and a second instalment of £2. 10*s*. on or before the 1st of October, 1836. No further call will be made on these shares until after the 1st of January, 1838.

The number of these additional shares being nearly completed, persons desirous of taking an interest in the Company should apply without delay.

The Report of the Directors is now published, and ready for delivery to the Subscribers.

EDWARD HILL, Sec. *pro tem.*

Applications to be made at the Office between the hours of 10 and 3.
London, June 6th.

WILL BE DESPATCHED IMMEDIATELY.

FOR HOBART TOWN AND SYDNEY, the fine British-built Ship TAM O'SHANTER, A 1., 500 tons burthen; WHITEMAN FREEMAN, Commander; lying in the St. Katharine Docks; has a poop, with elegant Accommodations for Passengers, and is well armed. For Freight or Passage apply to the Commander on board, or to GODWIN & LEE, 117, Bishopsgate-street Within.

This Ship is intended as a Colonial Trader, and will be open on her arrival at her port of destination to make arrangements with parties interested, to load Oil and Wool at Portland Bay, Van Diemen's Land, or elsewhere, as may be required.

BLACK AND ARMSTRONG, 8, Wellington-street North, COLONIAL PUBLISHERS, BOOKSELLERS, and STATIONERS to the Honourable the COLONIZATION COMMISSIONERS, and to the SOUTH AUSTRALIAN COMPANY, are ready to execute all Orders for Books and Paper, together with Miscellaneous Articles in Stationery, which may be required in the Colonies.

They keep a constant supply of Maps, Charts, and Publications connected with Colonial Information.

SOUTH AUSTRALIAN AGENCY OFFICE,
3, Austin Friars, London.

MR. JOHN GLIDDON, appointed by the Commissioners Agent for the Purchase of Land in South Australia, is in correspondence with some of the most respectable and influential among the Colonists (some of whom have already departed for the new Settlement), and has been intrusted with the entire management of their concerns in London.

Any business of a more private nature which may be confided to Mr. Gliddon, will be conducted with the same attention and zeal as if it were transacted by the parties themselves.

It is Mr. Gliddon's object to supply to settlers a means of safe and immediate communication with the mother country, by acting as an agent, to whom they may intrust any business, whether of the most minute, or of the most weighty and confidential kind. Mr. Gliddon is well known to most of the members of the executive Government and those interested in the formation of the colony, and he feels sure that the responsible references he can give, both in London and South Australia, and the mode in which his employers will find their interests advanced, will justify their fullest confidence.

ALLEN, BOTANIST, FRUIT, and KITCHEN GARDENER, Fellow of the Horticultural Society of London, late Chief Gardener to His Majesty William the Fourth, Landscape Gardener and Ground-workman to the Honourable Commissioners of His Majesty's Woods and Forests, in laying-out and planting St. James's and Regent's Parks; Botanist and Cultivator to the Australian Agricultural Company, New South Wales; appointed Gardener and Ground-workman to His Excellency the Governor Captain Hindmarsh, R.N.

N.B. T. ALLEN and SONS respectfully beg leave to offer their services to the Gentlemen Capitalists to select, enclose, lay-out, and plant their Gardens in the best manner, both for utility and ornament, on the most reasonable terms, and with the utmost despatch.

NO. I. of the SOUTH AUSTRALIAN GAZETTE and COLONIAL REGISTER, a Newspaper for the New Colony of South Australia, which is to be continued Weekly in the Colony, will be PUBLISHED on SATURDAY the 18th inst., at No. 13, Catherine-street, Strand, (with Stamped Numbers for Country Circulation, post free,) containing every species of intelligence that can be interesting to the Colony, now on the point of departing, to their friends at home, and to others who may wish to be acquainted with the principles, objects, and local circumstances of the Colony, and the actual doings thus far of the Colonists. No. II. of the SOUTH AUSTRALIAN GAZETTE will be published (being printed in the same Form and with the same Type as No. 1) immediately after the arrival of His Excellency the Governor in South Australia, who will sail from Portsmouth on the 28th inst., in command of His Majesty's Ship Buffalo, with the Officers and their Families. Price 6*d*. unstamped, and 9*d*. stamped. Orders received by all Newsvenders in town and country, and by Mr. Capper, at the South Australian Office, Adelphi-Terrace, Strand. Annual Subscription, paid in advance, £2. 2*s*. Early applications are requested.

COLONIZATION OF SOUTH AUSTRALIA.

This day is published, in one vol. price 12*s*.,

COLONIZATION OF SOUTH AUSTRALIA.
BY R. TORRENS, Esq., F.R.S.
Chairman of the Colonization Commission for South Australia.

"It is scarcely exaggeration to say that it is one of the most important practical expositions which have been made of late years in economical science. The chapter upon the effects of extended Colonization upon the agriculture of the United Kingdom is, however, the most important one in the volume."—*Spectator*.

"No man in Britain is more capable of wisely directing an enterprise of this important character, for no living writer has shown himself either better acquainted with what is due to the economical well-being of societies, or better qualified to enforce and gain general acceptance and respect for his profound and enlightened views."—*Fife Herald*.

"Colonel Torrens has written a useful work entitled 'Colonization of South Australia.' 'He avails himself,' says the editor of the 'Atlas,' 'upon the foundation of the new Colony in Southern Australia, to enter upon the whole question of Colonization, to examine into the means of best carrying it into effect, how it would be likely to influence the prosperity of the industrial classes, and what results it would produce to the trade of the mother country. He divides the subject into two parts: the first explains the object contemplated by the founders of the new Colony, the principles upon which its formation will proceed, the agricultural and commercial capabilities of Southern Australia, and its relative advantages compared with the British dependencies; the second part is dedicated to the elucidation of the efforts which systematic Colonization would be likely to have upon the trade and industry of the United Kingdom.'"—*Hobart Town Courier*.

"It is but justice to the talents of the gallant writer to commend his work of the knowledge and ability it displays. We are not aware of any work in which the views of the Colonization Society are more satisfactorily stated than in this volume."—*Atlas*.

London: Longman, Rees, Orme, and Co.

From a Correspondent.

WE avail ourselves of this our first publication to communicate to Parties proceeding to the Colony the facility of obtaining every description of suitable Agricultural Implements, Ironmongery, and Articles for Domestic Use, which have been with much care and attention selected by the parties who proceeded in the Cygnet, but more exclusively by the Buffalo, Tam O'Shanter, Africaine, &c. Provided by Messrs. H. H. MORTIMER and CO., Wholesale Ironmongers, 10, Bush Lane.

SOUTH AUSTRALIAN CHURCH.

COMMITTEE.

Rev. Henry Blunt.	P. St. Leger Grenfell, Esq.
J. S. Brownrigg, Esq. M.P.	John Labouchere, Esq.
Rev. A. M. Campbell.	John Shaw Lefevre, Esq.
John Capel, Esq.	Rev. Charles Miller.
The Dean of Chichester.	George Palmer, Esq. Jun.
J. W. Childers, Esq. M.P.	Capt. Sir Edward Parry, R.N.
Thomas Somers Cocks, Esq.	Rev. Henry Raikes.
Raikes Currie, Esq.	John Rundle, Esq. M.P.
Rev. Dr. Dealtry.	Abel Smith, Esq. M.P.
Rev. H. R. Dukinfield.	Wolryche Whitmore, Esq.

HON. SEC.
Charles Mann, Esq.

TREASURER.
Raikes Currie, Esq.

An Association has been formed, in connexion with the Society for the Propagation of the Gospel, to assist the Colonists, now settling in South Australia, in providing for themselves the means of Public Worship and Religious Instruction, according to the doctrines of the Church of England.

Measures are in progress for securing the erection of a Church, a residence for the Clergyman, and a School, in the new Settlement; but to accomplish these objects assistance from this country is absolutely necessary; and the Committee earnestly solicit the contributions of those who are alive to the great importance of making the introduction of the Christian Church co-ordinate with the first planting of a Colony which may hereafter, under the Divine blessing, be the centre of light and truth, as well as of commerce and the arts, to the vast regions in which it is placed.

The Rev. C. B. Howard, M.A., recommended by the Bishop of Chester, and approved by the Bishop of London, has been appointed to the Chaplaincy by Lord Glenelg.

SUBSCRIPTIONS.

	£.	s.	d.
Society for the Propagation of the Gospel	200	0	0
Society for Promoting Christian Knowledge	200	0	0
The Archbishop of Canterbury	20	0	0
The Bishop of London	20	0	0
The Bishop of Winchester	10	0	0
The Bishop of Australia	5	5	0
Abel Smith, Esq. M.P.	21	0	0
John Labouchere, Esq.	21	0	0
Raikes Currie, Esq.	21	0	0
Henry Currie, Esq.	10	10	0
Samuel George Smith, Esq.	10	0	0
George Robert Smith, Esq.	5	0	0
Oswald Smith, Esq.	5	0	0
The Hon. and Rev. G. Noel	10	0	0
The Dean of Chichester	5	5	0
The Rev. H. R. Dukinfield	5	5	0
The Rev. A. M. Campbell	5	5	0
Sir M. Blakeston, Bart.	10	0	0
The Hon. and Rev. L. Powys	5	5	0
P. St. Leger Grenfell, Esq., 1 acre of town land, 40 acres of country land—estimated value	70	0	0
Capt. H. O'Brien	2	0	0
Major Digby Mackworth	2	0	0
The Rev. Lister Isaac	1	0	0
George Palmer, Esq.	5	5	0
George Palmer, Esq. Jun.	5	5	0
G. F. Angas, Esq.	5	5	0
John Capel, Esq.	5	0	0
Rowland Hill, Esq.	3	3	0
O. Gilles, Esq. and the Miss Gilles	12	12	0
The Rev. Henry Blunt	5	5	0
The Rev. Horace Mann	2	0	0

Subscriptions received by Cocks & Co., Curries & Co., Esdailes & Co., Goslings & Co., and Williams & Co.

TO SOUTH AUSTRALIAN AGRICULTURISTS.

HYDRAULICS.—The attention of the Public interested in South Australia, is earnestly directed to the NEW PRINCIPLE in Pumps, called the PATENT FOUNTAIN PUMP. This invention is freed from the bad qualities of the common friction Pump. It requires no truly-bored cylinder, and one man working at the Patent Pump is able to perform the labour of three men when employed at the old Pump in short lifts. Any practical Party going out to South Australia, or any Gentleman having Property in this highly important and rising settlement, is invited to look in at the Works of the Patentee, JOHN BEARE, Civil Engineer, 7, Pall-Mall East, London.

For the purposes of Irrigation, these Pumps are indispensable. Plans, Drawings, &c., may be seen at Messrs. OAKDEN & Co's. South Australia.

LIST OF SHIPS THAT HAVE SAILED AND ARE ABOUT TO SAIL TO SOUTH AUSTRALIA.

Sailed.	Emigrants.	About to Sail.	Probable Number.
John Pirie	28	His Majesty's ship Buffalo	200
Duke of York	38	Africaine	60
Cygnet	84	Tam O'Shanter	30
Lady Mary Pelham	34	A Vessel by the South Australian Company	350
Emma	26		
Rapid	24		
	234		640

Actual Emigrants this Season . 874

The Colonial Register.

To print the first number of the South Australian Gazette and Colonial Register in the capital of the civilized world, with the intention of publishing its second number in a city of the wilderness of which the site is yet unknown, may appear to many more chimerical than interesting; but we trust to satisfy all who honour these pages with other than a casual glance that there is greater prudence and higher import in that intention than are apparent on the surface; and, moreover, that, without presumption or self-deceit, our scheme possesses none of the characteristics of the rash projector, but is the result of the patient investigation of men qualified by years and experience to form a sound judgment, and who, in all other relations of life, have acted on opinions cautiously adopted, deliberately confirmed, and fully capable of practical development.

That the plan for the colonization of South Australia is one of the nature we have described, we refer to the names of the individuals who constitute His Majesty's commissioners as gentlemen whose intelligence and honour are indisputed and indisputable. That it possesses the requisites by men of business deemed essential to the successful result of mercantile enterprise, no better assurance can be afforded than a reference to the gentlemen forming the Direction of the South Australian Company—an association on an extended scale for commercial purposes in the colony. The names of these gentlemen will be found in another part of this paper. Their extensive participation in the great trading interests of the empire, their characters for probity, and their general information on all subjects connected with mercantile matters, are too well known to the capitalists and merchants of England to require the aid of our humble testimony in their favour.

It may be thought that in a colony, the population of which at the outset must necessarily be limited, the establishment of a Journal like the present is premature. That we do not think so, the fact of types precisely similar to those which have printed what the reader now holds in his hands, printers, presses, paper, and the whole *matériel* of a newspaper, being already on shipboard, and bound to South Australia, sufficiently proves. But the history of the progress of a colony founded upon principles which are believed to be the true principles of colonization, ought, we think, to be a source of deep and permanent interest to every one who has at heart the welfare of our Poor and the increase of the prosperity of our country; and as our Journal is intended not as a vehicle for the diffusion of political or party opinions, but as the simple record of the proceedings of a new colony which professes to commence with the elements of society already formed, and society itself to a certain extent, matured, with a government organized and complete, and to be conducted on the principle of selling unoccupied land to the settler, and expending the price received for it in providing him with labourers to render it productive and valuable, we are led to the conclusion that our Register may find its way into the hands of the statesman and the philanthropist at home, by whom the importance of this experiment on society in England, and on the future well-being of all her colonial possessions, must be at once discovered.

As the official acts and orders of the Colonial Government will be published in this Journal, that portion of the paper containing these acts and orders will be called the Gazette. This circumstance renders it proper to state here, and once for all, that the Gazette alone is to be considered as recording the official acts and orders of the Colonial Government. The Register being devoted to the elucidation of the principles of colonization, to the record of the establishment and progress of the colony, and the general news of the place and of the day, is altogether *non-official*, and under independent control.

The first issue of South Australia's first newspaper was produced in London, six months before the colonists arrived in the new colony. Like other papers of the time, the front page included government announcements and advertising, with the addition of an explanation of the need for the paper.

24 The chart of advancing civilisation

Second issue of the *Melbourne Advertiser*, 1838

IN 1838, WITH NO PRINTING PRESS AVAILABLE, ENERGETIC ALL-ROUND NEWSPAPER PUBLISHER, EDITOR, WRITER AND HOTELIER JOHN PASCOE FAWKNER (1792–1869) SET ABOUT HAND WRITING THIRTY-TWO COPIES A WEEK OF HIS 'MANUSCRIPT NEWSPAPER'.

The stand-in newspaper—produced by the teetotaller Fawkner from the first established pub in Melbourne, Fawkner's Hotel—lasted nine issues during 1838, before Fawkner suspended publication. However, he soon returned to the newspaper scene armed with printing type from Tasmania to produce the *Port Phillip Patriot and Melbourne Advertiser* in 1839. In 1846 the *Advertiser* became the *Melbourne Argus*—a newspaper that dominated the Melbourne press for much of the late nineteenth and early twentieth centuries. Fawkner is regarded as its founder.

Melbourne's first newspaper reflects the tempestuous beginnings of the early colony at Port Phillip and Fawkner's role in the 're-establishment' of a colony near present-day Melbourne. As an 11-year-old transported to the colonies with his convict father, Fawkner had been part of the group of convicts and settlers under the first Tasmanian governor, David Collins (1756–1810), who had tried unsuccessfully in 1803 to establish a colony near present-day Sorrento. With failing crops and no supplies, Collins retreated back across Bass Strait to Tasmania.

Fawkner seems to have been much influenced by his experiences on the Victorian coast and continued efforts to re-establish a colony there. In 1835 a new expedition to settle the area was mounted from Tasmania. One of the expedition leaders John Batman (1801–1839) endeavoured to buy the land from the local Kulin people. The 'exchange' he offered was an annual rent of 40 blankets, 30 axes, 100 knives, 50 scissors, 30 mirrors, 200 handkerchiefs, 100 pounds of flour and 6 shirts. Governor Bourke had to remind the colonists that the land was not to be purchased, as it was in the first instance owned by the Crown. Bourke's proclamation of October 1835—aimed at limiting free settlers—introduced the idea of *terra nullius* by stating that in British legal terms, no-one had owned the land before the British arrived, effectively ignoring Aboriginal people's claims to land ownership.

Settlers had not only been quietly moving in to the area before the Port Phillip expedition, but one had been there since the first expedition of 1803. The 'Wild Man', William Buckley, had escaped and was effectively marooned when Collins's expedition left for Tasmania. He had lived among the Watourong Aboriginal people for thirty-two years before surrendering himself to the authorities, gradually re-learning English and, after a period as an interpreter, retiring to live in Tasmania.

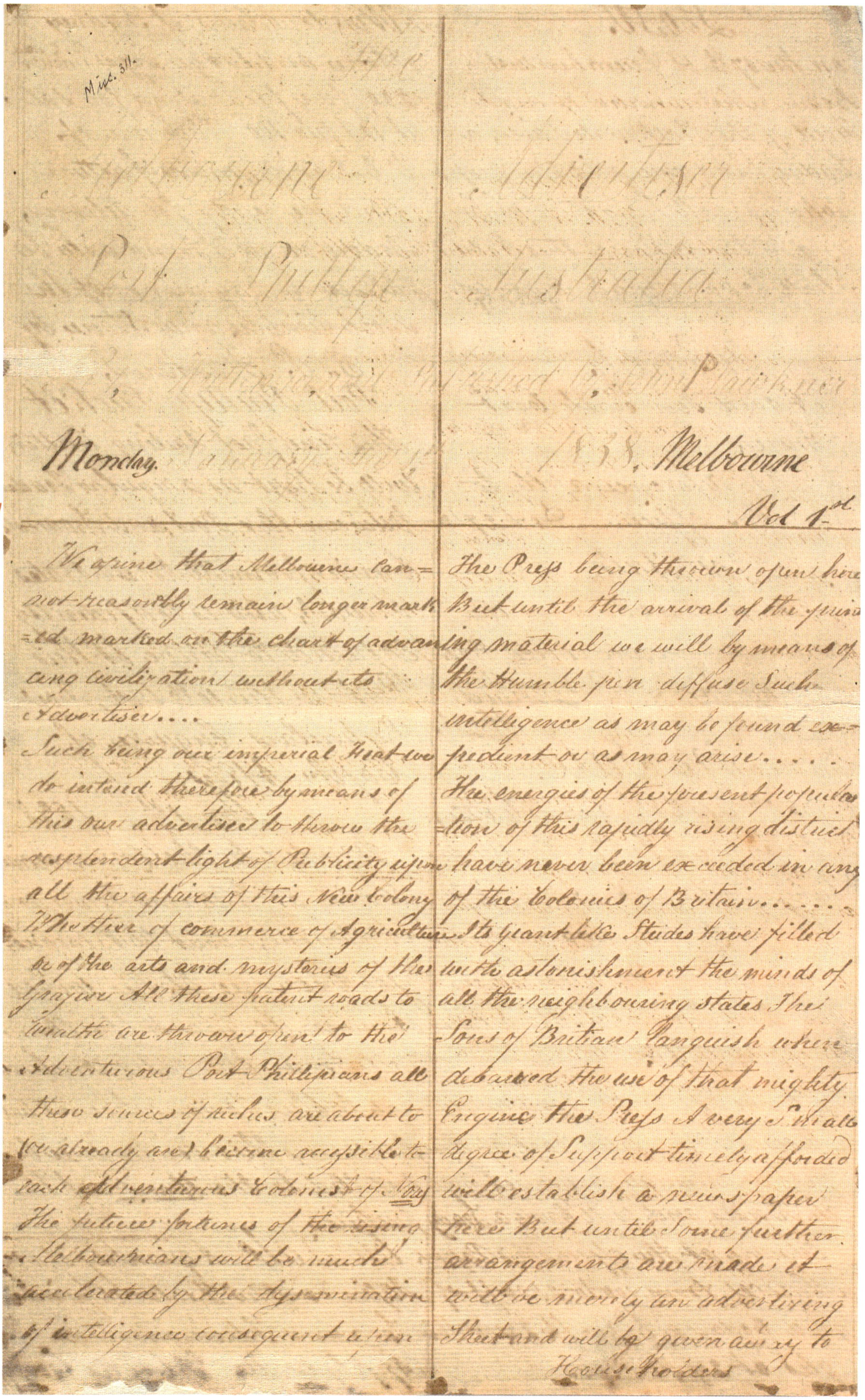

Melbourne Advertiser
Port Phillip Australia
Written and Published by John Fawkner
Monday January 1st 1838. Melbourne
Vol 1st

We opine that Melbourne cannot reasonbly remain longer mark
-ed marked on the chart of advan
cing civilization without its
Advertiser....
Such being our imperial Heat we
do intend therefore by means of
this our advertiser to throw the
resplendent light of Publicity upon
all the affairs of this New Colony
Whether of commerce of Agriculture
or of the arts and mysteries of the
Grazier All these patent roads to
wealth are thrown open to the
Adventurous Port Phillipians all
these sources of riches are about to
(or already are) become accessible to
each Adventurous Colonist of Nous
The future fortunes of the rising
Melbournians will be much
accelerated by the dissemination
of intelligence consequent upon

The Press being thrown open here
But until the arrival of the print
ing material we will by means of
the Humble pen diffuse such
intelligence as may be found expedient or as may arise....
The energies of the present popula
tion of this rapidly rising district
have never been exceeded in any
of the Colonies of Britain.....
Its giant like strides have filled
with astonishment the minds of
all the neighbouring states The
Sons of Britain languish when
debarred the use of that mighty
Engine the Press A very small
degree of Support timely afforded
will establish a newspaper
here But until some further
arrangements are made it
will be merely an advertising
Sheet and will be given away to
Householders

In the first issue of Fawkner's Advertiser *he rather grandly claimed that his hand-written paper would put Melbourne on the map of 'civilization', yet humbly concludes that, at first, his paper would be 'merely an advertising sheet and will be given away to Householders'.*

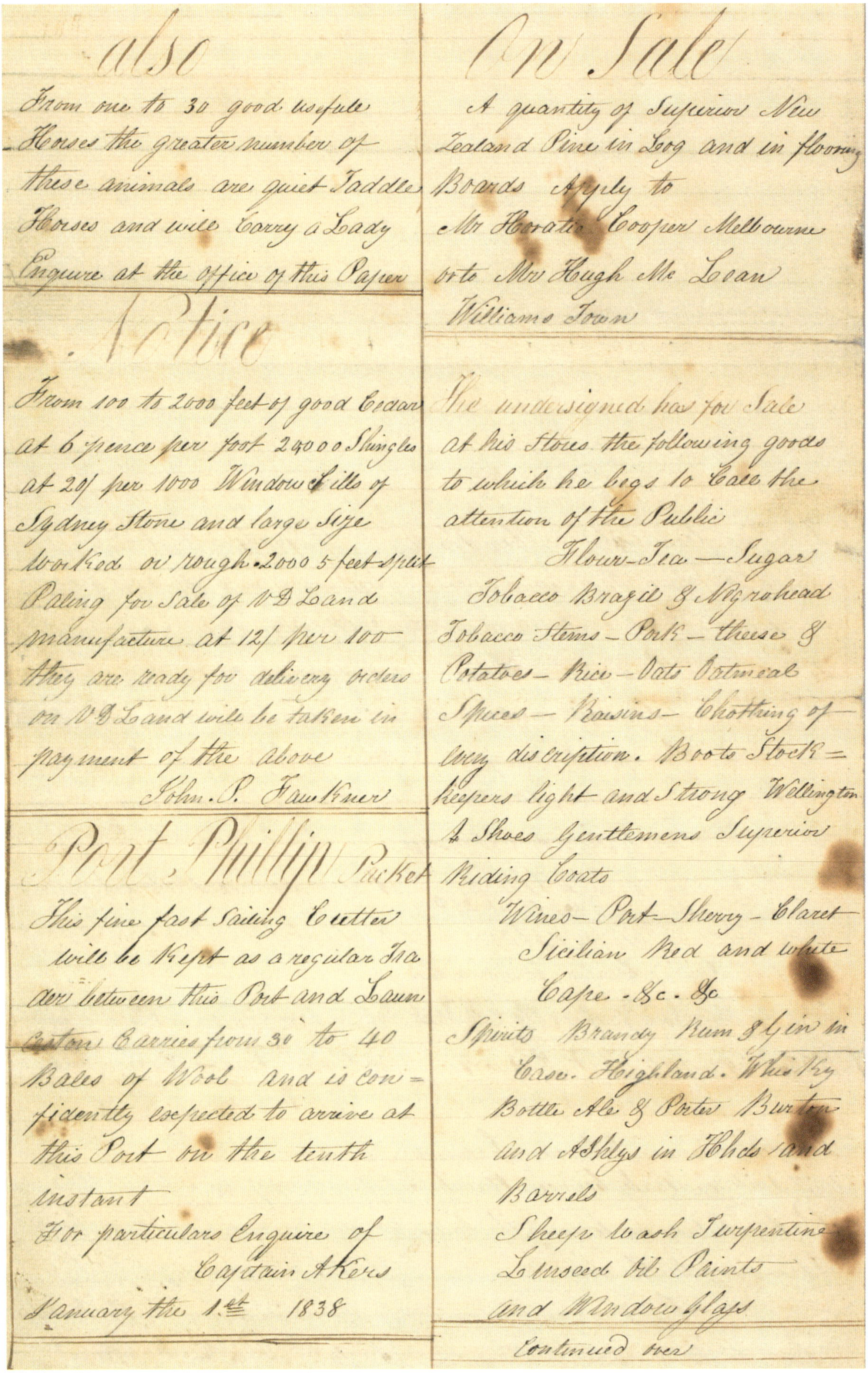

also

From one to 30 good usefule Horses the greater number of these animals are quiet Saddle Horses and will Carry a Lady Enquire at the office of this Paper

Notice

From 100 to 2000 feet of good Cedar at 6 pence per foot 24000 Shingles at 20/ per 1000 Window Sills of Sydney Stone and large Size Worked or rough. 2000 5 feet split Paling for Sale of V D Land manufacture at 12/ per 100 they are ready for delivery orders on V D Land will be taken in payment of the above

John. P. Fawkner

Port Phillip Packet

This fine fast sailing Cutter will be Kept as a regular Trader between this Port and Launceston Carries from 30 to 40 Bales of Wool and is confidently expected to arrive at this Port on the tenth instant

For particulars Enquire of Captain AKers

January the 1st 1838

On Sale

A quantity of Superior New Zealand Pine in Log and in flooring Boards Apply to Mr Horatio Cooper Melbourne or to Mr Hugh Mc Lean Williams Town

The undersigned has for Sale at his Stores the following goods to which he begs to Call the attention of the Public

Flour – Tea – Sugar
Tobacco Brazil & Negrohead
Tobacco Stems – Pork – Cheese & Potatoes – Rice – Oats Oatmeal Spices – Raisins – Clothing of every discription. Boots Stock=keepers light and Strong Wellington & Shoes Gentlemens Superior Riding Coats
Wines – Port – Sherry – Claret
Sicilian Red and white
Cape. &c. &c
Spirits Brandy Rum & Gin in Case. Highland. Whisky
Bottle Ale & Porter Burton and Ashlys in Hhds and Barrels
Sheep wash Turpentine
Linseed Oil Paints
and Window Glass

Continued over

The second page of the first Advertiser *shows Fawkner setting out his advertisements as they might have been in a typeset newspaper, with larger headings to catch the reader's attention. Vital shipping news, as well as lost, wanted and sale ads all appear.*

Monday

We opine that Melbourne cannot reasonably remain longer marked on the chart of advancing civilization without its Advertiser …

Such being our imperial Fiat we do intend therefore by means of this our advertiser to throw the resplendent light of Publicity upon all the affairs of this New Colony Whether of Commerce of Agriculture or of the arts and mysteries of the Grazier. All these patent roads to wealth are thrown open to the adventurous Port Phillipians. All these sources of riches are about to (or already are) become accessible to each adventurous Colonist of NOUS. The future fortunes of the rising Melbournians will be much accelerated by the dissemination of intelligence consequent upon The Press being thrown open here. But until the arrival of the printing materials we will by means of the Humble pen diffuse Such intelligence as may be found expedient or as may arise … The energies of the present population of this rapidly rising district have never been exceeded in any of the Colonies of Britain ... Its giant like Strides have filled with astonishment the minds of all the neighbouring states. The Sons of Britain languish when debarred the use of that mighty Engine the Press. A very Small degree of Support timely afforded will establish a newspaper here But until Some further arrangements are made it will be merely an advertising sheet and will be given away to Householders.

Melbourne as it appeared in 1840, not long after Fawkner began production of his typeset newspaper. The sketch was published in Australian Pictures *by Howard Willoughby, published by the Religious Tract Society, London, in 1886.*

25 *Massacre at Myall Creek*

Attacks on Australian Indigenous people, 1838

AS THE COLONY EXPANDED INLAND IN THE 1830S, CONFLICT AND VIOLENCE DEVELOPED ON THE FRONTIERS OF SETTLEMENT, AWAY FROM THE REACH OF BRITISH LAW. SOME SETTLERS RETALIATED HARSHLY TO REAL OR PERCEIVED THREATS TO THEIR STOCK. ABORIGINAL PEOPLE, WHO OFTEN WELCOMED SETTLERS INTO THEIR COUNTRY, TOOK SHEEP OR GRAIN AS THEIR PART OF THE BARGAIN, OR BECAUSE TRADITIONAL FOODS WERE DISAPPEARING.

Some punitive raids were sanctioned by authorities, such as the Appin Massacre at a Dharawal encampment south-west of Sydney in 1816. Others were unsanctioned, such as in Bathurst in 1824, when gangs of heavily armed convicts and settlers turned retaliation into indiscriminate massacres. The reports of such events were often hidden or limited, and historical evidence of the extent of massacres has been debated. However, the many well-documented cases, such as at Myall Creek, show a widespread pattern.

Myall Creek became infamous because it was the first frontier massacre where Europeans were tried under British law and hanged for their crimes. The trials and punishment ignited debate in a highly racist society where many people did not equate the murder of Aboriginal people with the murder of Europeans. A juror in the Myall Creek trial admitted to *The Australian* newspaper in November 1838 that he knew the men were guilty, but did not find them so because he could not stand to 'see a white man hanged for killing a black'.

In June 1838 a group of twelve stockmen in northern New South Wales, in retaliation for the theft of some cattle, decided to 'round up' any Aboriginal people they could find. They came across a camp of around forty to fifty Wirrayaraay people, then attacked and murdered many of them. The station manager reported the incident and eventually police investigated and found at least twenty-seven identifiable individuals among the charred remains where the stockmen had tried to get rid of the evidence.

Eleven of the stockmen were tried in Sydney in November 1838 and the jury took just fifteen minutes to acquit them—to popular acclaim. But Edward Smith Hall (1786–1860), editor of *The Sydney Monitor*, was incensed. Hall, a significant figure in early colonial society, is said to have initiated three major reforms in the colony: the introduction of trial by jury, freedom of the press and representative government. His report on the case in a special supplement to *The Sydney Monitor* of 19 November 1838 made a mockery of the trial. The stockmen were retried, and in December 1838 seven were found guilty of murder and hanged.

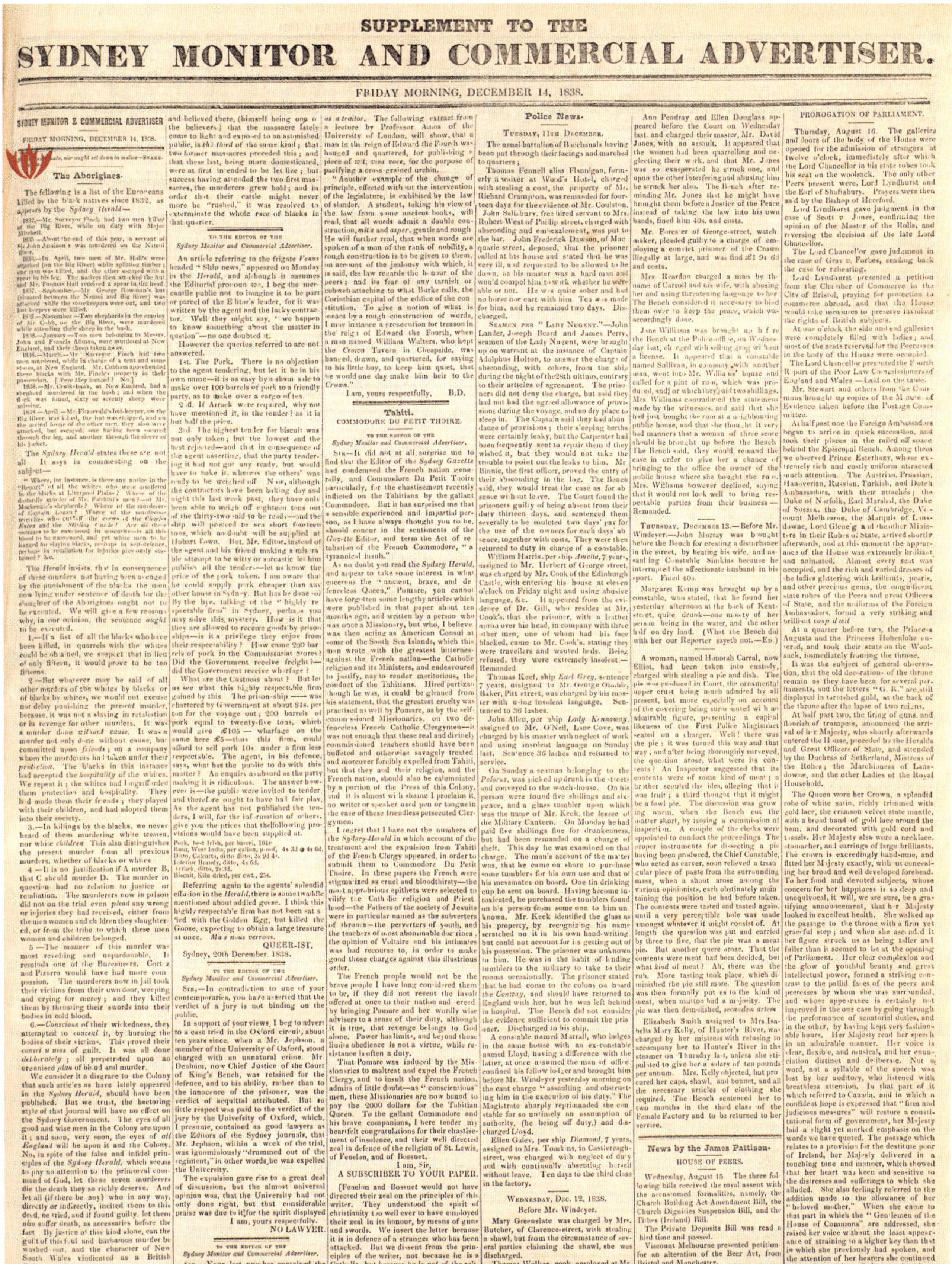

SUPPLEMENT TO THE

SYDNEY MONITOR AND COMMERCIAL ADVERTISER.

FRIDAY MORNING, DECEMBER 14, 1838.

The Aborigines.

Police News.

Tahiti.

News by the James Pattison.

PROROGATION OF PARLIAMENT.

The Sydney Monitor and Commercial Advertiser *under Edward Smith Hall was an important mouthpiece of dissent in the colony from 1826 to 1838.*

The aborigines.

The following is a list of the Europeans killed by the black natives since 1832, as appears by the *Sydney Herald*—

1832,—Mr. Surveyor Finch had two men killed at the Big River, while on duty with Major Mitchel.

1835,—About the end of this year, a servant of Sir John Jamison's was murdered on the Namoi River.

1836,— In April, two men of Mr. Hall's were attacked (on the Big River) while splitting timber; one man was killed, and the other escaped with a spear in his leg. The natives then attacked the hut and Mr. Thomas Hall received a spear in the head.

1837,—September.—Mr George Bowman's hut (situated between the Namoi and Big River) was attacked while the storekeepers were out, and two hut keepers were killed.

1837,—November—Two shepherds in the employ of Mr. Cobb, on the Big River, were murdered while attending their sheep in the bush.

1838,—January—Two men belonging to Messrs. John and Francis Allman, were murdered at New England, and their sheep taken away.

1838,—March.—Mr Surveyor Finch had two men murdered, while in charge of a tent and some stores, at New England. Mr. Cobham apprehended these blacks with Mr. Finch's property in their possession. [Were *they* hanged? No.]

1838,—Mr. Cruikshank, at New England, had a shepherd murdered in the bush; and when the flock was found, sixty or seventy sheep were missing.

1838,—April—Mr. Fitzgerald's hut-keeper, on the Big River, was killed, the hug was stripped, and on the arrival home of the other men, they also were attacked, but escaped, one having been speared through the leg, and another through the sleeve of his jacket.

The *Sydney Herald* states these are not all. It says in commenting the subject—

"Where, for instance, is there any notice in the "Report" of all the whites who were murdered by the blacks at Liverpool Plains? Where of the dastardly murder of Mr. Faithful's men?—of Mr. Mackenzie's shepherds? Where of the murderers of Captain Logan? Where of the murderous wretches who cut off the crews of the *Charles Eaton* and the *Stirling Castle*? Are all these outrages to be enveloped in obscurity—is all this blood to be unavenged, and yet white men to be hanged for slaying blacks, perhaps in self-defence, perhaps in retaliation for injuries previously sustained? &c.

The *Herald* insists, that in consequence of these murders not having been avenged by the punishment of the blacks the men now lying under sentence of death for the slaughter of the Aborigines ought not to be executed. We will give a few reasons why, in our opinion, the sentence *ought* to be executed.

1,—If a list of all the blacks who have been killed, in quarrels with the whites could be obtained, we suspect that in lieu of only fifteen, it would prove to be ten fifteens.

2 —But whatever may be said of all other murders of the whites by blacks or of blacks by whites, we would not excuse nor delay punishing the *present* murder, because, it was not a slaying in retaliation or in revenge for other murders. It was a murder done *without cause*. It was

a murder not only done without cause, but committed upon *friends*; on a company whom the murderers had taken under their *protection*. The blacks in this instance had accepted the *hospitality* of the whites. We repeat it; the whites had long afforded them protection and hospitality. The had made them their friends; they played with their children, and had adopted them into their society.

3.—In killings by blacks, we never heard of them murdering white *women*, nor white *children*. This also distinguishes the present murder from all previous murders, whether of blacks or whites.

4.—It is no justification if A murder B, that C should murder D. The murder in question had no relation to justice or retaliation. The murderers now in prison did not on the trial even *plead* any wrong or injuries they had received, either from the men women and children they slaughtered, or from the tribe to which these men women and children belonged.

5—The *manner* of this murder was most revolting and unpardonable. It reminds one of the Buccaneers. Cortez and Pizarro would have had more compassion. The murderers now in jail took their victims from their own door, weeping and crying for mercy; and they killed them by thrusting their swords into their bodies in cold blood.

6.—*Conscious* of their wickedness, they attempted to *conceal* it, by burning the bodies of their victims. This proved their *consciousness* of guilt. It was all done *deliberately*, all perpetrated upon an organised *plan* of blood and murder.

We consider it a disgrace to the Colony that such articles as have lately appeared in the *Sydney Herald*, should have been published. But we trust, the hectoring style of that journal will have no effect on the Sydney Government. The eyes of all good and wise men in the Colony are upon it: and soon, very soon, the eyes of *all England* will be upon it and the Colony. No, in spite of the false and infidel principles of the *Sydney Herald*, which seems to pay no attention to the primœval command of God, let these seven murderers die the death they so richly deserve. And let all (if there be any) who in any way, directly or indirectly, incited them to this deed, be tried, and if found guilty, let them *also* suffer death, as accessaries before the fact. By justice of this kind alone, can the guilt of this foul and barbarous murder be washed out, and the character of New South Wales vindicated as a British Colony.

But then it would be the most disgusting cant to brag of justice in putting these seven ignorant convicts to death, and then screen others of gentle blood who had incited them to the deed? if such there be.

We are informed, that Mr. Hobbs, one of the witnesses on the late trial, asserts, that it is rumoured at Liverpool Plains, and believed there, (himself being one of the believers) that the massacre lately come to light and exposed to an astonished public is *the third* of the same kind; that two former massacres preceded this; and that these last, being more domesticated, were at first intended to be let live; but success having attended the two first massacres, the murderers grew bold; and in order that their cattle might never more be "rushed," it was resolved to exterminate the whole race of blacks in that quarter.

26 *Separation at last!*

Victoria becomes a separate colony, 1850

BY THE LATE 1840S THE COLONIES OF NEW SOUTH WALES, SOUTH AUSTRALIA, WESTERN AUSTRALIA AND TASMANIA WERE ALL DEVELOPING RAPIDLY, PARTICULARLY THROUGH THE EXPANSION OF SHEEP GRAZING AROUND THE COUNTRY AND THE EXPORT OF WOOL. THE NEWSPAPER INDUSTRY HAD ALSO GROWN SIGNIFICANTLY, AND THE MAJOR POPULATION CENTRES EACH HAD SEVERAL COMPETING NEWSPAPERS.

While business and political interests around Melbourne were clamouring for a new colonial administration based in Melbourne, a new age of news was beginning, and the two collided in possibly the first journalistic scoop in Australian history. Perhaps most importantly for the development of the way news was communicated, this era also saw the first appearance of a true front page headline.

Almost from the time they had arrived at Port Phillip from the mid-1830s, colonists had been arguing for the creation of an independent colony, separate from New South Wales. Up to 1836 when South Australia was established, the colony of New South Wales stretched from the east coast of the continent to the boundary with present-day Western Australia, and from Cape York in the north to Port Phillip Bay in the south. Separation was seen as essential for a more effective administration of the areas south of the Murray River, but the demand was also a sign of growing political independence south of the border.

The British Parliament eventually agreed with the colonists and passed the Australian Colonies Act in August 1850. With shipping still taking several months to arrive from Europe, Melburnians remained ignorant of their status as an independent colony. That changed in early November, when one of the town's most colourful early reporters, Edmund Finn (1819–1898) took delivery of some overseas news from a recently arrived ship, and found mention of the passing of the Colonies Bill, tucked away among official notices, next to notice of a new Dog Act.

Finn realised that no-one in the government had yet been informed of this, and so he 'said nothing to anybody'. Not finding his editor 'immediately accessible', he 'assumed responsibility' for placing what he called an 'Extraordinary' in the hands of the printers. The result was a full-page headline in *The Melbourne Morning Herald*, informing the locals that they were now officially Victorians, as the Colonies Bill had been passed.

The separation of Victoria was momentous news, and it furthered the economic and political rivalry between Sydney and Melbourne that was to be a central feature of the next half-century. It was also quite timely, as the 1850s were to see a huge transformation of Australian society, with the reverberation of just one word—gold.

V R

THE MELBOURNE
MORNING HERALD
EXTRAORDINARY.

VOL. XI. MELBOURNE, MONDAY EVENING, NOVEMBER 11, 1850. No. 1508.

GLORIOUS NEWS!
SEPARATION
AT LAST!!

We Lose not a moment in communicating to the PUBLIC the Soul-stirring intelligence that
SEPARATION HAS COME AT LAST!!
The Australian Colonies' Bill,
WITH THE AMENDMENTS MADE IN THE LORDS, ON THE 5th JULY,
WAS AGREED TO IN THE COMMONS ON THE 1ST AUG.,
AND ONLY AWAITS THE QUEEN'S SIGNATURE TO BECOME
THE LAW OF THE LAND.
The long OPPRESSED, long BUFFETTED Port Phillip, is at length an
INDEPENDENT COLONY,
Gifted with the Royal name of VICTORIA, and endowed with a flourishing revenue and almost inexhaustible resources.
Let all classes of Colonists then lose not a moment in their hour of triumph in celebrating the Important Epoch in a suitable manner, and observing one
GENERAL JUBILEE.

The "Public Rejoicings" Committee lately nominated by the Citizens of Melbourne, will assemble without delay; let one and all co-operate with them heart and hand in giving due effect to the enthusiastic ovations of our
New-born Colony!
It is an ERA in the existence of our adopted Land which can never again occur; and the Glorious opportunity once past will be irrevocable.
COLONISTS, "now is the day and now is the hour!!" For this act of Justice to Port Phillip, and every other good gift, may
God Bless the Queen!!!

Printed and Published at the "Melbourne Morning Herald and General Daily Advertiser" Offices, Little Collins-street, Melbourne, New South Wales, by GEORGE CAVENAGH.

The Melbourne Morning Herald's *'Extraordinary'* was a one-page handbill that loudly and proudly claimed the scoop that the Australian Colonies Bill had been passed by the British Parliament.

1851–

Gold, bushrangers and rebels

-1880

The discovery of gold in central west New South Wales in 1851 was a key moment in Australian history. In just a few years a relatively isolated British colonial outpost was rapidly transformed into a seething hive of industry, largely propelled by non-British people from around the globe. The population expanded dramatically: in the newly established colony of Victoria, the number of inhabitants rose from 76,000 in 1850, before the discovery of gold around Ballarat and Bendigo, to more than 530,000 in 1859.

UNTIL THE GOLD RUSHES, ALMOST ALL FREE SETTLERS HAD COME FROM BRITAIN. THE AUSTRALIAN COLONIES PREVIOUSLY HAD LITTLE NEED TO PUT MUCH THOUGHT INTO RESTRICTING IMMIGRATION, SO THERE WERE NO REAL POLICIES OF EXCLUSION, AND IN 1852 PEOPLE CAME FROM EUROPE, THE AMERICAS AND CHINA TO SEEK GOLD IN THE AUSTRALIAN BUSH.

By 1850 the squatters had reached all the useful grasslands in Victoria and New South Wales. Queensland was not yet a separate colony and remained comparatively unexplored and unpopulated until the latter half of the nineteenth century. And most of the vast and drier north and west of the continent, apart from a handful of ports clinging to the coast for survival, were still the lands of traditional owners.

Essentially, the Australian colonies had conquered the areas of the continent where it seemed possible for agriculture and pastoralism to thrive. A squattocracy, or aristocracy of squatters, held sway in the interior and formed a powerful political interest group—where around 2000 squatters controlled about 30 million hectares of land.

But with the discovery of gold in the 1850s, all this was changed. Once news spread of six ships arriving in England in May 1852 laden with eight tons of gold from the Australian colonies, the rush was on to the goldfields of New South Wales and then Victoria. In 1851 the European population in Australia numbered 430,000; by 1871 it had quadrupled to 1.7 million.

However we might picture it, the first discoveries of gold were never front page news with bold headlines of GOLD DISCOVERED! In fact the rushes began via word of mouth, as the government was reluctant to release news of the discoveries—quite rightly fearing a mass exodus. Despite attempts to downplay the first news reports of the extent of the discoveries of May 1851, whole towns were almost deserted overnight by men heading to the goldfields.

One event on the goldfields, however, was to become headline news, dominating reports in all of the growing number of Australian newspapers in late 1854. Miners' protests against the licence and fee that the Victorian government had imposed turned into one of the most important events in Australian history, and one of the most significant moments of violent confrontation between the colonial authorities and their subjects. The fact that a large group of miners on the Ballarat goldfields had barricaded themselves in and refused to pay their mining licences was outright rebellion. But the shocking news of the military response, reported by some journalists as a massacre, had a huge impact across the colonies. It marked a significant turning point in the way the colonial authorities dealt with the political rights of their growing numbers of citizens and laid the foundations of a more representative government.

The gold rushes sparked another far-reaching political development—how to deal with the growing number of non-Anglo-Celtic people entering the country. Chinese goldminers arrived in great numbers in the 1850s and the first of many future immigration laws was passed in Victoria in 1855. Yet despite the limits to the number of Chinese people a ship could land with, and an arrival licence fee per head, the Chinese continued to flock to the goldfields. European miners' resentment of their Chinese counterparts came to a head in a series of anti-Chinese riots, the most famous of which occurred at Lambing Flat in 1861.

The rapidly expanding Australian colonies began to define who was to be included and who was to be excluded in their new populations. The locally born now outnumbered convicts and ex-convicts, and during the 1850s the push to end the transportation system succeeded (except for Western Australia). The days of being a convict colony were over.

Yet convicts had been a source of cheap labour that was difficult to replace. From the 1860s, labour-intensive industries, such as sugar-cane in Queensland, turned to the Pacific Islands for cheap workers and brought indentured workers into the colonies. Many Islanders were kidnapped from their homelands in a practice known as blackbirding. When some of the more deplorable cases made news headlines, there was an uproar by many who saw the system as being akin to slavery.

Although the number of newspapers increased as the population grew during and after the gold rushes, headlines or front page news reports were still rare. Most newspapers retained the age-old format of reporting news on the inside pages, with shipping and other public notices on the cover page. Almost as if emboldened by the dynamism of the gold rushes, during the 1860s the typefaces of news headings had grown larger, but readers still turned to pages 3 or 4 to find news stories.

The introduction of the telegraph system meant 'correspondents', or journalists, could send in reports in moments, rather than in days by mail. Although it took several years for the telegraph system to be built across the country, and even longer for the telegraph to bring news from overseas, the system began to transform the speed of news transmission and affect the way it was reported. In fact, from the 1860s news headlines were often reprints of simple telegraphs, written in point form. The front page headline appeared as part of a new period of Australian history—the modern, industrial age.

27 Gold fever

Gold discoveries near Bathurst, 1851

THE FIRST NEWS OF HARGRAVES' DISCOVERY OF GOLD IN NEW SOUTH WALES WAS KEPT FROM THE PUBLIC BY A GOVERNMENT CONCERNED THAT THE COLONIES WOULD EXPLODE IN A FRENZY OF GOLD FEVER, AS HAPPENED IN THE GOLD STRIKE IN CALIFORNIA IN 1849. HOWEVER, A SECRET THAT BIG COULD NOT BE KEPT—NOR COULD EFFORTS TO PREVENT THE MASS EXODUS FROM TOWNS AND CITIES THAT WAS TO FOLLOW.

The colonial government had offered a substantial reward of 10,000 pounds for the discovery of a payable goldfield, and the entrepreneurial Edward Hargraves (1816–1891), a businessman experienced in the Californian goldfields who was also an adept self-promoter, decided to search similar terrain in the central west of New South Wales—where finds of small amounts of gold had been reported.

When assured by the government of his reward, Hargraves announced to the press the areas around Bathurst where he had found gold. The first news reports from *The Sydney Morning Herald* in May 1851 were not encouraging, with the paper noting that the gold might not 'be in sufficient quantities to pay for the trouble of obtaining it'.

Yet with Hargraves' exaggerated descriptions of the richness of his discoveries, on 20 May the *Herald* devoted four columns to reports of a 'complete mental madness' that had 'paralysed' the township of Bathurst. The paper may not have helped limit the rush of people to the diggings with its opening remark on the 'fact' that 'the country from the mountain ranges to an indefinite extent into the interior is one immense goldfield'.

At first, parties of prospective diggers banded together and headed off down the main streets of towns, farewelled with great ceremony by their townsfolk. But soon reports arrived of country towns from Orange to Goulburn being almost deserted and, in Sydney, hundreds of families were reported to be 'abandoned, destitute and starving.

The gold rushes transformed Australian society and created new wealth for many, but news of the chaos and threat to society, rather than success at the diggings, was prominent. The *Herald* of 20 May noted that some had headed to the bush with only a blanket and shovel, 'such is the intensity of excitement that people appear almost regardless of their present comfort and think of nothing but gold'. The paper was correct in predicting that for many diggers 'of course, all this must end in disappointment'.

OPPOSITE
Just two weeks after it had reported Hargraves' finds and the news of the discovery of gold had become common knowledge, The Sydney Morning Herald *of 20 May 1851 wrote of the frenzy that had ensued. Despite the importance of the news, this report appeared on the inside pages of the newspaper.*

SHIPPING INTELLIGENCE.

ARRIVALS.

MAY 19.—Fanny Fisher, barque, 239 tons, Captain Harrold, from Launceston the 10th instant. Passengers—Mr. F. A. Du Croy, Lady, and two children, Mary Anne Wedlake, Mr. and Mrs. Perry.

May 19.—Alice, schooner, 88 tons, Captain Robertson, from Launceston the 12th instant.

DEPARTURES.

May 19.—Black Dog, schooner, 141 tons, Captain J. R. Garrick, for Port Ross, Auckland Islands. Passengers—Mr. C. M'Aking, Mr. J. R. Thompson, Mr. William Putt, Mr. George Collins, Mr. James Robertson, Mr. J. S. Roberts, Antonio Mistachio, Mr. Thomas O'Brien, Messrs. T. Erving, Charles Richards, John Thompson, William Jeyred, David Kelly, and William Casely.

May 19.—Thomas and Henry, brig, 235 tons, Captain Bennett, for Adelaide. Passengers—Mr. Featherstonhaugh, Mrs. Thompson, and child, Mr. and Mrs. M'Court and five daughters, W. Doyle, W. Perry, Mr. Redman, Mrs. Smith, Mrs. Graham, Miss Graham, Miss Redman.

May 19.—Prince of Wales, brig, 112 tons, Captain Gaunt, for Melbourne. Passengers—Mr. and Mrs. Longmore, Mr. Gray, Mr. J. Gunning, Mr. Rankins, Mr. and Mrs. Connell, Mr. Atkinson, Mr. Rose.

PROJECTED DEPARTURES.

THIS DAY.—Frances, for Guam; Oriental, Wellington via Newcastle; George Champlin, for the South Seas and Newcastle; Johnstone, for San Francisco; Eagle, steamer, for Moreton Bay, this evening, at eight o'clock.

CLEARANCE.

May 19.—Frances, ship, 334 tons, Captain Jones, for Guam, in ballast.

COASTERS INWARDS.

May 19.—Lucy Ann, 42, Eastland, from the Richmond, with 22,000 feet cedar; Primus, 36, Lever, from Newcastle, with 50 tons coals.

COASTERS OUTWARDS.

May 19.—Echo, 22, Robertson, for Shoalhaven, with sundries; Wave, 17, Lobb, for Kiama, with sundries; Beppo, 24, Patten, Primus, 36, Lever, and the Vision, 43, Mackenzie, all for Newcastle, with sundries; Thistle, steamer, 127, Mulhall, for Morpeth, with sundries; Sea Bird, 20, Miller, for Shoalhaven, with sundries.

IMPORTS.

May 19.—Fanny Fisher, from Launceston 2000 bushels wheat, 31 bags and 8 tons potatoes, Henry Fisher; 680 bushels wheat, T. W. Smart; 165 bags wheat, 60 tons potatoes, J. Grimwood; 35 tons bark, Darvall and Co.; 6 cases haberdashery, 5 bales calico, 1 trunk shoes, 1 keg wheat, Willis, Merry, and Co.; 1 case jams, Thompson; 1 cask fruit, Taylor; 2000 bushels wheat, 1 case jams, Order.

May 19.—Alice, from Launceston: 568 bags wheat, 209 bags flour, 20 bags biscuit, 2 cases fruit, Order.

SHIPS MAILS.

Mails will close at the Post Office as follow:—

FOR SAN FRANCISCO.—By the Johnstone, this day, at noon.

FOR AUCKLAND.—By the Emma, on Thursday, at noon.

FOR HOBART TOWN.—By the Brothers, on Thursday, at noon.

VAN DIEMEN'S LAND.

HOBART TOWN.—Arrivals: May 3. Barretta Junior, 523 tons, Huggins, from San Francisco, with 20 tons oil, and part of original cargo from Van Diemen's Land; Harriet Nathan, 126 tons, Bowden, from Melbourne. 4. Pilot, 91 tons, Shepherd, from Victoria; Albert Packet, 103 tons, Abson, from Port Albert; Jenny Lind, 135 tons, Stevenson, from Victoria. 6. Emma, 139 tons, Pockley, from Sydney; Circassian, 112 tons, Smith, from Victoria; Yarra, 139 tons, Robb, from Victoria; Miranda, 127 tons, Beatly, from Port Albert 3rd instant. 7. Swordfish, 160 tons, Clinch, from Launceston 4th instant. Sailed: April 29. Scotia, 112 tons, Plunkett, for Victoria; Dart, 134 tons, Sanson, for Victoria; Agenoria, 107 tons, Burt, for Port Albert; Free Trader, 149 tons, Adams, for Port Albert. May 1. Flying Squirrel, 87 tons, Thoms, for Geelong; John Bull, for Melbourne. 2. Annie, 178 tons, M'Leod, for Mauritius. 6. London, 611 tons, Scales, for Madras, with horses; Union, 160 tons, Spain, for Adelaide. 7. Cacique, 141 tons, Milne, for Victoria.

LAUNCESTON.—Arrivals: May 3. Schooner Samuel M. Fox, 257 tons, Pryde, from San Francisco. Passengers—Mr. Munn, Mr. Castello, Mr. Mann. 7. Brig Helen, 168 tons, Dale, from Adelaide. 8. Brig Peri, 145 tons, Tregurtha, from Adelaide; Brig Sir John Byng, 169 tons, Grainger, from Adelaide. 10. Brig City of Sydney, Fawthrop, from Portland Bay.

The brig Lawsons, from Launceston, bound to Calcutta, arrived at Koombanah Bay on the 19th February. She shipped forty-three horses at Launceston, sixteen of which were for the colony, but had lost three on the passage. She sailed on the 24th, having added six horses to her stock, purchased at Swan River.

LOSS OF THE GEORGE HOME.—This vessel, which left here about a fortnight ago, laden with copper ore for Swansea, sprung a leak when about 200 miles to the westward of Kangaroo Island, and in a very short time foundered. Part of the crew in the longboat reached Kangaroo Island in safety a few days ago, with the mail for England on board, but which, after their landing, was accidentally burnt. The George Home was built at Plymouth, in 1809. The last repairs described in *Lloyd's Register* for 1850, were in 1845, when she is stated to have undergone "some repairs, and sheathed with yellow metal," but no classification is given.—*South Australian Gazette.* —We are indebted to Captain Grainger of the Sir John Byng for the *South Australian Register* of 2nd instant, which furnishes a few more particulars respecting the illfated vessel:—"We are happy to announce that the Captain of the George Home landed with his party, all safe, at Brighton, about half-past eight o'clock on Wednesday night, but in a starved and miserable condition. His statement, which is somewhat contradictory to that previously given, is to the effect that on Thursday afternoon, 350 miles south-south-east of Kangaroo Island, the George Home was wrecked (?) The upper works parted from the lower in half an hour; divided the crew as follows:—ten men in the long boat, five in the gig, the Captain himself, wife, and child, and two seamen, in the jolly boat. The last party had two gallons of water and five lbs. bread; parted company with the other boats at six o'clock, and did not see them afterwards. They had been throwing overboard copper ore for two days previously. The statement given by the second officer of the ship is that, finding the ship in a sinking state, preparations were made to abandon her. After getting their clothes, such as could be collected, in the boat, they were sufficiently laden, and could not take the mail with them. The heads of the spirit casks on board were stove in, and the mails placed by the casks. They then set fire to the spirits and left the ship. This was done after dark in the evening. About nine o'clock P.M., they were not far from the ship, which had been burning from the time she was abandoned, and was well seen to disappear all at once."—*Launceston Examiner, May* 10.—The George Home arrived in Sydney, from Panama, via Tahiti, on the 28th November, 1850; she sailed for Newcastle, and took in coals for Adelaide.

The barque Alibi, 500 tons, Shepherd, from Calcutta 4th February, touching at Coringa, Madras, Pondicherry, and Point de Galle, arrived at Adelaide on the 28th April. Lieutenant Hayman, commanding a detachment of the 18th Royal Irish was on board in charge of sixteen convicts for Hobart Town.—*Courier.*

The brig William, hence, was going into Launceston on the 12th instant. The Swan, Captain Skey, was loading for Sydney, to sail in a few days after the Alice.

The Fanny Fisher and Alice, both from Launceston, met very bad weather on the passage, with a heavy cross sea running.

QUICK WORK.—The schooner Alice left Sydney Heads on the 20th April last, and after beating down to Cape Howe, arrived at Launceston on the 5th instant; discharged there a full cargo of cedar and sundries; loaded again with wheat and flour, sailed on the 12th instant, and encountered a heavy sea and strong gales from E.S.E. to N.E., and arrived safely in Sydney yesterday morning; thus completing the round to Launceston and back, including the discharge and taking in of a full cargo each way, in less than three weeks.

WATER POLICE OFFICE.—Yesterday, the proceedings were confined to hearing charges against several persons suspected of being runaway prisoners of the Crown. In each case, no substantial reason was shown by the apprehending constable for his suspicion; and the men complained bitterly of being dragged handcuffed through the streets. In one case, where the man resisted the constable, Captain Browne said, that the law of the colony authorised the police to take any persons into custody whom they might suspect to be runaways; and that resistance rendered the parties liable to punishment. He trusted this public caution would prevent any more cases of resisting constables being brought before him. The men were discharged.

DESERTION OF SEAMEN.—Warrants have been taken out for the apprehension of seven of the Oriental's crew; eight of the Challenger's; and four of the Seringapatam's, for leaving their ships. Three of the latter are in custody; the fourth swam on shore. Serious complaints are made by the captains in harbour, as to certain of the watermen hanging about their ships in the night time for the purpose of getting their men away. Vigilant watches are ordered, and the captains have expressed their determination to fire into any boats that may approach without authority.

THE ORIENTAL.—The complications in this long protracted case are increasing. On Friday last, in Chambers, upon reading the affidavit of Mr. Robert Johnson, and the several exhibits thereunto, and hearing that gentleman on the part of Thomas Kinnear, the steward of this vessel, his Honor the Chief Justice granted a rule, calling upon Captain Browne, J.P., and Captain Hyde, of the Oriental, to show cause why a writ of prohibition should not issue to restrain them from proceeding upon, or in respect of, the order made by Captain Browne on the 15th instant, upon the complaint preferred by Captain Hyde against Thomas Kinnear, of being unlawfully absent from the said ship; and, by which order, Captain Browne directed that Kinnear should be put on board again. The grounds upon which Mr. Johnson moved for the rule are as follow:—(1.) That Captain Browne allowed Captain Hyde to be examined as a witness, and to give evidence in support of his complaint. (2.) That he refused to allow Kinnear to be examined, or to give evidence in answer thereto. (3.) That he allowed Mr. G. R. Nichols, as advocate of the complainant, to make observations upon the law of the case, after the evidence for the defence had been given; and after the defendant's case had been closed. (4.) That the evidence adduced was such as to show, to the reasonable satisfaction of Captain Browne, sufficient reason for the absence of the said Kinnear from the said ship. (5.) That the order made by him was contrary to law.—The rule is returnable on the 11th of June proximo.

DIARY.

MEMORANDA TO NEXT PUBLICATION.

May.		SUN rises	SUN sets	HIGH WATER morn.	HIGH WATER even.
20	TUESDAY	6 50	5 2	11 14	11 37

Moon, Last Quarter 11·10 A.M., May 23.

ROYAL VICTORIA THEATRE.

THIS EVENING, MAY 20,

WILL be produced, (second time), a New Play, in 3 Acts, called GIRALDA; OR, THE MILLER'S WIFE. Gil, Mr. F. Howson; Lucio, Mr. Spencer; Don Japhet, Mr. Rogers; Don Manuel, Mr. Willis; Philip, Duke of Aragon, Mr. Hydes; Grand Duchess, Mrs. Willis; Giralda, Mrs. Guerin; Maria, Mrs. Hart; Teresa, Miss E. Griffiths; Paquita, Miss Hart; Louise, Miss F. Griffiths; Janet, Miss A. Hart. Pas de Deux, Miss F. Griffiths and Signor Carandini. After which, the favourite Interlude of FORTY AND FIFTY; OR, THE LILYWHITES. To conclude with the comedy entitled the TUTOR'S ASSISTANT.

THE

Sydney Morning Herald.

TUESDAY, MAY 20, 1851.

"*Sworn to no Master, of no Sect am I.*"

LATER NEWS.

WE are again tantalised by receiving later news by a circuitous route, and consequently imperfectly. By a vessel arrived at Adelaide from India, English news to the 24th January was received, and has come to hand here via Launceston. We have compiled the best summary from the papers before us. It will be seen that the state of trade was satisfactory, and that there was a probability of a break up of the Ministry, in consequence of Lord JOHN RUSSELL'S determination to bring in a measure to resist the aggresion of the Papal See. A vessel making a good run would bring dates to the 20th February—two months later than we have received direct.

VAN DIEMEN'S LAND.

WE have our Van Diemen's Land files to the 10th instant.

When the Electoral Bill came under consideration in the Legislative Council, Messrs. GREGSON and DRY moved that the second reading be postponed for a fortnight, in order that it might be fully considered, and that members might have the advantage of the discussions that would take place in Sydney on the Sydney and Port Phillip Bills. This proposal was objected to by the government, and was negatived by ten to five; upon which, Messrs. GREGSON, DRY, FENTON, and DUNN, left the Council Chamber, and the Council was adjourned to the following Monday. On the Monday, when the second reading of the Bill was called on, the motion for adjournment was again made, and carried by a majority of twelve to two, it being generally understood that the opposition members had come to an understanding with the government. The further consideration of the Bill was then postponed until Monday, the 19th instant, and after some minor matters had been disposed of, the Council was also adjourned.

With the exception of a few alterations of detail, it appeared probable the Bill, (which is almost a copy of the Sydney Bill) would be passed as prepared by the government.

CAPE OF GOOD HOPE.

NEWS from the Cape to the end of February has been received. The Kafirs still remained in force on the borders of the colony, and several companies of the Hottentots had deserted to them. There had been several skirmishes, but no important engagement. The Kafirs were so strong that the GOVERNOR was unable to get from King William's Town to Graham's Town. The greatest suffering was experienced by the people living near the frontiers; they had been obliged to desert all their property and retire to the towns. The war was expected to be a very long one, and unless the English Government sent out large reinforcements, it was evident that no decisive blow could be struck.

We must postpone our extracts until to-morrow.

SINGAPORE.

(*From the Adelaide Times, April* 26.)

BY the Esperanza, from Singapore, we have dates from that settlement to the 26th of February.

The interior of our island, says the *Singapore Free Press* of February 21st, is in fire and flame. The disturbances, robberies, and burglaries, have never before reached such a height, not even at the time of the unfortunate Hoh-kah's case, who, it will be remembered, was kidnapped and never heard of more. He was a material witness in a burglary case, and was carried away from the public road in broad daylight.

In the present case, there appears to exist a determination on the part of the heathen to expel the Christians from all the rural districts of our island. Everywhere, at Serangoon, Bukit Timah, Bookoh Khan, Lauw Choo-khan, Nam To-kang, Chan Chwee-kang, even at Kranjee Propo, and Benor, the bangsals and plantations of the Christians have been attacked by sets of twenty to fifty heathens, who rob all the property, and destroy what they cannot carry away. The Christians come to town from all parts of the country as to a place of refuge, and people yesterday in flourishing circumstances are to day reduced to the greatest misery. Not less than twenty-seven plantations have been attacked since my last report: and the list of planters ruined by these vagabonds on the same day, namely, last Sunday, proves that there exists a conspiracy throughout the whole island, following the directions of one set of heads, which on examination will be found to consist in the leading men of the secret society.

The market was cleared of Japan and Australian copper.

Tonnage was plentiful, measurement goods £2 10s. per cubic foot to London and Liverpool.

From Siam the dates were to the 3rd of February. Sugar was high, and the coming crop expected to be very small. All the European and American residents were on the point of leaving.

CHINA.

(*From the Adelaide Times, April* 24.)

THE China Overland Mail had been received in Singapore to January 29.

Bamboo Town at Whampoa had been totally destroyed by fire. The loss of property is supposed to have been very great; 40,000 dollars according to one estimate, and five times as much, according to another.

On Sunday, the 12th of January, Messrs. Odell and Holderness were ordained at Hongkong, deacons, by the Bishop of Victoria; and on the following Sunday his Lordship opened the Mariner's Bethel, to which Mr. Holderness is to be attached.

In the beginning of the month of January, the Governor of Hongkong addressed a circular to the Justices of the Peace, proposing to make over to them the control of the Police, and the maintenance of streets, roads, and bridges; but without providing sufficient means except by imposing new burdens on the community. The offer as made would, we understand, be declined by them; but the Justices in their reply would probably take the opportunity of pointing out the sources of income properly applicable to police purposes, amply sufficient for the maintenance of a much more efficient body, and better roads and streets than we have yet seen, and which if conceded by the Government, must be placed at the disposal of the community, and not of the Justices, who only form a small portion of it, some of them not being rate-payers, and having no great stake in the colony.

The reply would not be given in till after the departure of the Mail, so the Colonial Office would have an opportunity to boast of having made an office of municipal institutions, omitting probably to explain that the terms are such as to preclude their acceptance.

DOMESTIC INTELLIGENCE.

INSOLVENT COURT.

MONDAY.

MEETINGS TO MORROW.

In the estate of Samuel Terry Hughes, a special meeting, at 10 o'clock.

In the estate of James Smith and Son, a special meeting, at half-past 10.

CITY COUNCIL.

MONDAY.

PRESENT—The Mayor, Aldermen Broughton, Allen, and Egan; Councillors Moore, Driver, Thomas, Board, Weekes, Josephson, Simmons, Tierney, Peck, Roberts, Ryan, Thornton, Williams, and Lenehan.

WATER FOUNTAIN.

Mr. THOMAS drew attention to the bad repair of the water fountain at the corner of Market and Kent streets.

PETITIONS.

Mr. ROBERTS presented a petition from the carters in the employment of the Corporation, praying for some increase in their payment to meet the advanced prices of forage.—Read and received.

Mr. ROBERTS presented a petition from the stall-holders and retail fruit sellers in George-street Market, praying that steps might be taken to prevent any evening retail sale by the wholesale dealers in shed letter A.—Read and received.

THE MAYOR'S MINUTE.

The Acting Town CLERK read a lengthened minute from the Right Worshipful the Mayor, relative to the financial position and prospects of the Corporation, to the sanitary condition of the City, to the improvements imperatively necessary, to the want of sufficient means for effecting the most material of these improvements, to the executive department of the Corporation, and to civic works and civic affairs generally.

MISSING DOCUMENTS ENQUIRY.

The MAYOR laid before the Council a statement (called for by Mr. Weekes,) showing that the cost of the above enquiry was £7 10s.

PAYMENTS.

A report was read from the MAYOR, stating that payments had been ordered by him of certain accounts, amounting in the whole to £86 2s. 4d.

TOWN HALL.

The MAYOR reported that the City Surveyor, having represented the necessity of certain repairs to the Town Hall, he had written to the lessor, who had refused to execute these repairs, although they were said to be necessary in order to avert danger.

CITY WORKS.

Alderman BROUGHTON moved, that the Report of the Improvement Committee, dated 12th and received by the Council on the 17th March, recommending the performance of the undermentioned works, be adopted. Castlereagh-street to be formed and gravelled from Campbell-street to Goulburn-street, and from Park to Bathurst streets, by contract. George-street North to be formed and covered with blue stone metal from Queen's-place to Messrs. Gilchrist's stores, by contract. Erskine-street, to be formed and gravelled; the gravel to be supplied by the present contractor, and laid down under the direction of the City Surveyor.

Mr. RYAN seconded the motion, which was carried.

CHARLES M'SHANE.

Alderman BROUGHTON moved, that the sum of six pounds ten shillings be paid to Charles M'Shane, mason, being the amount recommended in the Report of the Improvement Committee; received by the Council on the 10th February last, to be paid as an advance in his wages from 4s. to 5s. per day, from 6th December, 1850, to 15th May, 1851.

Mr. DRIVER seconded the motion, which was put and passed.

MUNICIPAL FRANCHISE.

Mr. WEEKES withdrew the motion standing in his name with reference to the Report of the Select Committee on the Municipal Franchise. The notice of motion, he said, was erroneously drawn up, and had been placed upon the business paper without his being aware of it.

GEORGE-STREET MARKETS.

Mr. PEEK moved, that the report of the Market Committee, dated the 5th and received by the Council on 17th March, on the erection of urinaries and providing gates for the George-street Markets, be adopted. The report having been read, it appeared that the cost of the gate would be £160 and their object was to enclose the whole of the markets, so as to prevent robberies, &c.

Alderman BROUGHTON opposed this outlay as unnecessary and inexpedient.

Mr. JOSEPHSON opposed the motion upon similar grounds, and the motion was negatived on division, by a majority of nine to six.

CATTLE MARKET.

Mr. PEEK moved, that the report of the Market Committee, dated 15th, and received by the Council on 17th March, on certain repairs required for the Cattle Market, be adopted; and that the City Surveyor be instructed to carry out the same in accordance with his specification and estimate.

Mr. DRIVER seconded the motion.

The repairs alluded to were in the fencing, and the cost was estimated at £20.

The motion was passed without dissent.

HACKNEY CARRIAGES.

Mr. SIMMONS moved, that the report of the Hackney Carriage Committee, dated 12th and received by the Council on 17th March, recommending the removal of a certain portion of the Public Stand in George-street, be adopted.—Carried.

ADDITIONAL WATER MAINS.

Mr. Alderman ALLEN moved, that the report of the Water Committee, dated 7th and received by the Council on 10th February, on additional Water Mains to be laid in the city during the year 1851, be adopted. After detailing the localities in which additional pipes were to be laid, and stating that the estimated cost was £5000, the Alderman went on to remark that although this sum was £1000 less than the amount at the credit of the Water Committee, the discovery of gold in the interior might probably render labour dearer.

It being understood to be the wish of the Council that this matter should stand over for the present, the motion was withdrawn.

REDUCTION OF WATER RATES.

Alderman ALLEN moved, that the report of the Water Committee, dated and received by the Council on 10th February, recommending a reduction in the water rates of Messrs. R. Dawson, and J. R. and A. F. Wilshire, be adopted.—Carried.

PROPOSED RESERVOIR.

Alderman ALLEN withdrew for the present the motion standing in his name relative to the erection of a reservoir, the reason for such withdrawal being the uncertainty of the labour market, and prices under present circumstances.

SUPPLY OF WATER.

Alderman ALLEN moved, that the report of the Water Committee, dated 13th and received by the Council on 17th March, on the means of supplying certain portions of the city with water at different periods, be adopted.—Carried.

Alderman ALLEN moved, that the Report of the Water Committee, dated 12th and received by the Council on the 17th March, on a supply of water to Domain Terrace, be adopted.—Carried.

Alderman ALLEN moved, that the Report of the Water Committee, dated 13th and received by the Council on 17th March, recommending a three-inch main to be laid in Kent-street, be adopted.—Carried.

ACCOUNTS AND RATES.

Mr. ROBERTS moved, that the Report of the Mayor, read to the Council on the 31st March last, that in virtue of the 62nd section of the Act of Council, 14 Victoria, No. 41, he had ordered certain accounts for work done for the Corporation to be paid, and had appointed Mr. Windeyer temporarily to collect the outstanding rates in Macquarie and Phillip Wards, be adopted and entered on the minutes of the proceedings.

Alderman BROUGHTON contended that the appointment of Mr. Windeyer was unnecessary under present circumstances, as the work could be performed by the two clerks in the Treasurer's office. He concluded by moving an amendment to this effect, discontinuing the services of Mr. Windeyer after the end of the present month.

Mr. PEEK seconded the amendment.

Messrs. SIMMONS and WEEKES suggested a postponement of this matter until their next meeting, for further inquiry. After some further discussion this was agreed to.

OFFICERS OF THE CORPORATION.

Mr. DRIVER moved that a Committee of one Alderman and six Councillors, to be chosen by ballot, be appointed to enquire into and report upon the duties of all officers belonging to this Council.

Mr. THOMAS seconded the motion.

Mr. PEEK supported the proposition, considering that the enquiry was necessary.

Alderman EGAN opposed the motion. The superintendence of the Corporation officers was properly vested in the Mayor, who had ample power to define the duties of those under his orders, and could appeal to the Council in any question of difficulty.

Mr. SIMMONS supported the motion, as did also Messrs. JOSEPHSON, ROBERTS, WEEKES, and LENEHAN, and Alderman ALLEN. These gentlemen contended that the enquiry was necessary, even for the advantage of the officers themselves. Past experience and the statements in the admirable minute of the Mayor read on that day afforded sufficient reason for entering upon such an investigation.

The Council divided upon the motion, which was carried by 15 to 1, (the dissentient vote being Alderman Egan's).

A ballot having been taken, the following gentlemen were chosen to form the Committee, viz., the Mayor, Councillors Driver, Little, Peek, Roberts, Simmons, and Weekes.

FINANCE.

Mr. WILLIAMS moved, That the Report of the Finance Committee of date 9th of May, recommending the acceptance of Mr. Shoobert's offer of £50 per annum for a lease of the southern portion of the wharf at the bottom of Erskine-street, be adopted. The offer of Mr. Shoobert was for a five years' lease, but the mover proposed to limit the tenancy for one year only.

Alderman BROUGHTON explained that Mr. Shoobert proposed, if a longer lease was granted to him, to make certain improvements, which he would not make under an annual tenancy.

Mr. LENEHAN proposed to grant a three years' lease.

The MAYOR suggested that a covenant should be entered into by the lessee to complete these improvements.

Messrs. WEEKES and PEEK supported the lease for one year only, and it was finally decided to let for that period.

Mr. WILLIAMS moved, That the Report of the Finance Committee, of date 9th May, recommending the payment of Mr. Beaumont's account for alterations made in the offices of the Council Chambers, (£38 11s. 1d.) be adopted.—Carried.

Mr. WILLIAMS moved, That the Report of the Finance Committee, of date 9th of May, recommending the payment of sundry accounts amounting to £101 14s. 8d., be adopted.—Carried.

BY-LAWS.

Mr. JOSEPHSON moved, That the Report of the By-Laws Committee, of date 9th May, on the subject of making By-Laws for preventing mal-practices in the slaughtering of cattle, calves, and sheep, be approved.

The effect of this report was that the Committee had no power to make such by-laws.

Dr. TIERNEY moved, that in addition the report be printed, to show the public that the Council had not the power to remedy these evils, aid for which purpose had been refused by the Legislature.

After a brief conversation the amendment was withdrawn, and the original motion was put and passed.

PITT-STREET.

Dr. TIERNEY moved, That the Report of the Board of Health, of date May 9th, recommending the removal of a grating in Pitt-street, near Dr. Fullerton's premises, be adopted.

The Council, however, broke up for want of a quorum while the mover was yet on his legs.

Mr. Lyons reminds the public that he sells, this day at his mart, at 11 o'clock, sheepskins, Barclay and Perkins' bottled porter, porter in hogsheads, Guernsey frocks, waistcoats, counterpanes, drawers, superior cut glassware, electro-plated ware, eye glasses, spectacles, papier mâché boudoir tables, folios, waiters, trays, &c.—Communicated.

TO INTENDING GOLD FINDERS.

THAT there is gold in Ophir, and that the gold of that land is good, seems to be now determined. Whether it will pay for the finding is yet uncertain. But whatever view may be entertained of its probable abundance, its profitableness to work, it is obviously quite in vain to attempt by any arguments addressed to the fears or the reason of men to prevent numbers of adventurers from leaving their sure and honest employments and crowding to the Australian California. There are some considerations, however, which may be usefully submitted to every individual however sanguine, *qui sperat, rescius auræ fallacis*,—not to deter, but to guide him, in order that the evil of an unsuccessful exploration, if he be bent upon going to the diggings, may be somewhat alleviated. The following observations ought to be written in letters of gold, but as this would not suit the *Herald's* mechanical arrangement, I put them partly in small capitals.

I. Remember "THE WINTER IS COMING ON; and though the winters are not severe in this colony, as compared with those of the old country, or of California, still those of the interior are considerably more so than those of the sea-board. There they have ice and snow, and the water in the brooks flowing from the hills will be very cold to the gold washer standing in it up to the middle.

II. Remember "FLOUR IS SCARCE in the Gold Region." Previous to this discovery it was upwards of £20 a ton. The excitement and expected resort of strangers to a district not thickly peopled and not growing more wheat than was necessary for itself, has already prodigiously advanced the price, and if the apprehended result actually takes place, a famine must ensue: for no person can carry with him beyond a few days' provisions, and there are no sufficient means of supplying the anticipated demands of the auriferous district by carrying provisions thither from other places.

III. Remember, farmers, first to "SOW YOUR FARMS" before you go. The price of wheat will, no doubt, this year and next, be very high everywhere, in consequence of the influx of strangers. Your crops will be growing while you are in the mountains digging, and whether your search for gold should prove fortunate or the contrary, the produce of your fields will procure you golden coin in due season.

IV. If any of you have respectable, remunerating and certain employments, BEWARE HOW YOU DESERT YOUR POSTS, lest on your coming back from a wildgoose chase, you should find your places occupied by strangers, and you should seek in vain to resume your old avocations.

V. BEWARE HOW YOU BREAK YOUR LEGAL ENGAGEMENTS, OR DESERT YOUR WIVES AND FAMILIES. Such an occasion as this marks the difference between the honorable and the unprincipled man. Do not for the sake of the chance of a few pounds or hundreds of pounds destroy your character, burden your conscience, and ruin your happiness. Those who remain at their duties, will be most esteemed and trusted, and will receive an increased rate of wages by the departure of others. The gold will find its way into the hands of all—of him who stays by the baggage as well as of him who goes to the battle; always supposing there is gold to be got; but, if not, why then the home-stayer is the better off.

VI. Ask yourself, O thou who proposest to thyself to go and dig gold, dost thou know in what places thou shalt be likely to get it by digging, and wouldst thou know it when mixed with earth if thou shouldst see it? If not, thou mayest lose a week or two in learning the indications of its existence, the appearance of the article, and the trick of obtaining it in a measure enough to pay thy labour.

These, from thy assured friend,

POOR RICHARD.

VII. REMEMBER TO TAKE OUT YOUR LICENSE.

AUSTRALASIAN ANTHEM.

Dedicated to the League for the Prevention of Transportation to the Australian Colonies.

Let the song of joy arise!
Not in anger or in pride,
But in firm and high decree
Be it wafted to the skies,
O'er our shores and forests wide,
That our land must be free.

Though the laughing vine prevail
In the joyous sun's embrace,—
Though the olive load with treasure the tree,
What peace, if crime assail?
What joy, if shame deface,
The hearths of the free?

Though flocks on every hill
Mark the land as plenty's own,—
Though gold in the teeming soil we see,—
What mockery, if we still,
Hear the lash and the groan
'Midst the homes of the free.

Yet not with the sword,
Our fair land would we screen,—
For deaf to treason's voice are we,—
In the name of The Lord,
We call upon our Queen,
That her people may be free.

Sydney, May 17. H.

ABSTRACT OF SALES BY AUCTION THIS DAY.

MR. G. A. LLOYD.—On the Commercial Wharf, bottom of King-street, at 10 for half-past 10 o'clock, 6000 feet Cedar; in the Store, at the rear of the City Mart, at 11 o'clock, Stores, Groceries, Red Herrings, Beef and Suet, Casks, Puncheons, Iron Hoops, Phaeton, Lucerne and Oaten Hay.

MR. J. G. COHEN.—At his Rooms, at 11 o'clock, Shoemaker's Hemp, Vinegar, Pickles, Rope, Boots and Shoes, Wine, &c.

MR. S. LYONS.—At his Mart, at 11 o'clock, Porter, Cut Glass, Electro-plated Ware, Papier Mâché Boudoir Tables, Eye-glasses, Folios, Glass Chimneys for Lamps, White Counterpanes, Blue Striped Worsted Frocks, White Lambs'-wool Pantaloons, Thibet and Watered Poplin Waistcoats, Sheepskins, &c.

MESSRS. MORT AND BROWN.—At their Rooms, at 11 o'clock, New Zealand Rope, Wearing Apparel, Sundry Furniture, Nautical Instruments, Charts, Books, &c.; at 12 o'clock, a five years' Lease of the Corinda Estate, on the River Hunter, Five Houses at Redfern, Five Acres of Land at Lane Cove, Allotments in the Towns of Richmond and Parramatta.

MR. E. SALAMON.—At his Rooms, at 11 o'clock, New Books, Stationery, Account Books, &c.

MR. T. HUXLEY.—At the Haymarket, at 10 o'clock, Devonshire Bull, Household Furniture, Watches, Wearing Apparel, &c.

MR. G. SEYMOUR.—At the Haymarket, opposite the Picton Arms, at 12 o'clock, Stock and Dray Horses, Gig and Harness, Dray, Carts, Bullock Dray, and Tackle for twelve Bullocks.

MR. A. MOORE.—At the Labour Bazaar, at 11 o'clock, Household Furniture, Wearing Apparel, Watches, Pistols, Guns, &c.

MR. H. D. COCKBURN.—On the Premises of Mr. Russell, General Dealer, Brickfield Hill, at 11 o'clock, Stock in Trade of General Merchandise.

THE SHERIFF.—At No. 17, Domain Terrace, at 12 o'clock, Household Furniture, &c.

THE GOLD COUNTRY.—Mr. Wells has taken time by the forelock, and published a map of the district through which the gold district is supposed to extend. Irrespective of the temporary interest which belongs to it, it is a valuable map of a most important district in the colony, and will be useful to all interested in that part of the colony.

MEMBER FOR THE HAMLETS.—We are requested by Mr. R. Johnstone, of Annandale, to contradict the report that he is a candidate for the representation of the Sydney Hamlets.

HORSE STEALING.—Yesterday afternoon, a mare was stolen from the stable of Mr. Alexander Ross, of King-street. About seven o'clock last evening, Mr. W. A. Dick's horse, saddled and bridled, was stolen from the door of his office, in Elizabeth-street. As there will be a demand for this sort of animal by sundry of our population who may be inclined to try their luck at the diggings, owners should keep a bright look out.

THE ROAD TO THE DIGGINGS.—A selection of eighteen men has been taken from the city police force for the formation of a mounted patrol to be stationed along the road from Parramatta to the gold country, under the command of Mr. John R. Hardy. A dozen left Sydney with Mr. Hardy on Sunday evening, and the remainder will start this morning.

CORONER'S INQUEST.—Yesterday, an inquest was held by the Coroner, at the City Inn, Kent-street, on view of the body of James Pattison, who died suddenly, on Sunday afternoon. G. E. Warne stated, that he resided in Kent-street. On Saturday evening last, the deceased came to his house, and asked for a night's lodging. He consented, and deceased remained all night, and in the morning eat a hearty breakfast. He also had dinner, and seemed in perfect health. Between two and three in the afternoon, he complained of being very sick, as also of a pain in the stomach, but was moving about. Witness did not think there was any danger. Deceased vomited a little, and lay down, witness sent for a neighbour to assist him, but in a few minutes deceased died. He was about thirty years of age, and was quite sober when he came to witness' house. Deceased, and four others, had about four quarts of colonial ale amongst them to dinner, and deceased eat heartily. He had long been in the habit of drinking to excess. He was a very harmless man, and had quarrelled with no one. Latterly he drank a great deal of colonial ale. Mr. R. Thompson stated, that the deceased had been constantly employed by him as a messenger, since 1846, until a few months ago. He was a very hard drinker, and witness had frequently warned him as to the probable effect of his intemperate habits. During the time witness had known deceased, rum was his usual drink. He was a quiet inoffensive man. Dr. Tierney having made a *post mortem* examination of the body, stated that he found the pericardium filled with blood, the result of rupture of one of the blood vessels of the heart, which was the immediate cause of death. The lungs were diseased, and the liver enlarged, indicatory of previous habits of intemperance. There was a slight aneurism of one of the small blood vessels of the heart. The Coroner, in charging the Jury, said, that he was particularly desirous to offer a few remarks as to the supposition that in cases like this, colonial ale, being the beverage lately taken by the deceased, was the cause of death. Such, he believed, was a very erroneous conclusion. Men of the class of the deceased, in this instance, undermined their constitution in the prime of their lives, by excesses of all kinds; and it had been stated by Mr. Thompson, who had employed the deceased for the last five years, that, so long as he could afford it, he drank ardent spirits. When reduced in circumstances such men usually flew to a cheaper drink, but whether they drank colonial ale, or dearer liquors, the consequence was precisely the same. Death suddenly overtook them. He, the Coroner, was anxious to draw attention to this, because juries had frequently expressed their opinion, that drinking colonial ale had been the cause of death. Now, it was but justice to the Sydney brewers to state, that they had requested him (the Coroner) to analyse their beers, which he intended to have done at an early moment. In the unhappy case before them was found a man not more than thirty years of age, whose long career of intemperance rendered him peculiarly liable to sudden death, and it was sincerely to be hoped that so sad an example would not be without its effect. Verdict—Died from the rupture of a blood vessel.

FURIOUS RIDING.—Between six and seven o'clock on Sunday evening, Mr. and Mrs. White, of Sussex-street, were walking in George-street, near the Haymarket, when three persons on horseback came along at a furious rate. Before Mr. and Mrs. White could get out of the way, the latter was knocked down by one of the horses, inflicting a wound on her head, and two or three bruises on the arm. The fellows gallopped on, and although several persons endeavoured to stop them, they made their escape. We regret to learn that neither of the men was known to any of the parties who were witnesses of their reckless conduct.

CROWN LANDS.—Mr. Isaac Stansfield, butcher, yesterday appeared at the Police Office to answer an information filed by Mr. Simeon H. Pearce, Commissioner of Crown Lands for the county of Cumberland, for having on the 15th April, depastured a number of sheep on certain waste lands of the Crown, situate in the parish of Alexandria, contrary to the statute in that case made and provided. Mr. Nichols conducted the prosecution, and Mr. Little the defence. Richard Cross, Ranger of Crown Lands, deposed that on the day named he saw some sheep, perhaps 50, attended by a man who said he was in the employ of defendant, grazing on a portion of Crown land situate between Paddington and defendant's paddock; he pointed out the spot afterwards to Mr. Pearce. Mr. Pearce deposed, that the land in question was Crown land; he had several times seen sheep there, the property of Stansfield; he had several times spoken to the shepherd, intimating that he was trespassing, and was met by the reply that he was obliged to obey orders, or incur perhaps three months' imprisonment for neglect of duty; in his hired service he held the authority of his Excellency the Governor to proceed against all persons found in the unlawful occupation of Crown lands; the land in question is the property of the Queen. Mr. Little submitted that it was not competent to Mr. Pearce to prove whether the land was Crown land: on the authority of Hannam *v.* Chapman the surveyor who measured was the only competent witness on this point. Mr. Nichols replied, that in the case referred to the question was a right of road between two private individuals, and not at all parallel with the present. In this colony all lands are *prima facie* Crown lands, and therefore it was not necessary for him to prove that this was Crown land: the *onus probandi* to the contrary was on the other side. For the defence Mr. Little submitted, that no conviction could now be had by Mr. Pearce, inasmuch as the offence alleged was the unauthorised occupation of Crown lands, while the evidence set out what was evidently by the Act (9 and 10 Vict., cap. 104) contemplated as a different offence, namely, the unauthorised depasturing of stock on Crown lands. Moreover, the authority under the hand of the Governor, which had been put in did not give authority to proceed for the latter offence; it was not sufficiently extensive to include depasturing, and this case must therefore fail. Mr. Pearce would have to get enlarged powers before he could successfully institute such proceedings as this. Mr. Dowling overruled the objection and held the authority to be sufficient. Defendant did not attempt to rebut the charge on its merits, and was sentenced to pay a penalty of 10s. with 21s. costs.—An old man was sentenced to pay a penalty of 5s. with damages 1s. for destroying shrubs on the sand hills in the parish of Alexandria, to which he had pleaded guilty.

STEALING STONE.—The charge against George Melrose for stealing certain stones, the property of the Queen, was yesterday dismissed. The Bench held that the taking was clear enough, but not such a taking as would constitute larceny.

THE LATE MR. UNSWORTH.—Notwithstanding it was shown at the second inquest on the late Mr. Unsworth, and decided by the Jury, that not a tittle of foundation existed for the charge preferred against Mr. Farmer, he was not discharged from the George-street watch-house until yesterday morning, although the verdict was returned on Saturday evening. The Coroner has recommended the dismissal of Constable Egan; and legal proceedings will be taken against all parties concerned in Mr. Farmer's incarceration. He was in the watch-house from last Tuesday evening until yesterday.

SALE OF PROVISIONS AND SUNDRIES.—Mr. George A. Lloyd sells, this morning, at the City Mart stores, at eleven o'clock, a large quantity of provisions and other articles, particularly deserving the attention of ship owners, storekeepers, grocers, and others.—Communicated.

THE GOLD MINES.

To the Editors of the Sydney Morning Herald.

GENTLEMEN,—One would think the experience already derived from the past results of gold digging in South Australia would teach its lesson, and moderate the mania now existing in our territory. What was the fact and what the result there? After an expenditure of £20,000 in the purchase of the land from Government, it afforded so little remuneration to the miner, who could make thirty times the wages by raising copper upon tribute, that the mine is to this day abandoned, and the shares for which the original holders gave £100 bona fide sterling money, are at the present day literally worth nothing, and nominally at a discount of 70 per cent.

ARTHUR.

THE GOLD FEVER.

(*From the Bathurst Free Press of Saturday.*)

THE discovery of the fact by Mr. Hargraves that the country, from the Mountain Ranges to an indefinite extent into the interior, is one immense gold field, has produced a tremendous excitement in the town of Bathurst and the surrounding districts. For several days after our last publication, the business of the town was utterly paralysed. A complete mental madness appears to have seized almost every member of the community, and, as a natural consequence, there has been an universal rush to the diggings. Any attempt to describe the numberless scenes—grave, gay, and ludicrous—which have arisen out of this state of things, would require the graphic pen of a Dickens, and would exceed any limit which could be assigned to it in a newspaper. Groups of people were to be seen early on Monday morning at every corner of the streets, assembled in solemn conclave, debating both possibilities and impossibilities, and eager to pounce upon any human being who was likely to give any information about the diggings. People of all trades, callings, and pursuits, were quickly transformed into miners, and many a hand which had been trained to kid gloves, or accustomed to wield nothing heavier than the grey goose-quill, became nervous to clutch the pick and crow-bar, or "rock the cradle" at our infant mines. The blacksmiths of the town could not turn off the picks fast enough, and the manufacture of cradles was the second briskest business of the place. A few left town on Monday, equipped for the diggings; but on Tuesday, Wednesday, and Thursday, the roads to Summer Hill Creek became literally alive with new-made miners from every quarter, some armed with picks, others shouldering crowbars or shovels, and not a few strung round with wash-hand basins, tin pots, and cullinders, garden and agricultural implements of every variety, either hung from the saddle-bow, or dangled about the persons of the pilgrims to Ophir. Now and then a respectable tradesman, who had just left his bench or counter, would heave into sight, with a huge something in front of his horse, which he called a cradle, and with which he was about to rock himself into fortune. Some have rushed from their homes, provided with a blanket, a "damper," and a pick or grubbing hoe, full of hope that a day or two's labour would fill their pockets with the precious metal; and we have heard of a great number who have started without any provision but a blanket and some rude implement to dig with. Such is the intensity of the excitement, that people appear almost regardless of their present comfort, and think of nothing but gold. Of course all this must end in disappointment. The wet weather of the last two nights, with the damp ground for a bed, and the teeming clouds for a canopy, will do much towards damping the enthusiasm of numbers. We have the authority of an experienced man in stating that, from the imperfect and unsuitable implements used by all who have left for the diggings, coupled with their miserable provision in other respects, success is impossible; that the labour necessary to success is extremely severe, and he ventures, as his opinion, that no more than three per cent. will become permanent miners. One of the consequences has been a rapid rise in the price of provisions. Flour which ranged from 26s. to 28s. per 100 lbs., has been sold for 45s.; tea, sugar, and almost every other eatable commodity have advanced in equal proportion. A large amount of the wheat of the district is in the hands of a few speculators, who will maintain their hold in the hope of a golden harvest. But for the very extensive supplies now on their way from Sydney, flour would soon be at a famine price, and should a rush take place from below, as may be reasonably expected, it is to be hoped that there are capitalists enough to adventure in one of the safest speculations of the times—the purchase of flour for the supply of the district.

What assisted very materially to fan the excitement into a flame, was the arrival of a son of Mr. Neal, the brewer, with a piece of pure metal, weighing eleven ounces, which was purchased by Mr. Austin for £30, who started to Sydney by the following day's mail, with the gold and the news. Since that an old man arrived in town with several pieces in mass, weighing in all from two to three pounds. He also started for Sydney with his prize. Mr. Kennedy, the Manager of the Bathurst Branch of the Union Bank of Australia visited the diggings on Saturday last in company with Messrs. Hawkins and Green, each of these gentlemen picked up a small piece of the pure metal, and a few handsfull of the loose earth from the bed of the creek, which were brought home by Mr. Kennedy from motives of curiosity, have been since assayed by Mr. Kent, from Sydney, and a piece of gold extracted therefrom of the size of a small pea. Besides these we have not heard of any particular instances of success.

On Wednesday morning last, Mr. Hargraves accompanied Mr. Stutchbury, the Government geologist, went to the diggings, and with his own hands washed a pan of earth in his presence, from which twenty-one grains of fine gold were produced. He afterwards washed several baskets of earth, and produced gold therefrom. Mr. Stutchbury thereupon expressed his satisfaction, and immediately furnished him with credentials, which have since been forwarded to Government. The fact of the existence of gold is therefore clearly established, and whatever credit or emolument may arise therefrom, Mr. Hargraves is certainly the individual to whom it properly belongs. Should Government deem it necessary, as it most probably will, to appoint an inspector, superintendent, or commissioner, over the gold regions, in addition to the fact of Mr. Hargraves being the discoverer, his practical acquaintance with mining points him out as the most suitable and worthy person for the appointment.

We have very much more to say, but have not space to say it in.

A Mr. Rudder, an experienced California gold digger, is now at work at the diggings. There are also several magistrates plying their picks and cradles most laboriously, but we have not heard with what success. In fact there appears every probability of a complete social revolution in the course of time. Those who are not already departed, are making preparations. Servants of every description are leaving their various employments, and the employers are, *per necessitatem*, preparing to follow. But notwithstanding all this, we feel that a reaction will speedily take place. The approach of winter and wet weather will do something towards cooling the ardour of the excited multitude.

ORIGINAL CORRESPONDENCE.

[ADVERTISEMENT.]

To the Editors of the Sydney Morning Herald.

GENTLEMEN,—Permit me to offer a few remarks on a very ill-natured letter that appears in your paper of yesterday, regarding myself, from the pen of the Rev. H. R. Gilchrist, Moderator of the Synod of Australia. The particulars of the case to which Mr. Gilchrist refers are simply as follows:—

In the month of November last, I made a clerical visit to the Upper Hunter and the Manning River, to ascertain the condition and wants of the Scotch and other Presbyterian inhabitants of those districts in regard to the ordinances of religion. The result of that visit was the immediate settlement of the Rev. I. T. Carter, a zealous Presbyterian Minister, at the Manning River, and the subsequent settlement of the Rev. Alexander Black, an alumnus of the University of St. Andrew's, in the district of Scone and Murrurundi. Both of these settlements, I am happy to say, have been remarkably acceptable to the Christian people of the Presbyterian communion in these comparatively remote and isolated localities.

In passing to and from the Manning River, I stopped at the Agricultural Company's beautiful village of Stroud, and preached there by appointment on my return journey; and at that occasion I told the people who had assembled to hear me, both publicly and privately, that it was my intention, in conference with my brethren in Sydney, to send a minister to officiate regularly in that locality. I had been invited to do so indeed by some of the people themselves, of whom one respectable family at least had come out to the colony under my own charge.

On my return to Sydney, Mr. Patrick Fitzgerald, a native of Scotland, and a candidate for the ministry under the superintendence of

THE GOLD FEVER.

(From the Bathurst Free Press of Saturday.)

The discover of the fact by Mr. Hargraves that the country, form the Mountain Ranges to an indefinite extent into the interior, is one immense gold field, has produced a tremendous excitement in the town of Bathurst and the surrounding districts. For several days after our last publication, the business of the town was utterly paralysed. A complete mental madness appears to have seized almost every member of the community, and, as a natural consequence, there has been an universal rush to the diggings[.] Any attempt to describe the numberless scenes—grave, gay, and ludicrous—which have arisen out of this state of things, would require the graphic pen of a Dickens, and would exceed any limit which could be assigned to it in a [n]ewspaper. Groups of people were to be seen early on Monday morning at every corner of the streets, assembled in solemn conclave, debating both possibilities and impossibilities, and eager to pounce upon any human being who was likely to give any information about the diggings. People of all trades, callings, and pursuits, were quickly transformed into miners, and many a hand which [h]ad been trained to kid gloves, or accustomed to wield nothing heavier than the grey goose-quill, became nervous to clutch the pick and crow-bar, or "rock the cradle," at our infant mines. The blacksmiths of the town could not turn off the picks fast enough, and the manufacture of cradles was the second briskest business of the place. A few left town on Monday, equipped for the diggings; but on Tuesday, Wednesday, and Thursday, the roads to Summer Hill Creek became literally alive with new-made miners from every quarter, some armed with picks, others shouldering crowbars or shovels, and not a few strung round with wash-hand basins, tin pits, and cullinders, garden and agricultural implements of every variety, either hung from the saddle-bow, or dangled about the persons of the pilgrims to Ophir. Now and then a respectable tradesman, who had just left his bench or counter, would heave into sight, with a huge something in front of his horse, which he called a cradle, and with which he was about to rock himself into fortune. Scores have rushed form their homes, provided with a blanket, a "damper," and a pick or grubbing hoe, full of hope that a day or two's labour would fill their pockets with the precious metal; and we have heard of a great number who have started without any provision but a blanket and some rude implement to dig with. Such is the intensity of the excitement, that people appear almost regardless of their present comfort, and think of nothing but gold. Of course all this must end in disappointment. The wet weather of the last two night, with the damp ground for a bed, and the teeming clouds for a canopy, will do much towards damping the enthusiasm of numbers. We have the authority of an experienced man in stating that from the imperfect and unsuitable implements used by all who have left for the diggings, coupled with their miserable provision in other respects, success is impossible; that the labour necessary to success is extremely sever, and he ventures, as his opinion, that no more than three per cent. will become permanent miners. One of the consequences has been a rapid rise in the price of provisions. Flour which ranged from 26s. to 28s. per 100 lbs., has been sold for 45s.; tea, sugar, and almost every other eatable commodity have advanced in equal proportion. A large amount of the wheat of the district is in the hands of a few speculators, who will maintain their hold in the hope of a golden harvest. But for the very extensive supplies now on their way from Sydney, flour would soon be at a famine price, and should a rush take place from below, as may be reasonably expected, it is to be hoped that there are capitalists enough to adventure in one of the safest speculations of the times – the purchase of flour for the supply of the district.

What assisted very materially to fan the excitement into a flame, was the arrival of a son of Mr. Neal, the brewer, with a piece of pure metal, weighing eleven ounces, which was purchased by Mr. Austin for £30, who started to Sydney by the following day's mail, with the gold and the news. Since that an old man arrived in town with several pieces in mass, weighing in all from two to there pounds. He also started for Sydney with his prize. Mr. Kennedy, the Manager of the Bathurst Branch of the Union Bank of Au[s]tralia visited the diggings on Saturday last in company with Messrs. Hawkins and Green, each of these gentlemen picked up a small piece of the pure mental, and a few handsfull of the loose earth from the bed of the creek, which were brought home by Mr. Kennedy from motives of curiosity, have been since assayed by Mr. Korff, from Sydney, and a piece of gold extracted there from of the size of a pea. Besides these we have not heard of any particular instances of success.

On Wednesday morning last, Mr. Hargraves accompanied Mr. Stutchbury, the Government geologist, went to the diggings, and with his own hands washed a pan of earth in his presence, from which twenty-one grains of fine gold were produced. He afterwards washed several baskets of earth, and produced gold therefrom. Mr. Stutchbury hereupon expressed his satisfaction, and immediately furnished him with credentials, which have since been forwarded to Government. The fact of the existence of gold is therefore clearly established, and whatever the credit or emolument may arise therefrom. Mr. Hargraves is certainly the individual to whom it properly belongs. Should Government deem it necessary, as it most probably will, to appoint an inspector, superintendent, or commissioner, over the gold regions, in addition to the fact of Mr. Hargraves being the discoverer, his practical acquaintance with mining points him out as the most suitable and worthy person for the appointment.

We have very much more to say, but have not space to say it in.

A Mr. Rudder, an experienced California gold digger, is now at work at the diggings.— There are also several magistrates plying their picks and cradles most laboriously, but we have not heard with what success. In fact there appears every probability of a complete social revolution in the course of time. Those who are not already departed, are making preparations. Servants of every description are leaving their various employments, and the employers are, *per necessitatem*, preparing to follow. But notwithstanding all this, we feel that a reaction will speedily take place. The approach of winter and wet weather will do something towards cooling the ardour of the excited multitude.

28 *Evil-disposed persons*

The Eureka Stockade, 1854

AT FIRST NEWS OF GOLD IN THE BATHURST AREA, VICTORIANS HEADED INTO NEW SOUTH WALES, AND THE NEW COLONY BECAME CONCERNED ABOUT THE RUSH NORTH. BUT IN MID-1851 GOLD WAS DISCOVERED AT MOUNT ALEXANDER, THEN AT THE RICH FIELDS OF BENDIGO AND BALLARAT, AND VICTORIA ALSO BECAME INFECTED WITH GOLD FEVER. IN 1852 MORE THAN 100,000 PEOPLE FLOODED INTO THE COLONIES—LURED BY GOLD. PEOPLE ARRIVED FROM EUROPE AND NORTH AMERICA, AS WELL AS CHINA.

The colonial governments tried to regulate goldmining activities with a licence system, which soon became a revenue system. The Victorian government argued that it needed more money to run the rapidly growing colony and police the often violent and dangerous goldfields. For goldminers, or 'diggers' as they soon became known, evading the licence fee became a sport—and collecting the tax became a sport for many police.

'Monster rallies' and meetings protesting the infringement of the miners' rights and civil liberties were called on many goldfields. Eventually, in November 1854, things came to a head at the Ballarat fields, where diggers burned their hated licences and defied the authorities. After some heavy-handed policing, on 2 December around 1500 miners vowed to defend themselves, gathered weapons and constructed a stockade around their defiant Eureka flag.

In the early hours of Sunday, 3 December, only around 150 miners remained in the stockade—many had returned to their homes and tents on the Saturday night, not suspecting a police attack. On the Sunday, the largest battle between European Australians in Australian history occurred. Around 270 police and soldiers who had been called to the diggings to reinforce the local authorities, moved on what Police Commissioner Robert Rede (1815–1904) described as 'a large body of evil-disposed persons of various nations who had entrenched themselves in a stockade'. After a brief but bloody engagement, the military forces swamped the miners in their redoubt, and the second major rebellion in Australian history was over. At least twenty-two miners and four members of the government forces were killed.

News reports highlighted the callous nature of the military forces and saw the goldfield's authorities as 'wholly to blame' in provoking the diggers. Although the story of the battle at the Eureka Stockade was never printed as headline news, it was indeed momentous news that has been regarded as an important part of the political movement for full self-government in the country.

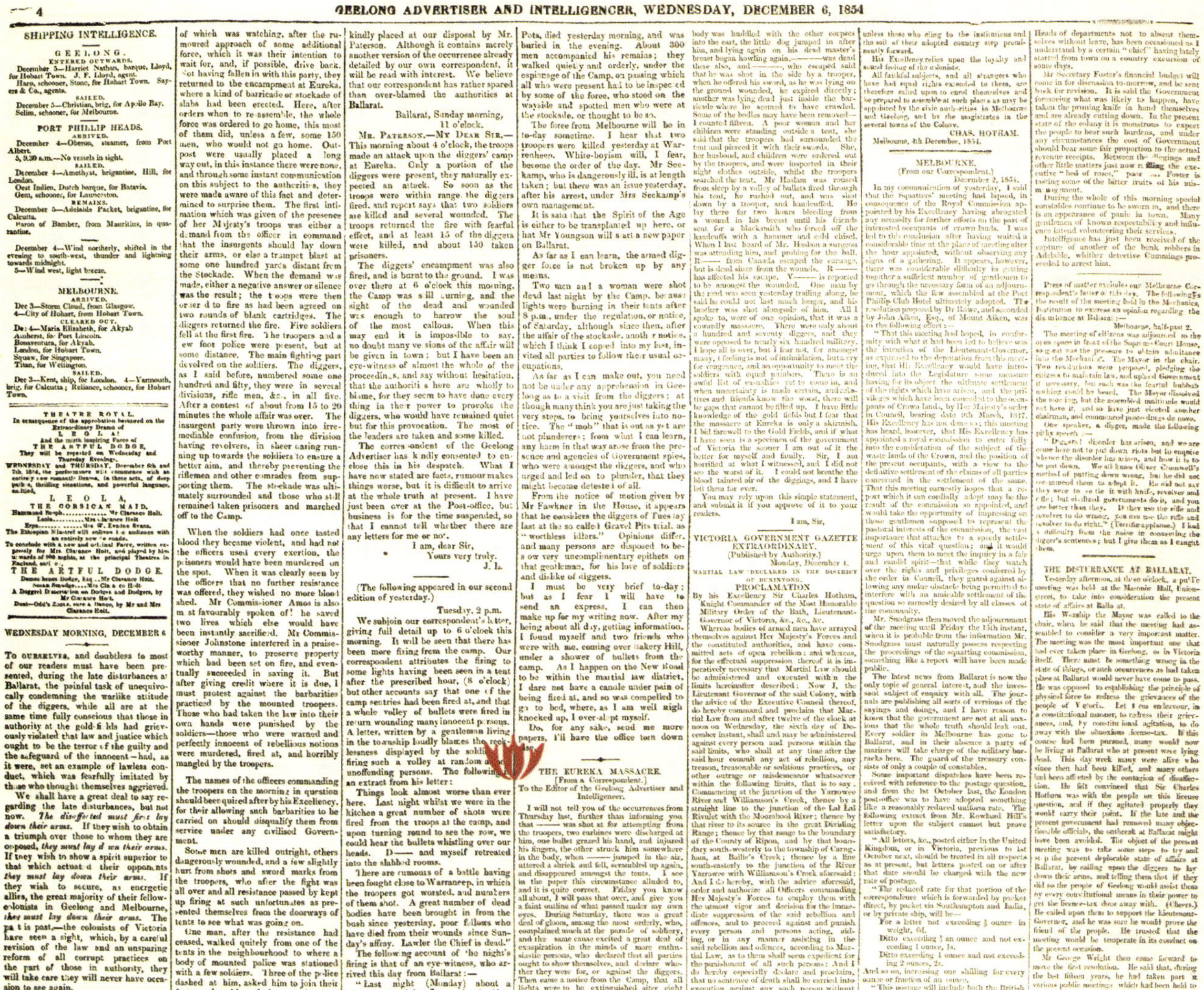

While one letter to the newspaper described events as 'The Eureka Massacre,' journalist Sam Irwin's report of events at the stockade for the Geelong Advertiser and Intelligencer *was regarded as one of the most accurate accounts of events. It was published on 6 December 1854. Another journalist on the spot, Frank Hasleham, reporting for the same newspaper, was shot and taken prisoner by the military when the stockade was stormed.*

THE EUREKA MASSACRE.

[From a Correspondent.]

To the Editor of the Geelong Advertiser and Intelligencer.

I will not tell you of the occurrences from Thursday last, further than informing you that— —was shot at for attempting from the troopers, two carbines were discharged at him, one bullet grazed his hand, and injured his fingers, the other struck him somewhere in the body, when— —jumped in the air, uttered a shriek and fell, scrambled up again, and disappeared amongst the tents. I see in the paper this circumstance alluded to, and it is quite correct. Friday you know all about, I will pass that over, and give you a faint outline of what passed under my own eyes. During Saturday, there was a great deal of gloom, among the most orderly, who, complained much at the parade of soldiery, and the same cause excited a great deal of exasperation in the minds of the more enthusiastic persons, who declared that all parties ought to show themselves, and declare whether they were for, or against the diggers. Then came a notice from the Camp, that all lights were to be extinguished after eight o'clock, within half a mile from the Camp. At this time it was reported that there two thousand organised men at Eureka barricade. I was sitting in my tent, and several neighbours dropped in to talk over affairs, and we sat down to tea, when a musket was heard to go off, and the bullet whizzed closed by us, I douced the light, and we crept out on our hands and knees, and looked about. Between the Camp and the Barricade there was a fire we had not seen before, and accasionally lights appeared to be hoisted, like signals, which attracted the attention of a good many, some of whom said that they new other lights like return signals. It grew late, I and R—— lay down in our clothes, according to our practice for a week past, and warn out with perpetual alarms, excitement and fatigue, fall fast asleep, I didn't wake up till 6 o'clock on Sunday morning. The first thing I saw was a number of diggers enclosed in a sort of hollow square, many of them were wounded, the blood dripping from them as they walked, some were walking lame, pricked on by the bayonets of soldiers bringing up the rear. The soldiers were much excited, and the troopers madly so, flourishing their swords and shouting out, "We have waked up Joe! and others replied, "and sent Joe to sleep again." The diggers standard was carried by in triumph to the Camp, waved about in the air, then pitched from one to another, thrown down, and trampled on. The scene was awful—two and threes gathered together, and all felt stupified—I went with R——to the barricade, the tents all around were in a blaze; I was about to go inside when a cry was raised that the troopers were coming again. They did come with carts to take away the bodies—I counted fifteen dead, one of them was C——, a fine well educated man, a great favorite; I recognised two others, but the spectacle was so ghastly that I felt a loathing at the remembrance. They all lay in a small space with their faces upwards, looking like lead; several of them were still heaving, and at every rise of their breasts, the blood spouted out of their wounds, or just bubbled out and trickled away. One man, a stout chested fine fellow, apparently about forty years old lay with a pike beside him, he had three contusions in the head, three strokes across the brow, a bayonet wound in the throat under the ear, and other wounds in the body—I counted fifteen wounds in that single carcase. Some were bringing handkerchiefs, others bed furniture, and mating to cover up the faces of the dead. O! God, Sir, it was a sight for a sabbath morn that I humbly implore Heaven may never be seen again.—Poor women crying for absent husbands, and children frightened into quietness. I, Sir, wright disinterestedly, but I hope my feelings rose from a true principle, and when I looked at that scene, my soul revolted at such means being so cruelly used by a Government to sustain the law. A little terrier sat on the breast of the man I spoke of, and kept up a continuous howl, it was removed but always returned again to the same spot, and when his master's body was huddled with the other corpses into the cart, the little dog jumped in after him, and lying again on his dead master's breast began howling again. —— was dead also, and ——, who escaped said he was shot in the side by a trooper, when he offered his sword, as he was lying on the ground wounded, he expired directly; another lying dead just inside the barricade where he seemed to have crawled. Some of the bodies may have been removed—I counted fifteen. A poor woman and her children were standing outside a tent, she said that the troopers had surrounded the tent and pierced it with their swords. She, her husband, and children were ordered out by the troopers, and were inspected in their night clothes outside, whilst the troopers searched the tent. Mr Haslam was roused from sleep by a volley of bullets fired through his tent, he rushed out, and was shot down by a trooper, and handcuffed. He lay there for two hours bleeding from a wound in his breast until his friends sent for a blacksmith who forced off the handcuffs with a hammer and cold chisel. When I last heard of Mr. Haslam a surgeon was attending him, and probing for the ball. R—— from Canada escaped the carnage, but is dead since from the wounds. R—— has affected his escape. V—— is reported to be amongst the wounded. One man by the road was seen yesterday trailing along, he said he could not last much longer, and his brother was shot alongside of him. All I spoke to, were of one opinion, that it was a cowardly massacre. There were only about a hundred and seventy diggers, and they were opposed to nearly six hundred military. I hope all is over, but I fear not, for amongst many, the feeling is not of intimidation, but a cry for vengeance, and an opportunity to meet the soldiers with equal numbers. There is an awful list of casualties yet to come in, and when uncertainty is made certain, and relatives and friends know the worst, there will be gaps that cannot be filled up. I have little knowledge of the gold fields but I fear that the massacre at Eureka is only a skirmish. I bid farewell to the Gold Fields, and if what I have seen is a specimen of the government of Victoria the sooner I am out of it the better for myself and my family. Sir, I am horrified at what I witnessed, and I did not see the worst of it. I could not breathe the blood tainted air of the diggings, and I have left them for ever.

You man rely upon this simple statement, and submit it if you approve of it to your readers.

I am, Sir,

29 The Continent Crossed

The Burke and Wills expedition, 1860

IT MAY BE HARD TO IMAGINE TODAY, BUT THE HYPE SURROUNDING THE BURKE AND WILLS EXPEDITION, WHICH AIMED TO CROSS CENTRAL AUSTRALIA FROM ITS SOUTHERN TO ITS NORTHERN COAST, WAS SOMETHING AKIN TO THE FIRST MOON LANDING OF 1969.

By 1860 much of the continent had been explored by Europeans, but the imagined difficulties of crossing the great expanses of dry and unforgiving desert in the interior were heightened in public imagination following a series of failed attempts, which had ended with spearing deaths or mysterious disappearances of explorers such as Ludwig Leichhardt (1813–1848).

As new technologies and developments of the modern, urban world began to dominate lives in the colonies, the mysteries of the 'untamed' Australian outback seemed to grow in stature. In the newspapers of the day, the fascination with the fate of explorers increased in proportion to the bungles and ineptitude of expeditions and their leaders.

Robert O'Hara Burke (1821–1861) and William Wills' (1834–1861) heavily laden expedition was plagued with quarrels, sackings, missed opportunities and misdirection. The fact that Burke and Wills made it to the Gulf of Carpentaria and then returned to their Coopers Creek meeting point to miss a rescue party by around nine hours added to the tragedy.

But the outback was not mysterious to many who had lived there for generations. Burke and Wills had learned some tricks from the local Yandruwandha people, but probably ate the nardoo seeds that Wills recorded as giving 'great satisfaction' without preparing them properly. As every local in the area well knew, nardoo seeds had to be ground and soaked to remove toxins before the flour made from them could be made in to a damper. It seems Burke and Wills tried to eat bush tucker to survive, but without proper knowledge, it led to their deaths.

The momentous nature of the deaths of Burke and Wills was reflected in Melbourne's *Argus* newspaper releasing a press sheet on 2 November 1861, which was a large page printed with the telegraph message it had received from its correspondent attached to the expedition, William Brahe (1835–1912). The headline overshadowed the Melbourne Cup race and brought the first news of the explorers' deaths to an audience that had been waiting for months to hear the fate of the expedition that seemed to have all but disappeared into the interior.

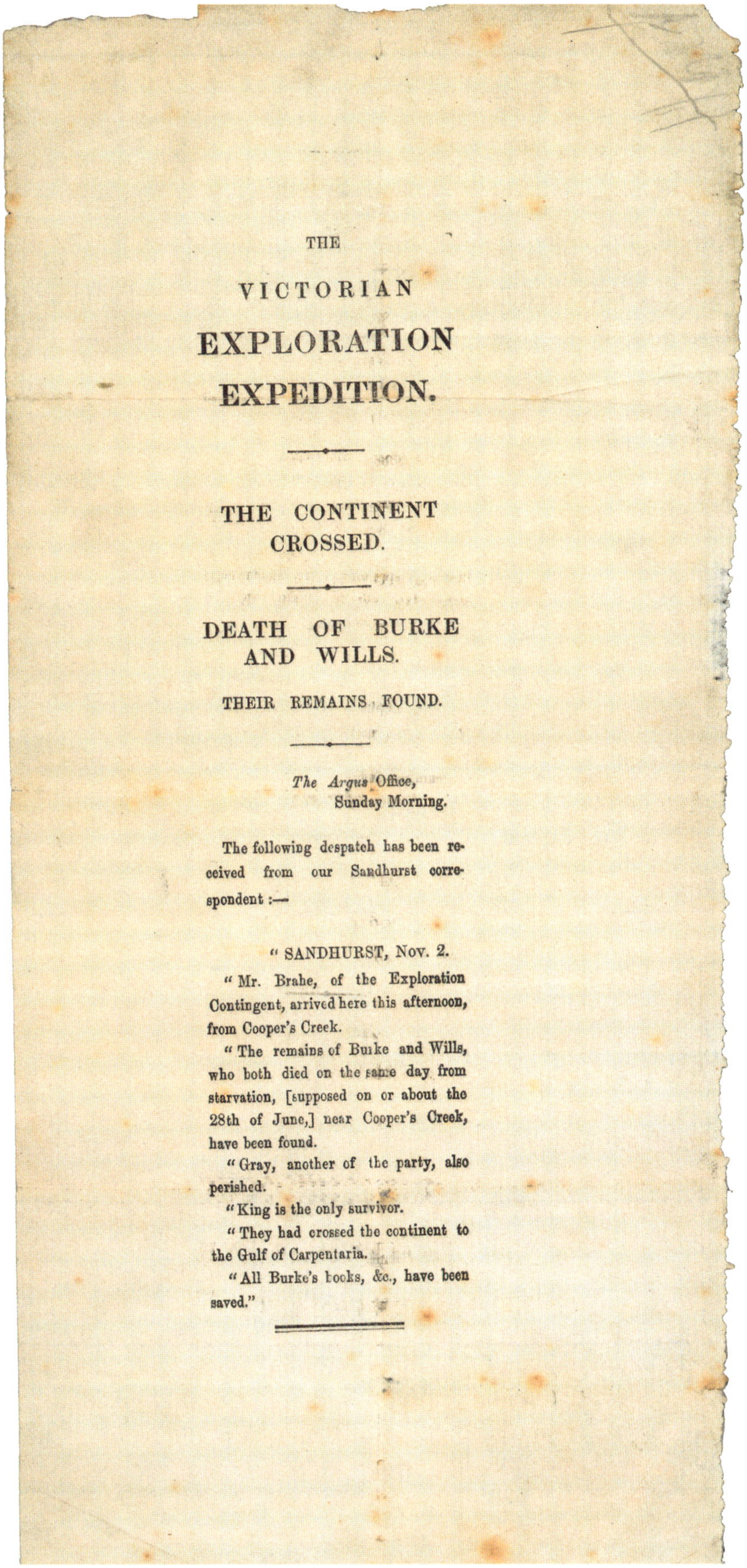

THE

VICTORIAN

EXPLORATION

EXPEDITION.

THE CONTINENT CROSSED.

DEATH OF BURKE AND WILLS.

THEIR REMAINS FOUND.

The Argus Office,
Sunday Morning.

The following despatch has been received from our Sandhurst correspondent :—

" SANDHURST, Nov. 2.

" Mr. Brahe, of the Exploration Contingent, arrived here this afternoon, from Cooper's Creek.

" The remains of Burke and Wills, who both died on the same day from starvation, [supposed on or about the 28th of June,] near Cooper's Creek, have been found.

" Gray, another of the party, also perished.

" King is the only survivor.

" They had crossed the continent to the Gulf of Carpentaria.

" All Burke's books, &c., have been saved."

When Argus correspondent William Brahe, who had been searching for the explorers for months, heard that John King, the only survivor of the expedition, had been found, he raced to the nearest telegraph office at Bendigo and sent what was to become the famous headlines 'The Continent Crossed. Death of Burke and Wills.' King survived after their supplies ran out because he had befriended a group of Indigenous people.

30 *No Chinese*

Race riots at Lambing Flat, 1861

THE EARLY COLONIES HAD FEW RESTRICTIONS ON IMMIGRATION. THEY WERE HARDLY NEEDED IN A REMOTE OUTPOST THAT RECEIVED SHIPLOADS OF BRITISH AND IRISH CONVICTS AND MIGRANTS. BUT THE GOLD RUSHES BROUGHT IMMIGRANTS FROM ALL OVER THE GLOBE. BY 1861, 38,000 CHINESE MEN (AND 11 WOMEN) FORMED THE LARGEST FOREIGN GROUP ON THE GOLDFIELDS. THEY WERE CULTURALLY VERY DIFFERENT FROM, AND INCREASINGLY SEEN AS A THREAT TO, THE BRITISH, EUROPEAN AND AMERICAN MINERS.

Chinese miners lived frugally on the diggings and worked together in disciplined teams. Many of the Chinese also began re-mining areas the Europeans had abandoned. After the initial rush, such mining methods usually provided better returns, but by 1860, most miners were struggling to make a living at all.

Anti-Chinese sentiment built up across many goldfields. From the early 1850s there had been fights between the Europeans and Chinese as well as 'incidents' where Europeans drove Chinese off fields the Chinese had claimed.

At the Burrangong goldfields, near Young in central west New South Wales, in 1861 agreed areas where the Chinese could work were established, and the large police presence was withdrawn. Then in June 1861 a 'roll up' or mass meeting was called under the banner of a 'No Chinese' slogan. By 30 June tensions had escalated and a mob of perhaps 3000 destroyed and looted the Chinese encampments, forcing around 1000 Chinese to abandon the diggings.

Perhaps in light of the overzealous policing of the goldfields in Victoria, the stand taken by police at the Lambing Flat riots has often been overlooked. When a small police force arrived in early July, they arrested some of the ringleaders of the attack, but on 14 July, about 1000 armed miners set upon the police. In a fight that appears to have been more like a battle than the suppression of a riot, police mounted sabre charges against their attackers and exchanged rifle fire for two hours. The rioters eventually withdrew. A detachment of nearly 300 soldiers reinforced the small police presence and restored control. The soldiers remained at Lambing Flat for the next twelve months.

Rioters were as much against the authorities as they were against the Chinese, but growing anti-Chinese attitudes led to the New South Wales *Chinese Immigration Restriction and Regulation Act 1861*, as well as a series of other acts of exclusion that underpinned the White Australia Policy of the twentieth century.

OPPOSITE
The unknown reporter of the 'Riot at Lambing Flat' in The Sydney Morning Herald *of 20 July 1861 created a vivid picture of the rioters' looting and subsequent attack on police.*

several additional parties have entered into tunnelling speculations, similar to those we have already alluded to. In some of these, the tunnels have been driven in for a distance of 450 feet, but as yet no deposit has been hit upon. We mentioned in our last summary that it had been asserted that the yield of the Bingera gold-field went to swell the escort from the Rocky River. This statement has been denied by a correspondent, in whose acquaintance with the subject there can be no doubt, who informs us that 100 ozs., received in January last was the only amount of Bengera gold received for transmission by the Rocky River escort.

The new fields on the table-land at the heads of the Clarence have been scarcely spoken of lately. No great finds are reported there, though it is said that the miners are all content.

It has been reported by the local paper that two auriferous and payable quartz reefs have been discovered within a few miles of Scone.

POLITICAL SUMMARY.

Parliament being in recess there is at present little excitement in political circles, the matters principally engaging public attention during the past month having been—the visit of the Governor to the Hunter, three or four elections for the Assembly, and the fatal disturbances at the Burrangong diggings.

We published in our last summary the names of the twenty-seven gentlemen who had received offers of seats in the new Legislative Council. Five of these at once refused Mr. Jones, Mr. Faucett, Mr. Marks, Mr. Close, and Mr. Oakes. A few days afterwards the members were gazetted, with the addition of Mr. A. M'Arthur and Captain Russell, but with the omission of Captain Lamb, who, refusing to accept a seat if his so doing would be regarded as fettering his conduct in the Council, was not appointed. It is understood that seats have been offered to Mr. Butler and Mr. Gordon, but have not yet been accepted. The following is a list of the members so far as at present appointed:—

Allen, George	Mitchell, James
Byrnes, William	Plunkett, John Hubert
Campbell, John	Robertson, John
Darvall, John Bayley	Robey, Ralph Meyer
Fitzgerald, Robert	Russell, Bourn
Hargrave, John Fletcher	Russell, William
Holden, George Kenyon	Scott, Alexander Walker
Kemp, Charles	Thomson, Edward Deas
Macarthur, Alexander	Ward, Edward Wolstenholme
Macfarlane, John	Watt, John Brown
Manning, Sir William Montagu	Wentworth, William Charles
Mereweather, Francis Lewis Shaw	Esquires.

It will be remembered that the offers of seats to these gentlemen were accompanied with a minute of the Executive Council, which stated that in making the appointments they regarded it as essential that the Land Bill should be passed in the same form as agreed to by the Assembly, and that the Legislative Council should be placed on an elective basis. Considerable uncertainty is entertained as to how far the members of the new House will be guided in their procedure by that minute; it is, however, clear their acceptance of seats is looked upon by the Government as intimating their willingness to perfect the Land Bill as passed by the Assembly, and to take into consideration a measure for making the Upper House elective; as a proof of which the Emigration Commissioners in England have been officially advised that the early passing of the Land Bill may be spoken of as a certainty. The conduct of those members of the new Council who in the late Chamber opposed some of the leading provisions of Mr. Robertson's Land Bill, will, no doubt be influenced by their knowledge that, in the event of their refusing to agree upon those points, another and more successful attempt than the last will probably be made to swamp the House. Some surprise has been expressed that they should consent to become parties to the passing of provisions of which they have shown their strong disapproval; but they have, no doubt, been led to look upon the adoption of these as inevitable, and have considered themselves bound to use their influence as far as possible, to mitigate their mischievous effects. The reconstruction of the Legislative Council is a measure to which the members have only committed themselves so far as regards the substitution of election for nomination, and they will direct their efforts to the construction of a Chamber that will constitute a balancing power in the State, which such a House as that determined on by the Assembly—elected by universal suffrage and without any property qualification—never could hope to be. The high character for statesmanship and independence of many of the members of the new House is a sure guarantee for their disagreement on a number of social questions with an Assembly, the members of which owed their elections in a great measure simply to their offering to support Mr. Robertson's Land Bill. It is easy, for instance, to foresee that the crude and dangerous Chinese Bill of Mr. Lucas, which the Assembly will, of course, again pass, will be thrown out by the Council; the Bill to declare the Church and School Lands waste lands of the Crown will share the same fate. The Government can at any time use the swamping power should the Council prove too independent; but they are not likely to exercise that power unless they are subjected to a very strong pressure from without, and as the passing of the Land Bill promises to give a temporary check to political agitation, the rejection of an Upper House Bill, or of a Chinese Bill would probably not create much public indignation. The Chinese have indeed been recently the victims of such brutal and unprovoked cruelty that a sympathy has been raised in their favour, which is not likely to render any legal persecution of them very popular. The unlikelihood of the present Council agreeing to any proposal of the Assembly for its reconstruction upon a purely democratic basis, coupled with the improbability that either upon that measure or upon the Chinese question the Government would recommend the swamping of the nominees, point rather strongly to the permanence, or at all events to a long existence, of the House now constituted; and the circumstance of some of the supporters of the Government in the Assembly resigning their seats for appointments to the Council seems to confirm that conclusion.

The recent election for East Sydney—in which Mr. Forster, the late Premier, polled nearly a hundred more votes than a candidate who was supported by the personal influence of the Ministry—was well followed up by the election, for the important suburban electorate of Newtown, of Mr. Holt, who will join the Opposition in the Assembly. These defeats are indications, not so much of the altered state of public feeling with regard to the Government, as of the widely entertained determination to elect men of tried ability and social position in preference to those ephemeral politicians who are ready to advocate any opinions that happen to be popular. This circumstance encourages the hope, that the men of intellect and character, whom several of the constituencies during the recent excitement about free selection refused to re-elect, will before long obtain seats in the Assembly.

The fatal disturbances at the Burrangong diggings, particulars respecting which will be found in another portion of our summary, will probably postpone for the present the intended visit of the Premier to Melbourne. The object of Mr. Cowper's visit was to endeavour to obtain a settlement of the difficult question of the Murray River Customs. It will be remembered that the Victorian Government refused to accede to the measures proposed by our Government for the collection of the duties paid in Victoria upon articles consumed in this colony. The amount [illegible] these duties is estimated at upwards of [illegible],000 per annum, by the collection of which the Victorian Government is benefited at the [illegible]ense of New South Wales. It was intended to [illegible] border custom-houses, at which the duties [illegible]ing to this colony should be collected; but their [illegible]tion proved very objectionable, and they were [illegible]tinued. Should the Victorian Government, [illegible] refuse to agree to some equitable arrange[illegible] appropriation of the duties, it is con[illegible] re-establishment of these custom[illegible] only alternative. [illegible] the intention of the Government [illegible] Parliament together on the 3rd of [illegible]

RIOT AT LAMBING FLAT.

Since the departure of the troops from Lambing Flat it has been evident to many persons resident there, that the strong feeling against the Chinese that had previously broken out in disorder had anything but subsided; and our Special Correspondent, who had been sent up purposely to watch the course of events, has over and over again pressed upon the public, through our columns, the necessity for largely increasing the police force on the Burrangong gold-fields, if it was intended to prevent the recurrence of scenes of brutality and violence, such as it had been his misfortune to have previously recorded. No attention was paid to these warnings, coming from all quarters; and so long as no actual disturbance took place, all was considered to be going on well. This fancied security received its first shock on the 18th of last month, on which date the cry of "Roll-up" was raised for the first time since the departure of the military.

It was successful to but a very small extent, bringing to the "No Chinese" standard some thirty Europeans only. These, however, were well armed with bludgeons and revolvers, the evident nucleus around which it was intended that a larger force should form. Contrary to their expectations, they were not joined by the numbers they anticipated, and their work was consequently carried on upon a comparatively minor scale of destructiveness. They attacked and drove off from the Flat, on which by the authority of the Commissioners they were encamped, a body of forty Chinese, and were about to burn the tents and other property of the Mongolians, when luckily Mr. Henley, the Chinese interpreter, arrived, and by his prompt interference and decided attitude saved the goods, and no doubt prevented scenes of violence and cruelty similar to those which subsequently occurred.

This outbreak was known to all on Lambing Flat, and was made public through the columns of the Press, and yet all those who alone were in a position to nip the evil in the bud, remained wilfully blind to the significant act here perpetrated. Everything was allowed to go on as usual; no attempt was made to strengthen the hands of those in authority on the ground; no step was taken to prepare for the concentration of such a force upon the ground as would have overawed the rioters who had thus shown themselves so persistent in their violence.

At last the storm, which had been so long seen, by all but those who should have been the most attentive in their examination of the social horizon, to be impending, broke with a violence that at once woke up the sleepers from their pleasant dreams. On Sunday, the 30th June, the residents of Tipperary Gully were aroused by the cries of "Roll up," and in the course of a very short time upwards of a thousand men, armed with bludgeons and pickhandles, no fire-arms as yet appearing, were assembled round the "No Chinese" standard. Forming themselves in a rude kind of order of march, and with a band of music, which appears to have been thoughtfully provided for the occasion by the leaders of the movement, at their head, shouting, yelling, and singing, the crowd of rioters took the road to Lambing Flat, a distance of some four or five miles. Arrived there, every Chinese resident in the township on whom hands could be laid was attacked and maltreated, the chief object of ambition being to secure the long tails of hair with which the Chinese are accustomed to ornament their heads. The main body was here joined by numerous others, who came flocking in from all quarters, until the number assembled amounted to at least 3000 persons. Finding themselves so strong, and being determined to make a clean sweep of the Mongolians now that they were about it, they now turned their attention to the Chinese camp, situated on the spot and within the area allocated to them by the Commissioner in accordance with the regulations previously made, and apparently agreed to by the diggers. This was at once attacked and carried, the Chinese being driven off, under circumstances of great barbarity in some cases, and in all cases without being permitted to take with them any portion of their property. It has been said also that many of them were robbed of various amounts of gold and cash; and that, mixed up with the crowd of rioters were numbers of women and children all actively engaged in plundering the property of the runaways of everything valuable, or convertible, prior to carrying the remainder to the enormous fires that were kept up with such kind of fuel. In the mean time the band, placed in a conspicuous position, enlivened the scene by playing spirit-stirring airs, to an accompaniment of yells and shouts that would have done credit to a New Zealand war dance. Excited with their triumph, heated with their violence towards unresisting captives, and possibly thirsting for the plunder, of which this last attack had given them a taste, a wild and savage yell of joy was raised, when some one suggested Back Creek as the next spot to visit. Shouting, firing (for guns were now pretty generally produced), singing, laughing, and cheering, the body of rioters moved off towards Back Creek, a locality about six miles from where they then were, and where it was known that there were several hundreds of Chinese at work. Information of the projected attack was, however, taken over to the Chinese in this locality, who, hastily packing up the most valuable and portable portions of their property, hurriedly made off from the spot. The rioters were not long behind them, and on coming up, a savage yell of disappointment rose up from the mob when they found that their prey had escaped. The tents, goods, &c., left behind were fired, after having been carefully looked over for plunder; and such articles as would not burn were destroyed by being broken with axes. Whilst this had been going on, a number of the rioters, who were mounted on horseback, galloped forward on the track of the retreating Mongols, overtook them, not much more than a mile away, headed them, and rounded them up in the same way as a shepherd-dog would do a flock of sheep. Information of the surround was sent off to those behind, who, eager for their prey, were already on the road. Here ensued a scene such as, thank heaven! it seldom falls to the lot of a British journalist to record. Unarmed, defenceless, and unresisting Chinese were struck down in the most brutal manner by bludgeons provided for the occasion, and by pick handles. The previous excitement had done its work, and now the wretched Mongols were openly and unblushingly searched for valuables, and robbery was committed without the slightest attempt at concealment. Very few of the poor creatures here attacked escaped with their pigtails, none of them without injury of some kind, whilst every article of the property they had endeavoured to take with them was plundered of all that was valuable, and then burnt. Some of the acts of barbarism said to have been committed here were such, that Englishmen can scarce be brought to credit that their countrymen could be guilty of them — for who amongst the British people could ever believe that men of their own country—Britons, would take the Chinese pigtails *with the scalp attached*. That this was done in more than one instance there can be no doubt, since the possessors of these trophies made no concealment of them, but rather prided themselves on their possession.

Some of the scenes that then took place are thus described by our special correspondent:—Men, or rather monsters, on horseback, armed with bludgeons and whips, with a fiend-like fury, securing the unfortunate creatures by taking hold of their tails and pulling their heads so that they came with their backs to the horse and their heads upon the saddle, and then cutting or rather sawing them off, and leaving them to the fury of others who surrounded them. One unfortunate Chinese boy went down upon his knees, the tears ran down his cheeks as he lifted his hands and pleaded for mercy; a ruffian, with a bludgeon sufficient to kill a giant, with one blow felled him to the ground. Another unfortunate creature, a cripple, was trying to crawl away into the bush—he could not walk—and endeavouring to take a blanket; it was ruthlessly torn from him, and carried to a fire where their property was being consumed Here was to be seen another propped up against a tree, his forehead laid open, and the blood running down his face—truly terrible to behold. But these details are sickening. I have only mentioned what came under my own notice. Were I to narrate only a tithe of the atrocities committed that day, that have been communicated to me, it would fill a volume. Mr. Henley, the Chinese interpreter, in a letter he has addressed to the Governor, detailing his view of this outrage, mentions the following:—A European woman with three small children, who is the wife of a Chinaman, was sitting in her tent rocking her baby in the cradle. The lawless mob burned down her tent, and the cradle wherein the infant was sleeping. Her own and children's clothes were torn to pieces by a lot of vagabonds, who counselled together for the violation of the woman and murder of the children, but were prevented by the timely interference of some of their number less hardened than the others.

With such facts before their very eyes, it is not to be wondered at that the feeling of the large bulk of the residents on the spot is greatly against the perpetrators of so gross an outrage, and that expressions of the utmost indignation have been most freely made use of.

So extensive and savage an outbreak could not fail in at once opening the eyes of all to the real position in which the authorities at Lambing Flat were placed, and now at last was done that which should have been done long before. The electric telegraph was set to work, and all the available police from the districts round about were ordered up to Burrangong. Captain Zouch, with the troopers of the mounted patrol, arrived there on the evening of the 6th instant. Several men of the foot police having come up from time to time, until the total number of the force, horse and foot, reached 57.

On the following day, Sunday, the 7th instant, there was a very large assemblage of diggers and others in the township, and though rather boisterous, there was no rioting.

Things remained in a perfect state of quiescence during the week, and it was imagined by some that this outrage, like those which had preceded it, was to be allowed to die quietly out of memory. But in the interim, explicit instructions had been received from the Government to enfore the law by apprehending every one of the ringleaders in the last riot who could be identified. No opportunity of carrying these instructions into execution, occurred until Sunday, the 14th instant, on which day, from the diggers being unemployed in their holes, and, therefore, out and about, and generally assembling in the township, the police identified and arrested three of the ringleaders in the late riot. The news of this arrest spread like wild fire along the diggings, and the cry of "Roll-up!" was quickly raised in Tipperary Gulley, which appears by all accounts to be the centre of all disturbance. The alarm thus raised quickly brought up an armed mob, the number in which has been variously estimated at from 500 to 1000 persons, which, under self-constituted leaders, who appeared to start up ready for the occasion at once marched up to the camp. Intelligence of the advance was given to the authorities, who speedily put the camp into a state of defence, and placed their men in such positions as to offer the most effectual resistance in the event of violence being attempted.

Shortly before eight p.m., the mob, all fully armed, drew up in front of the camp; but, before proceeding to extremities, sent in four delegates to have an interview with the Commissioners. They were met by Captain Zouch, of the mounted patrol, and Commissioner Griffin; and, in the first place, asked if any, and what number, had been arrested with respect to the late riots. They were informed that three were arrested; they then stated that they were requested to demand their release. Both Captain Zouch and Mr. Griffin firmly yet cooly declined to release the prisoners, informing the deputation at the same time that the law must take its course—that the parties arrested would be brought before the court on Monday morning, and would then be dealt with on the evidence produced against them. With this reply, the delegates went moodily back, but before Captain Zouch could get back, a volley was fired from the mob, at the Camp. Mr. Griffin then went forward and read the Riot Act, which was treated with derisive laughter by the mob, who still approached the camp, with cries of "Roll up," "Release the prisoners." Every endeavour was made and caution given that could be calculated to induce them to desist. Orders were at last given to fire, and then one volley was fired over their heads. This did not appear to intimidate them, and at last the mounted troopers were ordered to the front. They had scarcely drawn up when a volley was fired, and two of the troopers' horses fell. The excitement here became intense: and the troopers were ordered to charge, but not to fire. Shots were fired in continual succession at them, but in the coolest way they obeyed the orders they had received. The mob now closed in and approached the camp, evidently with the intention of rushing it. They were again cautioned, but heedless of this they endeavoured to make the rush. Orders were given to the foot police to fire, and two volleys were poured in steadily to the advancing masses, shivering the head of the attack, and causing it to fall back in disorder upon those behind. At this moment, the mounted men who had been posted at the rear of the camp were ordered to take advantage of this confusion, and make a final charge; and no sooner was the order issued than the cavalry were amongst the disorganised mass, galloping through and through it, sabreing on all sides, and driving the now helpless, but still vindictive, crowd back across the creek.

Captain Zouch's account of the conflict, as forwarded by telegram to the Government, is as follows:—

The mob came on the camp at a quarter to eight last night, after sending in four delegates to speak to Commissioner; demanded the release of the prisoners, and gradually moved forward, evidently intending to rush the place. A division of patrol under Mr. M'Lerie was ordered to clear the ground, and was immediately fired upon by the rioters. The patrol charged well, night though it was, and drove numbers over the banks of the creek. The foot patrol firing into the mob, but it was not till three charges had been delivered, and the firing at intervals continued for more than two hours, before the rioters withdrew. Every man did his duty as well as men could do it. Three men of the patrol were wounded—two gunshot wounds in one arm and one contused; one horse which dropped was recovered with four balls in him, and two horses missing wounded. Of the rioters, we know of one killed and several wounded. As soon as I can ascertain losses, I will inform you. The darkness prevented our making any prisoners.

After this defeat, the mob sullenly withdrew, with a threat, however, of returning on the following day, better armed and better prepared for their work. On the following morning, Monday, the three men who had been arrested, and for whose release so much blood had been shed, were brought up, examined, and committed for trial, but were subsequently admitted to bail. Of the course that Mr. Zouch afterwards found it necessary to pursue, he thus speaks, in a later telegram to the Government:—

The Camp was attacked for the purpose of rescuing three prisoners for Chinese riots. We fought them for two hours and more. Attack commenced at a quarter to eight o'clock, and by ten o'clock we drove them off, killing and wounding many. Three, we know, are dead, and we have heard of numbers wounded. My report will explain all. Seven special constables came to the camp—two only armed. There was no response to the call made to the respectable part of the community. Position, I found, untenable, against the numbers that were prepared to revenge the defeat of Sunday night. Some three thousand, better prepared and organised, were to attack, and had sworn to destroy the whole of us. I have brought away the whole force, wounded included.

When the police authorities determined upon evacuating their position, our Special Correspondent, whose life had been threatened by the ringleaders in the riot, on account of the too truthful way in which he had dealt with their proceedings, left Lambing Flat, and fell back upon Yass, and thus we are without positive information in regard to the subsequent proceedings of the rioters, or to the number of killed and wounded in the repulse of Sunday night; but this gentleman telegrams from Yass to say that three men killed on that night were buried on Tuesday, 16th, and that at the funeral of one of them, forty men bandaged for wounds were present, and that it was currently reported that over a hundred had been more or less wounded.

Immediately on the receipt of this intelligence by the Government the Commander of the Forces was communicated with, and orders were at once given to forward on to Burrangong, detachments of the 12th Regiment, of the Artillery, of mounted and foot police, and of blue jackets from H. M. S. Fawn (whose services were offered by Captain Kater), the various detachments amounting to 225 men, which, with the police of the district will give a total effective force of 280 men. Arrangements were made with the mail contractors to carry up to Goulburn in twenty-four hours fifty men per diem for such period as the Government may require. At Goulburn, the inhabitants have nobly come forward, and placed every means of conveyance in their possession, with horses and all requisites at the disposal of the Government for the conveyance of troops and police, and no time will consequently be lost in forwarding them on from Goulburn to Lambing Flat.

On Wednesday, a first detachment of infantry, artillery, and police left Sydney by rail, and was followed on the following day by seventy-five blue jackets under Captain Kater.

In the meantime, the Burrangong Gold Fields remain indisputably in the hands of the rioters. All those who have property to lose are leaving them as fast as they possibly can; the managers of the branches of the three banks established there having come into Yass on Wednesday, 17th, for security, bringing with them 4500 ounces of gold. No attack had been made upon the stores, though they had all been searched for arms and ammunition. Nothing else had been taken, as the leaders who now prominently direct every movement declare that they will not allow robbery. Business of every kind is suspended on the ground, and there appears to be a general impression that the rioters have determined upon holding out to the last.

THE INDUSTRIAL EXHIBITION OF 1862.

Considerable progress has been made by the Commissioners appointed to make arrangements for the representation of the colony at the forthcoming Great Exhibition of 1862. They have entered upon their duties with much energy; and, regarding the work as a labour of love, they are leaving nothing undone which can conduce in any way to the success of the mission which they have undertaken. In former summaries, we have chronicled their proceedings from time to time, as also the mode by which they hope to secure a fair display of our national products and industrial resources. The citizens, generally speaking, have not as yet been fully awakened to the importance of the event, but there is no doubt that as the period for the local exhibition, which it is proposed to hold in October draws nigh, the list of exhibitors will become exceedingly large. This would be the case under any circumstances, but when it is borne in mind that very liberal prizes are to be awarded in the various departments, we may rest assured that the skill and talent of our manufacturers will be brought into play, and that the natural and industrial resources of the colony will be fully pourtrayed. A capacious set of storerooms have been taken in new Pitt-street, for the reception of exhibits, and we need hardly say that every proper precaution is taken to guard against injury or damage of any kind. For every article sent, the commissioners issue a receipt signed by the secretary, so that the owner can experience no difficulty hereafter in respect to having his property returned, or in receiving the proceeds, in the event of his desiring to have it disposed of in London. By way of inciting others to come forward and assist in so desirable an undertaking, the commissioners consent to relieve the exhibitors from all expense for the conveyance of their respective exhibits. In this, we are happy to say they are liberally assisted by various individuals—the directors of the Clarence and Richmond River Steam Company, amongst others, having intimated their readiness to carry all articles which may be intended for the exhibition free of cost. The following is an alphabetical list of persons who have forwarded or promised to forward exhibits up to the present time, viz:—

Edward Baldwin, Hunter-street
Thomas Bandon, Clarence River
Henry Bell, Pitt-street
B. Bernasconi, Pitt-street
E. and C. Beckman, George-street
E. F. Blackett, Mort's-buildings
E. Blake, Australian Library
W. Blackwood, 328, George-street
Harold Brees, 95, Elizabeth-street
J. Brush, George-street
Broomfield and Whittaker, Albion Wharf
Brush and Mac Donnell, George-street
M. Campbell, Barker's Mills
W. J. Cates, George-street
W. G. Caporn, Fort-street
William Child, East Maitland
J. P. Christoe, Guyong
Rev. W. B. Clarke, St. Leonard's
Ingham S. Clements, Bathurst
J. R. Clarke, George-street
C. Croaker, Bathurst
Crawley and Sons, Market
E. Dalton, George-street
R. Dawson, 186, George-street
J. Degotardi
Elliott, Brothers, Pitt-street
George Taint, Armidale
Ferris and Sons, Pitt-street
Robert Fishlock, Wollongong
Flavelle Brothers, George-street
W. G. Freeman, George-street
A. J. D. Francis, Moruya
Mr. Futter, Bungonia
Mrs. Gordon, Goulburn
Thomas Samuel Gill
John Gosper, Colo
James Gow, George-street
J. Hovendon, Grafton
Hall and Alderson, Elizabeth-street
John Hagen, George-street
William Harbottle, George-street
G. J. Hamilton, Pitt-street
Mr. Hall, Parramatta
Mr. Herborn, Macleay River
E. S. Hill, Albion-street
Hill and Sons, King-street
M. G. Henfrey, Castlereagh-street
G. K. Holden, ditto
Julius Hogarth, Hunter-street
E. Hughes, Bathurst-street
Clark Irving, Sydney
William Jennings, George-street
David Jones and Co., ditto
J. Kellick, Phillip-street
William Keene, Newcastle
Kirchner and Co., Grafton
Edward Knox, Sugar Company
J. C. and C. W. Lloyd, Namoi River
E. H. Lloyd, ditto
J. V. Lavars, George-street
Thomas Leggatt, Clarence-street
A. Lenehan, Castlereagh-street
Charles Ledger, Arthursleigh
Sir W. Macarthur, Camden
Edye Manning, Phœnix Wharf
H. Milgrove, Park-street
Thomas S. Mort, Pitt-street
L. Moss, Hunter-street
J. H. Moss, Shoalhaven
J. Moore, George-street
C. Moore, Botanic Gardens
Mort and Co., Pitt-street
J. Nicholson, J.P., Little Plains
William Patten, Pitt-street
J. Paterson, A. S. N. Company
Hugh Paterson, George-street
J. H. Pearce, Randwick
S. R. Pembroke, Tuena
Richard Peek, Summerhill Mines
J. A. Portus, Raymond Terrace
Messrs. Portus, ditto
A. Riley, Tenterfield
Reading and Wellbank, Bridge-street
P. N. Russell, and Co., George-street
Captain Russell, Ravensfield
E. Rudder, Macleay River
S. Samuel, Pitt-street
Sands and Kenny, George-street
J. M. Sanger, Albury
J. Scott, Carrington
J. R. Severn, Royal Mint
Sheriff and Downing, George-street
W. H. Simpson, Mort's-buildings
W. Smith, Park-street
Captain Smith, Miller's Point
P. Snape, Stroud
George Stabler, Kent-street
The Surveyor-General
H. Terry, artist
Messrs. Thomson, Camden
William Tuckey, Newtown
Thomas Underwood, Sydney
Arthur Vyner, P.M., Tumut
R. J. Want, Pitt-street
Captain Ward, R.E., Royal Mint
J. W. Waugh, George-street
George Wacey, William-street
J. B. Winship, Newcastle
David Wilson, Adelong
George Wilkie, George-street
D. Wiley, Park-street
Wyndham and Lindeman, Exchange Cellars

In addition to gold, iron, copper, coal, and other natural products, the New South Wales contribution will include a great variety of interesting objects, as also many specimens of industrial skill. Without attempting to particularise, we may state that the contributions already sent in or promised, include nearly everything which can be supposed to represent the indigenous resources and manufacturing capabilities of the colony. In the department of minerals, we are promised contributions from all parts of the country, and as the list includes the names of the Rev. W. B. Clarke, Captain Ward, Mr. Keene, and other well known gentlemen, we can safely anticipate that a large and magnificent collection, will be got together. Our great staple, "the golden fleece," will be pourtrayed in all its qualities by the exhibits of Mr. Mort and other gentlemen who are either directly or indirectly concerned in pastoral pursuits. In the department of manufactures will be included specimens of colonial tweed and flannel, tobacco, wine, silk, pottery, jewellery, cutlery, models, cordials, manufactured skins and leather, pipes, furniture, and marble work, &c. The two departments of raw products and curiosities will include a goodly collection of specimens. For the information of friends at a distance, we proceed to notice a few of the more interesting articles and exhibits which have already been entrusted to the care of the commissioners

The superiority of our timber for purposes of ship-building is shown by a small block of blue gum from the framework of the steamer William IV., built by Messrs. Marshall and Lowe, on the Clyde River, in the year 1830. The wood is as sound and as hard as the day it was felled, notwithstanding that it has undergone the wear and tear and exposure of thirty-one years. This small and unpretending item will, no doubt, be viewed with much interest by the shipwrights of the mother country, and also by many old colonists who have travelled at one time or other in the steamer from which it is taken.

Mr. Scott, of Carrington, near Port Stephens, sends a rare and valuable specimen of the stilted plover, a bird now seldom to be met with. It is in fine condition, and when set up will be object of interest to all professional and amateur ornithologists.

A native cat-skin rug is contributed by Mr. David Jones, of George-street. This is chiefly noticeable as a specimen of what might be done in the way of a fur trade. The skins are beautifully marked, and have all the glossy softness of the chinchilla.

Mr. Peck, of Summerhill, forwards, with other articles, a block of steatite (soap stone); while several fine samples of our colonial white and coloured building stone are contributed by Mr. Blackett, the well-known architect. Some blocks of native meerschaum from the recently discovered quarries in the Clarence River district will also be sent home, together with some smoking pipes manufactured in the colony from the same commodity.

A Mr. Ferris, of Sydney, sends some superb specimens of carving in wood. One piece, representing "Cupid bound," is executed in a most elaborate and artistic manner. Four picture-frames in antique scrollwork, affords further evidence of Mr. Ferris's great skill, taste, and industry in this particular branch of human labour.

A door-bracket exhibited by Mr. Oram will serve to show both the beauty of our cedar, and the carver's skill in following that heavy Italian scroll pattern, which is so popular at the present time. Numerous articles of furniture from colonial wood will be forwarded by Messrs. Hill and Sons, and also by Mr. Lenehan, of Castlereagh-street.

Amongst the cereals, we find some cases of maize in cob, contributed by Mr. Underwood. These will compare favourably with any specimens that may be forthcoming from any other portion of the world, and will prove that, despite any drawbacks, our agricultural capabilities are not wholly overlooked.

A sword, manufactured, the blade by Mr. Jennings, and the hilt by Mr. Julius Hogarth, will also merit especial notice. The weapon will combine two of our great natural products, and at the same time show that our artists and handicraftsmen are not at all behind their fellow subjects in England or the workmen of the continent.

But one of the principal, if not the most interesting of the New South Wales exhibits will be a collection of stuffed skins, showing the various successful crosses of that valuable animal, the alpaca. The necessary authority having been given by the Government, Mr. Ledger purposes killing nine animals, from the increase of the flock since their arrival in the colony, the skins of which are to be carefully stuffed and set up, in order to show the quality of the fleece and also the results which have accrued from a systematic and judicious crossing or in-breeding. The tallow or lard taken from the animals (and which we believe has valuable medicinal properties) is also to be forwarded in glass jars for the inspection of those who may feel interested in the matter, while an opinion on the quality and nutritious properties of the flesh is to be elicited by the means of a distribution of venison to the different clubs of Sydney, and to such private individuals as may be desirous of giving a qualified opinion on the point. In his letter to the Commissioners, wherein he suggests the propriety of such an exhibition, after alluding to the comparatively small cost which it would entail, Mr. Ledger says:—"This would in all probability be covered by the sale of the specimens in London. I entertain no doubt but that they would command a high price, not only from the fact of their being the indication of a new source of valuable export from this colony, but for demonstrating the fallacy of hitherto erroneously advanced theory as to the sterility of the cross-breedings of this animal. Hybridisation assumes through them a complete change. The 'savans' will see that they have been in error for a very long period; and, moreover, the collection will be the first ever exhibited of the "Auchenia" in its varied crosses, and will be worthy a place in the National Museum."

Our colonial wines will form not the least important item in the New South Wales department of the Exhibition. Amongst the list of contributors we notice the following:—Captain Russell, Mr. Lindeman, Mr. Blake, Mr. Bettington, Mr. Lawson, and Mr. Sanger, of Albury.

The Commissioners will continue to receive exhibits up to the 18th September next, after which date they purpose holding a local exhibition of the selected articles in Sydney. This will extend over a month or six weeks, and the whole will then be sent on to London in January, under the care of competent persons appointed to arrange for their reception and display in London.

FINE ARTS.

MR. SMART'S GALLERY OF OIL PAINTINGS AT MONA.

The opening to the public on Saturday, the 13th instant, of Mr. Smart's Gallery of Paintings at Mona cannot but be viewed by every enlightened mind as a new and important epoch in our social progress—a precedent and an example calculated to produce the best possible effects in the elevation and refinement of the intellectual tastes of a large and important class in this community. Such a liberality on the part of wealthy and judicious lovers of the Fine Arts—who have gathered, one by one, many of the *chefs d'œuvre* of those glorious Old Masters whose names are household words to all that delight in the grand and beautiful—is, we are aware, by no means uncommon in the mother country and on the continent of Europe. Here, however, we may take leave to say, the pleasure of seeing anything of the sort is a most refreshing and attractive novelty,—a something unhoped-for that supplies a want which has long been felt, filling up the vacuum in such a manner that the privilege conceded will be very eagerly appreciated. It would, under existing circumstances, be a great boon to the rising families of the gentry and citizens of Sydney to have *any* gallery of good oil paintings thrown open (with all proper restrictions of course) for public inspection. Mr. Smart's Gallery at Mona, however, goes very far beyond satisfying what has hitherto been so much desiderated in this respect. Those amongst us once ever thoroughly familiar with the works of the Great Princes of the Pencil, who have long been revered in the History of Art, can here again renew their acquaintance with what (at a greater or less lapse of time) once delighted their taste, and more than gratified their judgment; and they may, with ease and unalloyed pleasure, kindly instruct those who have never enjoyed *their* advantages.

The gallery at Mona stands on the southern side of the magnificent residence of Mr T. W. Smart, M.P., situated at Darling Point, on a spot not less adorned by Nature than by Art. The views from this charming locality embrace such a combination of rocks, woods, houses, and waveless bays as could have been very happily transferred to canvas by many of those great artists whose works now adorn the walls of the gallery. After a long voyage over the trackless ocean, many thousands of miles further than any such a goodly company of paintings ever yet sailed in the history of the known world, the valuable works of many ancient and modern masters are now safely deposited in the gallery at Darling Point, where they have been judiciously hung under the careful superintendence of Mrs. Smart. The gallery itself is a handsome piece of masonry, sixty-five feet long by twenty-five feet wide, lighted in the proper manner, by clerestory windows in the roof. On entering from the corridor the "old world" visitor is forcibly struck with the majestic aspect of the paintings, the statuary, and the many other attractive objects, which there await his inspection. In the stillness of the place, and at the unwonted beauty of the *coup d'œil*, he is carried back to recollections of what he never expected to find realised in New South Wales. It seems hard for him to imagine that he is any longer in busy, struggling, mercantile Australia, when he looks on this large and valuable collection from the Venetian, Italian, Spanish, German, Dutch, Flemish, and English Schools of Painting. To recapitulate all the great artists which are honourably commemorated on the walls of the Mona Gallery would render it necessary for us to run through the catalogue. Suffice it to say that on the list will be found the names of Raffaelle, Rubens, Carlo Dolci, Ludovico Caracci, Annibale Carracci, Murillo, Mola, Guerchino, Salvator Rosa, Velasquez, Gaspar Poussin, Orizonti, Gainsborough, Albano, Van Dyck, Wouvermans, Canaletto, Guardi, Moreland, Teniers, Ostade, Cuyp, and many others; amongst which are the names of painters of very interesting and ancient pictures of the old German and Greek schools, and of numerous artists in oil of the present days. It is worthy of particular note that a great number of the most valuable of these paintings were purchased at the sale of the magnificent collection of the late Lord Northwick, who passed many years of his life in Italy, and was, as is well known, an enthusiastic and discriminating lover of the art.

Amongst the most remarkable pictures in this admirable collection attention has been particularly drawn to landscapes by the renowned Gaspar Poussin, by his celebrated Flemish Imitator Orizonti, by Swaneveldt, the favourite pupil of Claude, by our own great English painter Gainsborough (both in his Wynant's and his later style), and by a host of others, whose names stand high in the annals of fame and art. The Flemish and Dutch schools are both well represented; of the French and Spanish there are not so many exemplars, but what there is of each includes great names, such as Jouvenet, Murillo, and Velasquez. We have not space here to describe any of these in detail, or many in England would at once, doubtless, recognise some well remembered work of art. As a specimen, however, of the high character of these paintings, we may perhaps briefly refer to number 44, *The Magdalen in the Desert, from the Northwick Collection*, by Pietro Francesco Mola, that eminent Italian painter and imitator of Titian, who was born at Coldra, in the Milanese territory, in the year 1699. The subject treated of in this picture is brought out with a grandeur which is hardly surpassed by the best productions of Caracci and Domenichino. The penitent woman reclines in the foreground in an easy attitude, comforted by angelic visitants,—which may be supposed to represent the return of happier and less desponding thoughts. In the background are the trees and shrubs of a pathless forest, wrapped in a deep, warm, tranquilising gloom, —from which, and from the fading tints of the sky, it is obvious that the time is that of a soft summer evening. The foreshortening of the figure of Mary demands unqualified admiration. Her face has a sweet and thoughtful air, and is turned away towards the descending cherubs; all of which are painted in with a lightness, and softness, and ease which immediately arrest the eye. The knees, breast, and arms of the Magdalen are exquisitely drawn, and the colouring of the flesh is that of life itself. *Christ's Charge to St. Peter* by Ludovico Caracci, *a Holy Family* by Annibale Caracci; *another* (a small picture) *by the immortal Raffaelle* (from the Lucien Bonaparte Gallery) and a Carlo Dolci—*the Head of the Saviour breaking bread*, a *replica* of the Marquess of Exeter's picture at Burleigh—are amongst the many priceless gems which have thus been brought by our respected fellow-townsman to this colony, and are now liberally thrown open by Mr. Smart to the public. As we have said, it is, indeed, a new epoch in our social progress to have here amongst us such a noble collection as this—one of which the wealthiest and most discriminating of the patrons of art in England might well be proud.

THE GREENOAKS COLLECTION OF WATER-COLOUR PAINTINGS.

The magnificent water-colour paintings which, together with a number of valuable oil paintings, sculptures, and other works of art, Mr. T. S. Mort collected, during his recent residence in England, and brought with him to this colony, have recently been hung in a handsome gallery, built specially for their reception, at his residence at Greenoaks, Darling Point, and admission for their inspection has been kindly afforded to the public upon stated occasions. The collection, which numbers about a hundred and twenty pictures, all elegantly framed, contains some of the choicest productions of the most eminent artists of the English water-colour school, including Copley Fielding, David Cox, G. Cattermole, W. Hunt, J. B. Pyne, H. G. Willis, De Wint, S. Prout, and F. Tayler. The opportunity of inspecting these beautiful pictures has been freely appreciated and embraced by the public, and the gallery is, upon the days when it is thrown open, a well frequented resort, not only on account of the rarity of such exhibitions in this colony, but also because of the high merits and general attractiveness of the paintings.

TELEGRAPHS.

Of the telegraphic extensions carried out under the vote of the Legislature last year, only two remain unfinished, and these are in a very forward state. We reported last month the completion of the first portion of the northern extension, which carries the wire from Maitland to Murrurundi. The second portion which will connect that town with Maryland, on the Queensland frontier, is finished within a few miles; it would have been before this ready for opening but for the recent very bad weather. In about three weeks there will be a continuous wire from Adelaide through Victoria and this colony to the boundary of Queensland. There is no immediate urgency for the opening of the line beyond Armidale, as the wire is not likely to be much in requisition until it is connected with the Queensland telegraph, which was to have been ready at the same time as ours; it will, however, be three or four months before we shall be able to exchange instantaneous messages with Brisbane. When their line is finished the capitals of the four colonies will be connected by telegraph.

The southern extension which will connect Gundagai with Deniliquin, by way of Wagga Wagga, is finished, and Mr. Cracknell, the Superintendent of Telegraphs, has left Sydney for the purpose of opening the line, and also of arranging for the purchase of the private line between Deniliquin and Echuca. This extension joins at Echuca with the Victorian and South Australian systems by way of Castlemaine and Ballarat, and will afford a second channel of telegraphic communication between Adelaide and Sydney, in the event of any accident with the lines in Victoria or in this colony. Until, however, a second wire is stretched between Adelaide and Mount Gambier, there will not be two independent lines between South Australia and New South Wales.

The line between Goulburn and Braidwood—a distance of sixty miles—has been contracted for by Mr. Hatton, and has within the last week been commenced. About seven miles have been pegged out by the surveyors, a number of holes sunk, and the poles ready for fixing. The line is to be completed in April next.

No commencement has yet been made with the extension from Deniliquin to the frontier of South Australia, the preliminary negotiations not having, we understand, been completed.

RELIGIOUS MEMORANDA.

Church of England.—The Rev. E. Williams is about to take his departure for England. Prior to leaving his friends and congregation at Tamworth, he was presented with a testimonial and a purse of sovereigns as a token of respect.—The anniversary meeting of the Sydney Auxiliary of the Church Missionary Society to Africa and the East was held on the 24th ultimo, in the Church Society's House, Philip-street. The attendance was numerous, and the cause of the society was ably advocated by the several speakers present, viz., the Bishop of Sydney, Revs. Mayne, Moreton, the Dean of Sydney, and several lay gentlemen.—An auxiliary Church Society has been established at Berrima.—The Rev. H. Mayne has been appointed chaplain to the Burrangong gold-field.—The Rev. J. K. Tucker, agent of the British and Foreign Bible Society, has been licensed to officiate in the diocese of Sydney.—The Bishop of Sydney will hold confirmations in Sydney and the neighbourhood next month, and then proceed on a lengthened visitation tour to the south and south-west of the diocese.

Roman Catholic.—Archbishop Polding has been lately on a visitation through the Southern districts.—Among the recent appointments that have been made we find that the Rev. Fathers Hanley and O'Neill are to officiate in the Yass mission, Father D'Arcy at Queanbeyan, Father Dunne at Singleton, and Father M'Alroy and Lanigan at Goulburn.—The ceremony of professing two sisters of the Good Shepherd was lately celebrated at the Lower Pitt-street Convent. The ladies were, Miss Butler, who took the name of Sister Mary Frances; and Miss M'Donald, the name of Sister Mary Winifred.

Wesleyan.—A new chapel was opened at Hinton on the 30th ultimo, the Rev. J. Watsford preached before very large congregations. On the following evening a tea meeting was held to celebrate the occasion, afterwards a public meeting took place presided over by Mr. King. From the report which was read at the meeting, it appears that the land on which the new chapel is built was given by Mr. John Christian; the cost of the structure is about £200 which amount is nearly all paid by subscription from the residents.—The annual meeting of the Surry Hills branch of the Sustentation Fund society was held on the 1st instant. The committee's report for the past year showed that this branch society is in a very satisfactory condition.

Primitive Methodist.—Public tea meetings have been held during the month at the Newtown and Glebe chapels, for the purpose of raising funds in aid of the Circuit expenses. Sermons have also been preached for the same purpose. Both the above meetings were well attended, and the collections more than usually liberal.

Baptists.—A large tea meeting was given on the evening of the 24th ultimo, in the Odd Fellow's Hall, Sussex-street, in connection with the Particular Baptist Church to welcome the Rev. J. B. M'Cure and his family. The meeting was well attended, and several clergymen of various denominations were present and addressed the assemblage.

Presbyterian.—The ordination of the Rev. William Bain, to the pastorate of the Presbyterian Church of Eastern Australia was held on the 20th June, at the Oddfellows' Hall, Lake Macquarie Road. The Rev. Mr. M'Intyre, Mr. Hamilton (ruling elder), Rev. J. M'Culloch, Rev. A. M. Sheriff, and several ministers of other denominations were present. The hall was filled with a large and respectable congregation. The proceedings were opened by the Rev. Mr. M'Intyre by prayer. The sermon was preached by the Rev. Mr. M'Culloch, who gave a very instructive discourse which was listened to with marked attention. The Rev. Mr. Bain having answered the necessary questions according to the custom of the Presbyterian Church, and the Rev. Mr. Sheriff having stated that Mr. Bain had appeared before the Moderator at a meeting of the presbytery held in Maitland, and given satisfactory answers, the presbytery had therefore sanctioned his ordination for that evening, and as no one had objected to Mr. Bain as their pastor, they should therefore at once proceed to the performance of their sacred duties. The Rev. Mr. Bain then knelt down while the Rev. Mr. M'Culloch, assisted by the Rev. Mr. M'Intyre and the Rev. Mr. Sheriff, proceeded to the ceremony of laying on the hands and delivering a short prayer. Mr. Sheriff, in a very impressive address, delivered the charge to the new minister, and the Rev. Mr. M'Intyre addressed the congregation. The ceremony terminated by prayer at rather a late hour.—On Tuesday evening, 9th instant, a tea meeting was held in the Presbyterian Church, Palmer-street, Woolloomooloo, the occasion being the commemoration of the opening of that church. After tea, a public meeting was held, at which the Rev. J. M'Gibbon presided. In the course of the proceedings the Rev. Messrs. Robinson, Craig, Dr. Fullerton, W. Cuthbertson, and others addressed the meeting.—Since the removal of the Rev. James Coutts to Newcastle, the pulpit of the Scots Church, Parramatta, has been filled by several clergymen; on the 9th instant, a meeting of the members of that church was held and it was unanimously resolved to support a call to the Rev. Thomas Craig, of Essendon, Victoria. Subsequently a call, in the customary form of the Church of Scotland, was thereupon drawn up, and has been numerously signed.

Congregational.—The anniversary of the Sabbath school in connection with the Congregational church, Newtown, was commemorated on the evening of the 16th, by a tea meeting, and the claims of the school were subsequently enforced at a public meeting. There were present ministers of various denominations besides the pastors of several of the Congregational churches in and around Sydney. The chair was taken by the minister of the church, the Rev. S. C. Kent, who after a few appropriate observations, called upon the secretary to read the report. From this document it appeared that since the last report (August, 1859) there had been received into the school 179 children many of whom, however, had removed from the neighbourhood, and that there were at the present time 105 boys and 123 girls on the books, the average attendance being about 150. The Rev. Messrs. T. Johnson, W. Cuthbertson, W. Slatyer, S. Ironside, J. Langford, delivered addresses in testimony of the value of sabbath schools.—Sunday Schools, Pitt-street. The anniversary sermons were preached on Sunday last, by the pastor, the Rev. W. Cuthbertson, and the Rev. S. C. Kent. After both services collections were made, and amounted to the handsome sum of more than £70. These schools number at present about 400 scholars, and an infant class of 100. There are fifty teachers, fourteen of whom were once scholars in these schools. In consequence of the large attendance the Temperance Hall was taken, by which means a better classification was obtained. There are, as regular attendants, about 200 scholars over fifteen years of age, seventy of whom are over eighteen.

RIOT AT LAMBING FLAT.

...

At last the storm, which had been so long seen, by all but those who should have been the most attentive in their examination of the social horizon, to be impending, broke with a violence that at once woke up the sleepers from their pleasant dreams. On Sunday, the 30th June, the residents of Tipperary Gully were aroused by the cries of "Roll up", and in the course of a very short time upwards of a thousand men, armed with bludgeons and pickhandles, no firearms as yet appearing, were assembled round the "No Chinese" standard. Forming themselves in a rude kind of order of march, and with a band of music, which appears to have been thoughtfully provided for the occasion by the leaders of the movement, at their head, shouting, yelling, and singing, the crowd of rioters took the road to Lambing Flat, a distance of some four or five miles. Arrived there, every Chinese resident in the township on whom hands could be laid was attacked and maltreated, the chief object of ambition being to secure the long tails of hair with which the Chinese are accustomed to ornament their heads. The main body was here joined by numerous others, who came flocking in from all quarters, until the number assembled amounted to at least 3000 persons. Finding themselves so strong, and being determined to make a clean sweep of the Mongolians now that they were about it, they now turned their attention to the Chinese camp, situated on the spot and within the area allocated to them by the Commissioner in accordance with the regulations previously made, and apparently agreed to by the diggers. This was at once attacked and carried, the Chinese being driven off, under circumstances of great barbarity in some cases, and in all cases without being permitted to take with them any portion of their property. It has been said also that many of them were robbed of various amounts of gold and cash; and that, mixed up with the crowd of rioters were numbers of women and children all actively engaged in plundering the property of the runaways of everything valuable, or convertible, prior to carrying the remainder to the enormous fires that were kept up with such kind of fuel. In the mean time the band, placed in a conspicuous position, enlivened the scene by playing spirit-stirring airs, to an accompaniment of yells and shouts that would have done credit to a New Zealand war dance. Excited with their triumph, heated with their violence towards unresisting captives, and possibly thirsting for the plunder, of which this last attack had given them a taste, a wild savage yell of joy was raised, when some one suggested Back Creek as the next spot to visit. Shouting, firing (for guns were now pretty generally produced), singing, laughing, and cheering, the body of rioters moved off towards Back Creek, a locality about six miles from where they then were, and where it was known that there were several hundreds of Chinese at work. Information of the projected attack was, however, taken over to the Chinese in this locality, who, hastily packing up the most valuable and portable portions of their property, hurriedly made off from the spot. The rioters were not long behind them, and on coming up, a savage yell of disappointment rose up from the mob when they found that their pray had escaped. The tents, goods, &c., left behind were fired, after having been carefully looked over for plunder; and such articles as would not burn were destroyed by being broken with axes. Whilst this had been going on, a number of the rioters, who were mounted on horseback, galloped forward on the track of the retreating Mongols, overtook them, not much more than a mile away, headed them, and rounded them up in the same way as a shepherd-dog would do a flock of sheep. Information of the surround was sent off to those behind, who, eager for their prey, were already on the road. Here ensued a scene such as, thank heaven! it seldom falls to the lot of a British journalist to record. Unarmed, defenceless, and unresisting Chinese were struck down in the most brutal manner by bludgeons provided for the occasion, and by pick handles. The previous excitement had done its work, and now the wretched Mongols were openly and unblushingly searched for valuables, and robbery was committed without the slightest attempt at concealment. Very few of the poor creatures here attacked escaped with their pigtails, none of them without injury of some kind, whilst every article of the property they had endeavoured to take with them was plundered of all that was valuable, and then burnt. Some of the acts of barbarism said to have been committed here were such, that Englishmen can scarce be brought to credit that their countrymen could be guilty of them—for who amongst the British people could ever believe that men of their own country—Britons, would take Chinese pigtails *with the scalp attached.* That this was done in more than one instance there can be no doubt, since the possessors of these trophies made no concealment of them, but rather prided themselves on their possession.

This watercolour of a riot at Lambing Flat comes from a sketchbook produced by Dr J. T. Doyle, an amateur watercolourist, and S. T. Gill, a professional artist, with the aim of publication. Gill, often described as 'the artist of the goldfields,' joined the gold rush in Victoria from 1852, though he soon gave up mining and focused instead on drawing and painting images of life and events on the goldfields.

31 Triumph of British arms

Australia and the New Zealand Wars, 1863

AUSTRALIA'S LONG TRADITION OF FIGHTING WARS OVERSEAS IS OFTEN THOUGHT TO HAVE BEGUN WHEN MANY AUSTRALIANS JOINED THE BRITISH ARMY IN THE SUDAN WAR DURING THE 1880S. LESS WELL KNOWN IS THE FACT THAT SEVERAL THOUSAND AUSTRALIAN-BORN MEN SERVED EITHER IN BRITISH REGIMENTS OR AS 'VOLUNTEERS' IN THE NEW ZEALAND WARS OF 1845–1872.

In 1863, while the Civil War in the United States took some column space in Melbourne's *Argus* newspaper, reports of the British army fighting against Maori in New Zealand lodged by Australia's first war correspondent, Howard Willoughby (1839–1908), gained much greater coverage.

With a closely settled and relatively large population, New Zealand's Maori were able to conduct significant wars of resistance against settlers gradually taking their lands. Indeed, the British army saw some of its fiercest-ever fighting in the trenches and rifle pits constructed by the highly skilled Maori defence.

There had been several wars between Maori and the British during the nineteenth century but the invasion of Waikato in 1863—after Waikato Maori appointed their own king and seceded from New Zealand—was by far the largest campaign.

Britain had been trying to create a self-sufficient colony in New Zealand, just as in Australia, and it was reluctant to provide expensive military forces to the colony. The New Zealand colonial government, however, found willing help in Australia. Several thousand men volunteered for service in New Zealand, with the promise of a grant of Maori land as payment.

Howard Willoughby had a ringside seat as he watched the assault on the Maori Pa, or fortress, Rangariri from the deck of a warship anchored in a nearby lake, from which he recorded 'The most brilliant engagement of the war'.

Unfortunately the 'brilliant engagement' did not see the end of the New Zealand Wars. Fighting continued until the 1870s when Maori were finally exhausted by the sustained military campaigns—although minor conflicts lasted into the twentieth century. Many of the 2500 Australian 'military settlers' of the 1860s who were enticed to fight the Maori with the promise of a land grant were duly rewarded and stayed in New Zealand.

OPPOSITE
The Melbourne Argus *newspaper's extensive coverage of the New Zealand Wars on 12 December 1863 was provided by Howard Willoughby, arguably Australia's first war correspondent.*

deceased, that he was in an early stage of dementia. The verdict stated "That the deceased committed suicide by drowning himself while in a state of temporary insanity."

One of the army surgeons on duty at the Queen's Redoubt, Waikato, on 29th November last, writes as follows:—"Our wounded officers and men are doing well; as also the Maories wounded in our hands. I removed the arm of one yesterday; and to-day had to amputate another Maori's arm at the shoulder joint. They are well pleased and gratified at their treatment, and state they feel quite certain we are doing all for them for the best. It must be indeed to them a wonderful contrast to their treatment of any of our unfortunate men who fall into their hands wounded."

An application was made yesterday to Mr. Justice Barry, by the counsel who defended Goddard (one of the men convicted of the gross assault on the unfortunate Mary Fraser), for permission to call the attention of his Honour to some authorities, with the view of showing that the sentence passed upon Goddard and Branch the previous day, was greater than the law prescribed. Mr. Justice Barry expressed his opinion that little benefit would follow the proceeding. At the same time, he intimated his willingness to hear the learned counsel on the subject on the last day of the present special sittings.

The Philosophical Society of Queensland proposes the establishment in Brisbane of an institution somewhat resembling the Public Library of Melbourne. At the third annual meeting of the society in Brisbane, on the 1st instant, a lengthy letter was read on the subject, from his Honour Sir Redmond Barry, in reply to questions addressed to him by the secretary. The thanks of the society were voted to his Honour for his communication.

At the St. Kilda Police Court yesterday, Peter Le Page, a contractor, was brought up on remand, on a charge of aiding and abetting and being otherwise concerned in the unlawful manufacture of spirits. The defendant pleaded "Guilty;" upon which the inspector of distilleries, who prosecuted, stated that, since the charge was not denied, he would not press for anything beyond the lowest penalty which the magistrates had the power under the act to inflict. The defendant was then fined £50, or, in default, six months' imprisonment; three months to be allowed for payment of the fine on condition that one approved surety was found. The merits of the case were not gone into; but it appears that the spirits were being distilled in an empty house in Argyle-street, and when the premises were searched the police discovered two stills in full working order. They had apparently been erected about two months previously. A quantity of alcohol, in various stages of preparation, was also found. Of course these and the plant were seized by the police. Peter Lihon was next placed in the dock, on a similar charge. It appeared that Lihon had been in the employ of Le Page for a short time, and dreading detection himself, had sought to secure his own safety by giving information to the authorities. Having thus turned approver, the charge was not pressed against him, and he was set at liberty. A labouring man, named John Miller, was charged with stealing wearing apparel from the Grosvenor Arms Hotel, Brighton-road, on the morning of the 10th. The prisoner had taken lodgings in the house the night before, and on the morning named he was seen by some of the servants leaving the hotel at an early hour with the apparel in his possession. He was immediately followed and secured. The prisoner pleaded "Guilty;" but the magistrates declined to deal with the case, and committed the prisoner for trial. A servant-girl named Frances Goulden charged her mistress with having ill-used her. It appeared, however, that there were faults on both sides; and the defendant [illegible] week's wages, and let her go. The former had been engaged for three months, but had only served a week. A cabman, named John Frost, was fined 5s. for plying for hire off his stand. The presiding magistrates were Messrs. Cowderoy, Sydes, and Patterson.

The Botanical Museum received a very large addition of dried plants during the week, consisting of the whole collections accumulated by a renowned phytographer, the late Dr. Joachim Steetz, of Hamburg, during more than thirty years. This herbarium is especially valuable as containing sets of typical specimens, from which many descriptive works have been elaborated. It is, for instance, extremely rich in the collections of Ecklon and Zeyher of South Africa, in Tieber's various collections, in Mr. Moritzi's South American plants, Short's North American plants, Preiss' West Australian collections, Rochel's plants of the Banat; Russian plants by Turizaninow, Vahl's Arctic plants, Anderson's plants of the Gallopagos Islands, and many other important collections of celebrated travellers now no longer available. This new acquisition increases the species of plants preserved in our Botanical Museum to about 40,000.

A meeting will be held on Monday next, to consider a question which has become latterly of great importance in the mercantile world, the validity (where questionable) of deeds of assignment, &c., as affected by certain recent decisions in the Supreme Court. It appears that former decisions have been varied or reversed, and it is with a view that some settled law may be understood and established, if necessary by a new act of Parliament, that the meeting referred to has been called, at the Duke of Rothsay Hotel, on Monday afternoon, at three o'clock.

The *Sydney Morning Herald* has the following:—"Letters-patent have been received by Sir John Young, declaring that, whereas it may happen that guano and other fertilizing substances may be discovered on islands belonging to the Crown, but not within the jurisdiction of any colonial Government, and that it is expedient to make provision for the use and disposal of such islands, the Governor of the colony of New South Wales is empowered to make leases and other dispositions, for a term or terms of years, of any such islands, or part thereof, and to issue licences authorizing persons to take guano, &c., therefrom. These powers are to be exerciseable with respect to all such islands situate in that part of the Indian and South Pacific Oceans which is bounded as follows:—On the north by the tenth parallel of south latitude; on the east by the 170th meridian of west longitude; on the south by the Antarctic Circle; and on the west by the seventy-fifth meridian of east longitude."

We have received a sum of £2, collected from a few friends in St. Kilda, by Mr. A. Hamilton, for the Pearson fund.

The following corps of volunteers have been inspected since the 28th ultimo, and their strength ascertained to be as follow:—Sandridge Naval Brigade, 116—present at inspection, 100; Engineers, 63—present, 58; Williamstown Naval Brigade, 121—present, 102; Williamstown Artillery, 148—present, 131; Melbourne and North Melbourne Rifles, 187—present, 133; and the Carlton Rifles, 159—present, 147.

The *New Zealand Herald* (Auckland) of the 27th ult., writes as follows:—"We hear that General Cameron has been taking a reconnaissance further up the river than the last scene of action, and that he has marched forward with a considerable force at his disposal. It looks well to see the general act promptly, and follow up the rebels in their retreat. A few sharp actions like the last, and with the same result to the natives, will have the effect of soon showing who is the stronger—whether Queen Victoria or Potatau is to be the sovereign of these islands."

The City Court was occupied until an unusually late hour yesterday, disposing of its list of cases. The three females, Cook, Walsh, and Anderson, previously remanded on a charge of stealing £99 from a returned New Zealand miner, were now committed for trial. John Gledhill, lately employed by the Municipal Council of Sandridge as rate collector, was committed for trial, on a charge of embezzling money collected on behalf of the council. Edward Cutler, and Edward O. Cutler, son and father, respectively charged with stealing £52, and with feloniously receiving the same, were discharged, there being nothing in the circumstances of the case to support the charge.

Our Sydney correspondent writes:—"I have strong reason to believe that the Martin Ministry will be beaten on their budget, and will have to go out. Sir John Young's individual sympathies are against them, and he will not be disposed to aid them by dissolving, even if there could reasonably be a dissolution under such circumstances. In this case, Mr. Cowper is very likely to come back, and to form a coalition Ministry. At all events, the attempt will be made. I had some conversation with Mr. Cowper yesterday, and he told me that he intended to speak to-morrow evening in opposition. Arnold and Darvall are yet to be heard also, and will both 'come out strong;' so that, with the rejoinders on the other side, it is most likely the division will not be come to until very late on Thursday night. In the meantime, the collection of the duties is occasioning great discontent and confusion. The protectionist movement is not deep-seated, but will be made a great cry if we should have a Sydney election, on a change of Ministry, and may be found by Cowper a formidable obstacle."

A report from a select committee has been adopted, and ordered to be presented to the Governor, by the Parliament of New South Wales, on the subject of the lighting of the coast. The report recommends the erection of three lighthouses—one on the Seal Rock, another on South Solitary, and a third on Point Danger. Mr. Kemp, who submitted the motion, urged the necessity of proceeding with the first with as little delay as possible; the second was next in importance, though, perhaps, not so urgently required; and, with respect to the third, it was thought Queensland would share in the expense of erection and maintenance.

Emulous of the efforts being made by Ballarat, Castlemaine, Sandhurst, and other districts, to pit their cricketing talent against that of "All England," Maryborough, too, is anxious to secure a visit from the English champions, and overtures have already been made to Marshall on the matter. A sum of £100 cash has been guaranteed; together with all the proceeds of the ground; and it is looked upon as almost a certainty that the event will be speedily arranged. There are numerous outlying districts around Maryborough, the residents in which might find it a difficult matter to visit the "metropolis of the gold fields," or even the "great centre," or the "wayside village to Echuca;" and an excellent opportunity will thus be afforded them of witnessing in their midst such a display of cricket as may not be seen again for years.

We have our files to the following dates:—Sydney, December 8; Auckland, December 1; Brisbane, December 5; and Rockhampton, November 28.

We observe from the *New Zealander* that the House of Representatives has adopted a motion to the effect that the next meeting of the General Assembly should be held at Christchurch, if suitable buildings had not [illegible] Straits," which is to be selected as the new seat of Government.

No business could be transacted at the adjourned meeting of the East Collingwood Borough Municipal Council last night, in consequence of there again not being a quorum. Four members—Councillors Noon, Flockhart, Turnbull, and Petherick—were present, but, under the new Municipal Corporations Act, five are requisite to constitute a quorum. The meeting was further adjourned till Tuesday.

The annual cricket match between eleven representatives from each of the great social interests—the butchers and the licensed victuallers—was played on the Richmond Ground yesterday. The match was originally fixed for Thursday, but the copious supply of "heavy wet" on that day necessitated the postponement of the game until yesterday, which, although dubious at the outset, cleared up as the day wore on, and amply compensated for the disappointment of Thursday. The game was much more closely contested than the one played last season, and notwithstanding "mine hosts" were strengthened by the addition of Marshall, Bryant, and Greaves to their ranks, yet victory once more inclined to the "knights of the cleaver," who were the first to "shape" at the wickets. By good steady play, which, indeed, was the chief feature of their innings, they contrived to "run up a score" of eighty-four runs, of which twenty-two were credited to Ashton, fifteen to Bruce, and eleven to Oddy. The "bungs," as the licensed victuallers were somewhat irreverently designated by the lookers-on, seemed in a fair way of experiencing a signal defeat, until Marshall came to the rescue, and commenced scoring fast and free, to the immense delight of his party. After playing an exciting innings for forty-seven well-got runs, he lifted the ball with great force to the long field on, and was caught splendidly by Ashton, who had to run his "speedy utmost" for a considerable distance to secure the ball, which, by a most dexterous piece of fielding, he did, and with it another triumph for the butchers. Bryant, who was just getting well in, was completely "sold" by an ordinary-paced underhand ball, and had to retire after scoring seven runs. Hardham contributed five, and the others were nowhere. For the butchers, the lion's share of the bowling and wickets fell to Patterson, assisted by Willoughby; while Bryant and Greaves did duty for the publicans. There was a large attendance of the friends of both fraternities on the ground; and their presence contributed in no small degree to the jollity of the game. The second innings was begun, but more with a view of passing away the time until the hour for dinner than of playing out the game, which was decided by the result of the first innings. The twenty-two, and a large accession of friends, held their annual dinner afterwards at Bryant's Cricketers' Arms Hotel, and "Our next meeting" was by no means the least important toast of the evening.

The *Southern Cross* of the 27th ult., says:—"A letter has been received from Mr. Crosbie Ward by the last mail, stating that he had received an offer from the Intercolonial Royal Mail Company to provide boats that would run ten knots an hour, and make the passage in twenty-six days from Panama to New Zealand, for a subsidy of £60,000 per annum. The proportion which New Zealand would have to pay would be, by modifications of the present contract, and by the receipt for letters which would be handed over to this colony, about £30,000. The arrangement was not completed when the mail left, but we understand there is reason to suppose it would be completed." The *New Zealand Herald* (Auckland), of the 24th ult., says:—"The Intercolonial Royal Mail Steam Company have, we learn, taken up the Panama route, and intend at once to lay on a line of steamers to New Zealand. They have already secured several suitable vessels, and are in treaty for others."

The treasurer of the Melbourne Hospital begs to acknowledge receipt of £6 13s. 5d. from Mr. W. M. Fehon, of the railway department, as a donation to the institution.

To-day, at St. George's-hall "Christmas in Old England" will be given twice—in the afternoon and in the evening. Hitherto there has been nothing as regards the entrance to the hall to show that there was any such entertainment within; but a judicious change has been made in this respect. Now an illuminated copy of one of the admirable pictures of the diorama placed over the doorway, indicates the entrance to a place of popular amusement, and the "sign" may not be without its due effect. The whole entertainment goes more and more smoothly and successfully as it is repeated from evening to evening.

The programme at the Haymarket Theatre last evening was the same as on the previous night; and Mr. Barlow was again successful in his efforts to amuse his audience.

At the Theatre Royal, "The Stranger" drew a good house last evening, the never-failing attractions of this play losing nothing of their seeming perennial beauties for the admirers of domestic trials. Mr. Barry Sullivan played the Stranger, and Mrs. R. Heir was the Mrs. Haller of the evening. To-night, a grand complimentary benefit will be given to Mr. Sullivan, whose liberal management, not less than his great talents as an actor, entitle him to the earnest support of the patrons and lovers of the English drama, produced as the good old and the best new plays of the legitimate school have been during the period for which Mr. Barry Sullivan has been lessee of the principal theatre of this metropolis.

A concert in aid of the Melbourne Orphan Asylum, at the Botanical Gardens, advertised for this afternoon, offers a most attractive array of talent, both vocal and instrumental. It commences at three o'clock.

TELEGRAPHIC DESPATCHES.

(FROM OUR OWN CORRESPONDENTS.)

ECHUCA, FRIDAY.

Mr. Grassie's sheep crossed the Murray at Moama to-day, on free punt.

SYDNEY, THURSDAY.

Mr. Kean played "Hamlet" last night, to the largest house ever assembled in this city. Hundreds were turned away.

Mr. Silvester, the oldest reporter in the colony, died to-day.

The wool sales were inanimate, through the non-arrival of the English mail.

Escorts, 4,760oz.

The debate on the tariff continues, and is unlikely to finish this week.

Maize, 4s. 8d.

Sailed.—Urara, for Brisbane.

FRIDAY.

In *Mate v. Kidd*, of Albury, the judges have decided, on plaintiff's demurrer, that the mortgagee in possession could not accept surrender of the lease in prejudice of mortgagor's interest, and that action lies by the mortgagee against the lessees for rent.

A public meeting of the mercantile community was held to-day, at the Exchange, to consider the new tariff. A number of protectionist rowdies obtained admittance, and caused such annoyance that they were ejected. Resolutions condemning the *ad valorem* duties were passed.

Southern mail, near Yass. They coolly examined the letters, and abstracted the contents.

The Himalaya's mail closes at noon on Monday. The Wonga Wonga sails for Melbourne to-morrow. She will leave there again on Wednesday.

The tariff debate is unfinished; an amendment is proposed, adding agricultural produce to the list of dutiable goods.

Sailed.—Lindsay, for Otago; Kangaroo, for Auckland; Amherst, whaling.

BRISBANE, THURSDAY.

To-day being the anniversary of the Separation, public holiday is kept, and a Royal salute was fired. The anniversary regatta was very successful.

The erection of the telegraph line to Moreton Island is commenced.

Rockhampton advices state several acts of incendiarism have been discovered; and the recent fire was thus caused. The guilty party is not yet discovered.

The telegraph reports a vessel ashore on the bar of Richmond river.

ADELAIDE, FRIDAY.

The Governor returned last night.

A dangerous disease has appeared among the cattle at Mintaro. An inquiry is instituted.

Government, on considering the outrages by the blacks in the far north, are inclined to adopt the native police system. Magistrates and the protector of aborigines have been sent to inquire.

The Murray steamer Bunyip, with 500 bales, caught fire at Chambers's station, and was totally consumed. Three men were drowned, two were burnt to death, and several were severely burnt.

Arrived.—Nightingale, from Auckland.

WEEKLY ABSTRACT OF BIRTHS AND DEATHS.

Abstract of Births and Deaths Registered in the Metropolitan and Suburban Registration Districts during the week ending December 5, 1863:—

District.	Deputy Registrar.	Births.	Deaths.
Boroondara	J. D. Bragge	3	0
Brighton	S. P. Simmonds	4	0
Brunswick	Joseph George	3	1
Collingwood	Samuel Allen	24	11
Flemington	Joseph Paterson	3	0
Footscray	B. Robinson	1	0
Kew	F. Barnard	2	0
Melbourne, S.	Ellen Tierney	14	15
Melbourne, N.	G. F. Nagle	20	10
Prahran	John Tulloch	8	0
Richmond	W. H. Lagoe	11	3
Sandridge	Andrew Plummer	4	2
Emerald-hill	Andrew Plummer	9	2
South Yarra	E. B. Taylor	4	0
St. Kilda	F. T. van Hemert	2	0
Williamstown	Edmund Burke	3	2
		125	44

Cases of scarlet fever are reported from the districts of North Melbourne, Richmond, and South Yarra; but none have been fatal. At Brunswick there was one case of diphtheria, which ended fatally. The other districts are reported healthy.

WILLIAM HENRY ARCHER,
Registrar-General.
Registrar General's Office, Melbourne,
Dec. 10, 1863.

BY THE TELEGRAPH ACT, passed at the end of last session, a person in the employ of a telegraphic company who shall wilfully or negligently omit to transmit or deliver a message, or shall divulge the purport of one, is liable to a penalty of £20. The Board of Trade have powers to compel a company to erect a line of wire for the exclusive use of Her Majesty, and the Secretary of State, in case of an emergency, can issue a warrant, and obtain sole possession of the wires.—*London Paper.*

SPECIAL CRIMINAL SITTINGS.

NEW COURT-HOUSE.—FRIDAY, DEC. 11.
(Before his Honour Mr. Justice Barry.)
THE QUEEN V. GODDARD.

Dr. MACKAY made an application to the Court with reference to the sentence passed the previous day on Goddard and Branch, for assault with intent, &c., on Mary Fraser. He observed that, while entertaining the greatest respect for his Honour's opinion, and believing the sentence passed to be perfectly correct, it was his duty to ask permission to draw attention to authorities at some convenient period before the rising of the Court, or at the adjournment of the sittings, so that, if the sentence were accidentally or in any way erroneous, the Court might amend.

His HONOUR.—What is your view?

Dr. MACKAY.—Your Honour passed sentence of ten years' hard labour on the roads on each of the two prisoners. I am under the impression that the sentence should be two years' hard labour on the roads.

His HONOUR.—The course open to Goddard is to appeal.

Dr. MACKAY.—The only course would be by *certiorari* before the full Court. The reason I mention the matter now is, that should the sentence be erroneous—which I am not presumptuous enough to say is the case—and should the Court rise without attention being called to the subject, there would be no power to amend. There would then be a failure of justice.

His HONOUR.—I don't apprehend that, I assure you.

Dr. MACKAY.—If the prisoner were liable only to a certain modicum of punishment, it would be my duty to see that he received no greater sentence than the law prescribes.

His HONOUR.—I don't see what benefit will arise from the proceeding.

Dr. MACKAY.—Should I succeed in convincing your Honour's mind, by submitting authorities, that the sentence was erroneous, I presume your Honour would order the continuance of the sittings for the amendment of the sentence. Should I not succeed, the sentence would remain, and it would be open to the prisoner, if he felt aggrieved, to take any course that he might be advised afterwards.

His HONOUR.—Certainly. The Court can correct any errors which appear during the session; but it is not convenient to hear the argument now. I do not know what will be the last day of this session; it all depends upon the duration of the trial now proceeding.

Dr. MACKAY.—Perhaps your Honour will adjourn the case until the next session, and fix a day for the hearing of the argument.

His HONOUR.—I cannot do that, because I shall not sit then; but on the last day of this session the matter can be mentioned.

TRIAL OF THE PROVIDENT INSTITUTE DIRECTORS.—SECOND DAY.

THE QUEEN V. HANCOCK AND SAWELL.

The trial of Theodore Hancock and Henry Pownall Sawell, directors of the Provident Institute, for conspiracy to defraud, was resumed.

The counsel engaged in the case were—Mr. Adamson, for the prosecution; Mr. Dawson and Mr. Fellows for Hancock; Dr. Sewell and Mr. Hughes, for Sawell.

Mr. Pavey was examined at great length as to the contents of the directors' minute-books. He read entries of proceedings at meetings—some of which were signed by Sawell, and others by Hancock, as chairman—giving the names of the directors represented as being present at each meeting. On the reading of an entry, dated November 7, 1861, and signed, "J. G. Foxton, chairman,"

Mr. ADAMSON tendered the entries in the minute-books as evidence.

Mr. DAWSON objected to their reception as evidence, on the ground—first, that an entry in a book was not evidence that the directors named were present; and, secondly, that the directors could not be bound by any of the acts specified in the absence of proof that they were actually present.

Dr. SEWELL contended that the evidence was not admissible against the defendants, unless the person signing the minutes could be connected with them.

His HONOUR ruled that there was enough evidence to connect the defendants with the books, and, therefore, to warrant the admission of the books; and, further, that the evidence was launched sufficiently to allow of the use of the books as evidence of proceedings on occasions when defendants were not present. As to the effect of the evidence, that was a totally different matter.

Mr. Pavey was then examined as to further entries in the minute books. Among them were entries relating to the passing of the balance sheets, the purchase of Provident Institute shares, and advances on account of Enoch Chambers, the steamer Diamond, the St. Kilda and Brighton Railway shares, &c. The witness also spoke to entries in an agenda [illegible] book, and the capital ledger.

Cross-examined by Mr. FELLOWS.—I recollect [illegible] a special meeting in the Insolvent Court. I advised the official assignee not to consent unless the person asking for the meeting paid the expenses. I believe Mr. Hancock offered himself for examination only on one occasion, but when he was examined at our instance he was represented by counsel, and had opportunities, from time to time, of giving explanations. I recollect Mr. Hancock applying for a judge's order for a meeting. I took out a judge's summons to set aside that order, on the ground that such order ought not to be obtained, save by the official assignee. Hancock said he would pay the costs of calling the meeting, but no offer was made to pay the costs of the assignee for being represented at the meeting.

By Dr. SEWELL.—I was always anxious to protect the estate from expense. Our costs amount perhaps to between £3,000 and £4,000. A special act of Parliament was required, and there have been heavy insolvency proceedings. We were retained in this business on the 12th September, 1862—the day after the stoppage of the institute. The costs of the last trial amount, I believe, to between £1,000 and £2,000; but they have not yet been taxed. This prosecution was commenced by information filed by Mr. Langlands, the trade assignee, and did not come under the cognizance of the Crown until the parties were committed for trial.

Edward James Goold, a clerk to the St. Kilda and Brighton Railway Company, produced the subscription contract, dated the 7th February, 1861, for extending that railway. It was signed by the two defendants, and also by Arthur Anderson and J. G. Foxton, each person being represented as subscribing £4,000.

The next witness was Mr. Joseph Macardy, the founder of the Provident Institute, who was about giving evidence as to the circumstances under which the concern was established, when

Dr. SEWELL submitted that anything which occurred before the execution of the supplemental deed of settlement could not be taken as evidence against the defendants.

Mr. ADAMSON observed that the prosecution impugned the transactions of the defendants from beginning to end.

His HONOUR said the first count of the information accused the defendants of malpractices from the commencement of the institute in 1855 until the stoppage in 1862. However, he would take a note of the objection.

Mr. Macardy, examined.—The institute was started in June, 1856. The promoters were Messrs. Hellicar, Comer, Muir, Sawell, Hammill, Mackillop, Tootle, and Hancock. Each of these gentlemen, with the exception of Mr. Hancock, contributed £50 each towards establishing the institute, and Mr. Hancock rendered professional services which were considered equal to the amount. Messrs. Hellicar, Comer, Hammill, and Muir, afterwards retired, and were repaid the amounts which they respectively contributed. This left the capital of the institute £150. We had no other moneys than those which we received as deposits. Mr. Porter was afterwards brought in, but he paid nothing. He attended fifty board meetings; and being entitled to £1 for each meeting, he received a voucher for £50.

His HONOUR.—That did not increase the capital very much. It may not have diminished it.

Examination continued.—The preliminary expenses amounted, I suppose, to between £300 and £400. These expenses were paid out of moneys received as deposits. The society was a mutual society. During the time I was connected with the institute, investments were made only on freehold property, and never more than to one-third the value. The interest which we received varied from twelve and a-half to fifteen per cent. I remember Hancock mentioning at a board meeting, towards the close of 1857, that butter would be a good investment, but I instantly rose from the table and left the room. I retired from the institute in January, 1858.

Cross-examined by Mr. FELLOWS.—Depositors received ten per cent. No interest was allowed for a broken quarter. The deposits in the institute at the time I left amounted to £57,000, and they were increasing at the rate of £2,000 per week. When I retired Mr. Porter agreed to pay me £2,500.

By Dr. SEWELL.—When I left, the institute was perfectly solvent.

Mr. J. P. Mackillop.—I was auditing accountant to the Provident Institute from its formation up to 1859. The number of shares issued under the supplemental deed of settlement was 25,000; of these 8,500 were given to the promoters as paid-up shares. The remaining 16,500 were issued to the public, and calls to the amount of 10s. per share were paid. Of the 16,500 shares, 5,000 were taken by the directors (Hancock had 1,000 and Sawell 1,000), and the calls were paid "in account." The balance of profit to the end of June, 1859, when the old concern closed, was ascertained to be £3,019. This was divided among the proprietors, [illegible] were two. There was a balance sheet for the half year ending June 30, 1859, and it was passed about the following December. The money was paid to the several proprietors, or carried to their credit, in June.

Mr. ADAMSON observed that this was an irregularity, because the division took place by anticipation before the balance sheet was settled. It was also a fraud, because the deed of settlement of 1858 provided that the profits of the institute, after deducting the incidental expenses, should be divided rateably among the depositors.

Examination continued.—The amount paid by the directors up to the time of the stoppage, in the re-purchase of Provident Institute shares, was, according to the "capital ledger" produced, £12,537 10s. The effect of this re-purchase was to withdraw shares from the market and place them in the hands of the managing director. After these shares were re-purchased, they were credited with dividend, and the amount was placed to the credit of revenue. Some of the shares were re-purchased at a premium—some at par. The dividend, notwithstanding, was entered in the balance sheet in one bulk sum, as "Dividend to shareholders."

The witness was still under examination when the Court adjourned.

THE GAZETTE.

The following notifications appeared in the *Gazette* of yesterday:—

CORONER.—Edward William Plews, Esq., to be a coroner of Victoria, and to act at Newbury, Blue Mountain gold-field.

MANAGER OF A COMMON.—Peter M'Pherson to be a manager of the Bet-bet Farmers' Common No. 1, *vice* Thomas Wright, deceased.

COMMON SCHOOL COMMITTEE.—*Corrigendum.*—The name "Joshua Dryden," published in the *Government Gazette* of the 4th December, 1863, page 2,712, as a member of the Local Committee of the Pentland-hills School, No. 701, should be "John Dryden."

RESIGNATIONS.—Dennis Patrick Keogh, Esq., St. Kilda, as a magistrate; and Captain George Ryland, of his commission in the Castlemaine Volunteer Rifles.

MEDICAL BOARD OF VICTORIA.—Legally qualified medical practitioners, to whom certificates have been granted:—No. 409, 4th December, 1863, James Johnston, Carngham, Lic. Fac. Phys. Surg., Glasg., 1861; No. 409, 4th December, 1863, John Moore M'Neece, Lower Huntley, Lic. Fac. Phys. Surg., Glasg., 1854; No. 410, 4th December, 1863, John Rule, Maldstone, M.D. Univ. New York, U.S., 1862; Mem. R. Coll. Surg., Eng., 1806.

CONTRACTS ACCEPTED.—Ballarat to Ararat-road—supply of metal, £50, Andrew Dawse, jun.; Ballarat to Hamilton-road—constructing sixteen chains of road near Hamilton, £250, Thomas Clayton; Ararat to Raglan-road—rebuilding Dobie's-bridge, £134 14s., Thomas Walker; erection of bridge over west branch of the Goulburn, at Woods-point, £124 15s., G. W. Maxwell; erection of bridge over east branch of the Goulburn, at Woods-point, £75 5s., C. H. Edwards; Ballarat to Hamilton-road—rep[illegible] to bridge at Green-hill, £300, Daniel Barn; Ararat to Seaboard-road—repairs to Ross's bridge approaches over the Hopkins, £70, James Ladden; Ararat to Raglan-road—rebuilding Dobie's bridge, £350, Thos. Walker.

REFORM ASSOCIATION.

TO THE EDITOR OF THE ARGUS.

Sir,—With the discretion which characterizes the management of your paper, a full report was omitted of the proceedings last night at the Protestant-hall, but from the *résumé* in your news columns I judge that such material as was there spewed forth would form excellent stock for the "soup meagre" daily ladled out to suit the diseased palates of the readers of our sensation journals.

As an old colonist I beg leave to raise my voice, through the medium of *The Argus*, against the religious and class distinctions which, through such societies as the Reform Association, are endeavoured to be perpetuated in this sunny land of our adoption. Having witnessed and read of the Orange and like proceedings in Belfast, Liverpool, and North America, I deeply lament, with sane men squabbling as [illegible] and, following out egg should be broken [illegible] that the fire at the Protestant-hall should be put out by an intelligent press after the manner of our admired Gulliver.

As to the personal attack made by Mr. Jones, of Bourke-street (it's only known to Mr. Archer how many Joneses are in it) as to Mr. O'Shanassy's birth and parentage, *The Argus* has most properly treated the remark by placing it within quotation commas, as it will show what a consummate amount of impudence and misrepresentation a man can arrive at under a semi-tropical climate.

As in this colony, very wisely, each individual is treated upon his own deserts, we do not ask a man in the afternoon what he has had for breakfast, so I query through *The Argus* where Mr. Jones got the privilege of calling such a man as Mr. O'Shanassy a "low-born cur." In putting that question, Sir, I feel myself justified from the fact that I know from inquiry (perhaps impertinent) that he is the son of a most respectable middleman in county of Tipperary. He was educated, as I can learn, for the profession of surveyor or engineer, and by his steady industry and consistency has made himself a fortune and name under disadvantages which would discourage the Joneses.

While addressing the public through *The Argus*, it might be as well to say that every man of experience and honest feeling in this country has resolved to discountenance any war proposed to be waged against a race or class, and from the conduct of the Jewish community in not eating of this tempting apple of reform held out to them we may expect that those men whose only capital is to foist themselves into the notice of society by creating troubled routs in that society, may be found to turn round on their bigoted dupes, and say "It was I did it."

I send you my address for the information of Mr. Jones and his friends, and if the old *prestige* which Mr. O'Shanassy's name has earned in India, Australia, and Limerick, as well as on the fields of battle where the British won, is not sufficient to satisfy his taste for popularity, I beg leave to [illegible] *The Argus*, that I won't call him out.

Yours truly,
A PEACEABLE CITIZEN.
Hawthorn, Dec. 11.

THE FRENCH EMPEROR'S SHEEP.—It may be remembered that the French Emperor some time since sent to the Agricultural Exhibition and Cattle Show of Odensee (Denmark) a lot of sheep from the fold of Rambouillet, which excited general admiration. After the close of the exhibition, the Agricultural Society, as a mark of gratitude to His Majesty, sent him a gold medal accompanied by the following letter:—"Sire,—The agricultural population of Denmark have been justly proud of the high favour with which your Majesty has honoured them, by deigning to send to their exhibition a specimen of the celebrated flock of the Imperial fold of Rambouillet. They have regarded that gracious act not only as a mark of kindness towards agriculture in general, the development of which your Majesty so strongly encourages in France, but also as a mark of friendly interest for Denmark. They, and with them the entire country, have therefore felt a sentiment of deep gratitude, the homage of which, in the name of the society, I beg to lay at the feet of your Majesty. To perpetuate the remembrance of the exhibition of 1863, the society decided on striking off medals, two of them in gold—one intended for the King of Denmark, and the other for your Imperial Majesty. Our Sovereign has already deigned to accept this gift, and it is with his authorisation that I dare, Sire, to solicit the name of my fellow-countrymen, to solicit your Majesty's acceptance of this tribute of profound respect and of eternal gratitude.—I am, Sire, &c., T. FONNESBECH, President of the Agricultural Society."—*Express*, Sept. 18.

PETROLEUM.—Since the 1st of January last, up to June 1st, no less than 10,110,801 gallons of petroleum have been exported from New York to foreign parts, against 2,920,089 in 1862. In addition to the above 5,180,762 were exported from Baltimore, Philadelphia, Boston, and Portland, making a grand total of 15,221,572 gallons.

THE NEW ZEALAND WAR.

THE ENGAGEMENT AT RANGARIRI.

(FROM OUR SPECIAL CORRESPONDENT.)
RANGARIRI, Nov. 26.

The most brilliant engagement of the war took place at Rangariri, on Friday, the 20th inst., with a result which renders the triumph of the British arms secure. General Cameron assaulted the enemy's fortified position, and, after a heavy loss of 130 men killed and wounded, captured the stronghold. The event has taken the public here by surprise; but despite the price paid for it, the victory has been gladly hailed, for the hope is that it may save further effusions of the blood of our countrymen.

After their evacuation of Meremere last month, the hostile Maories retired to Rangariri, where they received such powerful reinforcements that at one time 2,000 men are believed to have been in the place. The difficulty of feeding so large a number was felt, however, and led to several bodies being moved into the country, to the eastward and southward. General Cameron, receiving private information to this effect, made his attack when the defenders did not muster half the number stated. Profiting by his experience at Meremere, and having the requisite forces at his command, he advanced a strong force with such secrecy and despatch as to take the enemy, well-informed and vigilant as they generally are, by surprise, and, cutting off their retreat by a skilful flank movement, he struck the heaviest blow they have yet experienced.

The rebels, when they retreated southwards up the Waikato river in the early part of the month, immediately commenced strengthening their position at Rangariri, where they had already erected formidable works. The Waikato, a river about as wide as the Yarra above Footscray, has lofty banks in the neighbourhood of Meremere; but twelve miles higher up the high land recedes away some nine or ten miles; and in the space between the river and the hills there is a lake named Waikare, four miles long by three in breadth. [illegible] on the most northern of those channels is Rangariri. The fortifications are constructed upon a hill overlooking the channel, and probably about eighty or ninety feet in height. It is half a mile from the river, and rises from a level plain, which may be said to be unwooded—for though there are fern and scrub, there are no trees. Approaching from the northward, up the river from Meremere, a flax-swamp is found to extend from the mouth of the channel inwards to the back of Rangariri, and the ground is further broken by a small backwater pond of the Waikato. In fact, the position is on a spot the only approach to which by land is on the Meremere side. Advancing in this direction a thick tea-tree scrub is met with, and this extends well-nigh down to the commencement of the rise. Beyond this point the ground is open. The peculiar configuration of the hill led the military authorities to under-estimate the strength of the position when they took their preliminary survey. They saw long lines of rifle-pits extending to the summit of the hill, flanked and protected with the greatest ingenuity, but they did not see that the hill after dipping to the lake rose again, and that here a formidable fortification had been constructed—a square redoubt, surrounded by a dry ditch nine feet wide, and with a total height from the parapet to the bottom of over eighteen feet. A work of this class could not be carried except by escalade, and no scaling ladders of sufficient length were provided. The rifle-pits should rather be called trenches. They are excavations some three feet wide, with the earth taken out, so as to make a shelving parapet eighteen inches high. The [illegible] leans over, and takes his aim in the most convenient position possible. Every dozen yards traverses—earthen mounds placed crosswise are erected—to confine the damage done by shells to a narrow space. The lines also are not straight, but form every variety of angle, so that the one may support the other, and at Rangariri, where there are many lines, a communication is opened with each by narrow passages, through which only one man can walk abreast. This opening allows the defenders to retire; while the attacking party, compelled to advance in single file, are liable to be literally mowed down. Had other proof been needed, the fortifications at Rangariri would show conclusively what adepts the natives are at field engineering. They were not nearly completed either, for at the river side extensive works were still in progress. An explanation, I feel, hardly conveys the idea of the strength of the position which at once strikes the onlooker. Looking at it, the wonder is, not that our loss was so heavy, but that our troops accomplished what they did. General Cameron says that with half the number of men the defenders had he would defy an army to take the position by storm, and I am sure military authorities must admit the success of the English forces to be a most brilliant feat of arms.

General Cameron's plan of action was to attack the enemy in front from the land, and simultaneously to land a force from the river to take the works at the rear, and cut off all retreat. For some days before troops were congregated at Meremere, and when, on Wednesday, Captain Mercer was ordered to the front with two Armstrong guns it began to be generally known that an assault upon the rebel position was in immediate contemplation. The troops, disappointed with the Meremere affair, and annoyed by the harassing bush duties imposed upon them, were eager to be led where they could meet their foe. As for the tars from the Curaçoa and Miranda, who manned the river flotilla, they were absolutely enthusiastic, and were to be seen sharpening their cutlasses and slashing away at trees for practice, in all directions. Events commenced early on Friday morning. By nine o'clock 1,145 men and forty-eight commissioned officers were on their way to the scene of action, independent of the marines and sailors, who would muster 250 men more. There were no volunteers engaged in the contest. General Cameron decided to act solely with troops of the line. The corps represented were—the Royal Artillery, under Captain Mercer; the Royal Engineers, under Colonel Mould; the 12th Regiment, under Captain Cole; the 14th, under Colonel Austin; the 40th, under Colonel Leslie; and the 65th, under Colonel Wyatt. Once more the brunt of the action fell upon the gallant 65th, who, after nearly seventeen years' service in the colony, have thus won another laurel.

The main body of the troops left Meremere soon after dawn on Friday morning, and halted eight miles from that place. Here they were joined by the general, who had come from head-quarters, at the Queen's Redoubt, in the steamer Pioneer. The Pioneer with the Avon, embarked also the detachment of the 40th regiment on duty, and proceeded with these troops up the river to the rebel stronghold. The four iron-plated gunboats, which had been armed each with a four and a-half inch howitzer, also went up in tow of the steamers; and so well were both advances timed, that when the flotilla came within range, at half-past three p.m., Captain Mercer was just placing his guns in position. Nothing was seen of the enemy either by river or on the march until Rangariri was nearly reached, when numbers of men were noticed flocking to the works; and the first gun fired was by the rebels, from the crest of the hill. Shell practice was at once commenced, from both howitzers and Armstrongs, and was continued for upwards of an hour, the enemy replying by volleys of musketry, which were quite harmless, as the troops were out of range. The bombardment did damage to the works, the shells bursting repeatedly right on them and sending up the loose earth in columns; but it is questionable whether it caused much loss to the defenders, who were too securely ensconced. At half-past four the steamers slackened their firing, as the signal for assault was made. Three hundred men of the 65th, with smaller detachments of the 12th and 14th, were told off for the storming party. The 65th advanced in four companies—the right under Captain Gresson, the centre (the ladder party) under Lieutenant Toker, the left under Lieutenant Talbot, and the reserve under Lieutenant Pennefather. From the flotilla the advance of the men could be plainly seen. First came the warning roll of the drums, and then on dashed our gallant soldiers from the thick tea-tree jungle through the scrub and fern, which was breast high, their arms glittering in the sun, and their cheers ringing down the breeze. The rugged ground broke their line, and the enemy's shot caused gaps, which could not always be closed. The men did not reach the work in field day order, but they dashed up to the rifle pits with unbroken spirit; and how can I describe the feelings of the spectators when the gallant band became lost in the white smoke which curled up from the ascent and from the brow of the hill, and when the crackling roll of musketry which followed told that the Maories were pouring in their fire from all their hiding-places? Their firing was better than on any previous occasion. It was evident that they had secured many rifles, and as they lay securely protected, they could take deliberate aim. Before the first work was reached, Captain Gresson had fallen, but Ensign Spiller was at once at the head of the company, cheering on the men. The first obstacle was a wide ditch, inside the parapet of which were the lines of rifle-pits. The ladder party rushed forward, bridged over the space, and, headed by Lieut. Talbot, who was first man on the rampart, sprang over into the trenches, while Private Gallagher planted the 65th's regimental colours on the work. Now the bayonets would have had full scope, but the Maories shrank from the charge, and fled with such precipitancy that but few met their death by this weapon. Chased impetuously by the storming party into the inner and flanking lines, the foe abandoned these also, numbers springing into the swamp and lake, and others seeking shelter in the inner and heretofore concealed works. Simultaneously with the advance of the land storming party, the 40th were put on shore—not without much difficulty, for the Pioneer seemed hard to manage—carried the unfinished works on the flat, and, sweeping round the base of the hill, joined the 65th in pouring in volleys upon the flying foe. The hill on this side sinks down almost precipitously to the flax swamp, but the Maories, in their desperation, hesitated not, but flung themselves down, and sought shelter from the deadly storm in grass and flax and suffocating mud. Many did escape, but the troops lining the edges of the gully, continued pouring in their fire while there was a foe to be seen, and from the space which had to be traversed, the execution done must have been most severe. On the lake there were several canoes, and the flying wretches in their mad terror crowded some of these till they were overturned, while a shell from Captain Mercer's battery [illegible] fragments from stem to stern.

The exterior lines thus fell into our hands without any great loss, but it was now that the strength of the inner position was discovered. A regular bastioned redoubt had been constructed, surrounded by a dry ditch nine feet wide, and having a height, as already remarked, of over eighteen feet from the ditch to the parapet. Orders were issued to storm the place, but the scaling-ladders were found to be too short, and the men fell back before the murderous fire of the Maories. The high ground to the left of the works was literally honeycombed with zig-zag rifle-pits, and the Maories, fairly brought to bay, fought with the utmost determination—a determination which rivalled that of our own forces. Had ladders been available, the place would have been stormed at once, but when two of the ordinary escalade ladders were lashed together, they did not reach within four feet of the top of the parapet. Three were planted in the ditch, and our men swarmed up them only to be picked off by the Maories as they showed above the crest. Here Lieut. Murphy received his death wound, and fell over into the enemy's works, so that his body could not be recovered at the time. Several of the men also fell over, and when the place was taken, three of them were found to have been stripped of their clothing. The only entrance to the redoubt was by one of the narrow passages already alluded to, and endeavours were next made to take the place by storm, through this approach. The 65th, the 40th, the 14th, the 12th, and the Artillery were led up by their officers again and again, and were as often repulsed. The Maories had all their rifles bearing on this spot. These rifles were those they had obtained from the 40th on the Drury road. They had also revolvers, with which they shot many of our men at close quarters, and they had bayonets lashed on to poles ten feet long. General Cameron had stationed himself near the battery during the early part of the day [illegible] occasion it may be question whether he was not too rash in exposing his person. One of his orderlies was shot down by his side. Lieutenant Talbot received his wound while leading one of the storming parties. Lieutenant Alexander, of the Curaçoa, and Midshipman Watkins, both fell in the same manner—the one severely, and the other mortally wounded. Captain Mercer made an attack at the head of his artillery corps, who were armed with revolvers. Cheering on his men, he dashed in so far that when he sank down, also with a mortal wound, he could not be recovered. He dragged himself to a corner of the trench, where he was screened from the enemy's fire, but no one could pass the line. After several had attempted it, Captain Mercer's servant, Gunner Colverwell, with devoted bravery, insisted upon rushing in to convey water to his officer. The second he showed upon the open ground he was brought down by a shot which passed through his body. Later on, Lieutenant Pickard crawled in the dusk on his belly to the fatal spot, and took water to the sufferer, who was in agonizing pain. Lieutenant Pickard saw by his daring visit that it was impossible for the place to be stormed, or Mercer relieved if the approach remained open. A sap was therefore commenced, and was covered with planks as it was continued. Captain Mercer was not reached until four hours after he had fallen, and during the whole of this time he was sensible, and endured the full horrors of his situation. Matters became so serious that the General despatched an orderly in hot haste to Commodore Wiseman, who was in personal command of the flotilla, to send up every available sailor and marine. The request was gladly complied with by both officers and men, and under the charge of Commander Mayne, of the Eclipse, the blue jackets dashed to the front. They rushed into the fatal passage, but even their spirit could not carry them through it; they tried again, and came back with their commander and Lieutenant Downes, of the Miranda, badly wounded. Again and again was beheld the unwonted spectacle of British troops having to retire before the fire of a savage foe. Darkness gradually came on, and the general gave orders to stay the assaults, in order that a properly arranged attack might be made by daylight. For the time, at this point, we were held in check. With the night-time came rain, and a cold biting wind, but no one could stop to think of discomfort; there was too much anxiety and misery for all for that. General Cameron was everywhere inspiriting the men and forming new arrangements. He determined to effect a breach by undermining the parapets of the works, and blowing them up. It was found, however, impossible to do this, the soil being so friable as to fall in wherever a drive was attempted. Still the height of the parapet was materially reduced. Guns were put into position to render the breach perfectly practicable, and a storming party was told off. The men not actually at work lay on their arms, completely surrounding the redoubt. The escape of the Maories was thus rendered impossible. They were conscious of the fact, but seemed defiant and determined to resist to the last. All night long they maintained a howling, so hideous at times that it was hard to believe that the sound proceeded from human beings. With daylight, when they saw the preparations made, and how their fate was certain, their spirit failed them, and the white flag was displayed. The general, with a Government interpreter at once communicated with the head chief, and informed him that no terms could be made, and that if the assault were not to be made, there must be an unconditional surrender. Without much consultation this was done; and, amid tumultuous cheering on the part of the troops, the Maories marched out of the place. Thus Rangariri passed into our hands, but at what a price! Our loss is as follows:—

Officers killed and mortally wounded	4
Men do.	35
	39
Officers wounded	11
Men do.	80
	130

The enemy's loss has not yet been dis-

THE NEW ZEALAND WAR.
THE ENGAGEMENT AT RANGARIRI.

...

The most brilliant engagement of the war took place at Rangariri, on Friday, the 20th inst., with a result which renders the triumph of the British arms secure. General Cameron assaulted the enemy's fortified position, and, after a heavy loss of 130 men killed and wounded, captured the stronghold. The event has taken the public here by surprise; but despite the price paid for it, the victory has been gladly hailed, for the hope is that it may save further effusions of the blood of our countrymen.

...

The main body of the troops left Meremere soon after dawn on Friday morning, and halted eight miles from that place. Here they were joined by the general, who had come from head-quarters, at the Queen's Redoubt, in the steamer Pioneer. The Pioneer with the Avon, embarked also the detachment of the 40th regiment on duty, and proceeded with these troops up the river to the rebel stronghold. The four iron-plated gunboats, which had been armed each with a four and a-half inch howitzer, also went up in tow of the steamers; and so well were both advances time, that when the flotilla came within range, at half-past three p.m., Caption Mercer was just placing his guns in position. Nothing was seen of the enemy either by river or on the march until Rangariri was nearly reached, when numbers of men were noticed flocking to the works; and the first gun fired was by the rebels, from the crest of the hill. Shell practice was at once commenced, from both howitzers and Armstrongs, and was continued for upwards of an hour, the enemy replying by volleys of musketry, which were quite harmless, as the troops were out of range. The bombardment did damage to the works, the shells bursting repeatedly right on them and sending up the loose earth in columns; but it is questionable whether it caused much loss to the defenders, who were too securely ensconced. At half-past four the steamers slackened their firing, as the signal for assault was made ... First came the warning roll of the drums, and then on dashed our gallant soldiers from the thick tea-tree jungle through the scrub and fern, which was breast high, their arms glittering in the sun, and their cheers ringing down the breeze. The rugged ground broke their line, and the enemy's shot caused gaps, which could not always be closed. The men did not reach the work in field day order, but they dashed up to the rifle pits with unbroken spirit; and how can I describe the feelings of the spectators when the gallant band became lost in the white smoke which curled up from the ascent and from the brow of the hill, and when the crackling roll of musketry which followed told that the Maories were pouring in their fire from all their hiding-places? Their firing was better than on any previous occasion. It was evident that they had secured many rifles, and as they lay securely protected, the could take deliberate aim ... Now the bayonets would have had full scope, but the Maories shrank from the charge, and fled with such precipitancy that but few met their death by this weapon. Chased impetuously by the storming party into the inner and flanking lines, the foe abandoned these also ...

Attempted assassination 32

Prince Alfred in Sydney, 1868

DESPITE A GROWING SENSE OF A DISTINCTLY AUSTRALIAN SOCIETY, SYDNEY IN 1868 REMAINED LOYAL TO THE BRITISH CROWN. IT CAME AS A DEEP SHOCK TO THE AUSTRALIAN COLONIES THAT A MUCH LONGED FOR AND FETED ROYAL TOUR BY PRINCE ALFRED—SECOND SON AND FOURTH CHILD OF QUEEN VICTORIA—ENDED IN AN ASSASSINATION ATTEMPT.

The prince was attending one of his many official engagements while in Sydney—a fund-raising picnic for the Sydney Sailors' Home at Clontarf on Sydney's north shore on 12 March 1868—when a member of the crowd suddenly pulled out a pistol and shot him in the back from close range. The assailant was quickly caught, but police could extract him only with difficulty from a mob that wanted to lynch him on the spot.

The prince recovered, but Sydney went into both soul-searching and scapegoating. The attacker, Henry O'Farrell, 'declared himself to be Irish', and he was at first assumed to be involved with the Fenian Irish independence movement. Although it was later found he was more, as his defence maintained, 'insane' than politically motivated, the divisions between the mostly Irish Catholics and non-Catholics in the colony were heightened even further. The newspapers fanned public indignation and anti-Irish sentiment boiled over even in parliament: the New South Wales government, including Henry Parkes (1815–1896), passed the *Treason Felony Act* a week later, making it an offence to refuse to drink a toast to the Queen's health.

The day after the assassination attempt nearly 20,000 Sydneysiders attended an 'indignation meeting' and the following week there were 'daily indignation meetings everywhere'. With the news of the world focused on Australia for a change—but for all the wrong reasons—people tried to show that the colony's loyalty to the British Empire was unquestionable.

One of the longer-term results of this display of loyalty was the public subscription fund that aimed 'to raise a permanent and substantial monument in testimony of the heartfelt gratitude of the community at the recovery of His Royal Highness'. The fund was used to build the Royal Prince Alfred Hospital in Sydney, which opened in 1882.

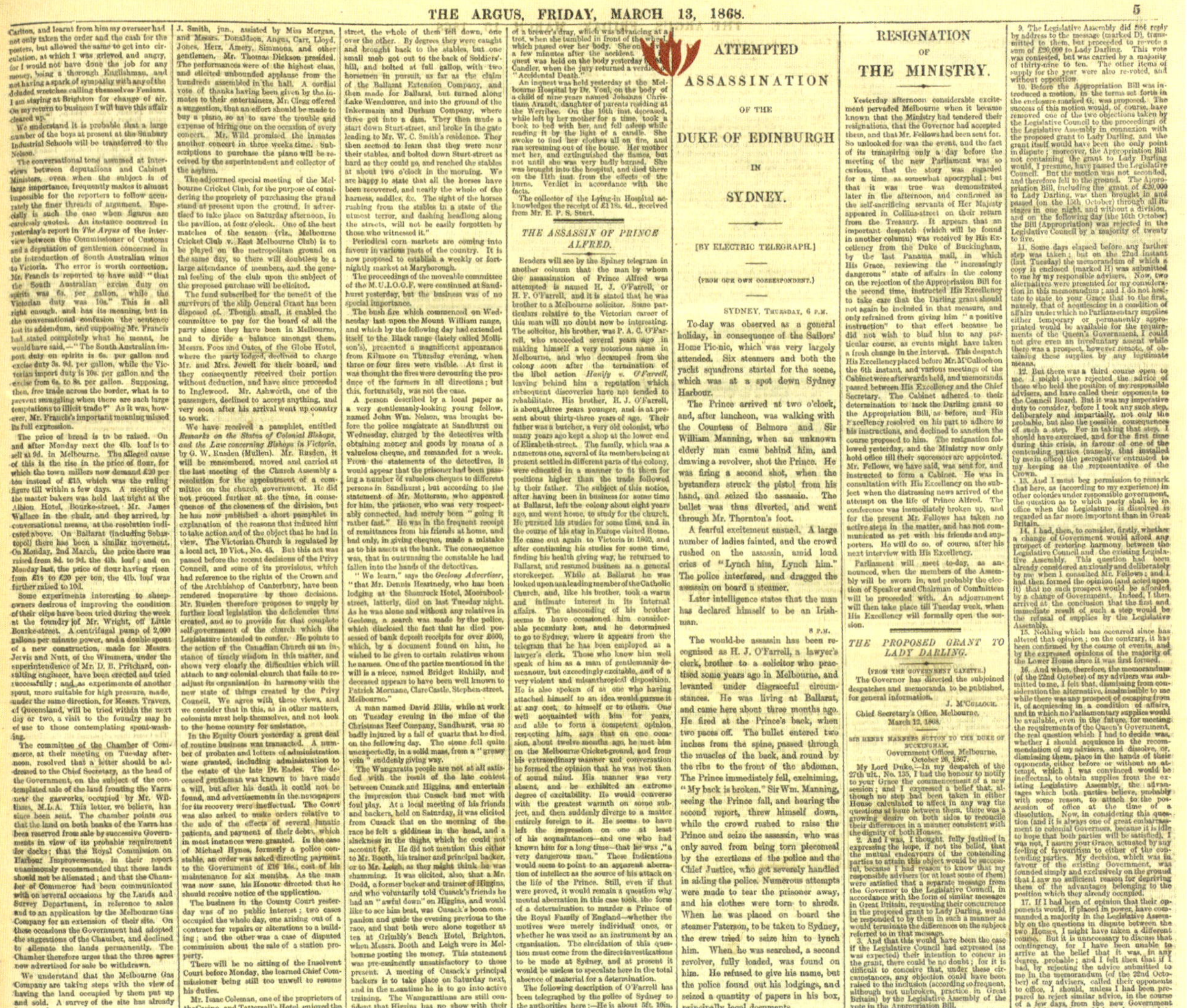
THE ARGUS, FRIDAY, MARCH 13, 1868. 5

ATTEMPTED ASSASSINATION OF THE DUKE OF EDINBURGH IN SYDNEY.

[BY ELECTRIC TELEGRAPH.]

RESIGNATION OF THE MINISTRY.

THE ASSASSIN OF PRINCE ALFRED.

TELEGRAPHIC DESPATCHES.

NEW INSOLVENTS.

LATEST BULLETIN.

THE PROPOSED GRANT TO LADY DARLING.

Reports of the assassination attempt in Melbourne's Argus *of 13 March 1868 had been relayed instantly from Sydney via Telegraphic Despatches. The speedy new service was at first slowed by the different systems used by the rival colonies of New South Wales and Victoria. At the border a written transcript was handed over for re-telegraphing.*

ATTEMPTED ASSASSINATION OF THE DUKE OF EDINBURGH IN SYDNEY.

...

The Prince arrived at two o'clock, and ... was walking with the Countess of Belmore and Sir William Manning, when an unknown elderly man came behind him, and drawing a revolver, shot the Prince. He was firing a second shot, when the bystanders struck the pistol from his had, and seized the assassin. The bullet was thus diverted, and went through Mr. Thornton's foot.

A fearful excitement ensued. A large number of ladies fainted, and the crowd rushed on the assassin, amid loud cries of "Lynch him, Lynch him." The police interfered, and dragged the assassin on board a steamer.

Later intelligence states that the man has declared himself to be an Irishman.

8 PM.

The would-be assassin has been recognised as H. J. O'Farrell, a lawyer's clerk, brother to a solicitor who practised some years ago in Melbourne, and levanted under disgraceful circumstances ... He fired at the Prince's back, when two paces off. The bullet entered two inches from the spine, passed through the muscles of the back, and round by the ribs to the front of the abdomen. The Prince immediately fell, exclaiming, "My back is broken."

This artist's impression of the attempted assassination of the Duke of Edinburgh appeared in the Illustrated Australian News *of 30 March 1868. One of Melbourne's major illustrated papers, it was published by the* Age. *Its monthly publication cycle allowed time for the labour-intensive production of woodblocks for the illustrations, which was impossible for the dailies.*

33 *Blackbirding in the Pacific*

The trial of the crew of the *Carl*, 1872

NEWSPAPERS THROUGHOUT THE COUNTRY CLOSELY FOLLOWED REPORTS OF THE TRIAL OF THE CREW OF THE BLACKBIRDING SHIP *CARL*. BLACKBIRDING WAS THE PRACTICE OF RECRUITING—EVEN KIDNAPPING—PACIFIC ISLANDERS TO WORK IN AUSTRALIA.

When the transportation of convicts to the eastern states ended in the 1850s, new sources of cheap labour were sought, particularly on labour-intensive cotton and sugar-cane plantations in the continent's north. While slavery wasn't officially known in Australia, the indentured or contracted labour practices of the 1860s and 1870s, especially in northern Queensland, came close. Unscrupulous contractors who captained or sent out ships to capture Pacific Islanders for work in Queensland were known as *blackbirders*.

Queensland planters followed the lead of European plantation owners in Fiji and New Caledonia, who from 1864 recruited labour from the Melanesian islands, such as the New Hebrides, the Solomon Islands and New Guinea. Many Islanders were indeed willing to work as indentured labourers for several years on Queensland plantations, given the promise of being taken home to their island at the end of their contract. At the height of the system in the 1880s, Queensland had more than 11,000 Islanders working there every year. However, particularly in the early days of the indentured labour system, there were many abuses by contractors who could make large profits from bringing workers to the colonies. Some labourers were tricked into coming aboard these ships; others were forced aboard; and in some cases ships' crews disguised themselves as missionaries, invited whole villages aboard for a religious service, and then set sail for Queensland.

Several ships were brought to court in the late 1860s, and their owners and crew tried under anti-slavery laws. After several cases failed in court because defence lawyers argued that the crews were not engaging in slavery, a new law was enacted to halt the abuses—the *Kidnapping Act 1872*, which was designed to deal specifically with 'practices scarcely to be distinguished from Slave Trading'.

One blackbirding episode that made headline news was the trial of the crew of the ship *Carl* in 1872. Melbourne's *Argus* printed a special supplement headed 'Carl Outrages', which detailed the forced capture of Islanders and a shipboard massacre. Two of the crew were convicted of manslaughter.

More than 60,000 Pacific Islanders were brought to Australia to work. Most who had not been returned home, as contracted in the indentured labour system, were repatriated in the early 1900s. But many chose to remain in Queensland.

OPPOSITE
The story of the Carl's *blackbirding season and the massacre on board the ship was provided by Seaman George Heath at the trial and reprinted in a special supplement to Melbourne's* Argus *of 21 December 1872. The extensive account reflects the high level of interest in the trial.*

The Argus Supplement.

No. 8,278. MELBOURNE, SATURDAY, DECEMBER 21, 1872. GRATIS.

THE CARL OUTRAGES.

TRIAL OF MOUNT AND MORRIS.

VERDICT OF MANSLAUGHTER.

The trial of Henry Clarke Mount and William Charles Morris for wilful murder on the high seas, was resumed yesterday, in the New Court-house, before his Honour the Chief Justice and a jury of twelve.

Mr. Adamson, assisted by Mr. Garnett and Mr M'Kinley, conducted the prosecution, and Mr. Ireland, Q.C., and Mr. Molesworth the defence.

James Fallon, seaman, whose examination-in-chief was finished the previous day, was placed in the box for cross-examination by Mr. Ireland. He deposed:—I heard about the captain and the mate of the ship being tried in Sydney. It was after that I gave information. It was about 10 or 11 months after I left the ship at Levuka. I saw Superintendent Winch in Sydney. I was going to be tried when I saw him, and I was in custody in the lock-up. I had made a confession to the inspector of police at Newcastle, before I saw Mr. Winch. It was before I was arrested. I was frightened if I told it before I might be done away with. That was why I did not tell it before. I did not place myself under the protection of the police, because they would not keep me all my life. I did not know any better. It was after the captain and mate were sentenced to be hung that I told my story. No bargain was made with me if I gave my evidence, and no promise was made. I don't expect to be tried after giving my evidence, but I may be. They could not find anything against me. I was forced to go in the vessel against my will. I do not remember calling the men up to fire down the hatch at the natives. I did not call Mount up, but may have called Devescovi, the cook. I may have told him that the natives were trying to get up the hatches, and that they would murder us all. I had no hand in firing down the hatch. I fired several shots during the night—two at the commencement. When the lieutenant of the Rosario boarded us I was at the wheel, but I did not tell him I was on board against my will. I would not have been allowed to tell him. I did not tell the consul when I got back to Levuka. It was reported that the first who said anything or got drunk when we got to Levuka would be shot. That was my reason for saying nothing. The statement I made at Newcastle was taken down in writing. After I was removed to Sydney Mr. Winch took down my statement in a room in the court-house. He asked me questions as I went along, but told me he did not want to know anything I did not like to tell him. He said he would not force me to tell him. I do not remember if I was asked any questions as we went along about Mount or Morris. I thought that my evidence was required for a trial at Melbourne, but I did not know against whom. I had not the slightest idea who the prisoners were. Dr. Murray ordered me to fire the shots I did. I did not tip over any canoes, but I sometimes picked up the natives. I was forced to go into the boats. I sometimes refused. The crew whitewashed the hold to prevent the smell. I don't remember that Mount was ill when the lieutenant of the Rosario boarded us. Morris was down in the forecabin when the firing through the auger holes was going on. I do not say he was firing. I think Mount was there also. I don't remember whether I told Mr. Winch this. He said nothing to me about Mount or Morris. I shipped on board the Carl as an ordinary seaman, at £2 10s. a month. We also had head money—2s. a head—for catching the niggers. I did not know I would get this money, and I never asked for it. I did get it. When the firing was going on through the bulk head I was on deck. The cook's galley is alongside the main hatch, perhaps three or four yards from the bulkheads. A man in the galley could not see what was going on in the forecabin. I could not swear I was not told that Mount and Morris were to be tried at Melbourne, and that evidence was wanted against them. When the natives were chucked overboard, the passengers were assembled on deck. I did not protest against that was being done. I had nothing to say. I had to sing small on board. I saw the boy with six fingers and six toes taken on deck, and believe he was thrown overboard, as I did not see him again. Morris was on deck when the Rosario boarded us, and I think Mount also, but I would not swear.

Re-examined by Mr. ADAMSON.—The Rosario was sighted about daylight. She did not come alongside for two hours after. I think Mount was about on deck during that time. We were heading for Apii when she sighted us. The man-of-war hoisted some flags, but Captain Armstrong could not make them out, and did not heave to until the Rosario fired two shots. The Rosario was a good way off when she fired. I don't remember seeing our flag hoisted. I made a statement at Newcastle to the police, but they did not then want to hear the biggest part I had to tell. I did not tell before, because I was frightened, as I heard from a man who knew Armstrong that if I did I should be shot. This was after the Sydney trials. I was discharged at the Sydney court. Dr. Murray was the only witness against me, except Captain Flynn, who did not go on the labour cruise at all. When I arrived at Levuka I applied for my discharge, as I heard the ship was going on a labour cruise. I applied to Armstrong, and he told me he had nothing to do with it, and referred me to Dr. Murray, who sent me back to the captain. I asked Murray who was the captain, and he said, "Armstrong." The latter told me to go ashore and see Consul March. I went to the consul's office, and Dr. Murray came with me. He shook hands with the consul's clerk, and accompanied him into a room alongside the office. When they came out the consul's clerk asked me what I wanted. I said, "I want my discharge." He told me I had signed for 12 months, and he read something from the articles that I cannot remember. He told me to go on board back to my work. I said I would not. He asked, "What's that you say?" and I repeated the words. He then said that if I told him that again he would get a boat, and put me on board very quick. He advised me when I got on board to do my work as I ought to. I went outside, and saw Captain Flynn. I told him I was going to run away, and he advised me not. He said that if I did a man-of-war would be in in a couple of days, and that the consul would then get me put on board and flogged. I then went on board the Carl. Wilson told me that if any one spoke of what had occurred when we reached Levuka, or got drunk there, he would be shot. I heard the same thing several times, and from Scott as well. It was stated to all the crew a couple of days before we reached Levuka, and was talked about during all the passage back. Dr. Murray ordered me to shoot on the night of the outbreak. I had to obey orders, or else I should have got shot myself. What I know of what occurred in the forecabin was from seeing those who fired coming up to load their muskets. I could not say that Mount was sick in bed, and delirious, at the time the Rosario boarded us. Mount was sick during the voyage, but not then, I think.

Re-cross-examined by Mr. IRELAND.—I could have called to Lieutenant Partridge when I was at the wheel, but if I had done so, I should never have seen Levuka.

Mr. ADAMSON proposed to call Superintendent Winch to prove that the last witness made his statement to him voluntarily.

The CHIEF JUSTICE.—That cannot possibly be evidence.

The evidence was not pressed.

George Heath, examined by Mr. GARNETT.—Was on board the brig Carl as seaman in June, 1871. Six of the crew and the cook, and Armstrong and Dowden, were on board at the time. I joined at Levuka. She was a British ship; had a British ensign on board. Dr. Murray, Scott, Wilson, and the prisoners, and Mr. and Mrs. Grut, Mr. Bell, and Mr. Smyth were on board as passengers. She was going on the labour trade. Sailed first to Suva, where we landed Smyth, then to Tanna, where we landed Mr. and Mrs. Grut, Mr. Bell, and Miss Chapman, who was also a passenger. Then we went to Havannah Harbour, where we took in yams and water; then to some small islands, and then to Apii. Dr. Murray and prisoners went ashore and bought land from natives, then to Mallicolo, where the ship anchored. A boat went ashore to look for better anchorage. Dr. Murray, the prisoners, Portuguese Joe, and the mate went. I did not. Some natives came off while the boat was away. In three-quarters of an hour the boat came back. As the boat came back the natives left the ship, and the boat fired on the canoes that were going ashore. Could not see who fired, but we heard the shots. Heard several. We could see the firing. The natives jumped into the water, and the other boat left the ship in pursuit. Can't say if an order was given. Took 10 natives there, and put them into the hold. There was a little resistance by them. Thence we went to the Solomon Islands. There we got to an island of which I don't know the name. Took natives. Two swam off. Others came in a canoe, and then went back again. After they went ashore they came off again. The wind was puffing at the time, and some of the canoes were swamped. We passed ropes to the natives that were in the water, and brought them up. I can't say if any were capsized in any other way. About a quarter of an hour after the canoes came they were capsized. Boats were got out. The prisoners and Wilson, Scott, and myself were in one boat; the crew was in the other boat in charge of the mate. Took 12 natives. There might have been firing, but I did not notice. I think there was a little struggling. Then went to Three Sisters Island, where we got cocoanuts, but there were no natives. At some of the islands the natives were armed with bows and arrows. Went to a larger island in the same group, where canoes were capsized by small cannon. Can't say how many were capsized. The cannon were fastened to the ship by ropes. The captain and the mate sank the canoes. The boats were lowered as usual. The same parties were in them. Some force was used. The natives would resist. The natives were struck with the oars. I was in one of the boats with the prisoners. They had revolvers. The natives could have swum ashore. Then went to Isabella Island. Canoes came off there, and were sunk as usual. Boats were lowered, and the men taken in the usual way. Then went cruising about different islands. At one a canoe with five men came off; the canoe was capsized, and the men were taken. Then to Bougainville. Did not anchor there. The canoes came off. We sunk them with cannon and pig iron. Were off the island three or four days. Were three or four miles off the island. Took 85 natives as near as I can recollect. There was a good deal of resistance. The same parties were in the boats as usual. The captain, with Murray, Lewis, and the cook, remained on board to keep the other natives in the hold. While off these islands we put to sea at night, and came back in the morning. After we got the 85 men we turned for Levuka. The first night there was a slight disturbance, and the natives were quieted by being sung out to. Did not hear a shot fired. Next night, about 9 o'clock, the row began again. They were quieted at first by being sung out to. The vessel had one hold, with three hatchways. Mount was on watch the night of the row. After the men were quieted, the row began again. All hands rushed on deck in consequence of some one crying out that the natives were trying to get up. Scott fired a revolver over the hatchway—not down it—to quiet them. They commenced fighting among themselves. Then all hands began to fire down the hatch. I saw Mount fire with the revolver. Morris was in the cabin loading the muskets most of the time. I did not see him fire. The firing was kept up all night. There was a light in the galley, and Mount used a bull's-eye lantern belonging to Morris. He held it down the hold. He kept doing this off and on all night. Can't say if he continued firing all the night. This was at the main hatchway. The firing stopped towards morning. We fired every time there was a fresh outbreak among the natives. At daylight Scott tried to get down the hatchway, but was repelled by the natives thrusting spears at him. Scott came on deck and went aft. Murray then came forward, and went down the forecabin with the two mates and three or four others, and commenced firing. Can't say who these others were. Don't know where the prisoners were. Saw the people firing at the bulkhead. This continued for about half an hour, and there might have been 15 or 20 shots fired. Murray was using two weapons, one a revolver and the other a sort of revolving musket. There were about 16 shots between the two. The revolver is 10 barrels and the musket 6. Recollect them coming up and going aft. The prisoners were at this time in the cabin. Murray joined them. They had a consultation, and shortly after Dr. Murray came forward, and a ladder was let down the hold. Those natives that could came up; those that could not were brought up with ropes. The natives were placed on deck. They were all wounded. Murray was standing at the fore part, overhauling the natives. He picked out 10 as not being badly wounded, and said they should be brought to Levuka. The others were put overboard. Some jumped overboard themselves. Can't say how many dead there were. Some of the wounds were fearful; they were all gunshot wounds. The saplings they were fighting with were pretty large poles, about as thick as my arm. The prisoners could not help seeing them being thrown overboard. During the disturbance the Bougainville men had got into the centre of the hold; others got near the forecabin; the crushing of the Bougainville natives driving the others forward forced up the hatch, and they came on deck. The Bougainville natives were trying to get up the main hatch. None of the friendly natives were killed or wounded. Some were skinned by being bruised against the hatch. The hold was whitewashed and cleaned up. Saw a couple of shot marks in the beams. The beams might be 3ft. 6in. from the ballast. The firing had been right down the hold. The 10 Bougainville natives were brought to Levuka. Met the Rosario at Apii. The lieutenant came on board. It had been blowing the day before we met the Rosario. Next morning the weather was fairer, and we were making sail. We then saw the ship, but could not make her out; she was making signals, but we could not understand them. She came up to us under steam, and then fired shots. We hove-to, and hoisted the English colours. The lieutenant overhauled the ship's papers and looked down the main hold. He then went aft again. Mount was sick at the time; but Morris was on deck. The lieutenant was on board three quarters of an hour. Did not see Morris speak to the lieutenant. He told us not to leave till he reported to his superior officer. Dr. Murray, Scott, and some New Hebrides natives left us at Apii. The Bougainville natives were taken to Levuka. We got there in December. Was paid off at Levuka. Came to Sydney with prisoners. The main hatch was four feet square. Saw a Chinese umbrella in Mount's cabin. Can't say if the passengers objected to the men being thrown overboard. The bulkhead was about an inch thick.

Cross-examined by Mr. IRELAND.—I can't say if Fallon called out for all hands to go on deck. Heard some one singing out that the natives were trying to get on deck. Can't say if water was thrown down the hatch. It might have been done. The fighting was stopped by half-past 4 or 5 o'clock. After the firing, Murray came forward to the main hatch and then went aft again. He then came forward again with two weapons. Lewis was forward. The mate went with him. Heard firing begin then. Could not say where the prisoners were. They were on deck after the firing was begun by Scott. I can't say if they were forward at the time the firing through the bulkhead began. I can't say where the prisoners were when Murray came from the forecabin, but I saw them standing aft shortly after. About five minutes after this we were at the galley getting tea or coffee. We all fired down the hatch. The only ones I recollect firing through the bulkheads were Murray, Lewis, and the mate. There may have been others. I can't recollect if Lewis or Murray said anything after this. Mount was ill for about a week before we met the Rosario. He had liver complaint, and was very ill. Murray was not treating him as he ought to have done. Never asked for assistance. I spoke to Mount the day before the Rosario met us. I saw him in the cabin, and he then said he was a little better. If Fallon says he was on deck at the time, that is not true.

Mr. ADAMSON.—Fallon only says he can't remember.

Cross-examination continued.—I know nothing about the consul or his clerk. We had a good many natives on board when we got to Levuka. The consul and his little boy came on board; the natives were called aft. He examined them, spoke to the captain, and shortly afterwards left. He said they were passed for three years. Next day left the vessel and came to Sydney. The price of labour at Fiji is £10 per head. Can't say the price given for labour. I thought when I joined we were to get them in a legitimate way. I had been in the trade before. I don't know that these men are obtained from the island for a bit of cloth, a fig of tobacco, or a toy. I never saw any of them paid, for I never was ashore when they were obtained. The big boat, called the Vulture, was sometimes, but not usually, used to protect the little boat.

Re-examined by Mr. GARNETT.—The firing through the bulkheads commenced about an hour and a half after all was quiet after the outbreak. I saw Mount aft, about five or ten minutes after Murray came out of the forecabin after the firing.

To a Juror.—I heard that some natives were shot from the ship when they were in the water, but I did not see it. I did not see Morris go down or come up with Murray and the mate when the firing through the bulkheads took place.

Charles Herbert Taylor, examined by Mr. M'Kinley, deposed.—I am senior lieutenant of H.M.S. Cossack. I met the brig Carl in Levuka last May. She is a brig of about 280 tons. She was fitted up like a labour vessel. Her hold was clear fore and aft, with the exception of the space occupied by the water tanks and the bulkheads of the cabin. It was fitted up in the ordinary way with bunks like other labour ships. The ship carried a large supply of water. The height of the hold was about 10ft. The tanks were in the fore part of the main hold, which was there three or four feet higher. There were three hatches in the main hold. The main hatch, which is the only one I particularly remember, was 6ft. or 7ft. broad and about 9ft. long. I examined the hold. From information received, we supposed that we might detect something, and I, as a member of the Naval Court held at Levuka, examined the hold. I found numerous shot and bullet marks. A carpenter who was with me cut out a bullet from the ship itself. It was similar to the one now produced, but I cannot swear it is the same, as it has been out of my possession for some time. The piece of wood produced was cut out in the attempt to find a bullet. No less than four shot in it were cut through with the chisel. Only one of them remains, as the wood has broken away. I traced the first bullet out by marks made in the stanchion. It must have been fired from the main hatch. All the marks of the bullets were covered with whitewash. There were shot-marks in the beams and in the mainmast, which were left untouched. The Carl flew the English flag. I did not see any marks of bullets in the opposite direction from the forecabin. The bulkhead was of plain fir, but I cannot say the thickness. There were about a dozen holes bored right along it. They were just large enough to pass a barrel of a single-barrel gun or rifle through.

Cross-examined by Mr. IRELAND.—The bullets I found were fired down the main hatch. If bullets were fired from the forecabin at people lying at the bottom of the hold I should think they would get lost amongst the dunnage and shingles. There may have been any quantity fired without my finding any of them.

Mr. IRELAND.—You did not see any indication of bullets at Apii?

Witness.—You are making a mistake. I did not make the examination you referred to.

The CHIEF JUSTICE.—A different vessel and a different man.

Witness.—Lieutenant Partridge, of the Rosario, went to England last April. I know something of the regulations for getting labour. Proper interpreters should accompany vessels, and a special licence from the consul or government at Levuka should be obtained. Certain regulations with regard to space should be complied with. The interpreters should be competent to make natives understand the agreements entered into that they should leave their homes. I cannot state how long such regulations have existed. Each vessel should start with interpreters from Levuka. There are different dialects for each group. They are so dissimilar that one interpreter could not act for all. It is supposed that there would be an interpreter for each native speaking a different language. I cannot say whether these regulations are practically complied with. There is no price given at the islands for men. The natives on returning to their homes are paid by the men who hire them as labour. They are paid nothing when they leave home. They get nothing at all from the men on the ship which takes them away. They should come voluntarily; and the custom is to pay them when they return. There are many natives who leave home voluntarily. Small presents—what is called "trade"—may be given before they leave, but they are never bought in that way.

Mr. IRELAND.—Would they come without it?

Witness.—Oh, yes, they would. In the case of the Mallicolo, which I inspected at Levuka, it was distinctly stated that the men came voluntarily.

Mr. IRELAND.—Who said that?

Witness.—Her captain.

Mr. IRELAND.—That will do.

Witness.—Oh, the ship was cleared.

Peter Daly, detective officer, stationed in Melbourne, deposed.—I arrested Morris on the 20th November. I read the warrant charging him with murder on the high seas. He said, "It is a frightful charge. I thought they might charge me with kidnapping, but I never thought they would charge me with murder." The next day I searched his place and found the document produced (a draft letter to Mount).

Cross-examined by Mr. IRELAND.—Raby Wilson has come from Sydney. He was at large, and not in charge of the police.

Felix Keon, constable, deposed.—I arrested Mount on the 19th November at the Buchan copper and silver mines, 50 miles from Bairnsdale. I read the warrant to him, and told him I arrested him for murder. After the lapse of a few seconds, he said, "Murder, eh? I think the Government have treated me badly, as I gave them all the information I could connected with the Carl case." I took him to his hut and found four letters there, two of which he gave me—one from Dr. Murray and the other from the prisoner Morris.

The letters referred to were put in and read. The draft of the letter found in Morris's possession was almost word for word the same as one of the letters handed by Mount to the constable, which was as follows:—

"Collingwood, 29th August, 1872.

"To H. Mount, Esq.

"Dear Mount,—I received a communication from your brother relative to the Fiji affair, and at once placed myself in communication with him. He advised that I should give you an epitome of the evidence I should give if necessary. Before I heard from your brother, Detective Daly waited upon me on behalf of the chief of police, to know what evidence I could give in relation to the affair, stating that the department had had a communication from you. I declined to state anything till I heard from you. Subsequent to this, however, at an interview with Captain Standish, he read a telegram from you stating that Armstrong was merely a tool, &c. I told him my statement would be similar. Captain Standish told me he would telegraph to the Sydney Government, and let me know the result in a day or two. This occurred last Monday, and is all I know at present of the affair, except that it is kicking up a devil of a dust, and Murray is carrying out his *rôle* as a thoroughpaced scoundrel. I think from hints that dropped from the detective and Standish that they're hunting up evidence against Murray. Now, with regard to the statement, the wisest philosophers have declared that honesty is the best policy, so I shall 'a plain unvarnished tale deliver,' of which the following is a brief:—That we—the party—agreed with Murray to occupy and form a cotton plantation on certain land in the N. Hebrides, to be pointed out by Murray; the land to be approved of by the party; that we were passengers only, having no connexion whatever with the ship or its trade; that Dr. Murray failed to perform his agreement with us, and deceived us in every way, leaving us no recourse than either to remain on a cannibal island, or to accompany the vessel till she arrived at Levuka; that we were not aware of the nature of the trade when we started; that men were taken from the Solomon Islands illegally by men jumping into the canoes or throwing weights into them; that Murray had the entire management of the ship, acting as supercargo, trading master, and captain; that we protested against the trade, both to Murray and Armstrong, but were unheeded; that the crew on several occasions demurred to the trade, but by Murray's representations were induced to continue; that the ship was almost destitute of provisions; that off the east coast of Bougainville a number of men were taken; that the crew objected to take these men, but were induced to do so by Murray; that Murray declared he would not return till he had men, but would proceed to New Guinea if necessary; that shortly after these men were taken, they endeavoured to fire and take the ship; that everything was done to induce them to be quiet, but without avail; that they were fired at, and quelled; that it was by Murray's order that the wounded were thrown overboard; that the crew refused to aid him, and he employed natives to do it; that the party expostulated, but without avail; that after this the crew came aft, and declared they would have nothing more to do with the labour trade; that Murray directed Armstrong to make the Cairoline Islands; that we obtained provisions at Seven Islands; that we touched at various groups, at all of which Murray endeavoured to obtain men, but failed, as the crew refused to aid; that when near the Marshall Group, north of the line, Murray directed the captain to make Pleasant Island; that from here we reached Duff's Group, and Murray asked the crew to take men, but they refused; that Murray addressed a circular letter to you, Wilson, and me, stating his intention of remaining at Apii, and requesting us to co-operate; that we declined, and demanded the return of money placed in his hands, as he had not performed his contract; that Murray and Scott remained at Apii with a number of natives; that we accompanied the vessel to Levuka; that Murray's agent at Levuka refused to recognise his order; that from this point our connexion with the vessel ceased. There, old fellow, if you think that correct, drop me a line. Address Post-office, Collingwood. I hear you're on a splendid spec, and hope it will turn out to the full as you expect. Wilson, I hear, is at Twofold Bay, N.S.W. Yours very truly,

"W. C. MORRIS."

The other letters put in were as follow:—

"Tattersall's Hotel, Sydney, Sept. 2.

"My Dear Mount,—I am now in town about this Carl case. I suppose you have read Murray's account of the affair, and how he has been trying to put it all on you, old Armstrong, and the crew, but I have put a different version on the matter. I have seen Sir W. Manning, and he has given me good advice on the matter. He says it is best to tell everything about the affair, and to tell how we was led into it, and to state that we had no interest in the vessel, only in cotton-planting. I saw the Crown solicitor yesterday, and he took down my evidence, in case anything should happen to me before the trial comes off in November next. I told them how I became connected with the Carl, and the account of the voyage, and also an account of that frightful night. I told them all the natives—I mean the quiet ones—would have been shot if it had not been for you opening the hatch behind the galley, and letting them up, and I told the Crown that you protested against the shooting into the hold of the vessel. I also told them you were very ill on the voyage, and Dr. Murray's treatment to you. I told also how Dr. M. went on during the night; how he walked up and down from the cabin to the hatch, singing 'Marching through Georgia;' and also his telling the crew that he was captain, and that Armstrong was only a sailing master under his orders. The inspector of police has got Dr. Murray's measure, and Mr. Williams, the Crown solicitor, says Murray is the man who ought to be punished. The Crown is going to bring you to Sydney as a witness in November. I will stay at Tattersall's. It is a nice place; so if you are in town you will no were to find me.—Yours, in haste,

"RABY WILSON."

"Tattersall's Hotel, Sept. 5 | 72.

"My Dear Mount,—Enclosed is my carte, which I promised you some time ago. I wrote you the other day about that unfortunate Carl case. I met that wretch Murray as I was going into the Crown solicitor's office yesterday. He walked up to me and said, 'Well, Wilson, old fellow, how are you?' I drew back, and said, 'Dr. Murray, I doant want to have anything to do with you; I doant wish to speak to you,' and passed on. Mr. Williams, the Crown solicitor, says he beleaves Murray is the man who ought to be punished, as he was the leader of the expedition. Sir W. Manning has been very kind to me, and also my Friend Charly Stiles. Sir W. Manning's partner, Clem Stiles, is on his way to Melbourne, to stay with his brother. I gave him a letter of introduction to you; he knowes all about the Carl case. I will tell you all about my doings at Begar. I have sellected 640 acres of land on the Benbooka run, and a grass right of about 1,200, which will make a fine property. Some day if I live I have a great mind, after all this Carl affair is over, to go up to the North or go to Ammerica. I told Charly Stiles I would. He was in a great scot, and said I should not. He says if I will get marrid and settle downe he will buye me a small station and give me so long to pay for it, but who the duce would marry a man who has been in the nigger trade. Do you know a girl who would, for I doant. If you come up to town on the trial in November, you will find me at Tattersall's Hotel. Write when you get this, and send me your carte.—Your sincere Fiend,

RABY WILSON."

"15th November, 1871. Brig Carl.

"Dear Mount,—I regret very much to perceive the disappointed tone of your letter, and the unfair view you have taken of my action. If it could serve any useful purpose, I would be able to show you, by taking up point after point, that I acted in every respect straightforwardly and with an honest intention to do justice to all, but this would now be useless, and I shall merely confine myself to repudiating the last insinuation contained in your letter—that of 'trickishness,' which in your inmost heart you know to be false as false can be. My means were not unknown to you in Melbourne, else why should I have sought the paltry aid of £50, and toiled for it. They were still less unknown to you at Levuka when you saw me borrowing small sums from Mr. Hennings. This, then, was the time to have spoken, and your money would in some way or other have been scraped together and refunded. But let this pass. Your better judgment will regret hereafter using such an expression to one who has never wronged anyone of a penny.

"To every other portion of your note reply is unnecessary, as matters of opinion and feeling do not admit of argument. I agree that we have not hit it, and it is idle to trace the cause.

"With regard to the money (£50) which you demand, you shall have it, although you have little idea of the straitened position such a payment will place me in. The necessary arrangements for its repayment will be at once entered upon. Your offer to transact any business of mine at Levuka or elsewhere I must beg respectfully to decline, with thanks. You will excuse me if I feel the disappointment of your action too keenly to disguise my feeling, for it is impossible that we could be ever again to each other in any other light than as strangers.

"Of course I wish you well, and hope you will be successful in what you next undertake.

"I remain, dear Mount, yours very sincerely,

"JAMES P. MURRAY."

Mr. ADAMSON remarked that Raby Wilson, who had been so frequently mentioned, was in attendance in case the counsel for the defence wished to call him. He now proposed to close the case for the Crown.

A few minutes later Mr. ADAMSON asked Mr. Ireland if he would prefer that the Crown placed Wilson in the box, so that he might cross-examine him, and on receiving a reply in the affirmative called

Raby Wilson, who was sworn.

Mr. ADAMSON thought it ought to be understood that he had the right of reply.

The CHIEF JUSTICE.—If you do not choose to call this man you need not.

Mr. ADAMSON submitted that under the circumstances the prosecuting counsel had the right of reply.

The CHIEF JUSTICE.—If you wished to have the right of reply you should not have called this witness. You have called him, and I cannot give you a reply.

The witness was then cross-examined by Mr. IRELAND. He deposed.—I am employed as superintendent on a station. I was on the Carl expedition with Dr. Murray. I went as a passenger under an agreement with Murray to start a cotton plantation at the New Hebrides or Fijis, or any island found suitable for the purpose. The land was to be selected subject to the approval of the party. The party consisted of Mount, Morris, Scott, Grut, and myself. Grut had his wife and child with him, intending to settle out there. A Miss Chapman, who was on board, was in partnership with Grut and Dr. Murray. She had some land at Tanna, and was under an agreement with Murray. Grut was going down to look after the land. Grut and his wife and child, with Miss Chapman and Bell got out at Tanna. Dr. Murray told him he could not carry out his agreement with them, that his wife and child were an incumbrance on the vessel; and we had no rations. We did nothing at Tanna about land; only yams and water were got there. Then we went to Havannah Harbour. We wanted to settle there, but Murray would not let us, and ordered the captain to go to Apii. At Apii Murray went on shore, and said he would like to buy land. We refused to go there, as we heard it was unhealthy. The captain of a vessel that was there lent Murray an interpreter, and he bought land against our wish. Went then to Palma, and got yams, but no natives. Murray said we must dress up as missionaries, but I said missionaries were not known there. Some of the crew were dressed as missionaries. Murray put a rug round me, as he said, to keep off the poisoned arrows. I took it off before I reached the island. I went in the boat with the captain. The natives were peaceable. The captain gave them beads. I asked him if he was going to kidnap them. He said no; that he only came off to please Murray. We got no natives there. Went then to Mallicolo. Then to Solomon Group—to an island called Santa Anna. Only three or four hours there. Only one boat was lowered there. I am sure of it. Poonah is the name of the township there. Dowden was in charge of the boat that was lowered. Never heard the longboat called the Vulture. It was the small boat that was lowered here. Could not say if Morris was in the boat. The boat was not out for long. They fired from the ship over the heads of the natives. One native was wounded, and he swam ashore. Dr. Murray always stood on the deck with a revolver, and repeating rifle. So did Lewis and Scott, and they fired over the canoes. Remember the night of the affair at Bougainville. I had turned in for the night; when some one cried, "All hands on deck." As I reached the deck, Scott fired over the hatch. Some of the friendly natives cried out, "Mate, mate," meaning they are killing us. I saw a fire. The other natives made a rush at it, and put it out. Murray ordered all hands on deck. The arms were also ordered up. Mount and others tried to quiet them. They tried to push up the hatches with the long poles. Murray then ordered the crew and passengers to fire down into the hold. This continued till half-past 12 o'clock. The Bougainville natives had forced up the fore hatch about 4ft. Mount protested against any more shooting, and wanted to lift the hatch to let up the quiet natives. Murray said that if anyone touched the hatch, he would blow his brains out. Mount then called on me to assist him, and he got a lever and forced up the hatch, and took them out. The firing then ceased. They appeared to be quiet. Murray then looked down the hatch, and said he would shoot everyone of them—that he knew the crew would help him to get more. Everything was quiet then, and most of us went below to get a rest. After a couple of hours' quietness some one gave the alarm that the natives were breaking out again. Murray rushed up again, and again fired down the main hatch. It continued till towards morning. The men fought desperately to force up the hatches, and I think they were fighting among themselves. At daylight the firing ceased. I had only been up once, and had gone below when the mate ordered me up on deck, and I refused to go. I went up at half past 8, and looked down the hatch. I saw very few, if at all, shot. Saw some wounded men. They all crowded over the side of the deck. I went and told Mount. He said, "That's a good job." Whilst we were talking we heard the firing again. Mount said, "What are they firing for now?" Some one came, and said that Murray and others had bored holes, and were shooting the natives as they lay along the hold. I don't know who was in the forecabin at this time. I was told there were three persons. Mount was below aft at the time. Morris was on deck.

To Mr. ADAMSON.—Mount and I were the only persons in the cabin at the time. We stayed there half an hour. He said he was very ill. I can't tell where Morris was. I can't say where Mount was at any time except during this half hour. I was examined at Sydney. I made a statement to the Crown solicitor there. I have remembered some things now I did not remember then. I made a statement to the Crown solicitor here.

Mr. ADAMSON.—How many things are there that you told us to-day that you did not tell us then? Did you say anything about taking up the land at Tanna, or about Grut being an encumbrance.

Witness.—I think I mentioned it in Sydney. I was very tired when I made the statement there. I told the Crown solicitor at Sydney it was against my will Murray purchased at Apii. At Palma, Murray did not go ashore. The mate had an oilskin coat on. I took off the rug Murray pinned on me, because I could not pull with it. I was not afraid of the poisoned arrows. Bob, the Kanaka man, put on the rug.

Mr. ADAMSON.—Do you expect anyone to believe your story? If two or three people swear you went as missionaries, what have you to say?

Witness.—I don't deny it. Murray said it would be a good thing to go as missionaries.

Mr. ADAMSON.—Then was the rug for the poisoned arrows?

Witness.—I did not believe it was. I knew what the rug was for. It was because Murray told us to dress up as missionaries.

Mr. ADAMSON.—Did you take any leaves or a book with you?

Witness.—I took a packet of pictures, of cattle, horses, &c. I took them out of the cabin. There was a little print on the pictures. The book I had was loose pictures. None of the natives were on their knees. They were sitting down. The natives all sang. We sang after them. We sang "Wait for the Turn of the Tide." I don't know that we sang "Marching through Georgia." Mount was on the ship with a red gown and Chinese umbrella. He had no book that I saw.

Mr. ADAMSON.—Were you not dressed up as missionaries?

Witness.—Mount was dressed up and so was I. At Santa Anna we got nine or ten men. Only one boat was lowered there.

Mr. ADAMSON asked the witness to read his statement in which he declared that two boats were used.

Witness.—That's a mistake. It refers to another island—the next one we went to after Santa Anna. Never heard the longboat called the Vulture. Never heard the expression, "Vulture's crew, ahoy." Morris used to be on the deck when Murray would fire over the canoes. Morris seldom went in the boats. When I looked in the hatch at half-past 8, before the firing through the auger holes, I saw people wounded. I can't say if any were dead. I saw some wounded moving; they were wounded with shot.

To Mr. IRELAND.—Dowden once said to Armstrong, "You ought to see that every man takes part in this." We were crossing to Bougainville at the time, and we were getting a glass of grog in the lazaret. Armstrong said, "There is no fear of that; if I thought any of them would not, I would shoot them or land them on some island. If anybody does not like it, he may go ashore at an island." I heard Dowden say to Murray that they ought to see no man escaped. Murray said, "I won't allow any one to put our heads into a rope; I'll let them land."

This concluded the evidence.

Mr. ADAMSON then summed up the case for the Crown. Commenting on the evidence given by Wilson, he remarked that he appeared to be influenced by a desire to shield the prisoner Mount, and pointed out that it was somewhat peculiar that Fallon occasionally exhibited a similar wish. The latter, when asked whether he could recollect whether on the voyage from Melbourne to Levuka the prisoners had said anything about establishing a cotton plantation, asserted that his memory failed him on the point. Subsequently, when asked as to whether the second boat was lowered, Fallon again asserted the same thing, and it was singular to observe that on the very same point, one which concerned the prisoner Mount materially, Wilson stumbled as well. The interest attaching to the trial was far beyond that attaching to ordinary trials, and it was possible some influence was brought to bear which would not be exercised on other occasions. Notwithstanding, however, that Wilson was a witness adverse to the Crown, it was rather in respect to his omissions to state what was done than his denials of what actually occurred, that his testimony was important. He had left all matters of the greatest importance, such as the presence or absence of Morris in the forecabin, open points. It was likely that it would be advanced for the defence, that all the natives who were killed were shot through the auger holes, and that the prisoners had nothing to do with it, but if such a theory were accepted, the jury would be more credulous than he thought them. It might also be argued that although it was necessarily a crime to shoot or murder the natives, yet that such people were of so inferior a race that to charge men who shot them with murder was an unreasonable and improper thing. He did not believe the jury would entertain such an opinion, and he merely mentioned it as he had heard such views expressed. If the islanders were not protected, an encouragement would be given to the perpetration of outrages such as that now under view. The prisoners were no more justified in taking the lives of the natives than he would be in killing anyone in court. The islanders, if lured on board by fraud or violence, were justified in effecting their escape, even if they used violence to do so, and to shoot them for doing so was nothing short of murder. It was said they had fired the ship, but Wilson was the only one who saw any light below. His evidence was open to great doubt. It might be asked what proof was there that any were really shot in the hold, and be argued that if any were killed it was by the firing through the auger holes. But was it reasonable to conclude that when firing was going on all night, by the light of two lanterns, in a crowded hold, that none of the natives were wounded and killed? What in that case induced them at dawn of day to become quiet, and how was it that that quiet was never afterwards disturbed? He did not wish to insist too strongly on any piece of evidence connecting the prisoners with participation in the forecabin affair, but one witness for the Crown distinctly swore that Morris was there, and not one would venture to deny that he might have been there. Fallon also said that he thought Mount was down there, and he gave one piece of evidence which seemed to make it conclusive that he was there. It was where he said that after the shooting, Mount threw down his revolver, saying he would have no more of this bloody work. It was impossible that all the natives who were injured could have been shot through the auger holes. It might be argued that the prisoners were forced into acting as they did, but he contended that the evidence showed that they were participators to the fullest extent in what went on. They might have prevented the last tragedy if all had they liked, but they stood by with revolvers in their hands and ammunition at their sides, and let the natives be thrown overboard. It was contended that Murray was the chief one to benefit by the labour cruise, but it was a noticeable fact that he left the vessel before she returned to Levuka. Who then had made the profit on the islanders which were sold there? In conclusion, the learned counsel warned the jury that they had a heavy responsibility resting on them, and expressed his conviction that they would bear that in mind in considering their verdict.

Mr. IRELAND, addressing the jury for the defence, remarked that the case was of no ordinary interest. Public indignation had been excited respecting it to a most extra ordinary pitch. The public press was teeming with denunciations of the slave trade carried on in the South Pacific. Within the last few days the topic had been alluded to in His Excellency's speech in prorogning Parliament; and one public print had given a pictorial representation of the scene supposed to have occurred on board the Carl, and had depicted numbers of the natives as being devoured by sharks. The Crown prosecutor, too, had exhibited an amount of animus which, combined with the fact that he had three or four informers at his back, certainly removed the case out of the ordinary category, and placed the prisoners at a disadvantage. Under all the circumstances, it behoved the jury to scrutinise the case narrowly, especially as no corroborative evidence had been offered of the main facts advanced. On that point Lord Abinger had stated that juries should not pay any respect to the testimony of an accomplice unless he was corroborated in some material circumstance that affected the identity of the party accused, as a man who had been guilty of a crime himself would always be able to relate the facts of the case, and if the confirmation were only on the truth of that history, without identifying the persons, that was really no corroboration at all. In this case the evidence of the informers was not corroborated at all. In regard to Fallon, every attempt had been made to frighten him into giving evidence. He was arrested on the capital charge himself, and was then brought to Melbourne, and though there was no contract under seal made with him for his life, he had a pretty shrewd notion that his life would be spared. To save his own life, he had no objection to swear away the lives of other people; for it was not till after people had been sentenced to be hanged, and after he had been arrested, that Fallon opened his mouth to further the administration of justice. What was the worth of evidence of that kind without corroboration. He dwelt upon the necessity of having corroboration, for if the rule of law were once broken through about requiring informers to be corroborated, no man would be safe. He did not care to offer severe criticism about the other witnesses, but there was one person of whom he was entitled to say something. He was entitled to ask, where was Murray? His learned friend said that he would not attempt to bring such a witness before them. But he had been brought before a Sydney jury, and two men were sentenced to be hanged upon his evidence. He could not tell what benefit he might have derived from Murray's evidence, but at all events he was entitled to have him there to see what could be got out of him. This man was the head and front of all, the chief offender, the concoctor of all. And was there ever a case like this heard of, where the principal was permitted to walk about free while his victims were placed upon their trial? His learned friend might ask, what could be got out of him? He was not entitled to give an answer further than that he might get something out of him; and sure he was of this, that if this man came here, the indignation of the jury would be centred upon him, and the others would be allowed to go free. They could have got him here if they liked, for the two Governments had been co-operating about these trials, and Murray could well have been sent on from New South Wales. At Sydney two men had been sacrificed, and thus the Victorian Government was vieing with the one in Sydney to make a similar sacrifice here. He implored the jury to stand between these men and the doom that awaited them, on evidence such as had been produced at this trial. Why had the witnesses that were examined been singled out as objects of clemency? Why were they the pets of the Government, and why should these two men be made the victims of Dr. Murray? These men left Victoria with the design of settling on some of the islands. They had no intention or desire at all to begin kidnapping, and it was not till they got to Palma that this system of kidnapping was commenced. The vessel was purchased in Melbourne by Murray; it was insinuated that the prisoners were his partners in that transaction. But there was nothing of the kind. The only arrangement made was that they should obtain land, and that Murray should supply the labour that was wanted. An attempt was made through the witness Binstead to show that from the very start the prisoners contemplated these transactions. He was told, he said, by one of them that they were going blackbirding. Now, there was no evidence as to the meaning of that; and it was an expression just as applicable to the lawful traffic as to the illicit trading. As to the arms that were put on board, why, every vessel that cleared out for that part of the world with any object was obliged to carry arms to protect the crew from the inhabitants of those islands. And with reference to these natives, as allusion had been made to the subject, he must say that so long as two races existed side by side, the one inferior to the other, the same course of dealing could not be pursued with the weaker race as with the stronger one. He did not defend the system, he was merely stating a fact—was merely stating what everybody knew to be a fact, and the British Government had recognised the fact, for it had passed a law legalising the traffic—had passed a law authorising the transfer of these natives from one island to another. They would not have done that had the men been whites, or the equals of whites. This was done to develope the resources of Queensland, and of some islands in the South Pacific occupied by whites. They thus recognised that the race which peopled this hemisphere were different from whites. This would show, then, that these prisoners were not the murderers and villains that they had been painted simply because they went into this business. The traffic was recognised by the British Government. A British consul issued licences for it. A British consul boarded the ships and inspected the natives, although what his inspection was worth might be judged of from the evidence that had been given on this trial, and British cruisers seemed only to make very cursory examinations of any ships they met. It seemed to him that the supervision began at the wrong end, and that instead of its beginning at Fiji, it should have been carried on at the islands. Regulations were talked about requiring interpreters for every language; but it was well known that there were nearly as many languages as there were islands, and that it was therefore impossible to obtain interpreters. It was nonsense, therefore, to talk of interpreters. And as the natives, if got at all, must be got without interpreters, the English Government, by sanctioning the traffic in the way they did, necessarily sanctioned whatever abuses had occurred. How were people to go to these islands, and without knowing the language, make the natives understand they were to be engaged for three years, and were to be sold for £10 per head? How many vessels could be freighted if every native was made to understand this? Force, therefore, was incidental to the system, and its use was connived at by the British Government. They recognised the traffic as an opening in which young and adventurous men might be employed. That the race of men who inhabited these islands were capable of a high degree of development he thoroughly admitted; and the cruelty of tearing them away from their homes was something detestable and abominable. He (Mr. Ireland) would not allow his learned friend to monopolise all the abhorrence of conduct like this of kidnapping. But it should not be forgotten that the men in their present state were all cannibals, and must be regarded as a low type of human nature. Of course that was no justification for treating them otherwise than as human beings. But even in this country how many were there—respectable people—who now rolled in their carriages who bought nothing in the early days of shooting down an aboriginal. He denied, therefore, that either Morris or Mount could be regarded as a murderer in the ordinary sense of the word. For there was something about this race that repelled us. Just fancy a cannibal husband and a cannibal wife—a cannibal baby on the breast of a cannibal mother. He admitted that the labour trade ought to be suppressed, but in order to develope the islands, he maintained that the natives should be deported from one island to another. Whilst on their own islands there was no inducement for them to work, but when transferred to another they were obliged to work. The missionaries had been dragged into this trial with the view, probably, of appealing to the religious sympathies of some of the jury, and it was spoken of as a terrible profaneness for these young men to personate a minister of the Gospel. But with the greatest possible regard for the missionaries, he must be allowed to say that the proper way to convert these men was to bring them in contact with civilisation. Their conversion would follow on their civilisation. The learned gentleman then proceeded to allude to the narrative given of the voyage of the Carl, and he asked what all that had to do with the charge against the prisoners. The accusation against them was for having committed a murder on 13th September, off the island of Bougainville. He pointed out that the prisoners had no object in wantonly committing murder; that it was to their benefit to get the natives alive and take them in safely to Levuka, where they would realise £10 per head. The prisoners were blamed for continuing in the ship after they knew what was to be done. But what were they to do? They could not leave it; it was useless to go on a desolate island, or an island where they would be eaten by cannibals. And in remaining, they had to do with a desperate man like Murray, a man who would stop at nothing, and who was utterly regardless of human life—on the contrary, who seemed rather to glory in sacrificing it. They were under him, they could not interfere; had they done so, he would have blown their brains out, as he threatened to do more than once. Well, on this night of the 13th September they had to deal with the Bougainvilleans, a set of ferocious cannibals. These men commenced a disturbance, and carried it on all night. He admitted they were on the ship in illegal custody, but what they did was not in pursuance of any plan of escape, or of any intention to escape. They merely wanted to get possession of the ship, and when they got possession of it there was little doubt as to what they would have done with the passengers and crew. It was impossible for the Bougainville men to escape, as they had then been two days at sea. Now, although the law was clear that when a man in escaping from illegal custody took life he would be guilty of manslaughter, and not murder, still it was nonsense to put these prisoners in the position that they must either be murdered by cannibals or be hung ashore. These men were in illegal custody, but they were not escaping from it; and it was recently held here (in the case of Weechurch) that where a man from vindictive motives attempted to kill another, even though he was in illegal custody, he would be guilty of a crime.

The CHIEF JUSTICE said the question of illegal or legal custody did not arise in that case.

Mr. IRELAND submitted that in that case it was laid down that a person, even though in illegal custody, must not act from revenge, and it was only when he was furthering his object of escape that he would be acquitted if he took life. A man, for instance, had no right to go into a room from which there was no chance of escape, and there stab the Crown solicitor.

Mr. ADAMSON.—Certainly not; and this case is just the other way round from what you have been arguing.

Mr. IRELAND then proceeded to contend that shots were fired down the hold not so much to shoot the natives as to keep the Bougainville islanders from under the main hatch, which they were desirous of forcing open. In the dead of the night, and when the ship was far out at sea, some 150 natives made an attempt, not to effect their escape, but to wreak revenge on their captors; and was it not excusable in the latter to use all reasonable force to prevent that catastrophe occurring. He did not mean to argue that the Crown was bound to pick out some man whom they could identify and charge the prisoners with murdering him, but the law required it to be shown that the person said to be murdered was dead, but there was not a tittle of evidence offered to show that such was the case. Unless it could be shown distinctly beyond all reasonable doubt that some one on that night, between the hours of half past 10 p.m. and 4 a.m., was killed by the firing down the hatch, the prisoners were entitled to an acquittal. Argument as to probabilities would not do. No evidence of the fact had been given. It was not shown that a single person was shot on that occasion. It was, however, stated in evidence given by one of the Crown witnesses that a man had gone to the cabin and said that nobody was shot in the hold, and that Mount had thereupon remarked, "A good job, too." Wilson, who seemed to be a confused sort of man, had said something about seeing a few men who were shot; but shooting a man and killing a man were very different things. The jury must not take away a man's life to satisfy public feeling. He asked for impartial and strict justice at their hands, and should, therefore, stand upon his rights. Those who fired were acting in self-defence; but whether they were or were not, so far as the firing on that night through the hatch was concerned, nobody was proved to have been killed, and the prisoner could be guilty neither of murder or manslaughter. For what happened afterwards the prisoners were not responsible. Although they might be considered answerable for each other's acts during the night, after the disturbance ceased and order was restored they could not be held accountable for the independent acts of any of the other passengers or crew. While Murray, with his bloodthirsty, tigerish instincts, wished to shoot down even the friendly natives, Mount stood forward, and at his peril protected them; and yet the jury were asked to believe he was a party to the detestable murder that took place later, when the firing through the auger holes com-

THE CARL OUTRAGES.
TRIAL OF MOUNT AND MORRIS.
VERDICT OF MANSLAUGHTER.

The trial of Henry Clark Mount and William Charles Morris for wilful murder on the high seas, was resumed yesterday, in the New Court-house, before his Honour the Chief Justice and a jury of twelve.

Mr. Adamson, assisted by Mr. Garnett and Mr M'Kinley, conducted the prosecution, and Mr. Ireland, Q.C., and Mr. Molesworth the defence.

James Falon, seaman, whose examination-in-chief was finished the prevsious day, was placed in the box for cross-examination by Mr. Ireland. He deposed:—I heard about the captain and the mate of the ship being tried in Sydney. It was after that I gave information. It was about 10 or 11 months after I left the ship at Levuka. I saw Superintendent Winch in Sydney. I was going to be tried when I saw him, and I was in custody in the lock-up. I had made a confession to the inspector of police at Newcastle, before I saw Mr. Winch. It was before I was arrested. I was frightened if I told it before I might be done away with. That was why I did not tell it before. I did not place myself under the protection of the police, because they would not keep me all my life. I did not know any better. It was after the captain and mate were sentenced to be hung that I told my story. No bargain was made with me if I gave my evidence, and no promise was made. I don't expect to be tried after giving my evidence, but I may be. They could not find anything against me. I was forced to go in the vessel against my will. I do not remember calling the men up to fire down the hatch at the natives. I did not call Mount up, but may have called Devescovi, the cook. I may have told him that the natives were tying to get up the hatches, and that they would murder us all. I had no hand in firing down the hatch. I fired several shots during the night—two at the commencement. When the lieutenant of the Rosario boarded us I was at the wheel, but I did not tell him I was on board against my will. I would not have been allowed to tell him. I did not tell the consul when I got back to Levuka. It was reported that the first who said anything or got drunk when we got to Levuka would be shot. That was my reason for saying nothing. The statement I made at Newcastle was taken down in writing. After I was removed to Sydney Mr. Winch took down my statement in a room in the court-house. He asked me questions as I went along, but told me he did not want to know anything I did not like to tell him. He said he would not force me to tell him. I do not remember if I was asked any questions as we went along about Mount or Morris. I thought that my evidence was required for a trial at Melbourne, but I did not know against whom. I had not the slightest idea who the prisoners were. Dr. Murray ordered me to fire the shots I did. I did not tip over any canoes, but I sometimes picked up the natives. I was forced to go into the boats. I sometimes refused. The crew whitewashed the hold to prevent the smell. I don't remember that Mount was ill when the lieutenant of the Rosario boarded us. Morris was down in the forecabin when the firing through the auger holes was going on. I do not say he was firing. I think Mount was there also. I don't remember whether I told Mr. Winch this.

Desperate encounter 34

Ned Kelly's last stand at Glenrowan, 1880

ONE OF THE GREAT AUSTRALIAN HEADLINES, 'DESTRUCTION OF THE KELLY GANG', MARKED THE LAST STAND OF THE MOST FAMOUS OF ALL AUSTRALIAN BUSHRANGING GANGS—AT THE SMALL TOWN OF GLENROWAN IN CENTRAL VICTORIA. NED KELLY'S ONE-MAN STAND AGAINST THE POLICE, IN HIS HOME-MADE SUIT OF METAL ARMOUR, HAS BECOME ONE OF THE MOST ENDURING AND LEGENDARY STORIES IN AUSTRALIAN HISTORY.

The Australian bush had provided a haven to convict bolters and so-called 'bush rangers' since the arrival of the First Fleet in 1788. There had been several waves of intense periods of bushranging, notably the 1830s and 1860s, when policing was limited and bushrangers were common.

Many were outright criminals and murderers, yet some, such as the Wild Colonial Boy or the 'gentleman bushrangers' of the 1860s, had a certain charm about them that fascinated urban newspaper audiences.

But by the 1870s, the rapid development of transport and communication technologies such as railways and the telegraph made policing the bush easier, and the days of bushranging seemed to be coming to a close. That was until the appearance of the Kelly gang and the apparent impunity with which they ranged the Victorian and New South Wales countryside.

Perhaps the Kelly story captivated audiences and lodged in the Australian consciousness because they were almost fighting the onslaught of modernity itself. Even with their suits of armour and rumoured hundreds of armed supporters, it was never a matter of whether the police would catch up with them, but when.

By 1880 Melbourne's *Argus* and other newspapers were moving closer to the headline style of news article we are familiar with today. Although the final stand of the Kelly gang had not yet displaced advertisements and notices from the front pages, the large eye-catching print in the local news sections began to reflect the importance of the news report.

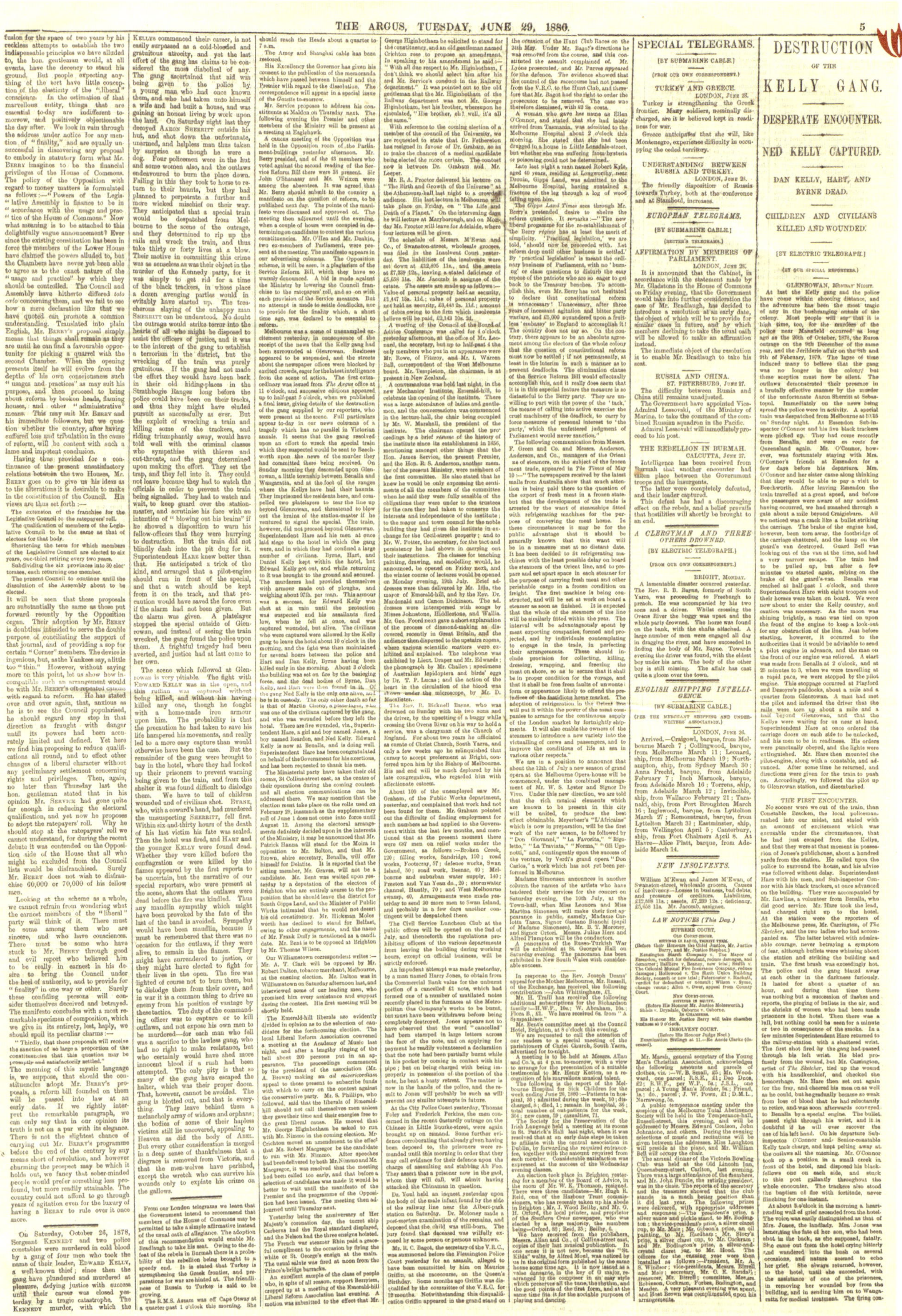
THE ARGUS, TUESDAY, JUNE 29, 1880.

DESTRUCTION OF THE KELLY GANG.

DESPERATE ENCOUNTER.

NED KELLY CAPTURED.

DAN KELLY, HART, AND BYRNE DEAD.

CHILDREN AND CIVILIANS KILLED AND WOUNDED.

[BY ELECTRIC TELEGRAPH.]

SPECIAL TELEGRAMS.

Melbourne's Argus of 29 June 1880 reported on the destruction of the Kelly gang. The story was relegated to the inside pages of the newspaper, but by now newspapers drew attention to significant news stories with headlines in larger type and several introductory or summarising statements ahead of the main story.

DESTRUCTION OF THE KELLY GANG.
DESPERATE ENCOUNTER.
NED KELLY CAPTURED.

...

GLENROWAN, MONDAY NIGHT

At last the Kelly gang and the police have come within shooting distance, and the adventure has been the most tragic of any in the bushranging annals fo the colony. Most people will say that it is high time, too, for the murders of the police near Mansfiled occurred as long ago as the 26th of October, 1878, the Euroa outrange on the 9th December of the same year, and the Jerilderie affair on the 8th and 9th February, 1879 ... We were now about to enter the Kelly country, and caution was necessary. As the moon was shining brightly, a man was tied on upon the front of the engine to keep a look-out for any obstruction of the line. Just before starting, however, it occurred to the authorities that it would be advisable to send a pilot engine in advance, and the man on the front of our engine was relieved. A start was made from Benalla at 2 o'clock, and at 25 minutes to 3, when we were travelling at a rapid pace, we were stopped by the pilot engine. This stoppage occurred at Playford and Desoyre's paddocks, about a mile and a quarter from Glenrowan. A man had met the pilot and informed the driver that the rails were torn up about a mile and a half beyond Glenrowan, and that the Kellys were waiting for us near at hand. Superintendent Hare at once ordered the carriage doors on each side to be unlocked, and his men to be in readiness. His orders were punctually obeyed, and the lights were extinguished. Mr. Hare then mounted the pilot-engine, along with a constable, and advanced. After some time he returned, and directions were given for the train to push on. Accordingly, we followed the pilot up to Glenrowan station, and disembarked.

THE FIRST ENCOUNTER

No sooner were we out of the train, than Constable Bracken, the local policeman, rushed into our midst, and stated with an amount of excitement which was excusable under the circumstances, that he had just escaped from the Kellys, and that they were at that moment in possession of Jones's publichouse, about a hundred yards from the station. He called upon the police to surround the house, and his advice was followed without delay. Superintendent Hare with his men, and Sub-inspector Connor with his black trackers, at once advanced on the building. They were accompanied by Mr. Rawlins, a volunteer from Benalla ... Mr. Hare took the lead, and charged right up to the hotel. At the station were the reporters of the Melbourne press, Mr. Carrington, of *The Sketcher*, and the two ladies ... The latter behaved with admirable courage, never betraying ... fear, although bullets were whizzing about the station and striking the building and train ... The police and the gang blazed away at each other in the darkness furiously. It lasted for about a quarter of an hour, and during that time there was nothing but a succession of flashes and reports, the pinging of bullets in the air, and the shrieks of women who had been made prisoners in the hotel. Then there was a lull, but nothing could be seen for a minute or two in consequence of the smoke.

1—GENERAL VIEW OF THE NIGHT ATTACK ON THE GLENROWAN HOTEL. 2—SCENE WH
THE MORNING. 4—THE BODIES OF HART

MR. T. CARRINGTON DURING THE ENCOUNTER.

July 10, 1880.

THE AUSTRALASIAN SKETCHER.

153

NED KELLY WAS SHOT. 3—THE SURRENDER OF THE 25 PRISONERS AT 10 O'CLOCK IN
DAN KELLY IN THE FLAMES.

By this time technology allowed the inclusion of artist's impressions of news events in the increasing numbers of pictorial papers. The Australasian Sketcher of 10 July 1880 showed the 'Destruction of the Kelly Gang. Drawn by Mr. T. Carrington during the encounter.' It presents several episodes from the gang's last stand.

Boom and bust

1881–

-1900

With the population explosion of the gold rushes in the 1850s, Australia's economy also began to expand. By the 1870s, steamship travel and telegraph systems ensured the once-isolated British colony was increasingly connected to the rest of the world. Accordingly, overseas economic investment in the country grew rapidly and created a period of economic boom in the 1880s.

During this period the colonies' pastoral industry consolidated squatted land into large acreages of leasehold, and in some areas freehold, title. Meanwhile in the growing cities of Melbourne and Sydney, especially, the early colonial estates that once sat on the outskirts of the urban areas were being subdivided for housing and industry. While urban development in the other colonial centres of Perth and Adelaide was comparatively slower, in 1859 Brisbane had become the capital city of the newly declared colony of Queensland. The 1860s and 1870s saw new discoveries create gold rushes in northern Queensland.

By 1880 nearly 70 per cent of the population of the Australian colonies lived in urban centres. The vast majority of Australians were not shearers or stockmen, but part of the increasing numbers of workers who lived in crowded inner-city areas near the busy ports, or caught trains and horse-drawn or steam trams to work from the outer suburbs. They worked on the docks or in the growing number of factories.

The boom period of the 1880s saw the growth of trade unions and relative prosperity among the working classes, as they were in an excellent position to bargain for rights and higher wages. However local manufacturing, which had developed to provide for a growing population and overseas export—critical for a growing economy—was still almost entirely dependent upon agriculture.

The 1890s, on the other hand, proved to be a harsh decade. Because of poor investment returns from the imbalance in local manufacturing and overseas export, as well as an economic downturn around the world, overseas investment in Australia began to dry up. The boom had bust, and following a series of bank collapses, an economic depression set in. During the 1880s the Australian colonies had been described as a 'workers paradise', but during the 1890s, depression ushered in a period of labour strikes, poverty and discontent.

In this time of urban growth, and boom and bust, an important phase of Australian nationalism developed. Perhaps surprisingly, considering that most of the population now lived in urban areas, an interest in what was beyond the urban sprawl—the bush—came to define 'Australia' for most people. With increasing urbanisation and the development of working-class slums in the cities, alongside the appearance of gangs of 'larrikins', roaming city streets, a faith in the iconic Australian bushman of the outback correspondingly increased.

At the same time, a growing movement towards some form of independence from Britain for Australia also began. This movement was often quite a contradictory desire to prove Australian nationhood, while also proving loyalty to the Mother Country and the British Empire—a tension that was to underlie Australian society for many years to come. In 1885, when the British army met some difficulty in its campaigns in the Sudan in Africa, an 'Australian contingent' was formed with some enthusaism to support the Empire in its time of need. Much of the energy behind this war effort was based on a desire for the colonies to be seen as Britain's equals, rather than feeling looked down upon as mere 'colonials'.

This insecurity and tension was vividly played out in the 1888 centennial year celebrations. The anniversary of the arrival of the First Fleet in 1788 was to be widely celebrated around the country with parades, pageants, monuments and other public works such as the creation of Centennial Park in Sydney. While it cemented 26 January as Australia's national day, Governor Phillip and the First Fleet were rarely seen in the anniversary symbolism. A much better set of 'origins', and a figure that had nothing to do with the anniversary, was Captain James Cook, whose visage appeared in parades and pageants everywhere. As Australians' sense of a national identity grew, it increasingly distanced itself from anything associated with convicts.

Throughout the late nineteenth century Australians found they could indeed be just like the British of the Mother Country. They had their own home-grown hero-adventurers, such as the intrepid journalist and explorer George Morrison, who hacked through jungles and fought off natives in New Guinea. Australians also found they could embark on their own colonising adventures. In 1883 the Queensland colonial authorities took 'possession' of New Guinea without waiting for the assent of the British Crown.

By the 1880s, distinctly Australian activities, characteristics and social habits had indeed developed. One characteristic was the widespread love of horse-racing, particularly, the great race—the Melbourne Cup. With the victory of Carbine—arguably the best horse ever to race in Australia—the Melbourne Cup of 1890 was a great distraction for all of the Australian colonies, even as discussions grew apace about their future independence from Britain.

The development of newspapers in this political and social milieu of the late nineteenth century Australian colonies was of critical importance. People in major towns and cities now

496 THE SYDNEY MAIL, SATURDAY, MARCH 7, 1885.

TROOPS FOR THE SOUDAN,—SCENE AT THE CIRCULAR QUAY.

By the 1880s the newspaper print production process was improving rapidly and images were becoming much less expensive to produce, and so more common. (See page 154 for the full story relating to this image.)

had several daily newspapers to choose from. Newspapers began to reflect a broader range of political opinions and also began to target different audiences. As the printing industry also developed, smaller newspapers catering to interest groups, such as trade unions or religious groups, began to appear. Regional centres often established local newspapers, such as the *Maitland Mercury and Hunter River General Advertiser*—the oldest regional newspaper, established in 1843—from the Hunter Valley area in New South Wales. Industries also established their own newspapers and some, such as the *Cumberland Argus and Fruit Growers Advocate* from western Sydney, combined local news with news relating to the predominant regional industry.

Newspapers also developed in terms of style and content. With new technologies and greater demand to see as well as read the news, more popular illustrated newspapers, such as the *Illustrated Sydney News* were in their heyday. The growing numbers of working-class people, who generally had only a basic education, formed an expanding and fertile market for these highly visual newspapers. These papers offered artists' impressions of events alongside much less wordy content than the broadsheets, such as *The Australian* or *The Sydney Morning Herald*. In Melbourne, the *Illustrated Australian News*, modelled on the *Illustrated London News*, provided a digest of news reports from its publisher, *The Age*, while the *Australasian Sketcher* performed the same role for *The Argus*.

In fact, imagery was to be the key to success in cornering the growing mass market of newspapers at the turn of the twentieth century. While the more conservative papers continued to refuse to change their production style, the more successful daily papers found headlines and images to be the new format for front page news. By 1900, the effects of the depression had worn off and Australians were ready for the modern technologies that a new century—with a new nation to be called Australia—promised.

35 Idle and depraved

The emergence of the larrikins, 1881

HEADLINES ANNOUNCING THAT YOUTH CULTURE IS A THREAT TO SOCIETY HAVE BEEN DOING THE ROUNDS SINCE AT LEAST THE 1880S. IN WHAT MUST SOUND VERY FAMILIAR, THE 'OUTRAGES' THAT IDLE YOUNG PEOPLE LOAFING AROUND THE STREETS WERE COMMITTING—PARTICULARLY DURING SCHOOL HOLIDAYS—FEATURED IN EDITORIALS IN THE 1880S. INDEED *THE BULLETIN* FOUND ROOM ON ITS FRONT PAGE OF 8 JANUARY 1881 TO TELL READERS THAT THE SCHOOL HOLIDAYS, A 'SEASON ONCE SACRED' WERE NOW MERELY A 'CARNIVAL TIME FOR LARRIKINDOM'.

In the late nineteenth century many saw larrikins as a threat to the moral and social fabric of society. The origin of the term is unknown, though it is possibly related to the word *larking*, as in *sky-larking*, but by the 1870s had come to mean young people who dressed 'sharply' and gathered in groups in public. Larrikins were generally from working-class backgrounds and some were—and many were assumed to be—petty criminals. Women who joined the gangs were called 'donahs' or larrikinesses. The larrikins' street presence dominated working-class suburbs in Sydney and Melbourne during the late nineteenth century. One of the most infamous larrikin gangs was the Millers Point Push, based in the Rocks area of Sydney.

The Bulletin, founded in 1880, was a weekly magazine and reflected the diversifying Sydney and regional newspaper scenes. It was nationalist and overtly racist, and became popular with working-class people, particularly workers in rural areas. Although it upheld a radical line of working-class politics, the magazine's position on 'decorum and youth' was especially scathing of the larrikin.

In January 1881, *The Bulletin* reported on a 'beach party' held at Clontarf. According to the report, ferry loads of 'too young' people attended. The newspaper claimed that all of those in attendance were larrikins, and the drinking and dancing was like a 'bacchanalian orgy'.

Unfortunately for *The Bulletin* and others concerned with 'proper' social behaviour at the time, the larrikins were to have the last laugh, as the word ultimately came to represent a streak of a supposedly distinctly and proudly Australian character—a joker or stirrer who cares little for authority. *Larrikin* was to become, perhaps somewhat ironically, a favourite appellation for the Australian troops during the First World War.

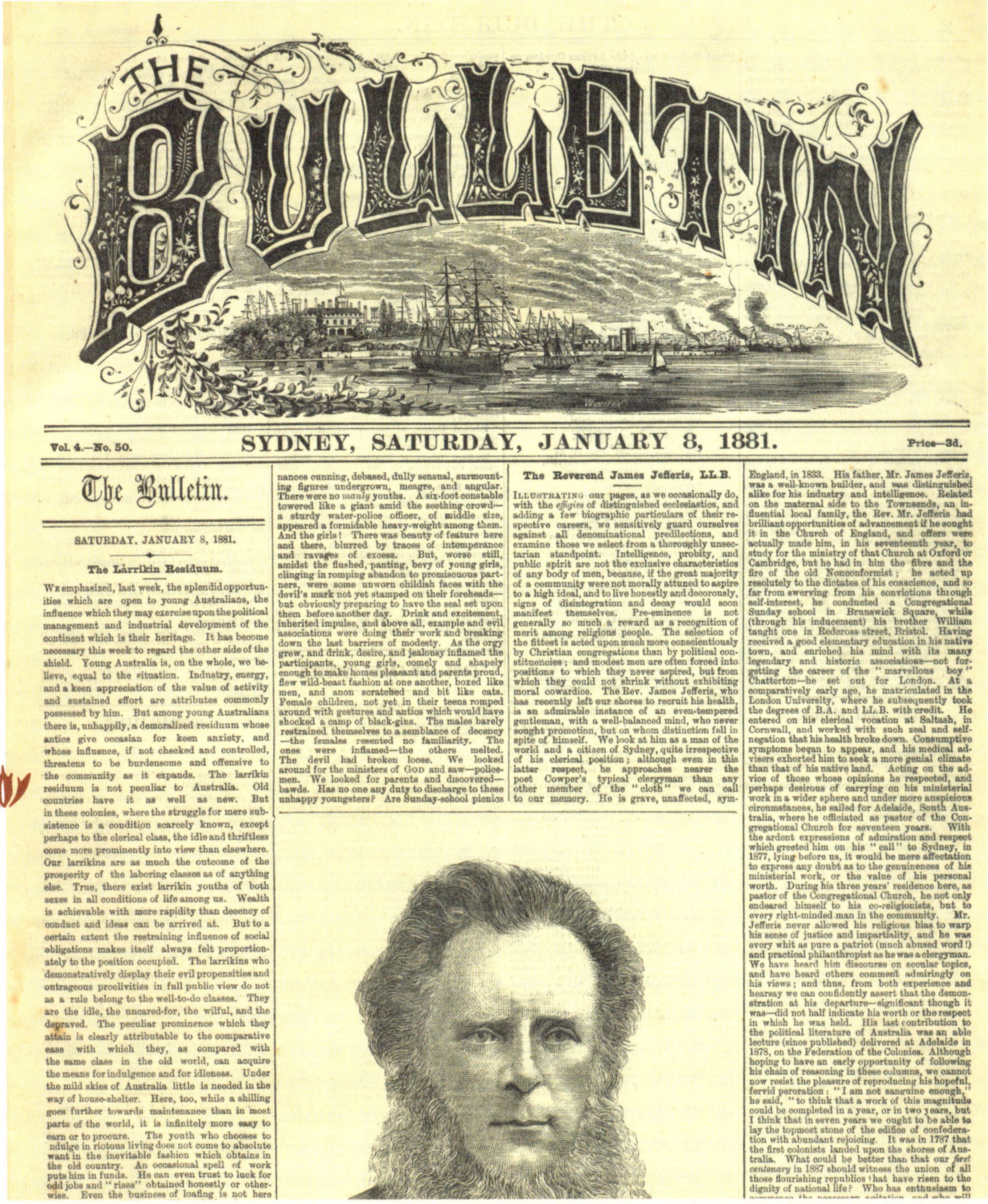

THE BULLETIN

Vol. 4.—No. 50. SYDNEY, SATURDAY, JANUARY 8, 1881. Price—3d.

The Bulletin.

SATURDAY, JANUARY 8, 1881.

The Larrikin Residuum.

WE emphasized, last week, the splendid opportunities which are open to young Australians, the influence which they may exercise upon the political management and industrial development of the continent which is their heritage. It has become necessary this week to regard the other side of the shield. Young Australia is, on the whole, we believe, equal to the situation. Industry, energy, and a keen appreciation of the value of activity and sustained effort are attributes commonly possessed by him. But among young Australians there is, unhappily, a demoralized residuum whose antics give occasian for keen anxiety, and whose influence, if not checked and controlled, threatens to be burdensome and offensive to the community as it expands. The larrikin residuum is not peculiar to Australia. Old countries have it as well as new. But in these colonies, where the struggle for mere subsistence is a condition scarcely known, except perhaps to the clerical class, the idle and thriftless come more prominently into view than elsewhere. Our larrikins are as much the outcome of the prosperity of the laboring classes as of anything else. True, there exist larrikin youths of both sexes in all conditions of life among us. Wealth is achievable with more rapidity than decency of conduct and ideas can be arrived at. But to a certain extent the restraining influence of social obligations makes itself always felt proportionately to the position occupied. The larrikins who demonstratively display their evil propensities and outrageous proclivities in full public view do not as a rule belong to the well-to-do classes. They are the idle, the uncared-for, the wilful, and the depraved. The peculiar prominence which they attain is clearly attributable to the comparative ease with which they, as compared with the same class in the old world, can acquire the means for indulgence and for idleness. Under the mild skies of Australia little is needed in the way of house-shelter. Here, too, while a shilling goes further towards maintenance than in most parts of the world, it is infinitely more easy to earn or to procure. The youth who chooses to ndulge in riotous living does not come to absolute want in the inevitable fashion which obtains in the old country. An occasional spell of work puts him in funds. He can even trust to luck for odd jobs and "rises" obtained honestly or otherwise. Even the business of loafing is not here

nances cunning, debased, dully sensual, surmounting figures undergrown, meagre, and angular. There were no *manly* youths. A six-foot constable towered like a giant amid the seething crowd—a sturdy water-police officer, of middle size, appeared a formidable heavy-weight among them. And the girls! There was beauty of feature here and there, blurred by traces of intemperance and ravages of excess. But, worse still, amidst the flushed, panting, bevy of young girls, clinging in romping abandon to promiscuous partners, were some unworn childish faces with the devil's mark not yet stamped on their foreheads—but obviously preparing to have the seal set upon them before another day. Drink and excitement, inherited impulse, and above all, example and evil associations were doing their work and breaking down the last barriers of modesty. As the orgy grew, and drink, desire, and jealousy inflamed the participants, young girls, comely and shapely enough to make homes pleasant and parents proud, flew wild-beast fashion at one another, boxed like men, and anon scratched and bit like cats. Female children, not yet in their teens romped around with gestures and antics which would have shocked a camp of black-gins. The males barely restrained themselves to a semblance of decency—the females resented no familiarity. The ones were inflamed—the others melted. The devil had broken loose. We looked around for the ministers of GOD and saw—policemen. We looked for parents and discovered—bawds. Has no one any duty to discharge to these unhappy youngsters? Are Sunday-school picnics

The Reverend James Jefferis, LL.B.

ILLUSTRATING our pages, as we occasionally do, with the *effigies* of distinguished ecclesiastics, and adding a few biographic particulars of their respective careers, we sensitively guard ourselves against all denominational predilections, and examine those we select from a thoroughly unsectarian standpoint. Intelligence, probity, and public spirit are not the exclusive characteristics of any body of men, because, if the great majority of a community were not morally attuned to aspire to a high ideal, and to live honestly and decorously, signs of disintegration and decay would soon manifest themselves. Pre-eminence is not generally so much a reward as a recognition of merit among religious people. The selection of the fittest is acted upon much more conscientiously by Christian congregations than by political constituencies; and modest men are often forced into positions to which they never aspired, but from which they could not shrink without exhibiting moral cowardice. The Rev. James Jefferis, who has recently left our shores to recruit his health, is an admirable instance of an even-tempered gentleman, with a well-balanced mind, who never sought promotion, but on whom distinction fell in spite of himself. We look at him as a man of the world and a citizen of Sydney, quite irrespective of his clerical position; although even in this latter respect, he approaches nearer the poet Cowper's typical clergyman than any other member of the "cloth" we can call to our memory. He is grave, unaffected, sym-

England, in 1833. His father, Mr. James Jefferis, was a well-known builder, and was distinguished alike for his industry and intelligence. Related on the maternal side to the Townsends, an influential local family, the Rev. Mr. Jefferis had brilliant opportunities of advancement if he sought it in the Church of England, and offers were actually made him, in his seventeenth year, to study for the ministry of that Church at Oxford or Cambridge, but he had in him the fibre and the fire of the old Nonconformist; he acted up resolutely to the dictates of his conscience, and so far from swerving from his convictions through self-interest, he conducted a Congregational Sunday school in Brunswick Square, while (through his inducement) his brother William taught one in Redcross street, Bristol. Having received a good elementary education in his native town, and enriched his mind with its many legendary and historic associations—not forgetting the career of the "marvellous boy" Chatterton—he set out for London. At a comparatively early age, he matriculated in the London University, where he subsequently took the degrees of B.A. and LL.B. with credit. He entered on his clerical vocation at Saltash, in Cornwall, and worked with such zeal and self-negation that his health broke down. Consumptive symptoms began to appear, and his medical advisers exhorted him to seek a more genial climate than that of his native land. Acting on the advice of those whose opinions he respected, and perhaps desirous of carrying on his ministerial work in a wider sphere and under more auspicious circumstances, he sailed for Adelaide, South Australia, where he officiated as pastor of the Congregational Church for seventeen years. With the ardent expressions of admiration and respect which greeted him on his "call" to Sydney, in 1877, lying before us, it would be mere affectation to express any doubt as to the genuineness of his ministerial work, or the value of his personal worth. During his three years' residence here, as pastor of the Congregational Church, he not only endeared himself to his co-religionists, but to every right-minded man in the community. Mr. Jefferis never allowed his religious bias to warp his sense of justice and impartiality, and he was every whit as pure a patriot (much abused word!) and practical philanthropist as he was a clergyman. We have heard him discourse on secular topics, and have heard others comment admiringly on his views; and thus, from both experience and hearsay we can confidently assert that the demonstration at his departure—significant though it was—did not half indicate his worth or the respect in which he was held. His last contribution to the political literature of Australia was an able lecture (since published) delivered at Adelaide in 1878, on the Federation of the Colonies. Although hoping to have an early opportunity of following his chain of reasoning in these columns, we cannot now resist the pleasure of reproducing his hopeful, fervid peroration: "I am not sanguine enough," he said, "to think that a work of this magnitude could be completed in a year, or in two years, but I think that in seven years we ought to be able to lay the topmost stone of the edifice of confederation with abundant rejoicing. It was in 1787 that the first colonists landed upon the shores of Australia. What could be better than that our *first centenary* in 1887 should witness the union of all those flourishing republics that have risen to the dignity of national life? Who has enthusiasm to

Transcription

The larrikin residuum is not particular to Australia. Old countries have it as well as new. But in these colonies, where the struggle for mere subsistence is a condition scarcely known, except perhaps to the clerical class, the idle and thriftless come more prominently into view than elsewhere. Our larrikins are as much the outcome of the prosperity of the labouring classes as of anything else. True, there exist larrikin youths of both sexes in all conditions of life among us. Wealth is achievable with more rapidity than decency of conduct and ideas can be arrived at. But to a certain extent the restraining influence of social obligations makes itself always felt proportionately to the position occupied. The larrikins who demonstratively display their evil propensities and outrageous proclivities in full public view do not as a rule belong to the well-to-do classes. They are idle, the uncared-for, the wilful, and the depraved. The peculiar prominence which they attain is clearly attributable to the comparative ease with which they, as compared with the same class in the old world, can acquire the means for indulgence and for idleness.

From its inception in 1880, The Bulletin *favoured leading with front page news, though without large headlines.*

36 *Attacked by natives*

Early exploration of New Guinea, 1883

ALTHOUGH MUCH OF THE ASIA–PACIFIC REGION HAD BEEN COLONISED BY EUROPEAN POWERS, IN THE 1880S THE ISLAND OF NEW GUINEA REMAINED BOTH 'UNPOSSESSED' AND UNEXPLORED. THE AUSTRALIAN COLONIES HAD BEEN URGING BRITAIN TO ANNEX NEW GUINEA SINCE AT LEAST 1875. A MINUTE TO THE SECRETARY OF STATE FOR THE COLONIES SUGGESTED GREAT BRITAIN TAKE POSSESSION OF NOT JUST NEW GUINEA BUT ALSO ALL THE CHAINS OF ISLANDS OF THE WESTERN PACIFIC.

'Annexing' New Guinea was also seen to be in the interest of Australian trade and defence and, it was hoped, would control or limit the growing trade in Islander labour. But an already overstretched British Empire was not very interested in taking on a large, mountainous island, which did not appear to offer much to a coloniser.

So in 1883, with the increasing threat of a newly powerful and actively colonising Germany taking control of its northern neighbour, the Queensland colonial government took possession of New Guinea—without waiting for consent from Great Britain. The Australian colonies had now themselves begun to colonise.

In an attempt to find out more precisely what Queensland had colonised, a young explorer–adventurer and journalist was sent by his paper, the Melbourne *Age*, to New Guinea. George Ernest Morrison (1862–1920) decided to try to walk across its unexplored mountains from coast to coast. Morrison, who was later to become famous for his reports to the London *Times* on the siege of Peking during the Boxer Rebellion in China in 1900, was an experienced traveller. By age 21 he had already walked from his home in Geelong to Adelaide, and from Normantown in north Queensland to Melbourne—a distance of 3270 kilometres in 123 days.

Yet his undoubted bush skills could not get his small exploring party more than 80 kilometres north of Port Moresby in thirty-eight days. Morrison was kept busy cutting a track through the jungles and ensuring the New Guinea warriors who kept barring his path were given presents they found useful. Morrison's welcome by New Guinea tribesmen came to an end when he was ambushed and two spears lodged in his body. One of his companions strapped Morrison to a horse to take him back to Port Moresby and on to a hospital at Cooktown in Queensland.

Morrison had reached further into the interior of New Guinea than any other European and his reports for *The Age* were eagerly received. The exploration and continuing attempts to gain control of New Guinea were to fascinate and frustrate Australians for many years to come.

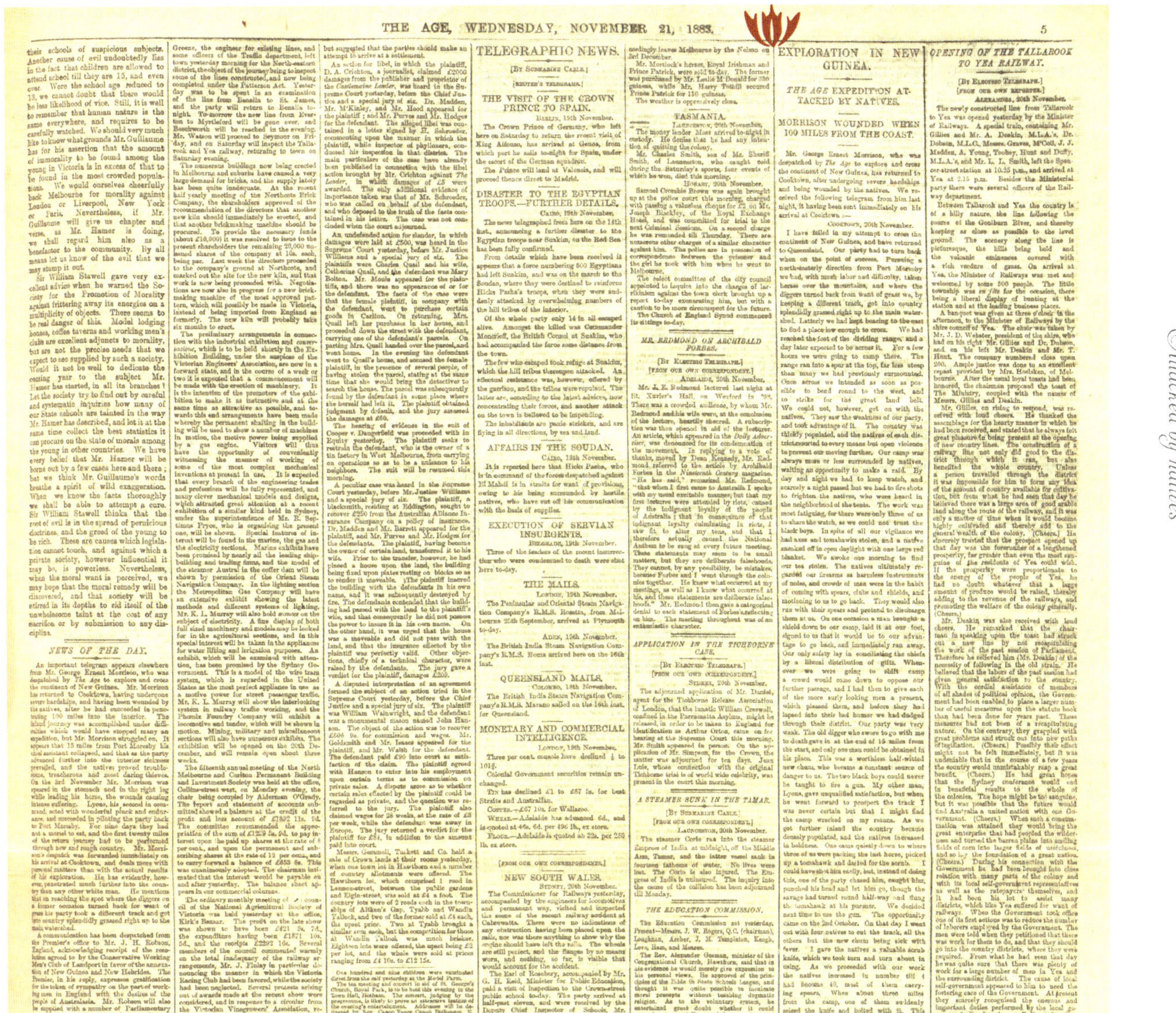

The Melbourne Age of 21 November 1883 reported the attack on Morrison and the failure of his expedition. His reports from New Guinea had been eagerly read by a fascinated Australian population.

THE AGE EXPEDITION ATTACKED BY NATIVES. MORRISON WOUNDED WHEN 100 MILES FROM THE COAST.

Mr. George Ernest Morrison, who was despatched by *The Age* to explore and cross the continent of New Guinea, has returned to Cooktown, after undergoing severe hardships and being wounded by the natives. We received the following telegram from him last night, it having been sent immediately on his arrival at Cooktown:—

COOKTOWN, 20th November.

I have failed in my attempt to cross the continent of New Guinea, and have returned to Queensland. Our party had to turn back when on the point of success. Pursuing a north-easterly direction from Port Moresby we had, with much labor and difficulty, taken horses over the mountains, and where the diggers turned back from want of grass we, by keeping a different track, got into country splendidly grassed right up to the main watershed. Latterly we had kept bearing to the east to find a place low enough to cross. We had reached the foot of the dividing range, and a day later expected to be across it. For a few hours we were going to camp there. The range ran into a spur at the top, far less steep than many we had previously surmounted. Once across we intended as soon as possible to bend round to the west, and to strike for the great land belt. We could not, however, get on with the natives. They saw the weakness of our party, and took advantage of it. The country was thickly populated, and the natives of each district resorted to every means but open violence to prevent our moving further. Our camp was always more or less surrounded by natives, waiting an opportunity to make a raid. By day and night we had to keep watch, and scarcely a night passed but we had to fire shots to frighten the natives, who were heard in the neighborhood of the tents. The work was most fatiguing, for there were only three of us to share the watch, as we could not trust the black boys. In spite of all our vigilance we had axes and tomahawks stolen, and a native sneaked off in open daylight with one large red blanket. We awoke one morning to find our tea stolen. The natives ultimately regarded our firearms as harmless instruments of noise, and crowds of men were in the habit of coming with spears, clubs and shields, and motioning to us to go back. They would also run with their spears and pretend to discharge them at us. On one occasion a man brought a shield down to our camp, laid it at our feet, signed to us that it would be to our advantage to go back, and immediately ran away. Our only safety lay in conciliating the chiefs by a liberal distribution of gifts. Whenever we were going to shift camp a crowd would come down to oppose our further passage, and I had then to give each of the more surly looking men a present, which pleased them, and before they had lapsed into their bad humor we had dodged through their district. Our party was very weak. The old digger who swore to go with me to death gave in at the end of 15 miles from the start, and only one man could be obtained in his place. This was a worthless half-witted new chum, who became a constant source of danger to us. The two black boys could never be taught to fire a gun. My other man, Lyons, gave unqualified satisfaction, but when he went forward to prospect the track I was never certain but that I might find the camp wrecked on my return. As we got further inland the country became densely populated, and the natives increased in boldness. One came quietly down to where three of us were packing the last horse, picked up a tomahawk and darted for the scrub. I could have shot him easily, but, instead of doing this, one of the party chased him, caught him, punched his head and let him go, though the savage had turned round half-way and flung the tomahawk at his pursuer. We decided next time to use the gun. The opportunity came on the 2nd October. On that day I went out with four natives to cut the track, all the others but the new chum being sick with fever. I gave the natives a valuable scrub knife, which we took turn and turn about in using. As we proceeded with our work the natives increased in number till 4 had become 40, most of them carrying spears. When about three miles from the camp, one of them suddenly seized the knife and bolted with it. This stealing was getting a farce, so I waited until the man had got such a distance that a shot would not inflict much injury, and I then gave him one charge in the back. Everyone declares that I made a mistake in not shooting the man dead, as I might then have effectually frightened the natives and given them an idea of our superior power. As it was they inferred that the worst our arms could do was to inflict but a temporary pain. That afternoon we could hear the news travelling everywhere, and see crowds of men collecting with piles of spears, and intently watching us. In the morning when I loaded up early, intending to shift the camp, warriors with heavy bundles of spears gathered in crowds at some points which we had to pass, until the long grass where they stood fully bristled with spears. Lyons was at this time very ill with fever and could hardly walk. We went on, however, exercising extreme caution till we reached the last rise we had to go up. I was leading the horse some distance ahead of the rest, and was just taking a steep step from the scrub into the long grass at the top when I was struck by two spears, one in the hollow of the right leg and the other in the stomach. The steep step saved me. I pulled the spears out, and fired a shot from my Winchester. I saw no men, though they must have been within four or five yards when I was struck. I had then to lie down, as blood flowed from me freely, and my stomach gave me great pain. When Lyons came up he thought I was mortally injured, for I was lying in a pool of blood, vomiting large quantities of blood, and suffering frightful pain. To save my life he resolved to abandon everything and bring me down to the coast. We were then over 100 miles from Port Moresby, but we could not return by the way we had travelled as we knew the natives were waiting for us. Over 50 spears in bundles were picked up near where I was wounded, showing the attack to have been premeditated but badly planned. Lyons, when packing the horses, could get no help from the new chum, who was paralysed with terror, and in consequence we retreated, leaving our stores behind, and escaped from the natives to nearly perish from starvation. For eight days I had not a morsel to eat, but the change of air healed my wounds, which are now quite well. Lyons, by the exercise of extraordinary courage and endurance, brought us safely into port. The first twenty miles of our return journey was through new and very rough country. For nine days Lyons was entirely without food, and but for his marvellous stamina I should now be rotting in the New Guinea bush.

37 *In aid of empire*

Sending troops to the Sudan Wars, 1885

IN THE EARLY 1880S THE BRITISH GOVERNMENT WAS RELUCTANTLY DRAWN INTO A CONFLICT WITH THE SUDAN, WHICH WAS IN REBELLION FROM EGYPT. AFTER SUDANESE FORCES DEFEATED EGYPTIAN TROOPS IN 1883, THE BRITISH AGREED TO POLICE AN EGYPTIAN WITHDRAWAL FROM THE AREA AND SENT THE POPULAR, THOUGH SOMEWHAT IMPETUOUS, GENERAL CHARLES GORDON (1833–1885) TO SUPERVISE. ALREADY A HEROIC FIGURE IN BRITAIN AFTER HIS EXPLOITS IN THE CHINESE OPIUM WARS (1839–1860) GORDON DECIDED TO DEFEND THE CITY OF KHARTOUM, AND IN MARCH 1884 THE SUDANESE FORCES DULY BESIEGED THE CITY.

After a drawn-out siege that excited the British and colonial newspapers, popular outcry demanding Gordon's rescue forced the British government to send a relief column, but it arrived on 28 January 1885, two days too late; the Sudanese had captured Khartoum and Gordon was dead. An outraged British public demanded Gordon's death be avenged, and the call was avidly taken up in the Australian colonies. Australians saw the expedition as offering them a chance to give the British Empire a contingent of Australian troops. Within just a few weeks, an infantry battalion of 522 men and 24 officers, as well as an artillery battery of 212 men, was ready to sail to Africa.

On 3 March 1885, to great public fanfare—enhanced no doubt by the declaration of a public holiday to farewell the troops—the Sudan contingent received a send-off at Circular Quay that was described as the most festive occasion in the colony's history. The contingent received a great deal of popular and government support, as this was the first time that troops in the pay of an Australian colony were to fight in a war in aid of the empire.

The raising of the Sudan contingent marked an important stage in the development of the Australian colonies' self-confidence. While it was also proof of an enduring link with Britain, there was some opposition in the colony to sending troops to foreign wars. When the contingent returned within a few months on 19 June having seen little military action and arriving when the fighting was almost over, they were lampooned in some sections of the press.

OUR STUDMASTERS.

Mr. Thomas Cook, Turonville, Scone.

No. XXXV.

Mr. Thomas Cook, of Turonville, Scone, Hunter River, was born in Canada, North America, in 1834. He arrived in the colony with his parents from St. Neotts, Cornwall, England, in 1837. St. Neotts was the birthplace of his parents. Mr. Cook was only 3 years old on arrival in this colony. From boyhood he has followed a bush life, and has been interested in and worked amongst stock ever since he was able to do so. He was about 20 years in the Tamworth district, and since then he has lived at Turonville, and on other properties on the Namoi, Thalaba, and Barwon rivers. The number of cattle on these runs is over 17,000 head, and they are considered equal to any herds in New South Wales. The brand is the well-known JBO brand, the JB being conjoined. About three years ago Mr. Cook sold the Barwon station, named Pockataroo, and the Thalaba Creek station, named Oreel; and has now the Namoi property, named Drildool, 30 miles below Wee Waa. This is chiefly stocked with sheep. Turonville and the adjoining lands consist of between 9000 and 10,000 acres. The flats are rich grazing land, and the ridges are well grassed and suitable for rearing horse stock. The stony ridges improve the hoofs of horses, and also their muscles. A considerable amount of money has been laid out on the estate in clearing off noxious plants, timber, &c. The owner contemplates making arrangements to raise water to irrigate land in dry seasons. Mr. Cook has now a large herd of horses, about 400 head of the number being brood mares. It would be a difficult matter to put such a lot of equal merit together. Within the last 12 months the owner has laid out over £1200 in the purchase of brood mares, and within the last three years in the purchase of stallions and mares over £3000. This season about 180 mares are breeding. At Turonville there are five stallions, besides several young stallion colts. The greater number of mares, say over 100 head, are in foal to Flying Shotand Cock of the Walk, imported Norfolk horses. Other sires include The Works, by Fireworks, by Kelpie; dam Baroness, by Boiardo; her dam Gannymede, bred by the late Mr. Austin, of Victoria; also Maroof, by Ameer, imported Arab; dam by Young Warwick, by Warwick (imp.); also a draught stallion. The stallions, the services of which have been obtained, include such well-known animals as "Goldsbrough," The Drummer, Splendour, Grandmaster, and Lightning—all thoroughbreds; Roscoe, an American trotter; Cherub, an English trotting cob. Mr. Cook has also a number of foals from mares purchased from the stud of Mr. A. Bowman by Sunlight, Athos, and Bulginbar; also from mares purchased from Mr. Walter Lamb, by Norfolk Jack, imported cob, and San Jose Patchen, an American Trotter. In the Turonville stud of horses the blood runs back to the old sires (imported) Waterloo, Mazeppa, Akbar, Mameluke, Scratch, Steeltrap, Toss, Reform, Warwick, Emigrant, and New Warrior; also, Yorkshire Hero, Sir Benjamin, and Confidence, all imported. In addition to the horse stock, there are 150 wellbred breeding cows kept on Turonville; and among the male stock is an English bull. Mr. Cook sold over £1000 worth of young bulls last year. The estate is a grand one for fattening purposes. Last winter 150 head of cattle were disposed of in the Sydney market at £15 per head. Mr. Cook visited England in 1867, and acquired a large amount of information regarding the most improved methods of horse and cattle breeding as practised in Great Britain and on the continent.

Patriotic Fund Committee.

The weekly meeting of the Patriotic Fund committee washeld on Wednesday afternoon at the Town Hall. There were present: The Hon. A. H. Jacob, M.L.C., chairman; the Hon. J. Macintosh, M.L.C.; Messrs. James R. Fairfax, hon. treasurer; R. B. Smith, M.L.A.; Captain Broomfield, Messrs. W. A. Hutchinson, M.L.A., hon. secretary; J. Pope, hon. treasurer; F. Bennett, W. P. Manning, and G. Pile.

Amongst the business transacted was the

THE N. S. WALES EXPEDITION TO THE SOUDAN.

Departure of the Troops.

Tuesday, the 3rd March, 1885, will be for ever a red-letter day in the history of New South Wales—the day on which this colony, not yet a hundred years old, put forth its claims to be recognised as an integral portion of the British Empire, just as much as if it had been situated in the county of Middlesex, instead of being at the very opposite side of the globe. That day marks an entirely new departure as regards the relations between the old country and her colonies. Hitherto the colonies have been regarded by many politicians as a drag upon the home country; and statesmen have been heard to say that the colonies of England were a source of weakness to her, and not of strength. The fallacy of such statements was demonstrated beyond dispute by the events of yesterday. If ever there was in the history of the world an occasion where everything that had been arranged was performed to the letter, if ever there was a day when a programme literally arranged was carried out satisfactorily, it was yesterday, when the chosen troops of New South Wales, the picked men of the colony, embarked for the purpose of assisting the British arms th e Soudan. We have on previous occasions recorded the enthusiasm with which the offer of our services was received; in fact, instead of having to invite applications, the authorities have been overwhelmed with them. The appearance of the men selected for this service, as they marched through the streets of the city yesterday, demonstrated that a very careful selection had been made; and there was only one feeling—very freely expressed by all who saw them—that they were just the very set of fellows to do credit alike to the colony and to the empire. There was no braggadocio among the men, but an earnestness of demeanour which plainly showed that they meant work, and none who saw them could doubt for a moment that they would give a good and conscientious account of themselves.

There may be some question as to the propriety of the step our Government has taken in dispatching troops to the Soudan, but there cannot be two opinions as to the skill and energy displayed by the Government in fitting-out the expedition. It must be remembered that this is entirely a new service here, and that our authorities had everything to learn in the matter, But in spite of this, everything has been carried out to the letter; our troops have been equipped in such a complete manner as perhaps no expedition in the world has ever been supplied with before, and everything was ready by the time named a fortnight ago, and our contingent for the Soudan started on their trip with all the punctuality of a suburban train. The greatest enthusiasm on the matter prevailed throughout the whole colony, as was testified by the enormous crowds who thronged the city yesterday. The day had been proclaimed a public

mission should be let into the Barracks but as one officer after another drove up, a section of the crowd in the road squeezed in behind the vehicle, and before the troops marched there were several thousands of people within the barrack walls. Many a pathetic scene occurred, as wives, mothers, or sisters took what might be the last farewell of the brave fellows going out to fight for the land of their fathers, and here and there an affecting parting between lovers obtruded itself upon the gaze of the passer-by. The few hours before noon must have been very trying to the members of the contingent, distracted as they were from quietly making their final preparations by the crying of women and the fervent valedictions of friends; but there was no disorder, and when the signal was given to fall in it was promptly obeyed. At half-past 11 the men dined, and afterwards there was a short interval before they were paraded, and at this time the square presented a phenomenal sight, the verandahs of the different buildings being packed with people, the walls half covered, and the ground thronged with soldiers and civilians, the bright uniforms of the former contrasting with the tasteful costumes of the ladies, who came to do them honour. A calm spirit dwelt over the scene, and all excitement was subdued until noon. Previous to that hour the men were formed into squads, and examined by Adjutant Bartlett and his subalterns with a view to ascertain that each had his accoutrements and was prepared to proceed to the point of embarkation. They were afterwards dismissed. It would be difficult to realise a more orderly set of men being got together than were these men the colony was sending forth to the field. They fraternised with the visitors and chatted sociably with their comrades, and seemed as light-hearted as though they were entering upon an Easter encampment. Suddenly the rattle of drums was heard, and the regular tramp of men accustomed to shoulder the rifle fell on the ear, and the sounds set the first great wave of excitement in motion, for it announced the period of the real business of the day. They came from the detachments from her Majesty's ships-of-war in the harbour, and as the gates were thrown wide open a body of pioneers marched in, heading 550 blue jackets, marine artillery, and marine infantry. The band played one of the liveliest marches, and the men trooped in, and by their bearing, their physique, and the smartness of their dress, at once challenged and won general admiration. The etachments had in their charge two Gardner guns, two field guns, and two Gatlings, and they made a stirring rattle as they quickly rolled these into their assigned positions. It fell to the lot of the squads in charge of the guns to clear a square in which the New South Wales troops might form into line, and much amusement was created by the impetuous sweep they gave the terrible instruments they were attached to. It was an absolute "scatter," and could not have been more complete had it been accomplished with rounds of ball cartridge. Another exciting sensation occurred when the newly-formed cavalry corps entered the square. Of this there were 50 members present, and they were under the command of Captain Macdonald. They rode splendid animals, and imparted an agreeable variety in the scene. Lastly, a considerable number of mounted troopers, under Captain Battye, filed in, and their animals also were sources of much admiration on account of the bone and muscle they displayed, and their splendid symmetry. His Excellency the Governor drove to the ground in his carriage, and was accompanied by the Hon. W. B. Dalley, Acting Colonial Secretary, Captain A. D. Loftus, A.D.C., and Mr. H. A. Unwin, private secretary. Amongst the other distinguished persons present were the Hon. J. S. Farnell, Minister for Lands; the Hon. F. A. Wright, Minister for Works; the Hon. G. R. Dibbs, Colonial Treasurer; the Hon. W. J. Trickett, Minister for Instruction; the Hon. H. E. Cohen, Minister for Justice; the Hon. J. Norton, Postmaster-General, the Hon. J. P. Abbott, Minister for Mines; Mr. E. Fosbery, Inspector-General of Police; Rear-Admiral Tryon; General Scratchley, High Commissioner for New Guinea, and Sir Edward Strickland. The crowd, which was exceedingly well behaved, was easily kept in order by Inspectors Anderson, Waters, Larkins, Lenthall, Lawless, Cotter, and M'Kay, and about 60 police under their charge. The route was divided into six sections, each of which was supervised by a sergeant, and all vehicular traffic was suspended by means of constables being placed in the side streets. Every arrangement was made to ensure a clear road for the troops, and happily they were most successful. Up to a quarter past 12 the local troops and the general public in the barracks were mingled with each other, and then the whole assemblage thrilled as the bugle for the last time in Sydney calls upon the troops to

Transcription

THE N.S. WALES EXPEDITION TO THE SOUDAN.

Departure of the Troops.

Tuesday, the 3rd March, 1885, will be for ever a red-letter day in the history of New South Wales—the day on which this colony, not yet a hundred years old, put forth its claims to be recognised as an integral portion of the British Empire, just as much as if it had been situated in the county of Middlesex, instead of being at the very opposite side of the globe. That day marks an entirely new departure as regards the relations between the old country and her colonies. Hitherto the colonies have been regarded by many politicians as a drag upon the home country; and statesmen have been heard to say that the colonies of England were a source of weakness to her, and not of strength. The fallacy of such statements was demonstrated beyond dispute by the events of yesterday ... when the chosen troops of New South Wales, the picked men of the colony, embarked for the purpose of assisting the British arms [in] the Soudan.

The Sydney Mail of 7 March 1885 reported on the departure of New South Wales troops for the war in the Sudan.

38 Celebrating 100 years

The centenary of settlement, 1888

THE AUSTRALIAN COLONIES SEARCHED FOR A DATE FOR THE CELEBRATION OF A 'FOUNDATION' MOMENT THROUGHOUT THE NINETEENTH CENTURY. IN THE 1860S, WITH THE IMPENDING CENTENARY OF CAPTAIN COOK'S ARRIVAL ON THE EAST COAST OF AUSTRALIA, SYDNEYSIDERS BECAME INTERESTED IN ESTABLISHING A GRAND MEMORIAL STATUE TO COOK IN HYDE PARK IN 1870. AND BY THE TIME THE CENTENARY OF GOVERNOR ARTHUR PHILLIP'S LANDING IN SYDNEY HARBOUR WITH THE FIRST FLEET ARRIVED IN 1888, IT WAS CAPTAIN COOK WHO STOLE THE SHOW.

The centenary celebrations were the first major commemorative events for Australians and they were conducted with gusto in Sydney and Melbourne. Decorations, balls and ceremonial dedications abounded. But most of the iconography produced for 26 January 1888 was devoted to James Cook, rather than Arthur Phillip.

Although there was some debate as to whether the first day of Cook's arrival at Botany Bay—29 April 1770—should be Australia's 'foundation day', it was hard to ignore the fact that the arrival of the First Fleet marked the origins of the colony. It was Governor Phillip and his officers who toasted the British flag on the shores of Sydney Cove.

Yet for many years Australians were reluctant to associate their past with convicts. Indeed in the parade for the 1938 sesquicentenary a timeline of Australian history did not represent convicts at all.

OPPOSITE
The Sydney Mail *produced a special edition centennial supplement on 21 January 1888 to celebrate the one hundredth anniversary of the arrival of the First Fleet and the foundation of the first colony in Australia.*

CONTENTS.

No. 1437............................Vol. XLII.

Page

Editorial : The Federal Council—Notes of the Week ... 123-24
Out and About 124
Gossip.—Melbourne Gossip 124
The Storyteller.—Miser Farebrother—Strange Adventures of a Houseboat 140-41-42
Natural History Association 153
Young Folks.—Good Night—A Boy who became Famous 144
Agricultural and Pastoral.—Meetings of Local Land Boards—Approaching Land Sales—Forthcoming Shows—Answers to Correspondents—Exhibition and Production—Agricultural Lectures—Work on the Acacia and Cognate Genera—Agricultural Societies—Breeders' Facts—Intercolonial Topics—The Rabbit Pest—The Clarence River Maize Crop—The Wheat Crop of Victoria—Schedule of Classes of Fencing in New South Wales—British and Foreign Gleanings—Judging Horses by Points—Preparation of Food for Dairy Cows—The Weather, Pastoral, Crops, &c.—The Land—Agricultural Items—The Work Done by Machinery—Encouragement of the Natural Enemies of Rabbits 119-20-21
Horticultural.—The Orchard—The Flower Garden—Greenhouse and Bushhouse—Garden Notes 121
Mining.—The Prospects of the Barrier Silver Mines—The Mount Morgan Appeal Case—Visit to the Fairfield Silver District—The Ruby Fields in South Australia—Queensland—The Barrier Mines—The Prices of Tin and Copper—Telegrams—Items 164
Country News.—Correspondents' Letters—Albury—Bombala—Deniliquin—Forbes—Glen Innes—Grafton—Goulburn—Kiama—Moama and Echuca—Mudgee—Parkes—Singleton—Temora—Telegrams 156-58
Commercial.—The Wool Trade—Stock and Share Market—Import Market—Weekly Review of the Produce Market—Latest Telegrams—Items—Stock, Station, and Produce Reports—Horse Market, &c. 127-28-29
General News.—Postal Conference—Parkes Fund—Victorian Railway Freight—The Federal Council—Through Railway Communication with Queensland—Military Matters—Northern Territory—Opening of the Railway to Rosehill Racecourse—Opening of the Tramway to Broken Hill—Civil Service Commission—Centennial Celebrations—Insolvency Court 155-56
Mail News—Our London Letter—Items by the English Mail 162
The Week 126-27
Sporting Notices 147
Racing.—Chronicle of Coming Events—Answers to Correspondents—Rosehill and Randwick—Turf Talk—Betting Market—Race Meetings—Entries for Coming Events, &c. 147-48-49-50
Athletic Sports.—Cricket Gossip—The International Cricket Match—Local Cricket Matches—Country Cricket—Pedestrianism—Cycling—Lawn Tennis—Athletic Mems—Shooting 150-51
Aquatics.—Rowing Notes—Sailing Notes—The Centennial Regatta—Swimming, &c. 152-53
Social Events 124-25
Music and Drama 125
Chess 144
For the Day of Rest : The Lily among Thorns 119
Intercolonial—Victoria—Queensland—South Australia—Tasmania—New Zealand—Fatal Coach Accident near Lorne 155
Correspondence.—Answers to Questions 125
Telegraphic.—Cable News 126
Miscellaneous.—Burning of the Barque J. T. Berry—Proposed New Fruit Markets—Late Country News—Temperature and Rainfall — Late Agriculture — Late Mining 154
New Publications 125
Our Illustrations.—Farm Cove and Government House—The Post Office—The Town Hall and the Centennial Hall—The University—Street View—The Harbour and Belle Vue Hill 137
The Humourist 144
Depth to Plant Potatoes 121
Historical Sketch of Australia 132-33-36
Our View of Sydney 136-37
A Few Statistics 136
Sydney Harbour 137
For the Gloves 137
Need of Practical Education 142
Fun and Fancy 142
Impoundings 166
Births, Marriages, and Deaths 166

ILLUSTRATIONS.

Sydney in the Centennial Year 131
The Colonial Secretary's Office 134
Town and Centennial Halls 134
View in Pitt-street 135
The University 138
Entrance to the Botanic Gardens 138
Sydney Harbour from Belle Vue Hill 138
Circular Quay 139
General Post Office, Sydney 139
Illustrated Stories 141-42
Key to Bird's-eye View of Sydney 136

SPECIAL SUPPLEMENT.

Bird's-eye View of Sydney

Abstract of Sales.

R. Goldsbrough and Co.—Early in February next, in Sydney, Dalkeith Station, Upper Hunter; on March 28, at Sydney Exchange, Alloway Bank Estate.

Alex. Wilson and Co.—In the middle of February, Gogelderie Station, Murrumbidgee.

Frank Wyndham.—On an early date, at Muswellbrook, 770 head of Store Cattle.

Nathan Cohen and Co.—On March 20, at Tamworth, 30 Splendid Rams.

Jenkins and Ray.—On a date to be named, Waterloo Station, Maranoa District.

Private Sales.—See page 118.

Astronomical Memoranda.

January.	Sun. Rises. h. m.	Sun. Sets. h. m.	Moon. Rises. h. m.	Moon. Sets. h. m.		Tides. Morn. h. m.	Tides. After. h. m.
22 Sun.	5 13	7 10	1 22	—	F. Q., 21st, 2.54 p.m.	1 48	2 12
23 Mon.	5 14	7 10	2 16	12 18		2 40	3 13
24 Tues.	5 15	7 9	3 11	12 54		3 46	4 21
25 Wed.	5 16	7 8	4 6	1 33		4 55	5 28
26 Thurs.	5 17	7 7	5 2	2 16		6 1	6 29
27 Fri.	5 18	7 7	5 56	3 4		6 57	7 22
28 Sat.	5 19	7 6	6 46	3 58		7 46	8 9

Planets Rising and Setting.	Rises.	Sets.	Daily Rate of Change. Rises.	Daily Rate of Change. Sets.
Mercury	5.7 a.m.	7.20 p.m.	4½ min. later	1¾ min. later
Venus	2.12 a.m.	4.14 p.m.	1 " "	1½ " "
Mars	11.5 p.m.	11.41 a.m.	3 min. earlier	2 " earlier.
Jupiter	1.1 a.m.	2.55 p.m.	3½ " "	3½ " "
Saturn	7.22 p.m.	5.32 a.m.	4½ " "	4½ " "

The English Mails.

Leave Sydney.

F. ... Jan. 25, Wednesday | P. ... Jan. 26, Thursday.
M. ... Jan. 25, Wednesday

The Sydney Mail.

SATURDAY, JANUARY 21, 1888.

The Federal Council.

The second session of the Federal Council was opened on Monday last at Hobart. There were present seven members, representing the colonies of Victoria, Queensland, Tasmania, and Western Australia. The title which belongs to the body by law is, therefore, still conspicuously out of harmony with the facts of the situation. As New South Wales, South Australia, and New Zealand have nothing to do with the council, its name, "The Federal Council of Australasia," is wanting in accuracy. This fact seems to have been uppermost in the minds of the members from the beginning. On the opening day the absence of representatives of the other colonies was a prominent subject in every speech. On the second day the question of the best means of securing the adhesion of the colonies not represented was referred by resolution to the standing committee. It is apparently recognised that the position now held by the Council is a false position. Under the Imperial statute the Council has to meet at least once in two years. As nearly two years have passed since the first meeting, this reassembling was a matter of necessity, even if it were nothing more than a matter of form. It had to take place to save the movement (in the words of one of the delegates) from "dying a natural death." The President (Sir S. Griffith) remarked, "If the council were allowed to fall into desuetude, it might be many years before the colonies would be induced to enter into such a combination again." As the colonies generally have not yet been induced to enter, the remark seems to indicate that those which have are not quite satisfied with the step they have taken, and would not be eager to take it again if they were set free. We can therefore understand the anxiety of the members of the Council to guard against the collapse of the whole undertaking.

But, probably, it would be the best thing in the interests of Australian federation if the Council were to die out, or if the Imperial statute, in which its constitution is set forth, were repealed. The standing committee has been directed to consider the best means of "securing the adhesion" of the other colonies. It is apparently supposed that the other colonies only want some alteration in the constitution of the Council to induce them to "adhere." There seems to be a belief that if the Council could only find out what it is that we desire, and could hold out a fair prospect of its attainment, we should be glad to accept the concession, and come in. The idea of increasing the number of representatives from each colony has been put forth. This could be done under the statute by her Majesty, at the request of the legislatures of the colonies. Would this satisfy us? If we are unwilling to affix ourselves to a federal legislature of less than a dozen members, are we ready to adhere to one consisting of two dozen, or of three?

It may be admitted that a considerable increase in the number of members of the Council would do something to save appearances. When seven gentlemen, meeting together, go through the formalities and give themselves the airs of a Parliament, the spectacle has a ludicrous aspect. The little gathering at Hobart was overweighted by its own standing orders. It is provided, for instance, that the bell shall be kept ringing for two minutes before a division is taken; that tellers shall be appointed and hand in lists of the members; and that in cases of confusion or error, which cannot be otherwise corrected, a second division shall be taken. Under other conditions these arrangements might be wise and salutary. We do not say that they are wholly unnecessary now. But there is a certain incongruity in carrying them into effect in an assembly of seven, with one of the number occupying the chair. We may just imagine four gentlemen sitting on one side of the chamber and two on the other in solemn silence for two minutes, while the bell was ringing and the lists were being made out; can we imagine a case of incorrigible error or confusion concerning the tellers' report? These performances would appear in better perspective in a chamber of twenty-four or thirty-six members. So much may be admitted at once.

But the reforms that are required should deal with fundamental principles, and not merely with appearances. The constitution of the Federal Council is fundamentally bad. It provides for the creation of a Federal Parliament, with immense contingent powers of legislation, but without any of the conditions that would entitle it to confidence or trust. The convention that drafted the constitution began on wrong principles and made a false start. An entirely fresh start should be made if that mistake is to be rectified.

Notes of the Week.

Our Centennium.

During the coming week the thoughts of all the colonists will be turned to the past. We are to have some national days of retrospection, to look back over the long space of a hundred years, to revive the recollection of our origin, and trace the course of our history. There is much in that history that we could no doubt wish to have been otherwise, but what is done cannot be undone. Errors and omissions have been neutralised by great efforts and great successes, and the ultimate result is such as none of us need be ashamed of. A hundred years ago, when Captain Phillip landed the "first fleeters," the world took very little heed of what was going on. Probably four-fifths of the English people did not know that such a fleet had ever left the mother country, and if they had known they would have had the vaguest possible ideas as to where Botany Bay was. The work was exclusively in official hands, and outside the Admiralty and the Prison Department few people concerned themselves in the matter. The young colony for the first few years of its life owed a good deal to the honesty and energy of its first Governor, whose name should always be mentioned with honour; but he worked under very discouraging circumstances, and though he might occasionally have cast a glance towards the future he would never, even in his most sanguine moments, have dreamed that in a hundred years three and a-half millions of people would be occupying Australia, and that Sydney would have stretched to Parramatta on the west and to George's River on the south. But the greater part of this work has been done not only within the hundred years, but within fifty. During the first twenty years the progress was hardly noticeable; everything was the results of English expenditure, and apart from that the colony had no foothold of its own. Sheep-farming was the real beginning of Australian development, and that had fortunately made a good start before mining followed on. As soon as the productiveness of Australia was thoroughly proved, then the penal expenditure became a matter of secondary importance, and the colony quickly outgrew its dependency on the British Treasury. The rate of progress during the next century will, as a matter of certainty, throw the work of the first century into the shade, and, standing where we do now, it is safe for us to be far more sanguine than even we see it would have been justifiable for Captain Phillip to be. We have as much reason to rejoice in what is going to be done as in what has been done.

Governor Bligh.

Sir Henry Parkes has published some documents forwarded by the widow of Captain Johnston, with reference to the arrest of Governor Bligh in 1808. Family documents are always of interest to historians who are trying to get at the facts of the past. Livy is said to have compiled a large part of his history from documents in possession of the Roman aristocracy. But then it should be remembered that documents of this kind should always be read with a little caution, because they were often originally designed either to praise or to vindicate some member of the family. Major Johnston was in charge of the New South Wales Corps at the time of the transaction referred to, and he was appealed to in a written document signed by John Macarthur and a hundred and fifty other persons to arrest Governor Bligh, on the ground that every man's property, liberty, and life were endangered. This document, oddly enough, was signed on January 26th, and therefore made the twentieth anniversary of the colony a very memorable one. Major Johnston did as he was requested, and on the following day received a memorial thanking him for what he had done. Another document is the deposition of Lance-corporal Marlborough, who takes oath that when ordered to search for Governor Bligh he poked him out with the point of his bayonet from underneath a bed upstairs in the servants' room. This statement, so derogatory to the Governor, it should be remembered, is distinctly denied on the testimony of other persons who were present at the capture. It was the interest of the insurrectionists not only to make out that the Governor deserved deposing, but that he knew it himself, and that conscience made him a coward. But Governor Bligh never showed himself a coward in any other transaction of his life. One point of great interest in connection with the lists of names appended to these documents is pointed out by Sir Henry Parkes—namely, that many of the founders of colonial families are among those whose names appear; but, so far as is known, the Hon. Edward Flood is the only person still living who is the son of one of those who supported the insurrection. Macarthur, John Blaxland, Simeon Lord, Thomas Jamieson, and others have scarcely any of their race left. It is very remarkable how many of them seem to have entirely disappeared from colonial knowledge. Scores of men who had the chance of founding families and of making fortunes in land seem to have made no mark. Why there should have been this infertility, we want some colonial Galton to find out; but the fact itself is a remarkable one. As respects Governor Bligh himself, it should, in fairness to his memory, be pointed out that the whole transaction was inquired into in England, and the conduct of those who deposed him was condemned.

Mining.

The last week has been remarkable for one of those sudden and spasmodic developments of speculation in mining shares, of which we have had several specimens in the past, and seem likely to have several more in the future. Mining in the colonies has been marked by sudden gains and wearing losses. If all the losses were put in one scale, and all the gains in another, the latter would not preponderate very largely; but the few great and rapid fortunes that have been made constitute an irresistible temptation to the adventurous. If it were only possible for mining to be carried out systematically, carefully, and after proper inquiry and tentative exploration, it would be as remunerative an industry as most others. To a large extent this has been the case with regard to coal-mining, and this has been the steadiest department of our mining industry, and has on the whole been remunerative, though there have been some exceptions when rashness has been punished; but with regard to gold and silver mining, speculators alternate between foolish neglect and equally foolish faith, so that valuable properties are for a long time spurned, and then worthless properties are bought at an extravagant price. It is not possible to take all the risk out of mining, because the most accomplished expert cannot judge from surface indications as to the deposit of ore below. Gold has been found in unlikely as well as in likely places, while good surface indications have often proved to be very misleading. In the early days of South Australia the great Burra mine was divided into two halves, the "nobs" and "snobs" drawing lots for the choice. The former secured pick, and chose the wrong half, misled by the specimens lying about. But, though no one can see into the bowels of the earth, it is quite possible to make sufficient exploration to prove that a payable mine exists before going into great expenses for plant; and it is possible for the public to refuse to buy an unproved mine at the price of a proved one. Mining captains can be got to report in very glowing language as to encouraging indications and splendid prospects and likely-looking ground; but reports of this kind should count for nothing. Promises are not worth paying for, or if people are asked to buy a purely speculative risk they should only be asked to pay a sporting price. But on the faith of glowing prospectuses and good names as provisional directors, many persons have parted with their money to find that they had simply purchased a liability to calls. If the public would not go mad about mining, but would exercise the same discretion that they have done in other businesses, by which they have made money, mining would be a great source of prosperity to the colony.

President Cleveland.

The President of the United States is reported to be ambitious of continuing his office for a second term, and in the message he has just sent to Congress he has certainly shown himself to be a man capable of bold and decisive steps, for he has spoken out plainly on the question which is just now the greatest one in America's internal politics, and that is the question of taxation and protection. He is indeed to some extent driven to a decision by circumstances which he could not control, because the present situation is one that cannot be continued. The American tariff is inconveniently productive of revenue, and there is a surplus of more than twenty-eight million; and as the Customs must be paid in gold, the Treasury vaults are full to bursting. One of two things must be done; either the revenue must be diminished, or some outlet must be found for the money. Mr. Cleveland, whether as a matter of policy or as a matter of conscience, has taken the ground that the people ought not to be taxed when there is no necessity for it, and that therefore the tariff ought to be reduced and the expenditure of every household lightened to that extent. His greatest antagonist for the next Presidency, Mr. Blaine, takes the opposite ground, and contends that the taxation ought to be kept up, and that some method should be found of spending the money. We know from our own small experience that it is quite possible to run through a surplus, when the people's representatives are deliberately asked to think in what way they can be extravagant; and we know also that such a policy is apt to lead to a reaction. Old-fashioned political economists have always contended that people can spend their money to the best advantage if left to their own judgment, and that, therefore, no more should be taken from them by the Treasury than is necessary for public purposes. But in these days this doctrine is very largely repudiated, and there is a school of politicians which contends that money could be more usefully spent under national direction for purposes which benefit the whole people than it could be spent by the people themselves in a peddling way. Any-one attempting to arbitrate between these two doctrines would find there was something to be said for each. There are some great undertakings which can only be carried out by the people collectively—that is, through their Government; but at the same time all experience goes to show that Governments when over-supplied with money are wasteful to the last degree.

Tapping the Water Springs.

The unprecedented volume of subterranean water recently brought to the surface of the ground in Queensland opens up a vast field for enterprise in artesian boring. Over half a million gallons per day pouring out over a country notorious for its aridity is almost impossible to realise. And yet from a depth of about 700ft. the gigantic spring has been released by the boring-rods, defying every attempt to keep it back by plugging. From the quality of the water it is surmised that it takes its source in some snow-clad range. But though its origin be shrouded in a mystery which we may not fathom, yet this discovery cannot fail to stimulate the search for similar subterranean rivers, in order to bring them up from their hidden depths to shed fertility around and turn the wilderness into a garden. What a serious loss of property might have been averted in the dry country to the west of Rockhampton had only this well been put down before the last disastrous drought. This discovery, too, bids fair to effect a great change in the method of boring hitherto adopted. Mr. Longhead has introduced the system of putting down a bore

134 THE SYDNEY MAIL, SATURDAY, JANUARY 21, 1888.

The Colonial Secretary's Office. Town and Centennial Hall.

PUBLIC ARCHITECTURE, 1888.

The centennial supplement of The Sydney Mail *of 21 January 1888 showed artists' impressions of Sydney scenes ahead of the celebrations. Within months the first newspaper photographs using the new halftone process appeared, and within a decade the illustrated papers had folded. The faster process meant the dailies could publish photographs that had been taken the day before.*

PITT-STREET LOOKING SOUTH FROM THE "SYDNEY MORNING HERALD," AND "SYDNEY MAIL" OFFICES, 1888.

Notes of the Week.
Our Centennium.

During the coming week the thoughts of all the colonists will be turned to the past. We are to have some national days of retrospection, to look back over the long spce of a hundred years, to revive the recollection of our origin, and trace the course of our history. There is much in that history that we could no doubt wish to have been otherwise, but what is done cannot be undone. Errors and omissions have been neutralised by great efforts and great successes, and the ultimate result is such as none of us need be ashamed of. A hundred years ago, when Captain Phillip landed the "first fleeters," the world took very little heed of what was going on. Probably four-fifths of the English people did not know that such a fleet had ever left the mother country, and if they had known they would have had the vaguest possible ideas as to where Botany Bay was. The work was exclusively in official hands, and outside the Admiralty and the Prison Department few people concerned themselves in the matter. The young colony for the first few years of its life owed a good deal to the honesty and energy of its first Governor, whose name should always be mentioned with honour ; but he worked under very discouraging circumstances, and though he might occasionally have cast a glance towards the future he would never, even in his most sanguine moments, have dreamed that in a hundred years three and a-half millions of people would be occupying Australia, and that Sydney would have stretched to Parramatta on the west and to George's River on the south. But the greater part of this work has been done not only within the hundred years, but within fifty. During the first twenty years the progress was hardly noticeable ; everything was the results of English expenditure, and apart from that the colony had no foothold of its own. Sheep-farming was the real beginning of Australian development, and that had fortunately made a good start before mining followed on. As soon as the productiveness of Australia was thoroughly proved, then the penal expenditure became a matter of secondary importance, and the colony quickly outgrew its dependency on the British Treasury. The rate of progress during the next century will, as a matter of certainty, throw the work of the first century into the shade, and, standing where we do now, it is safe for us to be far more sanguine that even we see it would have been justifiable for Captain Phillip to be. We have as much reason to rejoice in what is going to be done as in what has been done.

The greatest racehorse of all time 39

Carbine wins the Melbourne Cup, 1890

ON THE EVENING FOLLOWING THE MELBOURNE CUP HORSE RACE AT FLEMINGTON RACETRACK ON 4 NOVEMBER 1890, AN 'EVANGELISTIC AND SOCIAL MEETING' WAS HELD AT THE MELBOURNE TOWN HALL THAT DISCUSSED 'THE EVILS CAUSED BY GAMBLING'. THE REVEREND MR BLACKETT SPOKE ABOUT THE RACE MEETING HE HAD ATTENDED THAT DAY AND HE REPORTED THAT HE WAS VERY DISAPPOINTED TO SEE LARGE NUMBERS OF YOUNG MEN AND WOMEN THERE.

Few people attended the meeting with Mr Blackett and his supporters, for by 1890 the Melbourne Cup had become an institution for Melbourne, and wider colonial Australian society. The first Cup was run in 1861—with only a small crowd in attendance, as the news of the deaths of explorers Burke and Wills had just been telegraphed through two days before. The eventful race—won by Sydney outsider Archer—saw one horse bolt before the start and three others fall during the race.

With interstate rivalries between Sydney and Melbourne horses and large prize money on offer, the Cup quickly became so popular that by 1865 a half-day public holiday had been declared in Melbourne.

The 1890 Cup winner, Carbine, was a popular horse. From forty-three races Carbine had won thirty-three times and only once failed to gain a place. As *The Argus* reported, Carbine was 'a racehorse whose performances ... have certainly never been surpassed or even equalled in the history of racing in Australasia'. It was to take until the 1930s and a horse called Phar Lap to better Carbine's record, but no horse since has ever won with the 65.5 kilogram weight-for-age penalty that Carbine carried. Perhaps less well known is that both Carbine and Phar Lap were born in New Zealand.

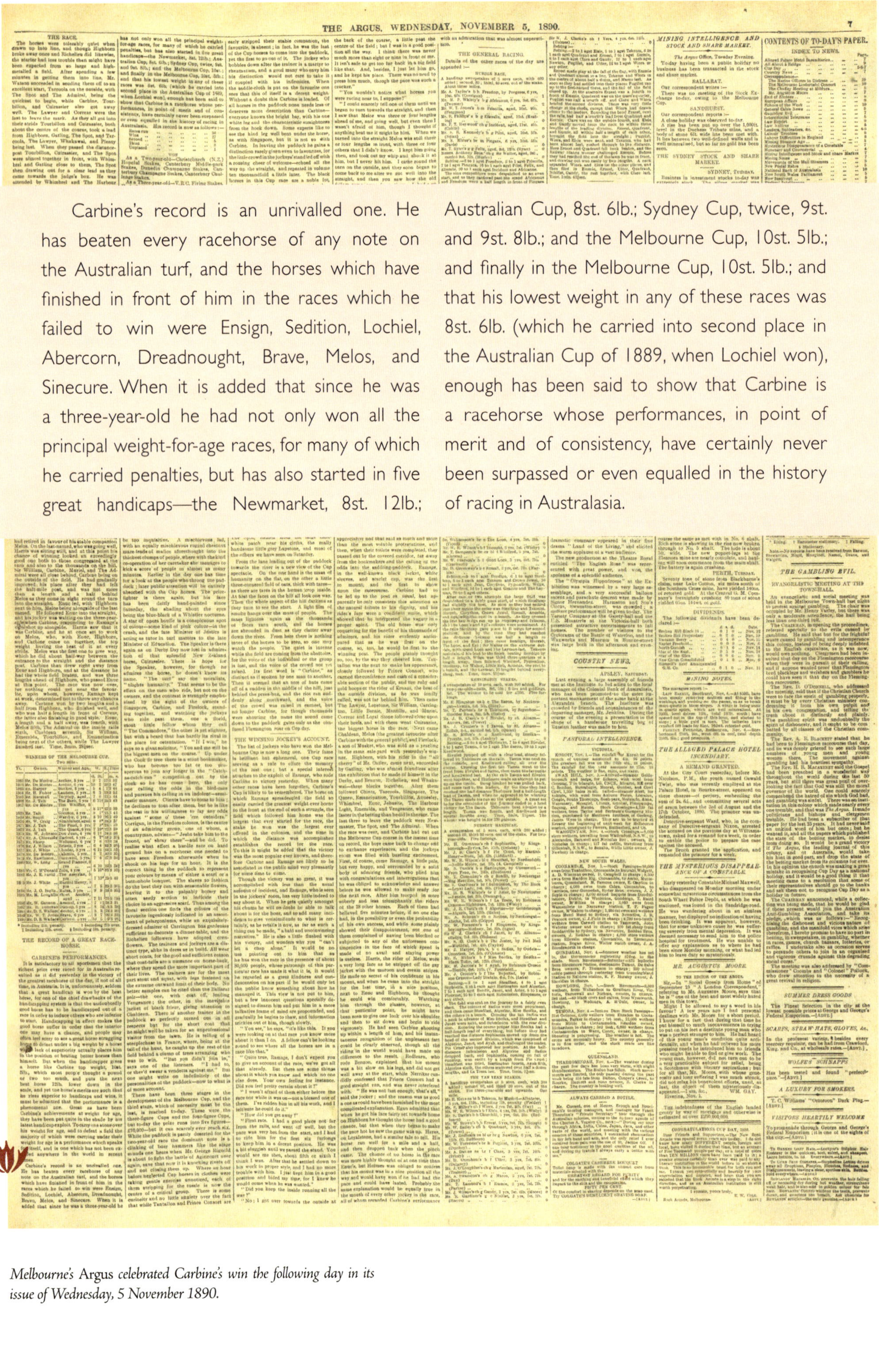

THE ARGUS, WEDNESDAY, NOVEMBER 5, 1890.

Transcription

Carbine's record is an unrivalled one. He has beaten every racehorse of any note on the Australian turf, and the horses which have finished in front of him in the races which he failed to win were Ensign, Sedition, Lochiel, Abercorn, Dreadnought, Brave, Melos, and Sinecure. When it is added that since he was a three-year-old he had not only won all the principal weight-for-age races, for many of which he carried penalties, but has also started in five great handicaps—the Newmarket, 8st. 12lb.; Australian Cup, 8st. 6lb.; Sydney Cup, twice, 9st. and 9st. 8lb.; and the Melbourne Cup, 10st. 5lb.; and finally in the Melbourne Cup, 10st. 5lb.; and that his lowest weight in any of these races was 8st. 6lb. (which he carried into second place in the Australian Cup of 1889, when Lochiel won), enough has been said to show that Carbine is a racehorse whose performances, in point of merit and of consistency, have certainly never been surpassed or even equalled in the history of racing in Australasia.

Melbourne's Argus celebrated Carbine's win the following day in its issue of Wednesday, 5 November 1890.

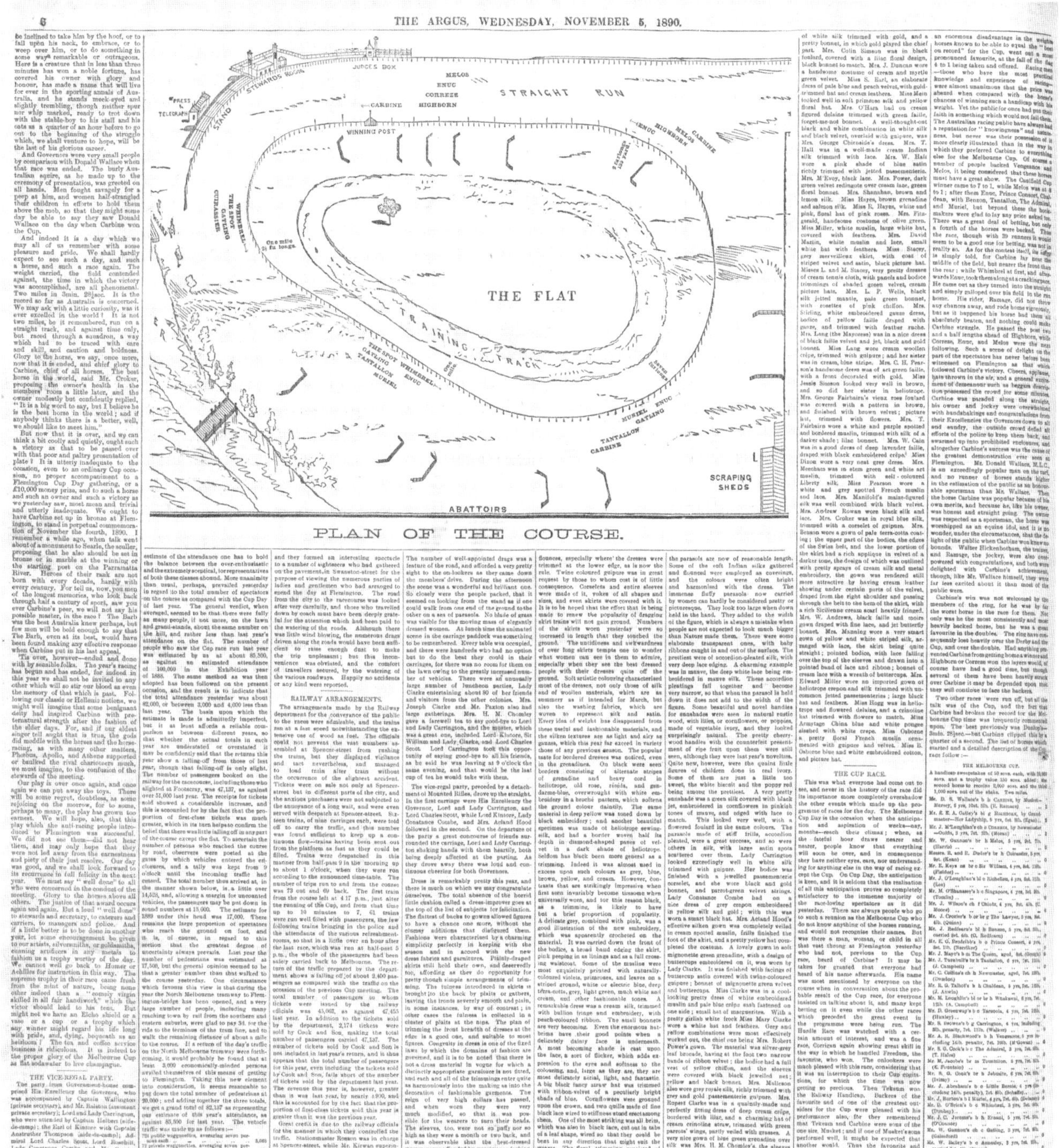

The hand-drawn course map printed in The Argus *for the post–Melbourne Cup day issue of 1890 shows the position of the horses at various points during the race.*

40 *A disastrous shock*

Bank crashes and depression, 1893

THE COLONIES OF AUSTRALIA HAD NOT FELT THE EFFECTS OF A SIGNIFICANT ECONOMIC RECESSION SINCE THE 1840S WHEN THE WOOL BOOM COLLAPSED. WHILE THE 1880S HAD SEEN AN ECONOMIC BOOM TIME FOLLOWING THE HUGE IMPACT OF THE GOLD RUSHES ON BOTH THE POPULATION AND THE ECONOMY, THE 1890S SAW A SEVERE ECONOMIC DOWNTURN.

Many industries had developed large workforces, particularly in shearing, mining and the maritime industry across the many ports in the colonies. Labour shortages meant higher wages were offered and many of these industries developed comparatively well-paid and skilled workers. From the 1870s their trade unions were successful in obtaining an eight-hour day and other benefits that were unheard of in Europe at the time. Australia earned a reputation as a 'working man's paradise'. But this changed dramatically in the early 1890s, when the boom of the eighties was replaced with the bust of the nineties.

The boom had attracted an influx of foreign investment and when returns began to fail, in 1891 several small Australian banks collapsed. When in 1893 a global economic downturn developed, an Australian banking crisis rapidly followed. The Federal Bank of Australia in Melbourne closed its doors, and many others suspended trading. In Victoria a five-day 'bank holiday' was declared to try to calm people down, who were in a rush to get at their savings before more banks fell.

A widespread economic decline followed, and employers were forced to cut wages. The workers' paradise of the 1880s was rapidly fading, and major strikes against declining wages and conditions in the large maritime and shearing workforces culminated in a series of bitter and bloody conflicts.

One significant development from this period was the emergence of political parties among the trade unions, including the Labour Party, first elected to government in Queensland in 1899—in fact it was the first such workers' political party elected in the world.

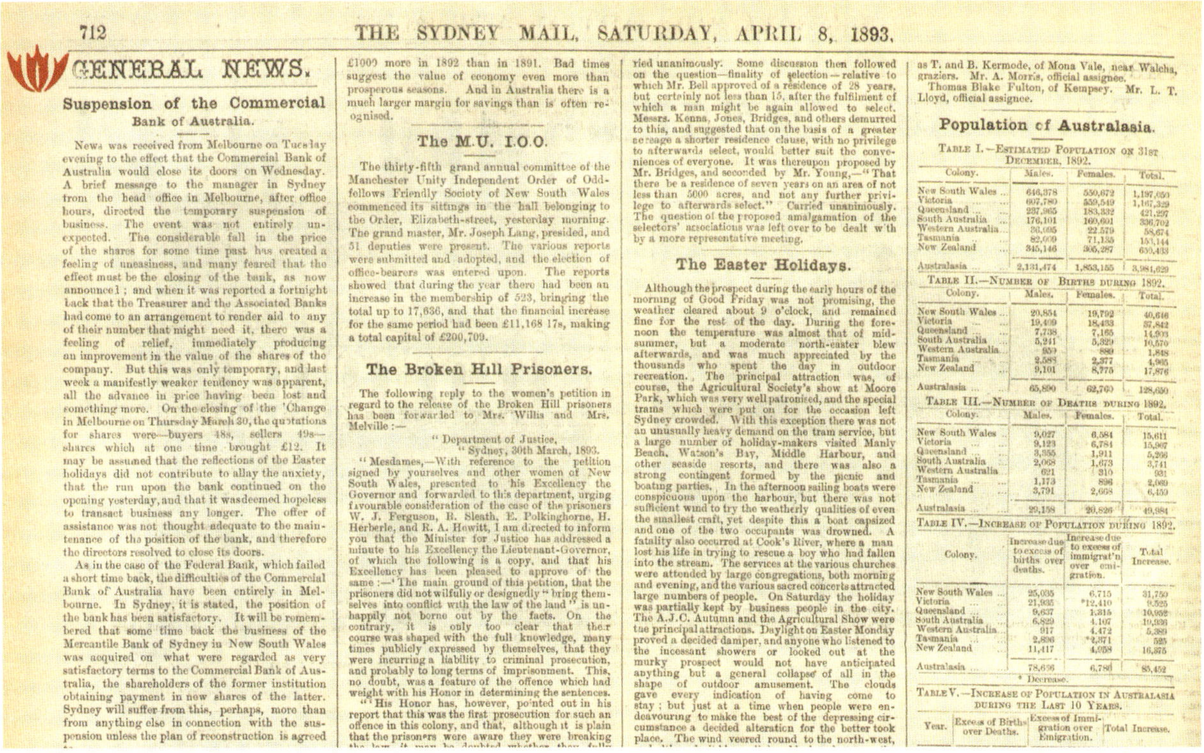

712 THE SYDNEY MAIL, SATURDAY, APRIL 8, 1893.

GENERAL NEWS.

Suspension of the Commercial Bank of Australia.

News was received from Melbourne on Tuesday evening to the effect that the Commercial Bank of Australia would close its doors on Wednesday. A brief message to the manager in Sydney from the head office in Melbourne, after office hours, directed the temporary suspension of business. The event was not entirely unexpected. The considerable fall in the price of the shares for some time past has created a feeling of uneasiness, and many feared that the effect must be the closing of the bank, as now announced; and when it was reported a fortnight back that the Treasurer and the Associated Banks had come to an arrangement to render aid to any of their number that might need it, there was a feeling of relief, immediately producing an improvement in the value of the shares of the company. But this was only temporary, and last week a manifestly weaker tendency was apparent, all the advance in price having been lost and something more. On the closing of the 'Change in Melbourne on Thursday March 30, the quotations for shares were—buyers 48s, sellers 49s—shares which at one time brought £12. It may be assumed that the reflections of the Easter holidays did not contribute to allay the anxiety, that the run upon the bank continued on the opening yesterday, and that it was deemed hopeless to transact business any longer. The offer of assistance was not thought adequate to the maintenance of the position of the bank, and therefore the directors resolved to close its doors.

As in the case of the Federal Bank, which failed a short time back, the difficulties of the Commercial Bank of Australia have been entirely in Melbourne. In Sydney, it is stated, the position of the bank has been satisfactory. It will be remembered that some time back the business of the Mercantile Bank of Sydney in New South Wales was acquired on what were regarded as very satisfactory terms to the Commercial Bank of Australia, the shareholders of the former institution obtaining payment in new shares of the latter. Sydney will suffer from this, perhaps, more than from anything else in connection with the suspension unless the plan of reconstruction is agreed

£1000 more in 1892 than in 1891. Bad times suggest the value of economy even more than prosperous seasons. And in Australia there is a much larger margin for savings than is often recognised.

The M.U. I.O.O.

The thirty-fifth grand annual committee of the Manchester Unity Independent Order of Oddfellows Friendly Society of New South Wales commenced its sittings in the hall belonging to the Order, Elizabeth-street, yesterday morning. The grand master, Mr. Joseph Lang, presided, and 51 deputies were present. The various reports were submitted and adopted, and the election of office-bearers was entered upon. The reports showed that during the year there had been an increase in the membership of 523, bringing the total up to 17,636, and that the financial increase for the same period had been £11,168 17s, making a total capital of £200,709.

The Broken Hill Prisoners.

The following reply to the women's petition in regard to the release of the Broken Hill prisoners has been forwarded to Mrs. Willis and Mrs. Melville:—

"Department of Justice,
"Sydney, 30th March, 1893.

"Mesdames,—With reference to the petition signed by yourselves and other women of New South Wales, presented to his Excellency the Governor and forwarded to this department, urging favourable consideration of the case of the prisoners W. J. Ferguson, R. Sleath, E. Polkinghorne, H. Herberle, and R. A. Hewitt, I am directed to inform you that the Minister for Justice has addressed a minute to his Excellency the Lieutenant-Governor, of which the following is a copy, and that his Excellency has been pleased to approve of the same:—'The main ground of this petition, that the prisoners did not wilfully or designedly "bring themselves into conflict with the law of the land" is unhappily not borne out by the facts. On the contrary, it is only too clear that their course was shaped with the full knowledge, many times publicly expressed by themselves, that they were incurring a liability to criminal prosecution, and probably to long terms of imprisonment. This, no doubt, was a feature of the offence which had weight with his Honor in determining the sentences.

"'His Honor has, however, pointed out in his report that this was the first prosecution for such an offence in this colony, and that, although it is plain that the prisoners were aware they were breaking

ried unanimously. Some discussion then followed on the question—finality of selection—relative to which Mr. Bell approved of a residence of 28 years, but certainly not less than 15, after the fulfilment of which a man might be again allowed to select. Messrs. Kenna, Jones, Bridges, and others demurred to this, and suggested that on the basis of a greater acreage a shorter residence clause, with no privilege to afterwards select, would better suit the conveniences of everyone. It was thereupon proposed by Mr. Bridges, and seconded by Mr. Young,—"That there be a residence of seven years on an area of not less than 5000 acres, and not any further privilege to afterwards select." Carried unanimously. The question of the proposed amalgamation of the selectors' associations was left over to be dealt with by a more representative meeting.

The Easter Holidays.

Although the prospect during the early hours of the morning of Good Friday was not promising, the weather cleared about 9 o'clock, and remained fine for the rest of the day. During the forenoon the temperature was almost that of midsummer, but a moderate north-easter blew afterwards, and was much appreciated by the thousands who spent the day in outdoor recreation. The principal attraction was, of course, the Agricultural Society's show at Moore Park, which was very well patronised, and the special trams which were put on for the occasion left Sydney crowded. With this exception there was not an unusually heavy demand on the tram service, but a large number of holiday-makers visited Manly Beach, Watson's Bay, Middle Harbour, and other seaside resorts, and there was also a strong contingent formed by the picnic and boating parties. In the afternoon sailing boats were conspicuous upon the harbour, but there was not sufficient wind to try the weatherly qualities of even the smallest craft, yet despite this a boat capsized and one of the two occupants was drowned. A fatality also occurred at Cook's River, where a man lost his life in trying to rescue a boy who had fallen into the stream. The services at the various churches were attended by large congregations, both morning and evening, and the various sacred concerts attracted large numbers of people. On Saturday the holiday was partially kept by business people in the city. The A.J.C. Autumn and the Agricultural Show were the principal attractions. Daylight on Easter Monday proved a decided damper, and anyone who listened to the incessant showers or looked out at the murky prospect would not have anticipated anything but a general collapse of all in the shape of outdoor amusement. The clouds gave every indication of having come to stay; but just at a time when people were endeavouring to make the best of the depressing circumstance a decided alteration for the better took place. The wind veered round to the north-west,

as T. and B. Kermode, of Mona Vale, near Walcha, graziers. Mr. A. Morris, official assignee.

Thomas Blake Fulton, of Kempsey. Mr. L. T. Lloyd, official assignee.

Population of Australasia.

TABLE I.—ESTIMATED POPULATION ON 31ST DECEMBER, 1892.

Colony.	Males.	Females.	Total.
New South Wales ...	646,378	550,672	1,197,050
Victoria	607,780	559,549	1,167,329
Queensland	237,965	183,332	421,297
South Australia ...	176,101	160,601	336,702
Western Australia...	36,095	22,579	58,674
Tasmania	82,009	71,135	153,144
New Zealand ...	345,146	305,287	650,433
Australasia ...	2,131,474	1,853,155	3,984,629

TABLE II.—NUMBER OF BIRTHS DURING 1892.

Colony.	Males.	Females.	Total.
New South Wales ...	20,854	19,792	40,646
Victoria	19,409	18,433	37,842
Queensland	7,738	7,165	14,903
South Australia ...	5,241	5,329	10,570
Western Australia...	959	889	1,848
Tasmania	2,588	2,377	4,965
New Zealand ...	9,101	8,775	17,876
Australasia ...	65,890	62,760	128,650

TABLE III.—NUMBER OF DEATHS DURING 1892.

Colony.	Males.	Females.	Total.
New South Wales ...	9,027	6,584	15,611
Victoria	9,123	6,784	15,907
Queensland	3,355	1,911	5,266
South Australia ...	2,068	1,673	3,741
Western Australia...	621	310	931
Tasmania	1,173	896	2,069
New Zealand ...	3,791	2,668	6,459
Australasia ...	29,158	20,826	49,984

TABLE IV.—INCREASE OF POPULATION DURING 1892.

Colony.	Increase due to excess of births over deaths.	Increase due to excess of immigrat'n over emigration.	Total Increase.
New South Wales ...	25,035	6,715	31,750
Victoria	21,935	*12,410	9,525
Queensland	9,637	1,315	10,952
South Australia ...	6,829	4,107	10,936
Western Australia...	917	4,472	5,389
Tasmania	2,896	*2,371	525
New Zealand ...	11,417	4,958	16,375
Australasia ...	78,696	6,786	85,452

* Decrease.

TABLE V.—INCREASE OF POPULATION IN AUSTRALASIA DURING THE LAST 10 YEARS.

Year.	Excess of Births over Deaths.	Excess of Immigration over Emigration.	Total Increase.

GENERAL NEWS.
Suspension of the Commercial Bank of Australia.

News was received from Melbourne on Tuesday evening to the effect that the Commercial Bank of Australia would close its doors on Wednesday. A brief message to the manager in Sydney from the head office in Melbourne, after office hours, directed the temporary suspension of business. The event was not entirely unexpected. The considerable fall in the price of the shares for some time past has created a felling of uneasiness, and may feared that the effect must be the closing of the bank, as now announced ...

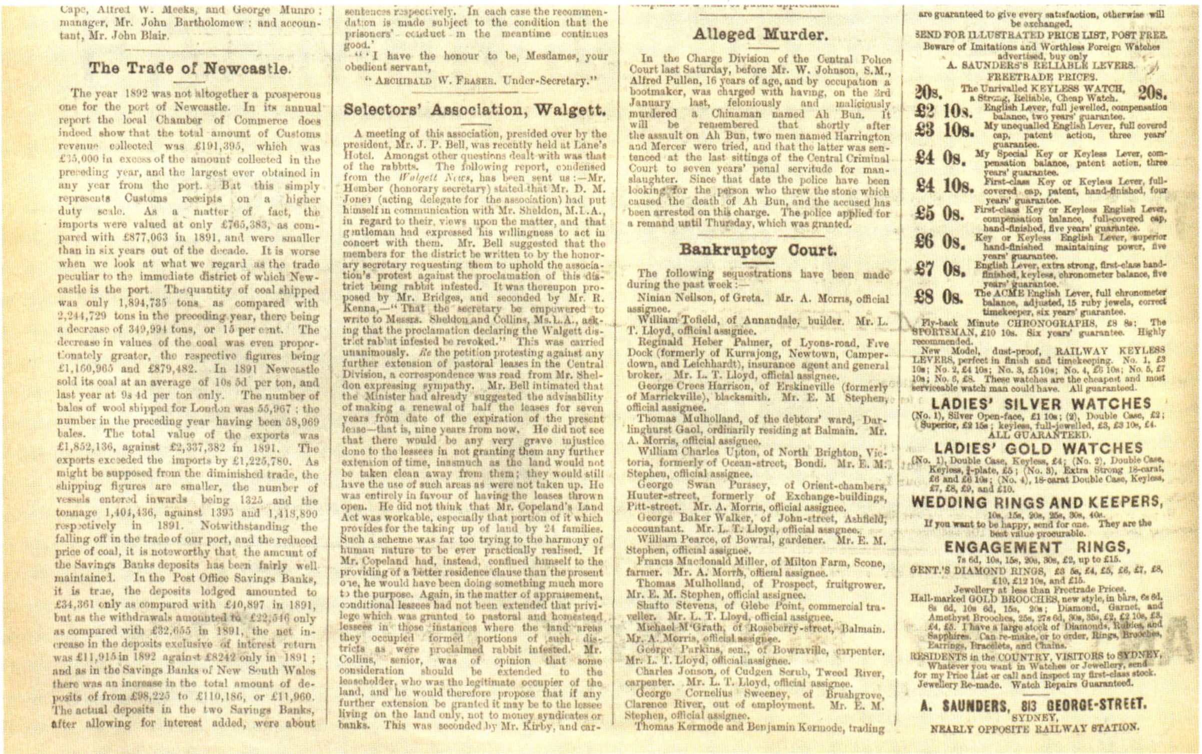

Cape, Alfred W. Meeks, and George Munro; manager, Mr. John Bartholomew; and accountant, Mr. John Blair.

The Trade of Newcastle.

The year 1892 was not altogether a prosperous one for the port of Newcastle. In its annual report the local Chamber of Commerce does indeed show that the total amount of Customs revenue collected was £191,395, which was £35,000 in excess of the amount collected in the preceding year, and the largest ever obtained in any year from the port. But this simply represents Customs receipts on a higher duty scale. As a matter of fact, the imports were valued at only £765,383, as compared with £877,063 in 1891, and were smaller than in six years out of the decade. It is worse when we look at what we regard as the trade peculiar to the immediate district of which Newcastle is the port. The quantity of coal shipped was only 1,894,735 tons as compared with 2,244,729 tons in the preceding year, there being a decrease of 349,994 tons, or 15 per cent. The decrease in values of the coal was even proportionately greater, the respective figures being £1,160,965 and £879,482. In 1891 Newcastle sold its coal at an average of 10s 5d per ton, and last year at 9s 4d per ton only. The number of bales of wool shipped for London was 55,967; the number in the preceding year having been 58,969 bales. The total value of the exports was £1,852,136, against £2,337,382 in 1891. The exports exceeded the imports by £1,225,780. As might be supposed from the diminished trade, the shipping figures are smaller, the number of vessels entered inwards being 1325 and the tonnage 1,401,436, against 1395 and 1,418,890 respectively in 1891. Notwithstanding the falling off in the trade of our port, and the reduced price of coal, it is noteworthy that the amount of the Savings Banks deposits has been fairly well maintained. In the Post Office Savings Banks, it is true, the deposits lodged amounted to £34,361 only as compared with £40,897 in 1891, but as the withdrawals amounted to £22,546 only as compared with £32,655 in 1891, the net increase in the deposits exclusive of interest return was £11,915 in 1892 against £8242 only in 1891; and as in the Savings Banks of New South Wales there was an increase in the total amount of deposits of from £98,225 to £110,186, or £11,960. The actual deposits in the two Savings Banks, after allowing for interest added, were about

sentences respectively. In each case the recommendation is made subject to the condition that the prisoners' conduct in the meantime continues good.'

"'I have the honour to be, Mesdames, your obedient servant,

"ARCHIBALD W. FRASER, Under-Secretary."

Selectors' Association, Walgett.

A meeting of this association, presided over by the president, Mr. J. P. Bell, was recently held at Lane's Hotel. Amongst other questions dealt with was that of the rabbits. The following report, condensed from the *Walgett News*, has been sent us:—Mr. Hember (honorary secretary) stated that Mr. D. M. Jones (acting delegate for the association) had put himself in communication with Mr. Sheldon, M.L.A., in regard to their views upon the matter, and that gentleman had expressed his willingness to act in concert with them. Mr. Bell suggested that the members for the district be written to by the honorary secretary requesting them to uphold the association's protest against the proclamation of this district being rabbit infested. It was thereupon proposed by Mr. Bridges, and seconded by Mr. R. Kenna,—"That the secretary be empowered to write to Messrs. Sheldon and Collins, Ms.L.A., asking that the proclamation declaring the Walgett district rabbit infested be revoked." This was carried unanimously. *Re* the petition protesting against any further extension of pastoral leases in the Central Division, a correspondence was read from Mr. Sheldon expressing sympathy. Mr. Bell intimated that the Minister had already suggested the advisability of making a renewal of half the leases for seven years from date of the expiration of the present lease—that is, nine years from now. He did not see that there would be any very grave injustice done to the lessees in not granting them any further extension of time, inasmuch as the land would not be taken clean away from them; they would still have the use of such areas as were not taken up. He was entirely in favour of having the leases thrown open. He did not think that Mr. Copeland's Land Act was workable, especially that portion of it which provides for the taking up of land by 24 families. Such a scheme was far too trying to the harmony of human nature to be ever practically realised. If Mr. Copeland had, instead, confined himself to the providing of a better residence clause than the present one, he would have been doing something much more to the purpose. Again, in the matter of appraisement, conditional lessees had not been extended that privilege which was granted to pastoral and homestead lessees in those instances where the land areas they occupied formed portions of such districts as were proclaimed rabbit infested. Mr. Collins, senior, was of opinion that some consideration should be extended to the leaseholder, who was the legitimate occupier of the land, and he would therefore propose that if any further extension be granted it may be to the lessee living on the land only, not to money syndicates or banks. This was seconded by Mr. Kirby, and car-

Alleged Murder.

In the Charge Division of the Central Police Court last Saturday, before Mr. W. Johnson, S.M., Alfred Pullen, 16 years of age, and by occupation a bootmaker, was charged with having, on the 3rd January last, feloniously and maliciously murdered a Chinaman named Ah Bun. It will be remembered that shortly after the assault on Ah Bun, two men named Harrington and Mercer were tried, and that the latter was sentenced at the last sittings of the Central Criminal Court to seven years' penal servitude for manslaughter. Since that date the police have been looking for the person who threw the stone which caused the death of Ah Bun, and the accused has been arrested on this charge. The police applied for a remand until Thursday, which was granted.

Bankruptcy Court.

The following sequestrations have been made during the past week:—

Ninian Neilson, of Greta. Mr. A. Morris, official assignee.

William Tofield, of Annandale, builder. Mr. L. T. Lloyd, official assignee.

Reginald Heber Palmer, of Lyons-road, Five Dock (formerly of Kurrajong, Newtown, Camperdown, and Leichhardt), insurance agent and general broker. Mr. L. T. Lloyd, official assignee.

George Crees Harrison, of Erskineville (formerly of Marrickville), blacksmith. Mr. E. M Stephen, official assignee.

Thomas Mulholland, of the debtors' ward, Darlinghurst Gaol, ordinarily residing at Balmain. Mr. A. Morris, official assignee.

William Charles Upton, of North Brighton, Victoria, formerly of Ocean-street, Bondi. Mr. E. M. Stephen, official assignee.

George Swan Pursey, of Orient-chambers, Hunter-street, formerly of Exchange-buildings, Pitt-street. Mr. A. Morris, official assignee.

George Baker Walker, of John-street, Ashfield, accountant. Mr. L. T. Lloyd, official assignee.

William Pearce, of Bowral, gardener. Mr. E. M. Stephen, official assignee.

Francis Macdonald Miller, of Milton Farm, Scone, farmer. Mr. A. Morris, official assignee.

Thomas Mulholland, of Prospect, fruitgrower. Mr. E. M. Stephen, official assignee.

Shafto Stevens, of Glebe Point, commercial traveller. Mr. L. T. Lloyd, official assignee.

Michael M'Grath, of Roseberry-street, Balmain. Mr. A. Morris, official assignee.

George Parkins, sen., of Bowraville, carpenter. Mr. L. T. Lloyd, official assignee.

Charles Jonson, of Cudgen Scrub, Tweed River, carpenter. Mr. L. T. Lloyd, official assignee.

George Cornelius Sweeney, of Brushgrove, Clarence River, out of employment. Mr. E. M. Stephen, official assignee.

Thomas Kermode and Benjamin Kermode, trading

The Sydney Mail of 8 April 1893 recorded the news of another bank in trouble. The Commercial Bank of Australia had suspended trading but intended a 'reconstruction' to ensure it could continue the business.

41 A cinematographe show

The first moving pictures, 1896

ALTHOUGH IT WAS NOT HEADLINE NEWS, THE FIRST REVIEW OF THE SCREENING OF A MOVIE IN AUSTRALIA MARKED A GROWING INTEREST IN THE CINEMATIC FORM. IN 1896 THE MELBOURNE *ARGUS* PRINTED THE FIRST REPORT OF A NEW INVENTION THAT WAS TO DOMINATE POPULAR CULTURE IN AUSTRALIA FOR THE NEXT CENTURY—THE CINEMATOGRAPHE.

Carl Hertz (1859–1924) was an American illusionist and magician who travelled the globe in the 1890s with a repertoire of magic tricks. Illusionists like Hertz were quick to take up the new moving pictures in the 1890s and add them to their shows. Although Thomas Edison's Kinetoscope, which showed sequential frames side by side through a viewing device for one person, had been shown in Australia, the enterprising Hertz is credited with the first screening of a true film, projected to an audience, in Australia.

Hertz had acquired a Theatrograph, one of the earliest screen projectors for moving images, and on 17 August 1896 he screened a film to an invited audience, and then a few days later to a paying public.

The Argus review of 24 August 1896 noted that Hertz's Theatrograph was much anticipated by the Melbourne Opera House audience, and that despite their tendency to criticise the performance, they were not disappointed. Although it certainly had some annoying 'mechanical defects', Hertz's Theatrograph screening was pronounced a 'veritable triumph'.

Entertainment promoter Harry Rickards (1843–1911), who had brought Carl Hertz to Melbourne, saw no future in the cinematographe, reportedly saying, 'I like 'em in the flesh'. Yet word had got out about the audiences' 'simmer of excitement' and the life-sized moving images.

An early Australian interest in film-making saw the local production of many major films up to 1914. In fact the world's first true feature film was produced in 1906 in Australia—*The Story of the Kelly Gang*. Unfortunately for the genre, police departments around the country claimed that films about bushrangers mocked the law and glorified criminal behaviour, and so bushranger films were officially banned in most states until the 1940s.

THEATRES AND ENTERTAINMENTS.

The announcement that Mr. Harry Rickards's fifteenth instalment of English artists would appear in the person of "The Beautiful Jessica," and that a new feature would be added to Mr. Carl Hertz's performance, sufficed to fill the Opera-house to overflowing on Saturday evening. With a house which, from the rise of the curtain, was in a pleasant simmer of excitement, success was practically a certainty, and thus the bright "first part," which Mr. Rickards has christened "The Æsthetics," possibly because the name looks as well on the bill as any other, "went" with enthusiasm from start to finish. In the olio Mr. Carl Hertz was accorded a great reception, and though an unfortunate accident prevented Mddle. D'Alton from appearing, the cleverly performed "handcuff" illusion—to our mind an even better variation of the familiar "disappearing trick"—was an efficient substitute for "Vanity Fair." "The Beautiful Jessica" proved to be a plump and pleasing person in adhesive fleshings, and her feats upon the slack wire were very graceful and easy. Still better was her serpentine dance on her aerial perch, but why Messrs. Tennyson and O'Gorman should come in dressed in a parody of the beauteous one's costume and "take" the end of the turn is a problem that the audience had better give up at once. The chief item of the evening was the cinematographe, which may be best explained by saying that it is the kinetoscope thrown upon a screen and life-size. In spite of mechanical defects—and they were many—with every disadvantage of lighting, with an audience disposed to criticise, not the astounding ingenuity of the invention, but the actions of the pictured performers, it may be said at once that the cinematographe achieved a veritable triumph, and that its introduction would confer honour upon any management. A matinee performance will be given on Wednesday next.

The revival of the once familiar drama "Romany Rye" has proved a successful enterprise on the part of Mr. George Rignold. The Theatre Royal was well filled on Saturday evening, when the play was repeated with all its thrilling and splendid effects. Mr. Rignold's company appeared to the greatest advantage, as "Romany Rye" gives ample scope for a multiplicity of talent, and the modern achievements in stagecraft are afforded many opportunities for display, which in the present representation are fully availed of.

On Thursday afternoon next Ovide Musin and his company will give a matinee at the Athenæum. The programme will comprise the most popular numbers of their large repertoire. This will positively be their last appearance in Melbourne, as the company leave for Sydney next day.

ORCHESTRAL CONCERT IN THE TOWN-HALL.

LEFT *The first Australian film review, of the cinematographe demonstration, was published in* The Argus *in August 1896.*

RIGHT *Carl Hertz and his Cinematographe were promoted as the two wonders of the world in this 1897 Melbourne poster.*

Nation, war, tragedy and race

1901–

-1929

At the beginning of the twentieth century, Australians greeted their new nation with gusto. For those who couldn't make the ceremony and celebrations in Sydney on 1 January 1901 (and over a quarter of a million people did) the news headlines informed everyone that, with Queen Victoria's assent, the Australian Commonwealth had been formed. Newspapers joined the celebrations with Federation supplements and images of the vast parade through Sydney streets. They also supported the highly symbolic nature of proceedings with many and varied artistic representations of the Nymph Australia—our equivalent to the female figure of Britannia.

FOR MOST AUSTRALIANS THERE WAS INDEED REASON TO CELEBRATE THE START OF THE NEW CENTURY AND THE BEGINNING OF THE NATION. THE ECONOMIC CRISIS OF THE 1890S HAD PASSED. BETTER WORKING CONDITIONS WERE AGAIN A FOCUS OF TRADE UNIONS, AND WORKERS' POLITICAL INTERESTS WERE NOW BEING REPRESENTED IN NATIONAL PARLIAMENT BY THE NEWLY FORMED AUSTRALIAN LABOUR PARTY (LATER THE AUSTRALIAN LABOR PARTY). WOMEN WERE ALSO BEING GRANTED THE RIGHT TO VOTE: AUSTRALIA WAS ONE OF THE FIRST COUNTRIES TO INTRODUCE VOTING RIGHTS FOR WOMEN, PROGRESSIVELY IN THE COLONIES AND THEN THE STATES BETWEEN 1894 AND 1926.

After the death of Queen Victoria in January 1901, the Victorian era that was named after her quickly faded in the early years of the twentieth century. New inventions, and growing social and political rights, as well as a faith in the rapid changes of a modern world occurred at the time the states unified and became a nation—and it was generally agreed that it was to be a *modern* nation.

Australia's economy was continuing to industrialise and diversify, and wool was not such a dominant export any more. Inventions, such as refrigeration technologies, meant food could now be transported long distances and Australia's exports began to include meat and other perishable produce. In a land of long distances, Australians were also quick to see the benefits of the new telephones, motorcars and, in particular, aeroplanes.

Yet underlying independence and growing modernity for Australia was an insecurity about the new nation being set adrift in a sea of Asian and Pacific countries, a long way from Britain. And so some of the first acts of the Australian government were to restrict who could live here. In northern Queensland, the gold rushes and development of agriculture, such as sugar-cane farming, in the late nineteenth century had attracted thousands of Chinese. By 1900, some areas, such as around Cairns and Innisfail, had majority Chinese populations, and thousands of Pacific Islanders, who had been brought to work on the canefields. Various immigration restriction acts not only 're-populated' Australia's north with European Australians, but also kept the majority of the overall population British, and therefore 'white'.

As the United States of America became a significant world power, Australians began to look across the Pacific Ocean for a new Western ally. The US government sent a fleet around the world on a goodwill mission, and when it arrived in Australia in 1908, front page headlines reflected the popular enthusiasm for the Americans, and editors splashed images and reports of the fleet's every move across their front pages. Painted white for effect, the Great White Fleet was for many Australians a 'great white hope'. In what has been a long tradition of welcoming great ships to their distant ports, Australians flocked to see the American battleships. An estimated 400,000 people—nearly twice the crowd for the Federation displays—lined the foreshores of Sydney Harbour to greet the fleet.

Perhaps a little more secure in their defensive position in the region, many Australians continued to believe that the true test of nationhood was a military one. The outbreak of the First World War in 1914 was quite enthusiastically met by those hoping to see Australian soldiers prove the Australian character and its nationhood on the battlefield. Unfortunately for some hundreds of thousands of soldiers and their families, their bravery was displayed in the misery and indiscriminate death that was trench warfare in the muddy battlefields of Europe.

A military sideshow—and a great disaster—became the focus of Australian soldiers' deeds during the First World War. The Australian and New Zealand Army Corps, or Anzacs, were part of an invasion force that landed in the Dardanelles in Turkey, and after eight months of difficult and ultimately fruitless fighting, they were forced to retreat. The Gallipoli campaign became the focus of future commemorations of a distinctly Australian military tradition. The perseverance of the Australians at Gallipoli came to symbolise not just Australian soldiers, but also the Australian people.

It did not take long for the early enthusiasm for war to wane, and with the stalemate of trench warfare in Turkey and in Europe, newspaper headlines had little to report—apart from regular and increasingly long lists of the Australian dead and wounded. After the withdrawal from Gallipoli in January 1916, the high casualty rate on the Western Front meant that losses in the Australian battalions could not be replaced quickly enough by volunteers. During 1916 and again in 1917, referendums were put to the Australian people to introduce conscription. After bitterly argued campaigns for and against, both referendums were defeated, and conscription was not introduced during the war of 1914–1918.

The 1920s saw a new period of relative growth and prosperity across the nation. Women, who had often helped out during the war or were increasingly being employed in

Sydneysiders watched, intrigued, as the engineering marvel of the Sydney Harbour Bridge gradually came together over a period of six years, finally being opened on 19 March 1932. It was designed by Public Works Department engineer John Bradfield (1867–1943), who also proposed the construction of an underground railway in Sydney and the electrification of its suburban railways.

the new department stores and in offices, were increasingly joining the workforce. Fashions also reflected the social changes taking place, and a less conservative female dress fashion reflected women's advances in Australian society, which were made possible by the work of early twentieth-century feminists.

Nonetheless, the changing moral standards and more liberal attitudes towards the rights of women did not transfer to Australian migration laws and racial attitudes. Arguably the defining factor of the cultural make-up of the modern Australian nation was the White Australia Policy. The policy found expression in a series of immigration restriction acts that were applied to, essentially, people from non-British and non-white places of origin. The visit of an African-American jazz band in 1928 caused a sensation, and they were deported by police. After the band had been allowed into the country, they were dogged and then 'exposed' by journalists from the Sydney *Truth*, a newspaper famous for its racism.

By this time, newspapers were also being transformed. New techniques introduced late in the nineteenth century allowed photographs to be reproduced on the printed page, and these became increasingly important in newspapers in the early decades of the twentieth century. Events were being captured on the spot by photojournalists and quickly turned into news. The extra time needed to create labour-intensive hand-engraved illustrations had given life to the weekly and monthly newspapers of the second half of the nineteenth century. By 1901 they had all disappeared, unable to compete with the immediacy of news illustrated with photographs in the daily newspapers.

The decade of the 1930s seemed to offer all Australians another new horizon of modernity. From the late 1920s, as people were fascinated by the construction of the Sydney Harbour Bridge, faith in industry and modernity could not have seemed misplaced. Yet this was to change with the onset of the worst economic collapse in Australian history in the Great Depression of the early 1930s.

42 *Pageants and parades*

Federation celebrations, 1901

EVEN THOUGH THE FOCUS OF FEDERATION DAY, 1 JANUARY 1901, WAS JUST A CEREMONY WHERE A PROCLAMATION OF AUSTRALIAN UNITY SIGNED BY QUEEN VICTORIA WAS READ OUT ON BEHALF OF THE QUEEN, AND THE NEW MINISTERS SWORE ALLEGIANCE TO THE CROWN AS WELL AS THE COUNTRY, THE EXCITEMENT GENERATED WAS PALPABLE. ACCORDING TO ONE JOURNALIST, PEOPLE LINING THE STREETS TO WATCH THE PARADE WENDING ITS WAY THROUGH SYDNEY TO THE CEREMONY AT CENTENNIAL PARK WERE WEEPING TEARS THEY COULD NOT EXPLAIN, OTHER THAN AS AN 'OVERWHELMING EXCESS OF PATRIOTISM'.

The long and laborious development and reflection of an Australian nation had at last been achieved. Sydneysiders were at the centre of the show and they threw a party the like of which the nation had never seen before. Spectators filled the specially built grandstands along Sydney streets to watch a grand parade that took nearly an hour to pass by. The whole town was decorated with banners and archways across the streets, with signs proclaiming both the unity of the colonies, and the unity of the new nation with the other nations of the world.

At the turn of the twentieth century, Greater Sydney had a population of 480,000. An estimated 250,000 people flocked into the city to see history in the making on 1 January 1901. Centennial Park was described as being a sea of people. According to one Melbourne journalist, 10,000 of them formed a choir of 'white muslin clad, sweet voiced little girls'.

With the passage of an act of the British Parliament, British subjects in the Australian colonies were, from 1 January 1901, Australian citizens.

Although it was widely believed that the perceived inferiority of being considered 'colonial' would now cease, this was not the case. Unfortunately for many young men and their families it was to take the military sacrifice of the First World War of 1914–1918 for many Australians to consider themselves to have truly entered the world stage.

The Sydney Mail's special Federation issue cover shows a 'Nymph' representing the spirit of Australia, reaching up, presumably to world affairs. Such symbolism and allegory were common to the Federation celebration imagery, particularly the use of a Britannia-like female figure, reminding people of the link with Britain, or the Mother Country.

43 *The Great White Fleet*

The US navy visits, 1908

IN A GRAND DISPLAY OF AMERICAN MILITARY POWER, IN 1907 PRESIDENT THEODORE ROOSEVELT (1858–1919) DECIDED TO ORDER A CIRCUMNAVIGATION OF THE GLOBE BY HIS NAVY'S BATTLE FLEET. FOUR SQUADRONS OF BATTLESHIPS AND THEIR ESCORTS LEFT THE UNITED STATES IN DECEMBER 1907 AND TRAVELLED THE WORLD FOR MORE THAN A YEAR. THE SHIPS' HULLS WERE ALL PAINTED WHITE FOR EFFECT, SO THE FLOTILLA WAS QUICKLY DUBBED THE 'GREAT WHITE FLEET'.

The opportunity to see a large fleet of modern (and some not so modern) battleships captured public imagination around the world and people flocked to see the fleet at each port of call. Sydney was no exception and people crowded the harbour foreshores when the fleet steamed in to Port Jackson on 20 August 1908.

As a new nation increasingly concerned about its own defence—particularly just after the Japanese navy had defeated Russia's Pacific Fleet in 1905—the visit of the Great White Fleet was reassuring for many Australians.

The visit of the fleet also spurred efforts to create an Australian navy. As part of the British Empire, the Australian government felt entitled to British support, but the appearance of what seemed to be an increasingly powerful American fleet in the Pacific began to shift perceptions of exactly who might be a useful ally in any future military conflict.

The reception of the Great White Fleet in Sydney Harbour was one of the biggest events in Australian history. An estimated 400,000 people, many of whom took the day off work to see the spectacle, welcomed the fleet to Sydney. The harbour itself was also crowded with spectator craft trying to get a glimpse of the ships and the 14,000 American sailors—some 300 of whom enjoyed the reception so much that they jumped ship.

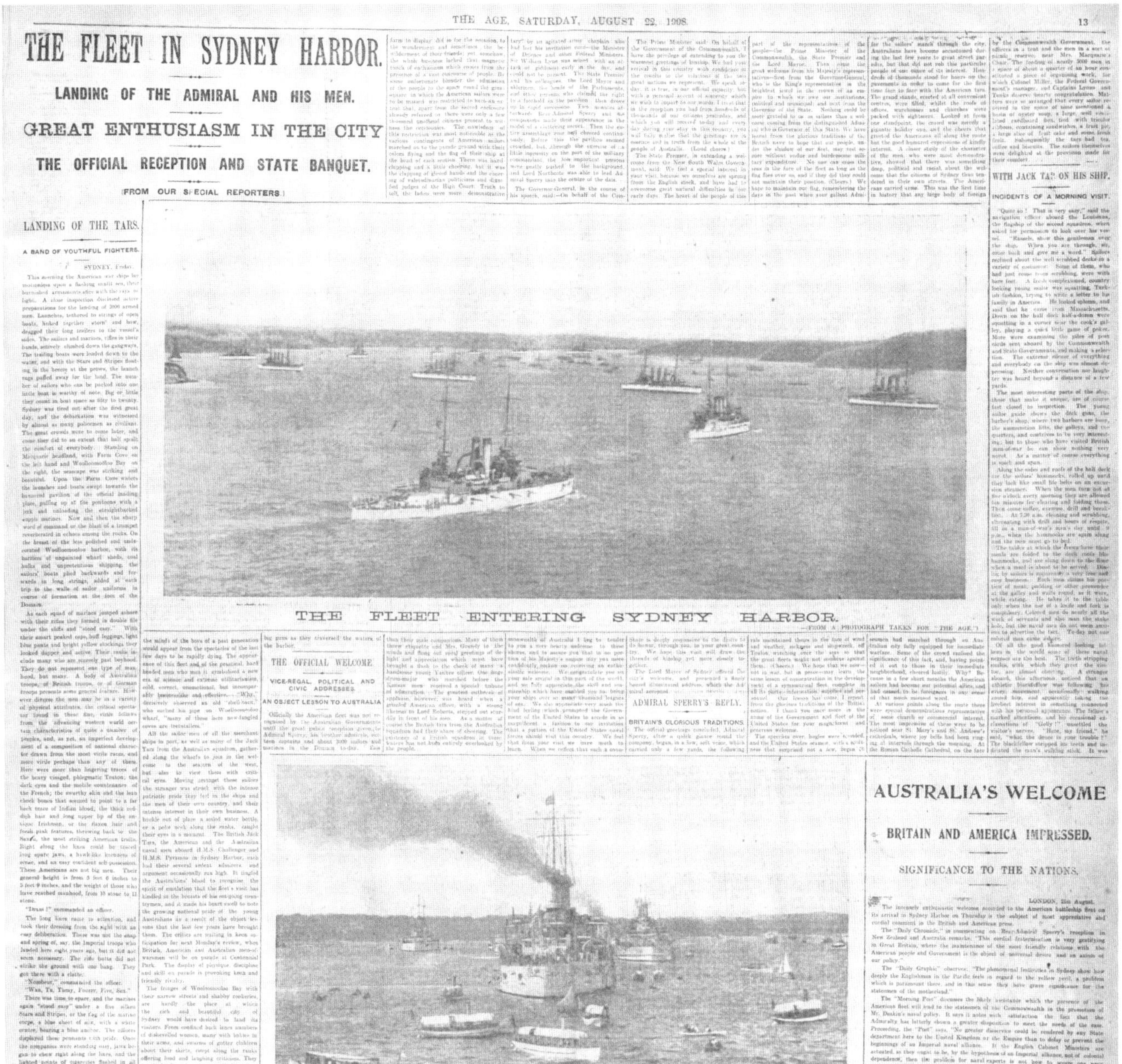

THE AGE, SATURDAY, AUGUST 22, 1908. 13

THE FLEET IN SYDNEY HARBOR.

LANDING OF THE ADMIRAL AND HIS MEN.

GREAT ENTHUSIASM IN THE CITY

THE OFFICIAL RECEPTION AND STATE BANQUET.

(FROM OUR SPECIAL REPORTERS.)

LANDING OF THE TARS.

A BAND OF YOUTHFUL FIGHTERS.

WITH JACK TAR ON HIS SHIP.

INCIDENTS OF A MORNING VISIT.

THE FLEET ENTERING SYDNEY HARBOR.

THE OFFICIAL WELCOME

VICE-REGAL, POLITICAL AND CIVIC ADDRESSES.

AN OBJECT LESSON TO AUSTRALIA

ADMIRAL SPERRY'S REPLY.

BRITAIN'S GLORIOUS TRADITIONS.

AUSTRALIA'S WELCOME

BRITAIN AND AMERICA IMPRESSED.

SIGNIFICANCE TO THE NATIONS.

AMERICAN PRESS DECLARATIONS.

THE FLEET AT ANCHOR IN SYDNEY HARBOR.

MARCH THROUGH THE CITY.

INTENSE ENTHUSIASM DISPLAYED.

FEEDING 3000 MEN.

The appearance of the Great White Fleet in Sydney Harbour was headline news around the country. Here it is reported in Melbourne's Age newspaper of 22 August 1908.

44 *Splendid conduct and bravery*

Anzac forces in the Dardanelles, 1915

SINCE THE SUDAN WARS IN THE 1880S, THERE HAD BEEN WIDE POLITICAL AND POPULAR SUPPORT BEHIND THE IDEA THAT A DISTINCTLY AUSTRALIAN NATION COULD BE FORGED—AS OTHER GREAT NATIONS HAD—THROUGH MILITARY SACRIFICE. IN MANY WAYS, PEOPLE WHO FELT THAT WAY WERE CORRECT, AS THE NEW COUNTRY WOULD INDEED FIND THE OPPORTUNITY TO LINK THE BIRTH OF THE AUSTRALIAN NATION WITH CONFLICT DURING THE FIRST WORLD WAR. EVEN THOUGH AUSTRALIA HAD BEEN DECLARED A NATION IN 1901, IN MANY EYES IT STILL NEEDED TO 'BLOOD' ITSELF TO PROVE ITS NATIONHOOD TO THE WORLD.

And so the First World War was initially met with great enthusiasm. It was seen as Australia's chance to perform on the world stage. From August 1914, many men volunteered for the Australian Imperial Force, with a huge weight of public expectation on their shoulders.

Considering the importance it later came to have for Australians, the initial newspaper reports to the Australian public of the Australian and New Zealand Army Corps, or Anzac, involvement in the Dardanelles campaign in Turkey in 1915, was a rather matter-of-fact 'headline'. The first official news of the landings was published on 30 April and *The Sydney Morning Herald*'s account was a carefully worded thanks to the Australian forces, for their 'splendid gallantry'.

The *Herald* also rather optimistically suggested that the Australian troops were 'still advancing'. In fact, during what was to be an eight-month campaign, little more ground was captured than had been taken on the first day of the landings.

KING'S CONGRATULATIONS
MELBOURNE, Friday

In the house of Representatives this morning the Prime Minister read the following cable, which had been received from the King:—

"I heartily congratulate you upon the splendid conduct and bravery displayed by the Australian troops in the operations at the Dardanelles, who have indeed proved themselves worthy sons of the Empire"

Signed GEORGE, R.I.

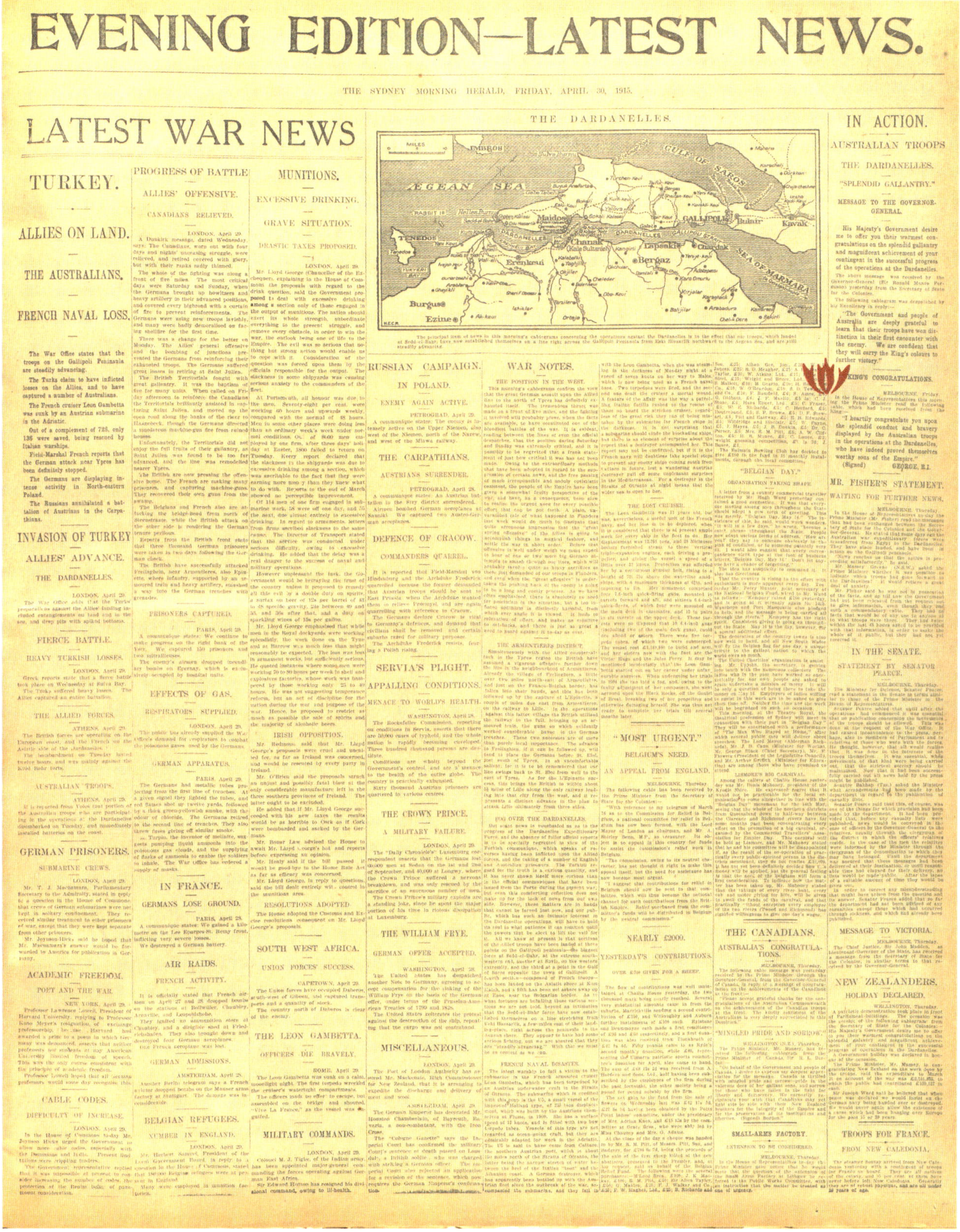

EVENING EDITION—LATEST NEWS.

THE SYDNEY MORNING HERALD, FRIDAY, APRIL 30, 1915.

LATEST WAR NEWS

TURKEY.

ALLIES ON LAND.

THE AUSTRALIANS.

FRENCH NAVAL LOSS.

INVASION OF TURKEY

ALLIES' ADVANCE.

FIERCE BATTLE.

GERMAN PRISONERS.

ACADEMIC FREEDOM.

PROGRESS OF BATTLE

ALLIES' OFFENSIVE.

IN FRANCE.

AIR RAIDS.

BELGIAN REFUGEES.

MUNITIONS.

EXCESSIVE DRINKING.

GRAVE SITUATION.

THE DARDANELLES.

RUSSIAN CAMPAIGN.

IN POLAND.

THE CARPATHIANS.

DEFENCE OF CRACOW.

SERVIA'S PLIGHT.

APPALLING CONDITIONS.

THE CROWN PRINCE.

THE WILLIAM FRYE.

SOUTH WEST AFRICA.

THE LEON GAMBETTA.

MISCELLANEOUS.

MILITARY COMMANDS.

WAR NOTES.

"MOST URGENT."

BELGIUM'S NEED.

NEARLY £2000.

IN ACTION.

AUSTRALIAN TROOPS

THE DARDANELLES.

"SPLENDID GALLANTRY."

MESSAGE TO THE GOVERNOR-GENERAL.

KING'S CONGRATULATIONS.

"I heartily congratulate you upon the splendid conduct and bravery displayed by the Australian troops in the operations at the Dardanelles, who have indeed proved themselves worthy sons of the Empire."

(Signed) GEORGE, R.I.

MR. FISHER'S STATEMENT.

IN THE SENATE.

THE CANADIANS.

NEW ZEALANDERS.

TROOPS FOR FRANCE.

Once the Anzac forces' destination was revealed, The Sydney Morning Herald *printed a map of the Dardanelles, which readers would get to know very well over the coming months as news of the war and casualty lists came in.*

45 News from the front

First World War casualty lists, 1916

AFTER THE GERMAN INVASION OF FRANCE IN 1914 HAD SLOWED INTO THE STALEMATE OF TRENCH WARFARE, THE WESTERN FRONT, WHERE MOST AUSTRALIAN TROOPS WERE SENT, TURNED INTO A SERIES OF DRAWN-OUT STRUGGLES FOR SOMETIMES JUST A FEW METRES OF GROUND. THE AUSTRALIAN PUBLIC WERE NOT USED TO BATTLES THAT LASTED FOR MONTHS, RATHER THAN DAYS, AND THIS SORT OF CONFLICT DID NOT MAKE GOOD HEADLINE NEWS.

Casualty reports were prominent in the newspapers of the day. At first, they often included detailed reports of soldiers killed in action, with short biographies of prominent officers, but as the number of casualties grew, the regular reports of casualties became no more than long lists of names.

Between July and August 1916, Australians fighting in France suffered heavily in the Somme Offensive, a major Allied massed attack designed to break through the German lines. In just six weeks, more Australian soldiers died in France than during the eight months of the Gallipoli campaign. Australian forces suffered 23,000 casualties in fighting at the Somme from 23 July to 8 August, and more than 6000 were killed in the space of a few weeks.

Most towns across the country were drastically affected by the number of soldiers killed, injured or disabled during the war; many of the injured were affected, not just by shrapnel and bullets, but also by the use of poisonous gas.

The Australian dead could not be returned home for burial and remained on the battlefields of France. Accordingly, in outpourings of grief, many communities, towns and work places began to erect monuments and memorials to these soldiers, almost as substitute grave markers. Many of the local monuments built were topped with the ubiquitous sculpture of an Australian infantryman, and most included long lists of names of locals who had served or were among 'the fallen'.

OPPOSITE On 15 December 1916 The Daily Telegraph *published the 250th casualty list from the war. It is typical of what became a regular feature in newspapers during the First World War.*

THE SOIL.

PRIMARY PRODUCERS' UNION.

FOCUSING THE FARMERS' VOICE.

The executive of the Primary Producers' Union has had a two-days' sitting in Sydney this week. Mr. C. J. M'Rae (Coraki) presided, and there were also present Messrs. R. W. Allison (Dungog), J. W. Banner (Billinudgel), D. Ferry (Woodville), D. Faulkiner (Singleton), G. W. Gordon (Raleigh), J. Healey (Port Macquarie), A. Mathieson (Tamworth), D. M'Intyre (Palmer's Island), J. T. Rogers (Bega), J. Stitt (Wingham), C. F. Williams (Copmanhurst), D. Ritchie (general organiser), and A. S. M'Kenzie (general secretary). Many questions affecting producers' interests were dealt with, and arrangements made for pushing on the work of organisation and consolidation. This being the last meeting of the provisional executive, matters in connection with the election of the permanent executive in February next were arranged.

The Coraki Co-operative Butter Company wrote, complaining of the inequality of treatment in connection with the Federal butter pool—New South Wales factories having to contribute 60 per cent. of their output for local consumption as against 25 per cent. contributed by factories in Victoria, the impression being that the pool, being a Federal matter, each State should contribute an equal percentage. It was decided to pass the matter on to the Butter Shippers' Association.

The secretary reported that he had been instrumental in having the inquiry before the Inter-State Commission in Melbourne with regard to the question of coloring margarine for export reopened, and that evidence had been given in opposition to the proposal by representatives of the Victorian butter producers. The commission could not see its way to accede to the request to reopen the inquiry in Sydney, but was willing to consider a written statement. The secretary was instructed to prepare a statement forthwith of the union's views in opposition, and submit it to the commission.

In regard to the recently issued claims of the A.W.U. (Rural Workers' Section) it was decided to appoint a sub-committee to work in conjunction with the secretary in compiling evidence in opposition to the claims, the committee to consist of Messrs. J. W. Banner, D. Ferry, R. Shepherd, J. T. Rogers, J. Binks (Berry), and a representative of the Mudgee branch. It was also resolved to ask the Milk Suppliers' Association to nominate a representative to join the committee.

The question of State embargoes on free Inter-State trade was discussed, on a request from the committe formed at a recent meeting at Bourke, at which a series of resolutions of protest were adopted, and the Federal Government urged to take steps to have the rights of the people preserved in this respect. It was resolved that the union co-operate in the movement to this end.

Representatives of the Butter Shippers' Association interviewed the executive and discussed several matters of mutual interest to the producers, more especially in relation to the handling of butter under the Federal pooling scheme, and it was agreed that it would strengthen the hands of both the producers and the butter advisory committee if a representative of the union acted in conjunction with the latter committee in any matter affecting prices before the Federal Commissioner for Price-Fixing. This arrangement was endorsed, and the secretary was appointed to represent the union.

The secretary was authorised to meet Mr. R. Shepherd, president of the Dairy Farmers' Association, with a view to arranging the basis of a conference on several matters affecting the welfare of the members of both organisations.

Messrs. Parkes, Mathieson, and Hayes, of Tamworth, representing the New South Wales Farmers' Union, attended to confer with the executive on the question of an amalgamation of the two bodies. The various phases of the proposal were fully discussed, and will be further considered by the executive of the Farmers' Union.

To give effect to the rule providing for sectional representative committees additional rules were adopted. In regard to the mode of election districts and industries will be allocated when required, and each district or industry shall then proceed to elect by its own organisation one or more representative delegates as may be authorised. When the delegates shall have been elected notification shall be sent to the general secretary, who shall convene and attend meetings of the sectional committees. One authorised delegate from a sectional committee may attend, and convey decisions to meetings of the central executive, or call for executive action. The sectional committees will not have power to deal with constitutional matter or pledge the union in any action, unless expressly authorised to do so by the central executive. The P.P.U. stands out to watch the interests of all producers, and the object of the sectional committees is to ensure experienced information.

The executive resolved that the union should be represented on all committees relative to price-fixing and other matters affecting the interests of the primary industries.

In responding to a vote of thanks, Mr. M'Rae expressed his indebtedness to his colleagues of the provisional executive for their assistance to him and the work they had accomplished in bringing the movement to a successful issue.

PASTORAL QUESTIONS.

At the monthly meeting of the executive of the Pasture Boards Council of Advice, Mr. F. A. Mackenzie presiding, a letter was received from the Railway Commissioners relative to the rates for the carriage of store stock, stating that "there is no present intention of abolishing the concession. In future the reduced rate will not be conceded unless the regulations covering them are complied with in their entirety, which is a reasonable proviso, in view of the facilities and concessions afforded stockowners."

In reply to a resolution from the Council of Advice, asking that the sale of phosphorus should be restricted, the Secretary for Defence forwarded regulations restricting dealing in phosphorus to authorised persons.

In reply to a letter from the council, asking whether the trustees of the late J. A. Gunn were still prepared to disclose to the Government the secret for the manufacture of anthrax vaccine for the benefit of the pastoral industry, Mrs. Gunn wrote stating that as soon as possible she would place the matter before her co-trustees, and would then give their decision on the matter. As far as she was personally concerned, all she wished was for it to pass into thoroughly scientific hands, which would make it, as it was in the past, a thoroughly reliable vaccine for the benefit of pastoralists.

AUSTRALIAN PRODUCE.

LONDON NOTES.

(FROM OUR CORRESPONDENT.)

BUTTER.

LONDON, November 2.—With only limited supplies coming on to the market butter prices continue to harden, and the Australian season, when it begins in earnest a month hence, is likely to break all opening records. Danish butter to-day is quoted 216s, New Zealand is nominally worth about 200s, there being more left in first hands, and Canadian up to 198s. As there is no prospect of any considerable quantity of butter being available until the end of this month, when fair-sized shipments of Australian and New Zealand are expected to arrive, the trade is getting somewhat concerned about what is going to happen in the interval. There are a few lucky people who have a few New Zealand butters left out of some recent arrivals, and I hear to-day of 212s per cwt. being paid for some of them by West End hotels, which must have the best butter whatever price they have to pay for it. Other consumers have to put up with inferior qualities, such as American, and pay high prices for them, or else take margarine. The latter article, it is perhaps unnecessary to say, is going ahead tremendously, and its makers must be making huge profits.

WHEAT.

More than three weeks have now elapsed since Mr. Runciman announced in the House of Commons that the wheat business of the country was being taken over by a Wheat Commission, but we are still without any information as to how the commission is going to work and on what terms the business will be done. Consequently the trade in cargoes is still in a state of stagnation. In parcels there has been a little business, and prices for these have continued to rise steadily, until to-day Australian near at hand is worth 77s 3d, as against about 73s at the beginning of the month. From this hardening of values it is only reasonable to infer that the trade does not anticipate that the Wheat Commission will bring about any reduction in values, and as Mr. Runciman seemed to imply in his speeches, the question of price is a secondary consideration, the point of primary importance being the securing of sufficient supplies to fill the requirements of the United Kingdom.

Yesterday the Wheat Commission posted on the Baltic a list of firms which had been appointed to act as Government selling agents for wheat from India, Argentina, the Pacific, United States of America, and Canada. It is announced that these firms will have to sell either direct to millers or through a broker, and that their remuneration will be at the rate of 3d per quarter. This can hardly be regarded as a very generous scale of payment, and it is reckoned to be only about two-thirds of what the sellers would receive if they sold, at present prices and received their old rate of commission. So it can hardly be said that there is very much enthusiasm about the business. Agents to sell Australian wheat have not yet been appointed, as there is practically nothing from Australia to be sold here yet, but it is not thought likely that the Wheat Commission will go outside the present Australian Wheat-selling Commission, which is doing its work very satisfactorily.

So far nothing definite is known as to how the commission is going to secure the tonnage which Mr. Runciman said the Government would obtain to lift the Australian crop. Many rumors are current on the Baltic and in other places where shipping men meet, but all that seems to be really authentic is that the Government has directed two or three steamers to Australia from the Cape and from Singapore. There is much talk about the engagement of a considerable quantity of neutral tonnage, and a Norwegian shipowner writes that he understands that a high rate will be paid for it—as much as 150s. This price has also been mentioned on the Baltic as the figure which the Government is prepared to pay, but no definite information can be obtained on this point. It is perfectly certain, however, that the price paid will be considerably above the rates at which a few patriotic shipowners allowed their steamers to be chartered for Australian wheat when Mr. Hughes was appealing for tonnage a few months ago, and will be somewhere about the parity of rates ruling for other parts of the world.

Some interesting comments on the Government scheme are made in "Fairplay" by a correspondent who calls himself "An Australian Merchant." In the course of his article he writes: "It was inevitable that the Government should take a hand in the wheat business, and, indeed, we are strongly of opinion that this ought to have been done two years ago. It would not have meant much to Great Britain to undertake to relieve Australia of all the wheat she could produce at a fixed f.o.b. price, and on the strength of such an undertaking farmers would have been better able to arrange to finance an increase in the acreage sown. Apparently we are not likely to benefit to anything like the full extent of present market conditions, judging from such details as are known of the recent purchase of half a million tons of wheat by the British Government. Our farmers would get their cash, of course, which, after all, is the main thing, but their net return is not likely to exceed half that of the British farmer. Yet the latter averages about 30 bushels of wheat to the acre, even with his unscientific methods, against an Australian average of about 12 bushels. Incidentally, it may be pointed out that the British Government do not stand to lose much money on its purchase of Australian wheat, for, on the basis of, say, 75s per quarter in Mark Lane it can afford to pay 125s homeward freight and still pocket about 60s per ton profit, or it can use the 60s to juggle with, and, perhaps, to cover up a little of the inevitable departmental bungling. The wheat importing problem is almost entirely a shipping one at the moment, and there need have been very little difficulty about it if the leading men in the shipping and grain trades had been switched on to the business, given a reasonably free hand, and simply told that it was their affair to bring wheat into the country."

TALLOW.

The Government has now made some relaxation in the stringent prohibition of the export of tallow, and some shipments to Allies have been permitted. This has brought about an improved demand, and though large offerings have been made at the public auctions during the past fortnight, only a comparatively small quantity has been left unsold, and prices have advanced. Last week 2081 casks were offered and 1779 sold at previous rates to 6d advance, and this week 1781 casks were sold out of an offering of 2207, at late rates to 3d advance. Recent quotations average to 50s 3d for mutton, and 56s for beef. On c.i.f. terms high prices are asked, and a considerable business has been done in beef at 49s and over.

FOR THE FRUITGROWER.

THE CASE QUESTION.

(By POMONA.)

The fruit case question has always been more or less a vexed one. In the past, the chief aim has been to secure a case of standard size, the cost not entering into consideration. This resulted in the passing of legislation governing the size of fruit cases. The difficulty this season lies in the fact that the cost of fruit cases has advanced enormously. The reasons for the advance are obvious. Why some organised effort on the part of fruit growers is not launched is hard to conceive. Surely the time has arrived when the requirements of each fruit district can be closely estimated. Branches of the Agricultural Bureau and fruit-growers' associations are distributed throughout the State, and it would not seem a difficult matter to co-ordinate and arrange for case supplies in bulk. The several systems of marketing are to an extent responsible no doubt for present conditions. Some growers receive their cases on loan from the agent; others, again, rely upon large quantities being returned. Then, again, others sell fruit and case outright. Some, of course, have a private order trade, and use second-hand dumps. There seem to be no definite method. The advantage of each system may be many, although they certainly tend to increase cost.

No doubt the further opening up of Crown lands by the Government, and the establishment of a Forestry Department will to some extent relieve the situation. It is largely a matter of some forward step, however, on the part of the grower. In the Batlow district, for instance, some hundreds of acres of fruit land are to be made available for returned soldiers. A great deal of the timber on the blocks is quite suitable for fruit cases. As a matter of fact, a first-class case can be cut at a cost of 8d per bushel case and 5d for half-bushel. If a demand is met the mills at work can utilise thousands of feet of timber which would otherwise be wasted. Local requirements are, of course, limited, although it is anticipated that in the near future many thousands of cases will be required annually. With such a source available for securing cases growers cannot complain if they do not avail themselves of the opportunity. Some growers in the past few seasons have gone so far as to import fruit-case timber from Japan, New Zealand, and Tasmania, on account of the high rates ruling locally. It is evident that with large timber resources at our disposal such a procedure is unwarranted. Needless to say, the timber mills cannot install expensive case-making machinery unless the expense is warranted. Orders must be of such dimensions that timber can be set aside for the purpose.

There is another aspect of the question, and that is the utilisation of the cardboard case. A leading Sydney firm of cardboard manufacturers recently made up sample cases of standard size to meet the requirements of retailers and those growers catering for the private order trade. The innovation has not met with success, although there are not sufficient growers acquainted of the fact.

It is necessary to cheapen production, and any reasonable means to this end should be given careful consideration. It may be necessary to depart from accepted practice. Even if there is a certain amount of risk with cardboard cases, it is thought the customary handling received on the railway would be a limiting factor. This could be overcome by supervision and an intimation to the railway authorities. The outstanding fact is that fruit cases have reached their maximum price, consistent with profit, and unless growers will face the situation and organise the industry must lose heavily.

NEWS AND NOTES.

Cultivation should be one of the principal operations of the orchardists at this season of the year. It is only on light, poor soils that team work is possible. The best implement to use when the weather takes up will be the plough. Spring-tooth and set-tooth cultivtaors can be brought into use at a later date.

Bandaging for codlin moth should be carried out as early as possible. Rough corn sacking or old bagging is most suitable. The bandage is made about 6in. to 8in. wide, and folded over to form a good lap on the underside against the tree. To fasten the bandage a 2in. copper nail is handy, the copper nail being used on account of non rusting.

Woolly aphis can still be treated. Commercial tobacco extracts are the most popular means of control. It is not advisable to use soap with the nicotine, as it is apt to stain the fruit.

Disbudding of young trees and topping young summer buds and grafts should be carried out. The growth this season is unusual, and a lot of inside sucker wood requires removing.

Anthracnose (black spot) on grape vines must still be treated. All efforts at control must be aimed at giving the foliage of the vine a thorough coating of the fungicide. Bordeaux mixture, summer strength, should be used for preference, although in the case of the fruit nearing the ripening stage ammonia carbonate of copper is best.

Second-crop oranges are falling badly. The unusual rainy season has brought about the drop. Now that the young crop is rapidly developing the dropping of the second crop is a blessing in disguise. As a matter of fact it would be an advantage to pick and market the fruit.

Lemons are showing well in the Cumberland hills district. The crops are generally heavy. The system of curing the fruit is not generally adopted. The Government orchard at Dural has lemon trees included in the citrus blocks. In handling the fruit from these trees it is customary to clip the fruit regularly every three and four weeks. The fruit is handled carefully and removed to the packing shed, where it is allowed to sweat. The fruit is then wrapped and placed in bushel cases. After several weeks it is found that the size has, to some extent, depreciated, the skin particularly fining up, leaving the fruit one complete mass of juice. The results of the system show that lemons grown on the coast can be successfully treated to ensure keeping, and also to improve the quality. From a commercial point of view, fruit treated in the above manner realises the highest prices on the market, even when competing against the Californian and Italian products.

Tableland districts are still receiving rain, thunderstorms occurring almost daily. The late cherry crop some few weeks ago promised a heavy yield. The wet season, however, is causing the fruit to split. The bulk of the crop will be worthless. The damage by hail too, has been greater than usual.

Peach crops in the cool districts are looking very well. The tableland districts are producing very fine peaches, due to the wet season. Cultivation, however, is out of the question, and spraying cannot be carried on. Unfortunately, fruit diseases, such as peach aphis, leaf curl, woolly aphis, and black spot are worse than usual. Up to the present codlin moth is not showing; perhaps, the wet season is holding back the egg-laying and hatching. It may be that spraying will have to be carried on later in the season.

The coastal orchards are to a large extent enjoying the wet season. Citrus have especially thriven under repeated falls of rain. Up to the present little complaint is heard of soil washing. Stone fruits are having a bad time, brown rot causing a lot of damage. In some orchards hail has destroyed the crop. Black spot of Bartlett pears is unusually prevalent. Careful application of lime-sulphur (commercial form) seems to have controlled the fungus. In seasons such as the present the orchardist is compelled to repeatedly spray to control fungus spread.

Batlow is experiencing an unusually wet season. The rainfall for the year has exceeded 70 inches. Fine weather is a thing of the past. Gooseberries and strawberries are being harvested. The crops are very poor indeed. Great interest centres upon the soldiers' settlement. A movement is on foot to aid the soldiers in clearing and fencing, and other operations incidental to the development of the block. Mill work has commenced on beautiful mountain gums, mountain ash, and messmate trees are being hauled to the mill. On each block 10 acres of land have been reserved for orchards, and the clearing work is being concentrated on the orchard section first.

The Hawkesbury district looks well. Peach crops are ripening. The size is not up to the usual standard, repeated rainstorms and cool weather having retarded development. Brown rot is commencing to develop, and growers are anxious concerning its spread. It is considered that if the rainy condition persist the crop will not be worth harvesting. Ground crops are backward, although looking well. One satisfactory feature of the season is the excellent amount of grass available for stock, and the good oat crops for hay. Young trees are developing rapidly, the growth this year being quite exceptional.

The back country districts are enjoying a good season for orchards. It is many years since trees showed to such advantage. In the Narromine district, for instance, the young orchards have made wonderful headway.

Owing to the infection of black spot in apples and pears in the Orange district, a large quantity of fruit not valuable for market will be available for pulping. It is the intention to commence pulping and canning operations. The present difficulty lies in the fact that a competent processor cannot be secured.

CROPS AND STOCK.

CAMDEN, Thursday.—Frequent heavy storms and continued wet weather are having a serious effect on the fruit crops that previously promised a heavy yield. Apricots and peaches are falling from the trees before maturing, and in some vineyards the grapes are showing signs of blight. Farming is being delayed, as the ground is too wet to plough. Several large crops of lucerne, cut prior to the rain, have had to be thrown away, having rotted in the paddocks.

CARCOAR, Thursday.—It is almost beyond doubt that serious loss will be experienced by district farmers owing to the continued wet weather. Crops in many cases are now on the verge of ruination. On some farms paddock after paddock can be seen of what promised to be record crops now destroyed and levelled to the ground. Taken all through, it can be safely estimated that the crop of hay in this district will be at least 33 per cent. lower than it was last year.

KIAMA, Thursday.—At a meeting of the Kiama P.P. Board the stock inspector (Mr. Hamilton) reported upon the splendid state of the pastures of the district, with plentiful grass and water on stock reserves and routes. No outbreaks of diseases had occurred, and the condition of stock was excellent.

YASS, Thursday.—Mr. Turner (district stock inspector) reports that the frequent rains have delayed the shearing, and some of the clips, as a consequence, will be caught with the grass seed. The wool is well-grown and bulky, but on the light side. Feed is in abundance everywhere. There has not been such a season for feed for many years. Rabbits are becoming numerous in places, and owing to the heavy coat of grass it is impossible to work poison carts with success. Stock are all in good condition, and no disease is reported.

APPEAL FOR MORE MEN.

LEADERS IN THE NEW RECRUITING CAMPAIGN.

Reading from left to right: MR. D. MACKINNON, M.L.A., PROFESSOR MACINTYRE, CAPTAIN COATES.

CASUALTIES.

THE 250TH LIST.

371 MEN WOUNDED.

The 250th list of Australian casualties was issued yesterday. It contains the names of 72 killed in action, and 371 wounded.

Following is a summary:—

—	Officers.	Others.
Killed in action	—	72
Died of wounds	—	14
Died (other causes)	—	5
Wounded	23	348
Missing	—	23
Sick	20	318
Injured	—	39
Prisoners of war	—	14
Total casualties	43	833
Returned to duty	3	72

NEW SOUTH WALES.

KILLED IN ACTION.

Gnr. C. L. STEWART, North Sydney.
Gnr. W. A. WRIGHT, Mosman.
Pte. R. A. GRACE, Tambar Springs.
Pte. J. HOGAN, S. Geelong, Vic.
Pte. E. J. BYRNE, Auburn.
L.-Sgt. A. P. HYDE, Croydon.
Pte. W. LAMPARD, England.
Pte. E. W. LAW, Moree.
Pte. T. JOYCE, Scotland.
Pte. A. LEVEY, England.
Pte. G. A. MATCHETT, Dubbo.
Pte. J. H. BIRD, Newtown.
Pte. H. C. MORRIS, Yass.
Pte. P. HILDER, Alexandria.
Pte. T. FAHEY, Carlton, Vic.
Pte. J. W. WAIN, North Sydney.
Pte. E. E. POTTER, Manly.

DIED OF WOUNDS.

Pte. A. G. SAUNDERS, Tingha.
Pte. B. THATCHER, Hurstville.
Pte. C. BRUCE, Tyaak, Vic.
Pte. J. D. DICKSON, Ultimo.
Pte. C. R. GIDDINGS, Gentle.
Sgt. J. W. KELLY, Hagowra.
Pte. J. B. CARROLL, Chatswood.

DIED (OTHER CAUSES).

Pte. J. F. HINES, Gilgai.

WOUNDED.

Gnr. W. A. FERGUSON, England.
Gnr. A. BRADFORD, Footscray, Vic. (severely).
Cpl. H. B. THROWER, Five Dock (severely).
2nd-Lt. K. M'K. FLETCHER, Roseville (severely).
Dvr. H. GARLAND, Hamilton.
Pte. A. TILLITZKI, Bexham.
Pte. J. A. RANDELL, Manly (severely).
Pte. P. J. SULLIVAN, Broadalbane (severely).
Pte. C. HARWOOD, England (severely).
Pte. P. DUNN, Leeton.
Pte. W. T. DENT, Randwick (and returned to duty).
T.-Cpl. E. C. HAMONET, East Maitland.
Pte. A. W. DIXON, Oxley Vale.
Sgt. G. BANCE, Centennial Park.
Pte. A. DICKINSON, England (severely).
Pte. R. W. FACKRELL, Murwillumbah (severely).
Pte. E. WINTHROP, Midland Junction, W.A. (and seriously ill).
Pte. K. R. S. RAMAGE, North Sydney (severely).
2nd-Lt. C. E. LUTEN, Stanmore (severely).
Cpl. E. T. LYONS, Forest Hill.
Sgt. C. R. CHRISTMAS, Neutral Bay.
Pte. R. W. E. THOMSON, Canada.
Pte. J. MANDEVILLE, England (and prisoner of war).
Pte. J. M'PHERSON, New Zealand (and prisoner of war).
Pte. N. D. MOTORIN, Russia.
Cpl. J. M. MAFFESONI, Chiltern Valley, Vic.
Pte. G. WHITTAKER, Mascot.
2nd-Lt. F. G. T. WALKER, North Sydney (severely).
Lt.-Col. F. W. G. ANNAND, Albion, Q. (severely).
Pte. G. CURRIE, Brisbane, Q.
Pte. J. J. CARROLL, Ireland.
Pte. J. E. KEOGH, Pyrmont.
Pte. J. W. NAYLOR, England.
Pte. W. J. WOOD, North Sydney.
Pte. D. J. CURNAN, Southport, Tas. (and prisoner of war).
Pte. A. MATTHIAS, Balmain East (severely).
Pte. A. V. HARRISON, Scone.
Pte. F. J. CANNON, Kurri Kurri.
Pte. G. H. RANDALL, Hunter's Hill.
Pte. H. G. M'KENZIE, Marrickville.
Pte. D. L. HARTWELL, Willoughby.
Cpl. H. L. HACK, Armidale.
Pte. W. MORTIMER, Sydney.
Sgt. A. PEARCE, Cardwell, Q.
Pte. W. J. GEORGE, Mascot.
Sgt. P. W. BURKE, Campbelltown.
Pte. J. L. NUNN, Burrinjuck.
Pte. F. ELLIS, Redfern.
Pte. A. M. ROBERTS, England.
Pte. F. EABLE, Lithgow.
Pte. G. F. H. DIXON, North Sydney (severely).
Pte. S. J. G. KELLY, Balmain.
Pte. S. L. ADAMS, Kogarah.
Pte. W. E. BAYLIS, Mascot.
Pte. E. F. M. FROST, Cabramatta.
Pte. J. J. COSGROVE, Bredbo.
Pte. H. R. AUSTIN, Darlinghurst.
Pte. J. A. ELLIS, Camperdown.
Pte. F. P. DAVIS, Marrickville.
L.-Cpl. E. A. CLEMENTS, Rockdale.
Pte. G. L. PRIOR, West Maitland.
Pte. W. J. KIRKUP, England.
Pte. C. M. CANDDELL, Balmain (severely).
Pte. T. T. DRAPER, Port Kembla.
Pte. F. CABLE, England.
2nd-Lt. P. Y. STORKEY, New Zealand (severely).
Pte. W. LOCHENS, Parramatta.
Pte. F. CURTIS, Surry Hills (severely).
Pte. G. A. DAVERS, Petersham.
Cpl. F. B. ADAMS, Paddington.
Sgt. E. D. TAYLOR, Newtown (severely).
Pte. C. V. PICKFORD, Newtown.
Pte. G. BATCHELOR, Surry Hills (and dangerously ill).
Cpl. E. M'NAB, Balmain (severely).
Pte. F. DIGWEED, Campsie (severely).
Pte. G. R. EVANS, Drummoyne (severely).
L.-Cpl. J. M. GOODMAN, West Wyalong (severely).
Pte. J. CHRISTIE, Narromine (severely).
Pte. J. BILSBORROW, Bathurst.
Pte. R. WHOLOHAN, Annandale.
Captain R. C. A. ANDERSON, Lindfield (severely).
Pte. S. D. O. CRAWFORD, England.
Pte. T. SMITH, Leeta (severely).
Pte. J. GALEA, Malta.
Pte. G. POND, Sydney.
Pte. D. W. CALLENSHIELDS, England.
Pte. F. H. SUTERS, Wauchope.
Lce.-Cpl. A. S. D. CROMBIE-BROWN, Enmore.
Lce.-Cpl. J. F. POULTER, Grong Grong (severely).
Pte. J. M'NEIL, Scotland (severely).
Pte. J. C. BARNES, Campsie (severely).
Pte. A. J. LAWSON, Blackburn, Vic. (severely).
Pte. T. HARRISON, Neutral Bay (severely).
Cpl. R. P. COLLINS, Grafton (severely).
Pte. J. H. ADDIS, Port Kembla, S.A. (and prisoner of war).
Temp.-Cpl. E. TURNER, Scotland.
Pte. E. P. K. ROBERTS, Gladesville (severely).
Cpl. J. D. RASHFORD, Waverley (severely).
Pte. G. CARRAGHTY, Beaumont (seriously).
Pte. J. ELLIOTT, England (severely).
Pte. P. LOGAN, England.
Pte. G. A. HAWES, Toowoomba (severely).
Pte. J. F. GLEESON, Gympie, Qld.
Pte. G. J. KING, Alexandria.
Lce.-Cpl. E. O. LYON, Botany.
Pte. W. D. HUTCHINSON, Cootamundra (severely).
Pte. E. M. STANFORD, Orange.
Pte. W. HILL, England (severely).
Pte. P. V. M'GRATH, Newtown (severely).
Pte. D. F. LEATHLEY, Katoomba.
Pte. M. HOUGH, Cowra (severely).
Pte. A. DUNKLEY, Parramatta (severely).
Pte. W. J. LOHSE, Tenterfield (severely).

MISSING.

Sgt. G. F. WELLS, New Zealand.
Pte. L. W. TIDEMAN, John's River.
Pte. S. C. TODD, Lidcombe.
Pte. C. A. N. POLLARD, Brewarrina.
Pte. W. F. PORTER, Pyrmont.
Pte. R. G. RUSSELL, Pyrmont.
Pte. T. RUTHERFORD, Paddington.
Pte. J. C. SIMINGTON, Newcastle.
Pte. H. N. SCHOFIELD, Riverstone.
Pte. W. H. SPARLING, England.
Pte. A. WILLIAMS, Woodstock.
Cpl. T. WHITTON, Annandale.
Pte. W. F. CONSTABLE, Narrabri.
Pte. V. R. STONE, Ballina.
Pte. C. A. WAGHORN, Petersham.
Pte. E. FANNING, North Lambton.
Pte. R. T. COSTELLOE, Coonabarabran.
Pte. J. FARLEY, Ireland.
Pte. A. GOVERS, Copeton.
Pte. R. E. HOLLINGWORTH, England.
Pte. W. C. RANKINE, Rooty Hill.

ILL.

Pte. E. W. KRAHE, Tenterfield (dangerously).
Dvr. K. A. BERRELL, Goulburn.
Bmdr. L. C. ELLIOTT, Haberfield.
Sgt. R. ADELT, Wollstonecraft (seriously).
Spr. S. C. BENNETT, Waterloo (seriously).
Pte. L. H. EDWARDS, Kiama.
Pte. K. EASTERBROOK, Manly.
Lieut. K. BAYLEY, North Sydney.
Pte. A. P. AUDET, Wee Waa (seriously).
Captain W. T. DICK, Waverley (seriously).
Cpl. D. S. GIBSON, Cambewarra.
Pte. W. COLLINSON, Leichhardt.
Pte. D. MASON, Merewether (dangerously).
Sgt. P. LONERGAN, Ireland (seriously).
Pte. J. F. COMYN, Riverstone (seriously).
Pte. T. G. WELLS, Port Macquarie.
Pte. H. J. EVANS, Alexandria.
Cpl. E. R. J. JOHNSON, Paddington.
Pte. W. B. EVANS, West Wallsend.
Lieut. C. T. AGASSIZ, Newtown.
Captain N. E. PLOMLEY, England.
Captain C. R. LUCAS, Waverley (seriously).
Pte. W. WILSON, England.
Pte. W. O. DEANE, Lidcombe.
Pte. G. MAPSTONE, Bombala.
Cpl. R. S. COLLER, Condobolin.
Pte. P. STEER, North Sydney.
Sgt. T. G. GOOLEY, Balmain.
Captain A. A. ABBOTT, England (seriously).
Pte. W. HOY, Surry Hills.
Pte. G. WOOD, Warren.
Pte. A. J. KLEIN, Middle Park, Vic.
Pte. P. P. JOLLY, Lismore.
Pte. F. R. HEATH, Surry Hills.
Pte. R. R. HELLYER, Coonabarabran.
Pte. J. M. HARMAN, Newcastle (seriously).
Pte. C. R. LELLIOTT, Woollahra (seriously).
Cpl. C. R. FINCH, England.
Pte. T. LEDDEN, Robinsville.
Pte. D. BACKUS, Surry Hills.
Pte. W. F. EATON, England.
Pte. J. P. COURTNEY, Sydney.
Pte. S. E. HARVEY, East Melbourne, V.
Pte. G. O. LIVINGSTONE, Tumbarumba.
Pte. G. F. JACKSON, England.
Pte. C. A. WYNDOW, St. Peters.
Pte. S. TAYLOR, Enfield (seriously).
Pte. C. T. ANDREWS, Redfern (seriously).
Pte. E. A. DAWSON, Burwood.
Pte. A. J. M'INNES, S. Lismore.
Pte. A. SUSAN, Glebe.
Pte. P. J. HORSNELL, Mosman.
Pte. E. ROBINSON, Waterloo.
Pte. F. P. WHITE, Dora Creek.
Pte. A. STOKES, England (seriously).
Pte. E. CURRIE, Double Bay (seriously).
Pte. W. A. DOYLE, Newtown.
Cpl. T. W. BAXTER, Drummoyne.
Pte. J. LEAN, Ultimo.
Pte. A. J. THOMPSON, Paddington.
Pte. C. COX, Newcastle.
Pte. T. A. DONOHOE, S. Kensington.
Pte. J. CHURCHILL, England.
Pte. W. LUNN, England.
Pte. P. A. DONOHOE, Quirindi.
Pte. J. W. DIMOND, Tumbling.
Pte. R. W. ALLEN, Ingleburn.
Second-lieut. E. O. BOUCHIERE, Kirribilli.
Second-lieut. A. W. DEVINE, Ashfield.
Cpl. T. L. DAVIS, Belmore.
Pte. J. A. MADDEN, Drummoyne.
Pte. J. T. DOHERTY, Glebe (seriously).
Pte. W. S. B. PRITZLER, Coramba.
L.-cpl. R. C. WORTHINGTON, Griffith.
Pte. W. O. WOMSLEY, Hurstville.
Pte. T. JACKSON, Arncliffe.
Sgt. W. T. WALTON, Port Melbourne, V.
Pte. R. WOODHOUSE, Guildford.
Pte. R. W. STRAFFORD, Miller's Point.
Pte. A. L. STEEL, Strood.
Pte. W. E. SMITH, Nevertire.
Pte. A. E. THOMPSON, Newtown.
Pte. J. GANNON, Binalong.
Pte. H. GREENSLADE, Townsville, Q.
Pte. C. E. BELY, Paddington.
Pte. W. G. HATTON, Lithgow.
Pte. S. J. HORSLEY, Guyra.
Pte. C. M. SMITH, Sydney (seriously).
Pte. J. F. SULLIVAN, Surry Hills.
Pte. G. H. COTTERILL, Yarram, Vic.
Pte. H. CARTER, Coonamble.
Pte. D. A. BAKER, W. Sydney (seriously).
Captain E. L. HENDERSON, Crow's Nest, Q. (seriously).
Pte. D. MORRISON, Pyrmont (seriously).
Pte. J. WILLIAMS, Pyrmont (seriously).
Pte. P. J. DALY, Albury.
Pte. F. V. DIXON, Turramurra.
Pte. B. GIBB, New Zealand.
Pte. A. FERGUSON, Marrickville.
Pte. H. W. HARRIS, Kogarah.
Pte. O. F. DUNSTAN, Sydney.
Pte. R. ROBERTS, Waverley.
Pte. T. HAYLAN, E. Sydney.
Pte. E. E. STOW, England (seriously).

INJURED.

Pte. J. H. BUSH, Cessnock (severely).
Pte. J. ISEDALE, Bell Bird (severely).
Cpl. A. COWDEN, Arncliffe.
Pte. W. T. MAYALL, Narrabri.

RETURNED TO DUTY.

Cpl. W. DICKSON, Scotland.
Pte. E. J. DREW, Auburn.
Pte. F. W. L. COOK, Redfern.
Pte. E. C. COOPER, Redfern.
Pte. S. E. ROPER, Granville.
Pte. J. A. REID, Scotland.
Pte. R. H. COWCROFT, Singleton.
C.S.M. T. R. CROOKS, New Lambton.
Pte. J. COOK, Annandale.
Pte. B. CONNELLY, Campsie.
Pte. E. CLARKE, England.
Second-lieut. L. H. BIGNELL, Bass, V.
Pte. H. P. BURNS, Wickham.
Pte. W. A. BAYNE, Scotland.
C.S.M. R. N. BROWN, England.
Pte. C. CAMPBELL, Orange.
Pte. J. E. CLARKE, Murdooran.
Cpl. F. T. N. FOXLEY, Erskineville.
Pte. A. J. BREAR, Lindfield.
Pte. G. HUMPHRIES, England.
Pte. J. CARTER, Stewart's Brook.
Pte. A. E. ROBINSON, Toowoomba, Q.

VICTORIA.

KILLED IN ACTION.—Dvr. J. J. Hanratty, Ptes. A. C. Burton, J. M. Morris, B. Bride, G. H. Simpson (Ballarat), J. Ahern, P. G. Stott, B. A. Freestone, C. A. Sonken, Cpl. F. E. Oates, Pte. H. Harding, Cpl. A. H. Edwards, Ptes. W. T. White, R. Toman, S. A. Olley, C. E. Brown, J. Brown, J. Nolan, H. Swanston, J. M. M'Kean, E. W. Lewis, H. R. Burton, H. M. Lennox, T. J. Ryan.

DIED OF WOUNDS.—Ptes. R. G. Dawes, G. F. Moore, W. G. Vienna.

DIED (OTHER CAUSES).—Pte. W. F. Hum.

WOUNDED.—Dvr. L. H. Matthews, Gnr. L. G. Somerville, Dvr. A. A. Cleveland, Bmdr. J. N. Hancock (severely), Gnr. A. H. Lane (severely), Bmdr. W. M'L. Robertson (severely), Trumpeter R. E. Conlon, Lieut. F. G. Lloyd (severely), Pte. R. M. Taylor, Spr. S. N. Phillips, Spr. T. Lees, Ptes. E. A. Cummins (severely), G. F. Love, J. Jenner, J. Donohue (severely), A. H. Carden, W. F. Russell, W. E. Bond, Capt. O. J. Thompson (severely), Cpl. J. C. Ferguson, Ptes. R. Jagnet (severely), E. J. Vaughan (severely), J. H. Mallett, W. V. Meakin, A. V. Brotherton, C. H. O'Farrell, Sgt. R. Goodall, Ptes. A. S. Hainsworth, J. A. Milbourn, J. Ingram, G. A. Davis, Lieut. H. M'Closkey, Pte. N. P. Bernard, Cpl. H. J. Parker, Spr. J. Phillips, Ptes. G. J. Fills, Lce.-Cpl. F. Matthews, Lce.-Cpl. M. Silvy, Pte. V. Elliott, Dvr. L. A. Whitfield, Sgt. S. B. Silvey, Sgt. I. M'L. Tulloh, Ptes. R. W. Allbutt, W. H. Boggler, L. C. Tonkins, H. J. Yorke, W. J. G. Louis, J. P. D. M. M'Mahon, W. L. A. Block, V. Vains, R. J. M'Waters, E. S. M'Phee, Sgt. C. Harcourt (Colac), Ptes. N. L. Martin, M. T. O'Donoghue, A. Jamieson, Sec.-Lieut. J. W. Winter, Pte. V. G. Burke, Lce.-Cpl. W. Boyle, Ptes. W. C. Jorgensen, A. Tillyer, J. T. Flanagan, J. Denman, S. W. Brownhill, A. J. Bracken, P. Breckenridge, Lieut. V. J. G. Coultie, Ptes. E. J. B. Newbold, B. H. Parrant, J. E. Williams, Cpl. S. R. Goldsmith, Sgt. L. Brette, Ptes. H. Gregory, A. Evans, R. Chadwick, Lce.-Cpl. W. S. Mallows, Ptes. C. W. Brown, A. Batters, F. A. Booker, F. W. Daniels, W. J. Farrell (and dangerously ill), H. A. Breen (and seriously ill), T. Halpin (severely), A. L. Robinson (and returned to duty), J. R. Clark (and returned to duty), T. H. Cartwright, L. J. Byrne, R. S. Stephens, W. Andiner (severely), W. J. Freeman, Sec.-Lieut. R. W. Coode, Sgt. J. F. Cronin, Ptes. F. Smith, W. H. Beament, A. E. H. Hughes, P. J. Daly (Deniliquin), V. A. Dawson, F. A. Murray, C. T. Sherwood, A. Johnsen, Sec.-Lieut. A. W. Smith, Ptes. S. A. Fraser, A. M'Alpine, A. C. Swaisey, Lce.-Cpl. L. W. MacDonald, Pte. T. Stanton.

MISSING.—Pte. A. Clark.

ILL.—Dvr. G. Cross, Lieut. C. Fiddle, Bdr. P. Quinn, Ptes. J. W. Comb, A. R. Walker, H. Nelson, A. A. Murphy, T. J. Bond, J. Douglas, J. G. Sullivan, D. Smith, R. J. Stevens, F. Nunn, J. Rice, L.-Cpl. J. E. Frisone, Sgt. R. M'Farlane, Ptes. H. R. Grisham, H. J. Spencer (dangerously), Capt. J. G. Bolton, 2nd-Lt. H. W. Goodwin, Ptes. A. Hawthorne, F. V. Peterson, Cpl. G. Hamilton, Pte. F. Curtis, L.-Cpl. D. H. Milliken, 2nd-Lt. H. A. Harrison, Ptes. G. P. Goode, T. Lakey, R. P. Edmonds, R. D. Chapman, G. Dean (Wagga), T. Coulson, L.-Cpl. L. Johnston, Ptes. C. T. Payne, C. R. Dixon, A. H. M'Kinstry, 2nd-Lt. A. O. Tubb, Ptes. R. H. Lambem, F. N. Walker (Wattamundara), H. Dingwall, A. F. Postlethwaite, A. M'Quade, Dvr. H. H. Hutchinson, Pte. G. Carroll, S.-Sgt. R. F. Crowley, Lieut. R. L. Smith, Pte. J. J. Cahill (seriously), Lieut. C. J. Jacobs, Pte. G. R. Osborne (seriously), H. W. Johnson, R. Hill, W. M. Hamilton, D. W. Mitchell, G. Roughan, D. T. Reynolds, A. Mounsey, Cpl. H. Giles, Pte. M. Murray, 2nd-Lt. O. M. Elliott, Ptes. C. W. Ross, R. Evans, Sgt. F. M. Dale, Ptes. C. R. Frencham, F. P. A. Fynch, L. Brokenwagen, L. D. Macdonald, J. H. Cribbins, A. W. Macauley, A.-Sgt. D. G. Fyffe, Pte. A. R. Barry, L.-Cpl. S. R. M'Combe, Ptes. W. Dalton, G. Hayes, E. T. M'Lean, E. Ryan, T. P. Leonard, L.-Cpl. W. J. Humphrey, Pte. W. C. Purcell, L.-Cpl. J. R. Porter.

INJURED.—Pte. E. P. Higgs (seriously), L.-Sgt. G. C. Oakley (Moama).

PRISONER OF WAR.—Pte. H. J. Rowgate.

RETURNED TO DUTY.—Dvr. A. M'Farland, Dvr. J. Nutt, Sgt. H. C. Byatt, 2nd-Cpl. P. L. Johnston, Sgt. H. R. Gallagher, Ptes. C. W. Brierley, R. E. Cross, G. Croft, E. L. Kubbecht, S. B. Edmondson, Lieut. E. T. Bander, Ptes. J. R. Kirkman, F. D. Furrows, F. J. Scanlon, A. Campbell, G. Swallow, A. G. Cartwright, R. Wilcock, H. G. Cook, A. S. Beck, R. F. Wintle, Q. C. Cardwell, Dvr. J. W. Marstin, L.-Cpl. G. M. Usher.

QUEENSLAND.

KILLED IN ACTION.—Dvr. W. G. Lilwall, T.-Cpl. W. H. Smith, Ptes. M. Aitken, J. F. Brosnder (Wardell), J. B. Donoghue (Macksville), W. H. Foggon (Balmain), T. Purcell (Walcha), A. Pitt, H. Stamp (Glen Wardell), A. R. Stoker (Ballina), P. Crosse, A. Chalmers, S. C. Crew, R. Brown, M. Walkoff, T. Wilson, A. R. Williams, J. Sutton, L. W. Smith, J. J. Smallhorn, W. J. Reid, E. Parsons, W. Paterson, J. D. Pearson (Casino), C. Hurt, G. Edwards.

DIED OF ILLNESS.—Pte. G. F. Cluberg, Cpl. D. J. Gillanders.

WOUNDED.—Gnr. A. Morgan, Pte. S. H. Edwards, Dvr. A. J. Purnwell, Gnr. E. C. Glue, Spr. G. Saunders, Pte. J. M'Kechnie, L.-Cpl. W. V. H. Johns, Ptes. F. Morrissey, C. P. Kelleher, L. Watkins, F. J. Rice, H. H. H. Hodges, W. Britten, W. H. Bolger, L.-Cpl. R. Batty, J. Byrne (Emmaville), Shoemaker-Sgt. B. Hopper (West Petersham), Cpl. N. Banks, Ptes. J. Mortimer, M. Dayman, D. E. Rundle, J. R. Jensen, J. I. Dryden, Dvr. J. P. Heber (Bellinger), Cpl. W. Cunningham, Ptes. E. C. Chaddock, P. Land (Casino), A. J. Taylor, E. Donoghue, G. Wells, J. C. M'Gregor (Casino), 2nd-Lieut. W. F. Hamilton, Ptes. R. J. Davis, F. Nicholas, L.-Cpl. P. Ainsworth (Ballina), Cpl. R. A. Wilkin (South Lismore), Pte. G. W. Kemp, Sgts. L. A. Davis, A. E. Spilling, Ptes. J. J. Harrison, W. B. Scholz, Sgt. R. Stockleton, Pte. R. D. M'Leod (Palmer's Island), Sgt. A. E. Hall, L.-Sgt. P. N. J. Crouch (Coombell), Ptes. H. W. E. Fuller, L. Hooper, J. J. Sayers, D. Sillars, A. White, L.-Cpl. J. J. Thomas, Cpl. W. George, 2nd-Lieutenant A. J. L. Coward (severely), Ptes. F. J. Williams (severely), W. J. Millen (severely), E. M. Riley (severely), F. C. Webb (severely), C. Aldred (severely), F. A. White, H. V. Vincicombe, B. Sigston, H. C. New, G. N. Carr, R. Cross, F. L. Claran (Cumbalum), A. R. Black (Beecroft), S. Grandon (2nd occasion), Cpl. J. A. Speechley (and prisoner of war), Pte. J. T. Wright (and prisoner of war).

ILL.—Ptes. A. Olsen, T. Dunn, H. S. H. M'Carroll, Dvr. C. W. Renouf, Pte. T. M'L. W. Howard, Gnr. L. G. M'Gown, Lieut. A. Lennan, Spr. G. J. Holmes, Spr. L. W. King, Spr. A. T. M'Namara, Ptes. F. M. Markwell, J. Doyle, W. Kirkwood, R. T. Caffey, E. R. Foreman, T. M. M'Cormack, D. M. Fraser, R. B. Cribb, E. A. Chapman, Sec.-Lieut. C. J. Blomfield, Ptes. L. S. B. Greenbury, S. H. Noble, A. Cowlin, Sgt. U. T. Burke, Ptes. B. Matthews, D. Hampson (Mudgee), E. W. G. Jenkins.

INJURED.—Ptes. J. A. Harrison (Burringbar), F. W. Farrington.

RETURNED TO DUTY.—Cpl. W. Winters, Ptes. A. H. Cox, F. Corcoran, T. A. Jones, R. G. Buchanan (Corrimal), A. C. Brooks, T. H. Boland (Murwillumbah), M. Barratt, S.Q.M.S. G. Hughes, Pte. A. Pountney.

RED CROSS INFORMATION BUREAU.

Dalton House, 115 Pitt Street, Sydney.

All who are anxious to seek news of sick, wounded, or missing men are invited to call at, or write to, the above address, and the Red Cross will try to help them.

LANGER OWEN.

AMELIORATION.

CASE OF IMPOSITION.

Mr. Justice Ferguson (chairman of the Australia Day Amelioration Committee) has authorised the following statement for publication:—"The Amelioration Committee at its weekly meeting on the 13th inst. investigated a number of cases where returned soldiers had endeavored to impose upon the fund. In some of these money was received as a result of representations which have since been proved to be of a wilfully false nature. The committee notes with regret the frequency with which these cases are recurring. It was resolved that such illegal practices must immediately cease. After a review of the position the committee decided, in view of the fact that they are dealing with sick and wounded soldiers, to issue a warning before taking legal proceedings. In future all attempts to impose upon the fund will be rigorously dealt with."

During last week the Amelioration Committee assisted 818 of the sick and wounded soldiers and sailors; 53 of these men were new applicants. The total number of cases to date which have received financial help is 5414, or about 88 per cent. of the total men returned to the State. Altogether £73,000 has been expended out of the Australia Day moneys in affording ameliorative help, and the total extent of payments during last week was £1562 6s 1d; 41,000 individual payments have been granted.

WRECK SOLD FOR £45.

The wreck of the steamer Belmore, at the Macleay River entrance, was sold at auction yesterday by Mr. F. R. Strange, and realised £45. Salvage operations will be started immediately to remove the wreck from the fairway. The sale was subject to the special condition that the purchasers have the responsibility and cost of removing the wreck to the satisfaction of the Department of Navigation. The purchasers were Messrs. Banks Bros.

BUILDING, TENDERS, AND PLANS.

DEPARTMENT OF EDUCATION.

Following are the tenders accepted for the week ended December 14:—

Berry.—Remodelling drainage: C. Donald, Marrickville, £98.

Blayney.—Alterations, etc.: J. Bridgman, sen., Blayney, £161/10/.

Thornleigh.—Improvements: E. Hewson, Auburn, £148.

Parkes.—Additions to closets: J. Job, Parkes, £116/10/.

Comleroy Road.—Repairs: Drayton and Silk, Richmond, £35.

Regentville.—Improvements: E. Everingham, Penrith, £82/14/6.

46 *White feathers and yellow streaks*

Conscription referendums, 1916–1917

UNIVERSAL MILITARY TRAINING HAD BEEN COMPULSORY IN AUSTRALIA SINCE 1911, BUT ONLY FOR SERVICE ON DOMESTIC SOIL. WHEN POLITICIANS CAMPAIGNED TO SET UP AUSTRALIA'S OWN ARMED FORCES, THE IDEA THAT THERE MIGHT EVER BE A NEED TO CONSCRIPT MEN FOR OVERSEAS SERVICE, RATHER THAN RELY ON ENTHUSIASTIC VOLUNTEERS, HAD NOT BEEN PART OF THE POLICY MAKERS' PLANS. STILL AT THE START OF THE FIRST WORLD WAR, DURING 1914 AND 1915, AUSTRALIAN TROOPS ENLISTED VOLUNTARILY IN LARGE NUMBERS.

But as the enormity of the casualties on the Western Front became known, volunteering rates dropped steadily. Patriotic advertising campaigns did not achieve the desired 5,000 enlistments per month that were needed to keep the Australian forces at combat strength.

Labor Prime Minister Billy Hughes (1862–1952) strongly campaigned for a referendum on the question of conscription for overseas service. The campaign included the production of a newsreel film of a speech by Hughes arguing the Yes case. The referendum held on 28 October 1916 asked Australians:

> *Are you in favour of the Government having, in this grave emergency, the same compulsory powers over citizens in regard to requiring their military service, for the term of this War, outside the Commonwealth, as it now has in regard to military service within the Commonwealth?*

The referendum was extremely divisive within Australian society and the arguments were passionate. How could Australian men not support their comrades fighting overseas? How could Australians send more men to their deaths? White feathers, a symbol of cowardice in Britain since the eighteenth century, were sent to many men who had not volunteered and to those who did not support conscription.

Newspaper headlines and editorials at the time of the referendum reflected this debate. To the surprise of many, the No vote won by 1,160,033 to 1,087,557. Another referendum in December 1917 (by which time Hughes was the Nationalist Party prime minister) was more soundly defeated, and the issue was over until the war's end in November 1918.

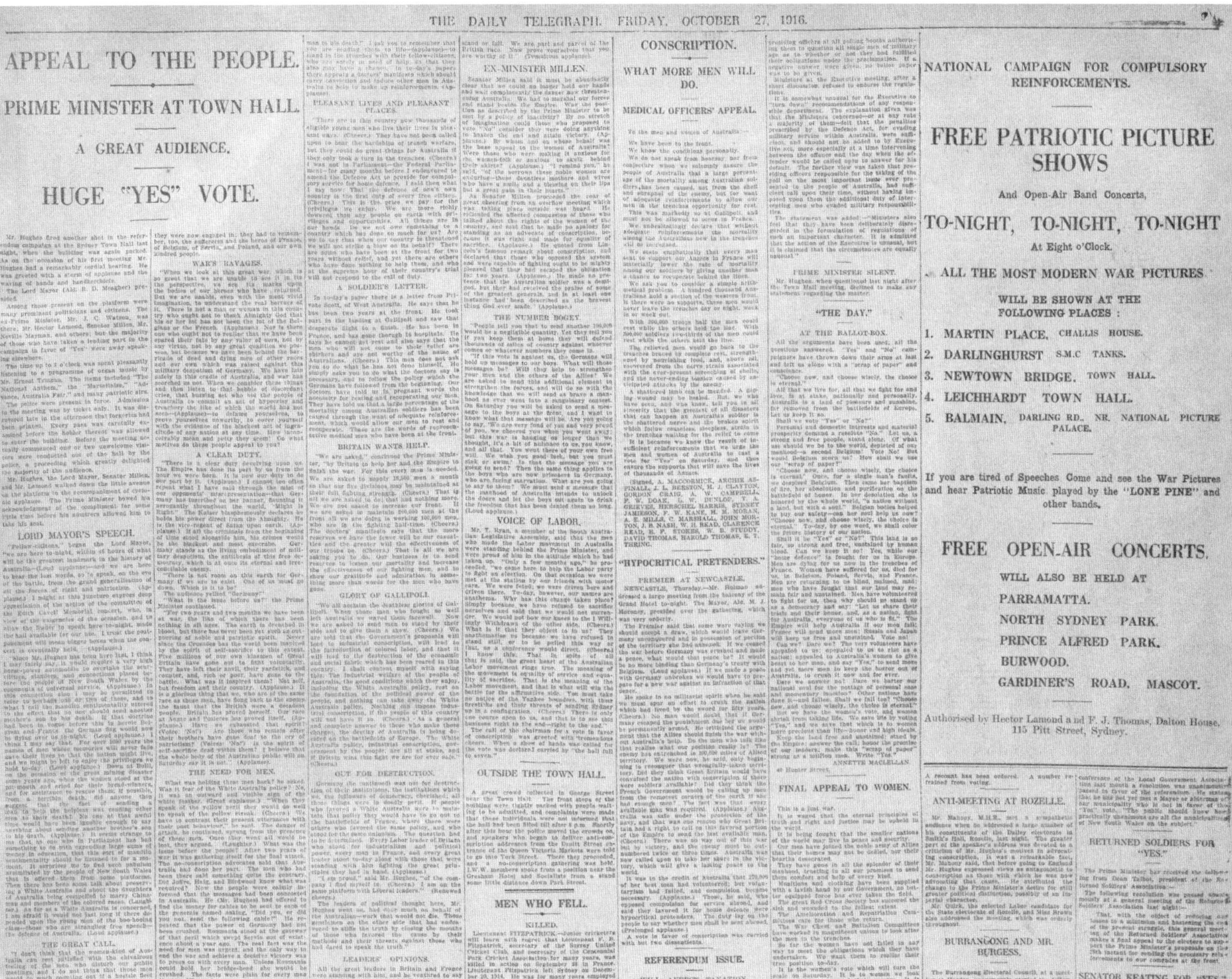
THE DAILY TELEGRAPH. FRIDAY, OCTOBER 27, 1916.

APPEAL TO THE PEOPLE.

PRIME MINISTER AT TOWN HALL.

A GREAT AUDIENCE.

HUGE "YES" VOTE.

CONSCRIPTION.

WHAT MORE MEN WILL DO.

MEDICAL OFFICERS' APPEAL.

NATIONAL CAMPAIGN FOR COMPULSORY REINFORCEMENTS.

FREE PATRIOTIC PICTURE SHOWS

And Open-Air Band Concerts,

TO-NIGHT, TO-NIGHT, TO-NIGHT

At Eight o'Clock.

ALL THE MOST MODERN WAR PICTURES

WILL BE SHOWN AT THE FOLLOWING PLACES:

1. MARTIN PLACE, CHALLIS HOUSE.
2. DARLINGHURST S.M.C TANKS.
3. NEWTOWN BRIDGE, TOWN HALL.
4. LEICHHARDT TOWN HALL.
5. BALMAIN, DARLING RD., NR. NATIONAL PICTURE PALACE.

If you are tired of Speeches Come and see the War Pictures and hear Patriotic Music played by the "LONE PINE" and other bands,

FREE OPEN-AIR CONCERTS.

WILL ALSO BE HELD AT

PARRAMATTA.

NORTH SYDNEY PARK.

PRINCE ALFRED PARK.

BURWOOD.

GARDINER'S ROAD, MASCOT.

Authorised by Hector Lamond and F. J. Thomas, Dalton House, 115 Pitt Street, Sydney.

The Daily Telegraph of 27 October 1916 reported on a rally for the first conscription referendum. While those on the spot voted in favour of conscription, a resounding No vote was delivered at the referendum itself.

10 THE DAILY TELEGRAPH, FRIDAY, OCTOBER 27, 1916.

FALLEN HEROES.

238TH LIST.

KILLED IN ACTION, 75.

TOTAL CASUALTIES, 491.

NEW SOUTH WALES.

KILLED IN ACTION.

DIED OF WOUNDS.

DIED OF ILLNESS.

DIED.

WOUNDED.

ILL.

QUEENSLAND.

VICTORIA.

PRISONERS OF WAR.

INJURED.

RETURNED TO DUTY.

PROGRESS.

HANDS UP FOR CONSCRIPTION.

Scene in Martin Place Yesterday. The lady standing is Miss Gladys Owen.

THE BATTLE CALL.

CHARGED WITH SABOTAGE.

CORRIGENDA

RED CROSS INFORMATION BUREAU.

NEXT-OF-KIN WANTED.

Y.M.C.A.

RECEPTION TO MR. VIRGO.

MR. VIRGO AT NEWCASTLE.

JAPANESE MAIL.

MILITARY CHANGES.

STATE ELECTIONS.

OFF TO THE WAR.

CONGREGATIONAL UNION.

VIOLENT SOUTHERLY SQUALL.

STEAMER KYARRA BLOWN ADRIFT.

A YACHT DISABLED.

EXEMPTION COURTS.

CENTRAL POLICE.

WATER POLICE.

PADDINGTON.

NORTH SYDNEY.

PARRAMATTA.

PARCELS TO SALONIKA.

[illegible]

Although The Daily Telegraph *had not yet moved headline stories to the front page, the paper had begun to use photographs in dramatic fashion. This image from page 10 of the 27 October 1916 issue shows a pro-conscription rally in Sydney. The image also promotes the pro-conscription stance taken by the* Telegraph, *reflected in its editorial of 28 October.*

Pulled from the monster's jaws 47

Coogee Beach shark attack, 1922

THE TRAGIC STORY OF MILTON COUGHLAN ECHOES A LONG HISTORY OF THE DANGERS THAT LIE BEHIND AUSTRALIA'S BEACH CULTURE. REPORTS OF SHARK ATTACKS HAVE MADE REGULAR HEADLINE NEWS THROUGHOUT AUSTRALIAN HISTORY, PARTICULARLY ATTACKS AT POPULAR SWIMMING PLACES SUCH AS THE SYDNEY BEACHES.

On 4 February 1922, 18-year-old Milton Coughlan was attacked by a shark at Coogee Beach, just south of Sydney. As attitudes towards public swimming and swimming attire began to change, surf life saving clubs and swimming carnivals had become increasingly popular from the early 1900s. At the Coogee carnival in 1922, an estimated 6000 people were waiting for the carnival to commence when they witnessed Coughlan being attacked. He fought off the shark until it had bitten both his arms. He was rescued by swimmers who plunged into the water, heedless of the danger, but he later died.

Coughlan's death was reportedly the first shark attack fatality on Sydney swimming beaches and from this time, many fenced-off baths were built in the harbour and on seaside beaches. During the early twentieth century, as the population of the city grew, people had increasing leisure time, and trains and trams made it easier for many to visit the beaches. Accordingly, as swimming and 'catching breakers' became more popular, the numbers of shark attacks rose.

Not all attacks were at the beach. In 1935 a 13-year-old girl, Berryl Morrin, was swimming at dusk in the Georges River, nearly 20 kilometres inland from the sea, and was attacked by a shark. Both her arms were bitten off, but she survived. Her story—including the process of fitting artificial limbs (which had been further developed due to the First World War)—was followed intensely by Australian and overseas media, and by a public shocked that predatory sharks could lurk in their rivers as well as their harbours and beaches.

THE SYDNEY MAIL, WEDNESDAY, FEBRUARY 8, 1922.—Page 10

Fight with a Shark: Tragedy at Coogee

One of the most sensational events in the history of surf-bathing and one of the most glorious deeds of gallantry ever recorded in Australia occurred at Coogee on Saturday when, in the presence of a large number of spectators assembled for a carnival, a youth named Milton Singleton Coughlan was attacked by a shark, and was pulled literally from the jaws of the monster by J. Chalmers, an ex-Digger and a member of the North Bondi Life-saving Club. Coughlan, who was only 18 years of age, died soon after being admitted to the Sydney Hospital.

MILTON SINGLETON COUGHLAN.
Who died from injuries inflicted by a shark.

THE victim of the tragic occurrence was the second youngest son of Mr. T. L. Coughlan, postmaster at Randwick. He was a prominent member of the Coogee Life-saving Club. A graphic story was related by Mr. T. F. Doran, who helped to give out the line to Chalmers when the latter swam out to the rescue of the plucky lad who, in his terrible struggle for life, was striving heroically—but, unfortunately, without avail—to drive off the shark.

"THE occasion" (said Mr. Doran) "marked a carnival for teams south of the Heads, in competition with a carnival at Manly for clubs north of the Heads. Many of the Coogee competitors were going to the other end of the beach for the purposes of the carnival, when Coughlan and two other members went in for a swim off what is popularly known as the reef, about 30 or 40 yards off the club-house rocks. They were all getting some fine

(*Continued on Page 21.*)

THE SCENE OF THE TRAGEDY.
Coughlan went for a swim at a spot which is commonly known as the reef, about 30 or 40 yards off the club-house rocks.

J. CHALMERS.
Whose magnificent heroism has made him famous throughout Australia. He is as modest as he is brave. In the war he served with the 45th Battalion.

THE FUNERAL OF MILTON S. COUGHLAN.
A very large number of surfers and the general public attended the funeral, which took place at Randwick on Monday. The picture shows the head of the cortege, with members of the Coogee Life-saving Club leading.

The Sydney Mail *of 8 February 1922 devoted a page of the newspaper to the story of the tragic death of a young swimmer, who had been about to take part in a swimming carnival at Coogee Beach. Despite being headline news, the story appeared on the inside pages of the paper, but as was now typical, it was illustrated with photographs. Portraits of both the victim and his rescuer, who was described as an 'ex-digger', appear.*

Hooligans take charge 48

Melbourne riots during a police strike, 1923

THE MELBOURNE DAILY NEWSPAPER *THE SUN NEWS-PICTORIAL* DESCRIBED THE RIOTING AND LOOTING THAT TOOK PLACE IN MELBOURNE ON THE WEEKEND OF 3–4 NOVEMBER 1923 AS 'AUSTRALIA'S WORST EPISODE', CONDUCTED BY 'OUR UNLEASHED SCUM' AND 'THE WORST DEMONSTRATION OF UTTER LAWLESSNESS EVER RECORDED IN AUSTRALIAN HISTORY'.

The paper was quite correct about the lawlessness. For three days and nights gangs effectively controlled the streets of Melbourne, derailing and trying to set fire to trams, smashing shop windows, fighting and looting. As the *Sun* noted, 'law and order in Melbourne has collapsed ... in a riotous orgy of looting, bullying and reckless street affrays'. The central district, around Swanston, Bourke and Elizabeth streets, was said to look 'like a sacked city' with windows smashed, street barricades erected, and thousands of men and women stealing what they could from shops.

Somehow, the idea that Melbourne's streets were not going to be patrolled because of a police strike fuelled a frenzy of opportunistic rioting and looting that became a semi-organised attempt to control the streets and steal anything that could be moved. Some 'rioters' roamed the city in packs just looking for fights, and the temporary 'special constables' were good targets. The special constables, many of whom were ex-soldiers quickly called in to restore order, responded in kind with some 'overzealous' baton work, and had to be restrained by the few remaining police. Hundreds of people were wounded in baton charges, bottle attacks and stonings. Soldiers were brought in, particularly to guard the city's banks, as well as to help restore order.

More than a third of the city's police force had walked off the job, just days before the Melbourne Cup was to be run. The police had many long-standing grievances with the Victorian government over poor pay and conditions, and especially the 'special supervisors', or 'spooks' as the police called them, who were appointed to secretly monitor police performance.

Order was restored after three days of rioting, but the Victorian premier, Harry Lawson, refused to reinstate a single one of the more than 600 striking police officers. But the conditions they fought for were soon granted to their replacements.

Special Edition 2.45 p.m. : Cabinet Decisions : Monash in Charge

A Later Edition will be issued containing strike developments as they occur

The Herald

Eighty-fourth Year

1½D.

No. 14,499. [Registered at General Post Office, Melbourne, for transmission by post as a Newspaper] MELBOURNNE, SUNDAY, NOVEMBER 4, 1923 (4 PAGES)

HUNDREDS OF CITIZENS ENROLLING FOR POLICE DUTY

BIG POLICE FORCE AVAILABLE TONIGHT

Generals Monash and Elliott Organising Mounted Patrols

STATE CABINET HOLDS SPECIAL SESSION

In view of the gravity of the situation caused by the police strike, a full meeting of the State Cabinet was held this morning to consider the whole position. The resolution of the Excutive of the Police Association, urging the police strikers to return to duty at once, was also discussed.

Within the recollection of the oldest politicians, there has been no similar Sunday Cabinet meeting in this State.

The Public Safety Committee is taking steps to call up light horsemen to act as mounted police, and promises stern measures.

A thousand special constables have been enrolled at the Melbourne Town Hall. Despite the grave warning from the police to citizens to stay at home today, crowds of sightseers began to pour into the city with the first trains this morning.

It is officially esimated that last night 410 members of the police force were on strike.

Information has been received from Ballarat to the effect that 30 members of the force in that district intend to go on strike at 7 o'clock on Monday morning unless a settlement is effeced in the meantime.

The police strikers are meeting at 3 o'clock this afternoon at the Trades Hall

Measures for the protection of the public during the police strike were taken by the Cabinet at special meetings held today. General Sir John Monash, formerly Commander of the Australian forces in France, was in attendance, and gave Ministers the benefit of his expert advice.

... was now well in hand. A large body of special constables, many of whom had had experience in the great war, was now available under the direction of General Sir John Monash. He had arranged for senior constables of experience to direct the operations of squads or contingents of special constables. He had also arranged for the assistance of mounted men who had had military experience. In other ways the police would be further reinforced.

"The public can rest assured," Mr Nicholson added, "that everything will be done for its protection. I appeal to the people to keep out of the city and not, through idle curiosity, to form a screen for the lawless section of the people."

NO CHURCH SERVICES TONIGHT

Owing to the stoppage of the trains and trams after a certain hour tonight, and the police strike, nearly all the churches in Melbourne, with the exception of St. Paul's Cathedral, will not hold services this evening.

MOUNTED POLICE

40 Expected Tomorrow

Official circles at police headquarters were optimistic this morning. Arrangements are being made to mount some police today, and it is expected that there will be 40 troopers on duty tomorrow.

In addition, there are said to be thousands of special constables, with hundreds of cars, ready for any emergency, and the order stopping trams after 6 p.m. and trains after 7 p.m. will keep all peace-loving citizens out of the streets.

"Those who do come in," say the police, "will be looking for trouble."

LIGHT HORSE PATROL

MEN TO BE CALLED UP

Stern Action Promised

The Public Safety Committee, acting under the advice of Generals Elliott and Monash, is creating the organisation for calling up Light Horsemen with experience to act as mounted police.

Two troops of former light horsemen were sworn in this morning as special constables under Brigadier-General J. K. Forsyth.

"We have horses ready for all who enroll," General Forsyth said. "They are real cavalry horses."

The light horsemen are enrolling in a special room at the Town Hall. General Forsyth hopes to have many troops formed before night.

"The people can rely upon the sternest possible measures against a repetition of last night's disgraceful scene," said General Elliott this morning. "We are now organising, and will be in a position by tonight to call up the equivalent of a brigade of infantry."

A fine type of recruit is offering at the Town Hall for special police duty. These men are being sworn in rapidly, equipped with arm badges and batons, and sent into the city.

The Town Hall is a scene of great activity, and in certain respects bears a resemblance to war time recruiting.

Outside the Town Hall a throng lined the footpaths, and the approach to the doors leading to the recruiting depot.

Within was a buzz of activity. Public school boys chatted seriously with middle-aged business men, and in the flagged courtyard stalwarts swung an experimental baton and made passes at an imaginary rioter.

The floor above was given over to the swearing-in ceremonies. As each ...

SIR JOHN MONASH, who is organising the forces to protect the community.

1368 SPECIALS ENROLLED

GUNS DRAWN

Shots at Suspects

HOT CHASE IN RUSSELL ST.

EVERY WINDOW SMASHED TO ATOMS

The Bourke Street frontage of the Leviathan Stores, after the rioters had completed their wanton destruction last night.

APPEAL FOR VOLUNTEERS

Ministry Issues Proclamation

"LAW AND ORDER" MUST BE MAINTAINED

The following proclamation was issued this morning by Sir Arthur Robinson, the Attorney-General, on behalf of the State Ministry:—

"The gravity of last night's events emphasises the seriousness of the position with which the community is faced. Never in the history of the State have such discreditable excesses occurred in the City of Melbourne. The responsibility for these excesses rests on those who have been false to their oath of duty. It now devolves upon every loyal citizen of military age to rally to the support of constituted authority and ordered Government.

"A resolute determination on the part of the public to maintain law and order can only have one ending—the complete rout of the mutineer. These have not shrunk, in breach of solemn trust, from leaving the city at the mercy of the worst elements of the underworld.

"This is no industrial dispute or class fight. The security of poor and rich alike depends upon the maintenance of law and order. If the basic principle upon which our civilised community life is founded is destroyed, what security is there for either the worker or the employer? It is not a question of the Government against the men, but the vital principle of ordered liberty against mutiny—of fidelity against rebellion.

"Knowing that there are many thousands of loyal Australians able and willing to serve the community in this crisis, arrangements have been made whereby special constables will be sworn in all day today at the Town Hall, and as long afterwards as may be necessary, and will be suitably organised. Sir John Monash, Brigadier-General Elliott, and other well-known Anzac leaders are as willing and as anxious to serve in the preservation of decency and order as they were to maintain our civilisation against a foreign foe. They will be in charge of this work at the Town Hall, and the Government relies confidently upon a full and ready response to this appeal to public-spirited citizens to serve under their direction.

"Citizens who are not capable of rend[illegible] physical aid can best serve the Government [illegible] away from the city, and by dissuading [illegible] from coming into the area where trouble may [illegible]. A crowd of sightseers only provides a sc[illegible] under cover of which desperadoes can indulge [illegible] and rioting, and hampers the efforts of th[illegible] engaged in the preservation of the public peace.

NO TRAMS AFTER 6 P.M.

Last Train Leaves City at 7 O'Clock

"With the object of limiting crowds in the city area in the evening, the Government has arranged that no trams will leave the city today after six o'clock and the last train will depart at seven o'clock It is essential, therefore, that travellers who spend the day in the country or at the seaside should time their return so as to reach the city before the hours named. The Government regrets any inconvenience that may be caused by the cessation of trams and trains, but it feels certain that the citizens will cheerfully accept these restrictions as providing for the public safety.

"A very difficult duty has fallen to the lot of those members of the police force who realised the sanctity of their oath and of their obligation to the community. They have faced grave danger with courage and restraint. The Government realises the services which they are rendering, and these services will neither be overlooked nor forgotten."

Country trains will run as usual.

EARLY MORNING WORK

Motor Patrols Busy

TRAMWAY TROUBLE

Board's Offer Rejected

STRIKE ON ALL LINES

The tramway regulation strike has been declared on again on all cable lines.

This decision was arrived at at a mass meeting of the tramway men this morning.

A very grave situation has now been created, and this is fully realised by the Trades Hall officials.

The men rejected the Tramway Board's offer to put 24 extra men on the lines forthwith, provided the strike was declared off on the Port Melbourne and Nicholson street lines. The Trades Hall Disputes Committee recommended the acceptance of this offer.

The motion for acceptance was defeated by an overwhelming majority, and the following amendment was carried:—

That the Board be asked to put into immediate operation a roster providing for a spread of 9½ hours for 60 per cent. of the men, and 10½ hours for 40 per cent. of the men. That until this is put into operation the regulation strike be enforced immediately upon all lines.

Lists of Arrests and Casnalties in Pagc 2

BROKEN WINDOWS

Damage, £7000

INSURANCE DOES NOT COVER "RIOTS"

Plate glass window experts toured the city early this morning to assess the damage caused to city shop windows.

Rapid estimates of glass stocks in hand satisfied the investigators that there was enough plate glass immediately available to repair all the broken windows, and men are being taken off all other building jobs to cope with the emergency.

Mr John Duff, of Duff Bros. Pty. Ltd., stated that some of the beautiful plate glass windows that have been destroyed cost as much as £1 a square foot.

It is estimated that the damage done to windows alone on Saturday night must amount to £6000 or £7000.

Traffic Stopped at Flinders Street

STOP PRESS

LIGHTHORSE WANTED

The Herald *printed a special edition on Sunday 4 November devoting several pages to reports of the violence across the city over the preceding two days during a police strike in the city.*

4 THE HERALD, SUNDAY, NOVEMBER 4, 1923

THE CITY UNDER THE RULE OF THE HOOLIGAN

SHOPS LOOTED IN LAST NIGHT'S RIOTS

Damage in City Exceeds £50,000

UNKNOWN MAN MURDERED

Police Charge With Batons

Taking advantage of the strike of metropolitan policemen, bands of hooligans ran amok, wrecking 300 yards of shop fronts and looting extensively.

It is estimated that the damage amounts to £50,000.

Eighty-nine windows of over 34 shops were smashed in the city. Destruction was also wrought in some of the more populous suburbs.

The first disturbances began about 4.30 p.m., and rioting continued until 11.30 p.m.

Never before has Melbourne witnessed such an outbreak of lawlessness.

Shortly after 6 p.m., when the hotels closed, a mob of 80 hooligans of the worst type—mostly of the criminal class, and many known to the police—began an attack upon jewellers' and clothiers' windows in Bourke street.

The shop windows were quickly despoiled of their choicest goods.

Within half an hour the mob was joined by about 200 young men not known individually to the police, but probably of the embryo criminal class.

This second mob completed the looting of the shops that had been already broken into and reduced the window fittings to ruins. They also filled their pockets with pieces of broken glass, which they used as missiles throughout the night.

The force of loyal police on duty fought the rioters until the last of them had disappeared from the streets.

Fifty-five arrests were made, and hardly a rioter escaped some injury from the police batons. Several policemen were injured during the riot, but none seriously.

LIKE FLANDERS — Glass Instead of Shrapnel — RIOTERS "COWARDS"

REVOLVER POINT — How Dunkling's Was Protected — VALUABLES SAVED

STREETS STREWN WITH BOXES — Women Fight for Loot — FLYING MEN ON GUARD

LARRIKINS BADLY BEATEN — Country Men With Ginger — SERGEANT LEADS THEM INTO THE FIGHT

Sir ARTHUR ROBINSON, Attorney-General.

MR NICHOLSON

JACK HOLDS BACK THE CROWD

Page 4 from the Herald's special edition continues with more reports of the riots, under the sensational headline: 'The City Under the Rule of the Hooligan'.

49 *The hearts of the people*

The US fleet visits in earnest, 1925

MELBOURNE'S *SUN NEWS-PICTORIAL* WAS ONE OF SEVERAL NEWSPAPERS ACROSS THE COUNTRY THAT FROM THE EARLY 1900S BEGAN TO FOCUS ON PHOTOGRAPHIC IMAGES RATHER THAN PRINTED NEWS. THE POPULARITY OF THE HIGHLY VISUAL FORMATS USED BY THE WEEKLY PICTORIALS LED MOST NEWSPAPERS TO FOLLOW SUIT IN SOME WAY OR OTHER. MAJOR NEWSPAPERS BEGAN TO INCLUDE MORE IMAGES, PARTICULARLY IN SPECIAL SUPPLEMENTS.

With rapid developments in photographic technology, spurred on by new film and materials such as plastics, photojournalism was becoming an important aspect of newspaper production. By now, the decision on which story would be headline news was increasingly determined by whether it was a photographic item or whether there was even a photograph of the event.

The visit of the United States battle fleet to Melbourne in July 1925 was an event that was particularly suited to the new pictorial style of news reporting. Melbourne had a long tradition of welcoming battleships to its ports. During the American Civil War of 1861–1865 crowds had flocked to see the Confederate raider *Shenandoah* docked in Melbourne on 25 January 1865, and the Great White Fleet's visit in 1908 had drawn huge crowds. The US navy had designated one ship for receptions and balls at each Pacific port on the fleet's tour, but in Melbourne they were forced to use three ships to satisfy the crowds.

The 1908 visit of the Great White Fleet had been an international political gesture, but it had involved just sixteen battleships and some escort vessels. The prime minister of the day, Alfred Deakin (1856–1919), was correct in observing that the visit would 'tend to knit [Australian and American] relations more closely'. The 1925 visit, which was described as a goodwill tour, was undertaken by a vast fleet of fifty-six vessels, including twelve battleships, and was very much concerned with strengthening bilateral relations.

Not that they needed strengthening if the popularity of the 1925 visit was anything to go by. The ships' crews were feted with balls, dances, sightseeing tours and entertainment, and more than one hundred American sailors found brides in Australia. But the tour achieved its aim in reminding Australians and Americans of their links in the face of an increasingly powerful and aggressive Japanese navy.

Richardson's Wines and Spirits, Single Bottle at wholesale price, delivered free to all Suburbs.

CONNOISSEURS ALWAYS ASK FOR HARVEY'S SPECIAL SCOTCH WHISKY

Forecast: Some coastal showers at first, becoming finer. Squally, but moderating.

The Sun

ABOVE ALL FOR AUSTRALIA

NEWS — PICTORIAL

CHILDRENS PADDLE BRAND COMFORT QUALITY BOOTS & SHOES

No. 894 Telephones, Cent. 9240, 18191 MELBOURNE: FRIDAY, JULY 24, 1925 (Registered at the G.P.O., Melbourne, for transmission by post as a newspaper.) 1½d.

TRIM AND SHAPELY THE SEATTLE LAY INERT ALONGSIDE PRINCE'S PIER yesterday, a few moments after she had left the head of the long line of ships that had followed her up the bay. The battleship Pennsylvania is shown edging in behind her. When the Oklahama and the Nevada had berthed on the other side of the pier, and the last 'plane had ceased stunting overhead, the gaze of the spectators became riveted upon the great grey flagship of Admiral Coontz. Melbourne's welcome then [illegible] in earnest, for the real berthing place of all the 44 ships of the Fleet is alongside the hearts of the people.

Headline news for The Sun News-Pictorial *of 24 July 1925 was the arrival of the US navy in Melbourne. Here the* Seattle *is shown alongside the pier, with the* Pennsylvania *nearby. More pictures were included on the inside pages and the fleet continued to be headline news next day.*

50 On the north-west frontier

The Forrest River massacre, 1926

AUSTRALIA'S HISTORY OF FRONTIER VIOLENCE WAS, PARTICULARLY IN THE REMOTE AREAS OF THE CONTINENT, A LONG ONE. THE KIMBERLEY REGION IN NORTH-WESTERN AUSTRALIA HAD SEEN MAJOR CONFLICT BETWEEN ABORIGINAL WARRIORS AND THE MILITARY AND POLICE INTO THE 1890S. THE BUNUBA WAR WAS INITIATED BY JANDAMARRA, THE LEADER OF A GROUP OF BUNUBA WARRIORS, WHO WERE ALL WERE ARMED WITH RIFLES. FROM 1894 THE GROUP RAIDED SETTLEMENTS ACROSS THE WINDJANA GORGE AREA UNTIL JANDAMARRA WAS KILLED BY POLICE IN 1897.

Massacres of Australian Indigenous people were often a response to such guerrilla warfare tactics of Aboriginal warriors, or to the murder of a European. But the last reported massacres of Aboriginal people in Australia occurred in Western Australia and the Northern Territory as late as the 1920s, when squatters were still opening up remote regions and taking more land for pasture. A series of droughts through the 1920s intensified the struggle to move Aboriginal people away from their traditional lands.

Although the veracity of the reports of the Forrest River massacre of 1926 has been questioned, a royal commission into the incident was established. Newspapers reporting the hearings of the commission stated that the bodies of sixteen 'natives' had been burned. The commission found that police had been involved, but the case against them was dismissed due to lack of evidence.

At the Coniston massacre in the Northern Territory in 1928, the wanton murder of numbers of Aboriginal people—though no-one was brought to justice for the crimes—led to more intense scrutiny of the policing of the area, and reflected a growing shift in European Australian attitudes to Indigenous people.

These were the final reports of massacres of Aboriginal people in Australian history. By the 1920s—particularly with the growth of newspapers in the country—the Australian public was much better informed about such events, and the national and international publicity they gained, ensured Coniston was the last of the massacres.

OPPOSITE
Although they were not dramatic headlines, both the Forrest River and Coniston massacres in the remote north-west of the continent were widely reported in most Australian newspapers. This page records evidence of the Forrest River massacre.

ALLEGED NATIVE KILLINGS.

FURTHER EVIDENCE.

Police Inspector's Report.

In a telegram to his chief, the Commissioner of Police, dated September 21, 1926, Inspector Douglas, of Broome, speaking of his investigations into the alleged killing of natives by a police party, declared: "Have returned from Forrest River locality. My investigations satisfy me that sixteen natives were burned in three lots—one, six and nine. Only fragments of bone, no larger than one inch, remain. I am endeavouring to locate certain police natives who can possibly give particulars. Some are three hundred miles away. Suggest you send two experienced detectives by the first boat to Broome."

This item from the departmental files, and also a written report made by the inspector about the same time, was produced yesterday when the Royal Commissioner (Mr. G. T. Wood, S.M.) took further evidence, at Parliament House, relative to the alleged killings. The Commissioner and party returned to Perth on Monday.

In his written report to the Commissioner of Police, Inspector Douglas detailed his investigations regarding the movements of the police expedition. He visited three camps. At the third he found indications that some natives had been chained up to a tree. "The native Sulieman" (one of the trackers) informed me that the party had camped here for two days, and had gone out in search of natives, and that he and other trackers had caught seven in a gorge and had brought them to the camp and chained them up with the two who had been brought along from the previous camp, making a total of nine. Sulieman states that in the afternoon Constables Regan, O'Leary and Murnane left camp with the nine natives, accompanied by native trackers Charlie and Frank, and that they took the natives back to the camp where they had been caught in a ravine some six miles away. On arrival there they sent Charlie and Frank back to the camp with the horses, but the three white men did not return to the camp that night. On the following morning they were picked up by the other members of the party on the top of this ravine. I visited this spot, and found the horse tracks leading in and out of the ravine where there had been a native camp. About fifty yards from the camp I found the remains of a large fire, and some thousands of fragments of bone in the ashes, and timber had been dragged from all around to the fire. No footprints were visible, the ground was sandy and rocky, and all footprints were obliterated by the wind and loose sand. By the size of the fire and quantity of bone fragments, I have no doubt but that the nine were cremated here."

"Matter Extremely Difficult."

The inspector's report continued: "In view of the serious aspect of the case, and the difficulties to be contended with in securing any definite evidence, I wired you suggesting that the assistance of detectives be sent. The native trackers who were out with the party are scattered in various directions. Three of them are in the Hall's Creek district, one is about Turkey Creek, two others are in the ranges somewhere within 50 miles of Wyndham, and friends of the party are making it their business to prevent some of them from being found. The whole matter is going to be extremely difficult. So far there is no proof that any particular native has been killed, or anything left to identify any particular person. Certain natives are missing, about thirty, but some of them may turn up later. As far as I can gather, no act of killing has been witnessed by any other than the principals, and I have not secured any evidence of the identity of any of the natives, other than the alleged identification of the tracks by mission natives, which is useless and only a fabrication."

At yesterday's sitting of the Commission the principal witness was Detective-Sergeant Manning, who, in October last, was sent North to assist in the investigation. With Inspector Douglas he took statements from the three trackers, Windie (alias Joe), Sulieman, and Comboroo (alias Frank), who had accompanied the police expedition sent out in June to capture the murderer of Frederick Wm. Hay. These three natives disappeared when the Commission arrived at Wyndham and just prior to the Commission's departure Inspector Douglas reported that he had been unable to secure their attendance to give evidence. A summary of the statement given by Sulieman to the Detective-Sergeant Manning appeared in the "West Australian" of April 20. Portions of the three statements differ materially from those tendered by and on behalf of the police. Each of the three trackers declared that he neither saw any killing of natives, nor heard of anything of the kind when at the Forrest River Mission.

Detective-Sergeant Manning said, in reply to the Commissioner, that no inducements were held out to the natives to make these statements. They showed no hesitancy in making them.

They did not require any prompting?—We had to question them. There were some discrepancies in their statements.

Are you satisfied that so far as you were able you got the truth from these natives?—Yes. We are quite satisfied that they told us practically what they knew.

Gin's Story of Shootings.

Witness produced also a statement taken from Lyddie, a native woman, who had been employed, she said, by Leo Overheu at Nulla Nulla Station for a long time. The Commissioner said that the evidence given by this witness later before the Commission coincided only in one or two particulars with her statement to the detective and Inspector Douglas. In the latter the following passage occurs relative to the police expedition: "The trackers bring all the bush blackfellows in on chain early in the afternoon. They had five men and five women on the chain, and about sundown Policeman Regan and Jack and white fellows Barney O'Leary, Dick and Dan, with trackers Joe, Sulieman and Frank all take the blackfellows on chain away from our camp. After some time they all come back without any blackfellows on chain. White fellow all about say they let the bush blackfellow go, but the trackers tell me that policeman and white fellows shoot all that bush blackfellow. I was at our camp with Leo Overheu, Tommy and Jacob and I did not see what they did with the blackfellows they took away. I did not hear them do any shooting while they were away neither did I see any big smokes go up. We then leave that camp and go farther into bush look out for blackfellow and one night we camp on a small river and the trackers go out and get a little lot of bush blackfellow and women and bring them in on the chain, and Regan have them on the chain in his camp when policeman Jack, Leo Overheu, white fellow Dan and trackers Tommy, Joe, Jacob and I all leave them and go back to Nulla Nulla Station; and Regan and his party were to go alonga Mission, and after we get some wheat at Nulla Nulla, Leo and Jack and all us natives were to go to Mission also. When we get to Nulla Nulla Dan he go back to Wyndham in a boat and we get some meat and then all go alonga Mission, and when we get to Mission Regan nothing got any blackfellows on the chain, and the trackers tell me that policeman and whitefellow all shoot that blackfellow while on the way to the Mission. Leo Overheu all the time tell policemen and whitefellow, 'You nothing take that bush blackfellow alonga gaol; you shoot them,' as he did not want them. I did not see the policeman or whitefellows shoot any blackfellows or burn them. I was always left at the camp when they went after blackfellows."

Mr. W. M. Nairn (representing individual members of the police and other parties interested): The woman Lyddie seemed to have a grievance against Overheu?

Witness: Yes, she seemed to think he was the man who killed her boy Tommy.

You have had a lot of experience with blacks?—Yes.

Are they in your experience trustworthy or untrustworthy?—Witness said that natives were peculiar. "If you let them think," he said, "that anything they will say will please you, they will continue in that strain. You have got to keep a serious face and must not let a native think you want anything special from him."

Inspector Mitchell (representing the Aborigines Department): Absolutely true.

Mr. Nairn (to witness): You would not place much reliance on the statements of mission natives?—I would not place much reliance on the statements of any natives.

Answering questions in regard to tracking by natives, witness said that if a native were shown a number of fresh tracks made by the "mob" among whom he had been reared he would be able to tell without fail the names of every man, woman and child making those impressions. But the tracks must be fresh. As a result of witness's inquiries into the allegations of killings by the police he had been unable to find any native who had seen anything. He had interviewed the wife of the Rev. James Noble at the Forrest River Mission. She had talked with the natives in their own language, but in the course of her inquiries, she told him, she had not come across any native who actually saw anything. No one could give any direct evidence.

Arming of Trackers.

Replying to the Commissioner, witness said that from 1898 to 1903 he had been stationed on the Nullagine, and in 1917 he was in West Kimberley in connection with the disappearance of Bowers.

"Would you take any considerable amount of ammunition on expeditions to arrest natives?" the Commissioner asked.

Witness replied affirmatively. When one got beyond the cattle country, he said, one had to depend on one's rifle for food for the party, and when starting on such an expedition one did not know whether it would last a fortnight, a month, or three months. They would take about 500 or 600 rounds.

The Commissioner: Would you have the native trackers armed?

Witness: Yes. My natives always had a rifle and a revolver. Otherwise you won't get them to go into strange country.

In your experience in the employment of armed trackers, were they ever allowed to get out of the control of their white officers?—Witness said that the tracker was often out of one's control. For instance, they would be out before daylight, after the horses. It was not practicable for the trackers to be always under their officers' control. One had to trust one's trackers. They could "clean up" the camp in the middle of the night if they liked. "I never talked to my boys," witness added. "Some people spoil good boys by making a fuss of them and treating them as equals."

The Commissioner: You don't think there is any substantial objection to the arming of police trackers?—No. You would practically do away with their usefulness if they were not armed.

Inspector Mitchell produced in evidence two stout sticks, each about four feet in length, which were found, he said, at Gotegotemerrie in the water hole among the debris. There was a big stone on top of them. They bore fire marks, and looked as if they had been used as pokers.

Asked by the Commissioner whether he would be calling any witnesses, Mr. Nairn said he preferred not to make a definite statement on the point. This morning at 10 o'clock the Chief Protector of Aborigines (Mr. A. O. Neville) will be questioned in regard to police methods with natives and the employment of armed black trackers to make arrests. The Commissioner of Police also will be present.

Alleged Use of Poison.

To the Editor.

Sir,—I wish to make a few remarks concerning the report of a deputation to the Minister for Home and Territories at Sydney on May 3, published in the "West Australian" of May 4. Mr. Aubrey Williams, who is reported to have travelled in the North-West of Western Australia, has heard rumours that when natives became what was considered to be a nuisance, cyanide was put in their meat or arsenic in their flour. Mr. Williams travelled from Darwin to Perth on the Bambra, on which I was a passenger last November. The Bambra, on this voyage, called for a few hours at ports and the only calling places at which Mr. Williams was able to land were at Wyndham, Port Hedland and Carnarvon. It must have been during those few hours in port or upon the ship itself that Mr. Williams heard the highly flamboyant rumours that squatters of the North-West of Western Australia were accustomed to wholesale murder of natives by the use of cyanide and arsenic. From the border of the Territory to Pilbarra in the west, it would probably be very difficult to rake up even one pound of cyanide, and in the good old days of the Kimberley goldfields, cyanide was not in use. Of arsenic there is a considerable quantity used for poisoning dogs, but the insinuation that our pioneers of the North are in the habit of utilising this for the destruction of natives will be rightly resented by all Western Australians who take pride in the men who have pioneered, and are pioneering, in the face of huge difficulties, the great open spaces of our inheritance. I travelled throughout the North-West and the Territory for over nine thousand miles, sometimes by car, sometimes by horse, and visited many stations through the Kimberley areas, where most of the aboriginals remaining are situated. I found on the stations, camps of natives who were for the most part happy, clothed and fed—very different indeed from the few bush natives which I saw, who had escaped what I presume Mr. Williams would call a disastrous contact with the settler. These natives, unemployed by the pastoralists, forgotten by a neglectful Government, are indeed a blot on the fair escutcheon of our land and a serious handicap to the development of the North, which all true Australians know to be essential to our future greatness. After many years, stationed as a political officer in West Africa among millions of natives, I am convinced from my observations of this fact—that the squatter in the North is a far greater gentleman than wandering tourists would have us believe, and that such statements as these should be checked at their outset before the insidious damage wrought by such rumours is accomplished.—Yours, etc.,

H. J. TINDALE.

Perth, May 4.

ALLEGED FRAUD.

Sale of Shares.

Sydney, May 5.

An extraordinary story was told at the Quarter Sessions before Judge Curlewis to-day, when Sydney Madden (23) and James Victor Turner (34) were charged with having conspired together to cheat and defraud Ernest Lauri and others of large areas of land at Sydney between January, 1926, and March, 1927.

In presenting the case to the jury, the Crown Prosecutor (Mr. N. McTague) said the allegation against the accused was that they had conspired to unload worthless shares in the Week-end Publishing Company, of which Madden was described as the managing director and Turner as the secretary, upon the public in exchange for valuable blocks of land. Lauri, an actor associated with the "Sweet Nell of Old Drury" company, was one of those attracted by the advertisements of the company, whose respectability was vouched for by its letter-heads, which gave the address of the company as Regent-street, opposite No. 2 Police Station. Lauri called at the company's office, where he saw Turner, who told him the capital of the company was £5,000 in paid-up shares. Turner represented the company to be in a most flourishing condition, adding that he held 1,600 shares.

Later on Lauri saw Madden, who bore out Turner's glowing account of the company's position. For 100 shares and £15 in cash Lauri transferred a block of land in the Pride of Mortdale Estate worth £115. As he received no dividend on the due date he interviewed Madden and Turner at their office, but they put him off for a time by stating that the balance sheet had been delayed by the auditors. Lauri soon ascertained that the shares were worthless, that the company owed debts everywhere, and that there was no prospect of its ever paying a dividend.

The hearing was adjourned till to-morrow.

STRANDED STEAMER.

Tasman's Passengers.

Sydney, May 5.

Arrangements have now been made by the Royal Packet Navigation Company for the Japanese mail steamer Aki Maru to proceed to the stranded steamer Tasman and take over the passengers who desire to tranship and the mails. The Aki Maru is bound from Yokohama to Australian ports, and will probably reach the scene to-morrow morning. After leaving the Tasman the Aki Maru will call at Townsville and Brisbane, and will then come on to Sydney.

The position of the Tasman is unaltered.

MISHAP TO STEAMER.

Propeller Fouls Mooring Chain.

London, May 4.

A message from Perim, an island in the Strait of Bab el Mandeb, at the entrance to the Red Sea, states that the steamer Transvaal en route from Fremantle to Britain fouled her propeller at a mooring buoy.

The mooring chain is now being cut, and a survey of the vessel will be made.

SOUTH AFRICAN PROBLEMS.

A Gloomy Outlook.

Views of Sir Granville Ryrie.

Sydney, May 5.

Sir Granville Ryrie, High Commissioner designate, to-day spoke gloomily of South Africa's problems to a huge assembly which the Royal Colonial Institute had gathered to a luncheon in his honour at the Hotel Australia.

At the end of a long catalogue of the Union's unhappy complications, he said: "I would not live there with a wife and family for all the tea in China. Away to the north hangs a great black cloud which is likely to roll down and engulf the Union at any time." He was speaking on observations he made when he visited South Africa with the Empire Parliamentary Delegation about two years ago.

A very serious problem in Natal, he found, was that of the Indians, who possessed one-third of the property, but they were British subjects who could not be

GENERAL SIR GRANVILLE RYRIE.

killed off or bundled out of the country. The one salvation seemed to be a payment of compensation for resumption of the property, and this would involve millions of pounds. Then, of course, there was the problem of the native races.

But what impressed him most of all was the problem that faced the 16,000 young men who were coming from the high schools and the universities. According to figures supplied to him, employment could be found for only 8,000 of these, so that 8,000 were condemned to drift into the ranks of the "poor whites." Any one who had not seen a "poor white" could scarcely grasp the tragedy of this situation. In the Union he had met many Australians who had left their country in the full athletic bloom of their youth, full of hopes for great success in South Africa, but they found that if they were not able to work as managers or clerks or administrators of one kind or other they could not work at all, for no white man worked with his hands in South Africa. No white man touched a shovel or a broom unless he was a "poor white."

MELBOURNE MOTOR SHOW.

Many British Models.

Melbourne, May 5.

Melbourne's international motor show, which is claimed to be the second in importance and second in size in the world, yielding first place only to that at Olympia, was officially opened by the State Governor (Lord Somers) in the Exhibition Building this afternoon. Motor vehicles valued at nearly £1,000,000 are exhibited and a record attendance is expected.

Never before has the British industry shown such keenness in the show, for of the 52 stands occupied by motor dealers 20 are displaying British automobiles. This interest is accounted for by the rapid growth in the British trade during the past year.

The enthusiasm of the exhibitors is indicated by the fact that a truck was despatched by road to Sydney to await the arrival of an overseas vessel and rush a special model to Melbourne in time for the show. This journey by road of over 1,000 miles is unique. The feature was an elaborate model Rolls Royce which is valued at £4,000. The exhibits were representative of practically every make in use in Australia. The show will be continued for two weeks.

TARIFF ON STOCKINGS.

German Competition.

Sydney, May 5.

The Tariff Board was asked to-day to impose such duties on imported socks and stockings as would provide effective protection for the hosiery industry. It was declared that Australian manufacturers produced a little more than 40 per cent. of the hosiery requirements of the Commonwealth, and this was said to be approximately only half of what it should be. The aim of the manufacturers was to obtain a measure of protection from foreign competition that would enable them to produce at least 80 per cent. of Australian requirements.

Mr. James L. Holt, assistant secretary of the Chamber of Manufactures, said Australian manufacturers submitted to no half measures in their manufacture. If an article was marked woollen the public could be assured that it contained 100 per cent. wool; if marked cotton it contained 100 per cent. cotton, and so on. It was estimated that the total value of hosiery produced in Australia at wholesale selling rates, inclusive of the contribution of the States, was about £2,100,000. Importations during 1925-26 were £1,645,644. To that should be added at least 60 per cent. to cover the charges of landing, including duty, making the total value approximately £2,600,000. That represented the actual value of imported hosiery landed in Australia.

The effect of foreign competition on the Australian hosiery industry was outlined by Mr. Rupert Neil McLean, director of George Bond and Co., hose manufacturers, who sounded a note of warning particularly against increasing importations from Germany. The retail stores of the capital cities of Australia, he said, showed more and more German hosiery, both cotton and silk. If the Germans were permitted to import into this country fully fashioned artificial silk hose to the extent that they had been doing during the last four months Australian manufacturers who had expended their capital in purchasing machinery to make this type of hose would have no market. The Australian manufacturers had the latest machinery in the world. Their workers were as efficient as any workers in the world. The wool was at their doorstep, and yet they were unable to compete owing to the fact that the English knitter of woollen hose had so perfected his manufacturing plans that he could produce cashmere hose from wool of a quality that was not only of no use in Australia, but which for the sake of his reputation the Australian manufacturer dare not look at. If the new tariff were granted the Australian manufacturers would immediately commence the manufacture of woollen hosiery for ladies, men and children at a price that would not be beyond the purchasing power of the community.

WAR SERVICE HOMES.

Inquiry into Difficulties.

Adelaide, May 5.

The annual interstate conference of the Soldiers and Sailors' Fathers' Association was continued to-day.

It was decided, on the motion of Mr. J. Clayton, seconded by Mr. Wm. Hopkins, that the State branches be requested to obtain the fullest information from their respective States of any difficulties which still exist in regard to the administration of the War Service Homes Commission and of any amendments in the Act or regulations which present experience shows to be necessary, and that information be collected and a precis thereof be transmitted to the State branches for consideration and recommendation as to further action, the president of the Victorian branch to carry out such collection and distribution.

Mr. Clayton moved that the association and branches individually put forward their best efforts for a continuance of the principle of preference for the qualified returned soldiers in all positions of employment, and that the earnest co-operation of all soldier organisations be invited and urged to attain that end.

Mr. J. Hennessy (W.A.) seconded the motion, which was carried. The business of the conference then ended.

TRAFFIC OFFENCES.

Harshness of the Court.

R.A.C. Deputation to Minister.

"While the law lays down that traffic accidents must be reported, the police do not use the third degree and cannot force people to make statements which may incriminate them. The sooner that is known to the general public the better."

In these words the Minister for Justice (Mr. J. C. Willcock) answered one of the points raised by a deputation from the Royal Automobile Club of W.A. which waited upon him yesterday. The deputation, which was introduced by Mr. H. W. Mann, M.L.A., consisted of Messrs. L. R. Butt (president), F. D. Sewell and G. McKay (vice-presidents), O. Zender (secretary), and J. R. W. Gardam. Several points were raised in criticism of the present Traffic Court administration, and it was argued that the presiding Magistrate should be a man having knowledge of motoring and its problems; that the taking of statements from persons concerned in traffic accidents, without first warning them that such statements would be used in evidence against them, was wrong in principle and unjust in practice; that penalties imposed were inconsistent and generally too heavy; and that, since costs against the police cannot be recovered in the event of the dismissal of a case it paid a motorist better to plead guilty to an offence and pay the consequent fine than to engage counsel to defend him.

Introducing the deputation and outlining these points, Mr. Mann said that the Automobile Club desired no leniency for wilful offenders, but it did desire to lay before the Minister certain disabilities under which motorists suffered, and to point out certain inconsistencies in the administration of the Traffic Court. At present motorists considered it cheaper to plead guilty and pay whatever fine was imposed than to defend a case.

The Minister: That is highly dangerous.

Mr. Mann: That is the view commonly taken, since it is, of course, impossible to get costs against the police. The deputation also desired to bring under the Minister's notice the matter of the King's Park toll.

Mr. L. R. Butt said that as matters stood the police should be very careful to take no action without being absolutely certain of their accuracy, because a motorist who was summoned before the Traffic Court knew that it was less costly to plead guilty than to defend his case. The word of a reputable citizen should be taken at least as freely as that of a constable. The Automobile Club desired to help the police, not—as was unfortunately the case in South Australia—to be constantly at variance with them. A man found drunk in charge of a car should be deprived of his licence and never permitted to drive again. Yet frequently such an individual was fined as little as £5, while a man who left his car at the kerb for 25 minutes might be fined very heavily.

The Minister: Oh, no!

Mr. Butt: Motor cyclists whose machines emit offensive noises are deprived of their licences. A person shaken by an accident was not fit to make a detailed statement to the police regarding it, and the police should certainly warn such persons that their statements might be used against them. The club was pleased with the appointment of Inspector Hunter to control the Traffic Department; he was a fair man. He (Mr. Butt) had known of instances in which a constable had warned a man that it would be better to plead guilty.

The Minister (quickly): I don't agree with that!

Mr. G. McKay said that he wished to speak of the toll levied by the King's Park Board upon motorists.

The Minister: Oh, well—I don't know that that concerns me. It is purely a matter for the board.

Mr. McKay: Our legal advisers hold that the toll is invalid. Only some 600 out of 7,000 metropolitan motorists have paid it, many of them at half the original rate, since the beginning of the year. That surely proves——

The Minister: The King's Park Board is entirely autonomous. I have no jurisdiction.

Mr. McKay: That will force the club into the position of having to cause a test case against the board.

Mr. O. Zender said that the present system of taking statements from persons involved in accidents made it possible to "frame a case" against a man. Motorists were obliged to undergo cross-examination by constables, and were not warned that their statements would be used against them.

The Minister: It is entirely at the option of the person concerned what statement he makes to the police. He may say "That's all I have to say," and sit tight on that.

A Member of the Deputation: But a policeman's argument is persuasive.

The Minister: I will give the police the credit of not wanting to fabricate cases. They do not use the third degree, and cannot force persons to make anything but a voluntary statement. The law says that one concerned in an accident must make a report as early as possible. People shaken by an accident do sometimes put themselves in a wrong light, and we do not want to incriminate innocent people. Often, however, it is in a man's own interest to make a statement that can be corroborated forthwith. If he holds it for the Court, perhaps a week later, corroboration may be lacking. On the point of inconsistency in penalties, that always occurs on the face of things, but if you heard all the evidence in each case you would find circumstances appearing in it which do not appear in the Press reports. It is not inconsistency, but difference in the facts of each case. We try to get all the traffic cases heard in one Court, by one individual, in order to secure uniformity. Mr. Horgan was appointed on the strength of his fair-mindedness and knowledge of the law, and he has given good results. The protection of life should be the outstanding consideration in any such court. Some responsibility rests with the pedestrian, and I think "jay-walking" regulations are necessary in Perth now.

Members of the Deputation: Hear, hear.

The Minister promised the deputation that he would discuss with the traffic police all the points raised, and see whether some fair way of dealing with the problems could be evolved. At the same time, he pointed out the difficulty of arriving at the facts concerning an accident unless statements were taken from those concerned.

Mr. Gardam complained that trivial traffic offences were being dealt with too heavily, and the Minister replied that lengthy records sometimes accounted for seeing harshness. He would consult with his officers on the points raised.

Motorists Again Warned.

Three motor cyclists were heavily fined, and the licence of one was suspended, by Mr. F. F. Horgan, Acting Assistant P.M., in the City Court yesterday. The Magistrate also issued a further warning to motorists, who, he said, did not appear to realise that under the provisions of the Traffic Act, persons twice convicted for driving dangerously or when under the influence of liquor, were liable to imprisonment without the option of a fine. Many motorists, he thought, were under the erroneous impression that a general fine of £20 covered all the more serious offences—even for second convictions.

Blowing People Off the Road.

During the hearing of a charge of dangerous driving laid against Frank Robert Stuart, an elderly witness said he thought he could run across the road safely before defendant's motor car reached him. The automobile was then 40 yards away, and travelling, in his estimation, at 20 miles an hour. "Are you aware," inquired Mr. T. S. Louch, defendant's counsel, drily, "that the car would take exactly three and a half seconds to travel 40 yards at 20 miles an hour? You must be a very fast runner."

"So I am. I win all the old buffers' races, I might tell you," replied witness promptly, amid laughter.

Evidence given by John Lyons, a pig farmer, of Belmont, showed that he was crossing the Guildford-road on April 2 to fill the radiator of his motor truck, when a car driven along the wrong side of the road by defendant knocked him down, dislocating his shoulder, and injuring his legs. Lyons admitted that defendant sounded his horn, and told witness afterwards that he swerved to the wrong side of the road to avoid striking him.

In the course of an address to the Bench, asking for a dismissal of the case, Mr. Louch contended that it was the duty of pedestrians not only to look both ways before crossing a road, but also while in the act of crossing. Moreover, authorities held that it was the duty of a driver to take the wrong side of the road if he thought he could avert an accident by doing so.

"Motorists must not think they can blow people off the road with their horns. The instrument is provided merely to sound a warning," replied Sergeant Houston.

The Magistrate reserved his decision.

Forty Miles An Hour.

Alfred Colley, who rode a motor cycle along St. George's-terrace (where the speed limit is 20 miles an hour) at 40 miles an hour when there was a fair amount of traffic about, was fined £10.

Edward L. Albrecht was fined £7 for having ridden a motor cycle along the Perth-Fremantle-road at the same speed. Constable Fletcher said defendant was travelling so fast over a rough part of the road that the front fork of his machine broke. There was not much traffic about at the time. The Magistrate remarked that the traffic which might reasonably be expected to be on the road must not be overlooked in these cases.

Leonard Worth was fined £3 for having ridden a motor cycle at 32 miles an hour on the Perth-Fremantle-road. Constable Fletcher provoked the Court to mirth when he said that defendant told him he was in a hurry to meet a young lady.

Noisy Motor Cycle.

In outlining a charge against Eric F. Steere of having emitted offensive noises from a motor cycle, Constable Fletcher said that defendant drove noisily along St. George's-terrace past three hospitals, mounted Malcolm-street, and made a terrific din when he reached the top. A notice, forbidding motor cyclists to travel up Malcolm-street, stood at the foot of the hill. Steere was fined £7, and his licence was suspended until June 30.

A Bandsman's Haste.

Clifford Jarratt was fined £3 for having ridden a motor cycle along Mount's Bay-road, without lighted lamps. Defendant told Constable Fletcher when he was stopped that he had run out of water for the lamps and was taking a risk. After adding that he was hastening to play in the band at White City he made off.

Charge Dismissed.

Eric P. Wheatley, through his counsel, Mr. A. G. Unmack, pleaded not guilty to a charge of having permitted a youth without a licence to drive a motor truck. Evidence for the prosecution showed that an apprentice employed by defendant, acting on his employer's instructions to see that the truck was delivered, drove it away himself, and was subsequently convicted for driving dangerously without a licence. Questioned by Mr. Unmack, the lad admitted that he received no definite instructions to drive the vehicle himself. The case was dismissed.

Miscellaneous Offences.

For various offences against the Act, George Jenkins, Dan Chipper, William Harper, John J. Kelly, Leonard Ephgrave, William Witten, Reuben Gudgeon, Maxwell C. Broadley, and Leslie W. Gandish were fined amounts ranging from 10s. to £5. John Nankivile was fined £1 for having overloaded a taxi at Cottesloe. A constable said that 10 persons were packed in the car, some with their legs dangling over the sides.

Fremantle Prosecutions.

Several offenders against the Traffic Act were fined by Mr. J. E. Geary, Acting P.M., in the Fremantle Police Court yesterday.

For having failed to keep his vehicle on the correct side of the road, William Bradburn was fined £4, with costs. Gilbert Henry Gaskin, who passed a vehicle on the wrong side was fined £2 10s., with costs and a similar penalty was inflicted on Harold Cheek, who drove a vehicle without having the necessary lights affixed. William Rose, who left his car in the one place for longer than was permitted was fined £3, with costs, and for similar offences Harry G. Lutey was fined £2, with costs, and Leonard Porter, £1 10s., with costs. For having used a dealers' identification tablet on Sunday, Frank L. Gard was fined £2 with costs. William E. Jones, who drove a motor vehicle at night without lights, was fined £1 10s., with costs, and Thomas Brown, Ernest William Woods, Jack C. Smith and William Arthur Cooper, all of whom rode bicycles without lights, were each fined 15s., with costs. Frank Luff, who drove a vehicle at night without a tail light, was fined £1, with costs. Because he did not have number plates affixed to his vehicle, Joseph Malacci was fined £1 5s., with costs. David H. Higgs, who failed to signal his intention of turning, was fined £1, with costs.

It was alleged against Otto Johnson that he knocked over a lad on a bicycle while driving his car across the bridge at North Fremantle. Johnson, for whom Mr. F. G. Unmack appeared, admitted that he was driving his car that night, but denied having hit or even seen any lad on a bicycle in the locality mentioned. The case was dismissed.

MELBOURNE EXPANSION.

High Values and High Buildings.

"Land in picked spots in the heart of Melbourne is now worth £3,000 a foot, and the result is that new city buildings soar to a great height. It is the only possible way in which to get an adequate return for invested capital. We no longer build office blocks there of less than 12 stories, and some of the facilities nowadays provided in such buildings would have amazed an older generation. Take, for instance, Temple Court, a fairly new building in Collins-street. It is worth £500,000, goes up twelve storeys, has seven electric lifts and a continuous hot water lavatory service throughout, and contains 4½ acres of office floor space. It is devoted purely to offices, and has such interior architectural facilities as letter-chutes and a heating system by means of hot water pipes throughout the building."

This description was given in the course of an interview, by Mr. Marcus R. Barlow, A.R.V.I.A., F.T.I.A., a partner in the firm of Barlow and Hawkins, architects and civil engineers, of Melbourne and Adelaide. Mr. Barlow arrived in Perth, by the Great Western express on Monday, upon a business visit.

"Recently," he resumed, "we erected a twelve-storey building on a piece of land having a 23ft. frontage and a depth of only 64ft. With land so precious, it pays to travel heavenward. Melbourne building by-laws are very stringent, and it is not possible nowadays to erect buildings there without including the most modern improvements. The traffic problem grows daily, the increase in the number of motor vehicles registered averaging approximately 1,700 a month. Parking in the city is, of course, a problem difficult of solution. We are solving it by erecting an 8-storey building solely for the purpose of parking cars. It is to have neither lifts nor stairs, but a ramp 23ft. wide, with a very easy gradient, up which the cars can ascend from floor to floor under their own power.

"Adelaide, too, is just waking up. Land in Rundle-street recently changed hands for £1,450 a foot, and we have built upon it a huge shop. It has a basement, a sub-basement, and eight storeys, and is independent of the city light and power supplies. In the sub-basement (the basement was too valuable for such use), besides furnaces, incinerators, and the usual paraphernalia, is a generating plant operated by a Diesel engine which burns crude oil. Every floor is brilliantly lit, the whole night through, and flood lights illuminate the walls. In case of emergency, the building is also connected with the city mains. The installation of this independent generating plant will save the owners some hundreds of pounds a year."

Turning to the subject of domestic architecture, Mr. Barlow said that enormous progress had been made in the design and building of homes in Melbourne. "Australians are developing an aesthetic sense, thanks to the increasing wealth of the country," he said, "and a great deal of literature dealing with domestic architectural problems has reached this country in recent years. The Americans being magnificent advertisers, this literature portrays the very best of their work, and its educational value is correspondingly high. Houses erected in Melbourne six years ago we now consider to be out of date, but the homes which are being built to-day will never be out of date, because they are true to architectural type. Not content with designing houses, leading architects now claim the right to design their setting—the gardens, which make a vast difference to the appearance of any home. The provision of internal colour schemes is now also a function of the architect."

"By the way," Mr. Barlow added as an afterthought, "Melbourne is to have a new theatre, on the site of the old 'Herald' building, which the 'Morning Post' recently sold, I believe at a handsome profit. The directorate of the latter paper, I understand, proposes to build afresh."

Topical Photographs.—"Snaps" of unusual incidents, accidents, etc., will be welcomed by the "Western Mail" if promptly delivered to the Editor. Here is a chance for the alert amateur who wishes to make money.

COMMONWEALTH-STATE FINANCE.

An Historical Review.

III.—Recent Developments.

(By H.J.L.)

The lukewarm endorsement given by some of the States in 1923 to the Federal Government's proposed substitute for the capitation payments gradually developed into open hostility. Thus it was that the 12 months' postponement of the scheme then agreed upon came to be indefinitely lengthened. Last year, however, the Commonwealth Government took a resolute stand, and Dr. Earle Page announced in unequivocal terms that the capitation payments must cease. Dr. Page, unlike Mr. Watt, did not ground his abolition scheme on the necessities of the Commonwealth, but on the postulate that, as between the Commonwealth and the States, there should be financial independence. The persistent increase in the yield from Customs and Excise, in defiance of all prophecies, had made the plea of necessity untenable. The States, too, changed their ground. As we have seen, in 1923 a majority of them had agreed, on certain conditions, to relinquish their claim to any share in the Customs and Excise revenue. At the conference to which they were invited by the Prime Minister in 1926, they took their stand immovably on their

Moral Right

to share in the yield from Customs and Excise. Commonwealth Ministers were equally emphatic that no such right existed—constitutional, legal, or moral.

In bare outline, the proposals put before last year's conference by the Federal Government were:—

1.—That the Commonwealth and State finances be now separated as far as possible, on the principle that, normally, indirect taxation is the proper field for the Commonwealth, and direct taxation the proper field for the States.

2.—That as a first stage towards this ideal the Commonwealth evacuate the field of taxation of incomes of individuals.

3.—That the capitation payments now made to the States under the Surplus Revenue Act be discontinued.

4.—That temporary financial assistance be given to the States to prevent undue dislocation of the State finances under the new arrangement.

5.—That for the development of the national resources the Commonwealth give financial assistance, without regard to State boundaries or population, in special cases where proper and necessary development cannot otherwise be secured.

The conference discussions of the details of the proposals were quite perfunctory. One reason was that insufficient time had been allowed the Premiers to make an exhaustive study of them, but the chief reason, as already indicated, was that the views of the Commonwealth and the States' representatives were

Fundamentally at Variance.

The Prime Minister and the Federal Treasurer refused to consider the continuance of the capitation payments; the State Premiers declined to entertain any proposals which involved their cessation. The conference was wholly abortive.

At issue as they were on root principles, further negotiation held no possibility of agreement between the representatives of the Commonwealth and the States. The legal and constitutional right of the Commonwealth to withdraw the payments was indisputable; on the arguable question of the States' moral right to a share of the Customs revenue the Commonwealth was its own Court of Appeal. The Federal Government adhered to its decision to abolish the capitation grants, and almost immediately after the conference rose the Treasurer placed before the House of Representatives his State Grants Bill with that object in view. But the compensatory provisions outlined by the Treasurer in putting forward the State Grants Bill differed widely from the scheme which had been submitted to the Premiers' Conference a week or two earlier. Instead of the abandonment of individual income taxation, the Government proposed to evacuate entirely the fields of taxation in regard to land, estate duties, and entertainments, and at the same time to remit taxation on companies or individuals to the extent of 40 per cent. The assumed

Effect on the States' Finances

of these proposals was set out in a table prepared by the Commonwealth Treasury officials. This table showed the estimated gain or loss to the various States if they forfeited the capitation payments, and re-imposed, for State purposes, the direct taxation surrendered by the Commonwealth. The gain to New South Wales was stated at £460,000; to Victoria, £126,000; and to South Australia, £28,000. Queensland would lose £238,000; Western Australia, £189,000; and Tasmania, £86,000. The States which showed a shortage were to be compensated by what were called "adjusting grants," and the net gain to the taxpayers of the several States was set out as follows:—New South Wales, £460,000; Victoria, £126,000; Queensland, £51,000; South Australia, £51,000; Western Australia, £413,000; Tasmania, £428,000.

This arrangement, it was proposed, should obtain for five years, but the adjusting grants (i.e., those grants which were intended to make up to the States which lost more in capitation payments than they could recover from the Federal taxation surrendered to them) were to be reviewed each year "in accordance with the position of the Commonwealth finances." It was claimed by the Commonwealth Treasurer that under the new scheme each State would be at least £50,000 a year better off than under the capitation system. A gain of that amount, it was held, would accrue to Queensland, South Australia, Western Australia, and Tasmania. In the table just referred to a much larger gain is shown to Western Australia and Tasmania (£413,000 to Western Australia, and £427,000 to Tasmania). This apparent discrepancy, however, is accounted for by the inclusion in the table of the disabilities grants, which were entirely independent of the scheme for the abolition of the capitation payments. It will be seen, therefore, that the chief beneficiaries under the scheme were New South Wales and Victoria, which gained £460,000 and £126,000, respectively, though one of the objections urged by the Commonwealth Government to the per capita method of payment was that it operated to the advantage of the larger and richer States, and to the detriment of the less populous and poorer ones.

The amended proposals under the State Grants Bill of 1926 were

Bitterly Assailed

by all the States. The accuracy of the Federal Treasury's calculations was challenged, and it was contended that it would be impossible for the States to raise, by increased land, income and entertainment taxes, and estate duties, anything approaching the amounts estimated. It was pointed out, moreover, that the scheme offered no guarantee of stability, and that the result would be a grave dislocation of the finances of all the States. Ultimately, consideration of the Bill was postponed until 1927.

The State Grants Bill was re-introduced by the Prime Minister in March of this year, and, after a stormy passage through both Houses, became law. It provides for the abolition as from June 30, 1927, of the payments of 25s. per head of population which have been receivable by the States from the Commonwealth since 1910. The Federal Government has invited representatives of the States to a conference to be held in June or July at which it is proposed that the whole question of Commonwealth and State financial relationships shall be reviewed in the light of the new situation which has been created. In order to guard against the financial embarrassment to which the States would otherwise be subject in the financial year 1927-28, clause 7 of the State Grants Act provides for the payment to the States in that year of amounts equivalent to the capitation grants.

Mr. Bruce's Undertaking.

In commending the State Grants Bill to the House of Representatives on March 2 last, the Prime Minister gave this assurance on behalf of the Government in regard to the forthcoming conference:—

On behalf of the Government I say that Ministers will go to that conference with absolutely open minds, and without prejudices respecting the scheme we have already submitted. We are prepared to consider any scheme and any method that may be suggested. The States should have confidence that they will receive fair and equitable treatment, because in the scheme which was proposed by the Commonwealth in 1924, there was a provision designed to make each State £100,000 better off than under the capitation arrangement, and the scheme now proposed would make each State £50,000 better off than it is at present. We have said frankly that if there is thought to be any mistake in the figures on which our calculations have been made we are prepared to appoint a commission of independent persons to consider them and to rectify them if, after investigation, they should be found to be wrong. We are prepared to consider the whole field of direct taxation, and not to limit the discussion to the particular methods that have already been suggested.

The State Debts.

There, for the present, the matter rests. One aspect of the problem that will certainly receive prominence at the forthcoming conference is the relation of Commonwealth and State finance on ordinary revenue account, to the whole question of Commonwealth and State loan indebtedness and their future borrowing policies. In the financial clauses of the Commonwealth Constitution, and in the subsequent agreement which resulted in the passing of the Surplus Revenue Act of 1910, the inter-relation of the two problems was recognised, and there was contemplated, as an alternative to the capitation payments, the assumption by the Commonwealth of the whole or portion of the State debts. Clause 105 of the Constitution provided:—

The Parliament may take over from the States their public debts as existing at the establishment of the Commonwealth, or a portion thereof according to the respective numbers of their people as shown by the latest statistics of the Commonwealth, and may convert, renew, or consolidate such debts, or any part thereof; and the States shall indemnify the Commonwealth in respect to the debts taken over, and thereafter the interest payable in respect of the debts shall be deducted and retained from the portions of the surplus revenue of the Commonwealth payable to the several States, or, if such surplus is insufficient, or if there is no surplus, then the deficiency or the whole amount shall be paid by the several States.

In 1910 a referendum of the people of Australia affirmed a proposed law for an amendment of the Constitution by omitting from section 105 the words "as existing at the establishment of the Commonwealth." This removed a limitation on the Federal power, and enables the Parliament to pass laws to take over from the States all their public debts, both those contracted before, as well as those contracted after the establishment of the Commonwealth.

No attempt has been made to use the power conferred by this section of the Constitution. In the meantime the public debts of the States have grown alarmingly. In 1900 they amounted to £195,000,000; in 1918 to £390,000,000; and in 1926 to £643,000,000—or, deducting the accumulated sinking funds of £21,000,000, to £622,000,000. In addition to this the Commonwealth has its own debt of upwards of £370,000,000.

THURSDAY'S WEATHER CHART.

Notes on Chart.

The same general features were present in yesterday's weather chart as in that of the previous day, but both the cyclonic development off the New South Wales coast and the southern "low" off our south-west coast had intensified. The former did not threaten to become a destructive storm, but it was responsible for increasing rain and rising winds and seas on south-eastern Australian coasts and was also retarding the eastward drift of the "high." This was partly responsible for the growing activity of the western "low," which promised much more extensive rains than at first anticipated.

LOCAL BUREAU'S REPORT.

A general cloudiness, extending to all sub-tropical areas, and showers on the south-west coast marked the opening hours of yesterday morning, and confirmed the impression gained from the previous day's reports that agricultural rainfall was developing. By 9 a.m. the showers had reached the city, where, however, the rainfall was only 3 points. Further south it was heavier, reaching a maximum of 108 points at Brunswick Junction. In the course of the day little further rain fell—a light misty shower in the city and a few points at Bunbury—but the barometer dropped steadily and the sky became increasingly gloomy, suggesting that the disturbance was more vigorous than at first supposed. Valuable agricultural rains are therefore expected.

TO-DAY'S FORECAST.

The forecast for to-day is:—

Unsettled generally south of the tropic, with rain over west and south-west coastal areas and the agricultural districts, extending to the south Coolgardie goldfields, with lighter showers over parts of the Gascoyne and northern goldfields. Squally north-west to south-west winds.

FORECASTS FOR OTHER STATES.

(Issued by the Commonwealth Meteorologist, Melbourne.)

South Australia.—Cloudy over settled areas and gradually becoming unsettled from west, with showers later. North winds chiefly and moderate temperatures.

Queensland.—A shower or two on north coast, and Peninsula, otherwise fine. Cool night temperatures, with some frosts in southern interior. South-east winds.

New South Wales.—Cloudy on south coast and southern tablelands, with some showers, but improving gradually. Fine elsewhere, cool night temperatures, many frosts and some morning fogs. West to south winds, freshening on South coast.

Victoria.—Cloudy in south and east, with some showers, but improving. Fine elsewhere. Cool night temperatures, some fogs and inland frosts.

Tasmania.—Some clearing showers in south but otherwise fine. South-west winds, becoming variable. Some frosts and morning fogs.

TEMPERATURES AT CAPITAL CITIES.

Thursday, May 5.

Perth, max. 73deg., min. 66deg.; Adelaide, 64, 43; Melbourne, 59, 48; Brisbane, 71, 54; Sydney, 63, 48; Hobart, 54, 43.

ASTRONOMICAL DATA.

To-day.—Sun rises at 6.38, sets at 5.1[illegible]; moon rises at 11.36 a.m., sets at [illegible] (first quarter on Sunday.)

AUSTRALIAN RAINFALL.

(For the 24 hours ended at 9 a.m. yesterday.)

Western Australia.

South-West Division.—Perth Gardens, [illegible] points; Perth Observatory, 3; Fremantle Oval, 6; Fremantle Signal Station, 7; [illegible], 2; Mandurah, 22; Collie, 11; Bunbury, 15; Donnybrook, 50; Bridgetown, 14; Busselton, 16; Cape Naturaliste, 4; Karridale, 65; Cape Leeuwin, 22; Albany, 4; Breaksea Island, 1; Esperance, 1; Wandering, [illegible]; Rockingham, 4; Pinjarra, 50; Brunswick, 108; Greenbushes, 10; Denmark, 7.

South Australia.

Robe, 6.

Queensland.

Thursday Island, 4; Mein, 1.

Victoria.

Cape Otway, 8; Melbourne, 14; Wilson's Promontory, 5; Omeo, 206; Sale, 11; Gabo Island, 164; Bruthen, 291.

New South Wales.

Dubbo, 4; Moruya, 34; Jervis Bay, 9.

Tasmania.

Hobart, 2; Bruni, 5; Oatlands, 4; Maydstone, 8; Swansea, 5.

MEASLES AT PAPUA.

Eight Deaths Reported.

Melbourne, May 4.

Advice has been received by the Minister for Home and Territories (Mr. Marr) from the Lieutenant-Governor of Papua (Sir Hubert Murray) concerning an outbreak of measles in the east end of the Territory. No deaths have been reported from Samarai, but eight deaths had occurred in the Mafulu district, 60 miles inland from Yule Island.

When the steamer Morinda arrived in Port Moresby on her return journey to Australia, she was allowed to berth alongside the wharf, and passengers for Port Moresby were allowed to land under surveillance. Passengers booked through to Australia were, however, kept aboard.

A YOUNG STATE.

Interesting Facts.

Australia probably knowing less of Czecho-Slovakia than Czecho-Slovakia knows of Australia, a chat with Mr. Z. D. Prager, manager of the football team that has just arrived from that country in Perth, was full of interest.

"Our Republic, created by the League of Nations," he said, "is as large as England and Wales, and has twice the population of Australia. It is the second largest sugar-producing country in Europe, and the first in sugar export. With malt and beer it supplies a large part of Europe, while its glass, textile goods, its toys, musical instruments, machinery and iron wares are exported to all parts of the world.

"This new State in the heart of Europe has great natural beauty and many historical sites. Prague, our capital, has well been called 'the history of the Czecho-Slovak nation in stone.' Its old-world character and wonderful architectural relics cause the visitor to imagine that he has strayed into some romantic scene of the Middle Ages. Prague has a population of three-quarters of a million. Its situation on the picturesque hills near the Vltava River has led to its being called the 'Rome of the North.'

"There are numerous other towns and places in the Republic that merit notice whether from a practical, commercial or industrial point of view, or on account of their natural beauties or historical significance. Among these are Pilzen, noted for its Skoda Works and the brewing of a beer exported to every quarter of the globe. The State also has mineral and medicinal springs of great variety. All told, we are very proud of our State, although it could be so easily lost in great, big, warm-hearted Australia."

FATAL BLOW.

Disturbance in Cafe.

Brisbane, May 5.

During a disturbance in a Greek cafe in Queen-street about 7 o'clock last night, Harold Edwin Freeman (28), single, of South Brisbane, was struck on the head with a bottle. Police were called in, and a man was arrested for creating a disturbance. Freeman was taken home in a car by a companion, and a doctor subsequently ordered his removal to hospital, where he died at 1 o'clock this morning.

This afternoon Peter Samels (39), a Greek, who gave his occupation as waiter, was brought before the Police Court on a charge of having unlawfully killed Edward Freeman.

Constable Quinn, giving evidence of arrest, said that when charged, the accused replied: "I did not kill him; he walked out of the shop." Accused, who, it was stated, had been 14 years in Brisbane, was remanded for a week on bail of £500, with two sureties of £250 each, conditional on his reporting daily to the police.

UNIVERSITY PLAYERS.

"Mary, Mary, Quite Contrary."

Mr. St. John Ervine's comedy, "Mary, Mary, Quite Contrary," is delightful not so much for its plot as for its characterisations. It is a study in types of character and on the interpretation of the characters the success of the play depends. The University Dramatic Society, which produced the comedy last night at the Assembly Hall, kept this fact in view and chose players who fitted the part admirably. The production was an entire success and Mr. T. S. Louch, the producer, is to be congratulated. Mr. Ervine has followed the tradition of the Irish National Theatre (of which he is a younger representative) in avoiding that almost worked-out vein of dramatic plot—material—the social problem. The play is all the more refreshing for the avoidance.

The whole piece hinges on the contrary disposition—she is engaged to two men at once, decides to marry each in turn, and then decides to marry neither—of Mrs. Westlake, a charming actress, who invades an English vicarage to give her opinion on the merits of a poetic play written by Geoffrey Considine, son of the canon. Among the unsophisticated retired members of the country household Mrs. Westlake descends like a moral thunderbolt and completely upsets the equanimity of the vicarage. Geoffrey and his uncle are soon in love with her and she, a woman of the world, charmingly leads them on. The part of the actress was admirably played by Miss Cecile Clarke. "If she behaved in a natural manner," says Hobbs, her cockney manager, "you would think she was putting it on." And so Miss Clarke displayed Mrs. Westlake's artificial vivacity and flourish of superficial sentiments and yet undeniable charm, with the energy and finesse of a professional actress. The other excellent actors were Mr. J. F. Virtue and Mr. A. E. Montefiore. Mr. Virtue displayed sympathetic imagination in his treatment of the halting, benign old-world canon, and Mr. Montefiore's role—that of the ex-Governor of Ambar, indignant, rheumatic and yet not lacking susceptibility to the flattery and the charms of woman—was well sustained. In the part of Hobbs, who is paid to take the blame for Mrs. Westlake's contrary assertions and actions Mr. K. Hadfield had a veritable mine of opportunities and he made fair use of them. Mr. H. E. Trenaman was well suited to the part of Geoffrey the poet. Miss Eleanor Lane took the part of Mrs. Considine; Miss Alix Parker that of Sheila (the artless lover of Geoffrey); Miss Frances Giles that of Miss Mimms (a girl guide commandant introduced as another delightful study in character); Miss Elsie Berry that of the maid, and Mr. D. C. Swan the character of Mr. Brodie, and the dramatist. A small orchestra from the University provided musical interludes. Mr. J. Paul acted as stage manager.

At the end of the entertainment many bouquets were handed to the lady members of the company. The play will be presented again to-night.

GENERAL NEWS.

Mr. Justice Burnside will sit in Chambers at 10.30 a.m. to-day.

A euchre tournament will be held at the R.S.L. Institute, South-terrace, Fremantle, to-night.

Advice has been received from the British postal authorities that mails for Australia left London on April 21 by the ss. Ferndale.

The quarterly ballot meeting of the Co-operative Building Society of Western Australia was held on Wednesday, when £2,700 was distributed amongst members.

When Harwood Jones, of John-street, Cottesloe, was cranking his motor car in Hay-street yesterday, the car, which apparently, had been put into gear, jumped forward and knocked him down. He was taken in the St. John ambulance to the Perth Hospital suffering from fractured ribs and shock.

Motorists, car and tractor owners, apprentices and others interested are notified that a new term for the motor mechanics class at the Perth Technical School is just commencing. New students should attend on Thursday, May 12, at 7 p.m., to enrol and arrange class nights.

Boys born in 1914 and who, therefore, reach the age of 13 during this year, are offered an excellent chance to become officers in the navy by entering the Naval College, Jervis Bay, as cadet midshipmen. Particulars are obtainable from the District Naval Officer, Fremantle.

At an inquest held yesterday concerning the death of Frederick C. Graham who fell from the balcony of the Criterion Hotel into the street on April 12, the Deputy Coroner (Mr. A. J. Sieber, J.P.) returned a verdict that death was due to a fractured skull caused by the fall, which was accidental. Sergeant Switzer examined the witnesses.

Detectives Pusey and McLernon yesterday arrested Arthur John Bowers (26), a railway porter, on a charge of being in the unlawful possession of a motor cycle tyre. Detectives Maingay and Trail arrested Allen Elliott Smith (18), a bag maker, on a charge of having stolen two pairs of socks, valued at 9s. 10d., the property of Boans, Ltd.

In connection with the Free Kindergarten for Subiaco, the Mayor of Subiaco (Mr. J. C. Boydhouse) invites all interested to be present at the Municipal Chambers, Subiaco, on Wednesday evening next.

An old-time dance will be conducted by the Ugly Men's Association in the Perth Town Hall to-night. The proceeds will go to the funds of the association.

MEETINGS.

The monthly meeting of the Victoria Park branch of the A.L.P. has been postponed.

ALLEGED NATIVE KILLINGS. FURTHER EVIDENCE. Police Inspector's Report.

In a telegram to his chief, the Commissioner of Police, dated Septemer 21, 1926, Inspector Douglas, of Broome, speaking of his investigations into the alleged killing of natives by a police party, declared: "Have returned from Forrest River locality. My investigations satisfy me that sixteen natives were burned in three lots—one, six and nine. Only fragments of bone, no larger than one inch, remain. I am endeavouring to locate certain police natives who can possibly give particulars. Some are three hundred miles away. Suggest you send two experienced detectives by the first boat to Broome."

This item from the departmental files, and also a written report made by the inspector about the same time, was produced yesterday, when the Royal Commissioner (Mr. G. T. Wood, SM.) took further evidence, at Parliament House, relative to the alleged killings. The Commissioner and party returned to Perth on Monday.

In his written report to the Commissioner of Police, Inspector Douglas detailed his investigations regarding the movements of the police expedition. He visited three camps. At the third he found indications that some natives had been chained up to a tree. "The native Suliemann" (one of the trackers) informed me that the party had camped here for two days, and had gone out in search of natives, and that he and other trackers had caught seven in a gorge and had brought them to the camp and chained them up with the two who had been brought along from the previous camp, making a total of nine. Suliemann states that in the afternoon Constables Regan, O'Leary and Murnane left the camp with the nine natives, accompanied by native trackers Charlie and Frank, and that they took the natives back to the camp where they had been caught in a ravine some six miles away. On arrival there they sent Charlie and Frank back to the camp with the horses, but the three white men did not return to the camp that night. On the following morning they were picked up by the other members of the party on the top of this ravine. I visited this spot, and found the horse tracks leading in and out of the ravine where there had been a native camp. About fifty yards from the camp I found the remains of a large fire, and some thousands of fragments of bone in the ashes, and timber had been dragged from all around to the fire. No footprints were visible, the ground was sandy and rocky, and all footprints were obliterated by the wind and loose sand. By the size of the fire and quantity of bone fragments, I have no doubt but that the nine were cremated here.

"Matter Extremely Difficult."

The inspector's report continued: "In view of the serious aspect of the case, and the difficulites to be contended with in securing any definite evidence, I wired you suggesting that the assistance of detectives be sent. The native trackers who were out with the party are scattered in various directions. Three of them are in the Hall's Creek district, one is about Turkey Creek, two others are in the ranges somewhere within 50 miles of Wyndham, and friends of the party are making it their business to prevent some of them being found ...

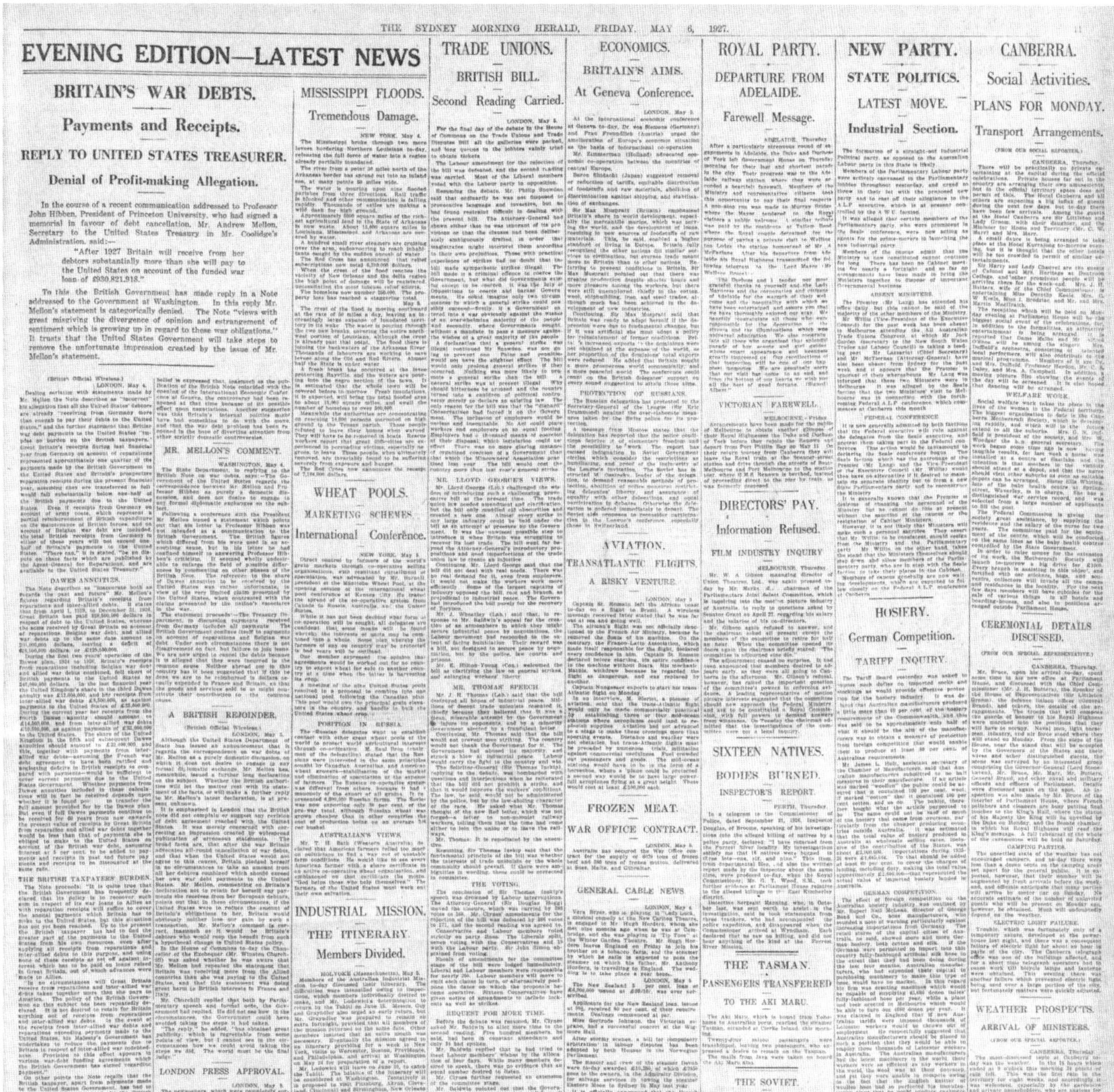
THE SYDNEY MORNING HERALD, FRIDAY, MAY 6, 1927.

EVENING EDITION—LATEST NEWS

BRITAIN'S WAR DEBTS.

Payments and Receipts.

REPLY TO UNITED STATES TREASURER.

Denial of Profit-making Allegation.

MISSISSIPPI FLOODS.

Tremendous Damage.

TRADE UNIONS.

BRITISH BILL.

Second Reading Carried.

ECONOMICS.

BRITAIN'S AIMS.

At Geneva Conference.

ROYAL PARTY.

DEPARTURE FROM ADELAIDE.

Farewell Message.

NEW PARTY.

STATE POLITICS.

LATEST MOVE.

Industrial Section.

CANBERRA.

Social Activities.

PLANS FOR MONDAY.

Transport Arrangements.

On 6 May 1927 The Sydney Morning Herald *recorded evidence of the Forrest River massacre presented in 1926 at the Royal Commission into the 'alleged killing and burning of Aborigines in East Kimberley and into police methods when effecting arrests'.*

51 Smashed and sunk

Greycliffe ferry disaster, 1927

ON THE FINE, SUNNY THURSDAY AFTERNOON OF 3 NOVEMBER 1927, SYDNEY HARBOUR WAS AT ITS SPARKLING BEST. FERRIES CARRYING WORKERS, TOURISTS AND SCHOOLCHILDREN PLIED THE BUSY WATERWAYS. THE LARGE MAIL AND PASSENGER SHIP *TAHITI* WAS HEADING DOWN THE HARBOUR, LEAVING SYDNEY FOR NEW ZEALAND. VISIBILITY WAS PERFECT THAT DAY.

Quite amazingly, the small ferry *Greycliffe*—nicknamed the 'schoolboat' for its regular 3 pm run to Watsons Bay—did not see the looming *Tahiti*. The *Greycliffe* ploughed into the *Tahiti*'s bow and was cut in two. In a matter of seconds the *Greycliffe* sank to the bottom of the harbour.

The tragedy did not just shock Sydneysiders—the horror of what remains Sydney Harbour's worst shipping accident, was felt around the country. The following day, newspapers were filled with stories of the 'Appalling Harbour Disaster'. Headlines described how people were 'Caught in Wreckage', or 'Crushed to Pieces' in 'Heartrending Scenes' of 'Great Confusion'.

Special edition newspapers were produced to provide readers with the growing casualty list, as well as the latest details. At first, eleven bodies were recovered and laid out in a temporary morgue at the tram sheds at Bennelong Point, now the site of the Sydney Opera House. Many other bodies later floated to the surface or were brought up by divers over the next few days. Several could be identified only from the papers in their pockets.

Twenty-six people were initially reported missing, and only after a few weeks was the death toll confirmed at forty people, with dozens more injured. Stories of survival were also featured: 14-year-old Ken Horler and three schoolmates survived only because they had taken seats at the back of the ferry so they could watch the progress of the construction of the Sydney Harbour Bridge.

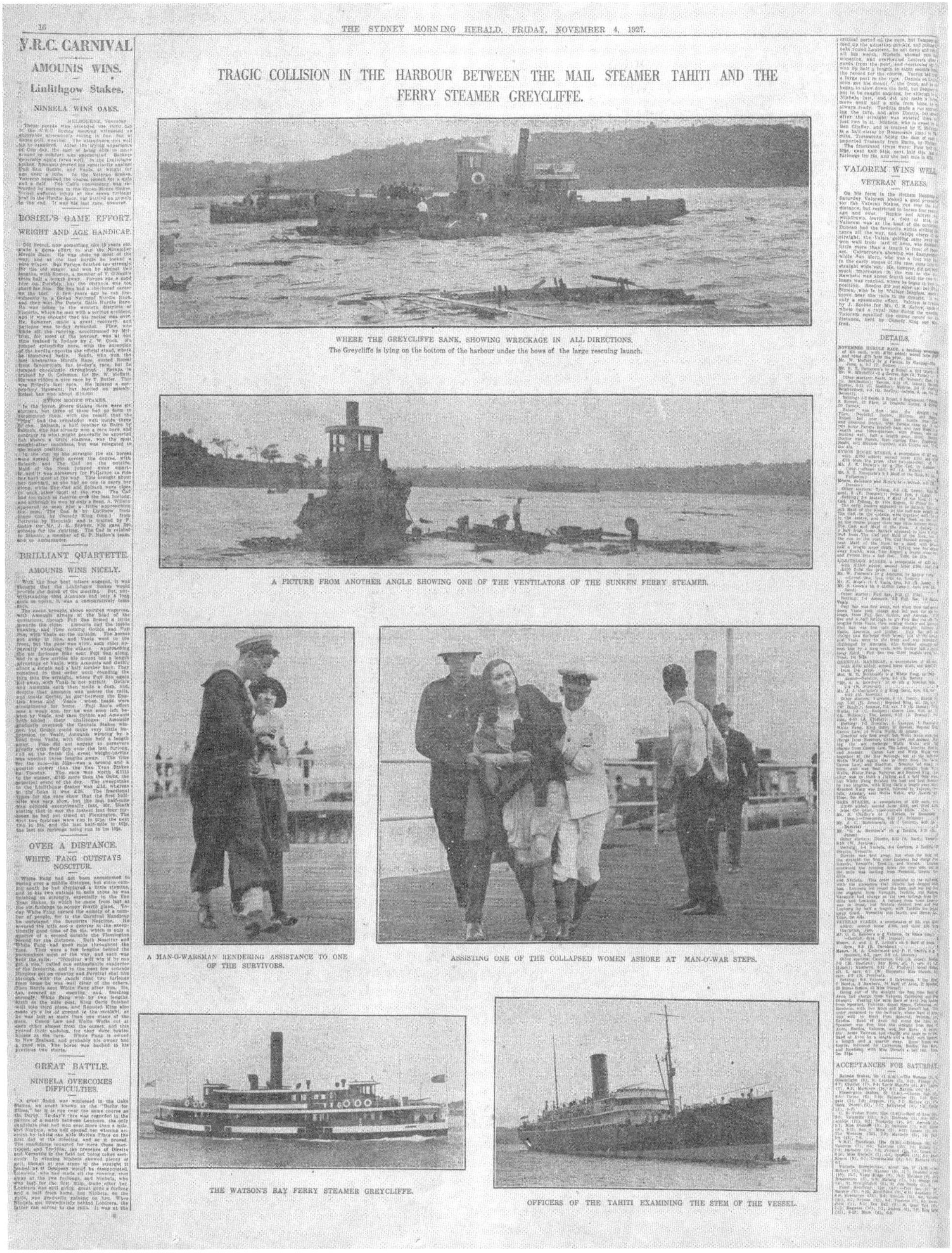

16 THE SYDNEY MORNING HERALD, FRIDAY, NOVEMBER 4, 1927.

V.R.C. CARNIVAL

AMOUNIS WINS.

Linlithgow Stakes.

NINBELA WINS OAKS.

ROSIEL'S GAME EFFORT.

WEIGHT AND AGE HANDICAP.

BRILLIANT QUARTETTE.

AMOUNIS WINS NICELY.

OVER A DISTANCE.

WHITE FANG OUTSTAYS NOSCITUR.

GREAT BATTLE.

NINBELA OVERCOMES DIFFICULTIES.

TRAGIC COLLISION IN THE HARBOUR BETWEEN THE MAIL STEAMER TAHITI AND THE FERRY STEAMER GREYCLIFFE.

WHERE THE GREYCLIFFE SANK, SHOWING WRECKAGE IN ALL DIRECTIONS.
The Greycliffe is lying on the bottom of the harbour under the bows of the large rescuing launch.

A PICTURE FROM ANOTHER ANGLE SHOWING ONE OF THE VENTILATORS OF THE SUNKEN FERRY STEAMER.

A MAN-O-WARSMAN RENDERING ASSISTANCE TO ONE OF THE SURVIVORS.

ASSISTING ONE OF THE COLLAPSED WOMEN ASHORE AT MAN-O'-WAR STEPS.

THE WATSON'S BAY FERRY STEAMER GREYCLIFFE.

OFFICERS OF THE TAHITI EXAMINING THE STEM OF THE VESSEL.

VALOREM WINS WELL.

VETERAN STAKES.

DETAILS.

ACCEPTANCES FOR SATURDAY.

Headline news was still appearing on the inside pages of The Sydney Morning Herald, *including the 4 November 1927 record of the collision of the steamer* Tahiti *and the* Greycliffe *ferry. By now, dramatic photographs of events had become a standard part of reporting the news in even the most serious of broadsheets.*

52 Colouring the Truth

Sonny Clay's jazz band and the White Australia Policy, 1928

SYDNEY'S *TRUTH* WAS AN INTERESTING NEWSPAPER THAT WAS IN MANY WAYS THE RESULT OF THE FREEDOM OF THE PRESS—AS WELL AS A GOOD REASON FOR CENSORSHIP ACCORDING TO SOME. DESCRIBING ITSELF AS THE 'PEOPLE'S PAPER' AND THE 'VOICE OF THE WORKING CLASSES', THE *TRUTH* WAS RENOWNED FOR ITS SENSATIONALIST HEADLINES AND OFTEN DEBATABLE 'NEWS'.

The *Truth* was one of the earliest of what were to be called tabloids—newspapers that were generally smaller in size, with larger and more sensational headlines and including multiple images with less text. Established first in Sydney in 1890 and then Melbourne, Brisbane and Perth in the early 1900s, it based its early reporting on the scandals of the divorce courts. During the twentieth century it continued its style of increasingly shocking headlines and articles, until the only version to survive past the 1950s, the Melbourne *Truth*, ceased publication in 1993.

One of the *Truth*'s more infamous moments was its response to the tour of the African-American jazz band Sonny Clay and the Colored Idea. In January and February of 1928, Sonny Clay's band performed with great success in Sydney and Melbourne, before *Truth* journalists informed police that the 'niggers' were partying and dancing late at night with 'scantily clad' white girls.

Despite their eager reception of the increasing number of recordings of African-American musicians from the United States, Australians retained strong fears of racial interrelations. Although its racism was obvious, the *Truth* was in fact pointing out the inconsistency in the application of Australia's own immigration laws. The White Australia Policy, according to the *Truth*, was a 'farce' if it allowed non-white people to even temporarily enter the country.

After a police raid on one of the band's after-performance parties, the troupe was duly deported and a government ban was placed on the entry of black musicians into the country. While audiences could listen to the recordings of the incomparable Louis Armstrong, they were not allowed to see him tour the country until changes were made to immigration policies in 1954.

A "Truth" in Every Home: Nett Sales Largest in Southern Hemisphere

FORECAST.—Mostly fine day; tendency to showers in evening.

Sporting: Page 2 and Following Pages

NEWCASTLE EDITION.

MONEY TO BE MADE. ENTER THE "SPORTSMAN'S" BIG COMPETITIONS.

Truth

THE PEOPLE'S PAPER.

No. 1995. Registered at the General Post Office, Sydney, for transmission by post as a newspaper. SYDNEY, SUNDAY, APRIL 1, 1928. (24 PAGES.) 3d.

MAN-WOMAN'S TRAGIC LIFE AND DEATH

AMAZING MYSTERY OF STATION COOK

Foster Sister and Spanish Friend Maintain He was a Girl—Doctor Says Normal Man

MAN HE SHOT REFUSES TO ANSWER QUESTIONS

(FROM "TRUTH'S" SPECIAL COMMISSIONER.)

WRAPPED in a grim death struggle, two forms fought frenziedly in a little stable. Then a revolver shot—the fourth—barked sharply, and the smaller, frailer form, sagged heavily to the straw-littered floor. Its life-blood trickled out upon a sheaf of hay, and the beautiful peacock on the homestead scuttled away in sudden fright.

THE life of Stanley Griffiths flickered and went out, and by his death has ended one of the strangest associations that ever endured between two young men—an association of two sweethearts based upon a foundation that should only have its being between sex opposites.

WERE Stanley Griffiths and Charles Hando sex opposites, the first a woman and the other a man? Charles Hando himself, under a gruelling cross-examination, during which he was protected by the sustained objections of his own counsel, refused to commit himself to speak upon his association with Griffiths on the grounds that his answer might incriminate him.

THE story thus unfolded through the death of Griffiths created a sensation that has startled the whole of the Commonwealth—a story which was further investigated when the inquest was resumed this week at Peak Hill before the District Coroner, Mr. Arthur Yeo, J.P.

Unpopular

Contradictions

Rushed Him

Open Verdict

"My Attitude?"

STANLEY GRIFFITHS, the Peak Hill cook, who, according to his foster-sister, was a girl, but who was said by the doctor to be a normal man, framed in the tail of a peacock which scuttled away on the Hando farm when the bullets from Griffiths' revolver rent the air.

BENEATH HIS MASCULINE GARMENTS, Stanley Griffiths, the unhappy Peak Hill cook, wore articles of feminine apparel, some of which he had made himself.

REFUSED TO ANSWER QUESTIONS on the ground that he might incriminate himself.—Charles Hando, with his trotting stallion, Machine Globe.

(CONTINUED ON PAGE 10.)

N.S.W. MONT DE PIETE D. and I. CO., LIMITED. SUBSCRIBED CAPITAL £300,000. 74 Castlereagh Street 74

Enter Now for Inglis New Competition "RUMPLED RIVERS" Handsome Cash Prizes to be won Goldenia Tea and The Billy Tea SAVE BONUS LABELS FOR VALUABLE PRESENTS.

For All Radio Requirements (at keenly cut prices). Price's Radio Service WINGELLO HOUSE, ANGEL PLACE, SYDNEY.

AUSTRALIA'S BEST RESCH'S RB THE GENUINE LAGER. DA DINNER ALE. ASK FOR THEM BY NAME.

Have an X-Ray Tooth Chart DENTIST PHILLIP MOSES

A CHILD DOESN'T LAUGH AND PLAY IF CONSTIPATED.

Every Woman Iron 'Jelloids'

CURZON HOTEL CURZON STREET, MAYFAIR, LONDON, W.1.

Pyorrhea?

TASMANIA IXL JAM AUSTRALIA'S BEST.

ASTHMA Catarrh, Bronchitis, Whooping Cough, Colds in the Head POTTER'S ASTHMA POWDER

To be healthy—drink HORLICK'S MALTED MILK the finest tonic food drink

WATCHES and JEWELLERY D. COLLINS

ONE AT A TIME ZIG-ZAG CIGARETTE PAPERS

DEAF? ACOUSTICON

LIDDY'S Shoe Stores 1/11 596 George St.

The front page of the Truth *issue 'exposing' Sonny Clay's band carried a typical* Truth *story as headline news—this one about the murder of a man who was apparently masquerading to 'her boyfriend' as a woman.*

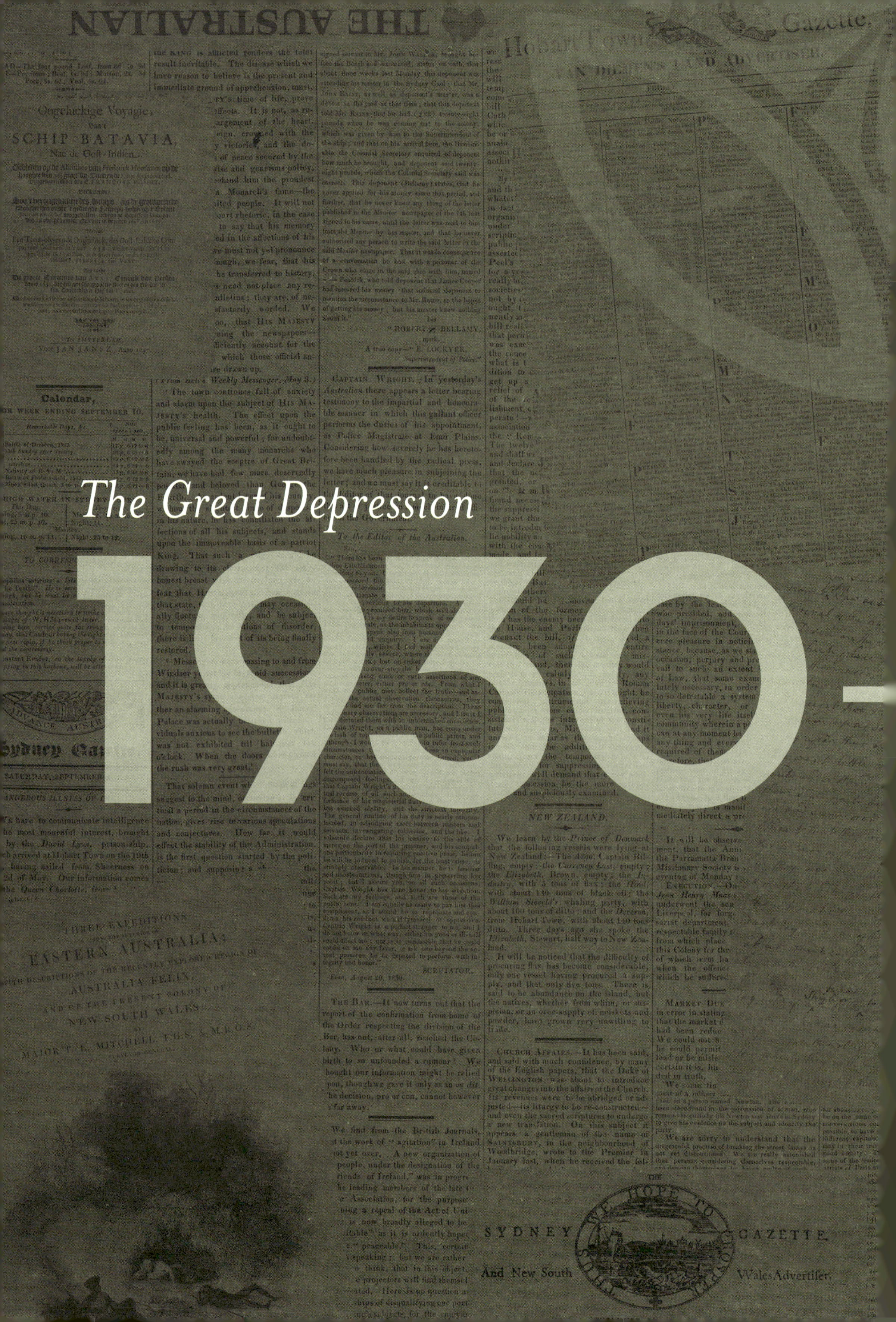

The Great Depression

1930–

–1939

In the early twentieth century Australians faced a series of events that were critical in shaping their new nation. The promise of economic and social growth that the federation of the colonies seemed to offer was followed by a war that deeply affected every family and town across the country. After a time of recovery in the 1920s, the trauma of the First World War began to fade. Yet the prosperity of this period became a stark contrast to the following decade, when 1929 saw the start of another event that affected all Australians—the Great Depression.

THE GLOBAL ECONOMIC COLLAPSE OF THE EARLY 1930S HIT AUSTRALIA PARTICULARLY HARD. IN FACT, THE ECONOMY HAD BEEN IN TROUBLE EVEN BEFORE THE 1929 STOCK MARKET CRASH IN NEW YORK—TRADITIONALLY THE MARK OF THE BEGINNING OF THE GREAT DEPRESSION.

Governments around the country were already investing in large-scale public projects, including the soldier settlement schemes to provide returned soldiers with land and housing, and they borrowed money from overseas to fund the projects. Combined with a continued dependence on exports of livestock and agricultural products, the Australian economy was vulnerable and weakening even before the great Wall Street crash.

By 1932 unemployment had risen to a record high of nearly 30 per cent. Many families could not pay their rent or mortgage and were evicted from their homes. Townships of homeless squatters began to appear on the fringes of urban areas, such as the shanty towns of La Perouse, a southern suburb of Sydney.

Although unemployment relief in the early days of the Depression favoured workers who had children, relief work for sustenance was highly sought after and not always available. Homelessness and poverty were demeaning experiences and suicide rates rose dramatically.

The Depression also generated left-wing radicalism, resulting in civil disturbances, protests and a surge in support for communism. The communists supported families facing eviction and barricaded themselves, with the affected families, in their houses. Violent battles between squatters and the police occurred.

Another political response during the Depression, as was happening overseas, notably in Germany, was a movement towards the far right. The fascist politics of Australia's New Guard movement attracted a surprising number of sympathisers. The New Guard claimed to have 50,000 members, and it threatened uprisings against what they called the 'socialist' Labor government in New South Wales. However, the New Guard was short-lived and their main legacy in Australian history was the slashing of the ribbon that was to open the Sydney Harbour Bridge.

Other responses to economic hardship took a racist turn. Australia's mining sector had continued to grow after the gold rushes. Coal and silver mining became important in the early twentieth century, and gold was still mined in Western Australia. Despite the White Australia policy, workers for this difficult and often skilled work came in from poor southern European countries. The Kalgoorlie goldmines used large numbers of Italians and workers from Slavic countries. When the Depression hit, they became the target of resentment, which erupted in the 1934 Kalgoorlie riots.

By the mid-1930s the Australian economy was slowly beginning to recover. A more optimistic national mood developed across the country as towns and cities prepared to celebrate their impending centenary and sesquicentenary anniversaries. A new interest in Australian history developed and, as the First World War became a more distant memory, there was also a growing focus on the commemoration of Anzac Day.

The 1938 celebrations of the 150th anniversary of the arrival of the First Fleet brought a new display of historical pageantry. The parades and festivals staged in Sydney later travelled to regional areas. They were designed to be a way for Australians to congratulate themselves on the establishment of a modern, Western nation. The symbolism of the heroic struggles of Australians helped create these 'colourful history lessons'.

The commemoration of the events of 1788 held a very different meaning for Indigenous Australians. As the parade of historical floats trailed through Sydney's streets on 26 January 1938, it passed a group of Aboriginal people holding a National Day of Mourning protest. In misguided efforts to assist Aboriginal people, since 1901 the Australian government had refused them the same citizenship rights as non-Indigenous Australians. The protest was a defining moment in the development of a national Aboriginal political movement that was to demand citizenship rights in their own country.

Still, such events were not headline news in the 1930s. Politics and sport were the mainstay of newspapers. This was a turbulent political period, where the premier of New South Wales was dismissed by the governor, and leaked secret cables brought the downfall of a federal government. But the rise of the great cricketer Don Bradman and the feats of the horse Phar Lap were popular distractions that often pushed politics from the front pages.

Newspapers were now becoming more like the papers we know today. Photographic and printing techniques improved, allowing the production of larger and better-quality images—which the tabloid papers readily took up, and the role of photojournalism became increasingly important.

Still, progress towards the front page headline format that we know today was slow. Many papers were still reluctant to run a large banner headline or a prominent image on the front page. But, from this time, graphic images of catastrophic news did appear as part of leading stories. In January 1939, on the eve of another war, headlines and images of destruction in the Black Friday bushfires shocked the nation.

53 Heroine of the air

Amy Johnson flies from England to Australia, 1930

CIVILIAN AIR FLIGHTS WERE STILL A NOVELTY IN THE 1920S AND 1930S, WHEN LONG-DISTANCE SOLO FLIGHTS WERE FOLLOWED AVIDLY IN THE NEWSPAPERS. SOLO FLIGHTS WERE PART OF A SERIES OF 'RECORD ATTEMPTS' IN AEROPLANE FLIGHT THAT FASCINATED AUDIENCES. HUGE CROWDS OFTEN GATHERED EXPECTANTLY AT AIRFIELDS TO WELCOME RECORD-BREAKING PILOTS.

Inexperienced British pilot Amy Johnson had flown from England to Darwin in a near record time of just nineteen days, at a time when ships, still the main form of travel were still taking three to four months to cover the distance. Johnson's feat was widely seen as remarkable because she was a woman, doing what was a dangerous job that had been, or should have been, the preserve of men. Such flights still traversed supposedly dangerous places, such as the 'jungles of Timor' where Johnson was forced to land and was surrounded by 'half-naked savages'.

Accidentally yet providentially, 'Johnnie' as she asked journalists to call her, landed in Darwin on 24 May, which was celebrated as Empire Day across the countries of the British Empire. Johnson stepped out of her Gypsy Moth plane to a ready-made celebration and was then feted by audiences in her six-week tour of Australia stopping at several regional towns and major cities around the country from Brisbane to Perth.

Johnson's achievements reflected the roles and views of women in Australian society that were changing during the 1920s. In fact Johnson was to fly non-combat aircraft in the Second World War, and died on an air mission in 1941—possibly shot down by British forces.

Johnson's Britain to Australia flight was also seen as a continued sign of 'Imperial unity', as *The Sydney Morning Herald* described it, during an increasingly unsettled period of international politics. So, too, Johnson's and other aviators' feats were popular among people looking for positive stories during an era of economic depression.

THE SYDNEY MAIL, WEDNESDAY, MAY 21, 1930.—Page 8

Amy Johnson—Heroine of the Air

A Recent Picture of Miss Johnson

The attempt of Miss Amy Johnson to establish a new record for the flight of a single-seater 'plane from England to Australia has stirred the whole world. With comparatively little, although careful, preparation and in a 'plane that had already seen a good deal of service, she set out from Croydon on the morning of May 5. An unfortunate accident on landing at Burma delayed her for two days, and removed any chance of breaking Hinkler's record solo flight from England to Australia.

A SECTION OF THE LANDING-PLACE AT DARWIN.
With the monument to Sir Ross Smith on the extreme right.

Miss Johnson is a slim, attractive girl, with bobbed hair and a winning smile. She was engaged for years in a solicitor's office, but was so keen on flying that she devoted all her spare time to the study and practise of the art until she secured both a pilot's and an engineer's certificate. Her father, who was a pioneer of the Klondyke goldfield, bought her a Gipsy Moth, which she christened Jason, and expressed his firm belief that she was capable of accomplishing her aim.

The Sydney Mail's *headlines on Amy Johnson's flight reflect the worldwide interest in her story, as well as the pleasure in the perceptions of an increasingly shortened transport link between the Mother Country and the isolated Australian continent.*

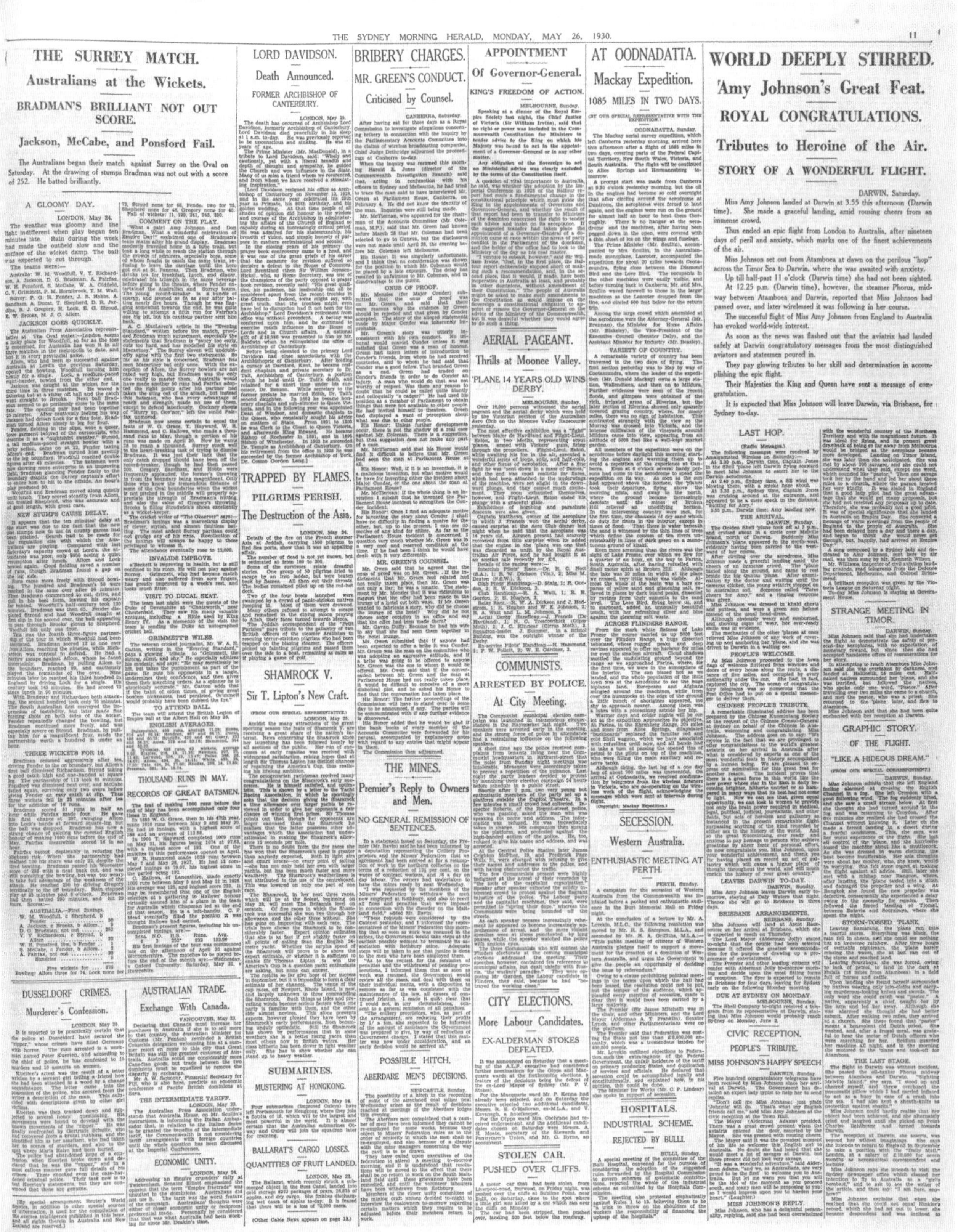
THE SYDNEY MORNING HERALD, MONDAY, MAY 26, 1930. 11

THE SURREY MATCH. Australians at the Wickets. BRADMAN'S BRILLIANT NOT OUT SCORE. Jackson, McCabe, and Ponsford Fail.

LORD DAVIDSON. Death Announced.

BRIBERY CHARGES. MR. GREEN'S CONDUCT. Criticised by Counsel.

APPOINTMENT Of Governor-General.

AT OODNADATTA. Mackay Expedition. 1085 MILES IN TWO DAYS.

WORLD DEEPLY STIRRED.

'Amy Johnson's Great Feat.

ROYAL CONGRATULATIONS.

Tributes to Heroine of the Air.

STORY OF A WONDERFUL FLIGHT.

DARWIN, Saturday.

Miss Amy Johnson landed at Darwin at 3.55 this afternoon (Darwin time). She made a graceful landing, amid rousing cheers from an immense crowd.

Thus ended an epic flight from London to Australia, after nineteen days of peril and anxiety, which marks one of the finest achievements of the air.

Miss Johnson set out from Atamboea at dawn on the perilous "hop" across the Timor Sea to Darwin, where she was awaited with anxiety.

Up till half-past 11 o'clock (Darwin time) she had not been sighted. At 12.25 p.m. (Darwin time), however, the steamer Phorus, midway between Atamboea and Darwin, reported that Miss Johnson had passed over, and later wirelessed it was following in her course.

The successful flight of Miss Amy Johnson from England to Australia has evoked world-wide interest.

As soon as the news was flashed out that the aviatrix had landed safely at Darwin congratulatory messages from the most distinguished aviators and statesmen poured in.

They pay glowing tributes to her skill and determination in accomplishing the epic flight.

Their Majesties the King and Queen have sent a message of congratulation.

It is expected that Miss Johnson will leave Darwin, via Brisbane, for Sydney to-day.

TRAPPED BY FLAMES. PILGRIMS PERISH. The Destruction of the Asia.

AERIAL PAGEANT. Thrills at Moonee Valley. PLANE 14 YEARS OLD WINS DERBY.

COMMUNISTS. ARRESTED BY POLICE. At City Meeting.

SHAMROCK V. Sir T. Lipton's New Craft.

THE MINES. Premier's Reply to Owners and Men.

SECESSION. Western Australia.

DUSSELDORF CRIMES. Murderer's Confession.

AUSTRALIAN TRADE. Exchange With Canada.

CITY ELECTIONS. More Labour Candidates.

STRANGE MEETING IN TIMOR.

GRAPHIC STORY. OF THE FLIGHT. "LIKE A HIDEOUS DREAM."

The Sydney Morning Herald of 26 May 1930 devoted columns of text to the story of Amy Johnson's flight, among varied short news reports. On the same page, one of the continuing good news stories of the Depression—Don Bradman's success playing cricket for Australia—also appeared.

Bradman breaks all records 54

Don Bradman in the Ashes, 1930

WHILE LONG-DISTANCE FLIGHT RECORDS WERE ONE FOCUS OF PUBLIC ATTENTION DURING THE YEARS OF THE GREAT DEPRESSION, ANOTHER WAS CRICKET. CONSIDERING THAT A 22-YEAR-OLD CRICKETER CALLED DONALD GEORGE BRADMAN (1908–2001) STARTED HIS FIRST ASHES TEST MATCH SERIES AGAINST ENGLAND IN 1930 AS A 'GOOD CHANCE', AND FINISHED THE SERIES AS A HOUSEHOLD NAME, THE ATTENTION IS QUITE UNDERSTANDABLE.

Bradman's feats and records were to make constant front page news through the 1930s Ashes series. He scored several double centuries and was at the batting crease so long, so many times, that when he scored 334 over two days in the July 1930 third test match at Leeds, one British evening newspaper, the *Star*, ran the simple and somewhat relieved two-word banner headline, 'He's Out!'

In the second test at Lords in June 1930, Bradman scored 254 in Australia's world record six for 729 runs. He was already being called a 'wonder bat', but perhaps the highlight of the 1930 tour was Bradman's 309 runs not out in one day in the third test at Leeds on 11 July. In this test Bradman achieved cricketing legend status by scoring 100 runs before lunch—and he remains the only person to have scored more than 300 runs in one day's play.

Bradman went on to captivate cricket audiences around the world and in a twenty-year career with a test batting average of 99.94—claimed to be statistically the greatest achievement in any major sport—he was widely acknowledged as the greatest batsman of all time.

Bradman's dominance at the batting crease led to a development in cricket that was to break into a furore between Britain and Australia. In the final test match of the famous 1930 Ashes series, from 16 to 22 August, English bowlers sought to get Bradman out with short-pitched deliveries, regarded as dangerous and unsporting by Australians. Regaining the Ashes was serious business.

NET SALES LARGER THAN THOSE OF ANY OTHER NEWSPAPER IN AUSTRALIA

FINAL EXTRA

THE SUN

ABOVE ALL FOR AUSTRALIA

FINE & MILD
CITY FORECAST: Fine, rather mild day; westerly breeze.

No. 6127 (Registered at the General Post Office, Sydney, for transmission by post as a newspaper.) SYDNEY : TUESDAY, JULY 1, 1930 PRICE 1d 'Phone: B.O. 333

Englishmen Now Compelled to Fight Rearguard Action

PLAYING UP

WICKET MAY TROUBLE BATSMEN

TWO OUT ALREADY

MANY RECORDS TOPPLE BEFORE BRADMAN'S FLASHING BAT

(From Our Special Representative)

LONDON, Monday.

On a wicket that is showing signs of wear, the Englishmen will have to fight desperately to avert defeat in the second Test Match, as, at the end of play to-day, two of their best batsmen, Hobbs and Woolley, were back in the pavilion, and at stumps England was still 206 runs behind Australia's first innings total.

The play to-day was marked by numerous records. Bradman crashed his way through so many that statisticians almost lost count, and, when he was out after compiling a magnificent 254, he received a wonderful ovation. Kippax was out soon afterwards, and then McCabe and Richardson, without waiting to dig in, flogged the bowling over the field. In McCabe's 44 there were eight fours, while Richardson hit a six. Even Oldfield had a go at the bowling, and the innings was closed at six wickets for 729—a world's record score in Test cricket history.

In the Englishmen's second innings Grimmett and Fairfax made full use of the tricky wicket.

THE SCORES

LACOSTE WEDS

Scramble at Service

Lacoste and his bride.

("Sun" Special)

PARIS, Monday.

GRAVE CASE

POPE DISCUSSES MALTA

"PEACE IMPOSSIBLE"

WORLD ACCLAIM

FLIERS AT WHITE HOUSE

CORDIAL HOOVER

("Sun" Special)

WASHINGTON (D.C.), Monday.

"Your flight has caught the admiration and imagination of the entire world," said the Assistant Secretary for War (Mr. Davison) in greeting Kingsford-Smith and his companions on their arrival at Bolling Field, Washington, amid cheering crowds.

The fliers made the trip to the capital to lunch with President Hoover at the White House.

President Hoover Sir Ronald Lindsay

PEACE WINS

End of the Occupation

AMID CHEERS

PRESS CONFERENCE ENDS

BISHOP'S FIANCEE

EMPIRE WIRELESS PLAN

INDIAN SITUATION

THE SUN STOP-PRESS

Round the World in One-Eighth Second

Scouts Blossom Into Hollywood Rivals

Arthur Mailey's Story and M. A. Noble's Comment on Page 14.

(Continued on Page 2).

Sydney's Sun well noted Bradman's 'flashing bat' during the second test of the 1930 series, where in just one test series he batted himself into the Australian public's imagination and onto the mantelpiece of legendary Australian figures.

The Maltese Voice in Australia 55

A foreign-language newspaper, 1930

FROM 1901 THE AUSTRALIAN PARLIAMENT'S INTRODUCTION OF THE IMMIGRATION RESTRICTION ACTS, CREATING THE WHITE AUSTRALIA POLICY, LIMITED THE OPPORTUNITIES FOR MANY NON-BRITISH PEOPLE TO MIGRATE TO AUSTRALIA. SOME IMMIGRANT GROUPS, SUCH AS THE GERMANS AND ITALIANS, WHO HAD ESTABLISHED THEMSELVES IN THE COUNTRY WELL BEFORE 1901, WERE ABLE TO CONTINUE TO BRING OUT THEIR FAMILIES THROUGH SPONSORED MIGRATION. BUT ANOTHER GROUP OF NON-BRITISH MIGRANTS CONTINUED TO ARRIVE IN THE COUNTRY IN SIGNIFICANT NUMBERS FOR A VERY DIFFERENT REASON.

Technically, the citizens of Britain's colonies were British subjects and so they were able to move between colonies in the British Empire. As subjects of Britain, many Maltese people took the opportunity of migrating to the Australian colonies and, after 1901, the Commonwealth of Australia.

From the 1880s, hundreds of Maltese families had settled in Australia, mostly in western Sydney and around Brisbane. In Queensland the men often took up backbreaking work as cane-cutters. In Sydney, many Maltese people found their farming skills in demand across the Cumberland Plain, which supplied the city with most of its fruit and vegetables. And as large farms in western Sydney were subdivided into small plots, their experience in intensive agriculture on the tiny Mediterranean island of Malta came to the fore. By the 1920s, several Maltese families had established the area's first major poultry farms around Pendle Hill, Blacktown and Fairfield in western Sydney.

Although *The Voice of the Maltese in Australia and Farmers' Advocate Weekly* lasted for only a year, the fact that a newspaper in a foreign language could be published and distributed in 1930s Australia reflects the long and often forgotten histories of non-English-speaking migrants in the country before the large-scale migration from the 1950s. In fact, there had been many foreign-language newspapers since the 1840s, such as the German language *Die Deutsche Post für die australischen Kolonien* published in Adelaide, South Australia, and in the 1850s the *English and Chinese Advertiser* published on the Ballarat goldfields in Victoria. Such community or ethnic newspapers were important information networks for many migrant groups throughout Australian history.

Jec trid Titghallem Bl'Inglis jew Bit-taljan ixtri il "Letard Conversation" f'Zewg Volumi jimbiegh 3/6 bil Posta ghand Giov Muscat 48 Sda Mercanti, Valletta, Malta.

The Voice of the Maltese in Australia AND Farmers' Advocate Weekly

Official Organ of the Maltese in Australasia.

Copyright—All Rights Reserved in A/sia. JULY 21, 1934. Vol. V.—No. 17.

Sell to the Thousands of Maltese in Australia USE THIS WEEKLY as Your Medium. IT PAYS!

Registered under the Newspaper Act as a Newspaper.

Head Office: No. 10, Second Floor, Union Bank Chambers, Queen Street, Brisbane. 'Phone: B 7547.

56 Stanley Street, West Melbourne. Sydney Office: 76 Pitt Street, Sydney.

FLILES MIN RAZZA LICTAR PRODUTTIVA.

Mil Bojod W.L. £3/10/- cul 100.
Suwed B.O. £4 cul 100.
Ferrovia imhalsa. Depostu Mal Ordni u Cumplament mal consenja.

P. U. GOOCH

Soldier Settlement, MOUNT GRAVATT.

S. KNOWLES & SONS

PTY. LTD.,

Mercanti tal Gawar u Jahdmu Deheb. Tiswiet ta Debeb u Arloggi Specialita Tana.

No. 11, Brisbane Arcade, QUEEN STREET - BRISBANE
G.P.O. Box 592 J. Telefon B 5948.
Sstabiliti 1878.

A. COUSNER,

Progressive Poultry Farm,

THE GAP — ASHGROVE,

BRISBANE.

FLILES, AWITAK U CUL XORTA TA TJUR TESTJATI EJJA ARA IL TJUR TANA.

Telefon: F 9078.

Mur Fil Royal Hotel

FINCH HATTON.

Biss lahjar licuri u xorb nofrulec Accommodazioni mil ahjar u Preziet moderatissimi.

Telefon 11.

ICTAR BAID-IGBAR PROFIT.

Billi Tghelef Sewwa.

Wahda mil manieri certi li tati risultati ahjar hua billi tghelef sewwa. Ghati il tjur tighec il ghalf sew biex jisviloppau il baid, huma jatulec. Tighom il proteins colla, minerali, vitamini u nutrimenti li andom bzon-tighom il EGGOLEEN.

EGGOLEEN hua ghal bilanciat bil xienza u fieh il minerali. Il 14 ingredient ta qualita isostnu sewwa il tigieg tighec u jatuc isfar li bmod iehor jigu mohlija imhabba li ma icol locx ghalf sewwa.. Biex tghamel razion bilanciat eccelenti, biss hallat 12 libra Eggoleen ma 60 libra smida u 30 nohhala. Eggoleen jaidlec il profit tighec, ghalec ordna xcora issa u uzah dejjem.
Ottenut min N.S.W. "Poultry" Newspaper, 13 Goulburn Street, Sydney. Priziet gio Victoria u N.S.W. 100 libra 15/6, 50 libra 8/-, 25 libra 4/3.

CLARK, KING & COY., PTY. LTD.
30-32 GUILDFORD LANE.
MELBOURNE.

MALTA TRIUMPHS. ENGLAND BEATEN IN INTERNATIONAL SOCCER.

Champion Central Europe Once More Defeated at Malta.

It is with great satisfaction we publish to-day the news that the Empire has once more triumphed against foreign nations and this time it was left to the Maltese to uplift the interest of International Soccer.

A very big surprise was the defeat of the English Eleven at Prague where they went down to the Czech. completely beaten by 2 goals to nil. Little, however, did the foreigners realise that they would be beaten by other Empire representatives, the Sliema Wanderers, Champion team of the Malta Football Association League and the Cassar Cup for which they have beaten the best of the Fleet and the Army.

The Maltese were superior in all phases of the game and resorted to their usual long passing which to a great extent upset the Czechs, so much that in the end they had to try and emulate this wonderful Maltese combination but without any success at all, because the Malta Champions had them completely off their legs most of the time.

This is the third occasion that the Maltese have won th Championship of Central Europe and they deserve, to be successful. A gloom was broadcasted when it was known that John Bull had gone down, but the Maltese as usual rose for the occasion and wiped out this gloom, by defeating John Bull's conquerors.

We from far distant Australia congratulate our brethren on their meritorious victory, one which will go down in history of soccer and fills up a page in the annals of Maltese sports.

KING ALFONSO OF SPAIN AS POLO REFEREE AT MALTA.

What may perhaps be a unique part was taken by ex-King Alfonso of Spain in May last when he refereed two polo matches at the Marsa Polo Ground in Malta. Lord Louis Mountbatten played for the Navy and showed remarkable improvement in his play. The spectators contained many high dignitaries of Malta and Europe.

The ex-King is a frequent visitor to Malta and a great lover of polo, which he always plays when in Malta. At one time he partnered His Royal Highness the Prince of Wales, when the latter was in Malta.

The ex-King has also presented a Cup which is known as "The King of Spain Cup." We wish our regular visitor a very pleasant and happy time.

MALTA TRIONFA. ENGILTERRA TITLEF FIL SOCCER INTERNAZIONALI.

Champions ta Centru tal Europa Mil Gdid Battuti gio Malta.

Hua blicbar sodisfazoni ahna nipublicau illum il ahbar li l'Imperu ghal da rba ohra itrionfa contra il Nazioniet stranieri u din il darba gie imholli lil Maltin biex jerfghou linteressi tal Soccer Internazionali.

Kata cbira bosta chinet dic li il hdax Inglisi tilfu gio Prague fein huma marru taht il Czecoslaviki li daun bateom ghal collox 2 goaliet bxein.

Ftit ma dan collu li stranieri hasbu li huma jigu battuti min Rapresentanti tal Imperu ohrain il Sliema Wanderers team Champion tal Malta Football Association League u il Tazza ta Cassar li ghalia huma battew lakwa fil Flotta u il Armata.

Il Maltin chienu superiuri fil fasi colla tal lghoba u zammew mal soltu tkassim fil tul tahhom li bicca cbira kalbet lil Czecs. hec tant flahhar li huma stess ipruvau jemulau din il meraviljusa combinazioni Maltia izda bla success ghal collox, aliex il Champions Maltin chinu zamewom ghal collox mitlufa il bicca cbira tal hin.

Din hia il tielet darba li il Maltin rephu il Championship tal Centru tal Europa u huma jisthokilom li ichunu succesevol. Dlam gie inferrex meta gi maruf li John Bull chien mar taht, izda il Maltin phal soltu telghou ghal occasioni u meshu dan il dlam billi battew lil dauc li chienu hacmu lil John Bull.

Ahna mil bghod distanti Australia nifirhu 11 hutna fil repha meritusa tahhom wahda li tmur imnizla flistoria tal ballun u timla pagina fil annali ta lghob gio Malta.

RE ALFONSO TA SPANJA REFEREE TAL POLO GIO MALTA.

Dac li forsi jista hua parti uniqa giet mehuda mil ex-Re Alfonsu ta Spanja f'Mejju li adda meta il referee zewg partiti tal polo fil Marsa polo round gio Malta. Lord Louis Mountbatten lghab mal Navy u wera improviment rimarcabili fil lghob tighou. Il nies li c ienu jarau chien hemm fighom bosta dinjitaiet ta Malta u Europa.

Il Ex-Re hua visitatur ta spiss gio Malta u mahbub cbir tal Polo li hua dejjem jilab meta ichun Malta. Darba wahda hua lghab mal Prince of Wales meta dan li semeina lahhar chien gio Malta.

Il Ex-Re ucholl ipresenta tazza li hia marufa phala "The King of Spain Cup" u competizioni ghalia issir cul sena.

Ahna nixteku lil visitatur tana zmien piacevoli u cuntent bosta.

CANNON & CRIPPS,

DIRETTURI TAL FUNERALI.
ADELAIDE STREET (kuddiem City Hall). Telefon B 1971.
WICKHAM STREET (fein Friendly Societies' Dispensary). Telefon B 1972.
STANLEY STREET (fein Vulture St., Sth. Brisbane). Telefon J 2007.

GULLIVERS GIONNA TA SIGIAR TA TAHWIL

TOWNSVILLE.

Andec Bzonn Xi Sigiar Tal Frott.

LARING, LUMI JEW MANDOLINA etc.

Jecc andec bzonn halli lordni tighec ma S. K. PAGE, Edith Street, Innisfail, Agent Locali.

FLILES TA GIURNATA

MIL BOJOD (W.L.) u MIL SUWED (B.L.).

Min tigieg vigorusi u robusti.
Il fliles colla garantiti mazula speciali mil nisel tighei stess.
MIL BOJOD £3 cul 100; £2/17/6 lot ta 500 u £2/15/- lot ta 1000 preziet cul mija.
MIL SUWED. £3/15/- cul 100; Lot ta 500 bil £3/12/6; lot ta 1000 bil £3/10/- cul mia.

Tifkis ta Baid 9/- cul 100.

C. W. DRUCE,

207 Old Prospect Road,
WENTWORTHVILLE.
Telefon UW 9171.
'Bus ta Parramatta jekak kudiemna.

M.I.B. FOODS

Ma Hemmx Ghalf Ictar Ahjar Mil Concentrati Mamula Mil Meat Industry Commission.

Uza il Meat Meal, Ox-a Vita, Bone Meal, Procalbone, etc.

MEAT INDUSTRY COMMISSION, State Abattoirs,

HOMEBUSH BAY, N.S.W.

Hia il Qualita li Jghod FLIBSA

Ahna inhitu blidein LILBIESI COLLA

Lictar Drapiet ta Moda Imfasla Sewwa

Min £6/6/- il wahda.

E. Borrows

Canberra Buildings

180 ANN ST., BRISBANE.

Icteb ghal Mostri u Formoli tal kies.

CHARLES INNES & SON

Diretturi tal Funerali
(Kabel chien ma Wm. Metcalfe & Co. Ltd.),
28 Darcy Street, PARRAMATTA.
Telefon: UW 9259.

Il Testment Tighec

hua document importanti u andu bzonn isir min esperti. Culhatt jista icollu dan il document u bla ebda spejjes ta xein. Treasferimenti ta propieta, raba, asseniazioni, crop liens, self ta flus xorta ohra u cul documenti ohra legali huma jigu preparati malli titlobom. Dan Officiu hua tal Cvern aliex tmur banda ohra. Icteb bil Malti jew bil Inglis al particolari compliti.

THE PUBLIC CURATOR.
Officiu Principali: Edward St., Brisbane. Agenziji gio Rockhampton, Townsville u Cairns

The Voice of the Maltese in Australia and Farmers' Advocate Weekly *was very much an industry journal that provided instructional articles on growing fruit trees and poultry farming techniques for readers, but it also included both Australian and Maltese news stories.*

Scullin's somersaults 56

Bringing down a Labor government, 1931

NEWSPAPER HEADLINES HAVE RARELY BEEN RESPONSIBLE FOR THE DOWNFALL OF A GOVERNMENT, BUT THE PUBLICATION OF PRIVATE CORRESPONDENCE HAS OFTEN SEEN THE DEMISE OF INDIVIDUAL POLITICIANS. DURING THE 1930S, WITH INCREASED COMPETITION AMONG THE GROWING NUMBER OF NEWSPAPERS FOR NEWS SCOOPS THAT MIGHT INCREASE DAILY SALES, JOURNALISTS BEGAN TO FOCUS MORE ON FINDING NEWS BEFORE IT BECAME NEWS.

In March 1931 Melbourne *Herald* journalist Joe Alexander was handed copies of private telegrams between then Labor Prime Minister James Scullin (1876–1953) and two of his ministers. Like the rest of the world, Australia was in the depths of the Great Depression and Scullin was in London seeking help for Australia's economy. His cables back to Acting Prime Minister James Fenton (1864–1950) and one of his senior ministers, Joseph Lyons (1879–1939), revealed a very different political opinion of the situation than the one that the Labor Party was officially and publicly running.

Joe Alexander's editor at the *Herald* did not initially publish the cables, but the question of whether official government correspondence could legally be published only momentarily held them back from the presses. They were such sensational news that very soon all the major newspapers ran stories quoting the 'secret cables' that showed 'Scullin's somersaults'.

Alexander's scoop was the beginning of the end for the Scullin government (1929–1932), riven by a division within the Labor Party over how to manage the Australian economy. Scullin's former minister Joseph Lyons left the party and led the United Australia Party to victory at an early election in December 1931.

The Labor Party was furious with Alexander, who refused to reveal his source of the leaked cables, and banned him from entering the House of Representatives for six months. However, Labor did not control the Senate at the time and could not pass a motion banning him from the Upper House. Alexander was allowed entry into one half of Parliament House, which meant he was not allowed to cross an imaginary line running down the centre of the main corridor of King's Hall.

No. 1459. (Registered at the General Post Office, Sydney, for transmission by post as a newspaper.) SYDNEY: SUNDAY, MARCH 15, 1931 'Phone: B.O. 333 36 Pages---Twopence

Secret Cables Tell of Scullin's Somersaults

OUTBURST WAS MOSTLY SMOKE

THREAT TO RESIGN OVER HIGH CT.

INFLATION WOBBLE

(From Our Special Representative)

CANBERRA, Saturday.

The secret cable messages that passed between Mr. Scullin, when he was in England, and Messrs. Lyons and Fenton, were made known to-day; and they show Mr. Scullin's indignation on the inflation and repudiation plan and the appointment of Mr. Evatt and Mr. McTiernan to the High Court bench—indignation that turned to gentle acquiesence when he came back to Australia and saw the disposition of his party.

Mr. Scullin even went so far as to threaten to resign if the High Court appointments were made.

Mr. Scullin

Mr. Lyons

On November 5, 1930, Mr. Scullin cabled Mr. Lyons from London.

The full message reads: "Banks are expected to carry any shortage in budget, also to underwrite loan conversion. That, together with responsibility to finance harvest, will be heavy strain on banks. To create credit for £20,000,000 for loan work is unsound, and I expect banks to refuse to do so. Government cannot deliberately coerce administration of banks. Such proposal means permanent inflation, which could not be checked, as is implied, and would demand further inflation. All this talk about creating credit and inflation is most damaging, and will seriously prejudice conversion maturing loans and treasury bills.

"Panic May Result"

"Since inflation was suggested efforts are being made by men here to withdraw their money from Australia, as they would lose by payment in a depreciated currency. Depreciation in currency would decrease values of savings banks deposits. Property would increase in price. There would be a rush to sell bonds for investment in property. Financial panic may result."

On November 7, Mr. Lyons had informed Mr. Scullin by cable of the Caucus resolution to compel holders of maturing loans to hold their bonds for a further period of 12 months.

"This is absolute repudiation," proceeded Mr. Lyons's message. "I immediately notified the party I would not be prepared to carry out their decision, but would communicate with you and ask you, if you approved their action, to relieve me of my position in the Cabinet and appoint successor to submit necessary legislation, which will inevitably crash credit of Australia.

"Repudiation Dishonest"

"Pending your decision, I propose to carry out my previous intention to recommend loan at meeting Loan Council Tuesday. During discussion effort was made, and received considerable support, to demand Commonwealth Bank to take up whole £27,000,000, failing which demands should be made that board resign. Fenton informed of this message."

To that cable Mr. Scullin replied: "Your wire 7th received. I do not approve, and will not support, revolution of party, which I agree is repudiation, which is dishonest and disastrous. Brennan and Moloney concur. We agree that you are right in recommending to Loan Council issue of loans, as party's resolution has demoralised Australian stocks here, and unless rescinded will render renewal of bills here, as well as conversions in Australia, impossible. Inform Fenton of this cable. Will telephone early as possible."

Hits Australia Hard

On November 10, Mr. Scullin sent the following cable message: "I appeal to the party to reconsider its resolution, which has demoralised Australian stock here, rendering renewal of Treasury bills impossible. I came to London with the consent of the party. Apart from the Imperial Conference, my most important mission was to restore Australian credit, so that we could fund floating debt, and, if possible, raise some new money to relieve our economic position. My efforts would have succeeded had party support been maintained. The world depression, affecting price of our exports, combined with inability to obtain loans, hits Australia very hard.

Door Still Open

Mr. Scullin's cable message to Mr. Lyons on November 10 continued:—

"I found in London a desire to assist, and plans were maturing to approach loan markets when budgets were balanced. Although there was disappointment in financial circles that our budget is not quite balanced, the door was not quite closed, and I still had hopes of success until the appalling resolution was passed last Thursday. That proposal was disastrous. It is a reversal of the Party's declared policy to honor national obligations, and no self-respecting Government could agree to it."

"Our Government floated loan and guaranteed the public a safe investment. Thousands of people withdrew their savings from the Savings Bank to assist the Labor Government. To default on this loan would weaken the value of their investments, would destroy public confidence, and delay for years the restoration of economic prosperity. If, however, wiser counsels prevail, and the Government is given a chance to obtain credit, a debacle may yet be avoided, but if we are frustrated by our own supporters by resolution or statement creating financial panic, our position becomes intolerable, and our efforts to govern in the people's interest hopeless.

Against Honor

"The Government proposal is to ask the bondholders voluntarily to renew their bonds. To enforce renewal by refusing to pay the debts for a year is repudiation. The law would not permit that in private transactions, and no one mindful of his personal honor would do it in private life. I know and share members' feelings regarding the sufferings of the unemployed, but the extension of our credit will spread that suffering tremendously. Brennan and Moloney concur."

On the same day Mr. Lyons sent a cable message to Mr. Scullin, in which he said that, while Messrs. Anstey and Beasley remained in the Government he was afraid there was little chance of re-establishing confidence.

Mr. Lyons added: "My position is made extremely difficult, having to meet opposition from these two Ministers in party meetings. You will need to consider this aspect as situations may develop early calling for drastic action on part yourself and moderate section."

"Astounds Us"

A flood of light is also thrown on the circumstances surrounding the appointment of two additional High Court judges by cable messages which Mr. Scullin sent to Messrs. Lyons and Fenton at the time.

In a message to Mr. Lyons, Mr. Scullin said: "See telegram sent to Fenton and Bailey regarding appointment of judges. For your personal information, I would go out of office if, under the circumstances, appointments were rushed through during our absence. Attorney-General takes same view. Appeal to you to avoid this."

A cable message from the Prime Minister to Mr. Fenton, read:—"Telegram from Vice-President Executive Council to Attorney-General, stating that steps being taken to appoint judges, astounds us. It is a reversal of Cabinet decision, and means that Cabinet accepts political direction on appointments to the High Court judiciary. Political interference, removing this matter from Cabinet responsibility, strikes fatally at the authority of the Court. Attorney-General and I will be no party to that. Number of judges adequate. Moreover, long vacation begins. We will return in three weeks. Why rush appointment and deny Prime Minister and Attorney-General opportunity to express strongly-held views? We have the right to take part in the discussion of this most vital question. We ask you to reconsider the appointments before it is too late."

Cabinet Surrenders

Another cable message from Mr. Scullin to Mr. Fenton, said: "Obliged for your message, stating that Party meeting rejected unanimous recommendation of the Cabinet to hold over the appointments to the High Court pending our return. I urge that Cabinet remain firm. It is a matter solely for Cabinet decision. Attorney-General and I hold views which we want to express, and cannot agree any appointment coming into force until our return. Grave principle involved."

Mr. Lyons, on December 30, cabled to Mr. Scullin, on board the Ormonde, as follows:—

"Following our cipher message regarding the appointment of High Court judges, I made representations to the Acting Prime Minister, and received the following reply: 'Prime Minister's telegram of December 19 received too late for consideration as Cabinet had already appointed Messrs. McTiernan and Evatt, and former had resigned seat. Therefore, consider only course now possible is to stand by Cabinet decision.'"

A radio message, sent subsequently by Mr. Lyons to Mr. Scullin, stated: "Cabinet agreed to dictation of Party during my absence from Canberra. I learned of Cabinet final decision from Press."

About this date, Mr. Lyons also telegraphed to Mr. Fenton, saying that he agreed entirely with the views expressed in Mr. Scullin's cable and urging that Cabinet should take full responsibility, and hold over the appointment, pending a further reconsideration when Mr. Scullin returned.

DESPERATE!

Hurling himself at the tape in the 100 metres decathlon championship, A. Batton (W.S.), managed to make a dead heat with W. H. Cooper. Note the tense expression.

Johnnie Jason taking the lead from Whittingham in the second division of the Juvenile Stakes at Rosehill yesterday.

SURFER ALMOST FRANTIC WITH AGONY

SWALLOWED BLUEBOTTLE

PLUCKY RACE FINISH

Half-way through the junior surf championship at the Bondi Beach carnival yesterday one of the competitors, Jack Craigie, swallowed a bluebottle.

He had a burning sensation in his throat and on his tongue, and he immediately dropped back. Recovering from the sudden shock he struck out again, and eventually finished fourth in the race.

On reaching the beach Craigie was in a bad way. However, he pluckily sprinted up to the finishing line, and then collapsed.

He was assisted to the beach ambulance station, and so serious was his condition that Dr. Ryan was sent for.

Though experiencing terrible pain, Craigie maintained consciousness, and an injection of morphia was administered to relieve his suffering.

Eastern Suburbs Ambulance then took him to St. Vincent's Hospital, where his suffering was further relieved.

Craigie, though very weak after his ordeal, had recovered sufficiently four hours later to return to his home.

EXHAUSTED!

Competitors who were exhausted at the finish of the junior surf race in yesterday's big carnival at Bondi.

ENOUGH!

MACHINE POLITICS

LYONS'S CRY

MELBOURNE, Saturday.

"Let us sink our minor differences, and unite, but above all things let us not build a new political machine to take the place of the old ones. Let us keep clear of machines altogether."

That declaration was made to-night by Mr. Lyons, formerly Acting-Treasurer, in a broadcast speech to three States.

The Best Needed

"We need to get the best out of every elected representative in times such as this," said Mr. Lyons, "and we can only do that if each representative is free. There is a real need for all who love Australia and desire her progress and prosperity to get together as the All For Australia organisation is doing."

Mr. Lyons pointed out that the result of the motion moved by Mr. Latham, although defeated, made it clear that the Scullin Government had lost the confidence of the House.

"If Australian citizens remain content to leave their destinies in the hands of foolish despots controlling the party political machine, nothing can avert complete disaster," he said.

Simple, Honest Plan

"The position of Australia is desperate, but it is not entirely hopeless if we will only follow the simple, honest plan of trying to pay our way. The present Government, through its Treasurer, continues to submit financial proposals one after another, each of which is merely a figment of a fertile imagination. There is nothing real or practical in any of them. The last one was apparently given a name difficult to pronounce, so that while we were struggling with the pronunciation we would overlook the fact that fiduciary currency merely means inflation."

Mr. Lyons said that such a visionary scheme could not save the country. Industry could only be rehabilitated and men and women employed with real money, not with bogus notes.

FOR LL.B.

Carlton's Choice

UNI. COURSE

EVERYONE has been wondering what Jim Carlton will do when he puts away his running spikes in the winter time.

Jim has solved the problem.

He intends to commence study in the Faculty of Law at the University.

FOUR YEARS' WORK

The co-operation of his employers has enabled Carlton to make this decision, and at the end of four years' work Carlton hopes to graduate with the degree of LL.B.

In the Lent term, which begins to-morrow, Carlton will make his first acquaintance with Roman law, constitutional law, and the law of contracts.

Three years ago the great sprinter won a public exhibition, tenable at the University. Because he was chosen to represent Australia at the Olympic Games, he was obliged to forfeit the exhibition. Now he will have to finance the course himself.

STUDENT DEAD

GAS-FILLED ROOM

Bursting into a gas-filled room in a residential in Glebe-road, Glebe, last night, police found John Maxwell Lefroy, 20, a student, sitting in a chair dead. A piece of gas tubing was on his lap.

Death had taken place about three hours previously.

Lefroy, it is stated, told his landlady that he came from New Zealand, and intended to enrol at the University.

SHE WON

Miss C. Dennis, winning the 500 metres breast-stroke scratch race at the Manly Baths yesterday.

SYDNEY HOMES PRAISED

Mr. T. A. E. Wells, managing director of a large New Zealand firm of house decorators, who returned from a tour by the Hobson's Bay yesterday, said that the futuristic type of decoration was generally favored on the Continent. However, Sydney's homes were equal to any he had seen.

Over The Breakers

Dee Why's start in its heat of the senior surf-boat race at the Australian championships at Bondi yesterday. This was a heat that kept the spectators on tip-toe with excitement, Dee Why winning narrowly from Queenscliff. See story on Page 18.

TRAGIC DEATH OF M.L.C.'s YOUNG CHILD

RUN DOWN IN STREET

TENNIS FRIENDS WAITED

A paragraph in last night's "Sun" led to the identification of Mary Murray, 15, daughter of Mr. Thomas G. Murray, M.L.C., of Lang-road, Centennial Park, who was knocked over and killed earlier in the day, when a motor van ran over her, in Oxford-street, Paddington.

The girl met a shocking end. She was running across the road to catch a 'bus, when the lorry struck her. One wheel passed over her chest, and the ribs, which were broken, penetrated her lungs and heart. She died almost instantly. She had left home to play tennis, and the racquet she carried held the only clue to her identification. It bore her name, and when Mrs. Murray read "The Sun" about 5 p.m., she received a severe shock. She thought her girl was playing tennis with friends.

Ran To Doctor

On the verge of collapse, she ran to Dr. Golding's surgery, next door, and told him. The body had by then been taken by the Central Ambulance to the Morgue, and Dr. Golding, who had hurried there with Sergeant Kelly, identified the body.

The dead girl was fond of sport, and she had many friends, who were waiting for her at the tennis court to take part in a game, all of whom were greatly affected when they learned of her death.

HUSS HURRIED

In 10 4-5 secs., S. Huss dashed over the 100 yards to win Northern Suburbs junior title yesterday.

SHOWERS

Week-end Westerlies

Surfers and sun-bakers will not applaud the week-end weather bulletin issued by Mr. Mares.

"The weather will be chiefly cloudy and cool throughout the week-end, with an occasional shower; fresh westerly to south westerly winds will prevail," it says.

"Sydney is on the outskirts of unsettled weather, and a general rain storm over the State during the previous 24 hours makes the weather more uncertain for week-end trips."

"NOT MUCH LONGER"

ENGLISH VIEW OF CRISIS

(Published in "The Times")

LONDON, Friday.

Mr. Scullin's victory is almost worse than defeat, as it was secured by an appeal to the seceders to stay and save the Government (says "The Times" in a leading article). But the left wingers cannot long be counted on to keep Mr. Scullin in office, owing to the campaign in New South Wales, especially against Mr. Theodore.

Thus Mr. Scullin is merely the leader of one section into which a strongly organised and severely disciplined party has broken. Under the stress due to the financial crisis the Government cannot hope to prolong its uneasy existence much longer.

With little concern for the consequences, as it turned out, the Sydney Sun *first published the startling headlines of 'Scullin's Somersaults' and the full transcripts of the secret cables that ultimately brought down the government.*

The battle of Union Street 57

Communists fight police in Newtown, Sydney, 1931

WITH TRENCHES, SANDBAGS, BARBED WIRE, BOMBS, TRAPS, POISONOUS GAS, CLUBS, RIFLES AND BAYONETS, THE BATTLE OF UNION STREET BETWEEN POLICE AND COMMUNISTS HAD ALL THE HALLMARKS OF A FIRST WORLD WAR BATTLEFIELD.

At the height of the Great Depression, with almost 60 per cent of male wage earners unemployed, many people were failing to make their rent and mortgage payments. Evicted families, with all their belongings piled up on the street in front of their home, became a common sight. As some families refused to leave their homes, landlords began to call the police to evict them—and residents gathered on the streets in support of their neighbours. At Lakemba in south-western Sydney in March 1931, a crowd of 1000 stopped the eviction of a First World War veteran.

Fostered by the poverty and hardship of the Depression, small left-wing political groups in Australia began to attract many new members seeking an alternative to the major political parties. The Communist Party of Australia, formed in 1920, had rapidly gained members during the Depression and was instrumental in directing the Unemployed Workers Movement, which gathered more than 60,000 members during the early 1930s.

These groups supported people who were facing eviction by occupying and barricading their houses against the police. Sensing the potential for a widespread increase in such occupations, the police reacted swiftly and harshly, particularly at Newtown and another occupation at Bankstown, and did not hesitate to fire their weapons.

At Bankstown on 17 June 1931, 120 police confronted 17 squatters. Two men were shot and all seventeen squatters were injured, some seriously, while only one of the one hundred and twenty police who stormed the house received serious injuries. Two days after the Bankstown affray, at another eviction in Union Street, Newtown, police were faced with a hostile crowd said to number 'many thousands'. Once again, police opened fire on the squatters and confronted the crowds with drawn revolvers. The heavy-handed police tactics ensured there were no further occupation battles. Only three weeks after 'the Battle of Union Street' the state Labor government under Jack Lang introduced changes to the *Landlords and Tenants Act*, which gave tenants some security in being allowed to remain in rented premises, rather than being summarily evicted.

THE SYDNEY MORNING HERALD, SATURDAY, JUNE 20, 1931.

13

DESPERATE FIGHTING.

Communists and Police.

BARRICADED HOUSE STORMED.

Barbed Wire Entanglements and Sandbags.

The most sensational eviction battle Sydney has ever known was fought between 40 policemen and 18 Communists at 143 Union-street, Newtown, yesterday morning. All the defenders were injured, some seriously, and at least 15 of the police were treated by ambulance officials.

Only one man was hit by bullets fired at the walls of the house by the police, and it is not known how the injury was inflicted. Probably the wounded man was struck by a bullet which had been deflected in its path.

Entrenched behind barbed wire and sandbags, the defenders rained stones weighing several pounds from the top floor of the building on to the heads of the attacking police, who were attempting to execute an eviction order.

After a desperate battle, in which iron bars, piping, rude bludgeons, and chairs were used by the defenders, and batons by the police, the defenders were dragged, almost insensible, to the waiting patrol waggons.

SHOWERS OF STONES.

The Sydney Morning Herald headlined the desperate fighting between 'communists and police,' even though many of the defenders were not members of the Communist Party.

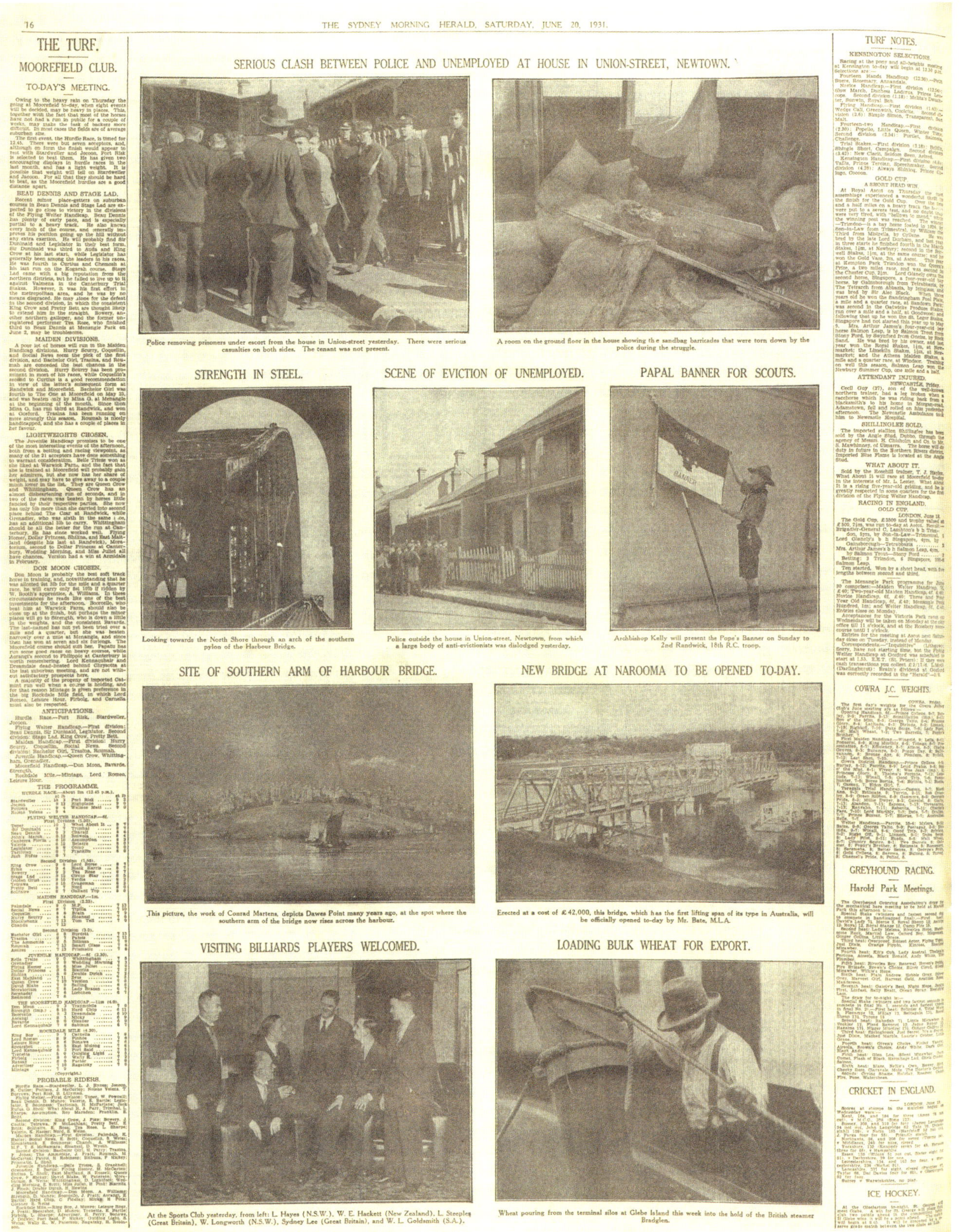

16 THE SYDNEY MORNING HERALD, SATURDAY, JUNE 20, 1931.

THE TURF.

MOOREFIELD CLUB.

TO-DAY'S MEETING.

BEAU DENNIS AND STAGE LAD.

MAIDEN DIVISIONS.

LIGHTWEIGHTS CHOSEN.

DON MOON CHOSEN.

ANTICIPATIONS.

THE PROGRAMME.

PROBABLE RIDERS.

SERIOUS CLASH BETWEEN POLICE AND UNEMPLOYED AT HOUSE IN UNION-STREET, NEWTOWN.

Police removing prisoners under escort from the house in Union-street yesterday. There were serious casualties on both sides. The tenant was not present.

A room on the ground floor in the house showing the sandbag barricades that were torn down by the police during the struggle.

STRENGTH IN STEEL.

Looking towards the North Shore through an arch of the southern pylon of the Harbour Bridge.

SCENE OF EVICTION OF UNEMPLOYED.

Police outside the house in Union-street, Newtown, from which a large body of anti-evictionists was dislodged yesterday.

PAPAL BANNER FOR SCOUTS.

Archbishop Kelly will present the Pope's Banner on Sunday to 2nd Randwick, 18th R.C. troop.

SITE OF SOUTHERN ARM OF HARBOUR BRIDGE.

This picture, the work of Conrad Martens, depicts Dawes Point many years ago, at the spot where the southern arm of the bridge now rises across the harbour.

NEW BRIDGE AT NAROOMA TO BE OPENED TO-DAY.

Erected at a cost of £42,000, this bridge, which has the first lifting span of its type in Australia, will be officially opened to-day by Mr. Bate, M.L.A.

VISITING BILLIARDS PLAYERS WELCOMED.

At the Sports Club yesterday, from left: L. Hayes (N.S.W.), W. E. Hackett (New Zealand), L. Steeples (Great Britain), W. Longworth (N.S.W.), Sydney Lee (Great Britain), and W. L. Goldsmith (S.A.).

LOADING BULK WHEAT FOR EXPORT.

Wheat pouring from the terminal silos at Glebe Island this week into the hold of the British steamer Bradglen.

TURF NOTES.

KENNINGTON SELECTIONS.

GOLD CUP.

A SHORT HEAD WIN.

ATTENDANT INJURED.

SHILLINGLEE SOLD.

WHAT ABOUT IT.

RACING IN ENGLAND.

COWRA J.C. WEIGHTS.

GREYHOUND RACING.

Harold Park Meetings.

CRICKET IN ENGLAND.

ICE HOCKEY.

The Sydney Morning Herald *of 20 June 1931 provided images relating to the Newtown 'battle', alongside other news photos of the day, including a view through the southern pylon of the Harbour Bridge and the papal banner to be presented to a scout group in Randwick, a suburb of Sydney.*

58 *Fascists open Sydney's bridge*

De Groot and the New Guard, 1932

WHILE THE COMMUNIST PARTY OF AUSTRALIA WAS GAINING POLITICAL GROUND DURING THE GREAT DEPRESSION, SO TOO WERE THEIR AVOWED ENEMIES. A MOVEMENT OSTENSIBLY FORMED TO OPPOSE THE THREAT OF COMMUNISM, THE NEW GUARD WAS EFFECTIVELY AUSTRALIA'S FASCIST PARTY OF THE 1930S.

In 1931 the New Guard formed units of a citizens' militia across the country, but it was particularly concerned about the left-wing politics of New South Wales Labor premier Jack Lang (1876–1975), which they feared would foster a communist takeover of the country. During the Depression, Lang had remained a popular leader in New South Wales as he focused on supporting the unemployed and workers, while refusing to repay interest on government loans to overseas banks. To the New Guard however, Lang's policies appeared to be more in line with socialism. The New Guard's membership had grown rapidly during the late 1920s, until they claimed to number 60,000 members, including many ex-servicemen who felt their war efforts were diminished by 'communists' such as Jack Lang.

Because the hated Jack Lang was to open the Sydney Harbour Bridge, the New Guard had threatened to disrupt proceedings. But Sydneysiders had invested a great deal of energy and anticipation into the arched bridge that they had watched slowly—and almost magically—come together from each side of the harbour. After several years of economic depression, by March 1932 the bridge had become a symbol not only of a modern Australian society, but also of the end of a period of significant hardship. The grand opening ceremony, scheduled for 19 March 1932, was not going to be derailed by anyone.

Intense security measures were put in place for the opening ceremony, but no-one could have predicted that an Irishman who was a uniformed war veteran, Francis de Groot, would ride up, cut the ribbon and steal Jack Lang's thunder. Although De Groot's actions were not the large-scale fascist riot that police were expecting, they had some impact. Rather than a celebratory headline that might have read 'Bridge Opened!', the Melbourne *Herald* led with 'New Guard Officer Cuts Bridge Ribbon'.

PHAR LAP OUT TO WIN — See Page 3

WEATHER FORECAST: Improving; southerly winds.

The Sun
DAILY AT DAWN
NEWS-PICTORIAL
WITH WHICH IS INCORPORATED
THE MORNING POST

No. 2968 | Registered at the G.P.O., Melbourne, for transmission by post as a newspaper. | MELBOURNE : MONDAY, MARCH 21, 1932 | (36 Pages) | 1½d.

NEW GUARD OFFICER "OPENS" BRIDGE WITH SWORD, AND IS ARRESTED

OPENING THE BRIDGE.—The Premier of N.S.W. (Mr. Lang) cutting the ribbon stretched across Sydney Harbor Bridge on Saturday. The ribbon was cut previously by Captain F. E. de Groot, of the New Guard.

CAPTAIN DE GROOT'S EXPLOIT in forestalling Mr. Lang by severing the ribbon with his sword formed a sensational incident in the official opening of Sydney Harbor Bridge on Saturday. Captain de Groot is shown being arrested by police officers after he had been dragged from horseback immediately after his unexpected coup. Right: A portrait of the officer, who made several ineffectual slashes at the ribbon before he cut it through.

SIR PHILIP GAME, Governor of N.S.W., reading the King's message from the official stand at the opening of the Harbor Bridge.

Newspapers were unexpectedly forced to report the disruption to the opening ceremony of the Sydney Harbour Bridge. This page of the Melbourne Sun News-Pictorial *must have seen some scrambling around press rooms and printing offices to mke last-minute changes.*

59 *A child of the modern world*

Radio sets and new technologies, 1932

IN JULY 1932, THE CONTROVERSIAL NEW SOUTH WALES PREMIER JACK LANG PRESIDED OVER THE OPENING OF ANOTHER AUSTRALIAN ICON, THE AUSTRALIAN BROADCASTING COMMISSION (ABC). AS RADIO TRANSMISSION TECHNOLOGY DEVELOPED, INCREASING NUMBERS OF AUSTRALIANS WERE RECEIVING THEIR NEWS ALMOST INSTANTANEOUSLY FROM RADIO SETS IN THEIR HOMES.

Despite the growing importance of radio, newspapers continued to remain popular. By the 1920s, developments in photography and printing meant more newsprint space could be devoted to intriguing and arresting images.

Front pages of the major newspapers now included photographs alongside increasingly bold headlines. The front-page formula of the bold headline and accompanying image arrived during the 1930s.

Not only did photographers now have a significant influence on what was being considered as news, but they also established their own news genre—photojournalism. Although not front page or headline news, 'human interest' stories and photographic studies became popular during the 1930s. This study of men in a Salvation Army home shows them listening intently to a 'child of the modern world'—a radio set that had been donated to the home.

Worried?—Consult the Stars

Week by week "The Sunday Sun" publishes a horoscope which is the guide of thousands of readers in their daily affairs—and on the racecourse!

BOOK YOUR "SUNDAY SUN" WITH YOUR NEWSAGENT.

The Daily Telegraph

MONDAY, APRIL 4, 1932

HERE'S A STRAIGHT TIP

Punters have learned to value the tips in the "Secrets of the Stable," published each week in "The Sunday Sun." They are tips that mean money to keen sportsmen.

BOOK YOUR "SUNDAY SUN" WITH YOUR NEWSAGENT.

ATTENTIVE, MEDITATIVE, REPOSEFULLY INQUIRING, as radio music blended its rich color, for the first time, into the softly glowing sunset of their life, old men of the Salvation Army Eventide Home, Collaroy, sat and listened. They welcomed the advent of a gay young child of the modern world. Sir Benjamin Fuller, on behalf of the A.B.C. Hospital Radio Fund, handed over the set.

Sydney's Daily Telegraph *of 4 April 1932 demonstrates the growing importance of photojournalism in this striking portrait of a group of men at the Collaroy Salvation Army Eventide Home listening intently to a radio.*

60 *A great shock to all Australians*

The death of Phar Lap, 1932

ON 6 APRIL 1932, AUSTRALIANS AROUND THE COUNTRY PICKED UP NEWSPAPERS ANNOUNCING THE SUDDEN DEATH OF A CHERISHED ICON. LIKE THE CRICKETER DON BRADMAN, A HORSE CALLED PHAR LAP HAD PROVIDED A MUCH-NEEDED DISTRACTION DURING THE DARK DAYS OF THE GREAT DEPRESSION.

Part of the popular interest in Phar Lap derived from his unmatched statistics—thirty-seven wins from fifty-one starts. But his legendary status also grew from the way he began racing, as an ungainly looking 'no hoper'. Perhaps his greatest triumph was his performance in the United States, where he had been taken to run in the lucrative Agua Caliente Handicap on 20 March 1932. Phar Lap came from second last to overtake the entire field, and then he staved off a final challenge to win. It seemed the entire Australian nation had been glued to their radio sets and celebrated Phar Lap's win in unison.

Shortly after, however, Phar Lap suddenly died. Initial reports suspected 'colic' or 'acute indigestion', but autopsies revealed no firm reason for the racehorse's death. Rumours and theories that he may have been poisoned quickly appeared. Many suspected 'the Americans' or that Mafia connections wanted to stop Phar Lap from racing again in the United States.

Just days after his death the skeleton of the great racehorse was already earmarked by the Institute of Anatomy for preservation for 'historic interest' and 'the study of comparative anatomy'. Phar Lap's pelt was also preserved, stuffed and displayed inside a glass case. Apart from finding an unusually large heart (which itself added to the legend) his preservation may not have greatly aided anatomical studies, but it did mean the mystery around Phar Lap's sudden death could later be 'solved'. Recent tests of his hair revealed the horse had ingested a large dose of arsenic just before his death. The early rumours appear to have been correct.

A great shock to all Australians

LARGEST NET SALE IN THE STATE — 182,293 DAILY

WEATHER FORECAST: UNSETTLED

The Herald

Ninety-third Year

No. 17,125 MELBOURNE, WEDNESDAY EVENING, APRIL 6, 1932 Price, 1½d. (18 PAGES)

GARNISHEE ACT VALID | PHAR LAP DEAD

HIGH COURT DECISION

Majority 4 to 2 Against Lang's Appeal

REASONS TO BE GIVEN LATER

From Our Special Representative

SYDNEY, Wednesday. — The High Court, by a majority of four to two, today held that the Financial Agreements Enforcement Act is valid.

The dissentients were the Chief Justice (Sir Frank Gavan Duffy) and Mr Justice Evatt.

As soon as the case was called, the Chief Justice made the following statement:—

"The Court has considered this case, and has reached a conclusion which I shall now state. The Members of the Court will give their reasons on a later date.

"Justice Evatt and I are of the opinion that Part 2 (enforcement against State revenue) of the Financial Agreements Enforcement Act 1932 is invalid.

"Justices Rich, Starke, Dixon and McTiernan are of the opinion that Part 2 (enforcement against State revenue) of the Financial Agreements Enforcement Act 1932 is a valid law of the Commonwealth, and that no declaration of invalidity should be made as claimed by the writ."

The next step in the Commonwealth's action against the New South Wales Premier (Mr Lang) will be the issue of a proclamation empowering the Commonwealth to seize certain New South Wales revenues—in the present instance, income tax.

FEDERAL MINISTERS MEET

When news of the judgment was received in Melbourne today, a hasty meeting of Ministers was held in the rooms of the Assistant Treasurer (Mr Bruce). Later, Mr Bruce conferred with the leader of the United Country Party (Dr. Earle Page) and Treasury officials.

Mr Bruce said that he could not say when the proclamation would be issued. He admitted that it was ready, and that, should the Government desire to issue it this afternoon, there were sufficient Ministers in Melbourne for a meeting of the Executive Council to be held.

The Governor-General, who must sign the proclamation, or appoint a deputy to do so, is at present not in Canberra, but it is understood that the Government has already been in touch with him. The Prime Minister (Mr Lyons) is today opening the agricultural show at Bathurst.

"I am delighted with the Court's decision," said Mr Lyons, on hearing the news.

"It is entirely satisfactory, and has vindicated the opinion of the Attorney-General, who has always maintained that the Act was valid."

The Federal Cabinet is to meet in Melbourne tomorrow afternoon.

FEDERAL SEIZURE PLANS READY

CANBERRA, Wednesday.—Officials of the Attorney-General's Department were elated when the news of the High Court's decision reached Canberra by telephone a few minutes after the judgment had been delivered.

In Canberra the judgment is regarded as a personal triumph for both the Attorney-General (Mr Latham) and the Solicitor-General (Mr Knowles), who collaborated in drafting the Bill, which was admittedly a daring innovation in ...

... members of the Court being equally divided.

If the High Court refused to grant Mr Lang a certificate he might still apply to the Privy Council for leave to appeal, but this could not be given unless the Privy Council decided in the first case that the High Court's decision—that the matter was "inter se"—was bad. The Privy Council would then decide whether or not it would give Mr Lang leave to appeal.

THE PROCLAMATION

Mr Lyons Anxious to Sign It

Question of Appeal

S.A. ADVICE TO N.S.W.

"Should Accept the Inevitable"

GOOD RAINS IN N.S.W.

NEWFOUNDLAND MOB

Storms Parliament House

See page 17

Phar Lap—His Last "Portrait"

PHAR LAP—HIS LAST "PORTRAIT": An exclusive study of the handsome head of Phar Lap, taken on the Agua Caliente racecourse, in Mexico, a few weeks ago.

STATE MINISTRY TO BE ASSAILED

Move Next Week

CHALLENGE ON RELIEF ACT

By Our Political Correspondent

Before the State Parliament opened today it was revealed that a definite challenge to the Hogan Government will be made next week, on a Bill to provide Supply for the remainder of the financial year.

The present intention is that the attack should be made in the form of an amendment to reduce the amount by £1.

THE United Australia Party, which met yesterday, discussed proposals for the launching of a direct censure motion, but it was felt that the challenge on Supply would be equally effective.

The United Country Party will be invited to join in the attack.

WORK FOR SUSTENANCE

The Government will be assailed on its administration of the Unemployment Relief Act, particularly in regard to its failure to give effect to the "work for sustenance" provision.

The opposition will declare that the Ministry, at the behest of outside bodies, deliberately flouted the will of Parliament. The expenditure of the whole of the money raised by taxation on the dole is regarded seriously, particularly since Parliament specifically directed that municipalities should be empowered to demand work for sustenance.

The charge will be made that the relief fund has been frittered away with-

ELECTION ISSUE

It was freely asserted in the lobbies today that the Government is anxious to go to the country at the earliest possible moment. This being the case, it will welcome a challenge on unemployment relief, making it one of the chief election issues.

The executive of the A.L.P. will consider the question of endorsing candidates tomorrow night. In the event of an emergency election it has the power to ...

BUSINESS MEN AT OTTAWA

Britain Favors Sending Advisers

LABOR DELEGATES TOO

Herald Special Representative

LONDON, April 5.

The British Government is in favor of attaching business advisers to the British delegation at the Ottawa Economic Conference. It is communicating with the Dominions on the matter.

THE Dominions Secretary (Mr Thomas) indicated the Government's attitude in reply to a question by Capt. P. MacDonald (Cons.) in the House of Commons.

Answering a question by Mr D. R. Grenfell (Lab.) Mr Thomas said that this was equally applicable to representatives of organised Labor.

CHOSEN BY GOVERNMENT

Britain's business men at the Ottawa Conference will be nominated by a joint panel of the Chamber of Shipping, the Federation of British Industries and the Associated Chambers of Commerce but, with a view to preventing dictation, the representatives will be selected by the Government.

They will act in an advisory capacity and will have no votes.

The Government hopes thus to prevent unlimited outside interests attending the Ottawa Conference for the purpose of lobbying.

It is expected that the Dominions will make similar appointments.

In Other Pages

Leader: "The High Court's Momentous Decision" ..	6
Sporting	2, 3
World Cables	7
Hiking Notes	8
Woman's World	10
Serial; Crosswords	12
Property Section	13
Radio Supplement	14, 15
Finance, Commerce, Stocks	16
Broadcasting; Shipping ..	17
Pictures in Back Page (Tomorrow: Investors' Guide; Touring Section)	

ABSOLUTION BY TELEPHONE

Bishop Blesses Dying Girl

Fog Delays Shipping

Lieut.-Governor At Opening Of State Parliament

The Lieutenant-Governor (Sir William Irvine) inspecting the guard of honor provided by the Air Force when State Parliament was opened this afternoon.

CHAMPION HORSE DIES OF ENTERITIS

Sudden Collapse

TRAINER STAGGERED BY LOSS

Herald Special Representative

Menlo Park, California.—Tuesday, 3.48 p.m.

Phar Lap, the Australian champion race-horse, died today.

Dr. Nielson, the Australian veterinary surgeon, conducted an autopsy, and certified that death was due to acute enteritis.

He and Dr. Caesar Masoero, of San Francisco, found that the stomach was highly inflamed and perforated, and agreed that the fatal illness had begun at least two days before the horse's death.

Dr. Nielson said that he believed that alfalfa or barley covered with dew in the stable yard had been eaten by Phar Lap and had caused poisoning because it was not properly prepared.

[Early messages gave the cause of death as colic and indigestion.]

TRAINER WOODCOCK HEARTBROKEN

PHAR LAP'S sudden end, after a successful operation for hoof trouble, staggered his trainer, Tom Woodcock, who is heartbroken over his loss.

The horse was off his feed early today. His illness developed rapidly, and the services of several veterinary surgeons were called in, but they were unable to save him. In a few hours he was dead.

Phar Lap had been brought up to the Tanforan track at Menlo Park, a suburb of San Francisco, just south of the Golden Gate city.

Dr. William Neilson, Phar Lap's special veterinary surgeon, last week performed a delicate hoof operation to cleanse a tiny crack which had been bothering the horse, following the bruise he suffered from a stone while training for the Agua Caliente Handicap.

Until today he was rounding finely into shape, and it was settled that he would run in the £5000 Handicap late this month.

Tom Woodcock, his trainer, expected Phar Lap to be at the top of his form by Friday or Saturday this week. He was getting very light exercise daily.

A special shoe had been designed for him for running in the coming race.

Woodcock was heartbroken when the great horse died at 2.30 p.m. today.

Everyone concerned in the care of the horse was carefully questioned and the whole of the circumstances examined before news of Phar Lap's death was announced. An hour elapsed before the farm telephone was allowed to be used to send a message into San Francisco.

Everyone concerned appeared to be stunned. "Yes, that's right. He's dead." This, with a sob, was all that could be learned by inquirers over the telephone for half an hour.

FOOD EXAMINED FOR POISON

Mr D. J. Davis had left Menlo Park for Los Angeles, and nobody wished to say anything until he could be found and told of his misfortune.

Early this morning the horse was slightly off his feed, and in the middle of the forenoon developed a high temperature.

Mr Neilson called in other veterinary surgeons, who worked hard, but they were unable to overcome the impaction (lodgment in the intestines).

Little, if any, American food had been given to Phar Lap since his arrival, according to the stable staff.

Rumors spread all over America that the horse had been poisoned, but these were immediately emphatically discounted by Dr. Nielson, Woodcock, and Elliot.

To remove all suspicion, Frank Love, police chief of Menlo Park, and Edward Farrell, police chief of Atherton, announced that they would have Phar Lap's oats examined.

About 20 sacks, the remainder of the original consignment brought from Australia, were stacked outside the horse's stall.

Phar Lap's illness was early kept a jealous secret.

Even a party of visiting journalists this morning was kept in the dark, but when they were refused permission to see Phar Lap they became suspicious, and an investigation began.

It was the afternoon before an accurate guess could be made as to the real trouble, and the query was put directly.

Members of the stable, with tears coursing down their cheeks, then confessed that Phar Lap was dead.

PIKE SHOCKED AND GRIEVED

Phar Lap's Jockey

SYDNEY, Wednesday.—Jim Pike, who rode Phar Lap to so many victories, heard the news at a barber's shop at South Kensington.

When he was told "Phar Lap is dead" he almost collapsed with shock and grief.

He sought details as to the cause of death. He could hardly speak for emotion.

"He was the greatest horse I have ever known," he said. "He was giving Australia the best advertisement it has ever had, and now this must happen."

"Phar Lap had everything before him in the States—he would have cleaned up every race he entered. What a shame he is dead.

"I formed a great attachment for him. I was only his rider, but one could not help liking such a marvellous horse. He will live in racing history forever. Kids growing up now will remember him when they are old men and will talk about him.

"They should bring him back to Australia and place his remains in the Museum."

Pike said that he felt sorry for Mr Telford.

Other References in Pages 5 and 11. Pictures in Back Page.

TRADE BALANCE

£26,162,000 On Right Side

8 MONTHS' FIGURES

The latest Commonwealth trade figures, in their bearing upon the financing of Australia's loan obligations in London and New York, present a very favorable aspect.

For the eight months to February 29 exports (including bullion and specie) exceed imports by £26,162,000.

This is within 2 millions of the estimated total amount required to meet interest on the external debt for the current financial year. The excess in outward trade includes a merchandise balance of £22,050,000.

40 PER CENT. DROP

The favorable merchandise balance accumulated within the past four months totals 10 millions, and the trade of the remaining four months of the fiscal year appears likely to show a similar result.

Imports for the eight months, compared with the figures for the corresponding period of the 1930-31 year, show a drop of 40 per cent., the totals being £28,277,000 against £47,236,000.

The value of merchandise imports is only 60 per cent. of that recorded for the eight months' period of 1930-31, machinery being only 33 p.c., alcoholic liquors 35 p.c., tobacco 37 p.c., jewellery and fancy goods 40 p.c., manufactured metals 46 p.c., leather 43 p.c., earthenware 49 p.c., and oils 53 p.c.

EXPORT INCREASES

Exports of merchandise for the eight months of 1931-32 totalled £64,117,000 in Australian currency, equivalent to £49,989,000 in sterling, compared with £58,272,000 in Australian currency, equivalent to £52,262,000 sterling, for the corresponding period of 1930-1.

Increases are shown this year in exports of wool, wheat, flour, butter, mutton and lamb, sugar, wine and tallow.

(Details in Page 18).

TODAY'S MARKETS

STERLING RATE: New York-London, 3.77¼ dol.

STOCK EXCHANGE: Further rises in Commonwealth bonds on High Court decision in "garnishee" case. Other sections slightly easier on small sales.

METALS: Market weakening again. Falls: Gold, 6d. to £5/9/5 an oz.; spot spelter, 5/ a ton; lead, 1/3; spot tin, 42/6.

WHEAT: Business small. City parcels, 3/1¼ to 3/2 a bushel.

PRODUCE: Potato prices, 5/ to 10/ a ton lower. Up to £15 a ton asked for best onions.

(Details in Page 18.)

BOND PRICES RISE

Favorable Effect On 'Change

Although a decision in favor of the Federal Government had been anticipated in recent market dealings, the judgment of the High Court upholding the validity of the Financial Agreement Enforcement Act led to a further rise in Commonwealth loans on the Stock Exchange today.

At the morning and noon calls rises ranging from 2/6 to 6/3 per cent. were recorded in nine of the Commonwealth consolidated 4 per cent. issues, with buyers supplying a strong increase in support for the market.

Because of limited offerings by sellers, these improvements were effected on comparatively small volumes of turnover, sales at the two calls totalling only £11,000.

The noon market closed on a very firm tone.

STOP PRESS

SUNBURY RACES

BETTING—SUNBURY PURSE

5/2 BEAU JOLAIS, 9/2 Cylight, 8/1 Great Bear — Evens to 15/1 others. Started 4.24.

LAST SUNBURY RACE

STARDOM (7/1), 1; Prince Rooks (7/1), 2; Present Again (3/1), 3. 4/4 to 10/1 others.

Non-starters: Lady Savanex, Del Riccio.

(Other Sunbury race results page 5)

ALBURY RACES

FLYING HANDICAP

TINWALD (5/1) 1, Baire 2, Lady Lavington 3.

LAST ALBURY RACE

EL COUCHE (3/2) 1, Poactherse 8/1 2, Ada Wood (5/2) 3

(Other Albury race results Page 5)

TODAY'S TEMPERATURES

Recorded up to noon

	Max.	Min.
Melbourne	71.1	52.2
Sydney	72.7	64
Canberra	74.9	52.2
Adelaide	66.8	54.7

On 7 April 1932, news stands around the country held placards with the simple message 'He's Dead'. The next day the Melbourne Herald, the Sun News-Pictorial and other newspapers ran large photographs of Phar Lap on the front page, recording the headline news of the day and as commemorative souvenirs.

PHAR LAP'S DEATH — LATEST POISON THEORIES. — Page 2

WEATHER FORECAST: Cloudy and unsettled.

The Sun NEWS-PICTORIAL

DAILY AT DAWN

WITH WHICH IS INCORPORATED

THE MORNING POST

No. 2982 | Registered at the G.P.O. Melbourne, for transmission by post as a newspaper. | MELBOURNE · THURSDAY, APRIL 7, 1932 | (32 Pages) | 1½d.

DEATH OF PHAR LAP :: STATE PARLIAMENT REOPENS

PHAR LAP, AUSTRALIA'S RACING IDOL, died suddenly of acute enteritis at Menlo Park, 50 miles south of San Francisco, on Tuesday. This picture shows the great gelding as Melbourne remembers him, with W. Elliott up and T. Woodcock, who trained him in America, leading him, after one of his many turf victories.

THE LIEUTENANT-GOVERNOR (Sir William Irvine) leaving Parliament House yesterday after he had opened the new session of the Legislative Council and the Legislative Assembly. Sir Frank Clarke (left), President of the Legislative Council, escorted him down the steps.

Newspapers marked the death of Phar Lap with commemorative images like this one. In 1930, when Phar Lap won the Melbourne Cup, he also won a race on three other days in that year's Spring Racing Carnival—an unequalled achievement.

The downfall of 'The Big Fella' 61

Jack Lang's government dismissed, 1932

THERE HAVE BEEN SEVERAL DISMISSALS OF GOVERNMENTS IN AUSTRALIAN HISTORY. IN 1932, THE GOVERNOR OF NEW SOUTH WALES, SIR PHILLIP GAME, DISMISSED JOHN THOMAS 'JACK' LANG'S GOVERNMENT, WHICH HAD BEEN IN OFFICE SINCE THEIR LANDSLIDE ELECTION IN OCTOBER 1930. GAME APPOINTED THE LEADER OF THE UNITED AUSTRALIA PARTY, BERTRAM STEVENS (1889–1973), AS PREMIER.

Known as the 'Big Fella' because of his large frame and powerful speaking skills, Lang ran his own economic agenda for the State of New South Wales during the Depression. Appropriately called the Lang Plan, it ran counter to the Premiers' Plan that the federal and the other state governments had agreed in 1930 and were pursuing in order to assist the Australian economy. Lang favoured not paying overseas debts until the economy improved, but in 1932, after Lang's stance had split the Labor Party and contributed to the fall of Scullin's federal Labor government, the new Joseph Lyons led United Australia Party government passed the *Financial Agreements Enforcement Act*, requiring the states to pay back their debts.

Lang insisted this would mean New South Wales government employees could not be paid, which would put the federal government in breach of the 1833 *Slavery Abolition Act*. Lang then took all of the state's funds from its bank accounts and held them in cash so the federal government could not access the money.

At this point the New South Wales governor decided Lang's actions were illegal and dismissed him from office on 13 May 1932. The Labor Party lost heavily in the election of 11 June, when Stevens' United Australia Party and Country Party coalition won government.

Lang later wrote a book about the politics of his time in office, aptly called *The Turbulent Years*.

CITY FORECAST: Cloudy, and Moderate.

PICK-ME-UP SAUCE — Makes all the Difference

The Daily Telegraph

WITH WHICH ARE INCORPORATED THE "DAILY GUARDIAN" AND THE "DAILY PICTORIAL"

Vol. 2.—No. 77 SATURDAY, MAY 14, 1932 PRICE, 1½d

TO-DAY:— "The LAW of the LARIAT" "THE WORLD'S NEWS"

LANG DISMISSED—NOW FOR ELECTION

SIR PHILIP GAME, Governor of N.S.W., who dismissed Mr. Lang.

GOVERNMENT PROVED GUILTY OF BREAKING THE LAW

STEVENS SWORN IN AS PREMIER

ELECTION IS LIKELY IN THREE TO FIVE WEEKS

FEDERAL GOVT. WILL HELP N.S. WALES TO RECOVERY

GOVR. ACTS ON OWN INITIATIVE

Yesterday afternoon the Lang Government was dismissed from office. An election will follow shortly.

It had been guilty of having issued a circular instructing its officers to break the Federal Government's Enforcement Act.

The State Governor, Sir Philip Game, dismissed the Premier after Mr. Lang had visited him, and had refused to resign.

Thus ended the regime which took office in 1930.

Mr. B. S. B. Stevens, Leader of the Opposition, was sworn-in as Premier last evening, having accepted the invitation of the Governor to form a Ministry.

His Cabinet will probably be announced at the beginning of next week.

It is thought that an election will be held within a few weeks. It is not expected that Parliament will meet before the election. Mr. Stevens will ask the Governor for a dissolution, which will be granted.

The dismissal of the Government will at once ease the position between the Federal and the State Governments, as N.S.W. now returns to the Premiers' Plan.

The attachment proclamations will be reviewed at a special meeting of Federal Ministers this morning. As Premier Stevens is committed to the Premiers' Plan, relief is certain.

The Federal Government will afford him every help in his task of restoring N.S.W. affairs.

Taxaxtion papers, both Federal and State, which were locked away by Mr. Lang, will be made available by the new Government on Monday morning.

The Federal Parliament, whose business for the current session has consisted almost entirely of legislation to deal with the N.S.W. crisis, will adjourn on Friday next.

A London message states that Sir Philip Game did not consult the British Government, but acted entirely on his own initiative.

MR. STEVENS, leaving Government House after his interview with Sir Philip Game.

CAREER OF THE GOVERNMENT

LEGAL HISTORY OF THE CRISIS

FEDERAL A.L.P. ACTIVITY

STADIUM

AFTER TWO YEARS

NO DISCUSSION BY A.L.P.

MEETING MONDAY TO CONSIDER POSITION

SWORN IN ALONE

GOVERNOR'S PART

LYONS' RELIEF

NEW HEADQUARTERS

LANG PREPARED

EFFECT ON FED. PARLIAMENT

SESSION MAY END ON FRIDAY

DEPARTURE

GYMNASTIC GOATS

:: THE CIRCULAR THAT WRECKED LANG'S GOVERNMENT ::

"the Government, it is the decision of Cabinet, for the guidance of, and as an instruction to, all Servants of the State and of State Statutory Bodies, in order that the essential and social services of the State of New South Wales may be carried on, that the method of collecting revenue and paying same shall be as outlined in the Treasury Circular of 13th April - Subject: "Collections and Expenditure - procedure to be followed" - and shall continue to be as directed by Treasury circular under Government instruction from time to time."

BECAUSE IT ADVISED State officials to disobey the law, the circular, of which a fragment is reproduced above, cost the Lang Government its existence. It was sent out by the Premier's Department, and demanded that members of the Public Service should deliberately flout the provisions of the Financial Agreement Enforcement Act.

The Daily Telegraph *of 14 May 1932 suggests a sense of relief that the political stalemate Lang had created was to lead to an early election in New South Wales.*

Just not cricket 62

The bodyline series, 1932–1933

SPORTING HEADLINES ARE PROMINENT IN AUSTRALIAN NEWSPAPER HISTORIES. THE INFAMOUS BODYLINE TEST CRICKET SERIES IN AUSTRALIA IN 1932–1933 BECAME THE FOCUS OF MANY FRONT PAGES, PARTICULARLY WHEN ARGUMENTS OVER THE TACTIC OF BOWLING SHORT-PITCHED DELIVERIES WENT BEYOND THE CRICKET FIELDS AND BECAME A DIPLOMATIC INCIDENT BETWEEN ARCH CRICKETING RIVALS AUSTRALIA AND ENGLAND.

After the English lost the 1930 Ashes series, largely because of the dominance of Don Bradman's batting, the team developed a plan to bowl to what they perceived to be Bradman's only weakness—the fast, rising ball on the leg side and aimed at the batsman's body. The tactic worked well, as most batsmen ducked and weaved when faced with these deliveries and failed to score runs. England regained the Ashes.

Yet most Australians found the tactic unsporting, and the Australian captain, Bill Woodfull (1897–1965), refused to use similar tactics in retaliation. In the third test in Adelaide, Woodfull, who had been hit by leg-side deliveries several times, famously told the English team manager 'There are two teams out there, one is playing cricket.'

While the English claimed the Australians were cowards and over-reacting to valid fast-bowling tactics, the Australian crowds jeered the English team and nearly rioted. Although the laws of cricket were eventually modified to reduce the effects of such bowling, the memory of the bodyline series continued to live in the minds of Australians.

The term was apparently first coined by a thrifty journalist who, in trying to keep the costs of his international telegram down, shortened 'in the line of the body' to 'bodyline'.

NET WEEKLY SALES LARGER THAN THOSE OF ANY OTHER NEWSPAPER IN AUSTRALIA

FINAL EXTRA

THE SUN

ABOVE ALL FOR AUSTRALIA

CLOUDY, SULTRY AND UNSETTLED

No. 7198 SYDNEY: TUESDAY, JANUARY 24, 1933 PRICE 1½d 'Phone: BO 333

Willing To Cancel Tests—M.C.C.'s. Offer

"CONFIDENCE IN OUR CAPTAIN"

REPLY TO BOARD

Spirited Defence Of Sportsmanship

CABLE 'DEPLORED'

("Sun" Special)

LONDON, Monday.

"WE, the Marylebone Club, deplore your cable and deprecate the opinion that there has been unsportsmanlike play. We have the fullest confidence in our captain, team, and managers, and are convinced that they would do nothing to infringe the laws of cricket, of the spirit of the game."

SUCH are the opening passages of the M.C.C. Committee's cabled reply to the Australian Board of Control's protest against "body-line" bowling.

THE concluding, but one of the most vital, passages of the cable says that if the Board of Control consider it desirable to cancel the remainder of the programme, the M.C.C. "would consent with great reluctance."

Lord Ullswater, wearing a top hat and a frock coat, was one of the early arrivals at the meeting at the M.C.C.

The Speedster

Larwood bowling at top.

Solemn Atmosphere

Historic Meeting

For Synod

WORLD ECONOMY

AND WAR DEBTS

Scope of New Talks

U.S. WISHES

("Sun" Special)

LONDON, Monday.

MR. ROOSEVELT wishes it to be understood that discussion of the war debts question with Britain must be concurrent with and conditional on discussion of world economic problems.

Mr. H. L. Stimson

(Continued on Page 12)

FLEW WELL

Lame Duck Amendment Carried

U.S. CONSTITUTION

("Sun" Special)

WASHINGTON, Monday.

ON THE "WET" WAY

FAVORS RUM RUNNER

New Decision of U.S. Court

("Sun" Special)

WASHINGTON, Monday.

THE U.S. Supreme Court ruled to-day that British or Canadian suspected rum-runners cannot legally be boarded, searched, or seized by coastguards when more than an hour's sailing distance from the shore.

U.S. Chief Justice, C. E. Hughes

STERLING UP

Reactions To New War Debts Proposals

("Sun" Special)

NEW YORK, Monday.

THE SUN STOP-PRESS

NEWCASTLE v. S. AUSTRALIA

OUTCOME STILL DOUBTFUL

Irish Election Forecasts

WIDE TIPS

(Published in "The Times")

LONDON, Monday.

Mr. Cosgrave

Gigantic Pushes

Cosgrave's Message

PRESS VIEWS

Board Should Accept Olive Branch

(Published in "The Times")

"Dignified Spirit"

Still Submerged

Trusting Captain

Leg Theory Film

Fender Glad

Yearling From N.Z.

Sydney's Sun *presents one of the many bodyline headlines in Australian newspapers during the 1932–33 test cricket season. Faced with the threat of the English team withdrawing and a British boycott of Australian trade, Australians were irate that the Australian Cricket Board was forced to withdraw its accusations of 'unsportsmanlike behaviour' before the fourth test.*

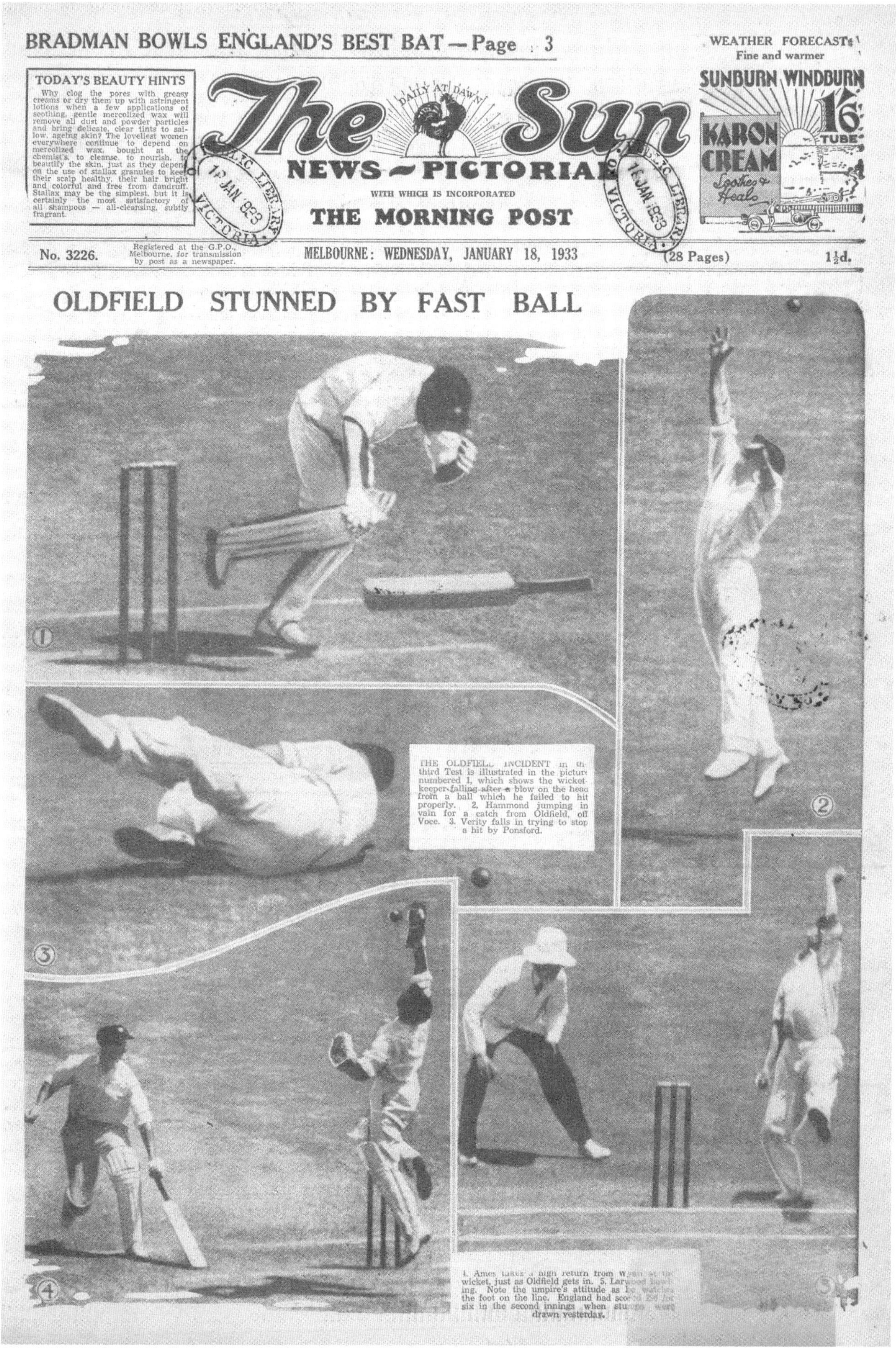

BRADMAN BOWLS ENGLAND'S BEST BAT — Page 3

WEATHER FORECAST: Fine and warmer

TODAY'S BEAUTY HINTS

Why clog the pores with greasy creams or dry them up with astringent lotions when a few applications of soothing, gentle mercolized wax will remove all dust and powder particles and bring delicate, clear tints to sallow, ageing skin? The loveliest women everywhere continue to depend on mercolized wax, bought at the chemist's, to cleanse, to nourish, to beautify the skin, just as they depend on the use of stallax granules to keep their scalp healthy, their hair bright and colorful and free from dandruff. Stallax may be the simplest, but it is certainly the most satisfactory of all shampoos — all-cleansing, subtly fragrant.

The Sun

DAILY AT DAWN

NEWS-PICTORIAL

WITH WHICH IS INCORPORATED

THE MORNING POST

SUNBURN WINDBURN

KARON CREAM

Soothes & Heals

1'6 TUBE

No. 3226. Registered at the G.P.O., Melbourne, for transmission by post as a newspaper. MELBOURNE: WEDNESDAY, JANUARY 18, 1933 (28 Pages) 1½d.

OLDFIELD STUNNED BY FAST BALL

THE OLDFIELD INCIDENT in the third Test is illustrated in the picture numbered 1, which shows the wicket-keeper falling after a blow on the head from a ball which he failed to hit properly. 2. Hammond jumping in vain for a catch from Oldfield, off Voce. 3. Verity falls in trying to stop a hit by Ponsford.

4. Ames takes a high return from W[illegible] wicket, just as Oldfield gets in. 5. Lar[illegible] ing. Note the umpire's attitude as [illegible] the foot on the line. England had sco[illegible] six in the second innings when stu[illegible] drawn yesterday.

Melbourne's Sun News-Pictorial *of 18 January 1933 shows the benefits of the improved newspaper technology, which allowed the inclusion of dramatic photos of the effects of bodyline bowling.*

63 Australia's wild west

Race riots in Kalgoorlie, 1934

THE MINING TOWN OF KALGOORLIE IN WESTERN AUSTRALIA HAD BEEN REGARDED AS A WILD WEST TOWNSHIP SINCE GOLD HAD BEEN DISCOVERED THERE IN 1893. LIKE OTHER MINING AREAS ACROSS THE COUNTRY, IT ATTRACTED MANY FOREIGN WORKERS, WHO MANAGED TO ENTER THE COUNTRY DESPITE THE OPERATION OF THE WHITE AUSTRALIA POLICY. ITALIANS AND OTHER SOUTHERN EUROPEANS FORMED PROMINENT COMMUNITIES IN KALGOORLIE DURING THE 1930S.

On the Australia Day weekend of 1934, a British miner died in a fight with an Italian, and rumours quickly spread that he had been murdered. The day after the funeral many people were gathered in town and drinking at wakes when a rock was thrown through the window of a migrant-run business, sparking off a night of rioting. Several buildings owned by southern Europeans were targeted and burned to the ground.

When miners declared a strike until all miners who had not been naturalised as Australian citizens were ejected from the mines, another night of rioting followed—involving non-miners as well. Two men were killed as the crowd rampaged through the largely migrant settlement of Dingbat Flat, targeting Italians and Slavs.

Rioting continued for a second night and, after two deaths, ceased. Order was restored several days later with promises by Kalgoorlie mining directors that a policy of 'British Preference' would be enforced in the mines—although they did not promise to dismiss all migrants currently employed as they needed the labour. The miners agreed to return to work after being given assurances that an English language test would be 'more carefully' administered to any future migrants—leaving it unclear how much the riots were based in racism, competition for work or simply the rage of a drunken mob.

Even after the riots, mine directors continued to seek the cheapest labour available, keeping the trade unions busy monitoring the companies' often corrupt hiring practices that still favoured offering work to the lowest bidder. At the same time, the local Returned Soldiers Leagues, which were eager to align the White Australia policy with 'what they had fought for' in the war, continued to publicly criticise non-British and non-Australian workers. This tension between employers encouraging the hiring of hard-working and cheap migrants, and workers who saw migrants as a threat to their jobs, created a contradictory situation that was typical of Australia's general attitude to migration and migrants for many years to come.

OPPOSITE The editor of The West Australian *on 30 January 1934 was outraged by the Kalgoorlie riots and the embarrassment resulting from international exposure.*

MOB VENGEANCE.

GOLDFIELDS ANTI-FOREIGN RIOTS.

1,000 MEN AMOK.

BUILDINGS LOOTED AND BURNT.

ESTIMATED DAMAGE £30,000.

A wild outbreak of mob vengeance against the foreign community in Kalgoorlie last night, later extending to Boulder, resulted in the wrecking, looting and burning of several buildings occupied or owned by foreigners. The damage is estimated at £30,000.

The cause of the outbreak was the death yesterday of George Edward Jordan from a fractured skull following an altercation with an Italian barman of the foreign-owned Home From Home Hotel in Hannan-street on Sunday night.

A mob of about 100 men gathered outside the hotel yesterday evening and, after a stone had been thrown through the bar window by a boy of 15, the building was raided and ruthlessly wrecked in an orgy of riotous passion which increased with the gradual strengthening of the mob to over 1,000 men.

Once started on a career of destruction and looting, the mob lost all control and raided other foreign premises, the wrecked buildings being set on fire, the police attacked and the fire brigade obstructed.

From Kalgoorlie the rioters turned their attention to Boulder, and, having commandeered trams and motor cars, continued their wrecking and burning there.

Before the mob dispersed shortly before 1 o'clock this morning, three hotels, a wine saloon, a two-storey boarding house, a brick club building, and 11 shops were either burnt to the ground or wrecked.

KALGOORLIE, Jan. 30.—To avenge the death of George Edward Jordan, who died in the Kalgoorlie Government Hospital at 4 o'clock yesterday morning from a fractured skull following an altercation with Cauldio Mattaboni, a barman at the Home from Home Hotel, at the western end of Hannan-street, Kalgoorlie, a body of men took the law into their own hands about 8 o'clock yesterday evening and commenced anti-foreign demonstrations reminiscent of the riots of 1919, when all foreigners were evicted from Kalgoorlie and Boulder following the death of a young man named Northwood, who was stabbed by a European.

The demonstrations rapidly developed into an orgy of rioting when about 100 men raided the Home From Home Hotel and began wrecking and looting. As the mob gradually increased to over 1,000, the field of destruction widened to include many other foreign premises, including shops, and several buildings were set alight and razed to the ground. The police were powerless to control the mob, which, later in the night, continued its wrecking, burning and pillaging at Boulder, the toll of damage being estimated at £30,000.

The western end of Hannan-street for the past few years has been mostly populated with foreigners, who have made the Home From Home Hotel, conducted by R. Gianatti, the Kalgoorlie Wine Saloon, and the All Nations Boarding House (on the opposite side of the street) their rendezvous.

Early Rumours Disregarded.

Rumours spread through Kalgoorlie today that an attempt would be made to avenge Jordan's death, but little credence was given to them, although the proprietors of the Home From Home Hotel, the Kalgoorlie Wine Saloon, and the All Nations Boarding House are stated to have received definite warning that an attack would be made on their premises.

The hotel and the wine saloon, which are within 100 yards of each other, opened as usual for business yesterday evening, but a few minutes before eight o'clock a body of men gathered outside the hotel. The first intimation of any trouble was the gathering crowd. After a few minutes' silence, a stone was thrown (by a 15-year-old boy, it is stated) through the window of the front bar of the hotel, which is a two-storey stone building with about 20 rooms. There were several foreigners in the bar, but they quickly disappeared through the rear of the premises.

Signal for the Assault.

The first stone was the signal for the assault, and a mob of young men, about 100 strong, swarmed through the front door. A crash of falling bottles followed. The bar counter was vaulted and choice spirits and wines, including bottles of champagne, were gathered up by some of the men or swept to the ground with a resounding crash by the more excitable. The fixtures of the bar were torn down, chairs were used to batter in mirrors and pictures, and advertisements were dragged from the walls. All the rooms on the ground floor were dismantled and furniture, including chairs, tables and settees, were broken by the ever-increasing mob. When the ground floor rooms were completely wrecked, the advance guard of the rioters rushed up the stairs and there repeated the attack upon the bedrooms and sitting room. Curtains were torn down from one of the front upstairs rooms opening on to a verandah which overhung the street, and one of the crowd, with a bucket of methylated spirit, poured some on to the curtains and pieces of broken chairs in an attempt to fire the premises. The material flamed for a time and lit up the whole of the front room but failed to ignite the building.

Liquor Pillaged.

Downstairs the wrecking had continued, and, from the roadway, which was beginning to run with broached casks of beer and bottles of wine and spirits, stones, empty bottles and all kinds of missiles were hurled through the broken front windows and doors. Men broke into the cellar and casks of beer were carried into the street, where they were opened or carried bodily away. The evidences of spoil could be seen on many men, whose shirts were filled with bottles.

Having thoroughly wrecked the hotel, the crowd, now about 1,000 strong, and reinforced with many sightseers, including women and children, turned its attention to the Kalgoorlie Wine Saloon, but not before the till of the hotel had been taken into the street and smashed open. There were only a few pounds in silver in the till, and the coins were eagerly pounced upon as they rolled into the gutter.

Wine Saloon Afire.

The Kalgoorlie Wine Saloon was a wood and iron building with a frontage of 120 feet, with the whole fronted with plate glass. Here, too, bottles and stones were hurled through the glass, which broke with a resounding crash, and 100 or more men forced their way into the front bar, where the cash box and the contents of the shelves were pillaged. A few men appeared with a flaring torch, and in the centre of the building furniture was piled into a heap and fired. Immediately the inflammable pile blazed to the ceiling, and within about five minutes the whole building was a roaring mass of flames, into which members of the crowd threw bottles and stones.

As there was a house adjoining the saloon on the eastern side and separated by only a small passage, the two fire brigades at Kalgoorlie and Boulder were summoned and arrived soon after. Willing helpers carried the furniture of the house into the roadway and out of danger while the firemen concentrated on diverting the flames. The saloon, which was only a one-storey building, was past saving and continued to burn.

Motor Car Set on Fire.

The road and footpath for several hundred yards were now crowded with people. With the saloon in flames attention was again focussed on setting alight to the Home From Home Hotel. While the crowd waited in the street to see what methods would be employed, several men discovered the proprietor's new sedan car in a garage opening on the roadway and set the machine on fire. Everyone drew back to the opposite side of the street expecting an explosion of petrol but the fire brigades, to save a dwelling on the western side of the garage, turned their hoses into the flaming mass amidst the derisive hoots and the jeers of some sections of the crowd.

To keep the crowd back the hose was turned from the building and the spray of water caused a stampede.

Police Attacked.

An ugly incident followed. Several policemen, including plainclothes constables who were attempting to save the wrecked hotel from further depredation, became the object of the crowd's attack and bottles and stones were rained upon them. They took what refuge they could from the missiles behind the posts of the verandah while bottles burst with a crash on the wall behind them. Eventually the rage of the mob calmed down and the attack ceased. The police were then surrounded by a shouting crowd urging them to give a reason for their action in preventing further looting.

In the attack upon the police, Constable Williams received a nasty cut over his eye and was taken to hospital.

The crowd was now out of hand and the police were unable to prevent further wrecking. One man appeared on the front verandah upstairs and threw down bedding and pillows, which were eagerly seized by some of the people. Then, in the street lights he was seen demolishing furniture.

During the past quarter of an hour a rumour had circulated among the crowd that an attempt would be made to blow up the building with dynamite and several rumours that a large case of fracteur had been fired in the rear of the premises caused a hasty retreat. Meanwhile another section of the crowd had broken down the iron fence surrounding the hotel and, making its way to a lane at the rear, prevented one of the fire engines in the lane from getting water by severing the hose with an axe.

Hotel Destroyed.

After repeated attempts to set fire to the hotel the rear of the building blazed up and the flames quickly spread to the front of the building. The man who had been seen on the front verandah upstairs again appeared in the light of the fire through the broken doorways and windows. Fearing that he might be trapped the crowd called to him, but several minutes passed before he discovered his plight. The staircase was already blazing before he reached the ground floor. The fire had now secured a good hold and soon dense clouds of smoke from blasting powder which had been used to fire the building issued in volumes through all apertures. About 10.15 o'clock the roof fell in.

While the hotel was being fired one portion of the crowd, many of whom were high-spirited from celebrating in the looted liquor, moved to the All Nations boarding house, almost opposite the hotel and a few yards from the wine saloon. The building was of stone and two storeys in height. For a while smoke rolled off the balcony, but an explosion at the back of the house, probably caused by miners' blasting powder, caused the flames to take a good hold. The front portion of the building was smashed in, and beds, bedding and furniture were added to the flames. Then the fowl run was raided, and the fowls were carried away.

Shops Looted.

The crowd having now wrecked this portion of the town and caused damage amounting to many thousands of pounds, left the two blazing buildings behind them and proceeded up Hannan-street wrecking and raiding the shops of foreigners as they went. The loot included the goods of the fish shops and tobacconists, and among the spoils one man found a cornet and led the band of men up Hannan-street. The smashing of the windows of shops owned by foreigners continued, as well as the looting. Five shops were treated in this manner, and the main street after the crowd had dispersed resembled a shambles. Splintered glass, ruined foodstuffs, and wrecked shop fittings strewed the footpaths of the main street.

At 11 o'clock the ever-increasing crowd commandeered the tramways and set out for Boulder, leaving wreckage and ruin behind them. Not one foreigner was seen in the streets.

Trams and Motor Cars Commandeered.

At 11.30 o'clock the crowd on tramcars and in packed motor cars streamed out to Boulder to continue the agitation against foreigners. Their first point of attack was in Burt-street, Boulder, where they wrecked two fish shops on either side of the street and a fruit shop in Lane-street. They then went to South Boulder and fired two hotels within 100 yards of each other—The Main Reef and the Cornwall Hotel. The Cornwall Hotel, which is the centre of a foreign community, is a two-storey structure and at midnight was blazing to destruction. The Main Reef has been rased to the ground.

At 12.15 a.m. the crowd turned its attention to the newly-opened International Club, which was recently opened to meet the needs of the large foreign population. The stone building, which was only opened in the last fortnight, has been completely destroyed. A posse of police arrived at the International Club but it was already demolished.

The crowd had now spent its fury and it appeared at 12.30 o'clock to be returning to Kalgoorlie.

The population of Kalgoorlie and Boulder now, at 12.40 a.m., is wide awake and the streets are packed with people in all sorts of attire. Many men could be seen making furtively homeward with their spoils, which included bottles of beer and spirits, fowls, a bucketful of crockery, nickel trays and bedding.

Skyline Glows Red.

The skyline on the west of Kalgoorlie and the south of Boulder is glowing red from the dying fires. There have been no actual personal conflicts with the foreigners and it is wondered what will happen when the mines open tomorrow morning, as there is a large foreign element in the mines.

The funeral of Mr. Jordan will take place at 4.30 o'clock this afternoon.

The Damage.

The damage to 1 o'clock this morning includes three hotels, one two-storey boarding house of brick, a brick and stone club building and a wine saloon as well as eleven shops. The damage is in the vicinity of £30,000.

As the result of the altercation in 1919 on the fields the All Nations boarding house, then an hotel was delicensed.

As far as can be ascertained, there have been no personal injuries, except that to the constable. One pathetic sight was the wife of the proprietor of the Home From Home, Kalgoorlie, viewing the destruction of her former home from a street corner several hundred yards away. No other foreigner has been sighted in either town. It is understood that two young men were arrested at Boulder as the result of being found in possession of articles from the wrecked premises. The whole of the crowd's attack was upon foreign property. It is estimated that about 1,800 foreigners, including Italians, Yugoslavs and Greeks live on the goldfields. The present trouble is said to equal that of 1919, although on that occasion, while the tenants were evicted and their premises were destroyed, there was not so much loss of property.

Mob Disperses.

Shortly before 1 o'clock this morning the men dispersed, and the trouble is over. Several men have been arrested.

The first to start the riot last night was a boy aged 15 at the Home From Home Hotel, who threw the first stone after members of the crowd had egged each other on for some time. Only about 100 men were at first concerned.

A police sergeant at Boulder addressed the crowd from a lorry and urged them to disperse. His words had some effect, as the crowd broke up a few minutes afterwards.

CAUSE OF THE RIOT.

MINER DIES IN HOSPITAL.

Italian Barman Arrested.

KALGOORLIE, Jan. 29.—As a result of an altercation with Claudio Mattaboni (34), an Italian barman at the Home from Home Hotel, Hannan-street, Kalgoorlie, last night, George Edward Jordan (29), married, of Lane-street, Boulder, a miner with three children, died in the Kalgoorlie Government Hospital at 4 o'clock this morning. Mattaboni was arrested by Detective Trist, and he appeared in the Kalgoorlie Police Court this morning before Mr. E. McGinn, R.M., when he was charged with having unlawfully killed Jordan. Mattaboni, who was not represented by counsel, was remanded for eight days, and bail was refused until further inquiries had been made.

The altercation apparently arose over the question of drinks and an argument started between Jordan, who was well known in Kalgoorlie and Boulder as captain of the South Kalgoorlie Volunteer Fire Brigade, and as a prominent member of the Mines Rovers Football Club, and Mattaboni, who was serving drinks in the bar of the hotel. The disagreement between the two men had apparently begun earlier in the day, for they came to blows at 7 o'clock in the evening when Mattaboni is stated to have punched Jordan on the nose. Jordan returned to the precincts of the hotel at about 8 o'clock, when Mattaboni left the bar went out on to the pavement in Hannan-street and met him. Mattaboni is stated to have punched Jordan in the face before a large crowd, the force of the blow causing Jordan, who was a well-built man, to fall backwards and strike his head on the concrete kerbing.

Jordan was immediately conveyed to the Kalgoorlie Government Hospital and at first his injury was not considered serious, but he failed to regain consciousness and died eight hours later. Further inquiries are being made by the detectives into the altercation, but as most of the witnesses were foreigners their investigations are hampered to some extent. The hotel is situated at the western end of Hannan-street, where many foreigners live, and is a common resort for Italians.

AMERICAN CURRENCY.

NEXT STEP AWAITED.

STABILISATION PLANS.

BRITAIN MAY BE APPROACHED

NEW YORK, Jan. 28.—The Washington correspondent of the "New York Times" says that President Roosevelt, according to informed sources, is expected soon to enter negotiations with Great Britain for modified stabilisation of the pound-dollar exchange as a natural sequel to the enactment of the Monetary Bill (which has passed both Houses of Congress and provides for the impounding of all monetary gold in the United States in the Treasury, empowers the President to devalue the dollar by at least 40 per cent, and, from the resultant profit, £400,000,000 at par is allocated to an exchange fund to peg the dollar exchange at the required level, this fund being controlled by the Secretary to the Treasury).

"There have been semi-official negotiations with Britain," stated the correspondent, "but the United States, reportedly, has been rebuffed. The President is expected in informed quarters as expecting quick results when the new negotiations start. The Administration's financial advisers are understood to feel that unless a currency war be prevented and foreign trade increased through the new gold policy, the Administration may face powerful demands for currency inflation. Therefore, Mr. Roosevelt is expected to decide at the proper time for currency stabilisation in the hope that the currencies of Britain and the United States may be held at a level which will encourage international trade beneficial to both countries.

"Mr. Roosevelt is also represented as feeling that it will be necessary to reduce the Hoover regime's tariff walls in order to promote a trade revival before undertaking negotiations with Britain. Mr. Roosevelt is expected to permit a trial period to intervene when the Government will attempt to demonstrate that the stabilisation fund authorised by the Monetary Bill makes the United States capable of holding her own in an international currency contest."

A United Press dispatch from Washington today states that Congressional leaders predict that a new White House proclamation will be issued soon to appease the growing demands for the wider use of silver as currency.

Senator Wheeler declared today that if Mr. Roosevelt did nothing, he would introduce another silver Bill. The Congressional leaders based their forecast that Mr. Roosevelt would issue a silver proclamation on the close vote on the silver amendment to the Monetary Bill in Congress on January 21. Some predicted that Mr. Roosevelt would proclaim the nationalisation of silver, as recommended by certain currency reform factions.

EFFECT OF A CURRENCY WAR.

Possible Foreign Measures.

WASHINGTON, Jan. 29.—The Foreign Policy Association, in a report on the Administration's gold policy, warns Americans that attempts to cheapen the dollar involve the danger of a currency warfare, bringing all the evils of uncontrolled inflation. The report cited three retaliatory measures that foreign countries might apply against the United States, including the imposition of a surtax to equal the difference between current exchange rates and the par value of the depreciated currency, various forms of quantitative trade regulation, and competitive currency depreciation.

BAD TEETH.

BRITISH MEDICAL RESEARCH.

The Importance of Diet.

LONDON, Jan. 29.—The Medical Research Council has issued an interesting report by Mrs. May Mellanby (a member of the Dental Disease Committee of the Council and an investigator for the Council on diet and teeth.

Mrs. Mellanby attributes bad teeth among civilised peoples to an excess of cereals in their diet, lack of sunshine, over-heavy clothes and too early weaning. "The most important items of diet from a dental standpoint," she says, "are calcium and phosphorus, plus an ample supply of vitamin D and the anti-infective vitamin A. Babies obtain these best from their mothers' milk, so that the longer a child is breast-fed, the better are its teeth. Cereals tend to neutralise the action of vitamin D, as shown by experiments with children at Sheffield and Birmingham."

The report suggests that the Eskimos and African natives have their magnificent teeth because the Eskimo diet is free from cereals, while, on the contrary, the sunshine of Africa supplies the vitamin D which counteracts the excess of cereals.

Mrs. Mellanby suggests that cod liver oil be given to all children. She adds that there is little evidence that tooth brushes prevent decay of teeth, though their aesthetic value cannot be denied.

WESTERNISING CHINA.

ABOLISHING LUNAR CALENDAR

Government's Unsuccessful Efforts.

SHANGHAI, Jan. 29.—Determined to enforce the abolition of the Chinese lunar new year, which is less than three weeks away, the National Government has renewed its campaign to compel the Chinese to adopt the western calendar.

The Ministry of Communications has instructed the post offices throughout the country to confiscate all greeting cards posted on the occasion of the lunar new year. The Ministry has also instructed the local authorities in each district to make a bonfire of seized mail to remind the people that the lunar calendar is abolished.

So far the Government's efforts to abolish the centuries old calendar by a stroke of the pen have proved futile. With the exception of the Government departments, the majority of Chinese continue their daily and seasonal reckonings by the moon cycles.

NAVAL CONFERENCE.

NO OFFICIAL STATEMENT.

Secrecy Regarding Proceedings.

SINGAPORE, Jan. 29.—The British, Australian and New Zealand naval officers who have been in conference here for several days decline to indicate the subjects of discussion and will disperse this week without issuing an official statement.

H.M.S. Hawkins left for Colombo today.

SMASH-AND-GRAB RAID

Clothing Material Stolen.

SYDNEY, Jan. 29.—Three young men escaped in a stolen motor car after having broken a window and stolen clothing material from Witts, Ltd., Camperdown, tonight. The motor car had been left in Clarence-street, City. The men evidently drove direct to the corner of Parramatta-road and Mallett-street, where the store is situated. One man remained in the car keeping the engine running, while his companions alighted. One of them threw a heavy stone through a window and both rushed forward and seized rolls of cloth. They jumped into the car and were driven away before the few spectators had recovered from their surprise.

CAPSIZE OF FERRY.

Women Trapped in Cabin.

TOKIO, Jan. 29.—Accounts vary regarding the total death roll, when at Nagasaki yesterday a municipal ferry capsized when heavily overcrowded. The workers, returning homeward, as usual, rushed to disembark when nearing the quayside, and this caused the ferry to overturn. The victims, which are believed to total about 20, included women sheltering from the cold in the cabin, where they were trapped.

LORD ALLENBY MENACED.

CONSPIRACY IN JAVA.

Special Guard Appointed.

("The Times" Special Service.)

THE HAGUE, Jan. 28.—The unexpected return to Singapore from the Dutch East Indies of Field Marshal Viscount Allenby was due to the discovery of a conspiracy against his life in Java. This necessitated a special guard being provided for him day and night. Three suspects were expelled from his hotel.

Lord Allenby wished to visit Bali, that romantic and unspoiled island, but a large special police force which had to be

VISCOUNT ALLENBY.

detailed to look after him proved so embarassing that he left by air for Madan, whence he departed incognito for Singapore.

GERMAN-POLISH PACT.

MISGIVINGS IN PARIS.

Hitler's Ultimate Aim Doubted.

PARIS, Jan. 29.—News of the signing by Poland and Germany of a non-aggression pact with a currency of ten years has been received with satisfaction tempered by misgivings regarding Germany's ultimate aims. The official view is that the fact promotes pacification in Eastern Europe, but does not affect existing agreements; but critics see in the treaty an opportunity for Germany to concentrate her attention on Austria and the Saar.

"EUROPEAN PEACE ENSURED."

Spiking the Guns of French Diplomacy

("The Times" Special Service.)

BERLIN, Jan. 28.—The entire Press voices dutiful satisfaction at the German-Polish pact, but it deserves unstinted praise because if words mean anything it ensures European peace for ten years and spokes the guns of French diplomacy, for who will now believe that Germany does not desire peace?

COMMERCIAL CONSEQUENCES.

Trade Treaty to Follow.

WARSAW, Jan. 29.—A logical development of the Germano-Polish non-aggression pact, which is further evidence of Marshal Pilsudsky's skill and vision, will soon be shown in the economic field. A direct Berlin-Warsaw commercial air service is being arranged, and a Germano-Polish commercial treaty terminating a nine-years' customs war is also being negotiated.

SCEPTICISM IN MOSCOW.

Germany's Sincerity Questioned.

MOSCOW, Jan. 29.—"Isvestia" throws doubt on Germany's sincerity in signing the Polish pact and says that Hitler's determination to sign it must call forth the question whether it means a real renunciation of war by Germany or is merely a political manoeuvre, and also what compensation (and at whose expense) Germany hopes to receive for renunciation of aggression.

CAUGHT RED-HANDED.

DRIVING TUNNEL INTO BANK.

American Socialist Arrested.

WINSLOW (Arizona), Jan. 29.—Oilworth Sumpter, an unsuccessful Congressional candidate at the last election, has confessed, according to the police, to attempting to rob a bank. A policeman surprised Sumpter digging a tunnel into the bank from another building. The authorities found a pick and shovel, drills and explosives.

Sumpter, who is destitute, declared, "The world owes me a living. Everything I have ever attempted went wrong and I made the usual mess of this job."

Sumpter polled more votes than any other Socialist in Arizona's history, exceeding the Republican candidate, although the Democrat won.

FRENCH IMPORTS.

THE BRITISH NOTE.

Official Circles Reticent.

PARIS, Jan. 29.—British official circles refuse to comment on the French newspapers' declaration that the British note handed to the Government yesterday demands the full restoration of the previous import quotas, otherwise Britain will institute reprisals and denounce the trade treaty between France and Britain.

CELLARS FLOODED.

STORM AT CHARLEVILLE.

Residents May Have to Move.

BRISBANE, Jan. 29.—A severe storm occurred at Charleville at 5.45 tonight when 470 points of rain fell in an hour and a half. Cellars in business premises and hotels were flooded and the fire brigade was requisitioned to pump the water out.

Bradley's Creek, which flows through the town, is in high flood and residents in the locality have been warned by the police to be ready to move.

SOCIAL SERVICE TO WORKLESS

Saving Men from the Scrap Heap.

LONDON, Jan. 28.—"The Times," in a leading article, quotes at length the broadcast speech in which the Prince of Wales reviewed the progress of the voluntary service movement to assist the unemployed. The article declares that social service for the unemployed is a proved necessity, demanding sustained effort which the Prince foresaw when he first aroused the nation to promote the welfare of those who feared they might be cast on the scrap heap. "Future social service," the article proceeds, "will require larger expenditure, organisation and development. The Prince's practical suggestions are part of a broad plan for equipping men for public life and leisure. While putting the provision of work first, it offers scope for the public spirit which keeps Britain the strong team it is today."

AUSTRIA'S FIGHT.

THE NAZI MENACE.

Heimwehr's Peace Terms.

VIENNA, Jan. 29.—Prince Starhemberg, leader of the Heimwehr (Austrian Fascists), in an address to the commanders of his organisation today, outlined the conditions upon which the conflict between Austria and Germany (involving the national independence of Austria in the face of the Nazi campaign against the Dollfuss Government) could be ended.

Prince Starhemberg said that the German Chancellor (Herr Hitler) must give a written declaration recognising Austria's sovereign independence; secondly, it must be recognised that Fascism in Austria was represented by the Heimwehr, so that the Nazi Party in Austria was superfluous; and, thirdly, Herr Hitler must give a written guarantee that he would never attempt to place non-Austrian Germans in leadership. "If Herr Hitler agrees to these conditions," he said, "I am prepared to say from Austria that I could support the German foreign policy." He added: "We back Dr. Dollfuss in a Fascist reconstruction of Austria."

[The Austrian Government recently addressed a Note to Germany requesting an assurance that the Nazi propaganda from Germany subversive to the interests of the Dollfuss Government would cease, as well as the smuggling of munitions and money for use by Austrian Nazis. According to Dr. Dollfuss, the alternative was an appeal to the League Council. There has yet been no German reply published.]

GOVERNMENT PRECAUTIONS.

An Early Attack Expected.

("The Times" Special Service.)

VIENNA, Jan. 29.—The Vice-Chancellor (Major Fey) told a semi-military assemblage yesterday that everything indicated that the Nazis would launch an early general attack. Austria would have finished the Nazis long ago, he said, but for the external help they received in the shape of propaganda and munitions. They were making a last attempt, but neither the spirit of Berlin nor of Moscow would prevail.

Major Fey added that he had called up fresh comrades and issued orders calculated to spoil the Nazis' fun. The agitators responsible for the precautions must bear the expense of them. Four Nazis would be interned for every detonator exploded. The loyal executive would be given a bonus in February.

O'DUFFY ACCLAIMED.

BIG BLUE SHIRT RALLY.

Opponents Attempt Obstruction.

DUBLIN, Jan. 29.—In the hope of preventing the holding of a meeting to be addressed by General O'Duffy (leader of the Blue Shirts and of the United Ireland Party) at Skibbereen yesterday, the telegraph wires in the vicinity of the town were cut and trees were felled across the roads, but volunteers soon cleared them.

Armed opponents of the Blue Shirts drove up in motor cars to the platform in the public square during the afternoon, levelled their rifles, and ordered two Civic Guards to put their hands up. The guards refused and blew their whistles. The invaders then sprinkled the platform with inflammable fluid, set fire to it, discharged their rifles in the air and drove off.

The fire was extinguished and, later, 3,000 blue-shirted men and 1,000 blue-bloused colleens triumphantly escorted General O'Duffy to the meeting place.

General O'Duffy made his customary attack on Mr. De Valera's policy. Mr. Dillon, another prominent Blue Shirt and a member of the Dail, urged the conclusion of an Anglo-Irish trade agreement.

In Dublin today, the leader of the Labour Party (Mr. Norton), who supports the Government, in reply to the statement by the British Secretary for the Dominions (Mr. Thomas) that the door was not closed to an Anglo-Irish settlement, said that Mr. Thomas should indicate his willingness to confer with representatives of the Free State to remove the causes of friction.

RICKSHAW MEN RIOT.

ATTACK ON GARAGE.

Fleet of Buses Wrecked.

SHANGHAI, Jan. 29.—Modern transportation and the introduction of a motor truck service at Chinkiang (a Yangtze port) has been responsible for serious rioting by rickshaw men who have been striking for the past few days.

Declaring that their livelihood had been ruined following the establishment of bus routes, approximately 1,000 men armed with iron bars and other wrecking weapons attacked the bus company garage, completely smashing the fleet of vehicles, and decamping before the police arrived.

An attempt to wreck the offices of the company resulted in a serious clash with the police and military forces, and many were injured on both sides.

The strike continues and street cleaners are being pressed in to maintain the rickshaw service.

LINER BUFFETED.

ATLANTIC TIDAL WAVES.

Twenty-eight Persons Injured.

ST. JOHN (New Brunswick), Jan. 28.—Three mountainous tidal waves, believed to have been caused by a submarine earthquake in mid-Atlantic, descended successively on the Canadian Pacific liner Duchess of York (20,021 tons) last Tuesday, smashing the ship's gear and injuring 25 of the crew and three passengers.

It was learned today, on the arrival of the vessel here, that the tidal waves followed a hurricane, during which the passengers were ordered to remain in their state rooms. The towering waves descended over the bridge and buffeted the vessel as though it were a straw.

While treating a seaman for a broken rib, the ship's surgeon, Dr. Morton, received a fractured arm. Another seaman is believed to have a fractured skull. The remaining injured persons were treated by the surgeon, despite his own injury.

AIRMEN OVERDUE.

SOUTH ATLANTIC CROSSING.

Faint Wireless Messages.

PERNAMBUCO (Brazil), Jan. 29.—The Italian aviator Commander Lombardi, who with three companions left Dakar in Senegal for Natal (Brazil) yesterday, is long overdue.

The last message from their wireless was intercepted at 12.30 o'clock this morning. It appeared to be somewhat weak, indicating that the aeroplane had strayed from the direct route. Reports from Fortaleza that the plane had been heard in that vicinity at 12.10 a.m. strengthened this impression.

Fortaleza is 300 miles north of Natal.

OVERWHELMED BY BLIZZARD.

Islanders' Bodies Recovered.

TOKIO, Jan. 29.—It is feared that the entire community on Utsuryo Island in the Japan Sea were overwhelmed by the recent blizzard. Searchers from the mainland of Korea report that they have already found 41 bodies buried in the snow.

By special arrangement, Reuter's world service, in addition to other special sources of information, is used in the compilation of the overseas intelligence published in this issue and all rights therein in Australia and New Zealand are reserved.

TWO BROTHERS MISSING.

Clothes Found on River Bank.

SYDNEY, Jan. 29.—Two brothers, Jack and Rae Ernst, have been missing from their home at Lamb's Creek, about 18 miles from Maitland, since they went for a swim late this afternoon, and it is feared that they have been drowned. The police were asked to assist in a search for the young men, one of whom is aged 21 years, and the other one 18 years. Clothes belonging to them were discovered on the bank of the Hunter River near the home of their father, Mr. J. J. Ernst, late this evening.

GRAZIER'S DEATH.

BROTHER ARRESTED.

Shooting in Country Road.

MELBOURNE, Jan. 29.—Following the shooting at Red Lion (in the Maryborough district) yesterday of Councillor Henry Vincecombe, J.P., a well-known grazier, William James Vincecombe, the dead man's brother, has been arrested and will appear in the Melbourne Police Court on February 1 on a charge of murder.

From police statements it appears that Councillor Vincecombe was confronted by a man who had apparently been hiding behind a tall hedge and was shot in the back of the head while riding to the home of a neighbour.

BOY SLIPS FROM PLATFORM.

Fatally Crushed by Train.

BRISBANE, Jan. 29.—Warwick Tuckerman (10), received severe injuries today when crushed between a train and the platform at Cambooya station and died shortly after admission to the Toowoomba hospital. It is understood that the lad slipped while opening a door as the train was entering the station. He was returning to Brisbane after spending a holiday with his grandfather at Tambo Park station, near Goomburra. His parents, it is understood, are en route to Perth.

The lad's father, Mr. R. Tuckerman, is a well-known business man in Sydney.

FRENCH CRISIS.

FORMING NEW MINISTRY.

M. Daladier Accepts Offer.

PARIS, Jan. 29.—Following the resignation of the Chautemps Ministry on Saturday as a result of pressure from the Socialists because of the Stavisky bond fraud scandal (in which the late Minister for Justice, M. Raynaldy, was allegedly implicated)—the President (M. Lebrun) invited the former Prime Minister (M. Daladier) to form a Cabinet.

After consulting his supporters, M. Daladier announced early this afternoon that he had accepted the offer of the Premiership. He is at present engaged in the task of selecting the personnel of a Government.

The previous Daladier Cabinet held office from January 31, 1933, to October 23, when it was defeated in the Chamber of Deputies on the Finance Bill, the particular clause on which the Government fell (owing to the opposition of a section of the Socialists), being that providing for a reduction in State salaries, allowances and pensions, and a special tax on stable incomes, the savings from which were designed to assist the Government's general plan to balance the Budget. The succeeding Sarraut Government was defeated on the same issue, but the Chautemps Government, which took office on November 27, succeeded in passing a Finance Bill which, it is hoped, would produce a balanced Budget. It failed, however, to weather the storm which followed the revelations of the Stavisky scandal. After M. Chautemps had submitted the resignation of the Government to the President

M. DALADIER.

on Saturday and declined to form a new Cabinet, a communique was issued stating that the Government was unable to perform its duty in the atmosphere of calm which the interests of the country required.

M. Daladier was Minister for War in both the Sarraut and Chautemps Ministries.

GERMAN PROTESTANTS.

NAZIS CRUSH OPPOSITION.

A Dictator for the Church.

("The Times" Special Service.)

BERLIN, Jan. 28.—The Nazis appear to have smashed church opposition and also monarchism at one blow, clearing the sky for the anniversary celebration on Tuesday of the Nazis' accession to power. With the aid of the Premier of Prussia (General Goering), the Reich Bishop (Dr. Mueller) has effectually declared himself dictator of the Prussian Church while the opposition clergy apparently have been routed, the non-Prussian churchmen who demanded Dr. Mueller's resignation having capitulated.

It is believed that President Von Hindenburg gave Herr Hitler authority to suppress Dr. Mueller but General Goering's intervention completely changed the situation. Pacification has been replaced with coercion. Many arrests have been made and 50 pastors have been suspended. There has been much stone-throwing by rowdies. Nevertheless the Nazis are aware of the effects of wholesale arrests on the religious life of the community. They have not only removed the restrictions on divine service but have declared that they were never imposed.

The entire property and funds of the People's Union for Catholic Germany of Munchen-Gladbach have been confiscated by the Prussian State. This is the final blow to the world's strongest Roman Catholic organisation.

Church Senate Suspended.

Determined to dominate the Prussian Church, Dr. Mueller has suspended the Church Senate and also deprived Dr. Niemoller of his pastorate. Dr. Mueller now rules 19,000,000 German Protestants and Nazi church leaders have announced their determination to support him.

SECRET POLICE ACTIVITIES.

Telephone Conversations Tapped.

LONDON, Jan. 29.—The Berlin correspondent of the "Daily Telegraph" states that Dr. Mueller has completely crushed the opposition, having promulgated a decree making himself dictator, to which the heads of the other churches have capitulated. An important factor has been the telephone-tapping activities of General Goering's secret police. The conversations of opposition pastors were tapped and phrases culled which were interpreted as showing disloyalty to Herr Hitler. The mass of the laity are in ignorance of the situation as no papers have been allowed to publish anything except Dr. Mueller's statements. Protests from pulpits and by meetings have also been forbidden.

KIDNAPPING THREAT.

Miss Pickford's Precautions.

NEW YORK, Jan. 28.—Miss Mary Pickford, the film actress, arrived here today guarded by four private detectives and immediately secluded herself in her hotel suite, where she personally inspected the placing of special locks on all the

MARY PICKFORD.

doors. Her publicity representative admitted that her life story would shortly be published in a popular magazine. Miss Pickford insisted emphatically that the threats to kidnap her were unimportant. The suspected person had been placed irrationally about "a message from the spirit world."

STATE DISABILITIES.

TASMANIA'S CASE OPENED.

Claim for £1,099,536.

HOBART, Jan. 29.—The Commonwealth Grants Commission commenced its sittings in Hobart today when documentary evidence was submitted in support of the claim of the less populous States for more adequate financial treatment on the part of the Federal Government. The case for Tasmania was submitted by the Chief Secretary (Mr. C. E. W. James).

The statement set out a claim for £1,099,536. It directed attention to the fact that the State had endeavoured to limit its loan expenditure to the bare minimum, the average of which for the last two years had been only 3/ a head of the population, while all the other States had spent on an average of £1/5/1, and Western Australia, £4/2/6. The Government's claim for £1,099,536 included £522,091, which was the amount estimated to cover the total revenue shortage.

Burden of Taxation.

The case dealt exhaustively with the handicaps which Tasmania had suffered under the Federation, particularly in relation to the tariff and the Navigation Act, and brought under notice the severity of taxation which, it stated, had during the last 10 years, been on an average from 35 to 40 per cent above the average of the other States. It stated that the high level of taxation in Tasmania was resented, and that the taxpayers were not in a position to stand the temporary effort to meet the emergency that taxpayers in the other States were capable of bearing. It pointed out that the per capita cost of the important functions of government was well below the average of the other States, and in no category was expenditure as high as 80 per cent of the average, and the total cost a head was only 63.4 of the average.

"During the year 1932-33," the statement proceeded, "Tasmanian social services, which were never generously catered for according to Australian standards, were too harshly treated when subjected under the Premiers' Plan to a reduction at least as severe as that of the other States, and more severe than some. It may, therefore, justly ask to be allowed more generous provision for some of these services. What has been said in previous claims concerning the necessity for a grant being made for more than one year at a time must be repeated. It is essential to financial stability that the Government should know with reasonable accuracy its expectations before it can draft its Budget. Grants for a year at a time are very often made after the beginning of the year, delaying the presentation of the Budget and causing embarrassment by the necessity of asking for supply for undue lengths of time. We would, therefore, ask that the Commission should recommend the grant which the State may expect for a definite period."

WELFARE FARM SCANDAL.

SCARS ON BOYS' FACES.

Statements at Sydney Inquiry.

SYDNEY, Jan. 29.—When the inquiry was resumed today by Mr. McCulock, S.M., into the truth of charges against Mr. A. W. Parsonage, superintendent of the Riverina boys' welfare farm at Yanco, evidence was given by William Allen Wearne, labourer, of Jennings-street, Matraville, concerning his visit to the farm to see his son William Christopher Anderson Wearne, who gave evidence last week of having been "court-martialled."

Mr. Wearne said that he reached the farm on December 1 or 2, about 14 days after the alleged events, and met Mr. Parsonage who by request sent for witness's son. After witness and his son had a conversation Mr. Parsonage took witness to the medical officer. Witness was sent to see the boy by the member for King. The boy was a little "broken up" and did not look well. He had a bad throat, an ear was scarred and there was a small scar over an eye.

Frederick Charles Mountford, president of the Willimbong Shire Council, said that for ten months he had been at the farm as foreman of the buildings in course of erection. He had seen a boy jumping and when he inquired the reason Mr. Parsonage said "Exercise—it will do him good!" He had also seen boys running round the playing ring and Mr. Parsonage had told him that this was a form of punishment.

Mr. Mountford said that he had seen Mr. Cattell (an employee of the farm) and Mr. Parsonage strike boys at different times. On October 10 he saw a boy named Dolan. Both his eyes were blackened, his right ear was out of shape and burst, his lips were swollen and the skin of the face was broken in several places. Witness questioned McVeigh (an employee of the farm) who said, "We set the boys on to him." Witness said, "It is a disgraceful and shocking state of affairs." McVeigh said, "We have to teach them not to run away." Later Melville, another farm employee, rode up to him and said, "They almost killed Wearne, he is in bed and his temperature is 100." Witness told Melville that he intended to throw the full responsibility for this on Melville's shoulders.

Witness said that he asked Parsonage if anything had happened to Wearne in No. 3 dormitory. Parsonage replied, "No, forget it." Later Parsonage rang up witness about what had been published. Witness asked, "Did this happen to Wearne?" Parsonage replied, "Yes, it did occur but it is the code of the boys." Witness remarked, "It is a rotten code."

Mr. Cater (for Parsonage): Were you aware that practically the whole of the boys had been placed on the farm because they were uncontrollable?

Witness: No, I did not know that.

Mr. Challoner, chief clerk of the Child Welfare Department, was examined by Mr. Cater.

Mr. Cater (to witness): It takes a specialist in child welfare to deal with these boys?

Witness: Yes.

Each boy requires different treatment?—Yes.

The inquiry was adjourned until tomorrow morning.

STUDENTS RIOT.

BOMBS DESTROY FURNITURE.

Ducking for Vice-Rector.

MADRID, Jan. 28.—Crying "Long Live the King," students rioted in Madrid today. They doused the university vice-rector with a bucket of water.

At Seville they smashed the furniture of the Republican Students' Union, resulting in several arrests and the closing of the university.

Small bombs were thrown into the university building at Valencia, destroying furniture.

ATTACK BY SHARK.

BOY'S CONDITION IMPROVES.

Mother Collapses on Hearing News

SYDNEY, Jan. 29.—It was reported tonight that the condition of Wallace John McCutcheon (15), who was attacked and severely injured by a shark in the George River, East Hills, on Saturday afternoon, was quite satisfactory. He was well enough this afternoon to see members of his family.

Mrs. J. McCutcheon, mother of the injured boy, had recently been ill and learned what had happened by accident. She collapsed and is suffering severely from shock.

Frank Spruce (23), who went to McCutcheon's assistance after he had been attacked said today that when McCutcheon dived in he noticed something peculiar. Instead of entering the water cleanly he fell in "all bunched up" as though he had tried to stop himself at the last moment. Spruce thought that he must have seen the shark just before he dived.

64 *The greatest Anzac gathering*

Commemorating Anzac Day, 1935

IN LONDON IN 1935, THE SPEAKER AT THE INAUGURAL LUNCHEON OF THE EMPIRE SERVICE CLUB, WAS THE 'GRAND OLD MAN OF GALLIPOLI', SIR IAN HAMILTON (1853–1947). IN HIS SPEECH HE PREDICTED THAT IN A THOUSAND YEARS AUSTRALIANS WOULD LEARN ABOUT THE LANDING AT GALLIPOLI ALONGSIDE THE LEGENDS OF HOMER'S *ILIAD*. HE ALSO PREDICTED THAT, IN THE FUTURE, PUBLIC INTEREST IN GALLIPOLI WOULD GROW RATHER THAN DIMINISH AND THAT AUSTRALIANS WOULD BE 'PROUDLY TRACING THEIR OWN DESCENT FROM ANZAC SOLDIERS'.

Although the first commemorations of 25 April were held in 1916 while the war was still being fought, these were very much recruitment campaigns. It was not until well after the war, in the 1930s, that all the rituals of the day had been developed.

Returned soldiers and the wider Australian public's interest in Anzac Day as a form of 'national day' was at first slow. Yet as the First World War began to recede into memory, 'immense crowds' began to attend Sydney ceremonies on 25 April, the day of the first landings of the Anzac soldiers on their ill-fated Gallipoli campaign in the Turkish Dardanelles.

The form of the early Anzac Day ceremonies was shaped by returned servicemen. With the choice of the day as a public holiday by several states in 1921, the introduction of soldier 'traditions', such as two-up gambling games, ensured the shape of commemorations would not be overly religious, and yet would hold a certain spirituality that would foster the widely popular dawn services, marches and battlefield visits of recent years.

NET WEEKLY SALES LARGER THAN THOSE OF ANY OTHER NEWSPAPER IN AUSTRALIA

FINAL EXTRA

THE SUN

ABOVE ALL FOR AUSTRALIA

No. 7898 SYDNEY: FRIDAY, APRIL 26, 1935 PRICE 1½d 'Phone: BO 333

Ottawa Will "Stand Pat" On Ottawa Pacts

1700 Guineas Colt

FOR PEACE

HOLY YEAR APPEAL

LOURDES CEREMONIES

POMP FOR LEGATE

No Debate After Jubilee

TRIP TO LONDON

Canada's P.M.

EYES ON ELECTIONS

("Sun" Special)

OTTAWA, Thursday.

If the Prime Ministers of Australia and New Zealand expect, as is reported, to sit at a round-table conference on leading Empire problems after the Jubilee celebrations in England, it is to be feared, according to advices current in Government circles here, that they are doomed to disappointment as far as Canada is concerned.

Miss Mildred Bennett

CLEAN-UP

PRIEST'S PLAN

U.S. Public Life

SOCIAL JUSTICE

'ARF A MO'

But the Tutor Would Not Wait

ALL NAZI

GERMAN PRESS

DRASTIC LAW

COMPANY PURGE

GONE WILD

Silverites

U.S. "BOOST"

FLYING GIRL

Hope of Record

Will Figure In Big Tourneys

Father Coughlin

EFFACE MEMORIES

French Objections

THE SUN STOP-PRESS

BELOW FORM

AUSTRALIANS' SINGLES

Won't Pay Ransom

WHY?

Artist's Query

ANZAC WILL BE A LEGEND

("Sun" Special)

LONDON, Thursday.

Sir Ian Hamilton, the "Grand Old Man of Gallipoli," to-day drew a comparison between the landing at Gallipoli and Homer's "Iliad."

"Good Old Birdie"

Killed Both Parents

("Sun" Special)

AUSTIN (Texas), Thursday.

Howard Pearson, aged 20, son of a judge of the Texas Supreme Court, confessed to-day to killing both his parents. He appears to be insane.

Seven h.p. (nominal) Develops 110 h.p.

MOTHER CHURCH

CANTERBURY GIFTS

The front page of Sydney's Sun *newspaper of 26 April 1935 reported on Anzac Day speeches in London. Elsewhere in the paper were to be found the images we still expect to see today of servicemen, ex-servicemen, commemorative services and marches.*

65 *Black Sunday at Bondi*

Mass surf rescues at Bondi Beach, 1938

ON SUNDAY THE SIXTH, A TYPICALLY HOT FEBRUARY DAY IN 1938, BONDI BEACH WAS PACKED WITH AN ESTIMATED 35,000 PEOPLE. THE WAVES WERE BREAKING REGULARLY AND THERE WAS NO SIGN OF ANY UNUSUAL SURF. AT AROUND 3 PM—FORTUNATELY, AS IT HAPPENED—SIXTY SURF CLUB MEMBERS HAD GATHERED ON THE BEACH, ABOUT TO START THEIR WEEKLY RACE EVENTS.

Suddenly, three huge waves rolled in to the beach in quick succession and, when they receded, hundreds of swimmers found themselves being swept into a deep channel out to sea. There was instant panic, and what journalists described as mass hysteria, as people on shore watched their friends and family members being dragged out into the ocean.

The Bondi surf club races suddenly turned into the biggest single surf rescue operation in Australian history. As lifesavers and surf club members began bringing people back to shore, the beach became a casualty clearing station. Around three hundred bathers were rescued, of whom sixty required attention, and thirty-five were rescued unconscious and subsequently revived. Five of those brought to shore were dead.

The rescue cemented lifesavers and their surf clubs in the national imagination as heroic figures. Interestingly, one news report mentioned that, on the beach that day, it was the men who panicked, while the women remained calm.

NET WEEKLY SALES LARGER THAN THOSE OF ANY OTHER NEWSPAPER IN AUSTRALIA

THE SUN

ABOVE ALL — FOR AUSTRALIA

COUNTRY EDITION

No. 8765 (Registered at the General Post Office, Sydney, for transmission by post as a newspaper) SYDNEY: MONDAY, FEBRUARY 7, 1938 PRICE 1½d Phone: BO 333

FORECAST
Warm—
Mainly fine—
Close night.

HEROISM IN THE SURF

BONDI DEATH WAVE

MAN DIED FOR ANOTHER

180 Rescued From Vicious Undertow

GRIM LESSONS

Reports prepared to-day by the police show that some extraordinary acts of heroism were performed during yesterday's surf catastrophe at Bondi, when four, and possibly five, persons were drowned and 180 brought ashore by 70 life-savers and others.

Carl Lenhart Saur, one of the four known victims, gave his life to save a girl whom he held up by the hair until he sank and was drowned. The girl was saved by others.

Important lessons emphasised by yesterday's tragic happenings, surf officials said to-day, were that no person should touch a lifeline during a beach rescue unless specifically asked to do so, and that all beaches should have loud-speakers for the better handling of excited crowds.

A still dangerous undertow to-day hampered the search for the body of a man yet unaccounted for.

"I've seen rescues and drownings in every part of the world, but never anything as magnificent as the job done by those lifesaving boys yesterday," said Mr. Francois Fouche, a French-Canadian wrestler, now in Sydney.

Mr. Fouche was at the water's edge, taking photographs, when the tragedy occurred.

"All at once, the water went quite flat," he said. "Then, before you knew it, those three great waves were there, and within five seconds hands were up everywhere." ...

... into action yesterday I saw just how much that drill had done for them. They were just great."

"There were so many heroes yesterday that it is difficult to mention any particular one," a police officer said to-day.

"Three young policemen revealed sterling qualities, but their acts of bravery were by no means the only efforts. They did no more than many others who repeatedly risked their lives in a terrible sea."

Sergeant Gorman, officer in charge of Bondi police, is preparing a special report on the bravery ...

"Going Down All Round"

Search for Body—Page 2, Columns 7 and 8.

A remarkable picture of one of the huge waves which yesterday at Bondi caused four, and possibly five, deaths, breaking over surfers. The photograph shows the immensity of the dumper. The cameraman was taking a snap of a girl bather by the waterside when the death-dealing wave suddenly came within range of the lens.

Resuscitation work being carried out by lifesavers and helpers on some of the men brought ashore yesterday in one of the most spectacular rescues in Australian surfing history.

JEWS FROM GERMANY

Given Permit To Settle

AUCKLAND, Monday.

Five German Jews on board the liner Niagara are on their way to settle in Australia.

Asked why they left Germany, they merely smiled, and said, "We are thinking of the future, not of the past."

From Our Special Representative CANBERRA, Monday.

An application by the Australian Jewish Welfare Society for permission for seven German-Jew youths to settle in Australia, has been approved by the Minister for the Interior (Mr. McEwen).

Mr. McEwen said that the youths were all between 16 and 18 years, and the society had made satisfactory arrangements for their training as rural workers.

No other landing permits had been granted for German Jews.

Further applications by the society for entry permits for five domestic workers, had not been approved, because no positions were awaiting them.

The society was now in touch with him regarding further immigration of German Jews.

In the case of aliens nominated by friends or relatives domiciled in Australia, satisfactory guarantees must be given by the nominators for the maintenance of new arrivals, and adult males must have £50 and guaranteed employment, which will not displace an Australian.

Where applications are made from overseas, the landing money required is £200.

JEWISH CHILDREN FOR AUSTRALIA

From Our Special Representative LONDON, Sunday.

The Berlin correspondent of the "Sunday Times" understands that the Commonwealth Government has agreed to accept 30 Jewish children as immigrants, following negotiations with German Jewish organisations.

Jews hope that the Commonwealth will allow a continued flow of relatives or friends to Australia.

League Team Control

A statement that "the agreement between the Rugby League managers and the Board of Control provides that the managers make all arrangements as to travelling accommodation while on tour" is made by Mr. H. Sunderland.

He says that if he had been as sure of the agreement while in France as he is now, he would have been saved a tremendous amount of worry. (See story Page 17.)

EXPLOSION IN AIR

FLYING-BOAT

Propeller Through Roof

MELBOURNE, Monday.

After a sharp report and a burst of smoke from the engines, a huge propeller from one of the visiting Royal Air Force flying-boats broke from its housing while the squadron was flying over the city just after noon to-day.

The main part of it fell 1000 feet and crashed through the roof of the Flinders-street railway station.

Thousands who were watching the squadron saw two of the three 6ft. steel blades of the propeller break away and fall.

One piece, six feet long, fell on the roof of the Metro Theatre in Collins-street, and missed by a few feet an electrician working there.

The other, which has not yet been found, may have dropped into the Yarra.

The accident occurred when a fault developed in the reduction gear, which gears the speed of the engine down to the speed of the propeller.

Apparently the propeller flew to pieces, one piece piercing the hull and another the wings.

Few of the crowd waiting on the pier at Williamstown for the flying-boat to land realised that anything had happened.

City watchers had seen the machine drop out of the formation and its companions veer away from it.

A split second afterwards the whole of the housing, with the third blade attached, broke away from the aircraft and buried itself in the Flinders-street platform.

The boat affected, No. 4 of the squadron, was piloted by Flight-Lieutenant H. N. T. Neugebauer. The controls were not affected, and the machine made a normal landing on the Bay where it taxied more than a mile to its moorings.

(Continued On Page 3.)

STRIKE AT DOCKS TO GO ON

Waterside engineers, who have been on strike for 26 weeks at Cockatoo Island and Mort's Dockyard, declined, at a meeting at Rozelle to-day, to return to work.

They rejected a recommendation from officers of the Amalgamated Engineers' Union and the Australian Society of Engineers that they should return to work forthwith.

The meeting was then adjourned for two weeks.

This period will take the dispute over the time limit set by Judge Beeby recently, when he allowed an order deregistering the union's concerned to stand over until midnight on February 13.

Between 130 and 140 engineers attended to-day's meeting.

RHINE FARMERS' NOTICE TO QUIT

"The Sun" Cable Service

LONDON, Sunday.

The Nazi authorities are compelling Alsatian farmers who have possessed the right since feudal times to 1000 acres on the German side of the Rhine to sell their property, the Strasburg correspondent of the "Daily Telegraph" states.

The reason is said to be that the building of a miniature Maginot line of fortifications opposite the French defences is contemplated.

IN OTHER PAGES

FLEET LEAVES FOR JERVIS BAY

H.M.S. Achilles Will Join In Exercises

The Royal Australian Navy, accompanied by H.M.S. Achilles, from the New Zealand station of the Royal Navy, left Sydney to-day for Jervis Bay, to carry out exercises.

The destroyers were first away and were followed half an hour later by the cruisers, led by the flagship of the Australian squadron, H.M.A.S. Canberra.

At 9.30 a.m., the destroyers began to move. They were led to sea by the flotilla leader, Stuart. Then followed the Vendetta, with the Waterhen next.

At 10 a.m. the cruisers cast off, their bands playing gaily on deck.

The Canberra was followed by the Australia, and then the Achilles.

The warships kept close in to the coast as they turned south. There was a gap of several miles between the destroyers and the cruisers.

A haze was hanging over the coast, and soon after they turned south the ships were lost to sight.

H.M.A.S. Sydney, the other cruiser of the Australian squadron, is at Jervis Bay, awaiting the arrival of the main force.

The sloop Swan is expected to leave Sydney this afternoon for Jervis Bay, with the gunnery target in tow. Her sister ship, the Yarra, is in dock, but is expected to follow later.

The R.A.F. flying-boats are expected to carry out manoeuvres with the warships off Jervis Bay. Four of the flying-boats were in the air soon after 6 a.m. to-day, flying over the Harbor and the city, "stretching their wings."

GAVEROYAL SALUTE WITH SIREN

The Dutch liner Nieuw Holland, which arrived here to-day honored the birth of a daughter to Princess Juliana with a royal salute.

The liner carried no gun, but 51 blasts of her siren frightened every seagull for miles around.

"We were coming down the Queensland coast on the night of January 31 and were close to Cooktown, when we received the news," said the commander of the Nieuw Holland, Captain J. Blaauboer, to-day.

"The hour was late, and we did not disturb the passengers by starting the celebrations at once.

"But at 8 a.m. next day the liner was dressed from end to end, and we gave 51 blasts on our siren.

Ensign Dipped

"When we came in sight of the signal station on Archer Point, no flags were flying.

"We thought the keeper should have had a flag up in honor of the little princess, so we blew our siren until the Australian blue ensign was run up on the flagstaff.

"The flag was dipped in our honor and we dipped in return, and steamed on."

It was a joyous day on the Nieuw Holland. A special "orange dinner" was served. The passengers and officers were given champagne and the native crew had soft drinks. A ball was held at night.

Australia's 150th birthday was also celebrated on board.

STOP-PRESS

EMPIRE GAMES BOWLS
Fours.—Round 2: T. Kinder (Aust.) 23 v. Donaldson (South Africa) 16; J. G. Cuthbert (Eng.) 25 v. R. Dobell (Fiji) 16.

EMPIRE GAMES ATHLETICS
Marathon: J. L. Coleman (Sth. Africa) 1; A. J. Norris (Eng.) 2; H. A. Gibson (Sth. Africa) 3. Time, 2.30.49.4 (Empire Games and Australian record.)

Editorial

Suppressing The Junkers

The High Command of the Army in Germany has always held great power.

It has influenced policy and swayed governments.

It has been the perquisite of the noble and very conservative families of Prussia.

Sooner or later this was bound to bring it into conflict with the Government it put into power to further its own purposes.

Herr Hitler, however, does not come of a noble family, and is the author and leader of National Socialism.

Recent events in Germany may be interpreted in terms of foreign policy according to the optimism or pessimism of the commentator.

The fact that stands out is that the Junkers who helped Hitler to power against the Republican forces, have now discovered that Hitler and his party propose to control Germany.

Says Our Exam. System Is "Childish"

"The Sun" Cable Service

LONDON, Sunday.

Criticism of the examination system in Australia is contained in an article published in this year's "Year Book of Education."

The headline news in the Sydney Sun of Monday, 7 February 1938 recorded the events of Bondi's Black Sunday, with dramatic pictures from the beach that day. Other front page stories foreshadow future events, recording Jewish refugees from Germany being allowed to settle in Australia, and naval exercises with the British.

Page 18 The Sydney Mail, Wednesday, February 9, 1938.

SURFING TRAGEDY AT BONDI

Resuscitating Exhausted Bathers on the Beach at Bondi

A treacherous undertow on Sunday suddenly swept nearly 200 surf-bathers out to sea, and, but for the Herculean efforts of the surf life-savers, more than a score must have been drowned. As it was, four lives were lost, despite great heroism on the part of the men with the lines and in the surf-boats. At one time no fewer than twenty were lying on the beach in an apparently drowned state, and here, again, magnificent work was done by the life-savers and others. An American medical man who witnessed the tragedy paid a glowing tribute to the rescuers. "I have never seen, and I never expect to see again," he said, "such magnificent work as was done by those life-savers. It is the most incredible work of love in the world." It is believed the tragedy was caused by a series of huge waves completely demolishing a sandbank.

The largest single surf rescue operation was photographed by eyewitnesses who increasingly carried their own cameras, such as the popular Kodak Box Brownie.

Nothing to do with missionaries 66

An Indigenous newspaper, 1938

IN JANUARY 1938 SYDNEY REJOICED IN CELEBRATION OF THE 150TH ANNIVERSARY OF THE ARRIVAL OF THE FIRST FLEET. DESPITE—OR PERHAPS BECAUSE OF—THE LOOMING CRISIS OF WAR IN EUROPE, PARADES, PAGEANTS AND RE-ENACTMENTS OF THE ARRIVAL OF GOVERNOR ARTHUR PHILLIP AND THE FIRST FLEET WERE HELD IN SYDNEY, AND ACROSS THE COUNTRY, THROUGH THE USE OF RECYCLABLE, MOTORISED FLOATS.

Meanwhile, Aboriginal people in Sydney had organised a symbolic protest and, quite bravely in the face of such an investment in the celebration of European history in Australia, called 26 January 1938 a National Day of Mourning. Around a hundred people gathered in the Australian Hall on Elizabeth Street, on the route of the grand parade of 'Australian history and progress' that was to wind its way through Sydney streets, through crowds of hundreds of thousands of spectators.

The activists who had called the meeting, including the footballer, pastor and later governor of South Australia, Douglas Nicholls (1906–1988), brought to prominence, among many grievances, the call for citizenship in their own country.

Australia's first Indigenous-run newspaper was produced to coincide with the National Day of Mourning protests. *The Australian Abo Call* was short lived, running to just six issues, but it was an important element of an emerging Indigenous political voice that was to continue through the twentieth century. As its title noted, it called for 'Education, Opportunity and Full Citizen Rights'.

Representing 80,000 Australian Aborigines

The Australian ABO CALL

THE VOICE OF THE ABORIGINES

EDITED BY J. T. PATTEN

We ask for Education, Opportunity, and Full Citizen Rights

No. 1. MONTHLY, 3d. APRIL, 1938.

To all Aborigines!

"The Abo Call" is our own paper.

It has been established to present the case for Aborigines, from the point of view of the Aborigines themselves.

This paper has nothing to do with missionaries, or anthropologists, or with anybody who looks down on Aborigines as an "inferior" race.

We are NOT an inferior race, we have merely been refused the chance of education that whites receive. "The Abo Call" will show that we do not want to go back to the Stone Age.

Representing 60,000 Full Bloods and 20,000 Halfcastes in Australia, we raise our voice to ask for Education, Equal Opportunity, and Full Citizen Rights.

"The Abo Call" will be published once a month. Price 3d.

The Editor asks all Aborigines and Halfcastes to support the paper, by buying it and also by acting as agents for sale to white friends and supporters.

Please send postal note when ordering copies.

Address all letters to:—

J. T. Patten, "The Abo Call", Box 1924 KK, General Post Office, Sydney, N.S.W.

Photo by courtesy "Man" Magazine.

AT THE CONFERENCE OF 26th JANUARY.

T. Foster (La Perouse), J. Kinchela (Coonabarabran), W. Cooper (Melbourne), D. Nicholls (Melbourne), J. T. Patten (La Perouse), W. Ferguson (Dubbo).

OUR TEN POINTS

Deputation to the Prime Minister

The following is a full copy of the statement made to the Prime Minister at the Deputation of Aborigines on 31st January last.

The Prime Minister was accompanied by Dame Enid Lyons and by Mr. McEwan, Minister of the Interior.

The Deputation consisted of twenty Aborigines, men and women, and Mr. Lyons gave a hearing of two hours to the statement of our case.

Please read these "ten points" carefully, as this is the only official statement of our aims and objects that has yet been made.

TO THE RIGHT HON. THE PRIME MINISTER OF AUSTRALIA.
MR. J. A. LYONS, P.C., C.H., M.H.R.

Sir,

In respectfully placing before you the following POLICY FOR ABORIGINES. We wish to state that this policy has been endorsed by a Conference of Aborigines, held in Sydney on 26th January of this year. This policy is the only policy which has the support of the Aborigines themselves.

URGENT INTERIM POLICY

Before placing before you a long-range policy for Aborigines, and while the long-range policy is under consideration, we ask as a matter of urgency:

That the Commonwealth Government should make a special financial grant to each of the State Governments, in proportion to the number of Aborigines in each State, to supplement existing grants for Aborigines. We ask that such aid should be applied to increasing the rations and improving the housing conditions of Aborigines at present under State control. We beg that this matter be treated urgently, as our people are being starved to death.

The following ten points embraces a LONG RANGE POLICY FOR ABORIGINES, endorsed by our Association.

A LONG RANGE POLICY FOR ABORIGINES.

1.—We respectfully request that there should be a National Policy for Aborigines. We advocate Commonwealth Government control of all Aboriginal affairs.

2.—We suggest the appointment of a Commonwealth Ministry for Aboriginal Affairs, the Minister to have full Cabinet rank.

3.—We suggest the appointment of an Administrative Head of the proposed Department of Aboriginal Affairs, the Administrator to be advised by an Advisory Board, consisting of six persons, three of whom at least should be of Aboriginal blood, to be nominated by the Aborigines Progressive Association.

4.—The aim of the Department of Aboriginal Affairs should be *to raise all Aborigines throughout the Commonwealth to full Citizen Status* and civil equality with the whites in Australia. In particular, and without delay, all Aborigines should be entitled:

(a) To receive the same educational opportunities as white people.

(b) To receive the benefits of labour legislation, including Arbitration Court Awards, on an equality with white workers.

(c) To receive the full benefits of workers' compensation and insurance.

(d) To receive the benefits of old-age and invalid pensions, whether living in Aboriginal settlements or not.

(e) To own land and property, and to be allowed to save money in personal banking accounts, and to come under the same laws regarding intestacy and transmission of property as the white population.

(f) To receive wages in cash, and not by orders, issue of rations, or apprenticeship systems.

5.—We recommend that Aborigines and Halfcastes should come under the same marriage laws as white people, and should be free to marry partners of their choice, irrespective of colour.

6.—We recommend that Aborigines should be entitled to the same privileges regarding housing as are white workers.

7.—We recommend that a special policy of Land Settlement for Aborigines should be put into operation, whereby Aborigines who desire to settle on the land should be given the same encouragement as that given to Immigrants or Soldier Settlers, with expert tuition in agriculture, and financial assistance to enable such settlers to become ultimately self-supporting.

8.—In regard to uncivilised and semi-civilised Aborigines, we suggest that patrol officers, nurses, and teachers, both men and women, of *Aboriginal blood*, should be specially trained by the Commonwealth Government as Aboriginal Officers, to bring the wild people into contact with civilisation.

9.—We recommend that all Aboriginal and Halfcaste women should be entitled to maternity and free hospital treatment during confinement, and that there should be no discrimination against Aboriginal women, who should be entitled to clinical instruction on baby welfare, similar to that given to white women.

10.—While opposing a policy of segregation, we urge that, during a period of transition, the present Aboriginal Reserves should be retained as a sanctuary for aged or incompetent Aborigines who may be unfitted to take their place in the white community, owing to the past policy of neglect.

DAY OF MOURNING

White people immediately realised that we Aborigines have no reason to rejoice at the 150th Anniversary of white settlement in this continent.

"THE ABO CALL".

Send us your order for a dozen copies of "The Abo Call" and give or sell them to friends and supporters.

Price to agents 2/- per dozen post free

Send cash with order to: "The Abo Call", Box 1924 KK, G.P.O., Sydney.

EASTER MEETING

A general meeting of Aborigines will be held at La Perouse Reserve on Easter Sunday (17th April).

The main purpose of the meeting is to adopt a Constitution and Rules for the Aborigines Progressive Association, also election of officers.

Please make a big effort to attend this important meeting, which will put our fight for Citizen Rights on a proper legal footing.

SELECT COMMITTEE

The Select Committee upon the Administration of the Aborigines Protection Board (New South Wales) took a lot of evidence, and then dissolved without making a report.

The Select Committee was a farce, as most of the evidence concerned the dismissal of Manager Brain from Brewarrina, and there was no time to present full evidence about the conditions of the 10,000 Aborigines and Halfcastes of New South Wales.

Parliament was more worried about one white man than about ten thousand blacks.

We call for a Royal Commission to investigate Aboriginal Administration in N.S.W.

We have a big lot of evidence, some of which will be published in "The Abo Call" in future numbers.

MR. BRUXNER'S PROMISE

In his policy speech in the N.S.W. Elections, the leader of the Country Party, Mr. M. F. Bruxner, promised "a new deal for Aborigines."

This is the same Mr. Bruxner who said to the Millions Club, Sydney, a few months ago, that "Jacky-Jacky is not a good advertisement for Australia."

In Mr. Bruxner's own electorate, near Tabulam, N.S.W., the Aborigines are living in dreadful conditions, which are a very bad advertisement for Mr. Bruxner.

We hope that his "New Deal" will be a better deal than we have had for the past 150 years.

PACKSADDLE

Our friends in Darwin inform us that a white man also was charged with rape at the same time as Packsaddle, but no mention was made of this in either Darwin or Sydney papers.

The first issue of the first Indigenous newspaper, The Australian Abo Call, *includes a list of demands for Aboriginal rights, many of which were slowly to become a reality.*

Black Friday 67

Deadly bushfires in Victoria, 1939

FRIDAY THE THIRTEENTH HAS LONG BEEN CALLED BLACK FRIDAY, BUT IN JANUARY 1939 THE TERM TOOK ON A NEW MEANING FOR MANY RESIDENTS OF VICTORIA. MORE THAN 1.5 MILLION HECTARES OF FOREST WERE BURNED DURING TWO DAYS OF INTENSE BUSHFIRES, WHICH ALSO DESTROYED AN ESTIMATED 1300 HOMES.

After a period of drought since 1937, in early January 1939 temperatures in Victoria reached over 45 degrees Celsius, and when a strong northerly wind hit on the thirteenth, several small existing fires rapidly converged. As the royal commissioner later wrote, 'it seemed like the whole state was on fire'.

The fires moved too quickly for many people, roaring down valleys at great speed. Witnesses saw brick houses explode from the intensity of the heat and large trees ripped from the soil by the high winds. Several towns across the state were completely destroyed. Ash from the fires drifted as far as New Zealand.

Seventy-one people died in what was, until recently, the most devastating bushfire in Australian history. The fires burned so intensely that it took decades for many of the affected areas to recover. Yet the fires of Black Friday brought about many reforms in the priorities and methods of fire protection and fire safety. The subsequent royal commission found there had been little preparation for such large-scale bushfires and was astounded that fires were often left unattended in remote areas. Fire towers, forest access trails and fire restrictions were among the many measures introduced after the Black Friday disaster.

AUSTRALIA'S LARGEST SALE—240,132 DAILY

The Sun NEWS ~ PICTORIAL

DAILY AT DAWN

With Which Is Incorporated The Morning Post

No. 5091 Registered at the G.P.O., Melbourne, for transmission by post as a newspaper. Melbourne: Monday, January 16, 1939 Telephone Nos.— Central 9240, Central 6853, Central 4641, J1322, J3191 (52 Pages) 1½d.

FULL HAVOC BY BUSH FIRES REVEALED

Some Rain at Last :: Relief For Several Areas

WOODS POINT IS A PLACE OF DESOLATION, and the main street is lined with ashes and twisted iron marking the sites of homes. This view shows the hotel ruins in the foreground, and a trail of destruction stretching to the end of Bridge Street, where two buildings were spared by a freak of Friday's bush fire.

HUGE LOSS OF LIFE AND PROPERTY ALL OVER STATE

WHEN the tragic story of Friday's bush fires was completed, yesterday, 45 deaths had been added to the 21 of the previous week-end, making a death total in Victoria of 66. Of these 11 were reported yesterday. The Friday fire list includes five women and four children. In addition, one child in Stawell Hospital is not expected to live and one man is missing and almost certainly dead. New South Wales reports five deaths in bush fires.

Although one or two more deaths may be reported, the list of missing people is now small, and there is some hope that cool south-easterly winds will help men in controlling what fires remain.

Breaking of Drought?

In some areas, fire-fighters were helped last night by rain which varied from light to occasionally heavy. A few outbreaks were extinguished. Heavier falls, however, are needed in the worst fire centres.

This was the first rain of any appreciable extent received in Victoria for about six weeks.

Details from the fire areas show that Friday's holocaust left a trail of destruction and desolation right across the State. The losses are beyond calculation. Hundreds of homes, sawmills, mineheads, and buildings have been destroyed in blazes which wiped out whole towns. There has been a terrible toll of horses, cattle and sheep. Native animals and birds probably have died in millions.

Yesterday the destruction of more than 30 buildings in Omeo was confirmed, but this paled before the complete destruction of Woods Point, where 750 people live normally and which might never be re-established. The damage here is estimated at £250,000.

Plans For Relief

Relief plans have been rushed through and hundreds of refugees from stricken areas are being cared for throughout the State. The military camp at Seymour was prepared overnight for the reception of a train-load of people from Woods Point who arrived to find a hot meal awaiting them early yesterday morning. Trucks and cars have carried supplies of food, clothing and furniture to dozens of burnt-out areas.

The public has contributed generously and promptly to the various appeals opened and tens of thousands of pounds have been subscribed to help in the relief and rehabilitation of the hundreds of victims.

BUSH FIRE DETAILS CONTINUED ON NEXT PAGE

Scenes and stories of the devastation of the Black Friday bushfires were printed in graphic detail as headline news across the country, shocking all Australians.

AUDITED DAILY NET SALES—212,229 (A.B.C. Certificate)

WEATHER FORECAST.—FINE ; SOUTHERLY WINDS.

BOOMERANG CIGARETTE PAPERS RICE STAINLESS

The Herald

One-Hundredth Year

STUMPS LAST EDITION SCORES

SPECIALISTS IN HOSIERY, GLOVES LINGERIE — SNAPPY LEGS PTY. LTD. MANCHESTER UNITY BLDG. SWANSTON ST MELB...

No. 19,239 | Registered at General Post Office, Melbourne, for transmission by post as a newspaper. | MELBOURNE, SATURDAY EVENING, JANUARY 14, 1939 | Postal Address: 62 Flinders Street, Melbourne, C.1. Tele: Cent. 4641; J3191; Circulation Dept.: F4663 | Price 1½d. 40 PAGES

42 MORE BURNED TO DEATH IN FIRES

Many Others Missing :: Victims Now Total 63

2 WOMEN & 20 MEN REPORTED DEAD AT WOOD'S PT.

From Our Special Reporters

Forty-two people lost their lives in the terrific bush fires whch raged throughout Victoria yesterday and last night. This brings the week's death roll to 63. Many others are feared to have perished, dozens being reported missing.

The victims included:

AT NOOJEE: A man, his wife and three children, a married couple and their baby, and a young man.

AT WOOD'S POINT: Two women and 20 men, 19 of whom are unidentified.

Of the 150 houses at Wood's Point, 143 are in ashes.

Noojee was wiped out late yesterday, and the victims there were burned to death in two timber mills. Three men were badly injured and several others suffered burns. Armed with axes, a party has left Warragul to recover the bodies.

An Italian, whose name is unknown, his wife and three children, are missing in the Noojee area. They are thought to have perished.

Noojee Wiped Out: Today's Vivid Picture

NOOJEE IN RUINS.—First picture to reach Melbourne of the remains of the mountain township after the holocaust yesterday. With other photographs on Back Page, it was sent to Melbourne today by a Herald photographer, who reached Noojee with searchers at 2 a.m., after a nightmare walk through falling and burning timber. Pathways had to be cut with axes.

CITY SOUVENIR-HUNTERS PILLAGE BURNT HOMES

Fourteen men were last seen at a timber mill at Matlock, crouching behind a sawdust heap, while flames encircled them. Their bodies were later found by a search party.

One of the two men saved was G. Sellars. He sheltered behind the boiler until the worst of the blaze had passed and then made a dash through the flames covered with wet bags.

All other mills between McVeigh's and Matlock have been destroyed. They include Porta's, Henderson's, W. Fitzpatrick's, and Richards.

The whole of the ranges between Warburton and Wood's Point have been devastated and dozens of houses have been destroyed.

At W. Fitzpatrick's mill, near Matlock, eight men escaped by sheltering in a dug-out all night.

In addition to the lives lost at the timber mills, it is feared that others have been killed in the fire which wiped out Wood's Point.

Many of them suffering agonies from burns, and all destitute, 500 people are waiting at Wood's Point for a convoy of 12 vehicles which left Melbourne early today with nurses, doctors, medical equipment, hospital tents, food and clothes.

Abandoning their belongings in a race for life, when fire struck Matlock last night, 500 men, women and children crowded into a Goulburn River water tunnel. The hospital was the first building struck by the flames.

Residents and fire fighters were amazed by streams of cars loaded with city sightseers who invaded the nearer fire districts this afternoon. Souvenir-hunters who began to pillage burnt homes in the Ringwood, Warrandyte and Kangaroo Grounds areas were warned off by angry owners of the ruins.

Noojee's disastrous fire leapt on the town with terrifying suddenness, giving the fighters no chance to save buildings, of which, today, only two still stand. Past Noojee, it destroyed the small settlements of Icy Creek and Fumina. Icy Creek and Vesper are cut off, and in both places there are numbers of people not yet accounted for.

There were grave fears for five men, a woman, and a child, at Brown's Mill, seven miles out from Noojee, but today they reached Warragul, after a terrifying night, spent by three of them in a dam, and by the other three in a dugout.

Benambra, more than 100 miles north of Bairnsdale, is in a desperate position and it is doubted whether fire-fighters who raced from Bairnsdale, can save it. Cassilis, in East Gippsland, has been wiped out.

32 HOUSES DESTROYED IN YARRA GLEN BLAZE

Fire swept into Omeo last night, wiped out a hotel, the hospital, 20 houses, and at least 11 shops.

Completely cut off by road and telephone, the town sent a dramatic broadcast today appealing for hospital and surgical equipment.

Yarra Glen lost 32 houses and guest houses in widespread fires today.

Although both the Ada Nos. 1 and 2 mills, 11 miles from Powelltown, were destroyed late yesterday, all the timber workers and their families are safe.

The fire which had been raging on the fringe of the Alps all the week did its most serious damage yesterday when it wiped out St. Bernard's Hospice and the highest house in the State, Hotham Heights Chalet.

The proprietor of St. Bernard's Hospice (Mr B. Bush), his wife, his daughter, and his mother-in-law escaped down the deep gorge into the Dargo River, where they are reported still to be marooned. A rescue party has left Harrietville.

Fires near Healesville freshened before the wind this afternoon. In a few minutes a puff of smoke in the distance blew up to choking clouds rolling through the town. Every available man is out fighting, and many who had retired exhausted have gone back to battle against the approaching fire.

In various parts of the State mill-workers and fire-fighters are reported missing, but many of them are probably safe.

There is yet no confirmation of a report, received in Moe, that 12 men were out in the bush without shelter in the fire that caused the Saxton's mill fatality.

In the Kiewa Valley, Mr J. Edney, who has been missing from the State Electricity Commission's camp since Wednesday, has still not been found by the search parties.

Relieving the deep tragedy of the State-wide disaster come occasional stories that have their touch of humor or rare courage. An 80-year-old man was found after the Goulburn Valley fire had passed sitting in the river smoking his pipe.

A 75-year-old woman, at Warrandyte, fought with a bucket of water to save her lonely home. She failed, but she saved her dog. It is now in the North Melbourne animal hospital.

In the Ovens Valley, Freeburgh, a township between Bright and Harrietville, is reported to have been wiped out. All communications are broken.

East Gippsland, where a hot northerly is still blowing, is ablaze and help is wanted everywhere. Omeo and Swift's Creek are still without sufficient man-power to fight.

SPECIAL GRANT BY FEDERAL GOVERNMENT

The Labor Party will ask the Premier (Mr Dunstan) to receive a deputation asking for a Royal Commission into the bush fires and allegations that insufficient safety measures were taken at some mills. Several members and a number of unions support the request.

In Devonport (Tas.) the Prime Minister (Mr Lyons) announced today that the Federal Government would make a special grant to relieve distress in fire areas. The amount would be decided by Cabinet when it met in Hobart early next month.

The Federal Government today placed at Victoria's disposal the resources of the Australian Army Medical Corps. The Relief Committee, working from Melbourne, is now caring for at least 1000 refugees.

Lorne's total loss yesterday was at least 20 houses and three mills. Heavy destruction in the Penshurst district included scores of haystacks, many miles of fencing and the loss of thousands of head of cattle, sheep and poultry. One man lost 6000 sheep.

More than 1200 volunteers were rushed to fire areas between 8 p.m. yesterday and 4 a.m. today. About 700 of these were from the city. The Forest Commission has been rushed with offers of cars and services, and has enrolled more than 1700 men.

Ben Mason, 17, who had been missing at Hall's Gap in the Grampians since Thursday night, was found alive today, although he was suffering severe burns on the legs.

FULL DETAILS IN PAGES 3, 6 AND 8

Latest Death Roll

REPORTED TODAY

FREDERICK TOPPING, 72, pensioner, Warrandyte.
— LAWRY, Buckland Valley, between Bright and Omeo (brother missing).
WILLIAM DOIG, Kyneton, died in hospital from burns.
MR AND MRS BEN SAXTON and their child, 2, Noojee.
MR AND MRS W. B. RAWLEY, Noojee.
THE RAWLEY CHILDREN—John, Ben and Agnes.
MICHAEL JOHN GORIN, 18, of Noojee.
At least 19 men at Wood's Point.

REPORTED LAST NIGHT

TERESA ROBINSON, 13, of Kawarren, near Colac.
MARY ROBINSON, 12, sister.
VERA ROBINSON, 10, another sister.
PAUL ROBINSON, 8, their brother.
W. J. LOOSEMORE, about 60, beekeeper, of Hillend, Gippsland.
ALBERT EDWARD McGINTY, a child, of Casterton.
— CASTONELLI, an elderly Italian, of Hillend.
ALBERT DUDLEY PENTREATH, retired journalist, of Strathewan.
THOMAS BERNARD CULLEN, Wood's Point.
MISS NELLIE O'KEEFE, of Wood's Point.
MRS MAYNARD, of Scotchmer Street, Fitzroy, chef at Yelland's Mill, Wood's Point.

MISSING

— LAWRY, between Bright and Harrietville.
J. EDNEY, Electricity Commission officer, Hinan's Gap, Kiewa Valley.
Three persons at Noojee (believed dead).
Two men at Jerralong, near Traralgon.
An Italian, name unknown, his wife, and three children, at Noojee.

Earlier Victims—Page 3

20 DEAD IN TWO MILLS

From Our Special Representative

MANSFIELD, Saturday. — A woman was burnt to death and another woman and 20 men are believed dead in the disastrous blaze which swept Wood's Point township and Matlock mills yesterday. One hundred homes, stores, the post-office, police station and the hospital were razed. Only nine houses are standing.

Two of the victims are Miss Nellie O'Keefe and Mrs Maynard, of Scotchmer Street, North Fitzroy, chef at Yelland Mill.

Fourteen men at Fitzpatrick's Mill and six men at Fitzpatrick's new mill—both at Matlock—have perished.

The last seen of the men at the first mill was late Friday afternoon, when they were crouching behind a sawdust heap, encircled by flames. The names of the men at both mills are unknown.

Mrs Maynard was trapped in her smoke-filled home alongside Yelland's Mill. The fire, which caused £50,000 in damage, to Woods Point alone, struck the town just before 3 p.m.

The fire which threatened the sawmills east of Mansfield is now burning away toward the east, and unless the wind changes to the north the mill should be safe.

The fire beyond Jamieson is still burning, but at present Jamieson is not in danger. Wood's Point has been wiped out, and there is a report that there has been additional considerable loss of life apart from the mill fatalities, but this has not been officially confirmed by the Mansfield police.

Mr Chas. Lloyd, 80, of Ten Mile, whose house was destroyed, was found after the fire sitting in the river calmly smoking his pipe.

The youngest refugee is the four-weeks-old child of Mrs Claire Clements. With other babies it was taken to the safety of the bridge over the Goulburn

(Continued in Page 3, Col. 7)

APPEAL BY PREMIER TO SUNDAY MOTORISTS

An appeal to motorists to keep out of the bush fire areas during the week-end was made today by the Premier (Mr Dunstan).

"Great disorganisation has been caused in many country districts by the fires, and I regret deeply the news today of further heavy loss of life," he said. "I, therefore, appeal to all sections of the community to do nothing which might hinder the work of those fighting the fires and providing relief for the sufferers.

"Motorists in particular can render a useful service by refraining from visiting any of the stricken areas during the week-end, unless they have urgent business to transact.

"Any large congregation of motor vehicles and people in those places will intensify a problem already great, and may lead to serious road congestion at a time when roadways comparatively free from traffic are urgently necessary.

"I make the appeal in the confident hope that the community generally will give the utmost co-operation, and so render less arduous the important work of bush fire prevention and relief."

BUSHFIRE SUFFERERS NEED YOUR AID

Nearly £10,000 had been subscribed to The Herald Bushfire Relief Fund when this edition went to press, and cash was still coming in with donations ranging from 1/- to £100.

Some firms who sent big amounts to the Herald list, which opened on Tuesday, have forwarded additional contributions because the loss of life, destruction to property, and pitiful conditions of hardship are much graver today than earlier in the week.

The people of Victoria, with characteristic promptness, have responded most generously to this call for help, but more money is needed urgently.

To read about this calamity gives some idea of the plight of those who have lost all they had possessed and—in many cases—their breadwinners.

COLLECTION BOXES

Those who have been near the scenes of the tragedies know that the distress and sadness which the fires are leaving in their trail are indescribable.

Whether your contribution to this worthy cause is large or small, the main thing is to send it to The Herald at the earliest possible moment.

For the benefit of those who cannot afford to send large amounts, collection boxes have been placed at all newsagents in the city and suburbs.

Donations, when this edition went to press, were:—

Previously acknowledged .. .. £[illegible]
J. McAlpin & Sons 100 0 0
Staffs of Shell Co. (Aust.) Ltd. Managerial and Office (£63), Newport Installation (£22) .. 85 0 0
Shell Co. of Aust. Ltd. (Second Contribution) .. 50 0 0
Vacuum Oil Co. Ltd. (Second Contribution) .. 50 0 0
Foy and Gibson Pty. Ltd. .. 50 0 0
Mr and Mrs A. Keilet .. 30 0 0
Crooks National Stores Pty. Ltd. .. 50 0 0
Employes of Crooks National Stores Pty. Ltd. .. 50 0 0
Silk Bros. Pty. Ltd. .. 50 0 0
Employes Bon Marche .. 30 0 0
Staffs of Foy & Gibson Stores .. 30 0 0
Vacuum Oil Co. (Second Contribution) .. 30 0 0
Staff and Factory, Brooks, McGlashan & McHarg Pty. Ltd. .. 30 0 0
Employes Headquarters Moran & Cato Pty. Ltd. .. 28 0 0
Melb. Office Staff Bank of New South Wales .. 27 18 0
[illegible]
(Continued in Page 7)

Cool, But No Rain Likely

Although Melbourne's temperature dropped from 114 yesterday to 71.5 today, no rain is in sight.

The Commonwealth Meteorologist (Mr Watt) said today he held little hope of the Western Australian depression coming here.

He forecast a cool week-end for Melbourne.

(Sydney's Record Heat.—Page 8.)

The front page of Melbourne's Herald *newspaper of 14 January 1939 reported the disastrous fires in Victoria as headline news.*

War and migrants

1940–

-1949

During the First World War, Australians had been eager to become involved in the fighting as a way of proving nationhood on a global stage. In the Second World War, however, not only was Australia itself under attack, it was also desperately trying to bring its forces back from overseas to defend itself against a possible invasion. The threat of the 'swarming' Japanese army as it advanced through the south-west Pacific during the 1940s was significant in shaping not only Australian politics, but also Australians' view of their place in the world, for many years to come.

The faith Australians had in the large British naval presence in the Asia–Pacific was shattered when the fortress of Singapore quickly fell to the Japanese in February 1942. With a sense of British abandonment while they focused on the war in Europe, Australians were forced to look to their own defence—and to other nations for assistance. Perhaps thankful that the Australian people had so warmly welcomed the United States navy in previous years, the Australian government now turned to the Americans for an alliance against the Japanese.

In 1942 Australians had never been under such threat of invasion since the arrival of the First Fleet in 1788. The threat of the Japanese forces—who attacked Australian shores with bombing raids and naval attacks from Sydney to Darwin—united the country as never before.

Reporting the news of war had always been important. As most of Australia's major military conflicts had occurred overseas, both official and unofficial war correspondents had been significant in relaying to Australians the experiences of their soldiers. But now in an age of radio communications, such reports could aid the enemy and so were severely censored. While newspapers were conscious of this and accepted censorship as part of the war effort, they were also very watchful of their right to report news, and they came into sharp conflict with both the Curtin and then Chifley Labor governments towards the end of the war. Interestingly, the conflict was over their right to report on the fact of their censorship.

With the demand for locally manufactured war material, Australia's manufacturing industries expanded in the 1940s. Ships, vehicles, planes and armaments were manufactured in great quantities across the country, and many women entered the workforce to replace the men who were joining the armed forces. Although there was an expectation that women would return to the home after the war, the fact that they could perform the usual work of men led to future significant changes in the workforce, and in the domestic and political lives of women.

When the war in the Pacific finally ended in August 1945, the tragedy of the war was still unfolding for many Australians. Newspapers began to report on what had happened to the thousands of civilians and military personnel who had been captured during the Japanese occupation of south-east Asia. Finally released from the hands of censors, newspapers were full of stories of the harsh treatment of prisoners, of massacres and other Japanese war atrocities.

Once again in Australian history, one of the key strategies planned for future national defence was to simply increase the population. This time, however, the countries of origin of the people being accepted into the country began to change. War refugees and orphaned children from Britain were encouraged, but more people than Britain could provide were needed to meet the need of a planned massive postwar economic program. Under international humanitarian agreements, Australia was quick to accept refugees or 'displaced persons' from Europe. Many of these were from eastern European countries. Others, such as Italians and Maltese, chose Australia because there were already small but significant migrant communities in the country.

The problem with such migration from southern European countries in particular was that it appeared to contradict the White Australia policy, and at first there was much opposition from all sides of politics. However, after the recent fears of invasion by the Japanese, and a climate of increasing political tension between Western nations on the one hand and the growing number of communist countries on the other—including China after the 1949 revolution—Australia's migration restrictions based on race finally began to change.

This far-reaching change was to take place during a period of a Liberal–Country Party government that was, like the Labor Party of the time, very supportive of the White Australia policy. Robert Menzies' election at the head of the Liberal and Country Party coalition in 1949 inaugurated a very long period of conservative politics in Australia. Yet at the same time it ushered in the largest intake of migrants from non-British countries of origin Australia had seen. The social and cultural make-up of Australia was to be dramatically transformed.

68 A strong force of Anzacs

Australians and New Zealanders in the battle for Crete, 1941

THE LEGEND OF THE FIRST ANZAC FORCE AT GALLIPOLI IN THE FIRST WORLD WAR REMAINS A PROMINENT PART OF AUSTRALIA'S NATIONAL MEMORY, BUT IT IS NOT COMMONLY KNOWN THAT ANOTHER ANZAC FORCE WAS FORMED IN THE SECOND WORLD WAR. ONCE AGAIN, TROOPS WERE SENT TO THE MEDITERRANEAN, AND ONCE AGAIN THEY WERE SOUNDLY DEFEATED.

In early 1941 the strategic decision to bolster the Greek army in the face of a likely German and Italian invasion was being closely followed in Australian newspapers. The Australian First Corps of the army was moved to Greece in April 1941, and as it included the New Zealand army's Second Division, the force was officially renamed the Anzac Corps.

The German army began the invasion of Greece on 6 April 1941 and, despite some strong opposition from the Greek, British and Anzac forces, they broke through and moved rapidly towards Athens. On 25 April that year, celebrating Anzac Day was not a priority in the minds of the Commonwealth forces, as their corps headquarters had already been evacuated and the 10,000 troops were boarding ships to leave Greece. The Germans had taken Athens, the Greek capital, by 27 April.

The large Anzac and British force that had been evacuated was sent to support British and Greek garrisons on the strategic island of Crete, and they soon came under attack by German paratroopers—the largest force of paratroopers yet assembled. After fierce resistance, which almost halted the airborne attack, the paratroopers were supported by fresh German troops and the Anzac, British and Greek forces were destroyed. Although the Germans were successful, their paratroopers suffered such heavy casualties they were never used again.

Although information was scarce, often censored and sometimes intentionally incorrect, the *Sun* of 21 May reported a message from 'official Greek sources' that was very wide of the mark; that the 'military authorities in Crete had completely mastered the situation' and that 'all the parachutists were dead or captured'.

NET WEEKLY SALES LARGER THAN THOSE OF ANY OTHER NEWSPAPER IN AUSTRALIA

SAVE THIS PAPER FOR THE WASTE COLLECTORS

THE SUN

ABOVE ALL — FOR AUSTRALIA

COUNTRY EDITION

CITY FORECAST Fine, mild day; Cool night.

No. 9789 — SYDNEY: WEDNESDAY, MAY 21, 1941 — PRICE 2d — Phone: BO 333

ANZAC TROOPS LAND IN CYPRUS

Vital Role Guarding Fleet

CRETE VICTORY REPORTED

'Parachutists Killed Or Captured'

Australain Associated Press.

LONDON, Tuesday.

A strong force of Anzac troops has landed on the Island of Cyprus, a most vital British outpost in the Eastern Mediterranean.

Cabling this news to London, the Cairo correspondent of "The Times" says that the Anzacs are to reinforce the existing British and Cypriot garrisons in defence of the island.

Cyprus is less than 200 miles from Alexandria, where the Mediterranean Fleet is based and a bare 60 miles from the Syrian coast.

Stuka dive-bombers based on Cyprus could possibly drive the Fleet from its main base as they are now trying to blast part of it out of Crete, 350 miles eastward, where New Zealanders are fighting a German parachute invasion.

A Free French Agency message from Cairo, quoting "official Greek circles" declared to-night: "The military authorities in Crete had completely mastered the situation by this afternoon. All parachutists have either been killed or captured."

Seven hundred German planes are reported to be concentrated at Greek air bases close to Crete, while intense enemy activity throughout Greece, the Dodecanese Islands and Syria is accepted here as preparation for an offensive against both Cyprus and Palestine.

Nazi Boast 'Over In Few Hours'

How complete are German preparations for a great drive through the Middle East is indicated by the following facts:—

German troops are heavily concentrated in Greek mainland ports and in the Aegean Islands east of Rhodes (Dodecanese), which partly outflanks Crete.

A large aerodrome at Aleppo is now completely in German hands. German technicians are billeted at many other airfields, equipment is being constantly ferried in by plane from the Dodecanese and large supplies of petrol are coming by train from Mosul, heart of the Iraki oilfields.

German experts are also reported as having taken over the Syrian railways and to be establishing large stores at all junctions.

Syria's High Commissioner, General Dentz has ordered all British Consuls to clear out of Syria and Lebanon within eight days.

High authorities at Vichy said to-night: "If Britain continues to bomb French aerodromes in Syria, then France will inevitably carry out reprisals."

The French Air Minister (General Bergeret) has flown into Syria, ostensibly to organise Syria's defences against air attack and to squash the de Gaulle movement. Several French pilots have flown their own machines into Palestine and joined the Free French.

Inside Syria, according to a traveller from Damascus, people are "huddling in nervous groups and discussing how to get away before the fighting begins."

"Must Expect To Be Shot"

The B.B.C. gave this warning to-night in a broadcast to Germany concerning Mr. Churchill's assertion that the parachutists who invaded Crete wore New Zealand uniforms.

"Every German soldier must know that whoever, in violation of the international law, fights in enemy uniform, must expect to be shot immediately when taken prisoner."

A B.B.C. military expert said: "The Germans in Crete, unsupported by their Panzer columns, are in for a bad time. They will have to fight for their lives in every valley and on every hill."

A Cairo message says that the parachute invasion of Crete—which is defended by New Zealanders, British and Greeks, under Major-General Freyberg, V.C.—began just before dawn.

"Provided we can get enough fighters to the scene to take care of enemy fighters, troop-carriers and dive-bombers simultaneously, our chances of beating off the invasion are good.

"A German occupation of Crete would not put Stuka dive-bombers within striking distance of Alexandria, because this would entail a return trip of nearly 1000 miles; but they would be able easily to hop to Tobruk (200 miles), thus creating another 'channel' more dangerous even than the Sicilian Channel" (90 miles between Sicily and Tunisia).

R.A.F. Again Faces Huge Task, Page 2.

"BLOW HER OUT OF THE WATER!" AND HERE IT IS!

THE SAILORS' SAYING: "We blew her out of the water," was literally true of this Italian destroyer Artigliere (1620 tons) as is shown by this remarkable series of pictures from the Mediterranean. The shell-hole that can be seen in this picture was only a prelude to—

THE DEATH BLOW dealt by H.M.S. York. Part of the destroyer's hull can be seen in mid-air on the extreme right of the picture. Then the mass of—

WATER, SMOKE AND WRECKAGE fell and the Artigliere was on her way to the bottom of the sea. All aboard had taken to the boats before the York's fatal shot.

Over Fiery Desert To Irak Victory

AUSTRALIAN ASSOCIATED PRESS

LONDON, Tuesday.

Behind the capture of Fallujah, Iraki fort 35 miles west of Bagdad guarding one of the crossings of the Euphrates, lies the story of an amazing forced march of 600 miles to Habbaniyah.

The march was made in five days by a column of hundreds of lorries, armored cars and guns, 300 miles of the distance being over waterless and roadless desert.

The temperature was 103 degrees in the shade, and metal inside the cars was so hot it could not be touched.

From Habbaniyah, the force made a wide detour around a vast stretch of desert, which the Irakis had flooded from the Euphrates.

The force split up west of the Euphrates, one half advancing to a bridge and the other crossing the river upstream. Simultaneously R.A.F. troop carriers arrived and landed troops east of Fallujah, barring the road to Bagdad.

STOP-PRESS

DEFEATED, DECORATED

NO PETROL IN CONTAINERS

BRISBANE RACES

SINKING OF U.S. SHIPS IN RED SEA FEARED

From Our Special Representative and Australian Associated Press

NEW YORK, Tuesday.

Sinking of the Egyptian liner Zamzam on her way to Alexandria with 142 American passengers and American ambulances has brought home vividly to the nation its nearness to open hostilities with Germany.

It is particularly significant that American freighters crammed to the gunwales with war materials, are now en route to the Red Sea, which the Germans have designated a combat area.

Washington is wondering now whether Germany was not bluffing but meant what she said when she announced that neutral ships entering combat zones will be attacked.

If a United States ship is sunk in the Red Sea it will bring America within sight of open war.

The State Department to-night declined to answer the question whether future movements of American ships will be affected.

Official circles in Berlin announced to-day that the Zamzam was sunk by a warship in the middle of last month.

The passengers and crew, for whose safety America had been gravely concerned, were rescued by the warship and landed from a German merchantman at a port in Western France, the Berlin statement added.

Alarm for the safety of the American passengers on the Zamzam crowded all other war news from the headlines here, but, with the German statement that the passengers and crew are safe, the chief interest of the State Department has shifted to the welfare and return of the American citizens.

U.S.A. Cables

Berlin For News

Contraband

Goods In Cargo

Envoy Protests Against U.S. Attitude To Vichy And Warns State Secretary Cordell Hull That—

France Will Fight To Keep Her Colonies

From Our Own Correspondent and Australian Associated Press

WASHINGTON, Tuesday.

The French Ambassador (M. Henry-Haye) informed the Secretary of State (Mr. Cordell Hull) to-day that France "will resist any attempt to take over any part of her Empire anywhere."

He protested against the United States' action in placing coastguards aboard 13 French ships, including the giant liner Normandie, in American ports last week.

Later, in a strong statement to the Press, M. Henry-Haye emphasised that France was determined to protect Dakar and Martinique from attack.

"I was painfully surprised by President Roosevelt's criticisms of Vichy," he said.

"I informed Mr. Hull that these were not justified, because Marshal Petain has not agreed to any modification of the Armistice, the terms of which permit the Germans to use Syrian aerodromes en route to Irak.

"I told Mr. Hull that our position was not ideal, but that we must adjust ourselves to defeat.

"We do not intend to re-enter the war, but we are determined to fight in defence of the French possessions."

The United Press reports that Mr. Hull told M. Henry-Haye that there will be no satisfactory relations between France and peaceful nations until Vichy proves it is not under German domination.

All peaceful nations are satisfied, he is reported to have added, that pro-Hitler elements are in control of the Vichy Government, and that it is up to the French to show that this impression is incorrect.

According to the Washington correspondent of the "New York Times," M. Henry-Haye concluded by informing Mr. Hull that the two American relief ships seized by the Vichy authorities would not be released until the United States released French ships.

There is a considerable division of opinion in official quarters regarding American policy towards France.

Some members of the Administration favor the most drastic measures before it is too late. The Navy Department is reported to be ready to take Martinique, Guadeloupe and French Guiana, but the State Department still exercises an effective veto.

This is not merely due to the reluctance to break finally with Petain, but also to a desire to make sure that such moves will be approved in Latin America.

The State Department is well aware that German propagandists would denounce American action in the Western Hemisphere as "Yankee Imperialism" throughout Latin America.

Therefore, the Secretary of State and the Assistant Secretary (Mr. Sumner Welles) will seek at least the secret approval of Latin America before they act.

Members of the State Department fear that precipitate action against France would immediately complicate the problem of lining up Latin America and obtaining bases there for "the long pull of war."

It would, however, be inaccurate to say that this postponement of vital decisions has left the State Department happy.

There are two opinions in the Department concerning the timing of decisive action against the Axis.

Mr. Hull is inclined to caution, but the younger members are holding that bold action is now more necessary than verbal philosophising.

The Army and Navy chiefs, whose standpoint ignores politics, believe that the sooner the United States gets hold of French bases the better.

Indications are that the Administration will endeavor to obtain French possessions by purchase.

Roosevelt Silent on Plans, Page 2.

Erroneous headlines like these, in this case reporting an Allied victory in Crete, were common during the Second World War.

69 *Japanese swarm down*

The fall of Singapore, 1942

IN FEBRUARY 1942 AUSTRALIANS WERE IN FOR A GREAT SHOCK. THE BRITISH STRONGHOLD OF THE FORTRESS OF SINGAPORE, THE 'GIBRALTAR OF THE EAST', HAD SWIFTLY AND UTTERLY FALLEN TO THE JAPANESE. NEVER BEFORE HAD THE BRITISH ARMY SEEN SUCH A CAPITULATION, EVEN THOUGH THEY OUTNUMBERED THE ATTACKING JAPANESE BY NEARLY THREE TO ONE.

In a lesson the Australian defence forces were quickly learning, Japanese air superiority was a decisive factor in the fall of Singapore. The Royal Navy could no longer be expected to hold its Pacific fortresses. Despite Britain's links with Australia, the young nation now found itself on its own.

Almost the entire Australian 8th Division of the army, numbering around 15,000 soldiers, was captured and many were imprisoned in a place that would later resonate deeply in Australian memory, Singapore's Changi Prison. Many other soldiers were used as forced labour and were shipped or marched to several other locations that would also be burned into Australian memories, particularly the Burma railway and the Sandakan airfield in Borneo.

While the horrors of these marches and prisons were not widely known until after the war, the intent of the Japanese occupation forces was apparent after a series of massacres in Singapore and elsewhere were reported. In early 1942, Australian newspaper headlines reflected the panic that spread across the nation.

Singapore had surrendered on 15 February 1942. On 19 February Australia suffered its heaviest wartime attack in history, as hundreds of Japanese aircraft bombed and strafed the port of Darwin in the Northern Territory. According to official estimates, 243 civilians and military personnel were killed and many more were wounded. Although news of the raid was reported in the press, the extent of the damage was suppressed, and the bombing of Darwin was not a significant headline in newspapers at the time.

OPPOSITE Brisbane's Courier-Mail showed graphically just how close the Japanese army had come to Australian shores as it moved past Singapore. The fall of Singapore and the Dutch East Indies (Indonesia) implanted a deep concern among Australians about invasion from Asian countries that had dire consequences in the 1960s.

GREATEST DAILY SALES IN QUEENSLAND

The Courier-Mail

No. 2638 - - (Registered in Australia for Transmission by Post as a Newspaper.) BRISBANE, TUESDAY, FEBRUARY 17, 1942. 8 PAGES—2d

JAPANESE SWARM DOWN ON DUTCH INDIES

Palembang Taken One Day After Fall Of Singapore

HARD on the heels of the fall of Singapore comes an official Dutch announcement that the Japanese have occupied Palembang, Sumatra's great oil centre.

In addition the Japanese are reported to have launched an attack on Java, where the Allied Supreme Commander in the south-west Pacific (General Wavell) has his headquarters.

Significance also attaches to Japan's capture of Banjermasin, capital of Borneo, as it is likely to be used as a centre from which to bomb Sourabaya, in Java, the Allies' only remaining naval base in the south-west Pacific.

The Japanese state that the surrender of Singapore was unconditional, and hostilities ceased at 10 p.m. on Sunday (1 a.m., Monday, Brisbane time).

The only official British announcement was that contained in Mr. Churchill's broadcast that the Malay Peninsula had been overrun and that Singapore had fallen.

Tokio radio announced that a Japanese armoured division entered Singapore at 8 a.m. local time yesterday.

Berlin radio says that the first Japanese warships entered Singapore Harbour on Sunday.

There is no confirmation of a Japanese claim to have cut off British troops who had landed on Sumatra from Singapore.

A land attack on Palembang on Sunday followed the failure of Japanese parachute troops to capture the oil installations on Saturday.

Then the Japanese began large-scale landing operations on Sunday the order was given to destroy all "vital points"—oil wells and refineries—near Palembang, and the order, it is stated officially, was fully executed.

Dutch bombers scored three direct hits yesterday on three Japanese transports near Muntok, on the Island of Banka.

Banjermasin, in Borneo, which has been captured by the Japanese, is 250 miles from Sourabaya and 500 miles from Batavia. Banjermasin's harbour is poor and is unlikely to provide a safe operating base for Japanese naval units, but as soon as its airfield is in order Java expects sustained aerial attacks from this quarter.

Tokio official radio claims that Japanese naval parachute troops were used for the first time in the occupation of Menado, in northern Celebes.

Huge Demolition

The destruction of the Palembang oilfields is the greatest instance of deliberate destruction in the world's history; beside it the Russians' destruction of the great Dnieper Dam last year was a splash in a bucket.

The output of these fields exceeded the entire output of Rumania. They produced nearly 4½ million tons yearly—more than half the entire Indies output.

The demolition was a gigantic task, but the Dutch had been preparing for it for two years. Their weapons were fire, dynamite, and cement, and, though the warning was short, the destruction is reported to have been thorough.

Large-scale Attack

Japanese land attacks on Palembang were on a large scale.

The Japanese first used parachute troops not only because they hoped to secure the Palembang oil refineries intact, but also because the country around Palembang, with its marshes and rice fields, looking from the air like a water-logged, moss-grown cheese board, could not be less suitable for land operations.

The Batavia communique announcing Palembang's fall stated: "After Japanese parachutist attacks started on Saturday strong action was taken. Towards Saturday evening a large part of the parachutists had been dealt with and the troops garrisoned in and around Palembang had the situation in hand.

"Meantime a strong enemy fleet was observed in Banka Straits.

"As a large-scale attack could be expected on Sunday, we proceeded, during Saturday night, to destroy completely the oil installations near Palembang.

"Early on Sunday morning large-scale bombardments on the Japanese fleet began and several successes were obtained. American, British, and Netherlands aircraft took part in these bombardments. Seven direct hits were scored.

Heavy Jap Losses

"In the Moesi Estuary the Japanese transferred their troops into all kinds of small craft—sloops, motor boats, sampans, and rowing boats. Then the craft sailed into various rivers and creeks, continually harassed by our very low-flying fighters and bombers, which played murderous havoc among the thousands of invaders.

"The enemy's attack was directed against the town of Palembang, which was occupied by the Japanese after fierce fighting.

"At present no further particulars can be given about the course of the fighting, which continues uninterruptedly.

"The Japanese are sustaining heavy losses.

"Our losses in aircraft and men at present are unknown, but it can be taken that they are considerably lower than the extent of this large action would make us expect.

"Fighting continues in south Celebes, especially near Macassar, and our troops are resisting with great stubbornness.

"Anambas Islands, east of Malaya, have been occupied by the Japanese."

Palembang's Value

Main reasons for the importance of Palembang, the big oil centre on the island of Sumatra, which the Japanese are attacking, are:

1. **It produces 60 per cent. of all the East Indies oil.**
2. **It is the site of the only really big oil refineries in the Indies still available to the Allies.**
3. **It has a big military and civil airfield.**
4. **It is at the head of a river flowing into Banka Straits.**
5. **It would provide a base from which Java could easily be bombed several times daily, the distance from Palembang to Batavia being only 250 miles.**

Dutch Will Defend Or Destroy

From DOUGLAS WILKIE, Special Correspondent of The Courier-Mail.

BATAVIA, February 16.—The Dutch will not consider any offer of a separate peace.

There is a unanimous determination by all groups, races, and classes to teach Japan that Indies' preparations, which already have been devastatingly effective at sea, is effective enough to cause enormous losses in an onslaught on Sumatra and Java.

After the heroic wholesale destruction by the Dutch of the price-less Borneo oilfields Palembang represents by far the most valuable prize left in the struggle for oil. This is the mainspring of the Japanese offensive, the reduction of Singapore being only an incidental necessity.

Previous Japanese belief that the Dutch might be persuaded to hand over at least a portion of the Indies' oil resources is reflected in Japan's reluctance to declare war against the Dutch until January 11, when the increased tempo of the Dutch sinkings of Japanese transports convinced even the Japanese that the Dutch are the most realistic and uncompromisingly determined of the united nations.

JAP THREAT TO AUSTRALIA

LONDON, February 16.—Speaking in the Japanese Diet to-day, the Japanese Premier (General Tojo) made a special reference to Australia.

"Australia and New Zealand should avoid a useless war by relying on Britain and America, on which no reliance can be placed," he said.

"Whether the peoples of Australia and New Zealand enjoy happiness depends on whether their Governments understand Japan's real intentions and her just attitude towards them."

The Tokio newspaper Nichi Nichi says that one of the aims of Japanese policy towards Australia will be the abolition of Australian laws which hitherto have practically prohibited Japanese immigration.

General Tojo declared that the Japanese war aim included a co-prosperity sphere under Japanese domination. Burma, India, and China were assured of happiness by Japanese co-operation, as also would Australia and New Zealand. This "happiness" would also apply to South America under Japanese co-operation. He warned the Japanese nation that there must be no slackening of morale if victory was to be gained.

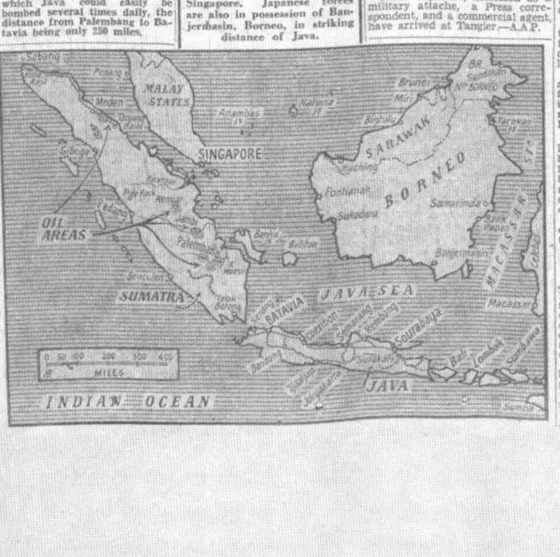

OIL LOSSES IN INDIES

BATAVIA, February 16.—The Dutch East Indies lost 22½ per cent. of their oil by the destruction of the Balik Papan and Tarakan fields. With the loss of the South Sumatra fields 88 per cent. altogether will have gone, leaving only 12 per cent. (produced in Java) for Allied use.

There are large stores in Java, but when these are exhausted production will be insufficient to maintain the Allied war machine here without bringing oil from the United States and the Persian Gulf.

The total Indies' oil production was eight million tons annually. Of this 4,300,000 tons was produced in Palembang and the nearby Djambi fields, from which it was pumped to Palembang.

The Palembang refineries surface workings alone were valued at £A70 million. Two big refineries adjoin, and together cover a block of four miles by three. The Standard Oil of New Jersey owns one and the Shell Oil Company the other.—A.A.P.

TASK NOW ON U.S.A.

NEW YORK, February 16.—Congressmen say that with the fall of Singapore the defence of the South Pacific now falls principally on the United States.

America's success in the task, they say, will depend on the speed with which reinforcements are rushed to the area.

Washington expects bitter fighting in the Batan Peninsula, in the Philippines, as the Japanese will seek to emulate their compatriots' feat at Singapore.

The military correspondent of the North American Newspaper Alliance (Colonel Palmer) says that the fierce hand-to-hand fighting in the Batan Peninsula, and Malaya is designed primarily to gain time to build up Australia as a great and impregnable base from which to launch future offensives.

"Darkest Hour"

In the considered judgment of responsible officials in Washington the fall of Singapore marks the darkest moment of the war for the united nations, says the New York Times' Washington correspondent.

"If there was any confidence here that Sumatra could hold out, the feeling would not be so pessimistic, but it is virtually conceded that Sumatra, too, must fall, cutting off the united nations from their main supply of petroleum in the south-west Pacific.

"It would also allow the Japanese free passage into the Indian Ocean, from where they could raid the Allied supply lines to China, Suez, and the Persian Gulf.

Swift Blows To South

PALEMBANG, Dutch oil refining centre in Sumatra, has fallen into Japanese hands one day after the surrender of Singapore. Japanese forces are also in possession of Banjermasin, Borneo, in striking distance of Java.

PALEMBANG: Looking across the River Moesi to the oil town of Palembang, which the Japanese have taken in the first sea and air attack on Sumatra. The wide, swift-flowing river is not spanned by any bridges, and water taxis (foreground) ferry pedestrians across the stream.

CHURCHILL'S GRIM PLEA FOR UNITY

LONDON, February 16.—The feature of Mr. Churchill's grim broadcast last night—it was the grimmest he has yet delivered—was his plea for closing the ranks and trusting the leaders.

It was the first time since he has assumed the leadership that he struck this grave note and the public quickly sensed the significance of it.

The succession of recent disasters has shaken the public more than anything else in the war. They see that the war can be lost and everyone is asking apprehensively and impatiently if the conduct of the war is all that it could be.

Russian Example

Mr. Churchill cited Russian unity in the face of disaster as a shining lesson, and his appeal was, above all, an urgent plea to the people to stand behind the Government whatever disasters befell the nation.

The most remarkable feature of Mr. Churchill's broadcast was the omission of any mention of the Scharnhorst armada's dramatic escape.

Having heard Mr. Churchill's recital of the war's developments since his last broadcast in August, setting beside each other the good and the bad—the former being America's entry and inestimable help, and Russia's marvellous come-back, and the latter being Japan's heavy marauding blows—listeners were staggered when Mr. Churchill abruptly broke off without a word about the German naval feat.

There also was a shocked feeling that Mr. Churchill did not provide even the most meagre preliminary details of the circumstances of Singapore's fall, merely describing it as a heavy and far-reaching military defeat.

Cabinet Change Urged

The Daily Telegraph and Lord Beaverbrook's newspaper, the Daily Express, wholeheartedly support Mr. Churchill's appeal for unity. The Daily Mail, although eulogising Mr. Churchill's leadership, demands reconstruction of the War Cabinet.

"The nation believes that no man can undertake all the responsibility for practically a world-wide war," points out the Daily Mail. "We believe that a War Cabinet of five or six men, without departmental duties, would be less likely to make mistakes than one man."

"Some criticisms have been misplaced," says The Times, "but their whole purpose is to stimulate greater and better co-ordinated effort. The British people demand that the Government match its own determination and express it in an unending and ruthless search for efficiency without regard to things or persons."

CHURCHILL SAID:

Points made by Mr. Churchill were:—

- **Japan was triumphant now, but he was sure history's verdict would be that the Japanese had committed an act of criminal madness.**
- Nobody must underrate any more the efficiency of the Japanese war machine.
- We must not undervalue the overwhelming forces aligned with us, which, when fully developed, would be capable of squaring all accounts.
- He had nothing to offer except "a hard adverse war for many months, many misfortunes, severe torturing losses, and remorseless anxieties before us."
- Every ship, plane, tank, and gun has been deployed against the enemy or is awaiting his attack.
- It was the duty of everybody to see that the Government had a solid foundation on which to act, and that the misfortunes and mistakes of the war were not exploited against the Government.
- **This was one of those moments when the British nation could show its quality.**
- **Let us draw from the heart of misfortune the vital impulse of victory.**

Page 2: Churchill's Plea For Unity Supported

New Drive Due On MacArthur

WASHINGTON, February 16.—Fighting in the Batan Peninsula in the Philippines is limited to local skirmishes, while the enemy obviously is regrouping to resume the offensive.

This information is given in a communique issued in Washington. It adds that General MacArthur is receiving frequent reports bearing out the hostile feelings of the Filipinos in the occupied areas against the Japanese.

Recently at a village in the Batangas area, a truck driver named Gueva volunteered to drive a Japanese army truck with 24 Japanese, but deliberately plunged the truck over the cliff, killing the passengers and himself.

A Japanese proclamation has barred the circulation of American currency by the occupied area, and has severely restricted withdrawals from bank accounts.

BOMB AT BRITISH TANGIER CONSULATE

LONDON, February 16.—The Daily Telegraph's Tangier correspondent says an unexploded bomb was found on Saturday morning on the balcony of an annexe to the British Consulate. Windows of a British chemist shop were broken at the same time.

Further anti-British demonstrations were expected, but the authorities apparently moved to prevent disturbances after representations from the British Consulate-General (Mr. Gascoigne).

Three Japanese, described as a military attache, a Press correspondent, and a commercial agent, have arrived at Tangier.—A.A.P.

Jap. Drive On Key Burma Town

LONDON, February 16.—Japanese motorised units, tanks, and infantry are pouring over the marshy rice fields on the Burma coast in an all-out drive to capture the key railway town of Thaton, says the Daily Express correspondent at Rangoon.

They would thus cut the railway communications between Rangoon and the Allied troops driven out of Martaban, he adds.

It was officially reported in Rangoon on Monday night that the British lines had been broken at several points.

The Associated Press correspondent in Rangoon says: "The battle for the control of the east coast of the Gulf of Martaban is reaching a decisive stage. The Japanese are attacking toward Thaton from the sea coast landing points and on a deep salient on the road between Paan and Thaton."

An earlier R.A.F. communique said: "In the past 24 hours Burma was again free from air attack. Our bombers, escorted by fighters, were again active on Saturday against Japanese dumps and war materials in the Paan and Martaban areas."

An army communique stated: "There were no further attacks on the Salween front, but reports indicate the enemy is preparing an attack in the area around Duyinzaik (12 miles west of Paan) and Thaton."

ROMMEL PLANS NEW LIBYA DRIVE

CAIRO, February 16.—Field-Marshal Rommel is believed to be preparing for a new push against Imperial positions in Libya between Gazala and Tobruk.

Latest reports received in London do not indicate that the battle is yet joined, but Rommel's forces, apparently having received supplies, are now on the move from the Tmimi-Makele line.

Rommel had 11 days in which to bring up supplies, and it is thought he may be ready to attempt to outflank the Imperial line south of Gazala.

Rommel's air activity suggests he has learned the lessons of last January, when he advanced for nine days without air support, at heavy cost in men and supplies.

His willingness to put so many machines into action also supports the belief that he intends to try to take the desert campaign to a new stage.—A.A.P.

Japs Attack Allied Ships In Timor Sea

MELBOURNE, Monday.—Japanese aircraft unsuccessfully attacked Allied shipping in Timor Sea (north-west of Darwin) to-day, according to an R.A.A.F. communique issued to-night by the Air Minister (Mr. Drakeford).

"R.A.A.F. reconnaissance of island bases in the Bismarck Archipelago at present occupied by the Japanese continued during the week-end," added the communique. "On Sunday small-scale Japanese reconnaissances were made along the south coast of Papua, but no bombs were dropped."

Australian anti-aircraft batteries at Port Moresby were in action yesterday for the first time against a Japanese reconnaissance long-distance bomber at midday.

The plane circled the port area at great height. After accurate fire by the anti-aircraft batteries it made off at high speed over the northern mountains towards Rabaul.

The Japanese plane wheeled leisurely under high clouds in bright sunshine. The guns burst into action suddenly, the shell bursts looming against the blue sky as black and white balls. Some of the shots went very near the enemy.

One anti-aircraft battery claimed a hit on the port wing of the Japanese machine.

Needed Soon

The appearance of the first Japanese land-based bomber over Port Moresby is considered significant. This and other evidence points to a concentration of Japanese forces in an effort to control the entire New Guinea area. Critical developments are expected in the next few days.

Only the Australian command knows New Guinea's place in the general Pacific scheme, but if any additional strength has been allotted it must arrive soon if it is to be used against the first Japanese thrust, resistance to which will decide immediately the control of the Torres Strait air bases from which the North Australian coast could be bombed by land-based planes.

The situation to-day is not complicated by civil considerations. The military authorities have taken over smoothly with the assistance of the younger administration men, who now are organising valuable native aid for the impending campaign.

Many natives have gone bush, but the better Papuan types have remained loyal and are enlisting in the Papuan infantry brigade, engineers, and artillery. Many of the natives are excellent snipers.

These should prove invaluable as guides and interpreters if a guerrilla campaign develops in the jungle-clad mountains of the hinterland.

They have stood up to the first bombing excellently, and are eager and excited at the prospect of fighting the Japanese.

News Awaited

The Papuan forces are awaiting eagerly release of news of the Rabaul forces, where many of their comrades are fighting. Details are being withheld for security reasons, but it is known that when the full story is told it will be one of the most heroic and desperate chapters of Pacific history.

The island force's message to Australia to-day is,

"Send every plane, gun, man, and crate of munitions not needed for more important operations. We know we are the sole guardians of the north-east gate. We will hold it with the resources at our disposal to the last."

No Big-scale Evacuation Of Australians Hoped For

IT is learned authoritatively in London that "There was no policy of evacuation from Singapore. The intention was to fight to the last. It would be misleading to suggest that there was any evacuation on a large scale.

The formations which participated in the fighting in Malaya consisted of about two-thirds of the Eighth Australian Division.

The Domei (Japanese) news agency asserted last night that the captured troops included 13,000 Australians.

It was revealed in Batavia yesterday that the Australian nurses were safely evacuated.

The Australian and Indian divisions had all been fighting on the mainland. They fought a rear-guard action for six weeks, with the enemy constantly landing behind them, and dive-bombing going on constantly.

These forces must have been severely weakened by casualties when they reached Singapore.

They put up a magnificent fight on the island. The Japanese say they fought "to the limits of human endurance."

They surrendered only when they were without food, water, and ammunition, and it was impossible to fight on any longer.

It is difficult to estimate the numbers involved in the surrender, and there is no check at present of the final numbers at the garrison.

Last Message

It is stated authoritatively in London that the last message received by the Supreme Commander in the South Pacific (General Wavell) from the Commander-in-Chief in Malaya (Major-General Percival) stated: "Because of heavy losses and the shortage of water, food, ammunition, and petrol it is impossible to carry on defence any longer."

"The original strength of the British formations in Singapore was about 55,000 troops without auxiliaries.

"There is no news of the number of the garrison in the final stages of the battle.

"It is believed that we lost very heavily in material and equipment. The evacuation of the women and children was probably almost complete, while some wounded also had been evacuated.

The Governor (Sir Shenton Thomas) and a number of officials are said to have left Singapore by air.

Tokio Radio says that under the terms of surrender 1000 British soldiers would retain their arms to maintain order in Singapore until the Japanese had completely occupied the city.

Berlin Radio, quoting the Tokio newspaper, Asahi, for the statement that British and Australian troops left Singapore on Friday night for Sumatra, said: "More than 30 ships, all of over 1000 tons, also one 10,000-ton cruiser were anchored at Singapore on Friday night, but all had gone next morning."

The announcer added that only Chinese and Malays remained in Singapore.

Describing the last phase of the battle, Tokio Radio said: "The blue sky is visible over Singapore for the first time for a week after the huge oil tanks had burned themselves out, but the tropical foliage of the landscape is still black with soot, which has settled down out of the black clouds."

The decisive blows were struck by the Japanese only last Saturday, said a Japanese commentator. On that day the Japanese occupied the water reservoirs—cutting off Singapore's water supply—and the Pyalebar radio station, where the British defenders fought fiercely and desperately until the lsat moment.

Meanwhile a second Japanese column struck southward to the coast, thus isolating the defenders and a stream of refugees from Changi fort, at the extreme northern end of the island.

A third column, after the occupation of Bukit Timah, completed the encirclement of the city and reached the Alexander Road.

SINGAPORE'S PYRE

Singapore had a funeral pyre in keeping with the tremendous significance of the event.

The Times' special correspondent graphically describes the tremendous destruction as a result of the "scorched earth" policy. When he left in a small freighter on Tuesday black smoke hung fatefully over the whole island.

"There had been enough oil in Singapore to fill Japan's war requirements for three months," he goes on, "but most of it is now ablaze. A great white column rose above a layer of black smoke, resembling a volcano against the sunny blue sky. The rumble of artillery fire was wafted across the waters from the deathly struggle in progress in rubber plantations, on tarred roads, in villages, and even in the streets of the city.

"Next morning we passed a peaceful and tropical island, but Singapore, although 120 miles away, did not allow itself to be forgotten.

"That 'volcano' was still erupting. Singapore was dying."

Stark Courage

The Daily Mail's special correspondent pays tribute to the stark courage of the women, children, and civilians under shellfire which "is imperishably written in the minds of all witnesses."

"The children were extraordinarily quiet," he continues, "hardly uttering a sound despite the constant roll of the guns and the thud of bombs along the battle front. The Government was then making bonfires of records, thus increasing the smoke from the burning buildings which choked one's throat and stung the eyes.

"The Japanese laid down incessant bombing and machine-gun attacks all along the line. It was only that night that the British were able to fight on anything like equal terms."

The correspondent adds: "Our convoy was bombed most of the way to Batavia. One 'strafe' lasted five hours, but the nurses' unremitting toil and the courage of the hundreds of women and children were marvellous.

"Four Australian nurses toiled below attending to the wounded.

"Men of the R.A.F. lined the decks using Lewis guns and tommy guns, and rifles, causing the Japanese to keep out of range and disturbing their bombing aim. The decks were continually flooded to prevent incendiary bombs setting fire to the ship."

Colonel Ohira, of the Imperial headquarters' Press section, in a broadcast to the Japanese nation, said: "The passing of Singapore into Japanese hands means not only the striking of a blow at the Allies, but seriously impedes communications between their territories and the Indian and Pacific oceans.

"Japan is now in a position to control the fate of India and Australia.

"Moreover, Chungking has been completely cut off from aid from Britain and America. In addition to Japanese military might British and American smugness and over-confidence were responsible for their successive setbacks."

He warned the people, however, that the fall of Singapore was only one phase in the war, which had a long way to go.

Japanese Imperial Headquarters claims that 32 Allied warships and transports were sunk south of Singapore during the last week. The vessels, the Japanese add, are believed to have included the 5220-ton British cruiser Arethusa, also a light cruiser, an auxiliary cruiser, a submarine, two gunboats, one "special" vessel, eight transports, including one of 30,000 tons, another of 8000 tons, and another of 5000 tons. Vessels damaged include a light cruiser, a destroyer, two "special" vessels, 10 transports, and one torpedo boat.

Effect On Sea Routes

"We will soon feel the great effects of a great loss," says the Manchester Guardian in an editorial analysing possibilities following the fall of Singapore.

"With the obstacle to the entry of the Japanese fleet into the Indian Ocean gone we must expect to see hostile warships sailing towards Rangoon, or at least along the sea routes to there from India.

"We may find Japanese cruisers invading the Cape route to Egypt, via the Red Sea, and to Russia, via the Persian Gulf."

The Daily Telegraph's naval correspondent says that through the fall of Singapore the Allies have lost their only base between Durban and Pearl Harbour with dry docks capable of taking a modern battleship.

BRITISH PRESENTS FOR SOVIET GENERAL

LONDON, February 16.—School children and theatre audiences throughout Britain have subscribed for the purchase of unusual presents for Marshal Timoshenko, whose birthday occurs on Wednesday.

The presents will go to Russia with the next shipment of war materials. The gifts include a saddle for Marshal Timoshenko's charger, but the bulk are in the form of comforts and medical aid for his troops.

SINGAPORE'S FATAL 4th ANNIVERSARY

LONDON, February 16.—Singapore fell on the fourth anniversary of the formal opening of the naval base by the Governor (Sir Shenton Thomas) in a worldwide broadcast.

TRAGEDY OF NO AIR AID

From GEOFFREY TEBBUTT, Courier-Mail War Correspondent

BATAVIA, February 16.—Singapore—the latest Crete—daily contributes more stories of tragedy.

Three Victorians—Roy Williams (Glen Iris), Lew Hillier (North Fitzroy), and Lance Rowe (Castertom)—left Keppel Harbour on Wednesday night when fighting was going on in the city of Singapore, with mortar fire, machine-gunning, and sniping in the streets near Raffles Hotel. The city was also being subjected to bombing and shelling, with especially heavy air attacks against ships and harbour works.

Their ship was attacked as they were embarking, but it did not experience any further bombing after it reached the open sea.

They passed the burning wreckage of several ships, including tankers. Other ships in their convoy picked up a number of survivors, some of them badly injured.

"We have grown so used to every bomber being a Japanese that we duck whenever we hear an aeroplane," said these escapees. "It was a terrible strain on the troops and civilians to be without air support.

"What happened in Singapore will happen in Australia unless the air arm is adequate. The Japanese swarmed over Singapore Island so quickly that the defending troops were repeatedly cut off. They seemed to be everywhere, giving the defenders no rest."

Evacuees Cared For

Australian evacuees from Singapore and Thailand, who have arrived in Java, are comfortably housed and well fed.

They are speedily recovering from their experiences in Malaya and three days' ordeal at sea.

All are in high spirits and have paid warm tributes to the speed and efficiency with which the Dutch organised accommodation, transport, and catering.

BERLIN SAYS BRITISH DESTROYER DAMAGED

LONDON, February 16.—Berlin news agency reports from Tangier that a British destroyer, badly damage by bombs amidships, has arrived at Gibraltar. Several were killed, and 15 wounded were put ashore.—A.A.P.

70 *Enemy submarines enter harbour*

Japanese midget subs attack Sydney, 1942

THE SECOND WORLD WAR CAME DIRECTLY TO SYDNEY ON THE NIGHT OF 31 MAY 1942, WHEN THREE MIDGET SUBMARINES STOLE INTO THE HARBOUR AND SET ABOUT DESTROYING SHIPPING. AROUND 10.30 PM ONE OF THE SUBMARINES WAS DISCOVERED CAUGHT IN HARBOUR NETTING AND THE GENERAL ALARM WAS SET OFF. CONFUSION REIGNED AS NO-ONE KNEW IF THERE WERE OTHER SUBS IN THE HARBOUR UNTIL A LOUD EXPLOSION WAS HEARD AND THE NAVAL DEPOT SHIP, AN EX-HARBOUR FERRY, *KUTTABUL*, WAS HIT BY A TORPEDO THAT WAS INTENDED FOR THE AMERICAN HEAVY CRUISER *CHICAGO*, LYING NEARBY.

Nineteen Australian and two British sailors were killed on board the *Kuttabul*. The other two submarines were either sunk or did not make it back to the three parent submarines that were awaiting their return just outside Port Hacking.

The parent submarines escaped to continue raiding shipping lanes. A week later, on 8 June, one of them returned to Sydney and just after midnight, surfaced outside the Sydney heads. The commander apparently ordered the crew to target the Sydney Harbour Bridge, but of ten rounds fired, nine landed across the eastern suburbs and one in the harbour. Several buildings were damaged but there were no casualties. The other submarine targeted Newcastle and fired thirty-four shells over a sixteen-minute period. Newcastle's Fort Scratchley unsuccessfully returned fire in the only time an Australian coastal defence fortification has engaged an enemy warship.

Understandably, many people hurriedly dug their own bomb shelters in backyards across coastal Australian towns and cities. The incident brought the reality of war to Sydneysiders, many of whom sent their children to relatives living away from the coast, but there were no further attacks during the war.

LATE EDITION

The Sydney Morning Herald.

PRICE, 2d
10 PAGES

No. 32,583 ONE HUNDRED AND TWELFTH YEAR OF PUBLICATION SYDNEY, TUESDAY, JUNE 2, 1942

SUBMARINE RAID IN HARBOUR

Three Japanese midget submarines, believed to have operated from a mother-ship somewhere off the Australian coast, entered Sydney Harbour late on Sunday night.

All are thought to have been destroyed. One submarine has been located at the bottom of the harbour. A hawser has been attached to it and efforts are being made to salvage it intact. (See page 5.)

Enemy submarines enter harbour

Transcription

SUBMARINE RAID IN HARBOUR

Three Japanese midget submarines, believed to have operated from a mother-ship somewhere off the Australian coast, entered Sydney Harbour late on Sunday night.

All are thought to have been destroyed. One submarine has been located at the bottom or the harbour. A hawser has been attached to it and efforts are being made to salvage it intact.

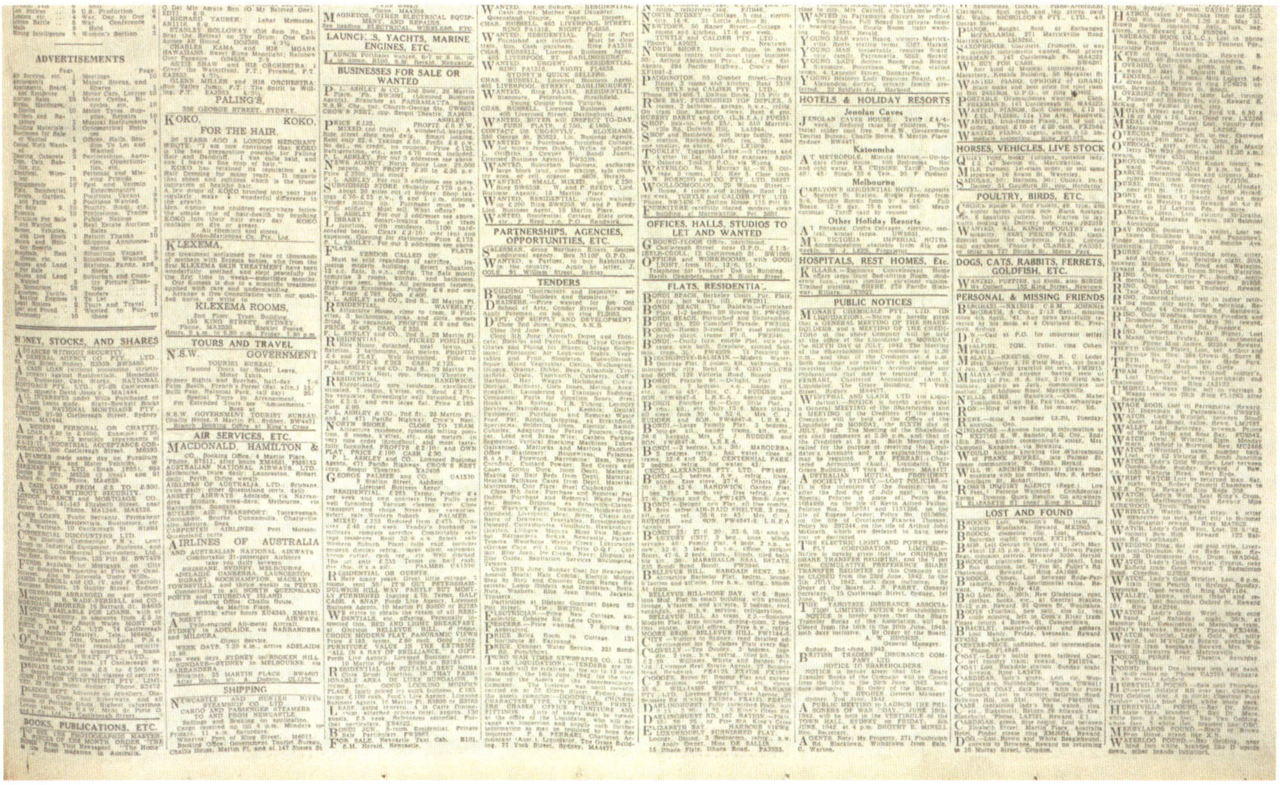

The Sydney Morning Herald *was almost forced to enlarge its front page news summary column during the Second World War with such dramatic events as the appearance of the midget subs in Sydney.*

This Paper is Needed for Our War Effort—Save It!

The Argus

LAST EDITION

No. 29,881 MELBOURNE, TUESDAY, JUNE 2, 1942 6 PAGES PRICE 2d.

3 MIDGET SUBS SUNK IN SYDNEY HARBOUR

SWIFT AIR SEARCH FOR MOTHER-SHIP

SWIFT ALLIED COUNTER-MEASURES HAVE FOLLOWED A DARING BUT FUTILE ATTEMPT BY JAPANESE MIDGET SUBMARINES TO PENETRATE DEFENCES OF SYDNEY HARBOUR AND ATTACK SHIPPING AT ANCHOR ON SUNDAY NIGHT.

As soon as the first submarine was sighted shore guns and naval units went into action and 3 attacking craft are believed to have been sunk—one by gunfire and 2 by depth charges.

Vigilance of defences prevented damage to any ships except one small harbour vessel of no military value.

Allied aircraft promptly embarked on a widespread series of sweeps over the Tasman Sea in search of the mother craft which is believed to have carried the submarines within range of their target.

A VIEW OF SYDNEY HEADS, ENTRANCE TO PORT JACKSON. Three midget enemy submarines entered through here on Sunday night and attempted to raid shipping.

THE FAMOUS BRIDGE makes a striking background for this fine photograph of Sydney Harbour. Its calm was shattered on Sunday night when the Japanese midget submarines were sunk by depth charges and gunfire.

SMALL VESSEL ONLY VICTIM OF RAID

Witnesses Tell Graphic Stories

SYDNEY, Monday: One submarine fired 2 torpedoes, one of which hit an old Sydney ferry used as a depot.

Naval authorities are anxious to take possession of one of the raiders intact, because, although they have been previously used by the Japanese, little is known by Australian authorities of the craft and their capabilities. A hawser has been attached to it with a view to salvaging it.

PLANNING VAST AIR OFFENSIVE

Part of U S Force

ROMMEL BREAKS OFF BATTLE IN LIBYA

Withdrawing Through Gaps

LONDON, Monday

Axis forces in Libya have had to break off the battle in which they hoped to drive on to Tobruk, and German armoured units are reported to be withdrawing through 2 exits in the vast British minefields in the El Adem sector.

Instead of German supply columns streaming eastward, the German Command now has tank units staggering westward under constant hammering by our air forces and artillery.

REDS AND GERMANS MASSING

Move Soon In Centre

LONDON, Monday

Important operations are believed to be imminent on the central front in Russia. The Germans are massing strong forces along the Smolensk-Viazma railway, and Russian preparations in this sector are also well advanced.

REPRISAL RAID ON CANTERBURY

Cathedral Was German Target

MASTER PLAN FOR PACIFIC STRATEGY

Mr Curtin's Talk With C-in-C

MIDGET SUBS IN GULF OF MEXICO

BRITISH PLANES ACTIVE IN MADAGASCAR

AMERICANS CRIED IN ANGER AT CORREGIDOR

WAVE INVADES HOLIDAY RESORT

CHINA DROMES 3 HOURS FROM JAPAN

Chiang Kai-shek's Plea for U S Planes

PLANNING PRODUCTION FOR VICTORY

AXIS COUNCIL TO MEET IN ROME

Japanese Report

JAPS CLAIM ADVANCE IN HUNAN

AIRCRAFT-CARRIER PROGRAMME FOR U S

RAID CALLED OFF BECAUSE OF BAD WEATHER

MORE AXIS SUPPLY SHIPS SUNK

BARRYMORE DIED A POOR MAN

ROMMEL'S FORCES are trying to fight their way out through gaps in British minefields in the El Adem sector of Libya. This map shows the battle area and other places.

DAY and NIGHT Production

Working to capacity, Radio Corporation Pty. Limited — makers of ASTOR FINE RADIO — is to-day answering the urgent needs of our armed forces. With all the vast technical and manufacturing resources of a huge organisation — with all the maturity of over 20 years' continuous development, ASTOR is playing a most vital part in a conflict demanding the utmost in radio communications.

ASTOR

A Product of RADIO CORPORATION PTY. LTD.

Melbourne's Argus newspaper of Tuesday, 2 June 1942, two days after the event, reported the extraordinary news of the midget submarine attacks in Sydney Harbour.

The great freedom of speech crisis 71

Riots over news censorship, 1944

IN THE EARLY HOURS OF SUNDAY, 16 APRIL 1944 COMMONWEALTH POLICE OFFICERS ARRIVED AT THE PRINTING PRESSES OF THE *SUNDAY TELEGRAPH* AND, WITH DRAWN REVOLVERS, BEGAN TO SEIZE ALL COPIES OF THE NEWSPAPER. IN EXTRAORDINARY SCENES REMINISCENT OF LIFE UNDER A DICTATORSHIP, ACCORDING TO NEWSPAPER COLUMNISTS, POLICE AROUND THE NATION ALSO SEIZED ALL COPIES OF THE *SUN, DAILY MIRROR, TELEGRAPH* AND *SYDNEY MORNING HERALD* IN SYDNEY, AS WELL AS THE MELBOURNE *HERALD* AND *ADELAIDE ADVERTISER.*

What the *Daily Mirror* labelled the 'great freedom of speech crisis' was in fact a crisis about what newspapers could report on the process of censorship. Strict rules had been imposed on newspapers at the start of the war through the establishment of the Department of Information. The government censor issued daily instructions to newspapers and radio stations. At the height of the war, this censorship was generally accepted. However in early 1944, as the Second World War seemed to be drawing to an end and American newspapers were relaxing their wartime censorship laws, the Australian press asked whether censorship would also be eased locally. Newspaper editors suspected that the government was using the laws to censor material that was not related to wartime information that could assist the enemy.

Arthur Calwell (1896–1973), Labor minister for information, responded that all news reports referring to censorship laws had to be submitted to the authorities for censorship. After an editorial on the subject from the *Telegraph* was returned with major changes, the editor decided to publish a newspaper with large blank spaces, on the grounds that the articles that were to appear there had been censored, rather than the censored articles. This deliberate challenge pushed the authorities into action, and they confiscated the blanked-out newspapers.

The strident and flamboyant editor of *The Daily Telegraph* Brian Penton (1904–1951) led the counter-charge against the censors and Arthur Calwell—who sued Penton for £25,000 damages in a libel suit that was eventually settled out of court. In a rare show of unity, the *Herald, Mirror* and *Telegraph* in Sydney requested an injunction against the Commonwealth government. When the High Court later agreed that the papers should not have been suppressed, the newspapers prominently promoted their role in defending Australians' freedom of speech. The heavy-handed action of suppression had backfired and ensured the future wariness of government attitudes to censorship of the press.

Last Ditch Axis Stand Before Sebastopol—Page 5

SUN ROSE 6.20 A.M., SETS 5.29 P.M. HIGH TIDES: 3.56 A.M. (4ft. 10in.), 4.55 P.M. (4ft.).

SYDNEY

DAILY MIRROR

Registered at the General Post Office, Sydney for transmission by post as a newspaper

Telephones: Business—BW3741 (6 lines).
Telephones: Editorial {FL3041 (10 lines). {FL5041 (10 lines).

LATE FINAL EXTRA

No. 915. SYDNEY, TUESDAY, APRIL 18, 1944. PRICE, 2d.

CENSOR RESTRAINED

Mr. Justice Sir Hayden Starke. Mr. Justice Sir George Rich. Chief Justice, Sir John Latham. Mr. Justice McTiernan. Mr. Justice Williams.

High Court Makes Order

A DAY which has had no equal in the newspaper history of this or any other British country culminated yesterday in suppressed newspapers in Sydney securing from the High Court an interim injunction forbidding interference by the Commonwealth with publication of the Sydney newspapers until Friday.

Before this injunction was granted late in the day all but a few of the citizens in three States were deprived of their evening newspapers.

FOLLOWING the banning of the Sydney morning newspapers, the Daily Mirror and the Sun also were suppressed, and in Melbourne the last editions of the Herald, and in Adelaide the late editions of the News suffered similarly.

As the latter two are the only evening newspapers in those cities, the bulk of home-going workers were without the news of the day.

Press Value Emphasised

The avidity with which the public in Sydney snatched up copies of the Mirror and the Sun which, containing the banned material referring to the dispute between the Minister for Information (Mr. Calwell) and the Australian Newspaper Proprietors' Association, managed to reach the streets, was a clear indication of what newspapers mean to the public.

What happened when the Commonwealth authorities visited the offices of the Daily Mirror was a parallel to events at the other newspaper offices.

At 10.55 a.m., little more than half an hour before the Mirror was due to go to press, a censor visited the editor and served a notice demanding that page-proofs of the Mirror be submitted for perusal.

With a thick blue pencil, the censor then set to work on the page-proofs. There were some columns of material referring to the Calwell dispute.

The censor was lavish in spreading his blue pencil markings. They ran down the pages from top to bottom, eliminating any reference, however small, to the dispute.

Blue Pencil Went Ahead

The pencil scored straight through a statement on the suppression which had been issued to all papers for publication by Calwell.

A little later the censor who visited the editor announced: "I prohibit publication."

The Commonwealth Peace Officer who was in attendance then announced: "You can't publish."

Copies of the Mirror did reach the public. So did copies of subsequent editions. So did copies of the afternoon editions of the Sun.

Commonwealth peace officers were posted about Kippax Street to see that no papers were distributed.

At one stage a Commonwealth peace officer drew his revolver.

A crowd that gathered in Kippax Street jeered and hooted the Commonwealth representatives, and cheered lustily each van load of papers that got through the cordon and sped for the city.

Throughout the day the battle of wits went on. During the afternoon more Commonwealth officers arrived on the scene. Some of the cars which brought the reinforcements bore Federal Capital Territory number-plates.

And throughout the day several thousands of copies of each edition of the Mirror continued to reach the public. Crowds struggled around the newsboys to purchase the papers as soon as they arrived.

Crowds Hoot Peace Officers

The Sun had similar difficulties. Crowds gathered in Phillip and Elizabeth Streets outside the Sun office before the first edition was printed.

Peace officers stood in front of the vans in the car docks to prevent them from moving. The crowd hissed and booed and there were cries of "Gestapo."

During the afternoon, papers and bundles of papers were thrown from windows of the Sun office to the crowd below.

Nimble-footed newsboys seized bundles and dashed away. Readers threw money at the newsboys and did not wait for their change.

● Continued on Page 3

UNIVERSITY STUDENTS, protesting against the censorship ban on Sydney newspapers, marched from the University to Martin Place yesterday and demonstrated against the suppression. Three were detained by the police, but subsequently released.

The censorship controversy was headline news across the country. The Sydney Daily Mirror *of 18 April 1944 records the newspapers' triumph in winning from the High Court an interim injunction for Sydney newspapers against the government.*

Inhuman barbarities 72

Japanese war atrocities revealed, 1945

ON 5 AUGUST 1944 MORE THAN 500 JAPANESE PRISONERS OF WAR BROKE OUT FROM THEIR PRISON CAMP IN COWRA IN NEW SOUTH WALES. FOUR AUSTRALIAN SOLDIERS WERE KILLED AND 231 JAPANESE DIED. WITH LITTLE CHANCE OF ESCAPING BACK TO JAPANESE TERRITORY ALL THE WAY FROM COWRA, IN THE JAPANESE CULTURE OF MILITARY HONOUR, MANY JOINED THE BREAKOUT SO THEY COULD DIE IN BATTLE, OR COMMIT RITUAL SUICIDE IN THE TRADITIONAL MANNER OF SEPPUKU, IN A PLACE THAT WAS OUTSIDE THE SHAMEFUL WALLS OF CAPTIVITY. AUSTRALIANS FOUND IT DIFFICULT TO UNDERSTAND THE JAPANESE SOLDIER.

After the atomic bombs had destroyed the Japanese cities of Hiroshima and Nagasaki, and Japan surrendered in August 1945, the task of finding and liberating Allied prisoners of war began. Australian and other Allied army personnel on this mission in Asia were accompanied by journalists, including Australian Wilfred Burchett (1911–1983), whose reports for London's *Daily Express* were the first to describe the devastation of Hiroshima. Burchett found it hard to comprehend the devastating destruction, particularly what he called the ongoing 'atomic plague' that was killing hundreds of people a day, even though they had been outside the immediate impact area of the nuclear bomb.

During September 1945 the true scale of Japanese war atrocities was being revealed daily in newspapers. A *Daily Telegraph* correspondent in Singapore found Australian Army nurse Vivian Bullwinkel (1915–2000), who told him that she was the only survivor of a massacre of twenty-one nurses and one elderly civilian woman on a beach on Bangka Island off the coast of Sumatra on 16 February 1942.

This was just one of the shocking stories emanating from the so-called 'death marches and camps' in Japanese-occupied south-east Asia. Others reported daily beatings, starvation, forced marches, summary executions and torture. The aftermath of the war in the east, as it had been in Europe with reports of Nazi concentration camps, was a period of tragic news headlines.

today's weather

State:
Fine,
mild;
few
N. Coast
showers.

Japs beheaded Australian V.C.—page 3.

Sunday Telegraph

OVER 300,000 SOLD WEEKLY

RACE FINISH PHOTOS Page 16

Vol. VI. No. 42 Telephone: M2406 SYDNEY, SUNDAY, SEPTEMBER 2, 1945 Registered at the G.P.O., Sydney, for transmission by post as a newspaper. Price 3d

MEN TORTURED, BEATEN

American troops ready to enter Japanese capital

SUNDAY TELEGRAPH SERVICE AND AAP

NEW YORK, Sat.—American troops now occupy almost the whole of the western side of Tokio Bay, and are awaiting the signal to enter Tokio.

Allied leaders in Yokohama (port of Tokio) are completing last-minute arrangements for the formal surrender of Japan on board the U.S. battleship Missouri, in Tokio Bay, tomorrow.

General MacArthur today refused a Japanese request that the ceremony be postponed until additional surrender talks had been held.

Exact time for the surrender signing has not yet been announced.

White House Secretary Charles Ross says that if the surrender is signed before 12 noon Tokio time (1 p.m. Sunday, Sydney time), President Truman will make a broadcast announcement immediately.

"If the ceremony is later than this, Truman will not broadcast until Sunday morning (Washington time)," Ross says.

Tokio at present is "out of bounds" to the main body of occupation troops, but U.S. soldiers are guarding the city's main public buildings.

Factories In Ruins

Allied correspondents allowed to enter Tokio with the U.S. vanguard report scenes of "almost indescribable desolation."

B.B.C. correspondent Douglas Willis says: "Two out of every three factories in Tokio are in ruins.

"About 900,000 houses in the city have been destroyed by Allied bombing, and 4,000,000 of the inhabitants have fled to the country."

New York Times correspondent Frank Kluckhohn, in a despatch from Tokio, says: "Japan is bitter in defeat. Everyone is so sorry. They say Japan did not lose the war, and that the atom bomb is to blame."

Kluckhohn says Japanese civilians in a train in which he rode from Yokohama to Tokio were openly hostile. In Tokio, he and other correspondents walked past thousands of glaring soldiers.

"People in Tokio either would not speak to us, or wanted to complain about the bombing," he adds.

"They wanted to know why we ripped Tokio to pieces, and even wanted to take us on sightseeing trips to show how unsportsmanlike we were.

"They considered Allied bomber flights over the Imperial Palace a direct insult."

Domei news agency president Inosuke Furuno said in Tokio today: "Danger period of the occupation is past. There is now little prospect of incidents.

"I am surprised that the occupation was accomplished with so little trouble."

Domei has provided Allied correspondents with special facilities, and promised to supply them with its foreign and domestic news services.

General Sir Thomas Blamey and R.A.A.F. Vice-Marshal Bostock have arrived in Yokohama, and joined the Allied delegation preparing for tomorrow's surrender ceremony.

More Jap atrocities revealed

SUNDAY TELEGRAPH SERVICE AND AAP

TOKIO, Sat. — More Japanese atrocities on Allied war prisoners are being revealed hourly as occupation forces drive deeper into Japan.

Liberated prisoners told how they lived in indescribable prison filth and were subjected to Gestapo-like interrogations by Japanese, who kicked and lashed them and mutilated their hands with thumb-screws.

One prisoner, describing the Japanese torture, said today: "I made my peace with God and prayed to die."

Evidence of prison deaths, beatings, and lack of medical care, will be given to Allied authorities responsible for pressing charges against Japanese war criminals.

Commander Harold Stassen, Admiral Halsey's special investigator dealing with Japanese prison camps, today revealed the existence of a central Japanese inquisition centre.

Liberated prisoners' stories:

Lieutenant John Laymon, 24, a Super-Fortress pilot, shot down on May 26 during a fire raid on Tokio, in which part of Emperor Hirohito's palace was destroyed:

"I hid all the first day in rice paddy-fields, but next day I was discovered by Japanese civilians.

"About 20 or 30 of them, wildly brandishing clubs, rushed at me, but when I made no move they did not hit me, but fingered my clothing and spat in my face.

"Then I was blindfolded, and my arms tied behind my back.

"They made me kneel, and one of them drew a sword across the back of my neck.

"I waited for what seemed an eternity, but nothing happened.

"Then, still blindfolded, I was led four miles through the streets. I was kicked and beaten all the way by civilians.

"After this, three Japanese soldiers—the first I had encountered—placed me in a motor cycle with a box attachment and took me to an inquisition centre.

"Here my blindfold was removed and a man in civilian clothes and a Japanese sergeant made me kneel between them.

"They accused me of deliberately trying to burn down the Emperor's Palace, and of murdering women and children.

"Every time I denied this they hit me on the jaw hard enough to send me sprawling on the floor."

Shot, Bayoneted

A U.S. Navy pilot, liberated from Ofuna Prison Camp, told correspondents today:

"When I was shot down over Formosa, my captors tied my arms behind my back and covered me with my parachute.

"I heard two shots. One entered my left shoulder, which was already full of shrapnel and hurting so much that I didn't feel the bullet.

"The second bullet went through the side of my chest.

"A Formosan soldier who thought I didn't move fast enough stuck me in the back with a bayonet.

"At the hospital the shrapnel and bullets were removed without anaesthetic."

A Scottish soldier, who had been imprisoned in Japan for nearly four years, said: "After every big Allied air-raid the Japanese administered severe beatings to helpless prisoners in retaliation for the damage.

"The Japanese women were worse than the men in their savage treatment of prisoners."

Jap drowned wounded prisoner

BRISBANE, Sat.—A Japanese guard put his foot on the head of a wounded prisoner and held it under water till he was drowned.

Ron Miscamble, of Brisbane, a gunner captured with the 8th Division, saw this in Singapore.

He was for two years and nine months a prisoner of the Japs, and is a survivor of the hell-ship sunk by an American submarine while taking prisoners of war to Japan.

Miscamble said the first job the A.I.F. got was to bury 200 Indians and Chinese who had been massacred.

These men had all been tied by the hands and let loose while the Japs had machine-gun practice.

The Australians were used to demine parts of Singapore. Then, after 11 days in a hell-ship, they were disembarked at Tavoy rice mill.

They were marched 25 miles to Tavoy drome.

Men collapsed on the march, and prisoners carried their exhausted cobbers for the last nine miles.

Any who collapsed were beaten unmercifully.

They were put on the infamous job of building the Thailand railway.

The Jap officer in command told them: "The railway must be completed on time, even if we have to use your skeletons as sleepers.

"You are only alive by the graciousness of the Emperor."

One Jap guard in this camp was nicknamed "Dillinger" by the men, because he shot an Australian at point-blank range three times for trying to escape.

The men sometimes got even with the guards by putting emery-powder in the engines of vehicles they were repairing.

"Eight men made a break, but were captured, brought back, and shot in front of us," he said. "We were made to bury them."

The Sunday Telegraph *reveals more Japanese atrocities on Allied war prisoners. Further descriptions appeared as headline news on the front pages of Australian newspapers for months to come.*

Aftermath of war and genocide 73

Jewish refugees arrive in Australia, 1947

AFTER THE SECOND WORLD WAR EUROPEAN REFUGEES, OR DISPLACED PERSONS AS THEY WERE ALSO CALLED, WERE BEING RESETTLED AROUND THE GLOBE UNDER INTERNATIONAL AND BILATERAL AGREEMENTS. AUSTRALIA OFFERED TO TAKE A SUBSTANTIAL SHARE OF THE MANY REFUGEES, EVEN THOUGH THE UNOFFICIAL WHITE AUSTRALIA POLICY WAS STILL EFFECTIVELY DRIVING THE *IMMIGRATION RESTRICTION ACT.*

Because of fears of restricting the entry of British Commonwealth subjects, the *Australian Immigration Act* did not specifically target or describe who could not enter. 'Undesirable aliens' could be from anywhere, but were generally people of non-British origin with different racial backgrounds. A dictation test in English (or any other language of the immigration officer's choosing) was applied when immigration officials felt the need to restrict an immigrant's entry.

Yet people who increasingly fell outside previous ideas of an 'acceptable' migrant, such as southern Europeans and Jewish people, were arriving. In somewhat of a contradiction they were being classed as 'desirable'. Historical Australian attitudes towards race were being transformed by the need for workers and to increase Australia's population. Even before the war had ended governments had begun planning Australia's postwar future, aiming to secure Australia against the possibility of invasion. The Curtin government's slogan ran 'populate or perish'. But the natural birth rate and migration from Britain were never going to achieve a rapid enough increase in Australia's population to satisfy the government. Immediately after the war, Australia's fear of Asia was greater than its fear of southern Europeans and Jewish immigrants, and from 1947, people from many non-British countries were beginning to be welcomed.

Still, while the arrival of a shipload of Jewish refugees in Cairns was not the headline news item of Brisbane's *Courier-Mail* of 13 March 1947, the tensions between the need for immigrants and the desire to keep Australia white are evident. It is not coincidental that, on the same page that the newspaper noted a report from the undersecretary of the federal Labour Department saying 'Australians must rigidly support the white Australia policy against all critics', it also included a story headlined 'Big Jew shipload at Cairns'.

NET SALES Exceed 160,000 DAILY

The Courier-Mail

'Phone B0111. BRISBANE, THURSDAY, MARCH 13, 1947. 12 PAGES—2d. (BY AIR—3d.)

LATE CITY

FOOD SET-UP: ONE CHANGE IS MADE, ANOTHER IS DEMANDED

APRIL 7 IS DEADLINE

Bread Strike Threat

QUEENSLAND bakers decided yesterday to stop making bread on April 7 unless Government action is taken to finalise price determinations and amend the Bread Delivery Act.

FISH BOARD TOLD TO SCRAP SALE SYSTEM

Check On Prices

THE Labour Minister (Mr. Gair) last night ordered the Fish Board chairman (Mr. R. F. Thompson) to scrap the existing system of selling fish at the South Brisbane fish market.

He told Mr. Thompson that at its meeting to-morrow the board must:

- Revert to a genuine auction of all fish instead of merely allocating to licensed buyers at ceiling prices.
- Abandon the recently introduced board instruction that mullet must be 13 inches instead of 11 inches as prescribed by the Fisheries Department.

ON THE EVE of his departure to-day for America on his loan financing mission, the Lord Mayor (Alderman J. B. Chandler) checked over at his home last night the voluminous documents he is taking with him.

15 New Men To Prevent Strikes

PREFERENCE IN EMPIRE TRADE CHANGE SEEN

CANBERRA, Wednesday.—In the view of at least some Dominions Britain, because of her economic circumstances, is not in a position to continue her exclusive Empire preference.

This was stated by the Prime Minister (Mr. Chifley) in the House of Representatives to-day in an outspoken review of Britain's economic situation.

HOUSES BURN IN PUNJAB

U.S. Fear Of Spies In Moscow

U.K. BLOCKADE BEATEN BY JEW SHIP

LONDON, March 12 (A.A.P.).—The first of a fleet of eight ships carrying illegal Jewish immigrants ran the British naval blockade of Palestine to-day.

BIG JEW SHIPLOAD AT CAIRNS

BIG ROLE FOR AUST. IN PACIFIC

'MUST STAND FIRM ON WHITE AUSTRALIA'

VICAR PUTS TIPS IN PARISH PAPER

LONDON, March 12 (Special).—Two tips for the Aintree Grand National Steeplechase on March 28 are given in this month's Parish magazine of St. Barnabas Church, Plymouth—and the tipster is the vicar, the Rev. John Stephenson Clarke.

NEWS TO HANLON

CHIFLEY TO PROBE MILK TROUBLE

"JERRY-BUILT HOUSES SHOULD GO"

EMPLOYEES, FRIENDS SHARE UNDER WILL

4 BOYS GUILTY IN MURDER CASE

The Courier-Mail of Brisbane might have made more of the fact that a ship with more than 700 Jewish refugees on board was anchored at Cairns if it had not been going on to Sydney and Melbourne. Signs of the beginning of the Cold War appear in a headline on the right, recording the US fear of spies in Moscow.

The Courier-Mail

No. 3217 'Phone B0111 BRISBANE, MONDAY, MARCH 17, 1947. 10 PAGES—2d. (BY AIR—3d.)

10,000 SQUARE MILE OIL SEARCH SOON

5 Companies To Drill at Roma

FOUR Australian oil companies will begin an oil search almost immediately in 6,400,000 acres (10,000 square miles) of the Roma district, Queensland.

In addition, the Vacuum Oil Company Pty. Ltd. stated last night that an intensive search for oil would be made soon in various parts of Australia, including Queensland.

It is believed that this will embrace the Roma area.

The four companies concentrating on the Roma field will have the co-operation of the State and Federal Governments.

REFUGEE SHIP REACHES PORT

REFUGEES crowd the deck of the Johan de Witt (top picture) as the ship berthed in Sydney Harbour yesterday afternoon. Lower picture: Passengers had to unload their own baggage because of the wharf labourers' strike.

FRANCE URGES MIGRATION TO PREVENT WAR

Wants German Population Cut

COURIER-MAIL FOREIGN SERVICE AND A.A.P.

LONDON, March 16.—Migration of Germans to other countries as an anti-war measure was advocated by M. Bidault, of France, at the Big Four Foreign Ministers' talks in Moscow to-day.

M. Bidault said France considered Germany's denseness of population, compared with the populations of neighbouring States, as a war potential.

The Allies, he said, should undertake an organised reduction of Germany's population through emigration.

PACT BY ARMIES IN JAVA

700 Jews Arrive, Bring Expensive Furs and Jewels

SYDNEY, Sunday.—Seven hundred Jewish refugees who arrived in the Dutch steamer Johan De Witt to-day brought hundreds of thousands of pounds' worth of personal belongings, including jewels, furs, and expensive cameras.

Customs officers think it will take about four days to clear their baggage.

Most of the refugees came from European concentration camps.

3 SHIPS TO BRING MIGRANTS

Launch, 2 Men, Missing

Robot May Read To Lazy People

MOTHER, CHILD BURNT

Spent 18 Hours In Agony

Flagstad In Minor Storm

Flashback

AWOKE TO FIND HOMES FLOODED

Jewish Ships Unsuitable

BIG ONES GOT AWAY

ROMA KEEN ON PLANS

EGG PRICE UP 3D. TO-DAY

KILLED IN INDIA RIOTS NOW 1036

BIG GUNS BY AIR NOW!

Dissolved Oral Vaccine Wages War On Catarrh

STORIES OF TWO DETERMINED WOMEN

PENSIONER BURNT TO DEATH IN BED

CHINESE HOPES FADE

Brisbane's Courier-Mail *of 17 March 1947 continued to make headline news of the arrival of Jewish refugees in Australia after the Second World War.*

74 *Long rule of the Liberals*

Liberal Party elected, 1949

AFTER THE SECOND WORLD WAR, THE LABOR GOVERNMENT UNDER BEN CHIFLEY (1885–1951) LOST MUCH OF ITS INITIAL POPULAR SUPPORT WHEN IT ATTEMPTED TO NATIONALISE THE BANKS, THE HEALTH SYSTEM, AND TRANSPORT AND COMMUNICATIONS.

Chifley's ideas about industrial relations backfired when the more militant trade unions, including the waterside workers, seamen, coalminers and metalworkers, were increasingly striking over wages and conditions—issues that had been put on hold through the Depression and Second World War. The nationalisation measures of the Chifley government made it an easy target for conservatives to paint it as a 'socialist' regime. After China became a communist nation in 1949, the fear of socialist 'reds' in Australian politics increased markedly and was highlighted by the conservative political parties.

In late 1944 Robert Menzies (1894–1978), who had been prime minister from 1939 to 1941 as leader of the United Australia Party (UAP) coalition, established the Liberal Party, combining the UAP and other smaller non-Labor groups. In a coalition formed with the Country Party (later to become the National Party), Menzies' Liberals were voted into power in the election of 10 December 1949, inaugurating a long period of Menzies-led government, with victory at the next five general elections from 1951 to 1963. As a result, Robert Menzies became Australia's longest serving prime minister.

Menzies continued many of the Chifley government's initiatives such as the Snowy Mountains hydroelectric scheme and expanded migration programs. In the context of the increasing tension of the growing Cold War between Western nations and the Soviet Union communist bloc, Menzies and his government were vehemently opposed to communism in Australia. In 1951 the Liberal Party supported a referendum to ban the Communist Party, which was defeated, despite the growing fear of communist influence, particularly in the trade union movement.

PHONE THE ARGUS F0411 —— CLASSIFIED ADS FJ9451

The Argus

No. 32,224 ☆ ☆ MELBOURNE, MONDAY, DECEMBER 12, 1949 20 PAGES PRICE 2d.

Registered at the General P.O., Melb., for transmission by post as a newspaper.

LANDSLIDE TO LIBERAL-COUNTRY PARTY DEFINITE

4 Ministers may go

THE Liberal and Country parties now appear to have won 66 of the 121 seats in the Federal Parliament.

Yesterday's counting confirmed the heavy election swing against the Labour Government, which has held office since 1941.

Labour now holds only 44 seats, but 11 are still doubtful.

Four of Mr Chifley's Ministers are in danger of losing their seats.

They are Mr J. J. Dedman (Corio), Mr C. Barnard (Bass), Mr N. Lemmon (Forrest), and Mr W. Scully (Gwydir).

When counting finished last night the position was

	LCP	Labour	Doubtful
NSW	22	22	3
Victoria	18	12	3
Western Australia	4	2	2
South Australia	6	4	..
Tasmania	3	1	1
Queensland	13	3	2
Totals	66	44	11

Menzies' majority

The Menzies Government will have a majority of about 19 seats in the new Parliament.

Victorian Senate voting indicates that four LCP Senators and three Labour Senators will be elected. The new system of proportional representation for Senate voting ensures minority representation in the Senate.

Mrs Ivy Wedgwood has a reasonable chance of being elected to the Senate. She was on the LCP ticket.

If elected she and Dame Enid Lyons (Lib, Tasmania), Senator Tangney (Lab), and Senator Rankin (Lib, Q) will be the only women in a Parliament of 183 members.

Members from the Australian Capital Territory and the Northern Territory only have votes on matters affecting their areas.

Dedman's fight

In Corio the Minister for Postwar Reconstruction, Mr Dedman, is trailing Hubert Opperman, former champion cyclist.

About 2,000 votes are yet to be counted in this electorate. At previous elections must of these votes have gone to the retiring member.

Mr D. McLeod, sitting Labour member for Wannon, has to depend on a drift in CP preferences to hold the seat.

Mr P. J. Clarey, former MLC and ex-president of the ACTU, is having a hard fight in Bendigo. When counting finished last night he was less than 300 behind Mr T. H. Grigg (Liberal). About 4,000 postal and absentee votes have yet to be counted.

Other victims

Sitting Labour members in other States who appear to have been defeated are:

Mr Hadley and Mr Conelan (Queensland); Mr Sheehy (South Australia).

Mr J. Lang (Lang Labour) and Mr M. Falstein (Independent Labour), NSW, were decisively defeated. Mrs D. Blackburn (Ind Lab) was beaten in Wills.

Mr L. Hamilton, CP member for Swan in the last Parliament, is in danger of defeat in the new seat of Canning.

So happy; So tired!

The strain of his election campaign touring......

......is apparent in this series of studies of Mr Menzies

....taken during his press conference held in Melb. yesterday.

By DULCIE FOARD

HE looked tired. He WAS tired. Tired but happy.

The Press—15 reporters—shot question after question at the Prime Minister-elect. He answered—or parried—them all.

"I'm in a bit of a coma today," he said. "I'm only mildly excited yet. I should be home in bed. After a night's sleep I'll probably begin to take in what's happened — about halfway through tomorrow.

"I didn't get to bed until 3am, after struggling with figures. And I'm not ashamed to confess that I stayed in bed all the morning—and let the world go by, sleeping the sleep which, in my experience, Nature sends to the just and the unjust alike."

And what had he done with his day since he got up, somebody asked Mr Menzies. The reply was prompt:

"Well, since then, I have been photographed in many postures, to an obligato by the telephone bell, which hasn't stopped since 6am.

"And I've seen my Kooyong electorate committee, and thanked them for increasing my record majority at the last poll to an even better figure on a pro rata basis."

He had also read lots of congratulatory telegrams.

The Argus EDITORIAL

Probe this smear—tell facts

AUSTRALIAN electors have purified public life by consigning Mr J. T. Lang and the Lang Labour Party to political oblivion.

By destroying Lang while returning Mr Menzies, electors have given a decision which even the most ardent member of the ALP will recognise as being clear, honest, and beyond dispute.

So far, so good.

There are, however, aspects of the Lang assault on Mr Chifley that still call for explanation.

The Lang story is alleged to have been offered to Mr S. M. Falstein by "a regular Press source." There are rumours suggesting that some metropolitan newspapers were in collaboration with Mr Lang to smear Australia's Prime Minister and influence the result of the Federal election by political muck-raking.

The facts should be probed and made public.

A probe would ensure that no political muck-raker would be likely to mar any future Federal election.

"The Argus" hopes that the new Government will probe the facts and make them public.

• Not wanted here, see Churches, P 8

P and A win to Coburg girl

Miss Margaret Holden, 25-year-old pianist from Coburg, last night won a trip to America award in Maples P and A Parade of 1949.

She also won the Open Instrumental section of the parade.

The trip to America is worth £500, and the first prize in the instrumental section £200.

"I'm so thrilled I don't know what to think," Miss Holden said after the announcement of the ward in 3KZ's studio.

She said she would not make any plans until she knew whether the new Government would make dollars available.

Piano teacher

Miss Holden is a teacher of pianoforte at the Melbourne Church of England Girls' Grammar School, Merton Hall, South Yarra.

Miss Holden is the first pianist in a Maples Parade to win the instrumental section, and it is also the first time that an instrumentalist has won the oversea trip award.

The full list of winners is:

Adult Vocal: Robert Simmons, baritone, 1; Betna Pontin, soprano, 2; Harry Mossfield, 3; Cliff Powell, 4; Beryl Dalley, 5.

Open Pops: John Oldnam, 1; Geoff Brooke, 2; Bill Harkin, 3; The Tune Twisters, 4; Kay Stavely, 5.

Open Instrumental and Novelty: Margaret Holden, 1; Desmond Bradley, violin, 2; Jim Jensen's Hawaiians, 3; Radio Swingette, 4.

Juvenile Vocal: Loris Ramskill, 1; Beryl Pearce, 2; Marie Paton, 3; Loris Sutton, 4.

Captain dies in cabin

Captain Adolf Wichstrom, 38, was burned to death in his cabin on the Norwegian freighter, "Silvana," at Victoria Dock yesterday.

Four hours earlier he had declined the invitation of visiting friends to spend the night at their home at Black Rock.

Police think Wichstrom was asphyxiated by smoke and fumes while trying to reach the doorway of his blazing cabin.

Spread stopped

The fire is believed to have started in or near the captain's bunk.

Fanned by a breeze through a porthole, it quickly gutted the cabin and adjoining office, but was checked by members of the crew before it could spread further.

Lief Westby, 20-year-old Norwegian wireless operator, whose cabin on the bridge deck is about 10 yards from the captain's quarters, was awakened at 6.30am by the crackling of flames.

Westby leapt from his bunk, threw open his cabin door, and was met by a wall of flames and smoke in the passageway.

He groped his way to a companionway outside the door and staggered down to the main deck to give the alarm to the sleeping crew.

"General Kenney Reports"

His book is to be serialised in THE ARGUS.

Watch for starting date

Interest overseas

Because of its implications as a move against Socialism, the result of the Australian elections attracted unusual attention in Britain, the United States, Canada and France.

In London it was front page news in most of the Sunday papers, and comments varied according to the individual paper's policy.

Right across Canada the news made front page banner headlines in Saturday afternoon's papers.

Mr Chifley ready to hand over

CANBERRA, Sun: The Chifley Labour Government wants to hand over to the new LCP Government as quickly as possible.

This was made clear tonight when Mr Chifley, Prime Minister returned to Canberra from Bathurst.

Mr Chifley declined to make any statement about his or the Government's intentions.

It was stated officially, however, that he is ready to vacate office immediately.

He will make an informal call on Mr McKell, Governor-General, early tomorrow morning, and then contact Mr Menzies by 'phone.

The resignation of the Chifley Government is expected on Wednesday after a final meeting of the present Cabinet. Mr Chifley will then advise the Governor-General and suggest that he send for Mr Menzies.

Normal procedure then would be for the Governor-General to commission Mr Menzies to form a government. Mr Menzies will probably be in a position to submit to Mr McKell the names of his Ministers on Thursday, and the new Ministry may be sworn in before the end of the week.

FORECAST

CITY: Cloudy, cool winds.

COUNTRY: Scattered showers in south, elsewhere fine. Cool winds.

(See Page 16.)

Menzies' election in 1949 marked an important shift in Australian politics and heralded a long period of conservative government, from 1949 to 1972 (although Menzies retired in 1966), which was buoyed by a growing economy.

Atomic bombs and opera houses

1950–

–1959

The 1950s are often recalled as a period of conservatism. The Liberal government led by Robert Menzies presided over much of the longest period of economic prosperity in Australia's history, lasting from the late 1940s to the early 1970s. This was a period of almost continual economic growth, rising standards of living and very low levels of unemployment.

The local manufacturing industry base that had expanded during the Second World War led to the growth of distinctly Australian products through the 1950s, with Holden cars, Victa lawn mowers and Hills Hoist clotheslines, to name a significant few. The 1950s was very much a period of consumerism—of modern goods that aimed to save time and effort for families who were beginning to have more time for leisure pursuits, spending time, for instance, at drive-in theatres and roller-skating rinks.

Yet it was also a period of social change and some surprisingly radical events. The choice of a design for the proposed Sydney Opera House flew in the face of convention—and engineering. So, too, the 1950s saw a significant shift in immigration policy. What became the largest migration intake program in Australian history began to accept migrants who were not of British origin and from a broader range of countries—although Asian and African people were not yet accepted as immigrants.

Migrants were critical for the massive infrastructure projects the Australian government had in mind. The Snowy Mountains scheme was an engineering and construction feat on an unheard of scale in Australian history—although after generating electricity 'for the nation', the other aim of the scheme, to divert Snowy River water flow to more arid western areas, met with less long-term success. The project was to take until the 1970s to complete and provided ready work for the large numbers of, generally, single male migrants entering the country during the 1950s and 1960s.

This period of development and population growth was still tied to broader political uncertainties. While international political tensions grew between the United States and the Soviet Union—heightened after the USSR tested its first nuclear weapon in August 1949—Australia was closer to the Cold War than its distance seemed to suggest. The 1950s was a period when Australia readily offered its expansive outback and uninhabited offshore islands to Britain as testing grounds for nuclear explosions.

So, too, as Cold War tensions developed, attempts were made to ban the Communist Party in Australia. The possibility of a Russian spy ring operating in the country, which was suggested during the Petrov Affair of 1954, fuelled the flames of anti-communism in the country.

Two major spectacles of pageantry in the mid-1950s distracted national attention from Cold War politics. These were the royal tour of the newly crowned Queen Elizabeth II in 1954 and the 1956 Melbourne Olympic Games. Quite typically in Australian history, at the same time as there was an outburst of Australian nationalism, an outpouring of sentiment for the British monarchy occurred—a strange tension in Australian society that was to continue well into the future.

The royal visit and the Melbourne Olympics were newspaper headlines across the country for weeks on end. By the 1950s, even the long-reluctant *Sydney Morning Herald* had finally put headline news on its front page. In an increasingly fierce climate of competition over readership and sales, growing numbers of newspapers offered readers images of the latest news, rather than merely text. Yet despite moving headlines to the front page, the divide between the broadsheets of the generally larger format, older papers, and the tabloids, with their smaller page size, bold headlines and extensive use of images, was to continue.

The final shape of the typical front page layout we are familiar with today was a result of these battles for readership as much as from advances in printing technologies. By the 1950s, although special inserts and cartoon strips in colour were popular, the introduction of regular colour images and print into newspapers was still a long way off. From the late 1950s, however, the introduction of competition in the form of television was to influence the importance of immediate and visual front page news, and would also see important news events become full-colour wrap-around spreads by the 1960s.

Ron Clarke, aged 19 and described as a promising middle and long-distance runner, lights the Olympic flame at the opening ceremony of the Melbourne Olympics on 22 November 1956. Despite international tensions, sometimes played out during these Olympics, they became known as the Friendly Games.

75 Montebello to Maralinga

Britain tests nuclear weapons in Australia, 1952

ON 3 OCTOBER 1952 BRITAIN SUCCESSFULLY CREATED AN ATOMIC EXPLOSION, MAKING IT THE THIRD NUCLEAR POWER IN THE WORLD, AFTER THE UNITED STATES AND THE USSR. MUCH MORE HAD BEEN LEARNED ABOUT NUCLEAR FALLOUT AFTER THE DESTRUCTION OF THE JAPANESE CITIES OF NAGASAKI AND HIROSHIMA, AND SO THE BRITISH GOVERNMENT HAD DECIDED THE EXPLOSION WOULD TAKE PLACE A LONG WAY FROM HOME. THE UNINHABITED MONTEBELLO ISLANDS, JUST 70 KILOMETRES OFF THE PILBARA REGION ON THE NORTH-WEST COAST OF WESTERN AUSTRALIA, WERE CHOSEN.

Perth's two daily newspapers, *The West Australian* and the *Daily News*, sent a team of reporters and photojournalists by jeep to set up a camp on the remote coastline near the small town of Onslow. From here they wrote their reports, photographed the huge atomic mushroom cloud and rushed the images by jeep and plane back to their newspapers.

The photographs of the nuclear cloud were an international scoop, because official pictures associated with the atomic tests were restricted. Importantly, the test explosion was widely seen as a reassertion of British military might after the dominance of the United States and the USSR during the Second World War.

Australia's involvement in the incredible atomic age was unstoppable. Not only did the tests offer a military reconnection with Britain, but also an opportunity for Australia to act on the world stage. The Australian government continued to offer what it saw as the deserted Australian landscape as nuclear testing grounds, and between 1953 and 1956 a further nine test explosions were conducted at Emu Field and Maralinga in South Australia.

The Montebello Islands were indeed uninhabited and the test conducted underwater, so the nuclear fallout did not affect many people—apart from those involved in the testing. However the Maralinga and Emu Field sites were not vacant desert, but were in fact occupied by the Pitjantjatjara and Yankunytjatjara peoples. It wasn't until the 1980s, when both Australian armed servicemen and Aboriginal people from the Maralinga area began to fall ill, that a Royal Commission of Inquiry was held and found there were still significant radiation hazards. The sites were more thoroughly cleaned and compensation awarded.

The West Australian

VOL. 68, No. 20,658. (Registered at the G.P.O., Perth, for transmission by post as a newspaper.) PERTH, SATURDAY, OCTOBER 4, 1952. TEL. B8161. 32 PAGES † PRICE 3d.

BRITAIN TESTS HER FIRST ATOMIC BOMB OFF W.A. COAST

(FROM OUR SPECIAL OBSERVERS.)

MT. POTTER, Friday.—With a brief lightning-like flash, Britain's first atomic weapon was exploded at 8 a.m. today in the Monte Bello Islands, off the north-west coast of Western Australia.

The flash was followed by a huge expanding cloud which reached a height of 12,000ft. within about three minutes of the explosion. By that time it was about a mile across at its widest part.

Although no official announcement has been made, it is believed that the explosion was from a tower either at Flag Island or at Hermite Island—the largest in the Monte Bello group.

The Press observation point is on the highest point in Rough Range, north of the Fortescue River, and is only 55 miles from the Monte Bello Islands.

No Ground Shock Felt

Observers here did not feel a ground shock, but a heavy air-pressure pulse hit the mainland four minutes and 15 seconds after the flash of the explosion, which occurred on the tick of 8 o'clock.

At the same time pressmen heard a report like a clap of thunder, followed by a prolonged rumble like that of a train going through a tunnel.

The air and ground shocks were sufficiently intense to cause slight pain in the ears.

The immediate flash resembled the top quarter of a setting sun.

A dense and magnificently turbulent cloud almost immediately shot to a height of 2,000ft.

At first deep pink, it quickly changed to mauve in the centre, with pink towards the outside and brilliantly white turbulent edges.

Within two minutes the cloud, which still was like a giant cauliflower, was 10,000ft. high. A small pure-white milling ball rested on top.

Though the day's wind was strong south-easterly, it changed to west for a brief moment as the shock went inland. By this time, the cloud was being torn about by winds at 2,000ft. and 10,000ft., but the intensely turbulent ball still rested on top.

A Faint Wisp Of Cloud

One hour after the explosion the atomic cloud—the only cloud in a clear blue sky—was beginning to take elongated stratus formation as strong upper winds whipped it north along the coast.

Within two hours the only evidence of the atomic explosion was a faint whisp of cloud a few miles above the horizon. Soon after, it disintegrated and disappeared.

The detonation glow seen by pressmen from their hilltop post was about as bright as, and of the same dimension as, the top segment of a setting sun.

A photographer who was looking directly towards the Monte Bellos when the explosion occurred said that the flash at first was deep orange-red.

Simultaneously a large sphere of flat smoke, estimated to be about one mile in diameter, shot up.

This puff immediately rocketed skywards at tremendous speed, closely followed by billowing white smoke.

Unfavourable weather conditions in the sub-stratosphere held up the tests for three days.

The test was originally listed for Wednesday but, since the scientists were ready, it was decided to explode a day early, on Tuesday.

Task For The R.A.A.F.

However, though it was a fine, clear day and all ships and scientists had taken test stations, it was found that an unfavourable wind was blowing in the sub-stratosphere and it was decided to postpone the test for a day.

On the following two days, however, conditions were again unfavourable.

Second only in importance to the actual explosion was the task of following the highly dangerous cloud of radio-active dust to find out where it finished.

This role was primarily allotted to a squadron of R.A.A.F. Lincoln bombers, specially flown to Broome from Amberley (Queensland).

It is believed that they were assisted, probably at low level, by Seafuries and Fireflies from the carrier Sydney

There has been no official indication that today's test completed Britain's atomic programme along this coastline, and there is conjecture on what any future tests may hold in store.

It is known that Hastings aircraft will be standing by from next Monday to take Britain's scientists from Onslow, so that any more tests involving atomic detonations would need to be within the next week.

(Details and Pictures, Pages 4, 5, 6 and 7.)

Cloud Billows High Over The Indian Ocean

Less than three minutes after Britain's first atomic weapon had exploded yesterday, this picture was taken with a specially-prepared telephoto camera from a coastal peak about 55 miles from the centre of the prohibited zone. The top of the cloud is continuing to rise and its centre to move away to the west. The cloud had reached 6,000 ft. one minute after the explosion and in another minute was 10,000ft. high. For the first few minutes the morning sun lit the top edges of the formation. Within a few minutes of the picture having been taken, it and others were being processed in a portable darkroom at the observation site. Soon after, the negatives were rushed to Mardie airstrip where a chartered Anson aircraft waited to begin an 850-mile flight to Perth. All was there in readiness to send the pictures to a waiting world.

"A POOR MAN'S BOMB" TO HARWELL MEN

LONDON, Fri.—At Harwell, where almost all nuclear research is done in Britain, they call the atomic weapon "the poor man's atomic bomb"—whether it is guided missile, shell or aircraft-carried bomb, says the "Daily Mail."

The reason is that Britain's atomic effort has been done comparatively cheaply.

Expenditure, at between £100,000,000 and £200,000,000 sterling, has been a mere fraction of what the United States has spent and, apart from the cost of the Australian test, very little money can said to have been "wasted" on purely war effort.

The atomic weapon, unlike the majority of other warlike instruments, has vast and valuable possibilities in peace.

Many of Britain's millions of pounds have gone into building huge plants for the production of uranium and plutonium.

These plants are necessary if we are to build a bomb; they are equally necessary if we envisage any future in the use of atomic power.

Most of the research into nuclear fission can be said to run concurrently whether it is for weapons or industry.

Only in the last stage of research processing do the two aims diverge, and before that most of the millions have been spent anyway.

News Travelled Faster Than Shock Wave

News of the explosion yesterday reached Perth—over 1,000 miles away—by telegraph one minute and 15 seconds before the shock wave from the blast was felt by journalists on the mainland—only 56 miles away.

This was because an almost instantaneous service was provided by the telegraph branch of the Postmaster-General's Department, under the direction of the Superintendent of Telegraphs (Mr. L. J. Clarke).

The first newsflash of the bomb explosion at 8 a.m. was received in Perth from Mt. Potter at 8.3 a.m. The shock-wave hit the coast 15 seconds after 8.4 a.m.

Keen cooperation by telegraph and telephone executives and workers permitted thousands of words of descriptive matter to be flashed from the Onslow area to Perth in record time.

The telegraph station from which the news was flashed to the world was situated on the back of a six-ton truck.

ADVERTISEMENT INDEX

Classified Advertisements	18
Shipping	23
Births, Deaths	32
In Memoriam	32

The West Australian of 4 October 1952 published its scoop of the atomic mushroom cloud that followed the first British test of nuclear weapons in Australia.

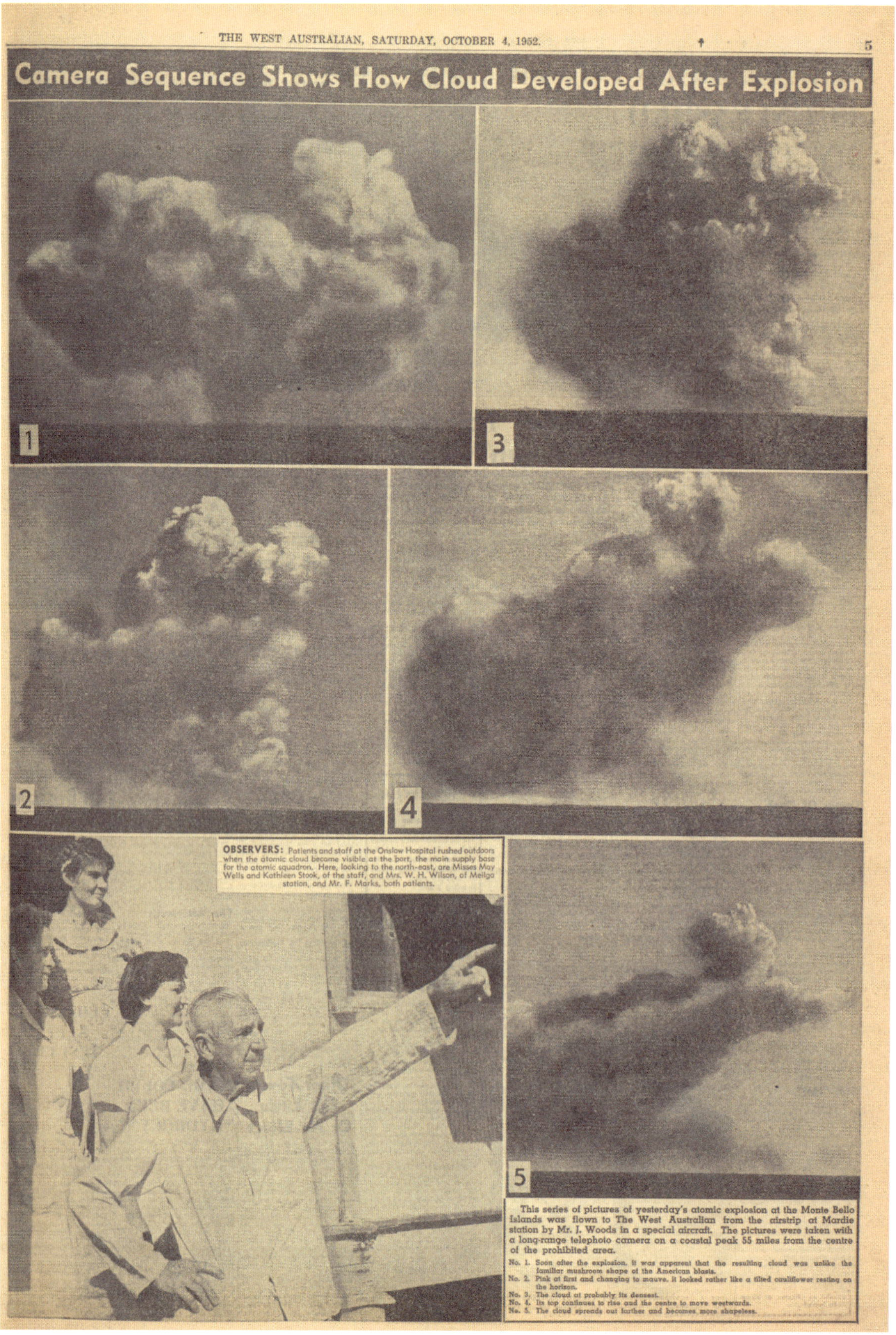

Camera Sequence Shows How Cloud Developed After Explosion

OBSERVERS: Patients and staff at the Onslow Hospital rushed outdoors when the atomic cloud became visible at the port, the main supply base for the atomic squadron. Here, looking to the north-east, are Misses May Wells and Kathleen Stook, of the staff, and Mrs. W. H. Wilson, of Meilga station, and Mr. F. Marks, both patients.

This series of pictures of yesterday's atomic explosion at the Monte Bello Islands was flown to The West Australian from the airstrip at Mardie station by Mr. J. Woods in a special aircraft. The pictures were taken with a long-range telephoto camera on a coastal peak 55 miles from the centre of the prohibited area.

No. 1. Soon after the explosion, it was apparent that the resulting cloud was unlike the familiar mushroom shape of the American blasts.
No. 2. Pink at first and changing to mauve. It looked rather like a tilted cauliflower resting on the horizon.
No. 3. The cloud at probably its densest.
No. 4. Its top continues to rise and the centre to move westwards.
No. 5. The cloud spreads out farther and becomes more shapeless.

Page 5 of The West Australian*'s issue of 4 October 1952 continued the story of the first atomic bomb test in Australia with a series of photos showing the development of the mushroom cloud that followed the test on the Montebello Islands.*

They've struck it! 76

Oil found at Exmouth, 1953

THE FIRST SUCCESSFUL DEEPWATER OFFSHORE OIL-DRILLING OPERATIONS IN THE WORLD WERE DEVELOPED IN THE GULF OF MEXICO IN THE LATE 1930S. BY 1940, WITH THE INCREASING WARTIME NEED FOR SELF-SUFFICIENCY IN OIL PRODUCTION, OIL COMPANIES WERE SCOURING PARTS OF THE AUSTRALIAN COASTLINE MOST LIKELY TO CONTAIN OIL DEPOSITS.

Oil exploration in Australia was interrupted by the war, but it continued on a small scale in the 1950s. Then, on 4 December 1953 West Australian Petroleum Pty Ltd announced that it had discovered high-grade crude oil in its Rough Range-1 exploration well, near Exmouth on the north-west coast of Western Australia.

This was the first oil flow recorded anywhere in Australia, and it caused jubilation throughout the country. The stock market boomed, and politicians and newspapers claimed that this could be Australia's most significant development of the twentieth century. Indeed, an American geologist claimed that it was the most important global oil development since oil had been discovered in the United States in 1859.

West Australians were euphoric about the discovery of oil. Australia had no domestic production of oil or gas at the time, and the costs of oil imports were a major burden on the economy. It seemed that the quiet backwater of Perth and Western Australia would soon be transformed into an industrial powerhouse. Locals were delighted that the attention given to the oil finds and subsequent drilling operations made it clear that their state was indeed important to the nation.

The discovery initiated a period of intensive oil and gas exploration, and another resources boom for the Australian economy.

The West Australian

VOL. 69. No. 21,022. (Registered at the G.P.O., Perth, for transmission by post as a newspaper.) • PERTH, SATURDAY, DECEMBER 5, 1953. • TEL. BA0161 • 36 PAGES † PRICE 3d.

STATE STRIKES OIL AT FIRST DRILLING

The headquarters office of Standard Oil of California announced from San Francisco yesterday that oil had been discovered in Australia at Exmouth Gulf, 600 to 700 miles north of Perth.

The statement said that "very high-grade crude oil" was discovered at a depth of 3,605 to 3,620ft.

The company ran a 25-hour test of this discovery and production was at the rate of 20 barrels an hour through a quarter-inch pipe.

[A barrel of oil contains approximately 40 U.S. gallons or 35 Imperial gallons. The 25-hour test, therefore, on the Rough Range well, yielded oil at the rate of 17,500 gallons for the period.]

Standard Oil said that the announcement had been made by the California Texas Corporation, which held an 80 per cent interest in West Australian Petroleum.

A 20 per cent interest was held by the Australian firm, Ampol.

Mr. R. G. Follis, chairman of the board of Standard Oil, said that the discovery appeared to be the first commercial quantities of crude oil ever found on the continent of Australia.

The discovery well, Rough Range, No. 1, was an exploratory venture of West Australian Petroleum Pty. Ltd., drilled to begin testing of more than 300,000 square miles held under long-term concession from the State of Western Australia.

Statement

The company's statement added: "Significance of the discovery is indicated by the fact that Australia now is using about 100,000 barrels of petroleum products daily all of which must be imported.

"Future plans for development of the concessionary areas include deeper drilling of the discovery well to test geological formations lying beneath the discovery sands and the drilling of other wells.

"The discovery well may be taken down as far as 15,000 feet."

The announcement by Standard Oil added:

"Oil showings in Australia. At Rough Range No. 1, its first wildcat, West Australian Petroleum Ltd. has been testing oil showings in sand at 3,605 to 3,620 ft.

"The well is located just inland from Exmouth Gulf in an isolated section of Australia's west coast, some 600 to 700 miles north of Perth.

"Tests at this depth have been completed and drilling resumed in accordance with original plans for deep testing.

Exploration

"Standard Oil Co. of California geologists, on behalf of Caltex, first began preliminary geological work in Western Australia in 1939.

"It was the extensive exploration efforts of Australia's Department of National Development, however, which led to the leasing of the widespread acreage now held by Caltex and Ampol.

"This work was what encouraged Caltex to return to Australia in the hope of bringing in the Commonwealth's first discovery.

"Caltex, which has widespread marketing outlets and refining facilities throughout the Eastern Hemisphere, now has under construction in Australia a 22,000-barrel refinery located near Sydney."

First Time

The managing-director of Ampol Petroleum Ltd. (Mr. W. G. Walkley) said tonight that it was the first time in Australia's history that there had been a strike like this one.

The oil was flowing at 20 barrels an hour and was of the finest grade paraffin base.

"All types of petroleum can be produced from it," he said.

"I will not predict the future, but this discovery may prove to be the most important in Australia's history.

"It could prove a terrific money saver and indirectly save Australia dollars."

The senior lecturer in economics at Sydney University (Mr. R. C. Gates) said last night that a major oil strike would have five vital effects on the Australian economy.

It would:

- Help greatly to solve the sterling area's dollar shortage.
- Justify the large expenditure in Australia for building oil refineries.
- Encourage investment in Australia by overseas countries
- Increase the general soundness of the Australian economy.
- Be a big help in developing Western Australia, previously a State without many rich resources.

Everything

The prominent nuclear physicist, Professor H. Messel, said news of the oil discovery in Western Australia was "simply marvellous."

"Now you have everything—water, uranium, and oil," he said.

"Over the last few years everything seems to have developed—the coal, water and now oil.

"It's just what the country needs."

News of the strike was not unexpected at Onslow.

Unofficial but authentic reports reaching the port for the past month had clearly indicated that the company had struck oil.

Local residents have been quietly purchasing small parcels of shares as available.

Strategy

It is believed that this vast sparsely populated area will come into strong focus with the Commonwealth Government from a strategic point of view.

Although it is thought that the oil discovery will have no immediate impact on Onslow it is considered generally that oil will be found in many other areas of the north, particularly in the country adjacent to Exmouth.

The consensus of opinion is that it would not be possible to erect a refinery in this area because of the lack of water and coal for power and of other natural resources needed.

It is considered significant that Kwinana was chosen as the site of the huge Anglo-Iranian refinery.

Carnarvon residents and people in the Gascoyne areas are jubilant.

Groups of people huddled in the streets discuss the possibilities of Carnarvon becoming a boom town as the trading centre for the oil wells.

Gusher Hope

Officials of the company in Perth yesterday had nothing to add to the official announcement. They had not been advised of the quality of the oil until they learnt of it in the news release from San Francisco.

The 17ft. of oil strata is regarded, in the oil world, as being a "relatively thin" in width.

Consequently, this will be sealed off while the company carries down the drill to the originally proposed depth of 12,000ft. in the hope a gusher will be struck.

If this should not occur, the company will carry out further tests on the 17ft. oil area to test the full value of the discovery and attempt to assess its oil-carrying capacity.

(Map and further reports, pages 6, 8 and 9.)

"THEY'VE STRUCK IT!"—AND SOME REJOICE, OTHERS WISH THEY HAD SHARES

ABOVE: "They've found oil!" An excited crowd gathers outside a city stockbroker's office as the news spreads round that the State's first oil drill has proved successful. Rapidly rising oil stock quotations were being posted on the board. RIGHT: The derrick which has been the focal point of the operation since September 5, when drilling commenced. BELOW: This black, sticky substance is a sample of the real thing—it may look like axle-grease, but in fact it is "black gold."—and it comes straight from Rough Range, 20 miles from Learmonth.

Brokers Flooded With Orders

Sharebrokers in Perth, immediately the news that oil had been found at Exmouth Gulf became public property, were flooded with orders yesterday.

They spent a frantic day coping with telephone calls, and many were working late last night to clean up the day's business.

All brokers admitted that they had never experienced anything like it since the gold boom days of the 1930's.

"The public was buying mad," one Perth broker said, "but most of them misjudged the speed with which the market would rise."

Some increased inquiry developed for Ampol Exploration among one or two brokers on Thursday, after the official call in Perth.

Yesterday morning it expanded to a torrent.

Late on Thursday, Ampol Exploration shares, which had been steady for over a week, moved up 2/ to 19/6.

At the official call yesterday, they soared to 55/ and 56/, but sellers were few and only about 500 or 600 changed hands.

Off-Room Sales

By the afternoon, in off-room sales, and stimulated by the reaction in the Eastern States, Perth brokers sold Ampol Exploration as high as £5, at which price 1,000 changed hands, while the sale of 500 was recorded at 95/.

In Melbourne, sales were as high as £6/15/, but the market closed at £6.

In Sydney, the day's selling finished at 95/ to 97/.

Ampol Petroleum Ltd. also participated in the boom.

On Thursday, sales had been made in Perth at 11/3 up to 11/6.

No official sales were made yesterday, but in the afternoon, on off-room sales, the shares sky-rocketed to 50/ for a parcel of 500.

Sales were also made at 41/.

In Sydney, sales of Ampol Petroleum were as high as 42/6, the closing price being 35/.

In Adelaide, these shares were sold at 33/6.

Well Held

Generally, the shares were well held, both for Ampol Exploration and Petroleum, and wide variations in prices reflected the thin market.

Holders had little intention of selling, and buying quotes for most of the day lagged behind sellers' ideas of prices.

Freney Oil reacted in sympathy. After sales at 8/3, 800 were sold at 19/4½.

Sydney prices were almost the same.

Oil Search also showed an improvement of a few shillings to 9/6 and 9/8.

Our Melbourne office reports that oil was the talk of stock exchanges in capital cities throughout Australia yesterday, and resulted in spectacular buying not seen for almost 50 years.

The most meteoric rises were seen on the Melbourne exchange.

Many Melbourne brokers were overwhelmed by telephone, telegraph and cable inquiries for Ampol Petroleum and Ampol Exploration shares.

London was in the market as a buyer, and some American orders came via London.

The turnover of Ampol Petroleum on the Melbourne exchange was 15,400.

There were wild scenes on the Melbourne stock exchange early in the day as car upon car became involved in a traffic jam outside the exchange.

Trading was electrical at the afternoon call.

Frantic afternoon trading on the Sydney stock exchange boosted Ampol Exploration to 98/.

On the Adelaide stock exchange, shares in Ampol Exploration recorded the most spectacular rise seen since the turn of the century.

Trading on the Brisbane stock exchange was brisk.

The secretary of the Sydney exchange (Mr. A. G. Wallace) warned investors to be guarded in oil share dealings.

LARGE FIELD IS "ALMOST A CERTAINTY"

CANBERRA, Fri.—A large oilfield almost certainly existed at Exmouth Gulf, the Secretary of the Department of National Development (Dr. H. Raggatt) said tonight.

Sands similar to those at Exmouth Gulf extended between Onslow and Carnarvon, indicating that the field could extend over many hundreds of miles, he said.

Dr. Raggatt said that to get even one cupful of oil a day from the first drill would have been remarkable.

But to get 28 barrels an hour was "miraculous."

The discovery vindicates the judgment of Dr. Raggatt and the Director of the Bureau of Mineral Resources (Dr. H. N. Fisher).

Indications

For years both have proclaimed the hidden wealth of Exmouth Gulf and their faith in the area has led materially to its selection for drilling.

"It is almost inconceivable that the first bore sunk in this area has tapped the only deposit," said Dr. Raggatt.

Dr. Fisher said that although the Bureau had supplied all the detailed surveys on which the drilling was based, he was unable to say whether more oil were lying beneath the first "strike."

There was every indication that further deposits would be found in the area.

Further north in the Kimberleys surveys had shown promising results.

Premier Says W.A. Will Benefit

Action would be taken to ensure that the State, and the people of the State as a whole, would receive some substantial benefit from what promised to be a very wonderful discovery of oil in Western Australia.

The Premier (Mr. Hawke) told this to a highly attentive Legislative Assembly yester-morning.

Mr. Ackland (C.P., Moore) had asked, if oil had been struck in Western Ausralia, whether Mr. Hawke would consider seeing that the State would receive benefits from that oil on lines similar to those in Alberta, Canada.

Alberta had been bankrupt in 1935, Mr. Ackland said.

It was now possibly the only credit State in the British Commonwealth because of the royalties collected for the State from oil.

Laws Studied

Mr. Hawke replied that the Minister for Mines (Mr. Kelly) and his officers already had given a fair amount of consideration to that angle, which was tremendously important for the people of Western Australia.

They had studied laws and practices which operated in Canada, including Alberta.

If hopes in connection with the news from the United States of America were met—that oil in payable quantities was available in the North-West—action would be taken to ensure that the State, and the people of the State as a whole, would receive some substantial benefit from what promised to be a wonderful discovery.

Value May Be Tremendous

The announcement that oil had been found in Western Australia was not only great news for the State and Australia generally, but also for the British Commonwealth, the Leader of the Opposition (Sir Ross McLarty) said yesterday.

Sir Ross said that it might be a little early to say whether the oil would be in payable quantities but the indications appeared favourable.

The fact that it had been discovered so soon augured well for the future of the field.

If all went as the people of the State hoped, the value to the State should prove tremendous, particularly as it would mean the advent of other great industries.

DRILLS WILL BE SENT STILL DEEPER

(Our Special Representative.)

CARNARVON, Friday.—Despite the presence of oil at 3,600ft. at Rough Range, No. 1 well, the search for additional oil penetrating beds at greater depth will be continued.

Drilling crews tonight are blanking off perforations in well casings out of which the crude oil samples that set Australia agog with excitement were first taken.

The general manager of W.A. Petroleum (Mr. J. W. Thomas) formerly of New York, who is in charge of present exploration, said: "We intend at present to explore all possibilities before exploitation.

"When blanking off operations are completed drills will start operating again and will follow the original programme of drilling to about 12,000ft. to make a thorough test of all possible oil-producing formations."

Promise

Mr. Thomas said that at present he was unable to determine the economic possibilities of formations so far encountered.

"Although we have not struck a bonanza, what we have struck shows promise and shows existence of oil bearing formations in W.A.

"Additional drilling will be required to determine the ecomomic possibilities of the area.

"Oil drilling crews included among others Americans, Australians and New Zealanders. All are jubilant at the news and are anxious to press on and find exactly what lies below the desolate countryside."

High Jinks In Pitt-street

SYDNEY, Fri.—The managing-director of Ampol Petroleum Ltd. (Mr. W. G. Walkley) today walked down Pitt-street, Sydney, wearing a red 10-gallon hat. Thus he kept a promise made at a Carnarvon (W.A.) hotel several weeks ago that he would do this if the drillers struck oil.

The West Australian of 5 December 1953 made headline news of the discovery of off-shore oil in Exmouth Gulf in Western Australia. Standard Oil, based in California, was one member of the joint venture exploration company of West Australian Petrolueum Pty Ltd.

Queen steps ashore 77

The royal tour, 1954

IN 1954 THE NEWLY CROWNED, YOUNG QUEEN ELIZABETH II VISITED AUSTRALIA AND WAS GREETED WITH UNPRECEDENTED CEREMONY, CELEBRATION AND CROWDS. ALTHOUGH ROYALS HAD VISITED AUSTRALIA BEFORE, ELIZABETH WAS THE FIRST REIGNING MONARCH TO TRAVEL THE LONG DISTANCE TO AUSTRALIA.

A somewhat restrained, but nonetheless pop-star-like hysteria swept the nation. Millions of Australians lined the streets to catch a glimpse of the queen's motorcade as it made appearances in the Australian Capital Territory, New South Wales, Tasmania, Victoria, Queensland, South Australia and Western Australia.

With the advent of television still a few years away, newspapers were the main source of news and images of the queen's comings and goings, and they produced massive souvenir spreads and issues. Every moment of the queen's day was photographed and every detail of what she wore each day was reported.

Despite the bodyline controversy, the fall of Singapore and Australian political independence, there was still a strong popular sentiment for what many Australians continued to believe was the Mother Country and its royal family. While the 1950s were to see a massive social and economic modernisation of Australia, a groundswell of nostalgia for Britain—in the form of the young Queen Elizabeth II—appeared almost in direct proportion to Australian independence and modernity.

OVER
Every moment of the queen's visit to Australia was reported on, especially her stepping ashore from the royal barge at Farm Cove in Sydney—somehow reminiscent of other great landing moments by Captain Cook and Governor Phillip.

THOUGHT FOR TO-DAY

Beauty can inspire miracles.
—Beaconsfield.

The Canberra Times

Price 3d.

To serve the National City, and through it the Nation

"The Canberra Times" is a subscriber to Australian Associated Press, which provides overseas news in this issue.

VOL. 28. No. 8,144. CANBERRA: THURSDAY, FEBRUARY 4, 1954. Registered at the G.P.O., Sydney, for transmission by Post as a Newspaper. EIGHT PAGES.

HISTORIC LANDING OF QUEEN AT FARM COVE

AT THE CENOTAPH

IN THE ONLY moments of silence throughout the Royal Progress the Queen and the Duke of Edinburgh laid a wreath on the Cenotaph in Martin Place.

Solemn Moment At Cenotaph

SYDNEY, Wednesday.

More than 50,000, who packed Martin Place from George Street to Macquarie Street to-day, saw the Queen and the Duke of Edinburgh place a wreath on the Cenotaph.

The wreath—heart shaped—of white chrysanthemums, red carnations, red roses and red gladioli, bore the simple inscription on a card: "From Elizabeth R. and the Duke of Edinburgh."

Many of the people had camped overnight on footpaths and G.P.O. steps to see the 5-minute ceremony—the only spot during the drive that the Royal Couple left the car.

Others swelled the throng of campers and early arrivals late in the morning when they streamed 40 abreast down Martin Place after watching the Royal Progress in Macquarie Street.

St. John Ambulance officers stationed in Martin Place treated more than 80 people who collapsed or fainted in the hot sun and the tightly-packed crowds.

Many people collapsed when the press of the crowd forced barriers to tip forward, threatening to throw people in the front rows onto their faces.

Although the custodian had appealed for silence during the ceremony, the crowds cheered madly when the Royal Car came into sight.

The cheering died down slowly as the Royal Couple alighted from the car.

The Duke and the Queen, each taking a side of the 4ft. 6in. long wreath, placed it on the G.P.O. side of the Cenotaph.

As the Duke saluted and the Queen stood silently, the crowd quietened down, realising the solemness of the occasion.

Then, as the Royal Couple turned to walk back to the car the cheering broke out again, and crowds between the Cenotaph and Pitt Street burst the barriers and streamed into the roadway.

The Queen, while returning to the car, acknowledged the cheers and waved to the crowd.

Cheering reached an all-time high when the Duke, before driving off, raised his right hand in salute to the crowd.

Moving Welcome By Sydney Throngs

(From Our Special Representative, Ian Healy)

SYDNEY, Wednesday.

In a scene of unforgettable beauty and pageantry, the Queen and the Duke of Edinburgh stepped ashore at historic Farm Cove at 10.33 a.m. to-day.

The Queen, looking incredibly young and fragile and more beautiful than any picture shows, has completely enchanted the city.

The greatest crowd in Australia's history joined in a tumultuous welcome at the landing and as the Royal Pair drove through the city.

More than a million people joined in the welcome, massing at every vantage point along the harbourside from the Heads to the Bridge and packing the Royal Progress so densely that in many places it was impossible to move.

As she stepped ashore in glorious sunshine, from the Royal Barge to the gleaming white landing pontoon, the Queen smiled with warm sincerity to those waiting to welcome her. She looked fresh and completely charming. Neither she nor the Duke showed the slightest sign of tiredness or strain after their five weeks in New Zealand and the rough Tasman crossing.

When the Queen walked to the welcoming dais, moving with natural grace, her first words to Australia were of happiness and thanks.

As she stepped on to the pontoon, to be welcomed first by the Governor-General, Sir William Slim, then by the State Governor Sir John Northcott, the Prime Minister, Mr. Menzies, and the State Premier, Mr. Cahill, the Royal Ensign was unfurled at the landing stage.

Royal Australian Artillery guns boomed out a 21-gun salute across the harbour and 18 Vampire jet aircraft flew over in faultless formation.

The pealing of church bells announcing her arrival through the city were lost in the thunderous noise of the crowd in the Cove.

Escorted by Vampire and Mustang aircraft and by four ships of the Royal Australian Navy the Royal Yacht Gothic passed through the heads at 8 a.m. making a majestic picture as she entered the harbour.

A pilot from the pilot ship Captain Cook, boarded Gothic off Cape Banks, about 10 miles south of the Heads, an hour and 10 minutes earlier.

As Gothic sailed through the Heads into one of the world's most beautiful harbours, artillery guns fired a Royal Salute from North Head.

Thousands on the headlands and around the bays, at windows and on rooftops of harbourside buildings watched through binoculars, cheered, waved and felt the first deep thrill of the Royal Visit.

Thousands more in decorated small craft and listing ferries waved and shouted greetings when the Queen and Duke were observed on the saluting deck.

The Royal Couple waved in acknowledgment.

At 9.20 an hour after Gothic had anchored, a naval launch drew alongside, and Sir William and Lady Slim went aboard the yacht to pay an official call on the Queen.

At 10-minute intervals, Sir John Northcott, Mr. Menzies and Dame Pattie Menzies, and the Premier arrived in other naval craft to pay similar calls.

The Royal Barge was lowered from the Gothic and at 10.20, when the official visitors had departed, the Queen and the Duke walked down the gangway to begin their journey to Farm Cove.

Around the full sweep of Farm Cove tens of thousands, many of whom had camped there overnight, thronged to barriers set back from the seawall and turned the lush gardens into a technicolour ocean.

TENSE EXCITEMEUT

As the hour of the landing approached, excitement became intense among those in the neighbourhood of the pontoon, and every new arrival with some official part in the ceremony was applauded and cheered with growing intensity.

By 9.15, when the Cove was a landscape of enormous crowds and dazzling colour, most of the dignitaries to meet the Queen were on the pontoon—Cabinet members and others in toppers, black mornings and morning suits, Church leaders, Service chiefs in uniform, and members of the judiciary in wigs and robes.

The first indication that the Royal Barge was on its way came with the echoing hoots and sirens of ships around the harbour.

Then a wave of cheers rolled in across the water when the barge became visible to those on the landing stage.

The excitement and cheering was almost overwhelming.

As the glistening, highly polished barge, preceded by an escort of police launches, drew alongside the pontoon, the first picture of the Royal Couple was one of sparkling youth—a beautiful, petite young woman in a light summer dress and a tall, handsome young man in white naval uniform.

After the first brief, smiling welcomes, the Queen, with the Duke on her left and slightly behind her, moved under the canopy on the pontoon, standing in shade as some 70 dignitaries were presented.

They were presented by Mr. Menzies and Mr. Cahill, moving in file to the canopy from their red leather and silver steel chairs.

As each dignitary was presented, bowing and shaking hands, the Queen and Duke smiled and spoke briefly to them.

After the presentations, Mr. Cahill escorted the Queen from the pontoon.

A naval guard presented arms in a Royal Salute as the R.A.N. Band from Nowra Naval Base played the National Anthem.

The Queen inspected the guard and then returned to mount the dais for the official welcome by the Lord Mayor.

The Queen's reply, given in a clear, well-modulated voice, brought a full-throated roar from the throng.

Ald. Hills then presented the city's aldermen. The aldermen, including the two Communist members of the council, added to the colour of the setting in black academic robes with light blue trimming.

Prolonged cheering, after silence throughout the presentation, began as the Royal Couple stepped down from the dais into their open car to set out on the 10-mile Royal Progress through the city.

Led by a police motor cycle escort, two cars carrying police and officials and an escort of mounted police, the procession of gleaming cars moved away from Farm Cove 10 minutes ahead of schedule.

The uninhibited welcome continued along the 10-mile route as the Royal Car, with the Queen's Standard flying, moved at an average speed of about eight miles an hour under the decorated arches and down the alleys of a more vivid spectacle than the city had ever seen.

Even in the industrialised stretches and along the slumside streets of Dowling and Cleveland the reception of the Royal Couple was as intense, vital and exciting as anywhere on the route.

Martin Place was one of the most packed areas. Here, a crush of about 60,000 watched in silence while the Queen paused in her progress to place a wreath on the Cenotaph.

When the Progress finally reached Government House, the grounds of the century-old stone building, built in the style of the earlier Elizabethan era, glowed with rich colour and beauty.

The Queen and Duke were welcomed in the grounds by Sir John Northcott, who presented his daughter, Miss Elizabeth Northcott, youngest vice-regal hostess to the Royal Couple during their stay in Australia.

After the Queen walked inside, crowds at the garden gates began chanting "We want the Queen."

MAJESTIC ENTRANCE OF GOTHIC INTO SYDNEY HARBOUR

Proud To Be Head Of Such A Nation

SYDNEY, Wednesday.

The Queen said to-day she was indeed proud to be at the head of a nation that had achieved so much. Her Majesty was replying to the Address of Welcome by the Lord Mayor of Sydney, Ald. Hills.

The Queen said "I thank you and your aldermen most sincerely for the welcome you have given me and my husband on behalf of the citizens of Sydney.

"I would like to take this opportunity of telling you how delighted we both were by the spectacular greeting given us this morning by the yachtsmen in the harbour and by the citizens on the shore.

"I have always looked forward to my visit to this country, but now there is the added satisfaction for me that I am able to meet my Australian people as their Queen.

"So this morning, as the Gothic moved up the great expanse of this magnificent harbour, and I saw before me the city of Sydney, I was filled with a sense of pride and expectation.

"Only 166 years ago the first settlement was made not far from where we stand by Captain Phillip and his small band of Englishmen and now there stands a fine city that has become famous throughout the world.

"In the same short space of time we have seen the rise of Australia as a great nation, taking her full share in the counsels of the British Commonwealth and of the world.

"I am proud indeed to be at the head of a nation that has achieved so much.

"Standing at last on Australian soil, on the spot that is the birthplace of the nation, I want to tell you all how happy I am to be amongst you and how much I look forward to my journey through Australia."

At the end of her speech, the people on the stand gave three loud cheers.

Ald. Hills said "We, the Lord Mayor of Sydney and aldermen, on behalf of the citizens of Sydney, loyal and dutiful subjects, desire to offer to Your Majesty and His Royal Highness the Duke of Edinburgh, our most sincere and affectionate welcome.

"We are ever mindful of the visit to this city in the year 1927 of his late Majesty King George VI and the Queen Mother and of the great pleasure such a visit gave to our citizens.

"We humbly pray that Divine Providence may be pleased to safeguard Your Majesty and His Royal Highness in your journeys in these distant parts, and that you may be granted the blessing of good health at all times."

Government House Dinner

SYDNEY, Wednesday.

The Queen and the Duke dined at Government House to-night with a few selected guests.

They included the Governor-General, Field-Marshal Slim, and Lady Slim, the Prime Minister, Mr. Menzies, and Dame Pattie Menzies, the Governor of New South Wales, Lieutenant-General Northcott, and the Premier, Mr. Cahill, and Mrs. Cahill.

After dinner, the Royal couple and their guests watched the display of fireworks on the harbour from the balcony of Government House.

BLIND "SAW" THEIR QUEEN

SYDNEY, Wednesday.

Hundreds of blind people today assembled in Cook Park to "see" their Queen.

Accompanied by relatives and friends they sat close to the roadway listening to the broadcast of the Royal Progress.

A special loud speaker was erected by the Royal Blind Society on the Australian Museum so that the blind people could hear the broadcast.

Russian spy ring in Australia 78

The Petrov Affair, 1954

BY THE MID-1950S THE COLD WAR BETWEEN THE WEST AND THE USSR AND COMMUNIST COUNTRIES OF EASTERN EUROPE, AS WELL AS FEAR OF COMMUNISM AND COMMUNIST SPIES, WAS REACHING NEW HEIGHTS. IN AUSTRALIA, IT WAS BROUGHT HOME ON 3 APRIL 1954 WHEN RUSSIAN DIPLOMAT VLADIMIR PETROV (1907–1991), FROM THE RUSSIAN EMBASSY IN CANBERRA, DEFECTED.

Petrov made contact with the Australian authorities and offered to provide evidence of Soviet espionage in exchange for political asylum. He feared being returned to the USSR and being 'purged' by the political successors of Joseph Stalin.

When Prime Minister Robert Menzies announced that the Australian government would offer protection to Petrov, the Russian government withdrew their Australian diplomats and expelled the Australian embassy on 29 April 1954. Official diplomatic links with the Soviet Union were not restored until 1959.

Petrov's wife, Evdokia, was apparently unaware of his intention to defect and the Soviet embassy staff quickly 'escorted' her to the airport to return her to the USSR before the rest of the embassy were due to leave. As news broke that Mrs Petrov was being driven from Canberra to Sydney, a crowd of several thousand people gathered at the airport, determined to show their opposition to her return to the USSR.

Newspapers had a field day with the Petrov case. Mrs Petrov was photographed being escorted to a waiting plane at Sydney airport crying and screaming, 'Help me, save me!', while being bustled away by Soviet officials. The crowd broke through barriers and tried to get at the hated Soviet officials, but without success.

It seemed that Evdokia Petrov was bound for Russia, but the situation changed when the plane stopped to refuel at Darwin airport. She was granted a long-distance phone call with her husband and then, much to the annoyance of the Soviet officials escorting her, dramatically decided to stay in Australia.

The photographs of Mrs Petrov that were splashed across newspapers became iconic Australian images of communism and Australia's own spy scandal of the 1950s. Vladimir Petrov's evidence of a Soviet spy ring in the country never actually amounted to anything—though the Menzies government certainly made much of the threat of communist infiltrators in the run-up to the 1954 elections. The Petrovs were given political asylum, changed their names and lived in relative obscurity in suburban Melbourne. Evdokia died in 2002.

FORECASTS (for 24 hours from 6 a.m.): CITY: Fine. Very warm day. Fresh NE winds during afternoon. N.S.W.: Fine very warm day with freshening Northerlies first. Patchy rain, isolated thunderstorms developing far West where slightly cooler W/SW winds later.

The Sydney Morning Herald.

PRICE, 4d

SUN: To-day rises 6.17, sets 5.34. MOON: Rises 3.19 p.m., sets 2.25 a.m. TIDES (Fort Denison): High, 5.46 a.m. (4ft 4in), 6.23 p.m. (4ft); low, 12.10 p.m. (11in).

No. 36,290 ONE HUNDRED AND TWENTY-THIRD YEAR OF PUBLICATION 40 PAGES SYDNEY, WEDNESDAY, APRIL 14, 1954

RUSSIAN SPY RING IN AUSTRALIA

EMBASSY MAN IN CANBERRA CROSSES TO WEST

Mr. Menzies Promises Full Judicial Inquiry

CANBERRA, Tuesday.—Mr. V. M. Petrov, Third Secretary of the Russian Embassy to Canberra and agent of the Russian secret police (M.V.D.) in Australia, has forsaken his Russian allegiance and been granted political asylum in Australia, the Prime Minister, Mr. Menzies, told the House of Representatives to-night.

Mr. Menzies said a Royal Commission would be appointed to investigate the systematic espionage and at least attempted subversion in Australia which Mr. Petrov had revealed to the Australian authorities.

He said Mr. Petrov had handed to Australian security authorities documents naming Australian citizens as contacts or co-operators in this espionage.

The information in these documents and verbal information Mr. Petrov was willing to give had not yet been completely assessed, Mr. Menzies said, but preliminary examination had disclosed that there were matters affecting Australian security which called for a judicial investigation.

Mr. Menzies said that Mr. Petrov had asked for asylum because he was disillusioned with the Communism of the Soviet leaders, and impressed with what he had seen of the Australian way of life.

Mr. Menzies's announcement came when the House had resumed after dinner. At 8 p.m. he rose and asked leave to make a statement.

Members heard the statement in stunned silence, punctuated by the "hear-hears" of Government members. As Mr. Menzies sat down the House broke into loud applause.

The Leader of the Opposition, Dr. Evatt, said later that the Labour Party would support the fullest inquiry into the circumstances raised by Mr. Menzies. The matter would be free from all questions of party politics.

"I NO LONGER BELIEVE"—PETROV

Petrov "Salted Away": Security Screen

QUEEN OPENS PARLIAMENT

The Queen and the Duke of Edinburgh passing through the Independence Memorial Hall when her Majesty arrived to open the Ceylon Parliament in Colombo on Monday. The walls and ceilings are decorated with 42,000 yards of coloured cloth, gathered like rosettes.

Espionage Ring

(From Col. 4)

Show Crowd Hoots After Polo Pony Breaks Leg

Crowds in the grandstand at the Royal Show hooted Queensland polo players when one of the team's ponies—a mare—broke its foreleg during the Inter-Dominion polo contest last night.

LATE NEWS

U.S. ATOMIC SCIENTIST SUSPENDED

NEW YORK, April 13 (A.A.P.). — The U.S. Atomic Energy Commission has suspended Dr. J. Robert Oppenheimer, who directed the making of the first atomic bomb.

The commission will investigate charges that he was sympathetic to the Communist cause, hired Communists or former Communists for the A-bomb project, and opposed development of the hydrogen bomb.

OPPOSITION TO H-BOMB

DR. J. ROBERT OPPENHEIMER

To-day At The Show

"Herald" On Good Friday

COLUMN 8

YESTERDAY I received a phone call from Government House to say that those London telephone directories, to which I've referred on two occasions, were never at Government House and therefore there could be no question of their return.

On Other Pages

The Sydney Morning Herald*'s headlines of 14 April 1954 confidently asserted the existence of a Russian spy ring in Australia, which was proven false fifty years later when official documents were released to the public.*

Power and multiculturalism 79

The Snowy Mountains Hydro-Electric Scheme, 1950s

ALTHOUGH IT DID NOT PRODUCE DRAMATIC HEADLINES, THE OPENING OF THE FIRST ELECTRICITY GENERATORS OF THE SNOWY MOUNTAINS HYDRO-ELECTRIC SCHEME REPRESENTED A SMALL MOMENT FROM MANY YEARS OF WORK. AUSTRALIA'S BIGGEST ENGINEERING PROJECT, THE SCHEME BEGAN OFFICIALLY IN 1949, BUT WAS NOT COMPLETED UNTIL 1974.

With the 'populate or perish' slogan of the postwar years came the need for the construction of major infrastructure projects and economic growth to accommodate the expected boom in population. The Snowy Mountains Hydro-Electric Scheme with sixteen major dams, a series of power-generating and pumping stations, and 225 kilometres of tunnels, pipelines and aqueducts, was the largest engineering feat in Australian history. It also fitted neatly with Australia's plans for postwar economic development and massive immigration. More than 70 per cent of the Snowy scheme workers were newly arrived migrants from more than thirty countries.

Part of the experiment in opening up restrictions to Australian immigration during the 1950s was the hope that migrants would 'assimilate'. Indeed, in 1952 the minister for immigration, Harold Holt, spoke of building 'a truly British nation on this side of the world' by imposing Australian customs and culture on all who wished to settle here, wherever they were from.

But the imposition was hardly necessary, as many Europeans, especially refugees who were just happy to have a job, such as working on the Snowy Scheme, were relatively quick to adapt to 'Australian ways'.

The water-driven Guthega power station, featured on the front page of *The Canberra Times* on 2 May 1955, generated a relatively small 60 megawatts of electricity, but the scheme's seven power stations across the Snowy Mountains, produced a total of around 4000 megawatts by the 1970s. The scheme still provides nearly three-quarters of the renewable energy sources for eastern Australia and one-third nation-wide. The scheme also planned the diversion of water for irrigation of inland New South Wales and Victoria. The iconic Snowy River, home to legendary stockmen, had almost all of its natural flow diverted, the effects of which are still being felt and heatedly debated today.

LATE EDITION

FORECASTS (for 24 hours from 6 a.m.): CITY: Fine, warm day. Afternoon NE breeze. Cool to mild night. N.S.W.: Isolated showers far North Coast. Fine elsewhere. Mild to warm day, cool to mild night. Light variable winds, smooth seas.

The Sydney Morning Herald

Price 2d

SUN: To-day, rises 5.12, sets 6.10. MOON: Rises 2.21 a.m., sets 12.44 p.m. TIDES (Fort Denison): High, 5.05 a.m. (3ft 8in), 5.08 p.m. (4ft 10in). Low, 10.46 a.m. (1ft), 11.40 p.m. (2in).

No. 34,890 ONE HUNDRED AND NINETEENTH YEAR OF PUBLICATION 16 PAGES SYDNEY, TUESDAY, OCTOBER 18, 1949

SNOWY PROJECT STARTED

Fated Town Celebrates

From Our Special Reporter

ADAMINABY, Monday.—With bunting aloft and big crowds of visitors in the streets, the town of Adaminaby celebrated its coming death, with the birth to-day of the £200 million Snowy Mountains hydro-electric project.

In the Eucumbene River gorge nearby the Governor-General exploded a charge of gelignite on the site of the first of the seven dams to pile up water under the scheme.

The Prime Minister, Mr. Chifley, said at the ceremony that he hoped the scheme would touch the imagination and hearts and enter into the spirit of the people of Australia so that they would give of their best in whatever jobs they were doing.

The scheme would bring to New South Wales and Victoria great quantities of power and water, he said, and provide the opportunity for important research in Canberra into atomic energy.

MANY AWAY: "NO BOYCOTT"

"LIMITLESS POSSIBILITIES"

Committee Sees Fight

All Miners Told To Protest On Sharkey

The Northern Miners Board of Management, meeting at Newcastle yesterday, directed all miners' lodges to send protests to the Prime Minister, Mr. Chifley, against the gaoling of Laurence Louis Sharkey.

APPEAL UNLIKELY

JUDGE'S COMMENT

You May Now Apply For Petrol Licence

SNOWY RIVER PROJECT OPENED

The Governor-General, Mr. W. J. McKell, started operations officially yesterday on the Snowy River hydro-electric and water conservation scheme. TOP: Mr. McKell presses the plunger. LOWER: The explosion, which moved the first earth from the site of the dam.

Weird Aboriginal Art: Young Scientists' Find

Weird aboriginal carvings caused a scientific sensation when they were unveiled at an exhibition in David Jones' Art Gallery yesterday.

Not 'Regular Customer'

PROTEST CABLE

German Shipyards Undercut Britain

CROWN PRINCE

EXTENSION OF BLOCKADE

Move By Chinese Nationalists

HONG KONG, Oct. 17 (A.A.P.-Reuter).—Chinese Communists now occupy the entire Chinese coast north of Hong Kong.

The Nationalist Government last night extended its blockade of the Communist-held China coast to Canton.

Thousands of peasants from border villages are moving with their cattle, pigs, and hens into Hong Kong, to save their stock from hungry Nationalist soldiers.

TELEGRAPH LINES OUT

FRONTIER CLOSED

ARTILLERY DUEL

PRESSING QUESTION

SEAMAN SHOT

Pensioner Charged

REVOLVER SEIZED

LATE NEWS

ASYLUM FOR 2 RUSSIANS

TWO MEN HELD

Turf Doping Alleged

FIRST OF KIND

QUESTION OF FRAUD

Air Liner Sets New Record

COLUMN 8

On Other Pages

The start of the Snowy Mountains Scheme was modestly headlined on the front page of *The Sydney Morning Herald* on 18 October 1949. The scheme's projects continued to generate news into the 1970s.

Over the twenty-five years of construction of the Snowy Mountains Hydro-Electric Scheme, few headlines were generated, but milestones were recorded as stages of the project were completed. The Canberra Times of 2 May 1955 featured Guthega Power Station, where a third generator was soon to join two already in operation.

80 *Lithe teenager wins gold*

The Melbourne Olympics, 1956

IN THE MID-1950S, WHAT WAS MEANT TO BE ANOTHER DEFINING MOMENT IN HOW AUSTRALIA WAS SEEN ON THE INTERNATIONAL STAGE LOOKED LIKE IT MIGHT BE A DISASTER. THE PREPARATIONS FOR THE MELBOURNE OLYMPICS WERE FRAUGHT WITH PROBLEMS. THE CONSTRUCTION OF THE FACILITIES WAS BEHIND SCHEDULE, AND THE INTERNATIONAL OLYMPIC COMMITTEE SUGGESTED ROME—WHICH WAS TO HOST THE 1960 OLYMPICS—WAS ALREADY IN A BETTER POSITION TO HOST THE GAMES THAN MELBOURNE.

The games seemed doomed when several Middle-Eastern countries also planned a boycott due to the Suez Crisis; some European countries withdrew in protest over the Soviet Union's crushing of the 1956 Hungarian Revolution; and China withdrew because of the participation of Formosa (Taiwan).

Yet the games were a great success. With a huge last-minute construction effort the scene was set for some tension-filled encounters between rival Cold War nations, the highlight of which was the infamous 'blood in the water' water-polo match between Hungary and the Soviet Union. And for the first time, an Olympic Games was captured using the new technology of television.

Australia came third in the medal tally, behind the United States and the Soviet Union, winning thirteen gold medals, with Murray Rose taking three of them in the swimming events.

Australians also witnessed the amazing feats of an 18-year-old Sydney woman called Betty Cuthbert. Cuthbert was unknown before the games—she rated her chances of even representing Australia so poorly that she had bought tickets to attend as a spectator.

Yet she began to show some form just before the games, was selected for the team and went on to overshadow her world-record-holding team-mates Shirley Strickland and Marlene Mathews. Over nine days Cuthbert won three sprinting gold medals, becoming the first Australian track athlete, male or female, to win three gold medals at a single Olympic Games.

Australian newspapers proudly splashed her new nickname across their front pages: Betty Cuthbert became the Golden Girl.

FORECAST: *MAINLY FINE.*

ST. AGNES BRANDY — ASK ALSO FOR ANGOVES WINES

The Age.

POSTAL ADDRESS: 233 COLLINS STREET, C.1. PHONES: MU 9731 (Ten Lines). CLASSIFIED ADVERTISING: MF 0381 (30 Lines).

No. 31,691 — [Registered at G.P.O., Melbourne, for Transmission by Post as a Newspaper] — MELBOURNE, TUESDAY, NOVEMBER 27, 1956 — 20 PAGES — PRICE 4d.

SKIN & SCALP DISEASES
★ Eczema ★ Baby Eczema
★ Acne ★ Dandruff
★ Psoriasis ★ Falling Hair
★ Dermatitis ★ Alopecia
★ Seborrhoea ★ Varicose Ulcers
Successfully Treated for Over 50 Years.
KLEXEMA SKIN CLINIC
A.N.Z. BANK BUILDING,
156 Swanston St., Melb. MF1913.

CLIMAX TO DAY OF RECORDS

4 I. DANIELS (U.S.A.) — 5 G. LEONE (ITALY) — 1 B. CUTHBERT (AUST.) — 3 M. MATTHEWS (AUST.) — 6 H. ARMITAGE (BRIT.) — 2 C. STUBNICK (GER.)

Lithe Teenager Our First Gold Medallist

IN a scatter of cinders and sawdust, one world record and four Olympic records were shattered at the Main Stadium yesterday.

But the records were small things to Australian eyes, which saw only a tousle-haired teenager named Betty Cuthbert, 18 years of age, and — since 5.21 p.m. yesterday—the fastest woman in the world.

With a short and nervous dash down the brick-red straight, she won fame, the women's 100 metres title and Australia's first Gold Medal of the 1956 Games.

Miss Cuthbert was ...ed at 11.5 seconds, ...tenth of a second ...wer than her heat ...e on Saturday, but ...t enough to equal ...rjorie Jackson's pre...us Olympic record.

During the afternoon ...l Danielsen, a lithe ...rwegian with a pro...dous throw, hurled a ...elin more than six feet ...t the existing world ...ord and nearly 40 ft. ...t the Olympic record.

In the 800 metres ...nal the first four ...acegetters finished in ...etter than Olympic ...cord time. The fifth ...an equalled the exist...g record.

American clergyman ...v. Bob Richards flew ...r 14 ft. 11½ ins. in the ...le vault to break his ...n Olympic record.

Two more world records ...mbled at the Exhibi...n Building. Weight...ters Tommy Kono ...S.A.) and Arkadii ...roviev (U.S.S.R.) both ... new figures in their ...sses.

...ore Action ...n Arena

There was tremendous ...ce in yesterday's Main ...adium events, pace ...at was not limited to ... competitors alone.

There seemed to be ...re action, more closely ...nned schedules, a ...gher pitch of concen...ated action.

But the added speed ...ailed to short-circuit ...he current of excite...ent that has been ...resent every day since ...he Games began.

The tense minutes be...re, and the joyous ...inutes after, the ...omen's 100 metres final ...ere as emotional as any ...e Games have pro...ded.

Every Australian in the Stadium—and there were close to 100,000 of them—seemed to share the weight of responsibility that belonged to Betty Cuthbert and Marlene Mathews.

They sat down to lace their running spikes and countless pairs of worried eyes followed every movement of their hands.

Once Betty Cuthbert appeared to trip on the kerb of the track. Calamity colored the sighs of all who saw it.

Yard Ahead of the Field

In the event, it was just the crack of the starter's pistol, a thankfully brief period of tension and a blonde head a yard ahead of the field. We need not have worried at all.

The enormous crash of sound that ran through the Stadium might have been tempered with regret that Marlene Mathews had come only third.

But Miss Mathews was so quick to congratulate her faster team-mate that the crowd took its tone from her and shouted its pride and joy.

Miss Cuthbert was all smiles. She waved just once to a person hidden in the stands. It was her mother.

She walked back down the track to the start and the smiles were replaced by tears; lots of them.

It was altogether too much for a mere girl. She cried for a long time.

Fine Weather Again Today

Melbourne is expected to have fine weather again today with temperatures little higher than yesterday.

The bureau said last night that the fine spell should last at least until tomorrow, with a general improvement and steadily rising temperatures.

Conditions today are likely to be similar to those of yesterday with southerly winds gradually strengthening during the afternoon.

The maximum temperature in Melbourne yesterday was 66.8 deg., 4.5 below normal.

5000 Metres Heat Wins

There were two secondary Australian triumphs, Allan Lawrence and Albert Thomas, disregarded as possibilities in top-class international fields, bolted with their heats of the 5000 metres.

Lawrence turned the tables on the relentless Russian Vladimir Kuts, winner of Friday's 10,000 metre classic.

Once again Kuts raced to the front and tried to make his own pace too fast for the field that trailed him. And it was too fast for everybody but Lawrence.

Doggedly he hung on until Kuts tired, swept past in the second-last lap and won clearly.

As the first five placegetters in each heat qualified for the final, Lawrence's win should be recorded with a few reservations. But it looked promising for Wednesday's final.

Thomas, almost an unknown, was almost out of sight of his opponents as he hit the tape in his heat.

Yachtsmen Sail Impressively

Australia's yachtsmen sailed impressively when the Olympics took to the water on Port Phillip Bay yesterday.

West Australian Roley Tasker scored a decisive win in the International 12 square metre Sharpie class and all other Australians finished in sound positions.

And Australian oarsmen have won the right to compete in five of the seven rowing finals at Lake Wendouree today.

Tatt's No. 351 Draw. Page 7

AUSTRALIA'S FIRST GOLD MEDAL at the 1956 Games went to 18-year-old Sydney girl, Betty Cuthbert, the youngest competitor to win an Olympic final. Here she is shown breasting the tape in the women's 100 metres sprint. The big crowd gave her a terrific ovation.

Lower: Miss Cuthbert proudly displaying her prize after the presentation.

Film Premiere for Duke

ISLAND BEND, Monday. — The film The Battle of The River Plate will have its Australian premiere tonight in the Australian Alps on the banks of the Snowy River.

A command performance will be put on for the Duke of Edinburgh.

The film was a Royal command show for the Queen after the Duke left England and evidently she has reported most favorably, as tonight will be the first Royal command film performance in Australia.

The film stars Australian Peter Finch and it will be shown to the Duke, members of his staff, the Minister for National Development (Senator Spooner), the Snowy Mountains Commissioner (Sir William Hudson) and senior members of the authority.

It will be shown at the commissioner's cottage, where the Duke is spending the night on the snow line.

(Duke Sees Snowy Project—See Page 5).

Classified Ad. Index, Page 3

Main Events on Today's Programme

BASKETBALL (Exhibition Building): 8 a.m.; 1.30 p.m.; 8 p.m., semi-finals.
ATHLETICS (Main Stadium): 10 a.m.: Qualifying trials of hop, step and jump, discus, long jump (women). 2.30 p.m.: 80 m. hurdles, (women's) 1st round; hop, step & jump final. 3 p.m.: 200 m. semi-finals. 3.20 p.m.: 110 m. hurdles, 1st round. 3.25 p.m.: Discus final. 4 p.m.: Steeplechase 1st round. 4.05 p.m.: Long jump, women, final. 5 p.m.: 200 m. final. 5.20 p.m.: 80 m. hurdles, (women's) semi-finals.
FENCING (St. Kilda Town Hall): 2.30 p.m.: Foil, individual final.
YACHTING (Port Phillip Bay): Noon: Large classes. 12.30 p.m.: Intermediate classes; 1 p.m.: Olympic dinghy class.
BOXING (Stadium): 2 p.m., 7.30 p.m.: elimination matches.
HOCKEY (Olympic Park): 2.30 p.m.
MODERN PENTATHLON (Swimming Stadium): 3 p.m.: Swimming.
ROWING (Lake Wendouree): Finals, 2.30 p.m.
FOOTBALL (Olympic Park): 4.30 p.m.

Seats Available

Football, 4.30 p.m., 500 reserved; standing room 20,000 (at gates).
Basketball, 8 a.m., 2000 reserved; 1.30 p.m. 1000; 8 p.m. 500 tickets (at doors).
Boxing, 2 p.m. 3500 reserved, 1900 unreserved seats; 7.30 p.m. 2000 reserved, 1900 unreserved seats.
Hockey, 350 reserved seats, 20,000 standing room.
Rowing, finals, seats sold out, 12,000 standing room.
Modern Pentathlon, swimming 3 p.m., 5000 unreserved.
Fencing, 600 seats (at gate).
Athletics, 10 a.m., 6000 reserved, 22,000 standing.

New York Makes Plea for United Front

NEW YORK, November 26.—As each of New York's four morning newspapers today reported mounting anti-American feeling in Britain, the "New York Times" declared it was time a united front was presented to the enemies of freedom.

The paper in its leading editorial said: "It is time that we put away childish things — in Washington as well as in London and Paris."

These comments followed an outline of the U.S. vote with Russia and Hungary against Britain and France in the United States on Saturday on a resolution calling for the immediate withdrawal of foreign troops from Egypt.

The "Times" quoted its Paris correspondent as saying the vote was seen in Paris as "a sign of continued division within the Western alliance."

Bitter attacks on United States policy over Egypt were made on Sunday in Paris by two British members of Parliament.

Mr. Julian Amery said at a banquet given by French Conservatives in the National Assembly:—"Never has any country been treated as an ally as we have been."

Mr. Amery said never in history had a Government been so threatened as that of Sir Anthony Eden.

"I am talking of an Allied threat, the threat of the Sixth United States fleet in the Mediterranean, and the threat of United States economic sanctions against us."

The other member of Parliament (Mr. John Biggs-Davison, asked whether United States wanted a Communist Middle East.

(Other References, Page 4.)

Weightlifting

Paul Anderson, United States, won the Olympic heavyweight weight lifting gold medal at 3 a.m. today.

Blue Eyes Shone With Happiness

BETTY CUTHBERT'S blue eyes always sparkle. Yesterday they filled and shone as a pretty girl suddenly became radiant.

She walked slowly from the white-hot tension of the Olympic track with a gold medal clutched in her hand and a smile etched into her face.

Betty had just received her Olympic medal from a fellow Australian (Mr. Hugh Weir).

Mr. Weir, who is senior I.O.C. member for Australia, said it was his proudest moment in 30 years of sporting administration.

She was a little nervous and is not yet accustomed to fame—and acts it. Also she seems the sort of girl who will always be that way.

How did she feel? "Wonderful!" answered the 18-year-old girl with the world of sport at her feet.

Was she confident? She thought so—but she had been worried about her team-mate, Marlene Mathews.

She talked of her future. Everybody who watched her dash into the record books had already thought of the 1958 Empire Games and the 1960 Olympics.

Betty had too. "I hope I'll be good enough," she said and there was a murmur of laughter. Only Betty had doubts.

She is fairly confident about the 200 metres later this week. "On times I should have a reasonable chance."

Even that seemed reasonable from a girl who had just proved herself the fastest over half that distance.

Betty Cuthbert shows off the first of the three gold medals she would win at the Melbourne Olympics, and the first Australian gold medal of the games, in The Age *of 27 November 1956.*

81 *One of the great buildings*

Designs for the Sydney Opera House revealed, 1957

EUGENE GOOSSENS (1893–1962), DIRECTOR OF THE NEW SOUTH WALES CONSERVATORIUM OF MUSIC AND CONDUCTOR OF THE SYDNEY SYMPHONY ORCHESTRA, LOBBIED THE NEW SOUTH WALES GOVERNMENT FOR THE DEVELOPMENT OF A PERFORMING ARTS CENTRE. HE ALSO SUGGESTED THE SELECTION OF A PROMINENT HARBOUR FORESHORE SITE.

By the time a competition for the design of an opera house was launched in 1955, the site of Bennelong Point had been chosen. Once dominated by a sandstone harbour fortress and named after the famous Aboriginal leader and statesman Bennelong, for the previous fifty years it had been the home of Sydney's tram sheds. But by the mid-1950s, the tram system was beginning to be replaced by buses, cars and highways, and the sheds on Bennelong Point were to be demolished.

On 19 January 1957 the winning design, by Danish architect Jørn Utzon (1918–2008), was revealed. The design appeared quite radical in the context of a generally conservative 1950s Australia, especially compared with the second and third prize-winning entries.

Utzon's design caused sensational news headlines across the country, but also a surprising amount of public acceptance. Thankfully for Sydney today, the judging committee were convinced that Utzon's sketches presented 'a concept of an Opera House which is capable of becoming one of the great buildings of the world'.

Turning the concept into reality was a greater struggle than anyone anticipated, and after initially solving some complex engineering solutions, budgetary constraints and disagreements meant a significantly altered version of Utzon's building was finally constructed, ten years late and without its original architect on board. In 1965 the minister for public works in the newly elected Liberal state government, Davis Hughes, was a vocal critic of the arts and the Opera House project in particular. He stopped payments to Utzon, who could not pay his staff and was forced to resign in 1966. Utzon left the country and never saw the completed building.

Despite its huge cost, too much had been invested for Hughes to stop the Opera House and it went on, much changed without Utzon's involvement. When the Opera House was finally opened by Queen Elizabeth II in 1973, Utzon was not invited to the ceremony, and his name was not mentioned.

PRICE, 4d

The Sydney Morning Herald.

SUN: To-day, rises 5.14, sets 7.02. MOON: Rises 4.29 a.m., sets 6.19 p.m. TIDES (Fort Denison): High, 8.00 a.m. (5ft 4in), 8.25 p.m. (4ft 1in), Low, 1.35 a.m. (1ft 2in), 2.35 p.m. (10in).

TELEPHONE: B0944 ONE HUNDRED AND TWENTY-SIXTH YEAR OF PUBLICATION 30 PAGES SYDNEY, WEDNESDAY, JANUARY 30, 1957

TOP: An impression of the winning entry in the Opera House competition, won by Joern Utzon, of Denmark. RIGHT: The second prize winning entry, by a group of American architects. LOWER RIGHT: The third prize winning entry, by a firm of English architects.

SYDNEY OPERA HOUSE CONTEST WON BY DANISH DESIGNER

Joern Utzon, 38, of Hellebaek, Denmark, has won the £5,000 first prize in a world-wide contest for a design for a National Opera House to be built at Benelong Point.

His Opera House, estimated to cost £3,500,000, would have an unusual roof consisting of a series of shell vaults of cement covered on the outside with white tiles.

The judges, in their report issued yesterday, said: "Because of its very originality, it is clearly a contraversial design. We are, however, absolutely convinced of its merits."

Controversy has already begun. One architect said last night that the winning design was "a piece of poetry . . . magnificent."

Another architect said the design looked like "an insect with a shell on its back which has crawled out from under a log."

"CHEAPEST TO BUILD"

"National Rather Than Parochial"

MR. J. UTZON

"One Of The Great Buildings Of World"

Movable Walls Planned

● Continued in page 3

WINNER HOPES TO LIVE HERE

Mr. Joern Utzon, the Dane who won the Sydney Opera House competition, is overjoyed by his success.

He told "The Sydney Morning Herald" in a radio-telephone interview last night that he hopes to settle in Sydney before the construction of the Opera House begins.

Mr. Utzon, who spoke from his home in Hellebaek, Denmark, said:—

"So far the Opera House committee has not contacted me, but I am expecting a cable at any moment.

"It depends on what they can advise me how soon I migrate.

"But I shouldn't think I would have a great deal of trouble getting a good position in Australia now, do you?

"It must be a wonderful country with plenty of what we have not been getting lately—sunshine."

"My wife is just as thrilled about the win as I am.

"I have won 20 prizes for architectural design before, in Denmark and Sweden, including six first prizes. But this is far and away the most important.

How Long Did He Spend On The Design?

"I spent about six months, from May to December, 1956, whenever I could get time off from my other work.

"I studied hundreds of pictures, photographs, and maps of the site. It is a very lovely position for an Opera House and most inspiring to any architect.

"But from this distance it naturally took a great feat of the imagination to 'see' it in its setting."

LATE NEWS

Boy Drowns After 25ft Fall In Pool

A 6-year-old boy was drowned when he fell 25 feet into a deep rock pool at Wahroonga yesterday afternoon.

He was Martin Noel Ramsay, of Chalis Avenue, Turramurra.

Slid, Rolled Down Rocks

Two States Swelter

Victoria and South Australia are sweltering in heatwaves and have been warned that the danger of bushfires is acute.

The Chief Officer of the Country Fire Authority in Victoria, Mr. C. A. Daw, said last night: "The next 24 hours should be the most dangerous so far this summer."

QLD. STUDY OF PETROL PRICE ORDERED

BRISBANE, Tuesday.—State Cabinet to-day instructed the Prices Commissioner, Mr. A. T. Fullagher, to make a petrol price determination based on information supplied by six oil companies.

● Companies blamed for delay, page 4.

Rocket Range Talks Started

WASHINGTON, Jan. 29 (A.A.P.).—The British and U.S. Defence Ministers yesterday discussed a British plan for the United States to share the Woomera rocket range.

Official sources reported this last night after the first day of talks between the Ministers, Mr. Duncan Sandys (Britain) and Mr. Charles Wilson (U.S.).

According to Reuters, the British delegation has given British Commonwealth representatives in Washington an outline of the views being put to the United States.

Woomera Longer Than U.S. Range

British Rocket Cut "Unlikely"

Fire Ban Ends In Central West

COLUMN 8

WHILE attending a C.M.F. conference at Singleton at the week-end, an N.C.O. heard an address by an officer on unit transport.

What made it memorable for him were the words trafficable, motorable and footable, which came tripping from the officer's tongue.

* * *

BIG CHANGE. After Mr. and Mrs. George Robinson, Cremorne, collected the £30,000 cheque for their lottery win the other day Mrs. Robinson hustled her husband into a department store to buy 25/ worth of dress material.

For a joke they persuaded the assistant, an old friend, to clip the giant cheque to the docket and chute it up to the accounts office.

Presently a perturbed office girl arrived and said: "It's a Government cheque, so it's okay. But we haven't got enough change!"

* * *

AMONG the new registrations of racehorses is a 5-year-old gelding called Problem Heir—by an unidentified sire from Leonine Lass.

* * *

A WHILE back the police warned motorists that they must take pedestrian crossings seriously.

I'm afraid they'll have to issue the warning again.

Both in city and suburbs—but more particularly in the suburbs—a great many motorists are challenging pedestrians to wait until they have gone through.

It's a risky business because it makes pedestrians dithery, and once that happens, they are half-way to death.

* * *

MRS. P. D. F. MURRAY, Vaucluse, has been adopted by a possum which, for the last two years, has arrived regularly for supper.

On Other Pages

The first public glimpse of the proposed Sydney Opera House made headlines across the nation.

BIGGEST WEEK-DAY SALES IN N.S.W.

LAST RACE MELB.

THE INDEPENDENT PAPER

Daily Mirror

OPERA HOUSE SOUVENIR

WEATHER: Fine

Phone 2 0924 Sydney, Saturday, October 20, 1973 No 10,059 — 7c*

'IT'S ONE OF THE WONDERS OF THE WORLD'

as they watched the spectacular Opera House opening. Full story, more pictures of the Queen in Sydney -- INSIDE.

DAILY MIRROR SPECIAL SOUVENIR SUPPLEMENT 1

Sydney's Daily Mirror *of 20 October 1973 devoted the front page of its souvenir issue to the spectacle of the opening of Sydney Opera House.*

A small group of malcontents 82

The Bonegilla riots, 1961

IN THE FIFTEEN YEARS FOLLOWING THE SECOND WORLD WAR, MORE THAN ONE AND A QUARTER MILLION MIGRANTS ARRIVED IN AUSTRALIA. TO PROVIDE HOUSING FOR THEM, AS WELL AS THE LARGE NUMBERS OF PEOPLE WAITING FOR PUBLIC HOUSING, MANY COMMONWEALTH MILITARY FACILITIES FROM THE WAR YEARS WERE QUICKLY ADAPTED. THEY WERE NOW BOTH EXCESS TO MILITARY NEEDS, AND QUICKLY AND EASILY CONVERTIBLE INTO TEMPORARY ACCOMMODATION CENTRES.

The Bonegilla Migrant Reception and Training Centre, near Wodonga in Victoria, was the largest of these facilities in the migration settlement system. Between 1947 and 1971 it housed more than 300,000 migrants while they were waiting to find jobs before moving into their own accommodation and wider Australian society.

Large numbers of immigrants were entering the country, but the government's intake and settlement program was being formulated along the way, rather than planned at the beginning. The result was that, by the early 1950s, many migrants were waiting for permission to work and confined to Bonegilla for long periods.

In 1952 a large group of mostly Italian men protested about the lack of work, and the poor food and facilities, which the press quickly labelled a 'riot'. Their actions were roundly criticised in many newspapers by those who believed the migrants should be grateful for what they had. That the army was called out at the time of the riot embarrassed the federal government, when international media reports focused on the poor living conditions at the Bonegilla camp.

Migrant experiences and reports on the conditions of the camp vary—some thought it was an excellent entry point to Australia, while others were reminded of concentration camps.

In 1961 riots were again reported, largely because of the difficulty of immigrants finding work, but also because few improvements to the austere army base had been made since the 1950s. Although the decade was largely a prosperous one, in both 1952 and 1961 Australia was experiencing relatively short economic recessions, which meant that migrants entering the country were likely to be the last to obtain jobs in a tight market.

Still by 1961, there was more sympathy for non-British European migrants in the wider Australian community. Despite the odd riot or two they had generally proven to be excellent contributors to Australian work and society.

'FEW' CAUSED CAMP RIOTS

The Herald 3d.

MF0211 MELBOURNE, TUESDAY, JULY 18, 1961 24 PAGES

FINAL 474,772 daily sales

Downer: I'll act firmly with them

CANBERRA, Today. – The Minister for Immigration, Mr Downer, blamed "a small group of malcontents" today for yesterday's riot at Bonegilla migrant camp.

He said he would "act firmly" against them, but did not say how.

"These people must understand that such behavior will not be tolerated in this country," he said.

His "firm action" would be carried out "in fairness to the great majority of migrants who have proved themselves responsible and law-abiding members of our community."

Mr Downer said he had received detailed reports of the events yesterday and it was clear that a relatively small group from only two accommodation blocks at the centre was responsible.

Most migrants at Bonegilla realised that present economic conditions in Australia were transitory, and they appreciated that the Government was doing everything possible to help them.

Police keep guard

Calmed by police

FIRST PARTY

Queensland raises speed limits

BRISBANE, Today. — Speed limits in Queensland will be increased from next Monday.

ALL QUIET AT BONEGILLA: Crowds were orderly today outside the employment office and canteen building. Both buildings were stoned in yesterday's rioting.– Picturegram sent by The Herald transmitter at Bonegilla.

POLICE GUNS STOLEN

A safe containing two police automatic pistols was stolen during the night from the Glenroy police station.

SHIVERS IN THE CITY

TRY FOR £4000

RADAR CHECK

FEATURES

VAN WAITED

Legal move threat on park bowling

Legal steps would be taken to stop the building of a bowling alley on public land in Albert Park, Mr G. E. Reimann-Basch said today.

Mr Reimann-Basch, State secretary of the Council of Progress Associations, criticised the attempted secrecy and speed with which about 40 trees on the site had been destroyed.

He said a meeting of the council tomorrow would discuss plans to stop the Albert Park committee from "handing over" parts of the people's park.

"The committee is guilty of gross mismanagement of a public trust," he said.

"The committee seems to be determined on a course of action opposed to the public interest."

Mr Reimann-Basch said that his council had the support of at least 150,000 ratepayers.

An executive of Civil and Civic Contractors Pty. Ltd. said today that building of the £200,000 bowling alley would definitely begin this week.

Trip for Bunty

BUNTY TURNER

Cigarettes go: £2600 raids

Thieves stole cigarettes valued at more than £2600 from two

Clear by tomorrow

"It's a good bargain"

GINA KISSES YURI

ITALIAN FILM star Gina Lollobrigida salutes Soviet space hero Yuri Gagarin with a kiss. Gina met Yuri when he returned from England. She is in Moscow for the Film Festival. — Radiophoto.

Big phone exchange for city

VIRGIL HAS TO WAIT A DAY

Australian Associated Press

NEW YORK, Mon.—Air Force Captain Virgil Grissom will have to wait another day before being shot into space.

3 CIRCUITS

Help them keep warm

Smiling U.S. astronaut Virgil Grissom, in space suit, prepares for his big adventure. — Radiophoto.

Fu-Fu was in fridge

I want to be warm, warm, warm

So it's this FJ double box pleated skirt for me . . . . it's so, so warm and pretty too! from £8.14.6.

FLETCHER JONES

Personal fittings only

1 QUEEN STREET, MELBOURNE

New SIMCA ARONDES BELOW WHOLESALE PRICE

Commonwealth Motors 111-125 a'Beckett St. FJ5136

Take selective action against COUGHS & COLDS

There's a special Sigma treatment for your symptoms.

SIGMA LINCTUS

SIGMA RELAXANT COUGH MIXTURE

SIGMA LINCTUS. Soothing sedative linctus for relief of dry coughs — especially at night.

SIGMA RELAXANT—with added Vitamin C. Fast-acting treatment for tight "chesty" coughs.

ASK YOUR CHEMIST HE'S QUALIFIED TO ADVISE YOU.

MANUFACTURED BY SIGMA COMPANY LIMITED.

BUREAU FORECAST: City. – Cold tonight with frosts, fogs. Fine tomorrow. – P 19.

Other reports in The Herald's *issue of 18 July 1961, like this one, detailed the frustrations that even British migrants faced in finding work, suggesting that the riots in fact had little to do with the migrants' countries of origin.*

Page 2 — The Herald, Tues., July 18, 1961

The Bonegilla story

Many UK migrants jobless

Many British migrants in Melbourne hostels told a Herald reporter today they sympathised with the Bonegilla demonstrators.

At Brooklyn hostel 30 per cent of the men are unemployed, and a further 20 per cent have only casual jobs. Some migrants who have been here for more than 12 months say they are planning to return to England.

A Herald reporter spoke to some unemployed migrants and their wives today. All said they wanted to get back home as soon as possible.

"It's not that we don't like the country. We just can't get jobs," one Holmesglen migrant said.

"We are desperately unhappy and miserable. The happy picture that was painted to us in England has faded completely," he added.

DITCH-DIGGERS

At Holmesglen, more than two-thirds of the women are unemployed. They say many of their husbands are skilled workers who are digging ditches.

"Most of us feel sorry for those at Bonegilla, but rioting won't help them," a woman who has been here two years, said.

Dozens of cars, many under hire purchase, line the narrow streets in the Brooklyn camp.

Most of the migrants say the unemployment situation is dashing their hopes to return to England because they had to pay all their back tariff as soon as any money came in.

'I'll tell,' says A.L.P. chief

PERTH, Today. — The Federal secretary of the A.L.P., Mr F. E. Chamberlain, said today he would tell European countries which supplied Australia with migrants that there was a "developing unemployment crisis" here.

"They're bringing people into Australia under false pretences, breeding bitterness both here and overseas and doing incalculable damage to Australia's prestige," he said.

"We don't play down the value of migration, but it is stupidity to go on with it while having no regard at all to our national economy."

POLICE on guard as migrants begin to assemble to discuss events. — Picturegram sent by The Herald transmitter at Bonegilla.

Thousands know it as first home

Bonegilla, where migrants rioted yesterday, is the largest of five similar immigration centres in Australia.

The only other Victorian one is Benalla, where there are about 600 migrants.

The people who go to these centres are mostly Europeans who do not speak English.

From Bonegilla they go to jobs in Victoria, New South Wales and Tasmania.

Among nationalities at Bonegilla at present are Italians, Germans, Yugoslavs, Austrians, Greeks and some Maltese.

British migrants go to suburban and country hostels run by the Commonwealth Government.

CASH FOR ALL

An official of the Immigration Department said today that all migrants at Bonegilla received unemployment benefits, but money was deducted to pay for their accommodation and food.

After these deductions had been made the head of a family or a single man was given £1 a week as pocket money.

The migrants received three reasonable meals each day and were not expected to do any work at the camp apart from looking after their army-type huts.

During the day classes were held to teach the adults English, the use of Australian money and Australian social customs.

SHORT STAY

Until recently most migrants spent only about two weeks at Bonegilla before going to jobs that had been found for them.

But some of the migrants in yesterday's riot had been at Bonegilla for more than three months.

The Immigration official said no curfew of any kind was imposed at the camp, but as it was 10 miles to Albury, the movement of migrants to and from the camp was limited.

AMENITIES

Kindergartens, nurseries and play centres are provided for children.

There also are sports centres and a camp picture theatre for adults.

The camp is run and maintained by a staff of 650.

The Immigration official said that some migrants had found the Bonegilla Camp very much like a European holiday camp.

"We have had letters from several migrants with good jobs, asking if it would be possible to return to the camp for their annual holidays," he added.

An official of the Department of Labor and National Service said unemployment benefits paid to newly-arrived migrants were the same as those paid to Australians.

Deductions were made according to a person's age and marital state to cover food and accommodation at the camp.

"BAD FOR US"

The Premier, Mr Bolte, said today: "Trouble at Bonegilla migrant camp is a very bad advertisement for Australia.

"But it is a Federal matter entirely. I don't know the conditions or the situation at Bonegilla."

The Victorian secretary of the Democratic Labor Party, Mr Frank Dowling, said more money should be released to municipal and semi-government bodies so that their public works programs would help to relieve unemployment.

Because of the language difficulty and because many of them were unskilled workers, migrants today were bearing the brunt of unemployment.

There were also important effects on Australia's whole migration program.

"With the European Common Market developing more rapidly than expected, migration between European countries will soon become free and open and the source of Australian migration will dry up," Mr Dowling said.

Mr Dowling said there was a strong case for compassionate allowances for unemployed workers facing particular difficulties, and that included many migrants.

He added that all unemployed workers would benefit from the immediate creation of a moratorium to protect house-payments and personal debts.

CONTINUED FROM PAGE 1

POLICE GUARD AT CAMP

The Police Commissioner, Mr Porter, arrived at Bonegilla this afternoon to "have a personal look at the situation."

With him is the chief of the CIB, **Supt. Hugh Clugston.**

Accommodation is being prepared at the camp for the Melbourne police, who were expected to stay for several days.

Yesterday's riots disrupted the camp for six hours, caused more than £1000 damage and injured a policeman.

The riot leaders kept away today from the crowded square in front of the employment service building. They were mainly 18 and 19-year-old German and Italian youths who have been at Bonegilla since March.

They have not been able to get jobs.

Wives and children

Most of the 3500 migrants at present in Bonegilla are wives, children and men working in nearby districts.

About 1200 are workers without jobs, and more than 900 of these have been at Bonegilla less than three weeks.

This morning, unemployed migrants were handed their weekly spending money—up to £1 for single migrants, about 30/- for couples and up to £2/10/- for families.

All jobless migrants at the camp get free meals and accommodation.

More than 200 migrants grouped around the pay office door. A dozen policemen stood nearby.

When the door opened the migrants moved quietly inside and collected their money.

Camp leader confident

The director of the Bonegilla centre, Mr Henry Guinn, said today he doubted that there would be any more rioting.

"Yesterday's trouble was caused by a small group of less than 60 whom the others, who had been merely spectators, joined" he said.

"I think the leaders are repentant this morning and have no wish to repeat their foolishness."

Mr Guinn said it was possible that yesterday's riot had been organised by agitators from Melbourne at the week-end.

He said there was nothing to stop such people walking into Bonegilla and he suspected that some had been there on Sunday.

"Jobs not so scarce"

A Commonwealth employment official said jobs had been hard to find for the Bonegilla migrants in recent months, but the position had improved since the beginning of July.

In the first hour the office was opened this morning, it got 23 requests for labor—the biggest number in a morning for a long time.

"The demonstrators picked a bad time for their riot, because the Bonegilla employment position is improving," the official said.

HSV7 news cameramen were at Bonegilla yesterday. Their first films will be shown in the news service at 6.45 tonight.

CHAPLIN ON WORLD TOUR

PARIS, Mon. — Charlie Chaplin left Paris today by air for Tokyo with his wife Oona and his son Michael.

Mr Chaplin arrived yesterday from Geneva. He plans to make a world tour. He is 72. — AAP.

Melbourne's Herald *headlines of 18 July 1961 did not reflect the investigative reporting of the Bonegilla riot story that appeared later in the same issue (see opposite).*

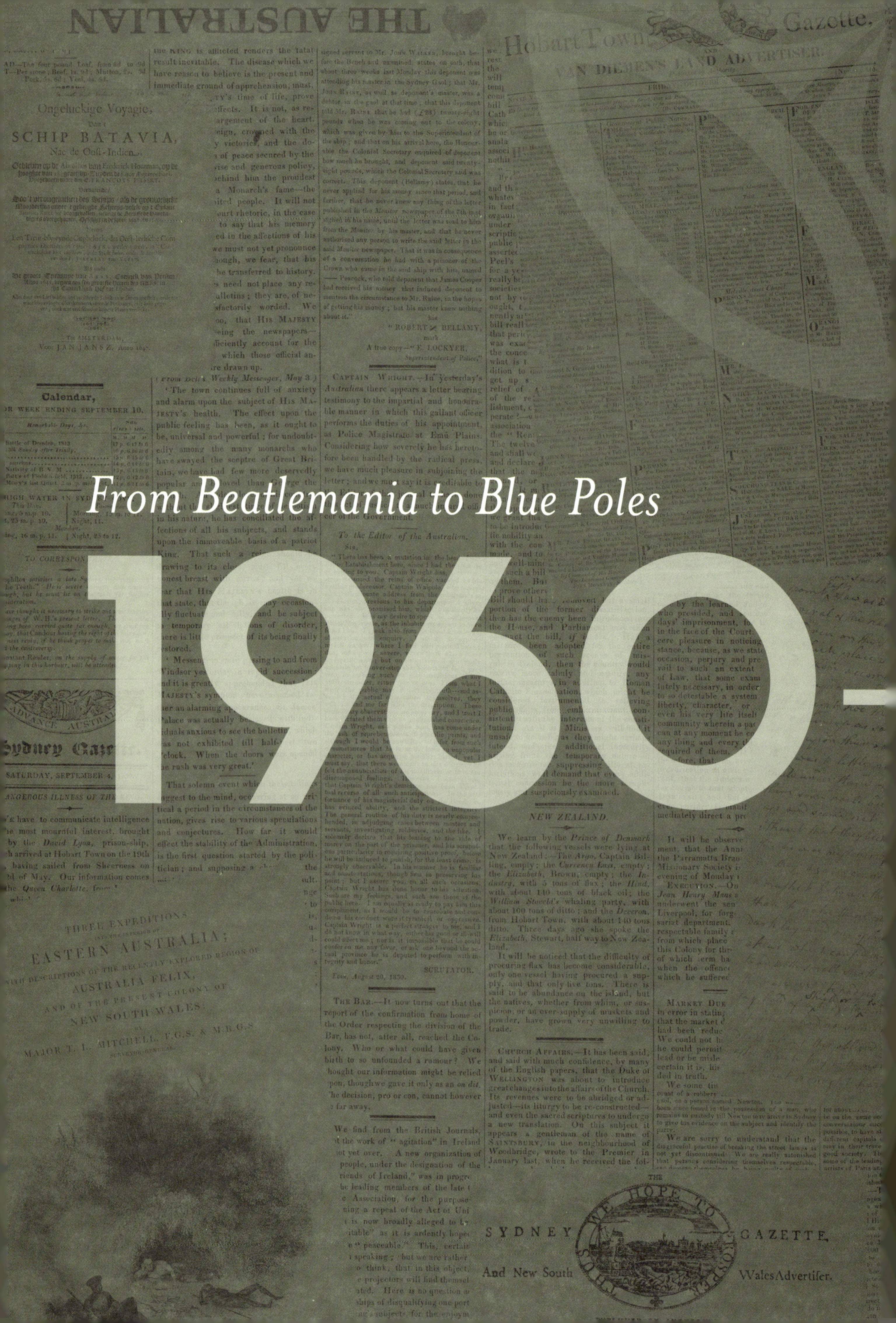

From Beatlemania to Blue Poles

1960–

-1973

Despite the fact that a conservative government remained in power during the 1960s, Australian society, like other Western societies, underwent a period of significant change during this decade. With increasing numbers of migrants, the cultural make-up of the country was being transformed. The era also saw the development of hippy culture. Finally, this was a critical period for women and Indigenous people, who made important gains in civil and political rights.

ONE INDICATION OF THE SOCIAL CHANGE SWEEPING THE NATION WAS REFLECTED IN WHAT BECAME NATIONAL HEADLINES IN JUNE 1964—THE ARRIVAL OF A BAND CALLED THE BEATLES. THE MASS HYSTERIA AMONG THE THOUSANDS OF TEENAGERS AND YOUNG PEOPLE WHO FLOCKED TO CATCH A GLIMPSE OF THE BAND DURING THEIR TOUR OF AUSTRALIA WAS QUITE A SHOCK TO OLDER GENERATIONS. ALTHOUGH YOUTH CULTURE ICONS AND BANDS HAD BEEN MOBBED BEFORE, THE AMOUNT OF ATTENTION FOCUSED ON THE BEATLES WAS UNPRECEDENTED. NEWSPAPERS HAD A FIELD DAY WITH SCENES OF YOUNG GIRLS SWOONING OR RIOTING OVER THE POPULAR BRITISH BAND.

The exuberance of a vibrant youth culture, however, was tempered by an increasing Australian involvement in the Vietnam War. Not long after the visit of the Beatles, Australians were informed by the Menzies Coalition government that all 20-year-old males were eligible for service in the armed forces and that conscription would be conducted by a lottery system. By 1965, increasing numbers of young men were fighting alongside US forces against the communists in Vietnam.

Opposition to the war in Vietnam heightened after the introduction of conscription and the division that erupted between supporters of the Vietnam War and protesters was to deeply affect Australians long after the war ended.

For many Australians, a notable feature of the 1960s decade was the introduction of new fashions, youth cultures and changing moral standards. This was highlighted by the media with the arrival of British model Jean Shrimpton at the Victorian Spring Racing Carnival, wearing a mini-dress reportedly 5 inches (about 13 centimetres) above her knees.

The political and social outlook of the nation was also being transformed. Although not a headline event, one of the signs of this change was the massive majority vote in the 1967 referendum to, among other things, include Indigenous people in the national census. Another sign of the times was the increasing protest against the apartheid regime in South Africa, which in Australia took the form of violent demonstrations and disruptions to touring South African rugby team matches.

Student political activists were among those who supported protests against Australia's own form of apartheid during the Freedom Rides of the mid-1960s. The segregation of Indigenous Australians from European Australians in cinemas, hotels and swimming pools in rural areas became the focus of a civil rights campaign that—particularly when it turned violent—received increasing media attention.

Still, the Freedom Rides did not achieve anything like the attention paid to the sudden and mysterious disappearance of Prime Minister Harold Holt in 1967. Holt had succeeded Sir Robert Menzies as Liberal leader, but after only two years in office, the keen swimmer was swept out to sea in rough surf, never to be seen again. Holt's disappearance was the subject of intense investigation and many subsequent theories about the circumstances of his death. It also marked the beginning of the end of the long period of conservative political party rule that was ultimately transformed with the election of the Labor Party under Gough Whitlam in 1972.

Although during the 1960s and early 1970s there had been a series of important social and political changes in Australian society, the transformation of artistic and other cultural activities was slower to follow suit. There was a rejuvenation of the Australian film industry, but a broader acceptance of modern art, for example, was not as forthcoming. The purchase by the Whitlam government of the Jackson Pollock painting *Blue Poles* in 1973 for 1.3 million dollars divided the nation. It was a huge sum for an artwork at the time. Indeed many did not regard Pollock's abstract impressionism as art at all, and the *Daily Mirror* famously headlined how 'drunks painted our $1m masterpiece!'

The 1970s might be regarded as the height of newspaper publication in the country. By this time, newspapers had finally settled into the front page formats that remain familiar to us today. Major daily newspapers were so important in communicating news events that many were published twice daily, capturing the huge market of commuters in capital cities in particular. Reading the news on the bus or train to work was a staple for many Australians. Yet the expansion of news presses could not continue and an era of consolidation soon followed. Combined with the increasingly competitive alternative medium of television, the face of Australian news was set to change once more.

83 *The big crush*

Riots when the Beatles arrive in Melbourne, 1964

WHEN THE ICONIC ENGLISH POP BAND THE BEATLES ARRIVED IN MELBOURNE IN JUNE 1964, AS PART OF THEIR AUSTRALIAN TOUR, NO-ONE HAD EXPECTED THE FRENZY THAT WOULD FOLLOW. POLICE WERE SWAMPED BY THOUSANDS OF FANS, MANY OF WHOM BRAWLED WITH EACH OTHER TO GET THE BEST VANTAGE POINTS, OR SIMPLY FAINTED.

After a mere 5000 fans had greeted the Beatles at the airport, another 20,000 people gathered around the Southern Cross Hotel where they were to stay. Police called on soldiers and sailors to help control the crowds, which even the Beatles described as 'the greatest reception they had received in any part of the world', if 'somewhat frightening'.

News headlines showed reporters were aghast at the scenes of rioting. People struggled to understand why young Australians reacted with what was described at the time, and medically treated, as 'hysteria'. The psychologist consulted by the Sydney *Daily Telegraph* after the 'great Beatle crush' in the streets of Melbourne suggested it was because the Beatles were 'a-sexual'—with their 'tight pants and long hair' they could apparently be either boys or girls' and thus they offered 'an attraction to both sexes'.

The Beatles' reception reflected a changing youth culture in broader Australian society that had been developing since the Second World War. The long period of economic prosperity through the 1950s meant that cars, movies, record players and rock and roll music had become accessible and desirable among such subcultures as the Bodgies and Widgies. Influenced by American style in fashion and film, such as the 'James Dean look', being able to buy cars and clothes became important to these 'rock and rollers' of the 1950s. By the 1960s, many young Australians began to turn away from modern society and were to be rebranded as counter culture, and the hippy movement began.

FORECAST: CITY: A Few Morning Showers. Fine Afternoon. Temp. 58.

Classified Index Page 13

The Age

POSTAL ADDRESS: 233 COLLINS STREET, C.1. TELEPHONES: 63 0241; CLASSIFIED ADVERTISING: 63 0301.

No. 34,040 MELBOURNE, MONDAY, JUNE 15, 1964 20 PAGES PRICE 4d.

LAWRENCE
DRY CLEANERS
Tailor Pressed—No Sleeve Creases
SAME DAY SERVICE—NO EXTRA COST

SKIN & SCALP DISEASES
treated by the successful Cu-Ex-Ma method at the modern skin clinic of the
NATIONAL SKIN INSTITUTE
165 COLLINS ST., MELB. (Next to Metro Theatre) 63 1272
Consultations Free—
Country Enquiries Invited
ECZEMA : BABY ECZEMA : ACNE : DERMATITIS : SEBORRHOEA : DANDRUFF : ALOPECIA : PSORIASIS : FALLING HAIR : VARICOSE ULCERS

50 TEENAGERS HURT IN WILD CITY CRUSH

Beatles' Welcoming Crowd Jams Streets

ABOUT fifty young people were taken to hospital yesterday after a near-chaotic welcome to the Beatles by 20,000 outside the Southern Cross Hotel.

Another 200 teenagers were treated on the spot, many of them in Red Cross stations set up in the hotel and in the Australian-American Club opposite.

The welcoming crowd jammed Exhibition Street from Bourke Street to Collins Street.

Between Bourke and Collins Streets, there was one solid, swaying, chanting mass of humanity.

...ch hysteria was never far away.

...ambulances ran a shuttle service to take casualties to the Royal Melbourne and St. Vincent's hospitals.

Hospitals reported the ...ed, none of whom were admitted, mainly suffering from faints, bruised ... and hysteria.

Police estimate 250,000 people welcomed the Beatles at the airport, along the route and in the city.

Barriers Down

As the crowd waited for the Beatles to appear on the hotel balcony overlooking Exhibition Street: ...ers to keep clear a section of the street in front of the hotel were swept away.

...s fainted but were carried along upright in the crush.

Police on horseback and on foot were sometimes powerless to halt the human tide.

...rous fights broke out but lasted only seconds.

A slightly built girl began hitting a man over the head with her stiletto shoe when he blocked her view.

Some fans climbed on top of cars; others scaled trees in the centre of the street. One fell 10 feet into the crowd when the branch of a tree snapped.

The Beatles, who had come from Melbourne Airport in a closed car, entered the hotel by a staff entrance in Little Collins Street.

Their welcome at the airport, by a crowd of 5000, was comparatively quiet.

Many of their young fans in Exhibition Street had been waiting for hours.

When the Beatles appeared eventually on the hotel balcony, cheering and chanting rose to a crescendo.

The Beatles joked and laughed with the crowd for several minutes. At one stage, they gave mock Nazi s a l u t e s because the scene must have reminded them—as it reminded many onlookers—of a Hitler youth rally.

When the Beatles went inside the hotel, the crowd soon dispersed.

All Right

Inspector L. M. Patterson, of Russell Street, who was in charge of police operations, said that despite the casualties "things went all right.

"It was hectic for everyone concerned from the airport into the city, but there were no bad incidents and no ill feeling either way," he said.

Inspector Patterson said more than 25 police cars and 300 policemen were used to supervise the crowds.

During the "big crush" the loungeroom floor of the Australian-American Club was like a battlefield strewn with bodies.

Crushing, foot and leg injuries and hysteria cases were laid out on blankets and carpets all over the floor and propped up in arm chairs lining the walls.

Steady Flow

They were brought in two entrances in a steady stream — s o m e on stretchers borne by police and ambulance-men, some supported by friends, others carried bodily.

Many were unconscious when brought in, while others sobbed in pain, or were hysterical with emotion.

Girls outnumbered boys by 10 to one in the casualty room.

First casualty was Marilyn Arthur, 14, of Nathalia, who screamed so hard at the earlier airport arrival of drummer Ringo Starr that she burst a blood vessel in her throat.

● Continued Page 3.
● Editorial, Page 2.

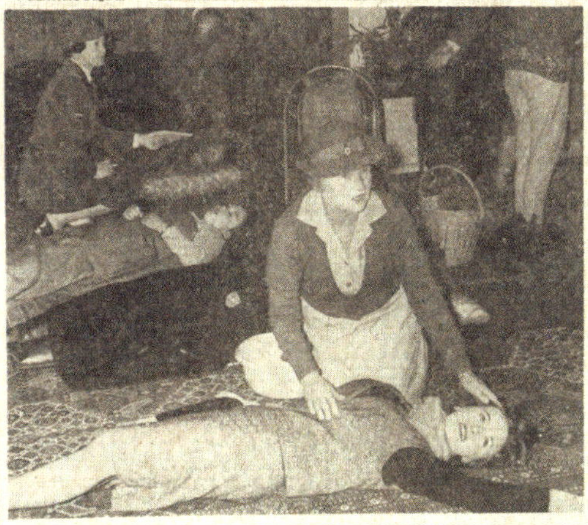

ABOVE: A mounted policeman carries an unconscious girl to a waiting ambulance while another officer helps an hysterical teenager from the pushing crowd waiting outside the Southern Cross Hotel yesterday for the Beatles.
LOWER: Several girls recover in the Australian - American club first-aid post.

Malaysian P.M. in Tokyo; Attempt to End Deadlock

From Australian Associated Press

TOKYO, June 14. — The Malaysian Prime Minister (Tunku Abdul Rahman) arrived in Tokyo by air tonight "in the hope of attending Summit talks with President Sukarno of Indonesia and President Macapagal of the Philippines."

Representatives of Indonesia and Malaysia were meeting late tonight for technical talks on the withdrawal of Indonesian guerillas from Malaysian Borneo.

Disagreement on the withdrawal issue has blocked agreement to a Summit although the leaders are now in Tokyo Indonesia, and President Macapagal, of the Philippines, preceded the Tunku to the Japanese capital.

The 10.30 p.m. (local time) technical meeting of border question specialists was to tackle differences between the two nations over the number and location of Thai checkpoints in the Sabah — Sarawak area of Malaysia.

The Philippines go-between Mr. Salvador Lopez, arranged the meeting—the first between the hostile countries in Tokyo —which originally was set for Monday.

"Any Time"

The change of plans was made after Mr. Lopez received a telephone call from the Indonesian Foreign Minister (Dr. Subandrio) saying the Indonesians were ready to talk "any time, including tonight."

Mr. Lopez immediately got in touch with the Malaysian Deputy Premier (Tun Abdul Razak), who suggested the 10.30 p.m. start. A couple of telephone calls later and the two parties gave the go-ahead signal.

"The sooner we get started the better," said Dr. Subandrio.

"I hope it will break the deadlock," Mr. Lopez said.

The deadlock was over whether four or five check points should be established by Thai observers in the Sarawak-Sabah area. Malaysia wanted five and Indonesia four.

At a stopover at Bangkok, the Tunku stressed that his condition for attending the Summit talks r e m a i n e d unchanged: the withdrawal of Indonesian troops would take place first simultaneously with a m i n i s t e r i a l meeting scheduled to precede the Summit.

"I cannot talk with a pistol pointed at my head," he said.

On arrival at Tokyo International Airport, he was met by Mr. Lopez, the Japanese Prime Minister (Mr. Hayato Ikeda), the Japanese Foreign Minister (Mr. Masayoshi Ohira) and the chief Cabinet secretary (Mr. Yasumi Kurogane).

● See Editorial, Page 2.

STOP PRESS

Miners Freed After Explosion

KABUL (Afghanistan), June 14.

Miners trapped after a coal mine explosion which killed 74 and injured six were all brought to safety yesterday. — A.A.P.-Reuters.

P.M. In Better Condition

CANBERRA. — The Prime Minister (Sir Robert Menzies) left his sick bed for several hours yesterday.

A medical bulletin says the P.M.'s health has continued to improve.

Sir Robert was ordered to bed on Friday with a recurrence of diverticulitis, an a b d o m i n a l disorder.

He was forced to postpone his departure for overseas and cancel a State visit to Israel.

It is believed that if the P.M.'s health continues to improve he may leave Australia late this week for talks with President Johnson in America.

Fine Afternoon for Football

Three League football matches will be a highlight of the Queen's Birthday holiday today. Fine weather is forecast after morning showers.

About 75,000 people are expected to go to the ... to watch traditional rivals Melbourne and Collingwood play.

In another important match, Geelong will be at home to Hawthorn.

Geelong half-forward John Sharrock has had to withdraw from the team because of a bruised thigh. John Brown, selected as 19th man, is likely to go into the side.

In the other game, North Melbourne plays South Melbourne at North.

Flemington

The second day of the V.R.C.'s holiday carnival will be held at Flemington, where the main events are the Marlborough Hurdle and the Royal Steeplechase.

In Brisbane, the Brisbane Cup will be run at Eagle Farm.

● See Sporting Pages.

Inside Today

NEWS:
Calwell on South Vietnam ... 3
...News ... 4
... Raises Two Ministers to Cabinet ... 5
...ship Bid in ... Election ... 6
... 16-20
FEATURES:
..., Crossword ... 12
...ials ... 2
... 5
... 11
The Churches ... 7
... 2
... 12
... of the Day ... 2
... Homes ... 10
...erty Sales ... 10, 11
...en's Page ... 8
SERVICES:
... 11
... 12
...er, Mails, Ships 11
Classified Advertisements Index, Page 13

Face Lift for Station

LONDON, June 14.

British Railways are renovating a disused railway station for a short visit by the Queen Mother next month.

Old Town, near Stratford-upon-Avon, has not been used for eight years and there are no plans to use it in the future.

During the Q u e e n Mother's visit to Stratford early in July, her Royal train will be stabled at Old Town.

The Queen Mother may spend one night in the train.—A.A.P.

U.K. Visit for Lord De L'Isle

CANBERRA. — The Governor-General (Viscount De L'Isle) and members of his family leave today for two m o n t h s leave in Britain.

"Drowned" Boy Lives

NINE - YEAR - OLD Trevor Hope of Dow Street, Port Melbourne was still alive last night after lying unconscious on the bed of the Yarra River for 10 minutes yesterday.

Trevor is in Prince Henry's Hospital in a critical condition.

Trevor fell into the water from a height of 30 feet after missing his footing on a pylon of Spencer Street bridge during a search for pigeons.

Bystanders who saw him fall called the police, who in turn contacted the Harbor Trust emergency service.

Within minutes, two of the trust's skin divers, Bill Mellis and Ted Howson, were speeding to Spencer Street.

They changed into their diving suits in the truck that drove them to the scene.

The big crowd standing around the bridge told the divers where the boy had fallen, and both Mr. Mellis and Mr. Howson jumped into the water at the spot.

Mr. Mellis said: "Within a minute of going down I found the boy on the bottom of the river. I got him to the surface as quickly as I could."

As soon as the boy was brought ashore two first-aid men applied mouth-to-mouth resuscitation and oxygen until an ambulance arrived.

Mr. MELLIS.

Firm Aust. Line on Vietnam Anti-Red Fight

SAIGON, June 14. — The Australian External Affairs Minister (Mr. Paul Hasluck) made a strong statement of Australian support for the anti-Communist struggle in South Vietnam as he left today after a brief visit.

"We know which side we are on and we are going to stick with that side," he told a press conference.

Mr. Hasluck left by a special Royal Australian Air Force Dakota for Vientiane.

Mr. Hasluck ruled out neutralisation for South-East Asia as proposed by President de Gaulle.

"I don't think you could get neutralisation in the p r e sent circumstances without yielding to the Communists," he said.

Outstanding

Mr. Hasluck said he found the Vietnamese Premier (Major-General Nguyen Khanh) "a leader of outstanding qualities."

He added, "In my talk with him and with other members of his Government, I made it clear that Australian support of Vietnam would be maintained. Australia believes that the struggle in Vietnam affects not only the future of the Vietnamese people but the people of Australia as well."

Sources said the firm stand taken by Mr. Hasluck today closely reflected his statements in a speech at a dinner given last night by the Vietnamese Foreign Minister (Dr. Phan Huy Quat).

Dr. Quat and other Foreign Ministry officials farewelled Mr Hasluck at the airport.

Mr. Hasluck had an honor guard of crack Vietnamese paratroops.

Mr. Hasluck told correspondents and a large number of American television representatives that victory in Vietnam "is something that's vital to our side."

Asked whether Australia would be willing to send combat troops to Vietnam if the situation continued to deteriorate, Mr. Hasluck replied. "I don't concede that it's going to deteriorate, so the premise is false."

Asked on Australia's attitude to General de Gaulle's proposals on neutralism Mr. Hasluck quickly replied: "We don't think it would work as this would involve yielding to the Communists."

(Continued on Page 4).

China Says Laos Now 'Critical'

PEKING, June 14.

China last night issued what observers in Peking saw as a near-ultimatum that she would take unilateral action over Laos if the 14-nation Geneva Conference was not reconvened in the near future.

It said events had reached "a critical juncture" and there was "a danger that the flames of war may spread to Indo China" if the U.S. was not prevented from "acting unscrupulously in defiance of the Geneva agreements."

A message from the Foreign Minister (Marshal Chen-Yi) to the British Foreign Secretary (Mr. R. A. Butler) and Soviet Foreign Minister (Mr. Andrei Gromyko) called on them to hold "emergency discussions" with other member nations to get the conference reconvened. Britain and Russia are co-chairmen of the Geneva conference.

BRASHS
FAMOUS NEW PIANOS
Select Your Piano from Melbourne's Largest Range of Quality Instruments.
NEW PIANOS:
August Forster
Gors & Kallmann
Thalberg
Wertheim
Rosler
Welmar
Gerbstadt
Belaire

Prices from
£198
or 25/ weekly.
Guaranteed reconditioned pianos from £145 or 12/6 week.
AT ALL 6 STORES
BRASHS
108 ELIZABETH ST., MELB. 63 6701
Chadstone, Frankston, Footscray, Dandenong, South Melbourne

Fletcher JONES
WORLD'S FINEST TROUSERS

Famous for Fit!
The perfect fit that only a range of 183 scientifically designed sizes can guarantee — that's why F.J. says:—"No man is hard to fit". Wonderful colours, styles, weaves and weights, priced from just £6.6.0.
FLETCHER JONES & STAFF
1 QUEEN STREET, MELBOURNE
Chadstone, Footscray, Frankston
Geelong, Ballarat, Morwell, Warrnambool, Hobart, Launceston, Adelaide, Sydney, Miranda Fair, Parramatta, Wollongong, Newcastle and Canberra

In scenes that were repeated at each stop in their tour of Australia, the Beatles were greeted by thousands of fans waiting outside their hotel, hoping for a glimpse of the band.

84 *Which Johnny goes to war?*

Conscription and the national service lottery, 1964

DURING THE 1950S AND EARLY 1960S THE COLD WAR AND THE PERCEIVED THREAT OF INCREASING COMMUNIST POLITICAL TAKEOVERS IN ASIAN COUNTRIES TO AUSTRALIA'S NORTH LED THE MENZIES COALITION GOVERNMENT TO INTRODUCE THE *NATIONAL SERVICE ACT* IN 1964.

The act required all 20-year-old males to register and be available to serve for two years in regular army units, followed by a further three years in the Army Reserve. As the number of men eligible for call-up far exceeded the number needed for military service, a twice-yearly ballot was drawn to select a number of dates of the year, and those whose birthdays fell on the dates were called up for national service.

As Sydney's *Daily Mirror* noted on 11 November 1964 when the act was introduced, the conscription system, or 'draft', was at first a 'great muddle', with confusion over who would be exempt from service and just how the ballot was intended to work.

By May 1965, the 1943 *Defence Act* was amended to allow for national servicemen—usually limited to serving only in Australian territories—to serve overseas. Many people began to fear the government was steadily progressing towards Australian participation alongside the United States in the growing conflict of the Vietnam War.

An increasing political resistance to Australian and United States involvement in the war between communist North Vietnam and democratic South Vietnam continued until the war ended in 1975 and was a significant element in the development of the 1960s counter culture.

Special lottery 1171, P. 23
Lottery 5440, P. 26.
TV news and opinion, P. 54
Finance, P. 56
Radio, P. 61

LAST RACE

Daily Mirror

THE INDEPENDENT PAPER

Registered at the G.P.O., Sydney, for transmission by post as a newspaper.

Printed and published by Mirror Newspapers Limited at the office of the company, Kippax and Holt Sts., Sydney.

Telephone: 2-0924 — Sydney, Wednesday, November 11, 1964 — No. 7284–Price 6d.

CLOUDY
Isolated showers.
• Weather Bureau details, page 61.

IS IT YOUR BOY?

Great muddle over call-up

From PETER SMARK

CANBERRA, Wednesday. — Confusion reigned in Canberra today over the compulsory call-up of 20-year-old youths announced by the Prime Minister, Sir Robert Menzies, last night.

Cabinet ministers are bewildered as to how the draft will work.

The only thing clear is that married men will be exempt and that university and technical college diploma students will be given automatic deferment of service obligation.

In some cases this could lead to total exemption.

That those who are to be conscripted will be chosen by a form of lottery seems certain.

But the question of who should be exempted from the ballot is completely unsettled.

Because of the age group selected, it is believed the Government will pay the conscripts the full military wage — £16/16/- a week plus free food and lodgings for unmarried men and £22/16/- a week for married men.

The decision to introduce conscription from the middle of next year, starting with the call-up of one 20-year-old man in every 20 for two years' service, was taken only in the past few days.

The complex administration of deciding how the scheme is to work, of balancing the needs of the economy and determining what is fair in relation to the needs of the scheme, is only in the early stages of discussion.

The conscription plan provides for:

- Registration of all youths in the year they turn 20.
- A call-up of 4200 youths in the second half of next year and a call-up of about 6900 youths in each succeeding year for three years.
- Protection of civilian jobs during the two-year draft period.

It was learned today from informed Government sources that Cabinet has decided that a wide range of exemptions should be allowed.

Those exempted are expected to include apprentices in protected industry and a range of other classifications.

But in specific terms there has been no clear decision on what is to be named a protected industry or what the other classifications for exemption will be.

Which Johnny goes to war?

Sir Robert Menzies last night gave a pledge that the civilian employment of conscripted youths will be protected.

But how this is to apply to apprentices not in industries classified as protected has not been decided.

The ministers now have to decide what is to be done at the end of a two-year service term for young men taken away from their civilian jobs in the middle of an apprenticeship course.

Obviously these young men cannot be expected to return to their old jobs to work at apprentices' wages until their training period is completed.

Some form of government subsidy to employers may be decided on, to enable the returning young men to be paid full tradesmen's wages—or close to this figure—while they finish their apprenticeships.

The Government is believed to be considering a proposal that exemptions should be made on compassionate grounds in some cases.

This, if agreed to, would particularly apply to young men who are the sole supporters of widowed or deserted mothers with large families.

The Government will be under the scrutiny of the whole of Australia as it establishes how the conscription system will work.

Any sign of political favor to any group in the community will bring a storm of protest down on the Government.

Government officials say the Country Party wants primary industry to be declared a protected industry with workers on the land immune from the draft.

But claims by all sections of industry for special protection are expected to flood the Cabinet room, and there is no certainty that this special status will be given to rural workers.

Out of this swamp of confusion and contradiction only one thing is sure — the unskilled city worker aged 20 will not be given exemption.

Decision on migrants: P2

With the introduction of the law establishing a ballot system for the draft in November 1964, the Daily Mirror *emphasised the family impact of the 'lottery of death', even before Australia had committed combat troops to Vietnam. The headlines also presaged the formation of a group of concerned mothers called Save Our Sons, who were to be involved in later protests against conscription for the Vietnam War.*

85 *Shocking Melbourne*

The Shrimp in a mini-skirt at the Spring Racing Carnival, 1965

ONE OF THE BAROMETERS OF THE SIGNIFICANT SOCIAL CHANGES IN AUSTRALIAN SOCIETY DURING THE 1960S WAS THE LENGTH OF WOMEN'S DRESSES. ALONG WITH DENIM JEANS AND LONG HAIR FOR MEN, MINI-SKIRTS AND MINI-DRESSES BECAME A MEDIA ATTRACTION AFTER THE VISIT OF AN ENGLISH MODEL TO THE MELBOURNE SPRING RACING CARNIVAL.

The carnival—focused on the Melbourne Cup—had long been an event for parading new fashions. But in 1965 Melbourne society was not quite prepared for the mini-dress worn by 22-year-old Jean Shrimpton to Derby Day at Flemington racecourse. Known as The Shrimp, and described as the first super-model, Jean Shrimpton was a guest of the Victorian Racing Club, and her dress was said to be a shocking 5 inches (13 centimetres) above her knees.

The furore that erupted over Shrimpton's short dress—as well as her lack of hat, stockings and gloves—was a reflection of what was soon to be called the generation gap. To the anguish of many parents, young women were already wearing mini-skirts—but for Shrimpton to wear one to the Melbourne races was regarded by many as outrageous.

Short dresses and mini-skirts made good news headlines and great photographic images. Photojournalists had a field day capturing The Shrimp in her mini-dress at Derby Day. One typical comment— showing ignorance of the fact that London had become the 1960s fashion capital—came from a former Lady Mayoress of Melbourne, who suggested that if Jean Shrimpton wanted to wear skirts 'four inches above the knee in London, that's her business, but it's not done here.'

Jean ruefully observed that Melbourne 'wasn't ready' for her just yet and that it seemed 'years behind London'.

Weather:

BUREAU SAYS: CITY: Cool. A shower or two.

- Expected top temperature: 60 deg.
- Weather details are on Page 19.

617,863 AVERAGE DAILY SALE

The Sun NEWS-PICTORIAL

44 FLINDERS ST. Registered in Australia for transmission by post as a newspaper. PHONE 63-0211

4d. By Air 6d.

13,444 Melbourne, Monday, November 1, 1965 48 Pages

VALUATE'S CUP RUN CHANCES SLIM

By JACK McPHERSON

LAST night there appeared little chance of Valuate getting a run in the £30,750 Melbourne Cup tomorrow.

Valuate, second favorite and backed to win £200,000, was left out of the field when named only third emergency on Saturday night.

He was placed among the four emergencies when the Victoria Racing Club committee determined the 26 runners at a 70-minute meeting.

All 26 were listed as certain starters last night.

Three scratchings would be needed to get Valuate a run.

REGRETS

Valuate's lessee-trainer, **Mr V. P. "Mo" Bernard**, said last night that he was disappointed that Valuate was not in the field, but had not given up hope.

The chairman of the VRC, **Mr Ross Grey Smith**, said last night that he did not think the committee would require a veterinary certificate to justify any scratching from the Cup before 9.30 a.m. tomorrow, when permission of the stewards would be necessary.

I believe that the VRC committee did the right thing in sticking to their balloting rules, although it is bad luck for the backers of Valuate.

But possibly the committee should have given the public an advance warning of what it proposed to do.

A special Melbourne Cup forecast says that tomorrow's weather will be mainly fine, but cool.

- **The Cup field, market, barriers — Back Page.**
- **Cup day early guide — Page 44.**

The Shrimp ➧ shocked them

By BARRIE WATTS

THERE she was, the world's highest-paid model, snubbing the iron-clad conventions of fashionable Flemington in a dress five inches above the knee, NO hat, NO gloves and NO stockings!

The shockwaves were still rumbling round fashionable Melbourne last night when Jean Shrimpton—The Shrimp — swore she hadn't realised she was setting off such an outraged upheaval at Flemington on Saturday.

"I don't see what was wrong with the way I looked," she said. "I wouldn't have dressed differently for any race meeting anywhere else in the world."

For my money, she looked tremendous — but Flemington was not amused. Fashion-conscious Derby Day racegoers were horrified.

"Insulting . . .," "a disgrace . . .," "How dare she . . .!" If the skies had rained acid not a well-dressed woman there would have given The Shrimp an umbrella.

For hours, Flemington had waited and sweltered in 94-deg. heat, waiting for the late arrival **of the English girl billed as the most beautiful on earth.**

She walked in serene and poised, dressed in this ultra-short shift she designed herself, showing a lovely amount of lissom leg totally unhindered by nylon. Her long hair swung about in the hot wind.

Strolling behind her came her friend, English actor **Terence Stamp** — in a navy-blue suit.

Fashionably - dressed ladies who had been dying to see what heavenly outfit Jean would be wearing seemed very angry.

It was hardly the sort of costume they must have expected — especially as the VRC flew Jean out here from America to present Fashions on the Field prizes.

Last night, 22-year-old Jean said she hadn't known that Melbourne placed such heavy emphasis on conformity.

"I haven't decided what to wear to the Melbourne Cup," she said. "I suppose I'll have to give it a lot more thought . . ."

- **Reds control big Java area: Page 2**
- **Dawn raids for "Mafia": Page 3**

Melbourne's Sun News-Pictorial *of 1 November 1965 shows English model Jean Shrimpton, hatless and gloveless, wearing the mini-dress that shocked Melbourne—and in the background the stunned faces of Melbourne matrons looking on in disapproval.*

86 Vote Yes for Aborigines

A referendum to change the Constitution, 1967

CONSIDERING THE 1967 REFERENDUM ON THE TREATMENT OF INDIGENOUS PEOPLE IN THE AUSTRALIAN CONSTITUTION HAS BEEN REGARDED AS A HUGE MILESTONE IN ABORIGINAL RIGHTS IN AUSTRALIA, THE EVENT ATTRACTED COMPARATIVELY LITTLE MEDIA ATTENTION AT THE TIME.

Newspaper reports of the referendum devoted much more space to the other referendum question—whether the numbers of members of the parliamentary House of Representatives 'may be increased without necessarily increasing the number of Senators'. This question was an attempt to 'balance' the numbers in the two houses of Parliament and was not passed.

However, the question of altering the Constitution to include Aboriginal people in federal rather than state government legislation, and to include them in the federal census, was passed with a historic majority of nearly 90 per cent.

The referendum was a culmination of several years of political agitation by Aboriginal people and their supporters. Particularly important was the media attention given to the 1965 Freedom Rides, a series of bus tours that highlighted discrimination against Australian Indigenous people—especially in rural and regional areas that still had policies of segregation between Aboriginal and non-Aboriginal people.

The referendum may not have made headline news, and it was several years before any effects of the change were really felt, but it allowed the introduction of important legislative changes over discriminatory practices, financial assistance, the preservation of cultural heritage and recognition of land rights for Indigenous Australians. Although often conflated with the granting of citizenship and voting rights (which had been granted at various times between 1948 and 1962), the referendum quickly acquired a wider symbolic meaning for Aboriginal people.

OPPOSITE
The Australian of 29 May 1967 recorded the defeat of the referendum question on the number of members of the House of Representatives and the overwhelming vote in favour of changing the Constitution so the federal government could legislate on behalf of Aboriginal people and count them in the national census.

THE AUSTRALIAN

NUMBER 906 — MONDAY MAY 29 1967 — PRICE FIVE CENTS
Registered in Australia for transmission by post as a newspaper

NSW ONLY STATE TO SAY YES ON SENATE REFERENDUM

Holt: "A victory for prejudice"

But 89.34 per cent vote for Aboriginals

By ALAN RAMSEY

Bitterly disappointed at the No vote in the referendum on the nexus, the Prime Minister, Mr Holt, commented last night: "I said prior to the poll that a majority for No would be a victory for prejudice and misrepresentation against calm reasoning and good sense. I still hold that view."

Mr Holt, who was speaking at Sydney Airport before he left on an overseas tour, said: "There is no doubt in my mind that there must be a redistribution in the life of this Parliament."

He did not wish to go into another general election without a "more equitable distribution of representation."

In Saturday's referendum, a majority of more than a million voters rejected the proposal to break the nexus, but voters overwhelmingly supported two constitutional amendments that will allow Aboriginals to be counted in a census and give the Federal Government wide powers to legislate for Aboriginals.

When counting closed yesterday, the vote on the Aboriginal question was 4,738,701 in favor to 478,931 against. The national Yes vote percentage was 89.34.

Only New South Wales supported the referendum proposal to break the numerical link which ties together the sizes of the two Houses of the national Parliament. It did so by a majority of 42,000.

In the other five States the No vote percentage ranged from 55.28 in Queensland to a massive 75.66 per cent in Tasmania — three to one against. In Victoria, home State of Mr Holt, the No vote swamped the Yes vote by more than half a million.

Mr Whitlam, speaking before leaving on a tour of the Northern Territory, said the No campaign of "no more politicians" had superficially been extremely effective.

But in fact it would not mean fewer politicians but more, but the electorate generally had not listened to this argument.

SEATS IN DANGER

Mr Holt said in a statement yesterday: "The majority of electors chose to ignore the advice of those to whom they normally look for guidance on political issues."

The defeat of the nexus proposal leaves him with a pressing political problem to solve on his return home.

He must decide whether to go ahead with some twin increase in the two Houses of Parliament, or carry out a long-overdue redistribution of electoral boundaries on the present size of the 124-member House of Representatives.

If he adopts the latter course, it will almost certainly mean that a number of Liberal-held seats in densely - populated Sydney will be lost to the Government.

There has not been a redistribution for 12 years. In 1961, Sir Robert Menzies was forced to abandon redistribution plans when his coalition partner, the Country Party, refused to support his redrawing of boundaries.

Had the nexus proposal succeeded, this would have allowed Mr Holt to increase the Lower House by 11 to 13 members, and solved his redistribution headache.

But the only equitable number by which Parliament can be increased under the nexus formula is 72 — 24 more senators and another 48 members of the House of Representatives.

In his statement, Mr Holt gave a broad hint that such a radical increase — in fact, any increase — would not take place until 1969.

"This view (that a No vote meant no more politicians), however ill-advised we might regard it to be, nevertheless must be accepted as representing a strong persuasive force, at least during the life of the present Parliament.

"I shall be consulting with my colleagues after my return from overseas as to the course that should be followed."

Of the success of the second referendum proposal, Mr Holt said: "I am delighted with the overwhelming vote in every State favoring the elimination of those references in the Constitution which smack of discrimination."

CONTINUED ON PAGE 2

TAA clerks plan protest strikes

AA clerks are plan- strikes in major Aus- an cities this week to est against the down- ding of top women members.

e Federated Clerks n claims TAA is try- to offset general pay eases won by the n earlier this year.

e union sees the -gradings as an at- by TAA to get nd the terms of an ement which fol- several months of trial unrest among ls employed by the r domestic airlines. e clerks held a series toppages in Sydney, ourne, Adelaide, ane, Hobart, Perth Canberra before clerks won in- es from $170 to $275 ar.

e new rates—recom- ded by industrial missioner, Mr J. H. s—were accepted by union at the end of h.

subsequent confer- TAA and Ansett- agreed to an exten- of the grading sys- for women clerks, an additional scale ding male margins ine occupations. omen employees certain classifica- were to be given in- es, while others were e reclassified under ew scale.

NEW RATES

e new rates for en were paid to oyees of Ansett-ANA the first time last

t last Monday TAA duced an adjust- to senior female ifications — down- ing all top grade , with the excep- of a few employed e head office in Mel- ne.

ey will drop about a year under the agreement. Among down-graded was secretary to the nsland manager of , Mr R. G. Cochrane. ployees were notifi- the adjustment the before TAA was to Brisbane officials of Clerks Union to dis- general problems reclassifications for en in the new award. e union claimed the tment prevented the otion of lower-grade s whose position ld normally have reviewed under the scale.

ATE NEWS

CAMPAIGN FOR HELP SEEMS CERTAIN

By JOHN STUBBS

Strong pressure for Commonwealth help for Aboriginals is certain to follow the sweeping Yes vote on the Aboriginal issue in Saturday's referendum.

The success on this question will mean that two discriminating references to Aboriginals will be removed from the Constitution.

As a side-effect it will also give the Commonwealth power to make special laws for Aboriginals in all States.

Senior officials of the Social Services, Education and Health departments have confirmed that there were no plans for the Federal Government to take advantage of its new powers.

But commentators said yesterday that the referendum vote gave the Government an overwhelming mandate to play a much greater role in Aboriginal affairs in the States.

Some went as far as suggesting the creation of a new department, similar to the Repatriation Department, to help in Aboriginal housing, health, education, employment and other problems, in association with State government departments.

The Yes vote on the Aboriginal question averaged 89.34 per cent.

The percentage was highest — 93.51 — in Victoria, and lowest—78.71 —in Western Australia.

'OVERWHELMING'

There were strong indications of discrimination and racial bias in the votes in some areas of NSW, Western Australia, South Australia and Queensland — particularly in areas with a proportionately high Aboriginal population.

The highest No vote percentage was registered in the Kalgoorlie electorate, of Western Australia, which takes in most of the inland areas of that State including the north-west.

In that electorate there were 7434 No votes and 17,468 Yes votes.

Mr G. M. Bryant, a Victorian Labor MHR who has been one of Parliament's most active supporters of the Aboriginals' cause, said yesterday he would move in Parliament for a select committee to investigate and recommend the most effective help the Commonwealth could give to Aboriginals.

He said: "The vote is an overwhelming endorsement of the view that it is time for national action.

"The Government cannot hide behind constitutional inhibitions, nor can it hide behind a faith in public apathy. This vote represents a great national demand for action.

Mr Bryant said few States had anything that could be described as a comprehensive programme to help Aboriginals.

A SHAGGY DOG gets a pat on the head from the Prime Minister, Mr Holt, as he leaves Sydney Airport last night for his four-week tour of America and Europe. Mr Holt made a brief statement before he left saying that his trip was one of the most important undertaken by a Prime Minister of Australia.

Holt leaves for talks 'to decide our future'

The Prime Minister, Mr Holt, last night described his four-week overseas visit as among the most significant of any Australian Prime Minister.

While in America, Canada and Britain he would discuss a wide range of subjects important to Australia.

Mr Holt was making a brief statement at Sydney Airport before boarding a BOAC airliner for Los Angeles.

From Los Angeles he will travel to New York and Washington before flying to Canada, where he will visit Expo '67.

FUTURE ROLE

Before going to London for talks with the British Prime Minister, Mr Wilson, he will meet President Johnson and the Canadian Prime Minister, Mr Pearson.

On his return journey will spend a weekend at the LBJ Ranch in Texas.

Mr Holt said last night that in his talks with President Johnson, Vietnam would loom large while his talks with Mr Wilson would centre on Britain's military presence east of Suez and its projected entry into the Common Market.

With Mr Pearson he would discuss the future role of Australia and Canada as senior members of the Commonwealth.

Both countries could influence the course of events, Mr Holt said.

He looked forward to being at Expo 67 on the day — June 6 — set aside to celebrate Australia's presense at the exhibition.

While in London he would discuss the global role in which Britain saw herself in the years ahead.

His talks in all countries would be important in trade and economic fields.

He had several important speaking engagements in the U.S.

"I hope to convey Australian views which will have great impact on the policies these countries are pursuing," Mr Holt said.

ROYAL LUNCH

In Britain, he would talk to the Chancellor of the Exchequer, and the ministers for Defence, Commonwealth Relations and Trade.

While in Britain he will have lunch with the Queen at Buckingham Palace.

He will be accompanied throughout the tour by Mrs Holt and a team of senior government officials, and will be joined by the Defence Minister, Mr Fairhall, in London.

The Prime Minister and Mrs Holt will return to Australia on June 22.

GIPSY DELAYED

PLYMOUTH, SUNDAY

A sudden wind drop has delayed Sir Francis Chichester's arrival in Plymouth.

His ketch, Gipsy Moth IV, was expected to enter Plymouth Sound at 9 o'clock tonight, Australian eastern time, to end his lone voyage around the world.

But the wind dropped and, with only 150 miles to go, Sir Francis radioed this message to the reception committee: "I am very sorry that I will not be in Plymouth by my Sunday deadline. I would need a 20-knot breeze to be on time."

Over the ship-to-ship telephone, he told the captain of one of the navy vessels escorting Gipsy Moth: "I am a little worried about my slow speed. But I am more concerned about all the people who are waiting to see my arrival."

Kenneth Clarke, of the London Sunday Telegraph, who is in a convoy of welcoming Press and television boats, reports: Gipsy Moth looks spick and span enough, despite some streaks of rust along the hull.

My first sight of Gipsy Moth drove home the full significance of one man's endeavor.

Two days at sea and my first introduction to the utter, bleak despair of bad seasickness make Sir Francis's single-handed voyage round the world in a 53ft boat made of plywood seem a superhuman task.

United Press International

Man gaoled over drugs

A 22-year-old man was sentenced to 12 months' gaol on charges of drug-taking, in Central Court, Sydney, yesterday.

The man, Peter Maurice Hardage, a laborer, of Darlinghurst, pleaded guilty before Mr J. C. Teece SM, to two charges of administering drugs to himself and one charge of having Indian hemp in his possession.

NASSER ASKS UN FOR URGENT MEETING

NEW YORK, SUNDAY

World interest in the Middle East crisis has swung back to the United Nations where the security Council will meet soon after an Egyptian request for an urgent meeting.

The 10-non-permanent council members have already met to discuss when the council should meet.

The UAR Ambassador, Mr Mohammed Awad el Kony, submitted his request to the Security Council chairman, Mr Liu Chieh, of Taiwan, fours hours after the UN Secretary - General, U Thant, had submitted his report on his Cairo visit.

TENSION EASES

The Egyptian request and U Thant's report have slightly eased the tension.

But against this, the Cairo newspaper, Al Ahram, regarded as the voice of President Nasser, said that the UAR had ordered the expulsion of 600 Canadian UN troops from El Arish and Rafah.

A dangerous incident, the type which U Thant had warned against as possibly leading to war, was reported yesterday by Israel.

It said an Israeli truck had been blown up on the southern Gaza strip border by an Egyptian mine.

UN officials said it might be possible to convene a Security Council today or tomorrow, but members might prefer longer time to study U Thant's report. The UAR did not specify an immediate meeting.

UN officials said today that Israel might also urge a meeting so that the Israeli case could also be inscribed on the council agenda.

United Press International

U THANT SEEKS BREATHING SPELL — PAGE 4.

CIVIL WAR FEARED IN NIGERIA BREAK-UP CRISIS

LAGOS, SUNDAY

Nigeria's central government declared a state of emergency last night after the radio station in the rebellious eastern region announced the area had declared itself independent.

The move raised fears of civil war.

An early radio broadcast from Enugu, the eastern region capital 250 miles east of Lagos, announced the secession. A later broadcast said the region's Consultative Assembly had not made a decision to break away, but was going to meet again later today.

The conflicting broadcasts confused the nation.

Immediately after the original broadcast from Enugu, Nigeria's military ruler, Lieutenant-Colonel Gowon, said he had assumed powers as commander-in-chief for "the short period necessary" to counter the announced secession.

Colonel Gowon banned all political activity, meaning that the assembly in the eastern region would have to defy the order to meet again.

The earlier broadcast from Enugu said the eastern region, led by its Governor, Lieutenant-Colonel O. Ojuku, was breaking away from the northern-led military government. The broadcast said the assembly had voted to establish the separate Democratic Republic of Biafra.

WARNING

Colonel Gowon pledged last week to use force if necessary to keep Nigeria intact.

"What we do in the next few days will be decisive," he said.

"What is at stake is the very survival of Nigeria as one political and economic unit."

Colonel Gowon accused the eastern region of pushing the country toward total disintegration and possible civil war and bloodshed.

Complicating the crisis is a threat by Nigeria's western region to split away from the federation and follow the secession of the eastern region.

RICH IN OIL

The eastern region has vast oil resources in the swampy delta of the Niger River. American, British and French petroleum companies have big stakes in the area.

These firms are expected to come under heavy pressure to pay revenues to the Eastern Region Treasury.

Nigeria, with more than 55 million people, is Africa's most populous nation. It is about the size of South Australia.

Nigeria has four regions — the eastern, the northern, the western and the mid-west. Only the mid-west has remained neutral in the present crisis.

Menzies ends silence

WELLINGTON, SUNDAY

Sir Robert Menzies, who has refused to speak on politics while in New Zealand, broke his sound barrier in Hamilton yesterday afternoon when he opened Waikato winter show.

Sir Robert said Britain's attempt to join the European Economic Community would prove a great opportunity for Australia and New Zealand to work together on matters of common interest.

He was optimistic about New Zealand's chances to achieve a balanced economy. "I am quite sure that the future of New Zealand has no ascertainable limits," Sir Robert said.

Since he arrived in New Zealand last Thursday he had refused to make any political sounds at all and the barrier was dropped again after his formal speech in Hamilton.

University man gets top ABC job

Sir Robert Madgwick, 62, a former vice-chancellor of the University of New England, will succeed Dr J. R. Darling as chairman of the ABC on July 1.

Sir Robert, who retired from the university and moved to Canberra at the beginning of this year, strongly emphasised last night that he had no political affiliations.

SIR ROBERT MADGWICK, new chairman of the ABC.

He said that he would be particularly interested in the educational role played by the ABC, but he hoped not at the expense of its functions in other fields.

The decision was announced in Canberra yesterday by the Postmaster-General, Mr Hulme.

The appointment of a successor to Dr Darling, who will be 68 next month, caused some political controversy in Canberra last month when it was suggested that the Government intended to strengthen its political influence over the ABC.

Dr Darling's second three-year term ends on July 1.

Last night, Sir Robert would not say when he was first approached by the Government to take the position.

FULLTIME JOB

"I haven't been actively involved in politics in the slightest degree, ever," Sir Robert said. "Being chief executive officer of a university, as I have for the last 20 years, effectively prevents any political involvement."

Since moving to Canberra in February Sir Robert has been devoting most of his time to organising a Commonwealth university congress to be held in August next year.

He is also on the council of the Australian National University and on the interim council of the proposed College of Advanced Education in Canberra.

He said he would be forced to give up some of these responsibilities because of his new appointment, and at the beginning would regard chairmanship of the ABC as a fulltime job.

"Once I know more about what it involves I may be able to reduce it to, say, three days a week," he said. "but this depends on how I find the job."

He had no firm ideas of any changes he would like to see made in the ABC.

"Fundamentally I regard the mass media as one of the most significant forces in the nation. They reflect public opinion and in reflecting it help to make it.

"I suspect that, of the mass media, television and radio are becoming more and more important.

"The ABC is one of the most significant educational influences in the nation—I realise it is also a lot more than that, but that would be the first aspect of its operations I would be interested in looking at."

Sir Robert was born in Sydney on May 10, 1905, and educated at North Sydney Boys High School, Sydney University and Oxford. He was afterwards a research fellow at Melbourne University and a senior lecturer in economic history at Sydney University.

FORECAST

MELBOURNE:	SYDNEY:	CANBERRA:	ADELAIDE:	BRISBANE:	HOBART:	PERTH:	DARWIN:
Fine. Becoming cloudy. Northerly winds. Max: 60.	Fine. Cool. Light winds. Max: 64.	Sunny day. North-west winds. Max: 57.	Unsettled. Windy. Max: 61.	Fine. Sunny. Max: 72.	Fine. Freshening winds. Max: 60.	Showers. Max: 64.	Sunny. Afternoon sea breeze. Max: 84.

87 *Whirled out to sea like a leaf*

The death of Prime Minister Harold Holt, 1967

ONE DECEMBER MORNING IN 1967, AUSTRALIANS PICKED UP THEIR DAILY NEWSPAPERS TO READ THAT THEIR PRIME MINISTER HAD DISAPPEARED AT SEA. ON 17 DECEMBER, HAROLD HOLT (1908–1967), THE SUCCESSOR TO SIR ROBERT MENZIES AS LEADER OF THE FEDERAL LIBERAL PARTY, WENT FOR A SWIM AT CHEVIOT BEACH NEAR PORTSEA IN VICTORIA. HE PLUNGED INTO WHAT WAS DESCRIBED BY WITNESSES AS 'TURBULENT SURF' AT A BEACH NOTED FOR ITS STRONG CURRENTS. HE WAS NEVER SEEN AGAIN.

The news that a serving prime minister had disappeared while swimming was a great shock to Australians from all sides of politics. Yet again Australia's iconic beach life had revealed its dangerous side. Newspapers headlined the extensive and ultimately fruitless search for Holt's body. Holt was a strong swimmer and avid skin-diver, although the 59-year-old was said to have been showing signs of deteriorating health by 1967.

Yet his swimming prowess and the fact that the prime minister's body was never found fuelled many theories about his death, including one that he had been taken to a waiting Chinese submarine. His wife, Dame Zara Holt (1909–1989), however, noted that Harold didn't even like Chinese cooking.

Holt's period of political office was brief, but in his two years as prime minister he oversaw several major developments, including significant changes to the White Australia Policy, increased Australian involvement in the Vietnam War and the referendum that changed the Australian Constitution to reduce discrimination against Indigenous Australians.

SEA 'WHIRLED HOLT OUT LIKE LEAF'

The Herald

FINAL

502,046 daily sales

63 0211 MELBOURNE, MONDAY, DECEMBER 18, 1967 28 PAGES

5c by Air 4c

TEMPERATURES TODAY

9 a.m.	65
Noon	59
3 p.m.	63
4 p.m.	63

A Man We Understood

TO Australians everywhere, there was a grievous shock yesterday in the first reports that the Prime Minister, Harold Holt, was missing and believed drowned in the sea at Portsea. Since then, the hours of massive searching have reduced any hope of his survival to vanishing point.

The first thought of everyone at this time is the ordeal that has come to Mrs Holt and her family. The people's deepest sympathy goes out to them.

Their loss is the heaviest, but ours is also very deep. Harold Holt was Prime Minister for less than two years. It was long enough for his country to widen its knowledge of the man with the silver-grey hair and the friendly smile.

KINDLINESS

It was said, at the time of the Senate elections last month, that his advisers had warned him not to smile so much. Perhaps the friendliness that was so essentially a part of Harold Holt's character could have created difficulties for a Prime Minister in some situations. He was never a man who could be ruthless, either along the way to the political summit or in dealing with others when he had a leader's power and responsibility.

The tougher school in politics may have seen it as a weakness that he was a man who wanted to be liked, and who seemed never to build up lasting resentment or bitterness against those who attacked him. Yet he could fight strongly for the things he believed in. He seemed to put a tireless, sunny enthusiasm into his work.

TOUCHED PEOPLE

In his Ministerial experience, which began nearly 30 years ago, his work gave wide scope to his ability to get on with people. In his first Labor Department portfolio he won the respect and liking of union leaders as well as employers. It was a good start.

As Prime Minister, he had begun to touch the international scene with his human qualities. Our relations with our Asian neighbors grew warmer through the personal contacts he made. He strengthened our accord with the United States, although some critics at home thought his methods too fulsome.

His term has been too brief to show if the test of leadership would have made him a great Prime Minister. But he had qualities that all of us could like. Millions here and abroad will mourn the man who worked so hard and whose zest for adventure took him once too often to the sea he loved.

...says woman who was there

"Nobody could have done a thing. He was like a leaf being taken out. It was so quick and so final."

Mrs Winton Gillespie, who was with Mr Holt just before he was swept out to sea yesterday, said this in a statement today.

The statement was given to reporters by Mr Holt's Press secretary, Mr Tony Eggleton.

"I knew there was nothing, nothing anyone could do even if you had all the life-savers there. It was too late then," Mrs Gillespie said.

Mrs Gillespie, who lives next door to the Holts at Portsea, said that she, Mr Holt, Mr Alan Stewart and a couple of others left the house at 11.15 a.m. yesterday in a party.

They went through the gates of the Portsea Officers' School and along to the end of Point Nepean.

"A little swim ..."

Mrs Gillespie, the only eye-witness who has so far spoken on the tragedy, went on:

"We went slowly, and were wondering where we would go because it was not a good morning.

"There was no question of snorkling. We were just going for a little swim or sun bathe.

"We went right to the very end to see the yachtsman Rose, and we all got out of the car and watched for a moment.

"Then we returned, thinking it might be better on Geyser Beach, which is on the Bay side.

"But Harold said, 'Oh, let's go to Cheviot.' He always goes there because it's more fun.

"So we pulled into the usual corner and ran down the beach. It's a long walk — right to the end of the beach — and it was very high tide with masses of floating wood.

"I had never seen it like that before, because usually when he is snorkeling it is low.

"We all dropped back very quickly, stumbling down with the wood and waves, and Harold went on ahead.

"Alan said to me, 'The Prime Minister must be a lot fitter than we are. There he goes striding along like Marco Polo.'

"We had practically lost sight of him by then. He strode ahead of us.

"It was cloudy and we were hoping the sun would come out in a minute.

"I said, 'I think I'll go for a paddle,' and left them at that stage, talking in a group up at the back of the beach.

"I went a long way down to the very end, and it was divine and flat in that corner. You could paddle around and walk for miles.

"When I was coming back — I was perhaps three-quarters of the way back — I saw Harold detach himself from the group where he had been talking.

"He went purposefully striding off down the beach — not towards me but towards the water. He didn't look towards me.

"He just went purposefully down to the water for a quick plunge in his customary manner. If I had been a bit closer I think I would have called and said, 'For goodness sake don't go into that.'

"But where he went in it was flat, with no waves breaking.

"And as **Vyner** (Mrs Gillespie's daughter) said, a moment before on the beach, he said to them, 'I know this beach like the back of my hand.'

Went out rapidly

"I think he thought he would go for a quick plunge where there weren't any rocks.

"We had all been out there the week-end before with **Pauly and Christopher** (Mr Holt's grandsons) and we had all been swimming there in a rock pool. It was beautiful and calm then.

"But I took one look at it (yesterday) and wasn't interested to put more than my toe in.

"However, he plunged in and I just watched a moment and went on up towards where our things were. When I looked back I could see that he was swimming in this broad stretch of swirly sort of water.

"I think he must have got to the stage where he tried to stand up and there was nothing. He seemed to be going out fairly rapidly and yet he was still swimming happily.

"I ran down to where Alan was standing on the edge of the water, not really wanting to go in.

"He said to me: 'If Mr Holt can take it, I'd better go in too' and he went into the water.

"But Harold was getting farther and farther away and suddenly I had the most terrible feeling and said, 'Come back, come back!'

"But by then he was too far to see or hear. We could still see his head — he was swimming. Alan said, 'Does he often stay in this long?'

"I knew it wasn't all right but there was nothing Alan or anybody could do at this stage.

"As we watched, the waves became violent and boiled up as it does when the tide is turning.

"It boiled up into a fury and we lost sight of Harold.

"I knew then there was nothing, nothing anyone could do even if you had had all the lifesavers there.

"It was too late then.

Swimming well

"He did swim for quite some time, it seemed to me, but I suppose it was only a couple of minutes. He seemed to be swimming with his head above water quite well — I suppose desperately trying, thinking at this stage that if he swam he might catch a wave back.

"But then after this boiling up, it all subsided and there wasn't a sign.

"Alan and I went and stood on a rock, and I don't think Alan realised what had happened.

"But nobody could have done a thing. It was like a leaf being taken out. It was so quick and as final.

"I said to Alan, 'You had better go and tell somebody and get help,' and he went off up the beach.

"This decision took only about the time it took us to be sure that he had gone," Mrs Gillespie said.

MR ALAN STEWART, one of the Prime Minister's companions yesterday on the beach at Portsea after he raised the alarm that Mr Holt had disappeared.

Police give silent swimmer's story

A police inspector read out to reporters this afternoon a statement made by Alan Charles Stewart, one of the party that accompanied Mr Holt to Cheviot Beach yesterday morning.

Reporters have not so far been able to interview Mr Stewart. He was not present at the Press conference this afternoon.

Insp. J. Newell, the search co-ordinator produced the statement from his pocket after reporters asked if police had taken a written account of the tragedy from Mr Stewart.

In the statement, Stewart said he was a company director, living in Elm Grove, Armadale.

He said he was invited last Saturday to stay with the Gillespie family at their house in Portsea Rd.

He said he arrived at the house about 2 p.m., spent the rest of the day with the Gillespie family, and slept at the house on Saturday night.

On Sunday morning, about 10 a.m., Mr Holt came to the house and invited Mrs Gillespie and other members of the family to go with him to the back beach at the quarantine station.

Stewart said he went with the others to the quarantine station, about 11 a.m.

SAME CAR

Mrs Gillespie travelled in the same car as Mr Holt. The rest of the party went in another car.

They parked the two cars about 50 yd. off the bitumen road, and walked down to the beach, arriving there about 11.30 a.m.

Stewart said no mention was made of skin-diving, and no-one took any diving equipment.

He said a high tide was running. The surf was wild, and the water turbulent.

After a talk, Mr Holt entered the water.

Stewart said he went out only a short distance. Mr Holt was farther out at that stage.

Stewart said he stayed in the water for only five or 10 minutes, and when he returned to the beach, Mr Holt was still swimming away from the beach.

Mrs Gillespie also entered the water, but left after a short time.

Soon after Stewart left the water, he looked out to sea, but could not see Mr Holt.

He climbed on to a rock to get a better view.

The four people on the beach looked for Mr Holt for some time, but could not see him in the heavy surf.

Stewart said he then decided to go for help. He drove to the main gate, and told an officer what had happened.

He tried to contact the local police by telephone, but the number was engaged, so he rang D24 in Melbourne.

"Mr Holt was in good spirits, and made no complaints about feeling unwell," Mr Stewart's statement said.

"I am a reasonably competent swimmer, but I did not feel I could handle the conditions."

He said he could see pieces of driftwood or kelp up to 5 ft. long in the water.

INSIDE

ON PAGE 2
- Shake-up likely on protection for PM.

ON PAGE 3
- Search picture.
- My modest pal, the PM.

ON PAGE 4
- E. W. Tipping writes about the Holt enigma.
- E. H. Cox discusses the changes Holt made.

ON PAGE 5
- LBJ may fly to Australia.

Hunt for Holt stepped up

By Herald reporters Alan Stewart, Graeme Kennedy and Kevin Randall

The air and sea search for Australia's missing Prime Minister, Mr Holt, was resumed this afternoon after being suspended because of heavy rain and big surf.

A minsweeper has been called in. And a Dakota has joined the air search.

Three hundred men, four helicopters and three boats went out at first light today to search the coast as far afield as Cape Schanck and Anglesea, about 40 miles apart.

But the weather got worse and worse. Steady rain cut down visibility particularly for the helicopters. And 15-foot breakers driven by 30-knot gusts of wind, pounded the coast.

All 38 divers taking part were ordered from the sea. One was treated for cuts after waves hurled him against rocks. The helicopters were grounded.

But then conditions improved and the search was back on.

Late this afternoon, two helicopters were still patrolling the area but all divers had left the water.

Mrs Zara Holt was due to visit the beach this afternoon to thank the searchers. She spent a comfortable night under sedation at the Holts' Portsea house.

Minesweeper

The 360-ton minesweeper HMAS Snipe left Sydney this afternoon to join the search. She is expected to reach Portsea tomorrow.

A TAA Dakota is patrolling between Cape Schanck and the western tip of Phillip Island. It has fuel for six hours and is carrying dye-markers and binoculars.

The Prime Minister's Press secretary, Mr Tony Eggleton, told a Press conference this morning: "We are all hanging on to a shred of hope that Mr Holt is still alive."

A big shark was sighted this morning about 500 yards from the beach at London Bridge, two and a half miles from Cheviot Hill Beach, where Mr Holt, 59, entered the water yesterday.

President Johnson and his wife have sent a message of sympathy to Mrs Holt.

It read: "The world is a lonelier place today. Our hearts and our thoughts are with you. Lady Bird and Lyndon Johnson."

Mr Eggleton revealed for the first time this morning that four people went with Mr Holt to the beach before he swam.

They were Melbourne businessman Mr Alan Stewart, earlier described as a quarantine officer; Mr Holt's Portsea neighbor, Mrs Winton Gillespie, her daughter, Vyner, 20, and Martin Simpson, 20, Vyner's boyfriend.

Mr Eggleton said Mr Holt and Mr Stewart were keen to go swimming. They strode ahead of the other three, who decided the water was too rough for them to swim.

When Mr Stewart became alarmed about the Prime Minister, he spoke to Mrs Gillespie who agreed that help should be sought.

The 300 men in the search today include police, soldiers, sailors, airmen, Department of Civil Aviation employes, St John Ambulance men and civilians.

The search co-ordinator, Inspector J. Newell, told this morning's Press conference he was "fairly satisfied" that the Prime Minister's body was not in the large hole in the rocks near where the PM entered the water.

He said a thorough search was made of the hole yesterday and today.

Police said today if Mr Holt's body was found it would probably be taken to Melbourne, where an autopsy might need to be held. Deaths in the area where Mr Holt disappeared are generally inquired into by the Melbourne City Coroner.

• Continued on Page 3

McEWEN PM TOMORROW?

From E. H. COX

CANBERRA. — The Governor-General, Lord Casey, made plans today to ask the Leader of the Country Party, Mr McEwen, to take over as Prime Minister tomorrow morning.

The plans are not likely to be changed unless Mr Holt's body is found before then.

Should this happen, Lord Casey would probably appoint Mr McEwen immediately.

A special gazette will be issued tomorrow.

It will announce that on the presumption Mr Holt has died, Mr McEwen has been appointed Prime Minister and has formed a government.

Commonwealth lawyers were today working out formalities to be followed in the situation.

Lord Casey will need official information upon which to base his presumption that Mr Holt is dead.

JUDGE

Commonwealth police are collecting facts on the case.

These may be presented to a Supreme Court judge with a request for a finding by the judge of presumption of death.

Alternatively, Lord Casey may himself act on the official reports when they are completed.

It is the responsibility of the Governor-General to ensure that the position of Prime Minister, as head of the administration, is always filled.

If tradition is followed — and this is expected — Mr McEwen, the next senior member of the Government to Mr Holt, will accept the commission to be Prime Minister.

There will be a proviso that he may resign when the Liberal Party has chosen a new leader.

He would then advise the Governor-General to offer the post to the new leader of the Liberal Party.

TWO POSTS

If Mr McEwen forms a caretaker government it is not likely that he will make any changes in the duties of the present Ministers.

Nor is it likely that he will make a ministerial appointment to fill the vacancy left by Mr Holt.

He is expected to fill both the post of Prime Minister and his present post as Minister for Trade during the caretaker term.

The deputy leader of the Liberal Party, Mr McMahon, will call an emergency meeting of the Parliamentary Liberal Party to choose a new leader as soon as possible.

It is not yet certain whether the meeting will be before or after the holidays.

A preliminary meeting may be held on Thursday.

• Continued on Page 3

• Public notices 22
• Films, shows, dining out 24,25
• Wealth Words 25

FORECAST: City.—Cool. Windy. Occasional showers today. Mostly fine tomorrow.—P. 23.

No. 27,341. — Registered in Australia for transmission by post as a newspaper.

Holt's death led to a rhyming slang expression 'to do the Harold Holt', meaning to do a bolt, but perhaps even more wry amusement has been gained from the fact a memorial swimming pool was named after the Australian prime minister who had drowned.

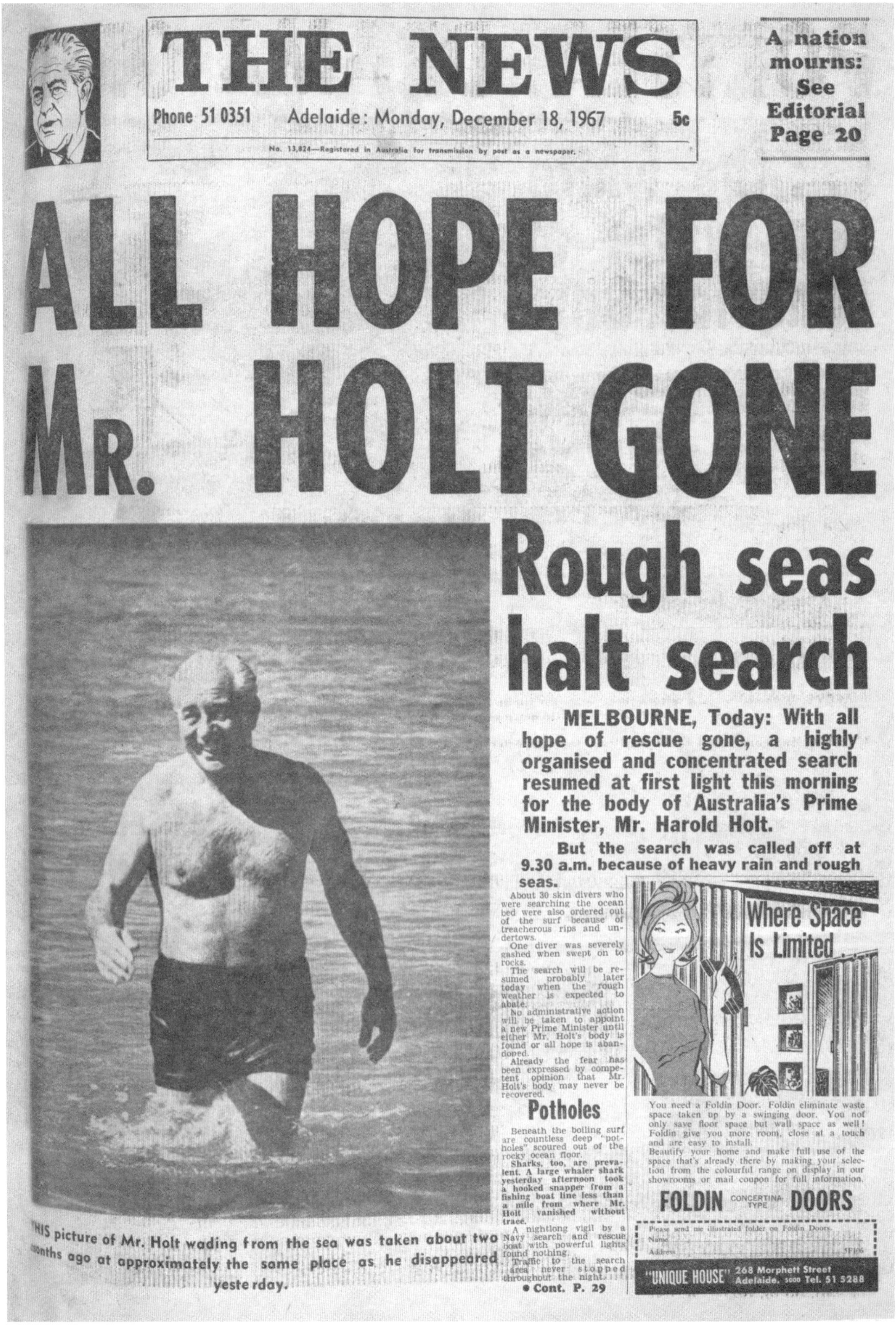

THE NEWS

Phone 51 0351 Adelaide: Monday, December 18, 1967 5c

No. 13,824—Registered in Australia for transmission by post as a newspaper.

A nation mourns: See Editorial Page 20

ALL HOPE FOR Mr. HOLT GONE

Rough seas halt search

MELBOURNE, Today: With all hope of rescue gone, a highly organised and concentrated search resumed at first light this morning for the body of Australia's Prime Minister, Mr. Harold Holt.

But the search was called off at 9.30 a.m. because of heavy rain and rough seas.

About 30 skin divers who were searching the ocean bed were also ordered out of the surf because of treacherous rips and undertows.

One diver was severely gashed when swept on to rocks.

The search will be resumed probably later today when the rough weather is expected to abate.

No administrative action will be taken to appoint a new Prime Minister until either Mr. Holt's body is found or all hope is abandoned.

Already the fear has been expressed by competent opinion that Mr. Holt's body may never be recovered.

Potholes

Beneath the boiling surf are countless deep "potholes" scoured out of the rocky ocean floor.

Sharks, too, are prevalent. A large whaler shark yesterday afternoon took a hooked snapper from a fishing boat line less than a mile from where Mr. Holt vanished without trace.

A nightlong vigil by a Navy search and rescue boat with powerful lights found nothing.

Traffic to the search area never stopped throughout the night.

• Cont. P. 29

THIS picture of Mr. Holt wading from the sea was taken about two months ago at approximately the same place as he disappeared yesterday.

Adelaide newspaper The News of 18 December 1967 recorded the end of the search for Harold Holt after he had disappeared off Cheviot Beach and was presumed drowned in the heavy seas.

Bungers versus batons 88

Anti-apartheid demonstrations at rugby matches, 1971

EVEN BEFORE THE 1948 APARTHEID LAWS THAT INSTITUTIONALISED RACISM IN SOUTH AFRICA, INTERNATIONAL SPORTING TEAMS VISITING THE COUNTRY WERE COMPELLED TO EXCLUDE NON-WHITE PLAYERS FROM THEIR RANKS. IN THE 1920S NEW ZEALAND NATIONAL RUGBY TEAMS HAD EXCLUDED MAORI PLAYERS, THOUGH THERE HAD BEEN LITTLE PUBLIC COMMENT AT THE TIME.

By the early 1960s, however, the exclusion of non-white players was increasingly being questioned. When the 1960 New Zealand team due to play South Africa included Maoris and it was thought the South African authorities might stop them from playing in South Africa, a public campaign commenced in New Zealand based on the slogan 'No Maori, No Tour'. The 1960 Sharpeville Massacre, where South African police opened fire on a crowd of black protesters and killed sixty-nine people, heightened international protest over the apartheid system. South African sporting teams touring overseas increasingly became the focus of protester anger, particularly in Britain, New Zealand and Australia.

In 1963, the first Aboriginal player to be selected for the Australian rugby union team the Wallabies, Lloyd McDermott, was unable to tour South Africa because of the apartheid regulations.

By 1970, the South African rugby team, the Springboks, were forced to play some tour matches in New Zealand behind barbed-wire fences due to fear of protesters disrupting the games. In 1971 the Springboks toured Australia and there were significant protests in Adelaide and Perth. At the third test match, held in Melbourne, Victorian police were well prepared to deal with the thousands of protesters (mainly students), and surrounded the Olympic Park Stadium before the game. The students, however, were also well prepared, with such things as smoke bombs and 'bunger' fireworks.

The subsequent confrontation saw a violent conflict and polarised support for anti-apartheid protests. Indeed, for the Queensland match of the Springbok tour, then premier, Joh Bjelke-Petersen (1911–2005), well known for his conservatism and for running what many Australians considered to be a police state, ensured the rugby test match would go ahead by not only erecting barricades around the stadium, but also declaring a month-long state of emergency.

The protests, however, were quite successful overall. There were no further Springbok tours to Australia for twenty years—until after the apartheid system was brought down in the early 1990s.

THE AGE

Monday, July 5, 1971 250 Spencer St., Melbourne 60 0421 (Classified 60 0611) 117th year 20 Pages 6c

'It happened because of the larrikins and louts' – Bolte

'I am appalled at the extent of police violence' – Holding

Violence wracks the city

Holding calls for Royal Commission

Mass violence flared twice in Melbourne at the weekend. And last night the Premier (Sir Henry Bolte) and the Opposition Leader (Mr. Holding) disagreed bitterly on what had happened and what should be done.

Sir Henry Bolte congratulated the police on the way they handled "louts and larrikins" at Olympic Park on Saturday.

Mr. Holding called for a Royal Commission into the clashes. He said: "I am appalled at the extent of violence on the part of police at Olympic Park".

And in Perth the Prime Minister (Mr. McMahon) said last night the South African rugby and cricket tours would go on and all matches scheduled would be played.

Last night foot police wielding batons attacked and dispersed about 200 demonstrators outside the U.S. Consulate. Mounted police charged the crowd.

On Saturday afternoon at Olympic Park about 3000 anti-apartheid demonstrators and several hundred police struggled fiercely for nearly four hours.

Foot police hit many people with their batons. Mounted police rode into masses of people at least a dozen times — inside and outside the ground.

Police arrested 217 demonstrators and charged 139.

Asked if he was concerned at the number of people hurt in brushes with police at Olympic Park Sir Henry replied:

"Too bad. Didn't they go there wanting to get hurt?

"They went there to upset the game and if in the process they were stopped I give the police full marks.

"They provoked the situation and if they came out second best that's just too bad."

Sir Henry said he had been at Flemington at the time and that people near him watching TV had cheered every time they saw "a lout or a larrikin" being taken away.

He said: "The police have to handle situations as they come up. If louts and larrikins run on to the ground, then the police have to handle it.

Spur of moment

"They've got to handle it on the spur of the moment as they see it."

He said the police had not created the Olympic Park situation.

"Whatever happened, happened because of the larrikins and louts who went there to break up the game," Sir Henry said.

"That is where the squeal is coming from.

"And nothing would have pleased 'The Age' newspaper more than for the game to have been stopped half-way through.

"It wasn't. And that was only due to the action of the police."

Mr. Holding said the Royal Commission should be held to establish why the violence had occurred and whether the police had had definite orders to disperse the demonstration at any cost.

He said: "If reports are correct that the white South African rugby team was entertained at the police officers' club after the match, one then must speculate as to the real nature of the police involvement in this demonstration".

(About half a dozen members of the Springbok team were entertained by police on Saturday night in the Police Association Club at the back of police headquarters.)

Horrified

Mr. Holding said the Governor (Sir Rohan Delacombe) had given Vice-Regal patronage to racialism by attending the match. His reported congratulations to the police afterwards could only serve to establish the name of Victoria as a racist State.

"Ordinary Victorian who saw the incidents on television and in newspaper photographs must be horrified at the way the police handled the demonstrators," he said.

"It is even worse when one realises this brutal action was taken against Victorians in the defence of the racist policies of another country.

Many of the Saturday demonstrators at Olympic Park were determined to stop the Springboks-Victoria Rugby Union match. The police were determined that they should not.

Twenty-nine demonstrators and other civilians were hurt, most not seriously.

St. John ambulancemen treated more than 25 people on the spot for face, body, groin and leg injuries, and burns.

Continued — 4.
• More reports, pictures— 4, 5.
• Editorial—9.
• Match report—19.

Newcombe's third Wimbledon title

Australian John Newcombe won his third Wimbledon men's singles championship within five years on Saturday.

Full report, page 20.

Riders outed

The riders of the three placegetters in Saturday's Doomben Ten Thousand, including champion jockey George Moore, were each suspended for a month for causing interference in the race.

Report, page 20.

High jump

American Pat Matzdorf broke Valery Brumel's eight-year-old world high jump record on Saturday. He jumped 7 ft. 6¼ in. to break the Russian's record by half an inch.

Report, page 16.

Raelene

Victorian Raelene Boyle won the 200 metres event at the U.S.-Soviet Union track and field meet at Berkeley on Saturday. Earlier she was second in the 100 metres.

Report, page 20.

5.15 p.m. Sunday: A July 4 demonstrator hits the ground near Queen's road. BELOW: Demonstrators in full flight in Queen's Road near St. Kilda junction.

Batons halt protest

Baton-wielding police and mounted troopers smashed into 200 July 4 demonstrators yesterday afternoon — bringing the protest to a sudden and bloody halt.

The 200 demonstrators — part of a 700 strong group — were cut off by police after windows were smashed and smoke bombs thrown at the South African Trade Commission building in St. Kilda Road.

Mounted and foot police pressed the demonstrators from behind and mobile police units came in along nearby Queens Rd. to close the gaps.

Then police drew batons on command and moved into the crowd.

Demonstrators were punched and thrown after mounted police broke them into small groups.

At least nine people were taken to the nearby Prince Henry and Alfred hospitals. They were all treated and later allowed to leave.

Three "Age" reporters on duty at the demonstration were struck by police batons.

Demonstrators attacked the South African Trade Commission with stones and smoke bombs after police thwarted attempts on the U.S. consulate in Commercial Road.

Police moved in after fleeing demonstrators jumped a fence into a car park at the Southern Command Army club in Queens Rd.

About 20 demonstrators broke from the march and hurled stonces through several windows and tossed smoke bombs.

The battle with police happened in Queens Road, just off Union Street, about 100 yards from the trade commission building.

Seven demonstrators were arrested and were later charged at Prahran watch house with assault and esisting arrest.

NEWS SUMMARY

AGE POLL — Who should lead the world? – 8

BOMB BLAST
Part of St. George's Free Serbian Orthodox Church in St. Albans was damaged by a gelignite blast.
—PAGE 2

SCIENTIFIC
Scientists still rely on intuition or faith in the supernatural, a survey by a NSW university lecturer in education shows.
—PAGE 2.

FEES LIST
A list showing what it should cost to see a doctor is available at post offices and health funds from today.
—PAGE 2.

$250,000
Shepparton window cleaner, Mr. Bill Thorne, and his wife, won $250,000 in Tattersall's Grand National consultation and plan to retire.
—PAGE 3

UNIONS HIT
Action by trade unions against apartheid is an unwarranted intrusion into areas of Government responsibility, according to the Minister for Labor and National Service (Mr. Lynch).
—PAGE 3.

NG MURDERS
Police questioned hundreds of New Guinea Highlanders following two murders on Friday.
—PAGE 3.

RACISM
Victorians practise racial discrimination by refusing houses and jobs to Aborigines, says the State Director of Aboriginal Affairs (Mr. Worthy).
—PAGE 3.

ELECTION
The Government-backed Sekber Golkar coalition appears to be heading for a landslide victory in Indonesia's elections.
—PAGE 6

PEACE PLAN
A split has appeared between Saigon's top two leaders over the Viet Cong's new peace proposals.
—PAGE 7

CHINA WAGES
Chinese workers who complain about low wages first have their "political consciousness' increased — sometimes a pay rise follows, our Chief Political Correspondent, Allan Barnes, has found.
—PAGE 9

● ODD SPOT
Hermione Gingold, 74, is to marry an antique dealer she has known for 20 years. "He loves antiques and I think that's why he fell for me," said the British commedienne.

Page index

WEATHER

VICTORIA: Early frosts eastern highlands. A little rain in the western half. Otherwise fine.

Details — 16

Wheat: a point to Labor

From ALLAN BARNES, our chief political correspondent, who is travelling with the Labor delegation.

PEKING, July 4. — The Labor Party delegation to China — in its first day in Peking — has scored a significant political point against the McMahon Government.

The delegation, led by Mr. Gough Whitlam, ha gained official evidence that China ha been giving preferences to Canada in the purchase of wheat because of the establishment of diplomatic relations between the two countries.

This refutes claims by the Prime Minister (Mr. McMahon) and the Minister for Trade (Mr. Anthony) that the main reason for China's failure to order wheat from Australia this year was because of record internal grain crops.

The loss of the Chinese market has cost Australia up to $100 million in wheat sales — the average level of Chinese purchases over the past nine years.

The A.L.P. delegation also learned officially that, with the establishment of diplomatic relations, China would continue to expand trade, economic and other relations with Canada.

The Labor group gained this evidence of Chinese intentions from a communique issued in Peking last night after talks with the Canadian Trade Minister (Mr. Pepin).

The Chinese attitude towards non-recognising countries was confirmed at talks which Labor had in Peking this morning with the Acting Foreign Minister (Mr. Chi Peng-fei).

The delegation had a two and a half hour meeting with Mr. Chi at which a wide range of trade, economics, political and diplomatic interests was discussed.

Members of the delegation refused to discuss the talks afterwards.

But it is clear they were left in no doubt that China would continue to give trade preferences to those countries with which she has diplomatic relations.

This means that the Labor visit will not achieve any specific gains for Australia for the time being.

But the information the group will gain will become the subject of political debate in Australia between now and the next Federal elections.

Registered for posting as a newspaper. — Category B.

The front page of Melbourne's Age *newspaper noted the government's view that violence at the Melbourne anti-apartheid protests was initiated by the protesters—who held a very different view of proceedings.*

THE AGE, Monday, July 5, 1971 HOME NEWS 5

It was bungers versus batons

By STAFF REPORTERS

It began in the quiet of Treasury Gardens, a little before noon on Saturday.

People gathered. Speeches were made. The police watched. There was no violence, but violence was not far off.

Police say they confiscated this string of nails at the Springbok rugby match.

Superintendent Holland

After the speeches—which were fiery enough—3000 demonstrators started their march to Olympic Park. Every step took them closer to a massive police task force.

The violence came only minutes after the marchers arrived in the part of Swan Street which runs along the front of the Olympic Park No. 2 ground.

Lead-encased crackers, rocks, marbles and eggs were hurled at foot and mounted police who blocked the two Swan Street entrances.

It was still only 1 p.m. or a little earlier — a good two hours before the Springboks were due to take the field.

Police tolerated the barrage for about 10 minutes, then moved in with batons and horses.

Mounted police drove a wedge through the demonstrators forcing them off the road.

Three protesters, including former State A.L.P. secretary (Mr. Hartley) were arrested.

Protesters reformed and started moving towards Batman Avenue to try gates at the rear of the ground.

'Fascist pigs'

Mounted and foot police again moved on the crowd to stop them.

Police threw demonstration leaders off the back of a truck carrying public address equipment. Police tore out wires of the public address system.

The demonstrators regrouped and marched along Batman Avenue to the rear gates which had been sealed off by extra police.

Fights between police and protesters broke out again when the marchers tried to tear down the security fence.

There were cries of "police brutality" and "fascist pigs" as demonstrators were beaten to the ground and dragged away to prison vans.

Mounted police formed at the rear of the crowd and kept it moving all the time. Protesters who resisted were arrested and thrown into a following prison van.

At one stage prisoners in the van began rocking it by running from side to side inside.

Demonstrators pelted police with rocks from the river bank when a small group was arrested.

March marshals called to demonstrators to break up about 1.30 p.m. and enter the ground individually.

At the gates in Swan Street police and policewomen searched everyone going in.

They took several knives, bundles of crackers, marbles, packets of tacks, pieces of lead, smoke bombs and cans of beer.

Demonstrators formed a queue almost 400 yards long outside the gates waiting for tickets.

Despite the stringent police search many demonstrators smuggled in crackers and smoke bombs which were later thrown at police lining the inside of the ground.

About 2000 demonstrators managed to get into the ground before the game started.

The rest pressed against security fences and yelled at police as they ejected demonstrators through the main gates.

Trouble started as soon as the players ran on to the field. Soon it was obvious that if the crowd was to surge onto the field it would do so from one of two places, perhaps both. There is a grassy rise at each end of the ground and each was thick with people.

Crackers

Within minutes the first punches were thrown, the first crackers hurled, the first arrests made.

The violence inside the ground was to last the whole of the match, ebbing and flowing, but always there.

Several youth got over the dog track to the grass and even on to the field. But the degree of penetration was nothing like as strong as at Norwood Oval, in Adelaide, last Wednesday night.

During the second half police were hurling demonstrators down the steep slope at the back of the knoll.

Below the slope, big prison vans waited — well out of sight of most spectators.

A young girl was dragged by her hair down the slope, across the gravel past the prison vans and thrown through the river-entrance gates.

'Enjoying it'

At this stage police were arresting some people and ejecting others—sometimes by throwing them out bodily.

Much of the violence late in the game took place in this area.

Mrs. Susan Hancock, a young lecturer at La Trobe University saw a man being batoned after he had stopped struggling.

Mrs. Hancock, close to tears, was shocked by the policeman's action. "He was really enjoying it," she said.

A reporter from "The Age" saw the same incident.

About the time the game finished 12 police horses charged upwards into the crowd on the grassy knoll.

Youths and girls were knocked down. At least one young woman was given first aid by St. John Ambulance men.

Silence shrouds S'boks

The Springboks left Melbourne for Sydney yesterday afternoon under the same cloak-and-dagger atmosphere which has surrounded their Australian tour so far.

Instead of an international sporting style farewell, they were whisked to the end of a runway at Tullamarine airport and boarded six twin-engined light planes.

These six tiny planes, the only aircraft available to the South Africans, left in relays with international and domestic airline jets between 1 p.m. and 1.30.

Only a few police and airport officials knew of the departure point.

Police guarded the team's entrance to Tullamarine.

Demonstrators who spotted their arrival at the airport could not get within several hundred yards of the Springboks as they boarded their planes.

These were scenes at Olympic Park No. 2 oval on Saturday as police fought with demonstrators protesting against the Springbok-Victoria rugby union match

ABOVE: A rugby player tackles a demonstrator who ran on to the playing ground while police close in from two sides.

BELOW: A demonstrator in the hands of police.

Worse than UK — Springbok

The Springbok vice-captain Tommy Bedford said after the match: "Most South Africans think this is a rugby tour. It's not like they think, it's more than that."

"A tour with a difference. The whole way things are happening. When you're out here you really do appreciate home. This tour is pretty hard work.

"Things are so difficult. You're living under such pressure. In Adelaide we never slept.

"In Melbourne we have been able to catch up on our sleep.

"The protests we've struck are as bad as England in 1969-70 and at times worse.

"We don't feel any antagonism towards Australia or Australians," he said.

"They feel antagonistic towards us."

Confiscated at the turnstiles

These are some of the missiles which police say they confiscated at the gates of Olympic Park No. 2 — firecrackers and stones with nails and other metal objects attached.

The Age of 5 July 1971 continued its account of the anti-apartheid protests in Melbourne with more extensive reports on the inside pages of the newspaper.

89 *Whitlam takes over*

Whitlam Labor government elected, 1972

THE ELECTION OF THE LABOR PARTY TO FEDERAL GOVERNMENT IN 1972 WAS A SIGNIFICANT MOMENT FOR MANY AUSTRALIANS. IT BROUGHT ABOUT WHAT MANY HOPED WOULD BE A PERIOD OF SOCIAL AND POLITICAL CHANGE AFTER TWENTY-THREE YEARS OF UNBROKEN CONSERVATIVE GOVERNMENT UNDER THE LIBERAL–NATIONAL PARTY COALITION.

While the result was not unexpected, it was surprisingly narrow, with the new Labor government under Gough Whitlam (b. 1916) achieving a reasonable working majority of nine seats in the House of Representatives, but facing a 'hostile senate', where the Liberal–Country Party coalition and the Democratic Labor Party (DLP) held sway. The DLP, which had split from the Australian Labor Party in 1954, was driven by Catholic ideologists and an uncompromising anti-communist stance. Their tactics were to support the Liberal Party against Labor until an acceptable reconciliation occurred. When Labor attained government in its own right, the DLP quickly disintegrated and ceased to exist in 1978.

Although the road ahead looked difficult, Whitlam and his government entered power with enthusiasm and strong expectations from supporters who had been 'in the wilderness' for the twenty-three years of Liberal coalition governments. Some electorates were still counting votes, but Whitlam decided to start governing the country without waiting for final results and appointing ministers. He created a 'duumvirate' with Deputy Prime Minister Lance Barnard (1919–1997), and the two of them held twenty-seven government portfolios for five days and used the opportunity to introduce several of Labor's more symbolic planned changes. He famously ordered the return of the remaining Australian troops in Vietnam, barred racially discriminating sport teams from Australia and instructed the Australian delegation at the United Nations to vote in favour of sanctions against apartheid countries South Africa and Rhodesia.

Combined with growing social movements during the 1960s and 1970s, such as the rise of environmental groups and a new wave of feminism, there was a great deal of momentum behind the new Labor government that, to many, held much promise. While the conservative parties still focused on Australian defence and security in the wake of the end of the Vietnam War, the Whitlam government promised to focus on 'cities, schools and hospitals'.

Such was the momentum behind Whitlam's Labor Party in 1972 that it was even supported by some of the usually more conservative elements of the media and press, also swept up in the Labor Party election slogan 'It's Time!'

SUNDAY MIRROR

PRINTED AND PUBLISHED BY MIRROR NEWSPAPERS LIMITED AT THE OFFICE OF THE COMPANY, 20-24 HOLT ST, SURRY HILLS, N.S.W. 2010.

No 707 DECEMBER 3, 1972 Phone 20924 NSW Price: 10c*
INTERSTATE 10c; DARWIN 20c; NEW GUINEA 25c; NEW ZEALAND 10c (NZ)

time!

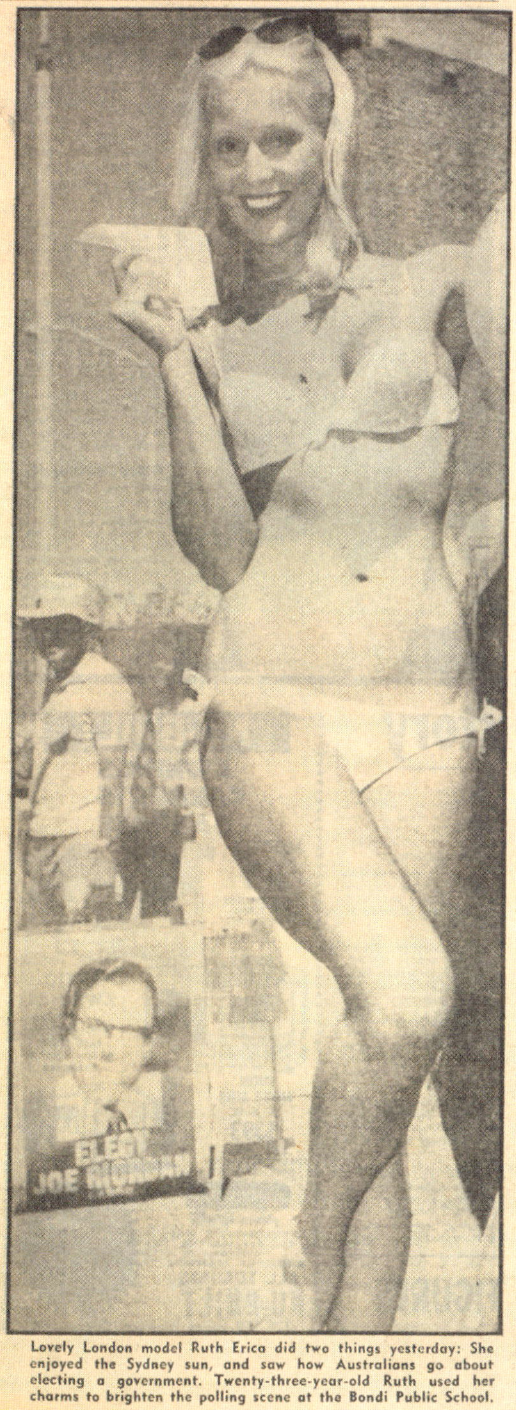

Lovely London model Ruth Erica did two things yesterday: She enjoyed the Sydney sun, and saw how Australians go about electing a government. Twenty-three-year-old Ruth used her charms to brighten the polling scene at the Bondi Public School.

LABOR KO'S LIBS

The McMahon Government was swept out of office yesterday by a swing which will give Labor a majority of at least 10 seats in the House of Representatives.

A spectacular feature of the voting was the crash of the DLP in Victoria, where early voting showed a swing of six per cent.

The Speaker, Sir William Astton, and three ministers have been defeated and three other ministers are in danger of losing their seats.

The strength of the anti-Government swing in Victoria was indicated by the fact that the Minister for Labor, Mr Lynch, was trailing the Labor candidate in the former Liberal stronghold of Flinders.

Even in Wannon, the Minister for Education, Mr Fraser, was trailing.

CONTINUED PAGE TWO

Popular Australian newspapers had changed the layout and style of their front pages significantly since the 1960s. In the 1970s the Sunday Mirror *published pictures of attractive cover girls, who on this day sat alongside the bold headline announcing the 1972 election victory of the Labor Party.*

90 *Drunks did it!*

The *Blue Poles* furore, 1973

IT DID NOT TAKE VERY LONG FOR THE NEW WHITLAM LABOR GOVERNMENT'S POLICIES TO BEGIN DRAWING CRITICISM. PUBLIC ANGER OVER THE PURCHASE OF AN EXPENSIVE PAINTING BY THE FEDERAL GOVERNMENT WAS TYPICAL OF THE PROBLEMS THE NEW GOVERNMENT FACED DURING THE BRIEF WHITLAM ERA.

The government quickly announced that it would devote more energy and money to the arts sector and it intended to increase acquisitions of important artworks. The recently established Australian National Gallery (later renamed the National Gallery of Australia) was given a large budget and specifically sought out 'masterpieces', rather than mere 'important works'. The economy was buoyant and it was intended that Australia would no longer be regarded as something of a cultural backwater.

But when the gallery announced that it intended to buy a painting by North American abstract artist Jackson Pollock (1912–1956) for $1.3 million—the highest price paid for a modern painting to that time—there was a public outcry. A report by an artist who said he had worked on the canvas on which Pollock created *Blue Poles* in 1952, also said they had been drinking when the artwork was begun, provided perfect ammunition for the tabloid papers. On 23 October 1973 Sydney's *Daily Mirror* blared one of its most memorable headlines: 'Drunks did it!' Opinion was bitterly divided as to whether this form of abstract art—where the traditional subject and tools of the artist were abandoned in favour of what appeared to many to be randomly throwing house paint onto canvas—was in fact art at all.

Whatever the case, Pollock's work was highly significant in the art market and it is now ranked among the highest achievements of twentieth-century art. The investment of $1.3 million has been well returned, with estimates of its current value approaching $100 million—despite, or perhaps partly because of, the infamous headlines it provoked.

BIGGEST WEEK-DAY SALES IN N.S.W.

LATE FINAL EXTRA

THE INDEPENDENT PAPER

Daily Mirror

INSIDE THE BEAUTY GAME P12 –13

Phone 2 0924 Sydney, Tuesday, October 23, 1973 No. 10,061 — 7c*

● Lotteries: Jackpot 638, P58, Ordinary 6778, P62 ● Historical Feature, P38 ● TV P34, P35 ● Finance, P64, P65 ● Weather: mild

ART BUY SENSATION

Barefoot drunks painted our $1m masterpiece!

'Like, it was quick-drying paint — and the bottles just stuck . . .'

Australia's new $1.3 million art treasure, Blue Poles, was created during a drinking binge with artists splashing paint over the canvas in their bare feet.

This sensational allegation was made today by Stanley Friedman, who once worked on a biography of Jackson Pollock, creator of the painting.

JACKSON POLLOCK

DETAIL FROM BLUE POLES

From RAY KERRISON in New York

His account of the painting of Blue Poles is the cover story in the influential New York magazine.

The Australian Government bought Blue Poles for the National Gallery in Canberra — and paid $U.S.2 million, the highest price ever for an American painting.

Friedman said that one of Pollock's closest friends, Tony Smith, actually started painting Blue Poles.

He said that in researching the book on Pollock, Smith gave him the background on the painting.

Smith said that Pollock, early in 1952, called him on the phone to say he was about to kill himself.

"I went out to see him at his home," Smith told Friedman.

"When I got there he had this long carving knife. He looked terrible and I was afraid.

"But after Jackson and I had been drinking, we decided to paint something together.

"I wanted to get him out of himself and into color again."

Smith said that he and Pollock spread out a long piece of belgian linen.

"It must have taken an hour, because it was wrapped in a canvas sack and inside it was wrapped in a kind of wax paper," he said.

"Jackson started taking down paint. Tube after tube of cadmium red.

"Jackson said, 'I can't start a painting in red.'

"So I said I'd start. And by luck, the next tube was cadmium orange.

"So I squiggled it on. And then I laid the wax paper over the squiggles because they were just lines, and I walked on the paper.

"I flattened the paint out and then I took the wax paper off."

● Cont. Page 3

WHAT THE CRITICS SAID:

QUOTE: In Blue Poles Pollock gave us one of the great masterpieces of Western art. It is our Raft of the Medusa and our Embarkation for Cythera in one . . . It is the drama of an American conscience, lavish, bountiful and rigid. It contains everything within itself, begging no quarter: a world of sentiment implied but denied; a map of sensual freedom, fenced; a careening licentiousness, guarded by eight totems native to its origins . . . What is expressed here is not only basic to his work as a whole, but it is final. — FRANK O'HARA, American critic.

QUOTE: It stinks — SALI HERMAN, Australian artist.

QUOTE: Outrageous. — SENATOR LAUCKE, Lib. SA.

OUR DREAM HOME WINNER ANNOUNCED—P 3

On 23 October 1973 the Daily Mirror's *headline criticism of the government's purchase of Jackson Pollock's* Blue Poles *was counterbalanced by the opinions of art critics, but it was a long time before the nation could think of the painting as a masterpiece.*

Vietnam War to Black Saturday

Since

1974

When Australian involvement in the Vietnam War ended in 1973, its impact on Australian society was to be felt for many years afterwards. The war had divided Australians and anti-Vietnam War protest marches and rallies drew huge numbers of supporters. In such a climate, soldiers did not experience the great welcome parades returning war veterans in the past had seen, and they were unceremoniously ushered back into the country. Many soldiers and their families were to suffer from the effects of this, the first time participation in an overseas war had been strongly condemned by Australian society.

THE VIETNAM WAR ALSO LED TO SOME SIGNIFICANT CHANGES IN THE SOCIAL MAKE-UP OF AUSTRALIAN SOCIETY. THE AUSTRALIAN GOVERNMENT ACCEPTED RESPONSIBILITY FOR THE RESETTLEMENT OF NUMBERS OF REFUGEES FROM THE WAR, AND SO IT WIDENED IMMIGRATION POLICIES TO INCLUDE, RATHER THAN EXCLUDE, ASIAN PEOPLE. FROM THE MID-1970S MASSIVE NUMBERS OF DISPLACED SOUTH-EAST ASIANS FLEEING PERSECUTION AFTER THE WAR IN VIETNAM WERE TO BE FOUND IN REFUGEE CAMPS ACROSS ASIA AND MANY BEGAN TO BE ACCEPTED INTO AUSTRALIA.

Australia's White Australia policy had been gradually dismantled since 1966, when the Holt Liberal government's review of immigration policies eased restrictions on non-European immigration: it would no longer be confined to what was described as 'well-qualified' non-Europeans. Then, in 1973, the Whitlam Labor government ratified international agreements relating to immigration and race. The government legislated that all migrants, regardless of origin, were eligible to obtain citizenship after three years of permanent residence.

Still, large increases in the number and percentage of migrants from non-European countries did not take place until after the Fraser Liberal government came into office in 1975. Political turmoil in south-east Asia following the Vietnam War generated a growing tide of refugees seeking asylum in Australia by fleeing in crowded boats and arriving on Australia's north-western coastline. Considering Australia's long history of racism towards non-European people, there was a surprising level of acceptance of Asian immigration and refugees during this period, although political debate over the arrival of 'asylum seekers' on Australian shores had begun to make headlines that continue to the present day.

The election of the Whitlam-led Labor government in 1972 was a watershed in what had been a long period of conservative governments. Many greeted the election result as a sign of major shifts in Australian society. However, after a brief period of power that did see many important changes in government policy, one event shocked the nation. In November 1975 Prime Minister Gough Whitlam was dismissed by the governor-general, Sir John Kerr—the representative of the British Crown. The Labor Party was swept out of office in subsequent elections. Few people had contemplated the possibility of such an event and the sacking of the prime minister was to ignite continuing debate over whether Australia should become a republic, breaking its final ties with Britain.

The late 1970s were to see an economic downturn, but by the early 1980s a new boom period was on the horizon. Often labelled the decade of greed, the 1980s were a heady mix of economic boom followed by collapse. The mining sector had become the new mainstay of the economy and again Australia was to become over-dependent on a single export industry in a pattern that was to be repeated in the following two decades.

Perhaps almost in spite of the wild economic ride, one of the most consistent headlines and most closely followed news stories of the 1980s was the trial of Michael and Lindy Chamberlain. Gaoled and then set free, the saga of Lindy Chamberlain's case of wrongful imprisonment for the murder of her child produced arguably Australia's most famous headline, 'A dingo stole my baby'.

The 1980s culminated in what was billed as the greatest ever celebration of Australian history—the 1988 bicentenary of the arrival of the First Fleet. In fact, 26 January bicentennial events across the country reflected many of the underlying tensions in Australian society and politics of

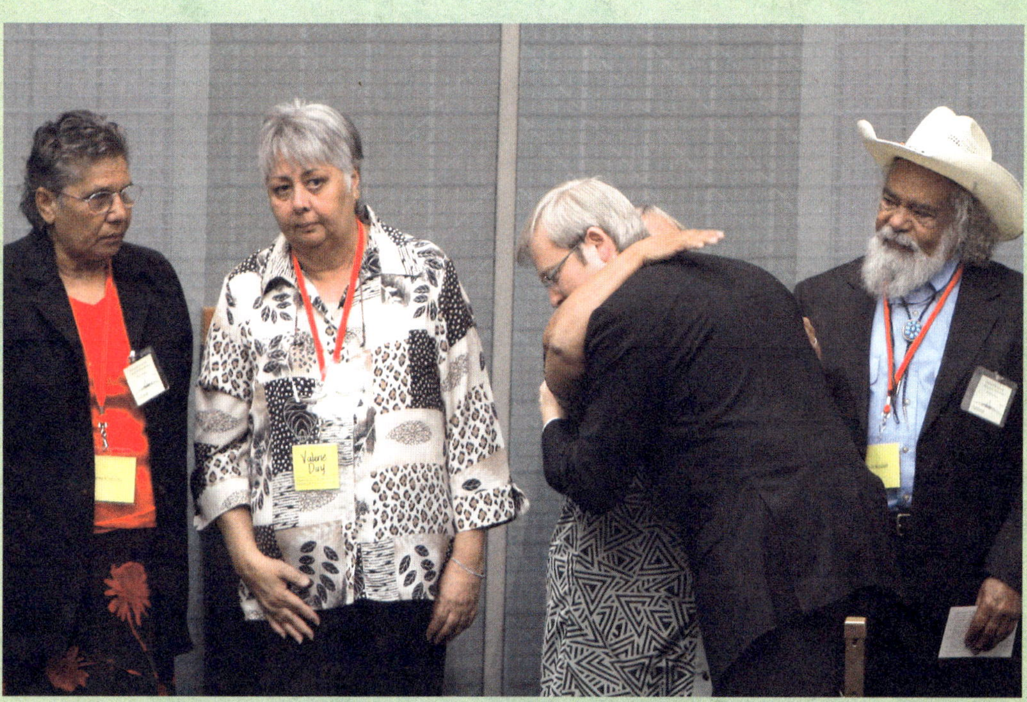

Australian Labor prime minister Kevin Rudd hugs a member of the Stolen Generations after his landmark apology to Indigenous Australians in Parliament on 13 February 2008. Tens of thousands of Indigenous children had been forcibly removed from their families over decades, and the campaign for a government apology had gathered momentum since a report on these children had been published in 1995.

the time. Although many activities commemorated the arrival of the British colonisers, the celebrations were also meant to incorporate the country's growing multiculturalism, rather than its largely mono-cultural history. But throughout his time, Indigenous people and their supporters continued to campaign strongly against the event, as it represented the day their country was invaded by Europeans.

The next two decades were to see the increasing prominence of Indigenous affairs. From the 1970s various state and federal governments introduced land rights legislation for Aboriginal people. In the 1990s, the Mabo court case forced the recognition of what was called 'native title', or prior occupancy of the land before the arrival of Europeans. Subsequent arguments, court cases and legislation over where this Indigenous land title might still exist, or has been extinguished, have continued.

Throughout the 1990s Indigenous Australians looked towards a new recognition in Australian society. A reconciliation movement began and stories of past injustices towards what had been labelled the Stolen Generations were publicly aired. The call steadily grew for a national government apology for the past treatment of Indigenous Australians, and this was taken up by the Rudd Labor government in 2008.

Yet despite important social and political gains, many Indigenous Australians still lived in poverty, greatly affected by drugs and crime. In 2007, revelations of the sexual abuse and neglect of children in Northern Territory Aboriginal communities shocked the nation. The Liberal government under John Howard ordered a National Emergency Response, which was quickly labelled 'the intervention'. It brought defence personnel into remote Aboriginal communities to assist. But in a pattern that has been common throughout Australian history, the intervention was seen by many as government patronisingly acting for Aboriginal people, without consultation.

The Northern Territory response was one of a number of federal interventions at this time. Other areas of state government responsibility that the Howard government targeted were seaports, work place relations and the growing environmental disaster of the Murray–Darling river system. The 1990s had seen a long period of drought that dramatically affected rural Australians. It also brought into focus the increasing recognition by scientists of steadily higher average temperatures around the globe and the first official moves to study what was being called climate change. The impacts of climate change were to be at times vehemently debated by Australians, though increasingly accepted as real.

One of the most obvious effects of changing weather patterns associated with climate change was the frequency of extreme weather events. Bushfires in Victoria in 2009—on what was soon labelled Black Saturday—had rapidly developed into a firestorm generated by a rare combination of wind, heat and humidity. The fires were made worse, some believed, by past fire-management practices and the increasing amount of bushland reserved as parks. The fires were the subject of tragic headlines as newspapers brought the extent of the death and destruction to the Australian public through some of the most graphic and memorable front pages of Australian history.

Over the previous fifty or so years, the format of daily newspapers had been transformed by the increasing prominence of bold headlines and pictorial front pages. Rapid communication of important news events had become the most important function of the daily newspapers. New technologies also allowed increasingly elaborate, as well as immediate publication of news, as well as more detailed features, supplements, comics, and social and sporting pages. But the headline still ruled as the way to sell a newspaper.

From the 1990s, the cheaper production processes offered by digital technologies helped newspapers to survive, but in many ways the new media were also in direct competition with newspapers. While daily and weekly newspapers added magazines and supplements to help them retain readers, holding them back from switching to television and online news sites, the digital age has appeared to spell the death of the newspaper and print-based formats. The immediacy of communication by email, internet and social networking sites has forced significant changes in the way news is communicated.

Still, as with the fear of the potential loss of the printed book to e-books and the internet, with some significant changes in both production and sales, the printed newspaper seems somewhat resilient. Free-of-charge commuter papers, for example, have proved successful in recent years.

How we will communicate and receive news events in years to come is difficult to predict. We may not see the familiar bold headlines splashed across front pages, or perhaps this style will continue in different forms. Whatever the case, it will be interesting to recall that the development of headline news on the front pages of newspapers in Australia was a long process over time that both reflected Australian history, and also helped to shape it.

91 *The agony is over*

End of the Vietnam War, 1973

AUSTRALIAN CASUALTIES IN THE WAR HAD INCREASED FROM JUST TWO IN 1962 TO OVER 100 DEATHS AND NEARLY 800 WOUNDED IN 1969. WHEN AUSTRALIA'S COMMITMENT TO THE WAR BEGAN TO INCLUDE 20-YEAR-OLD NATIONAL SERVICEMEN CONSCRIPTED BY BALLOT, WIDESPREAD OPPOSITION TO PARTICIPATION IN THE WAR DEVELOPED. AFTER THE MY LAI MASSACRE—WHERE AMERICAN TROOPS KILLED MORE THAN 300 UNARMED CIVILIANS—CAME TO LIGHT IN NOVEMBER 1969, REPRESENTATIVES OF MAJOR ANTI-WAR GROUPS DECIDED TO HOLD A MORATORIUM, OR PROTEST RALLY, MODELLED ON THOSE OCCURRING IN THE UNITED STATES.

On 8 and 9 May 1970 more than 200,000 people across the country marched in peaceful anti-war demonstrations. It was a defining moment for many Australians who had never openly supported peace groups, or who were defying their families, friends or jeopardising their employment by protesting against the war. Some wore disguises so they could not be recognised.

The protests were divisive. The second Vietnam Moratorium in September 1970 saw only 50,000 participate, but many violent incidents. Two hundred people were arrested in Sydney alone. However, support for a third Moratorium in June 1971 grew. In Melbourne nearly 100,000 people joined the march and the centre of the city was closed down. By this time, public opinion had turned significantly against participation in the war. Graphic nightly news broadcasts of the conflict in Vietnam played an important role.

In January 1972 the United States and North Vietnam had signed a peace agreement and were negotiating what President Richard Nixon (1913–1994) called 'Peace with honour'. It wasn't until 27 January 1973, however, that a full cease-fire commenced and the war could truly said to be over.

The announcement was still significant as it meant the beginning of an end to the division and conflict within Australian society about its role in Vietnam—a division that was to last much longer for, and have profound effects upon, many Australians, especially those who had fought in Vietnam.

THE AUSTRALIAN

NUMBER 2661 THURSDAY JANUARY 25 1973 SEVEN CENTS* WESTERN AUSTRALIA 10 CENTS

PEACE

President Nixon after announcing the ceasefire with (left) Secretary of State William Rogers and Defence Secretary Melvin Laird.

Vietnam war to stop on Sunday

The agony is over, Nixon tells the world

From SAM LIPSKI: WASHINGTON, WEDNESDAY

PRESIDENT Nixon broadcast to the world last night that he had reached a ceasefire agreement with North Vietnam which would "end the war and bring peace with honor in Vietnam and South-East Asia."

The agreement will be signed in Paris on Saturday.

The firing will stop on Sunday morning, Australian time.

It ends American military involvement in the Indo-China war and guarantees the return of all U.S. prisoners within 60 days.

South Vietnam and the Viet Cong provisional Government will also sign the agreement.

Simultaneous announcements from Hanoi and Saigon also reported the agreement, which was initialled by Mr Nixon's adviser, Dr Henry Kissinger, and Hanoi's chief negotiator, Mr Le Duc Tho, at a meeting in Paris on Tuesday.

In Hanoi, the North Vietnamese Prime Minister, Mr Pham Van Dong, said the peace agreement was a "great victory" for the Vietnamese people.

"But we shall carry forward the struggle to complete the revolutionary cause of the Vietnamese people," he said.

The ceasefire will be supervised by an international force from Indonesia, Canada, Poland and Hungary.

The four governments have been asked to place their troops on a three-day alert.

Indonesia's contingent of 250 officers and 1000 men is expected to be the first to arrive in Vietnam.

AIRLIFT

President Nixon gave only limited details of the provisions in the agreement.

The White House announced later that Dr Kissinger would hold a Press conference today, an hour after the release of the full text of the agreement and the accompanying protocols.

Authoritative sources in the Nixon Administration said the draft agreement reached in October was still the basic core of the accords.

That agreement called for accompanying ceasefires in Laos and Cambodia, creation of a national council of reconciliation and concord, and allowed the North Vietnamese to retain their forces in South Vietnam.

President Nixon did not refer directly to these points last night.

He emphasised the end of the long, agonishing American involvement in the war and the return of the POWs.

If the agreements work, the remaining 24,000 American troops and the 587 prisoners will be returned by the end of March.

The U.S. Defence Secretary, Mr Laird, said nearly 6000 doctors, nurses and psychiatrists were standing by to look after the released prisoners.

If necessary, American planes may land at Hanoi to evacuate the more seriously ill prisoners, some of whom could be on their way home within five days of the ceasefire.

In his speech, President Nixon defended the late President Lyndon Johnson, whose body arrives in Washington this morning for a funeral service and to lie in state.

He said Mr Johnson was attacked for his role in the Vietnam war, but nothing would have pleased Mr Johnson more than to have made peace.

The initial reaction in Washington to Mr Nixon's announcement of an end to the nation's longest and most divisive war was one of relief and gratitude.

CHALLENGE

"Thank God," said Senator Claiborne Pell (Democrat). "I hope it sticks."

Senator Hubert Humphrey said: "At last, the killing will be stopped."

Senator Edward Kennedy said: "My feeling is one of thanks and profound relief that these long years of national sacrifice, tragedy and bitterness are over."

The Senate Republican leader, Senator Hugh Scott, said: "Now is the time of conciliation and reconciliation. Peace has come. May peace remain."

Other Republican congressmen, including Senator Barry Goldwater, said Americans owed Mr Nixon a deep debt of gratitude and his critics owed him an apology.

Mr Nixon is unlikely to get an apology from his Congressional opponents, but the final breakthrough is likely to help him politically.

It will create a better atmosphere and soften much of the criticism.

But opposition on a wide range of domestic issues remains.

Vietnam, however, will dominate the public awareness in the United States in the days and weeks ahead.

In his speech last night, Mr Nixon did not refer directly to his critics but spoke to his own political constituency when he said: "Let us be proud that America did not settle for a peace that would have betrayed our allies.

"Let us be proud that America did not settle for a peace that would have abandoned our prisoners."

But, although Mr Nixon said the agreements would ensure that South Vietnam would be able to determine its own future without outside interference, the main question in Washington was whether the Saigon Government would have the military and political strength to cope with the expected challenge from Hanoi.

Such a challenge is expected, irrespective of the formal agreements to be signed in Paris.

The two key factors are expected to be the role of Moscow and Peking and the ability of the South Vietnamese army to absorb the large amounts of military material the United States has provided recently as a ceasefire agreement loomed closer.

President Nixon referred to Russia and China in his speech, making it clear he expected both powers "to exercise restraint." The main area of concern is arms supplies.

Some analysts in Washington believe North Vietnam will avoid early major military action in order to recover from the heavy bombing in the north and regroup its forces in the south.

Until recently, President Thieu of South Vietnam insisted he would not sign an agreement which allowed the north to retain troops in South Vietnam.

But last night President Nixon said President Thieu accepted the accords and that they met his goals.

CONCESSION

It is believed in Washington that the South Vietnamese agreed only after the United States won a major concession from Hanoi — to allow the Thieu Government to stay in power and not insist on a coalition government, including communists, as an early replacement.

Diplomats said this could be apparent from the text of the agreement and protocols, but it would more probably be part of the verbal understandings between Washington and Hanoi which were crucial in the last round of talks leading to the initialling of the agreement.

The secret ceremony on Tuesday took place after a 3hr 45min meeting between Dr Kissinger and Mr Tho at the Hotel Majestic in Paris, where the formal signing will take place on Saturday.

The Secretary of State, Mr Rogers, will sign for the United States, and the foreign ministers of the three other parties to the agreement will follow.

Speculation that the agreement had been concluded began sweeping Washington yesterday as soon as news came that Dr Kissinger was returning to see Mr Nixon.

Because of the time difference — Paris is five hours ahead of Washington — Tuesday became a long day as Dr Kissinger returned in the early evening, saw Mr Nixon and prepared to hold his Press conference later today.

Australia says it is ready to help rebuilding

AUSTRALIA is ready to generously support international efforts to rebuild all the countries of South-East Asia, the Prime Minister, Mr Whitlam, said last night.

He said Mr Nixon's announcement of a ceasefire agreement in Vietnam was a 'hopeful first step towards eventual reconciliation between the contending forces."

The achievement of a ceasefire had established Mr Nixon in the foremost ranks of modern statesmanship.

Mr Whitlam said months of patient negotiation would be needed before peace could be achieved.

He said: "The divisions caused by years of hatred, bitterness and mutual suspicion will add to the difficulties of an already complex task.

"As the fighting recedes, opportunities will emerge for relief and reconstruction work in the devastated areas of Vietnam — North and South — and in Indo-China as a whole.

"It is in this field that the Australian Government sees itself as making a particular contribution."

Mr Whitlam said that it was still too soon for detailed aid programmes and machinery to have been worked out.

"But, as I agreed with Mr Kirk (the NZ Prime Minister) in Wellington at the weekend, Australia, along with New Zealand, is prepared to take part in an international rehabilitation programme throughout Indo-China."

MR WHITLAM . . . "hopeful first step."

The Minister for Overseas Trade, Dr Cairns, one of Australia's most outspoken critics of the war, issued a statement in Canberra describing the ceasefire as "wonderful news."

He said those who had resisted the war had hastened an end to U.S. intervention and reduced the suffering of the people of Indo-China.

Dr Cairns said they would have the gratitude of the people of Indo-China, and of all those who stood for peace.

DIVISIVE

He said: "It is a source of gratitude and relief to know the suffering that has been imposed on the people of Indo-China by massive bombing and other forms of massive warfare, seems to be now at an end."

Dr Cairns said he hoped the political settlement would lead to a reduction of conflict in the area.

The Leader of the Country Party, Mr Anthony, welcomed the end to a conflict that had divided the world, and hoped the energy used to carry on the war could now be used to salvage the lives of the Vietnamese.

The Federal secretary of the DLP, Senator Kane, said the most important point was that the north had accepted an agreement based on U.S. recognition of the Saigon Government as the only legitimate government in South Vietnam.

Registered for posting as a newspaper Category "B"

LATE NEWS

INSIDE

Now the Vietnamese will fight it out — Page 8

Editorial — Page 8

Background — Page 7

The end of the beginning — Page 9

War cost lives of 475 Diggers

AUSTRALIA'S 10½-year military involvement in the Vietnam war cost the lives of 475 Australian soldiers.

Of these, 276 were regular soldiers and 198 national servicemen. One CMF soldier was killed in the conflict.

Of the deaths, 415 were battle casualties, and 60 resulted from non-battle accidents.

Among the 276 regular soldiers killed, 232 were in battle and 44 were non-battle deaths. A total of 182 national servicemen died in combat and 16 were killed in other accidents.

The army yesterday made available a State breakdown of the Vietnam deaths. They were:

NSW: 160 killed. Of these, 94 were regular soldiers (79 battle casualties, 15 non-battle) and 66 were national servicemen (63 battle, 3 non-battle).

VICTORIA: 103 dead. 54 regular soldiers (41 battle, 13 non-battle) and 49 national servicemen (40 battle, nine non-battle).

QUEENSLAND: 87 dead. 57 regulars (48 battle, nine non-battle) and 30 conscripts (all in battle).

SOUTH AUSTRALIA: 56 dead. 31 regulars (29 battle, two non-battle) and 25 conscripts (21 battle, four non-battle).

WESTERN AUSTRALIA: 56 dead. 34 regulars (30 battle, four non-battle).

TASMANIA: 11 dead. Five regulars (four battle, one non-battle) and six national servicemen (all in battle).

NORTHERN TERRITORY: One dead. A regular soldier, killed in action.

There were 3/16 non-fatal casualties — 2348 in battle and 668 in non-combat accidents.

Oil hopes rise as Hawke flies to talks

By MALCOLM COLLESS

Hopes for an early end to the six-day petrol strike in New South Wales rose last night following moves by the president of the ACTU, Mr R. J. Hawke.

Mr Hawke flew to Sydney yesterday and is understood to have discussed the strike with Mr Justice Moore of the Commonwealth Arbitration Commission.

The strike by petrol tanker drivers and aircraft refuellers has caused several companies to shut down and is threatening the jobs of more than 50,000 workers.

At a hearing in the Arbitration Commission in Sydney today, the Transport Workers Union of Australia, oil companies and the ACTU will try to find a solution to the strike.

The ACTU is believed to have worked out a compromise proposal which it will put to today's hearing.

Under the proposal, the ACTU would appear for NSW tanker drivers.

Officials of the Federal TWU are understood to have told the ACTU they will not object to this arrangement.

The ACTU considers it is entitled to appear for the NSW Transport Workers Union because the union is affiliated with the NSW Labor Council, a State branch of the ACTU.

Officials of the ACTU hope this will overcome the basic cause of the strike which is a clash between the NSW union and the Federal TWU over representation at negotiations for a new award to cover all tanker drivers in the oil industry.

DELEGATES MEET

The Federal TWU has refused to sit at the same negotiating table as a representative of the NSW union.

On January 17, Mr Justice Moore ruled that the oil companies should negotiate only with the Federal union.

This precipitated the strike by NSW tanker drivers.

The secretary of the NSW Union, Mr E. C. McBeatty, has said his union will agree to being represented at the negotiations by the ACTU.

Union delegates from all oil depots in Sydney will meet today to review fuel supplies for essential services.

It was strongly rumored last night that as a result of yesterdays moves by the ACTU a return to work would be called.

ACTU in workshop insurance this year

By KEN HICKEY

THE ACTU is likely to start its own life insurance company this year.

A meeting of the ACTU executive in Melbourne next week is expected to approve the venture in principle.

The new company could be operating by the middle of the year if it wins support from the larger unions.

One proposal is that shop stewards or other representatives of the union company should sell policies at the workplace.

Feasibility studies were carried out last year by delegations from the trade union movements in West Germany and Israel.

The delegations prepared reports into the possibility of the Australian unions entering insurance, consumer credit and housing.

The German unions have been operating their own insurance company Volksfursorge, for 50 years.

The Germans have no mandate to invest funds in the Australian insurance venture but the Israeli trade union movement may help.

The Germans will send experts to Australia to train personnel to run the company or provide training for them in Germany.

The success of the venture will depend on the financial and practical support of the big unions.

Stand-down threat to 20,000

THE THREAT of large-scale stand-downs of Victorian building workers increased last night after the Australian Workers Union rejected a peace plan on the State's cement dispute.

Mr Justice Aird of the Arbitration Commission said yesterday he would begin hearing a dispute between the Building and Construction Workers Union and the Pioneer Company if the union partially lifted its bans on ready-mixed concrete. He said the AWU should also lift its bans on the supply of cement.

The industrial officer for the Master Builders Association, Mr R. Luckman, said last night: "By next week builders will be forced to stand-down at least 20,000 workers if the dispute is not settled."

Bonnett defeats Killen in ballot

By PAUL WEBSTER

MOST of the interim executive chosen by the Leader of the Opposition, Mr Snedden, were re-elected when Liberal members met in Canberra yesterday.

A complicated voting system, described by the party as "secret exhaustive," was employed in the Liberals' first use of a voting system to choose its executive.

On Tuesday, the party took away the leader's right to choose his own executive and Cabinet. Eleven positions in the 17-member executive were to be filled by voting last night.

The first newcomer to the executive is Queensland member, Mr R. N. Bonnett.

Under the voting system every State must be represented and there must be five senators and 10 members of the House of Representatives and the two former Prime Ministers, Mr Gorton and Mr McMahon.

Mr Bonnett was elected as the Queensland representative, defeating former Navy Minister, Mr Killen, who was chosen Mr Snedden's executive. Mr Killen competed in later ballots.

FOUR BALLOTS

Those elected for States were: Tasmania, Senator Rae; Queensland, Mr Bonnett; NSW, Mr Bowen; South Australia, Dr A. J. Forbes.

Victoria and Western Australia were already represented among the party leaders.

Ballots were then general with as many as 18 members putting their names forward. Several former ministers, including Mr Wentworth, Senator Anderson and Senator Wright did not stand.

After four ballots posts went to: Senator R. Cotton, Mr J. M. Fraser, Mr A. S. Peacock and Senator C. L. Laucke. All of whom were in the original interim executive.

After a day-long meeting, the party met again last night to fill the last three posts.

The first went to the former Minister for Customs, Mr Chipp.

The others went to Mr D. E. Fairbairn and Mr A. A. Street.

Portfolios in the executive will still be distributed by Mr Snedden.

'Don't export gas to the U.S.'

CENTRAL Australia's natural gas is desperately needed in Western Australia and should not be exported to the United States, the WA Minister for Mines, Mr May said yesterday.

Mr May said Perth and outlying areas already had a critical energy shortage, and this could only get worse in the next few years.

His comments followed threats by the president of Pacific Lighting Corporation of Los Angeles, Mr J. Rensch, that his company would not continue providing finance for the Palm Valley fields unless the Federal Government indicated it would permit exports.

The U.S. firm is lending Magellan Petroleum Australia Limited $2.76 million to evaluate reserves in the Northern Territory.

It hopes to buy 500 million cubic feet of gas a day from the Palm Valley field.

But Mr Rensch said on Monday that his company's needs must only be surplus gas and that Australia's domestic market should be serviced first.

He said he wanted the gas to off-set America's growing energy crisis. His company did not want equity participation in the project, but would fund any shortfall in the estimated $1000 million project, Mr Rensch said.

Yesterday Mr May said he met the Federal Minister for Fuel and Energy, Mr Connor, last week and pointed out the need for a pipeline from Palm Valley to Perth — about 1200 miles.

Since then he had given Mr Connor projected gas needs for Perth and the eastern goldfields for the next 20 years.

He said that by 1980 these areas would require 357 million cubic feet of gas a day. The small field of Dongara, which is satisfying part of Perth's present needs, can only supply around 90 million cubic feet a day.

Mr May said yesterday the Government would be meeting with the Australian Gas Light Company next week to discuss who would own and build the South Australian-Sydney pipeline.

SIX PAGES OF BUSINESS and INVESTMENT BEGIN PAGE 10

FORECAST	SYDNEY:	MELBOURNE:	CANBERRA:	ADELAIDE:	BRISBANE:	HOBART:	PERTH:	DARWIN:
	Unsettled. Late change. Max 35	Fine. Mild. Max 23	Change coming. Max 30	Cloudy periods. Max 25	Rain periods. Max 27	Cloudy periods. Max 18	Fine. Max 29	Rain periods. Max 30

The Australian newspaper of 25 January 1973 announced the final cease fire in Vietnam and Australia's promises of help to rebuild the Asian countries affected by the war.

92 *It's time for reason*

Dismissal of the Labor government, 1975

THE SYDNEY *SUN* NEWSPAPER EDITORIAL FOR 12 NOVEMBER 1975—WITH ITS CALL FOR CALM AND REASON—WAS QUITE UNUSUALLY PUSHED TO THE FRONT PAGE. THE PREVIOUS DAY HAD SEEN UNPRECEDENTED SCENES IN AUSTRALIAN POLITICAL HISTORY AS AUSTRALIA'S PRIME MINISTER, GOUGH WHITLAM, WAS DISMISSED BY THE QUEEN'S REPRESENTATIVE, THE GOVERNOR-GENERAL, SIR JOHN KERR (1914–1991). THE LEADER OF THE COALITION AND OPPOSITION, MALCOLM FRASER (B. 1930), HAD BEEN INSTALLED AS CARETAKER PRIME MINISTER.

While there had been increasingly heated political debate about the brief and increasingly controversial tenure of the Labor government from December 1972 to 11 November 1975, there was also what the editor of the *Sun* called a 'despondency' over the ongoing crisis of a government that had run out of money. The government did not have the support of the Senate, which blocked the necessary bills of financial supply, essential for running the country, and some ministers had turned to international loan sharks for funds.

For many people, the dismissal at least broke the deadlock and elections could be called. Others felt betrayed and angry, particularly by the fact that the representative of the British monarchy still had the power to dismiss a government elected by Australian citizens. Protests quickly broke out across the country, demanding Whitlam's reinstatement.

At the subsequent election, Malcolm Fraser's Liberal and Country Party coalition was victorious, but the events of 11 November 1975 continues to be regarded as the most controversial political event in Australian history. Some more provocative analysts even suggested the United States secret service had a hand in helping to install a government more sympathetic to allowing the construction of US military facilities on Australian soil.

LATE CITY

$10,000 HOME GIFTS

NAME THE GREY-HOUND CONTEST

No. 21,401 WEDNESDAY, NOVEMBER 12, 1975 Twelve cents*

THE SUN

ELECTION CRISIS SPECIAL

Telephone 2 0944. Letters to Box 506, GPO, Sydney, 2001. 108 Pages

CITY FORECAST: Showers. • LOTTERY: Special 2670, P 100. • FINANCE: P 98. • HISTORY: P 12. • TV: P 95.

THE STRUGGLE FOR POWER

CITY BRAWLS

RAMPAGE AT 'CHANGE

ANGRY protestors fought through police lines and swarmed into Sydney Stock Exchange today.

Brawls broke out as the demonstrators barged through the front door of the Exchange chanting "We want Gough."

The demonstrators had broken away from a city march by 4,000 people, unionists mainly, protesting about the dismissal of Mr Whitlam.

It was the first big demonstration in Sydney and follows similar protests in Canberra and Melbourne late yesterday.

Police fought a rearguard action as hundreds of demonstrators tried to force their way into the Exchanges.

Police reinforcements came from the rear of the Stock Exchange to join the surging mass in the foyer.

Office staff stood on the balcony watching the struggle below while some women Stock Exchange clerks locked themselves in their rooms.

PHOTOS — PAGE 3

The demonstrators included many women.

The storming of the Exchange came at 12.10 pm.

Earlier, striking Waterside Workers Federation members, seamen and workers from Cockatoo and Garden Island dockyards caused traffic chaos with marches through the City.

Twelve abreast, the main group marched along George, Park, Castlereagh, Pitt and Hunter Streets chanting "We want Gough — out Fraser."

A policeman was hit on the head with a stone when the demonstrators later moved on State Parliament House in Macquarie Street.

The crowd gathered outside the House shouting slogans but there were no other incidents.

During the march through the City, police did not try to halt or divert the demonstrators.

At the Liberal Party office the demonstrators were confronted by shut wooden doors and a line of police.

Ash Street soon became choked with dem-

• CONTINUED PAGE 3

EDITORIAL

It's Time—for law and reason

The first momentous decision is made. Now for the one that really matters.

Does Mr Whitlam go back? Or is it time, as they say, for a change?

Was the Labor Government coping with inflation, unemployment and national despondency?

Or could a new broom do better?

These realities of life today will outweigh the academic argument over the sacking of Mr Whitlam.

Mr Whitlam was removed from office — by his own appointee — because he refused to take second place to the Constitution.

The Governor - General had no other choice. His decision rescued Australia from a political deathlock.

It has never happened before because never before has Australia had a Prime Minister so determined to hang on to power.

Is this political courage?

Or is it a Nixonian demonstration of one man's conviction in his right to rule?

People will vote as they see it in the backdrop to the coming campaign.

One thing must be clear: This is not a vote for or against the Governor-General.

Not a vote to change the past.

It is a vote for this country's future at a critical time.

Politicians, unionists and activists in this campaign bear a great reponsibility in the next few weeks.

Loyalties must not degenerate into loutishness.

It's time for reason, not rowdyism. Restraint, not recklessness.

So far, the law and commonsense have triumphed.

It's a crackling climate for a fight. But only numbers count in the end.

Australian history has generally been described as having been relatively peaceful, but there have been many times of violent protest, such as when outrage was expressed at the dismissal of Gough Whitlam's Labor government in 1975.

KERR SACKS WHITLAM

Mr Fraser in Canberra today.

Now Fraser is the PM

The Herald
Air Freight Extra 8c
FINAL EXTRA
63-0211 Classified 63-0351 MELBOURNE, TUESDAY, NOVEMBER 11, 1975 28 PAGES
456,646 daily sales

CANBERRA. – The Governor-General, Sir John Kerr, today sacked Mr Gough Whitlam as Prime Minister.

Within an hour, Mr Malcolm Fraser was sworn in as the new Prime Minister of Australia.

Sir John Kerr announced he had terminated Mr Whitlam's commission soon after Mr Whitlam had gone to Government House to seek a half Senate election.

At 2.30 p.m., Mr Fraser told a packed House of Representatives that he was the Prime Minister of Australia.

He said: "This afternoon the Governor-General commissioned me to form a Government until elections can be held."

Mr Fraser said the purpose of the commission was to permit a deadlock between the two Houses of Parliament to be resolved and to return Australia to stable government.

Five minutes before Mr Fraser's announcement in the House the Senate passed the Budget Bills on the voices. The Senate then adjourned.

Warning

In the House, there were loud and continuous interjections from members sitting behind Mr Whitlam as Mr Fraser spoke.

WHITLAM FIGHTS BACK

CANBERRA. — Mr Whitlam made a bid to recapture the Prime Ministership late this afternoon.

Mr Whitlam on his way to see the Governor-General.

WHAT SIR JOHN SAID

CANBERRA. — In a detailed statement on the reason for his decision, Sir John Kerr said:

Sir John Kerr . . . "no other decision open."

Powers

Denied

Cont. Page 3

Hell! It's incredible

"Hell! This is bloody unbelievable" — that was the shocked reaction of Melbourne Chamber of Commerce executive director, Mr Lovell, to today's momentous leadership upheaval.

Record

Unions plan strikes

SYDNEY. — Leaders of building, waterside and engineering unions forecast massive protest strikes within a few hours of Mr Whitlam's dismissal.

Cont. Page 3

BUREAU FORECAST: City. – Cloudy periods, light winds. – Page 20

Melbourne's Herald *of 11 November 1975 headlined Sir John Kerr's sacking of the Whitlam government and the installation of Liberal leader Malcolm Fraser as caretaker prime minister.*

Destination Darwin 93

Refugees and boat people, 1977

THE GRADUAL DISMANTLING OF THE WHITE AUSTRALIA POLICY SINCE THE LATE 1940S BY SUCCESSIVE GOVERNMENTS EAGER FOR MORE MIGRANTS AND THE END OF THE VIETNAM WAR IN 1973 TOGETHER BROUGHT ABOUT THE MORE SERIOUS ENGAGEMENT OF AUSTRALIA WITH ASIA.

From the mid-1970s, when the government took up what was a popular and widely felt responsibility to assist refugees from war-torn south-east Asia, claims of queue jumping by refugees started to appear. Millions of displaced persons escaping conflict in Cambodia, Vietnam and Laos, in particular, were moving to refugee camps around the world. Many began to try to reach Australian shores outside official channels in dangerously overcrowded and often leaky boats.

Considering Australia's long history of racism and fear of being swamped by what was once referred to as the 'yellow peril' and the 'Asian hordes to the north', the acceptance of Asian refugees and Australia's political engagement with Asia from this period onwards was remarkable.

But the arrival of what were soon labelled 'boat people' caused widespread concern. In the late 1970s, refugee boats heading for Australian waters made great headline news material. They played upon age-old fears of the country being inundated with Asian people. The issue has continued to feature strongly in Australian political debates ever since.

TUESDAY, NOVEMBER 29, 1977

HOSPITAL BLACK LIST REVEALED — Page 3

The Sydney Morning Herald

FIRST PUBLISHED 1831

13 CENTS* 24 PAGES

$78m plan to bring games to SCG

A $78 million scheme to bring the Sydney Cricket Ground area to Olympic standards was announced yesterday.

The president of the SCG Trust, Mr Pat Hills, who is also the Minister for Industrial Relations, announced this in the State Legislative Assembly yesterday.

Speaking during the second reading of the Sydney Cricket and Sports Ground Bill, Mr Hills said: "I advocate that NSW and Sydney ought to go flat out for the 1988 Olympic Games."

He also announced that a tender for $5.6 million had been let yesterday for the construction of the new Brewongle Stand at the SCG. This would include a television and communications centre capable of handling Olympic-scale media coverage.

Destination Darwin for 180 refugees...

Vietnamese refugees wave from the Darwin-bound Song Be 12 yesterday. The picture was taken from a Navy Grumman Tracker aircraft.

Navy patrol will escort Viet ship

The Navy sent the patrol boat Ardent yesterday to intercept the refugee ship Song Be 12 and escort it into Darwin.

High fire danger today

Cyclist, 16, falls after race, dies

Fraser, Hunt differ on health charge

From MIKE STEKETEE

Challenges fail

13 stranded

Still closed

429 die on US roads

TODAY'S WEATHER

Late news

Tremor in Greece

COLUMN 8

The Sydney Morning Herald of 29 November 1977 *offered just one of many headlines announcing the arrival of another boat from south-east Asia, bringing what became known as 'boat people' escaping the aftermath of war and seeking settlement in Australia.*

THE AUSTRALIAN

NUMBER 4158 TUESDAY NOVEMBER 29 1977 20 CENTS* FREIGHT EXTRA

Business & Finance BEGINS: PAGE 10

Talk-back is in, but Mr Whitlam cries 'foul'

Navy spots new trawler on its way to Darwin

VIETNAMESE refugee boats beached near Darwin's quarantine station.

Industry boosts capital spending by 14pc

By BILL MULDREW

THE manufacturing sector sharply increased new capital spending during the September quarter.

HAWKE: RETURN BOGUS REFUGEES

Viet boats sail into row

By Our Political Staff

THE Vietnamese refugee boat Song Be 12, carrying 182 people who are reported to include three captured government soldiers, will land in Darwin today amid burgeoning controversy over the admission of illegal immigrants to Australia.

The 120-tonne trawler, sighted 250 nautical miles north-west of Darwin by an R.A.N. Grumman Tracker aircraft yesterday, will be intercepted by an armed patrol boat, HMAS Ardent. It will be boarded by immigration and health officials immediately it berths in Darwin.

The Song Be 12, which will become the 10th refugee ship to land in Darwin since November 15, faces a hostile reception from unionists. And in Hobart yesterday the A.L.P. and ACTU president, Mr Bob Hawke, demanded that the Government make a clear statement that illegal immigrants had no rights to land.

Mr Hawke said if refugees arrived without government approval they should be sent back. He said it should be made clear "to these people that this country has laws relating to refugees and they cannot break these laws with impunity."

'Jumping the queue'

EVONNE BOUNCES BACK AFTER KELLY'S BIRTH

EVONNE Cawley during a winning burst at Kooyong yesterday.

Second big win in battle for comeback

PM quizzed over rise in health fees

Shares rally on poll hopes

PICKED UP

ALCOHOL

CONTINUED ON PAGE 2

LATE NEWS

Japan to take more beef

General Credits

EARN UP TO 12% P.A.

AVIS SPONSORED Weather Forecast

The Australian of 29 November 1977 headlines Bob Hawke, as president of the ACTU (Australian Council of Trade Unions), joining the call to reject refugees arriving by boat.

94 Died on the job

The death of Billy Snedden, 1978

SIR WILLIAM 'BILLY' SNEDDEN (1926–1987) WAS A LIBERAL PARTY POLITICIAN AND LONG-SERVING MINISTER IN THE MENZIES AND SUCCESSIVE LIBERAL GOVERNMENTS, BECOMING LEADER OF THE OPPOSITION AFTER THE WHITLAM-LED LABOR PARTY VICTORY OF 1972. HE WAS REPLACED AS LEADER BY MALCOLM FRASER IN MARCH 1975 AND BECAME SPEAKER OF THE HOUSE OF REPRESENTATIVES FROM 1976 TO 1983. SNEDDEN WAS REGARDED AS A DIGNIFIED SPEAKER OF THE HOUSE AND WAS KNIGHTED IN 1978.

On 27 June 1987, just hours after he had attended John Howard's election campaign launch, Snedden's body was found in a Sydney motel. *The Sydney Morning Herald* reported that police noted he was still wearing a condom.

Snedden had suffered a fatal heart attack and it was obvious that the woman involved had fled the scene to avoid being caught up in a scandal. It wasn't until 2006 that Snedden's son revealed that the mystery woman was in fact his own ex-girlfriend, half the age of his 61-year-old father.

The major newspapers of the day did not sensationalise Snedden's death. However the then struggling *Truth* newspaper remained as controversial as ever, and in one of its most famous headlines announced Billy Snedden's death as 'Snedden "Died on the job"'.

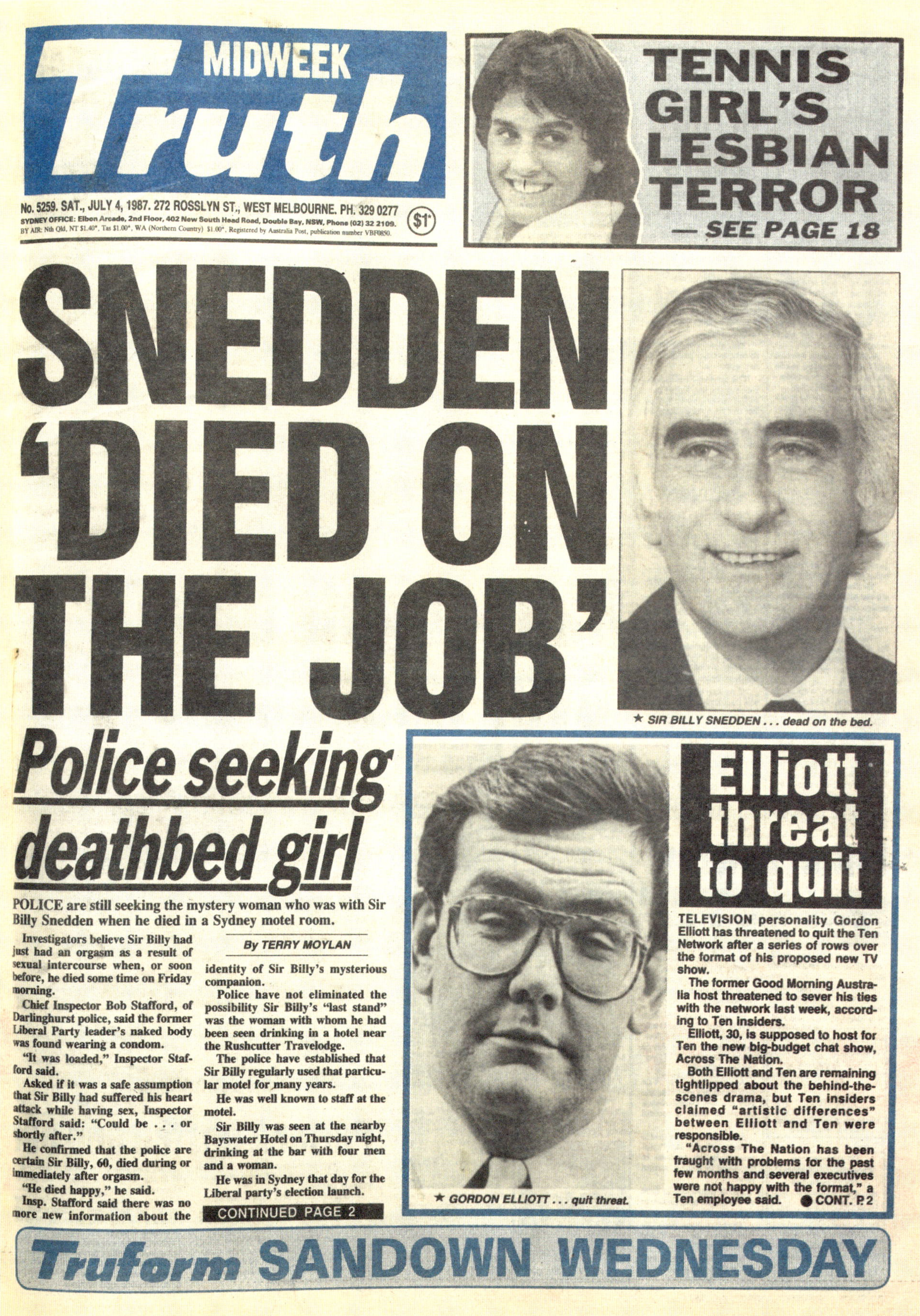

MIDWEEK
Truth

No. 5259. SAT., JULY 4, 1987. 272 ROSSLYN ST., WEST MELBOURNE. PH. 329 0277
SYDNEY OFFICE: Elbon Arcade, 2nd Floor, 402 New South Head Road, Double Bay, NSW, Phone (02) 32 2109.
BY AIR: Nth Qld, NT $1.40*, Tas $1.00*, WA (Northern Country) $1.00*. Registered by Australia Post, publication number VBF0850.
$1*

TENNIS GIRL'S LESBIAN TERROR
— SEE PAGE 18

SNEDDEN 'DIED ON THE JOB'

★ SIR BILLY SNEDDEN . . . dead on the bed.

Police seeking deathbed girl

POLICE are still seeking the mystery woman who was with Sir Billy Snedden when he died in a Sydney motel room.

By TERRY MOYLAN

Investigators believe Sir Billy had just had an orgasm as a result of sexual intercourse when, or soon before, he died some time on Friday morning.

Chief Inspector Bob Stafford, of Darlinghurst police, said the former Liberal Party leader's naked body was found wearing a condom.

"It was loaded," Inspector Stafford said.

Asked if it was a safe assumption that Sir Billy had suffered his heart attack while having sex, Inspector Stafford said: "Could be . . . or shortly after."

He confirmed that the police are certain Sir Billy, 60, died during or immediately after orgasm.

"He died happy," he said.

Insp. Stafford said there was no more new information about the identity of Sir Billy's mysterious companion.

Police have not eliminated the possibility Sir Billy's "last stand" was the woman with whom he had been seen drinking in a hotel near the Rushcutter Travelodge.

The police have established that Sir Billy regularly used that particular motel for many years.

He was well known to staff at the motel.

Sir Billy was seen at the nearby Bayswater Hotel on Thursday night, drinking at the bar with four men and a woman.

He was in Sydney that day for the Liberal party's election launch.

CONTINUED PAGE 2

Elliott threat to quit

TELEVISION personality Gordon Elliott has threatened to quit the Ten Network after a series of rows over the format of his proposed new TV show.

The former Good Morning Australia host threatened to sever his ties with the network last week, according to Ten insiders.

Elliott, 30, is supposed to host for Ten the new big-budget chat show, Across The Nation.

Both Elliott and Ten are remaining tightlipped about the behind-the-scenes drama, but Ten insiders claimed "artistic differences" between Elliott and Ten were responsible.

"Across The Nation has been fraught with problems for the past few months and several executives were not happy with the format," a Ten employee said. ● CONT. P.2

★ GORDON ELLIOTT . . . quit threat.

The Melbourne Truth *reported the death of Billy Snedden, a former leader of the Liberal Party, in the style for which the paper was renowned, on Saturday, 4 July 1987.*

95 *The dingo has got my baby*

The Azaria Chamberlain case, 1980

AUSTRALIANS HAVE BEEN FASCINATED BY STORIES OF MURDER TRIALS, MISSING PEOPLE OR THE DISCOVERY OF UNIDENTIFIED BODIES. THE CASE OF THE PYJAMA GIRL—THE BODY OF A WOMAN FOUND BY THE SIDE OF A ROAD IN 1934 AND NOT IDENTIFIED UNTIL TEN YEARS LATER—HELD NATIONAL INTEREST FOR MANY YEARS, EVEN WELL AFTER THE CASE HAD APPARENTLY BEEN SOLVED. BUT NO CASE HAS ATTRACTED THE ATTENTION OF THE NATION AS MUCH AS THE DISAPPEARANCE OF AZARIA CHAMBERLAIN.

On Tuesday 19 August 1980 newspapers around the country headlined the tragic story of a family camped at Uluru (Ayers Rock) in central Australia whose 10-week-old baby was taken from their tent by a dingo.

A long-standing urban Australian fascination with the harsh outback probably added to the mystery to the story. Several other factors fuelled rumours and opinion on the case. Azaria's mother, Lindy Chamberlain (b. 1948), showed little emotion when interviewed and was widely reported in the press as not behaving as a grieving mother should. The remains of the baby's body were never found and at the time most people had no knowledge of the fact that dingoes could indeed attack or take small children. A lack of understanding of the Chamberlains' Seventh Day Adventist religious beliefs also contributed to Australians' attitudes to the case.

After the first coroner's report found no case for trial, a second was ordered and the Chamberlains were brought to trial in September 1982. The jury was convinced of the Chamberlains' guilt, despite what was later described as a gross lack of evidence. by a judicial inquiry into the case. Lindy Chamberlain was charged with murder and, after several inquests, was convicted and sentenced to life imprisonment in October 1982. Her husband Michael (b. 1944) was convicted as an accessory after the fact and given a suspended sentence.

The Chamberlains unsuccessfully appealed several times, but in 1986 the chance finding of a piece of Azaria's clothing near a dingo lair at Uluru led to Lindy's immediate release and then full exoneration in 1988. The Chamberlain trial was the most publicised in Australian history and it is now held up as an example of how the media can adversely affect a trial.

IGHEST MORNING SALE IN N.S.W. (ABC AUDIT)

The Daily Telegraph

MORE BUDGET LEAKS —Page 2

WEATHER
SYDNEY: Fine
City 20, L'pool 21
STATE: Showers
Details — page 29

hone 2 0924 SYDNEY, TUESDAY, AUGUST 19, 1980 Price 20c*

(Interstate freight extra)

Anguished mum tells

I SAW MY BABY STOLEN BY DINGO

An anguished mother told last night how she chased a dingo which snatched her baby daughter from a tent near Ayers Rock.

By GEOFF de LUCA

Lindy Chamberlain said: "At first I thought the dingo might have bitten my baby, Azaria, and taken something else from the tent.

"I ran toward the tent and yelled at the dingo: 'Get out.'

"I dived into the tent. I saw the baby had gone.

"I felt desperately among the bedding — and I then realised the dog had my baby.

"I ran outside and screamed: 'The dingo has got my baby.'

"Then I shouted for anyone who had a torch to help try to find the dog.

"I chased it into the scrub . . . but it disappeared in the darkness."

An all-day hunt by hundreds of people yesterday failed to find any trace of the 10-week-old girl.

The searchers, helped by Aboriginal trackers, hunted through sandhills round the famous rock.

Barbecue

Azaria was taken by the dingo on Sunday night while she was sleeping in a small tent at the Ayers Rock camping ground.

She was with her two brothers in the small tent when the dingo snatched her from her carry-basket.

Her parents, Michael Chamberlain, 36, Seventh Day Adventist minister from Mt Isa, and Lindy, 32, were about 20 metres from the tent at a barbecue site when the dingo struck.

The family had arrived at the camping ground on Saturday night.

The distraught parents said yesterday they would erect a small monument to Azaria in the camping grounds.

"We have given up any hope for our baby girl," Mr Chamberlain said.

"In fact, we realised on Sunday night there was no hope for her.

"We have been terribly upset by this ordeal but I have to control myself and practice my faith.

"I am used to counselling people in these situations . . . I hope I can cope with it myself."

About 30 local people, tourists, police and rangers searched round the campsite on Sunday night but found no trace of the child.

Continued Page 3

Mrs Chamberlain . . . distraught

Baby Azaria . . . seized from tent by a dingo

CRONIN, REDDY OUT — Back Page

LOTTO P. 9. Lotteries: Opera House 701, P. 34; Jackpot 1766, P. 35. TV, P. 4. Finance, P. 17. Tele-Trading 2 0924

One of the most famous of recent Australian headlines was The Daily Telegraph's *first report of the Azaria Chamberlain case on 19 August 1980.*

LAND BUYING Where to get the money, P81

The Sydney Morning Herald

No. 45,190 First Published 1831 Telephone: Business 2 0944; Classifieds 282 1122 108 pages 30 cents Saturday, October 30, 1982

TODAY IN THE GOOD WEEKEND

THE MARATHON MACHINE — What makes Robert de Castella run? An exclusive series starts today

THE FALKLANDS: IN MEMORIAM — The last letters of a sailor to his wife before he was killed by an Exocet

DIPHTHERIA — Apathy, ignorance and some fear are to blame for very low levels of immunity

MONDAY — Come Racing for The Cup — Your complete guide to the big race with all the runners, tips and a sweepstake

COLUMN 8

Azaria: parents both guilty

From MALCOLM BROWN

Lindy: Life jail
Michael: Remanded

DARWIN. — Mrs Lindy Chamberlain was found guilty last night of the murder of her baby Azaria and sentenced to life jail with hard labour.

Her husband, Michael Chamberlain, was found guilty of being an accessory after the fact of murder.

He was remanded to appear in the Supreme Court at 2 pm on Monday when legal submissions will be made on his behalf.

The verdict at 8.37 pm Darwin time (9.07 pm Sydney time), stunned the packed court.

Mr and Mrs Chamberlain, who sat in the dock facing the jury showed no emotion. However Mr Chamberlain sat shaking his head from side to side.

Mrs Chamberlain is due to give birth to her fourth child very soon.

But one woman juror in the back row of the jury box hid her face in her hands and wept.

The jury had taken just over six and a quarter hours to reach its verdict after having been sent by Justice Muirhead to consider its verdict early in the afternoon.

Justice Muirhead thanked the jury and excused them from service for 10 years.

The crowd, which had built up to about 60 in the long hours of waiting outside the court had been discussing the likelihood of a divided jury.

When the jury foreman announced "guilty" to both charges, there was a dead silence in the court.

Mrs Chamberlain, 34, was found guilty of the murder of her daughter, Azaria Chantel Loren Chamberlain, aged nine weeks and four days, at the Ayers Rock camping ground on August 17, 1980.

Mr Chamberlain, 38, was found guilty of being an accessory after the fact of his child's murder.

When the verdicts were announced Justice Muirhead said: "Mr Phillips [the Chamberlains' counsel], as you are probably aware there is only one verdict I can pass by the law of this Territory and I feel I can pass this on Mrs Chamberlain and I will remand Mr Chamberlain for submissions.

"Alice Lynne Chamberlain, you have been found guilty of murder by virtue of the jury. There is only one sentence I can pass on you. The sentence is that you be imprisoned with hard labour for life.

"Michael Chamberlain, I remand you so that submissions on your behalf may be made at 2 pm next Monday."

Justice Muirhead told Chamberlain that he would be remanding him on bail of $5,000 on the same terms as he had been on bail during the seven-week trial.

He told the jury: "Mr foreman, ladies and gentlemen, on September 13 last I informed you that this would be a long and difficult trial and I asked for your patience and understanding and your forbearance.

"I can say on behalf of myself and members of the Bar that we have done everything possible for you."

Justice Muirhead thanked the barristers and left the courtroom.

As the jury filed from the courtroom, Mr Chamberlain rose and held his wife by the hand. They were taken from the courtroom by officers of the Northern Territory Department of Correctional Services.

Journalists then ran from the court all the way to the media room to phone the verdict to their newsrooms.

Mrs Chamberlain is likely to spend her sentence at Berrimah Jail on the outskirts of Darwin.

The prison was opened in 1979 and was designed for 150 inmates including 10 females.

This week, there were 131 prisoners in the jail including women, but a spokesman for the Northern Teritory Chief Minister, Mr Paul Everingham, said the breakdown of male to female in the jail was not available.

Prisoners work in the motor work shop, laundry, food services, at carpentry, metal working and agriculture. Women take part in craft activities.

PAGE 2: Judge's summing up.

Pastor Michael Chamberlain and Lindy Chamberlain enter the courtroom yesterday morning for the last time.

Bridge-tunnel crossing favoured by Govt study

By MIKE STEKETEE, State Political Correspondent

HERALD EXCLUSIVE

$½m taken by Maher, Crown says

From ANDREW STONE

BHP steel price up 3.9pc

The prices of Australian-made cars, refrigerators, washing machines and a range of other consumer products will almost certainly rise following a 3.9 per cent increase in the price of steel announced by BHP yesterday.

The increase will take effect on November 8.

It is the fourth rise in the last 12 months and brings the increase in that time to 15.6 per cent, well ahead of the 12.3 per cent inflation rate.

Kemira miners end stay-down

By JACK TAYLOR, Industrial Reporter, and ANNA MURDOCH in Wollongong

LATE NEWS

Grassby dropped · Debating threat · Shake-up near · Socialists in

NEWSBRIEF

MONEYBRIEF — Handling debts

SPORTSBRIEF — Grosvenor well · Tough test

ENTERTAINMENT GUIDE — Pages 77-80, Section 3

INSIDE

WEATHER

TODAY'S CLASSIFIEDS

TODAY ● 20 million people by 2001, Page 3 ● Nurses to act over pay cut, Page 5 ● Foot sees a Labour revival, Page 8

The Sydney Morning Herald *of 30 October 1982 recorded the guilty verdicts against Lindy and Michael Chamberlain for the death of their daughter Azaria more than two years before. It was another six years before they were finally exonerated.*

Yuppie Armageddon 96

Financial crash, 1987

THE 1980S HAS BEEN REFERRED TO AS THE DECADE OF GREED. IT ALL CAME TO A HEAD WITH THE SHARE MARKET COLLAPSE OF OCTOBER 1987. ON 19 OCTOBER 1987—LATER CALLED BLACK MONDAY—FINANCIAL MARKETS AROUND THE GLOBE CRASHED DRAMATICALLY. THE RELATIVELY CONSTANT ECONOMIC GROWTH THAT HAD CHARACTERISED GLOBAL ECONOMIES THROUGHOUT THE 1980S SUDDENLY STOPPED, AND SHARE TRADERS TRIED DESPERATELY TO SELL BEFORE PRICES COLLAPSED—WHICH INCREASED THE PANIC AND THE FALL IN SHARE PRICES.

If the 1970s could be characterised by anti-war protest marches and alternative lifestyle 'hippies', the 1980s was typified by the young urban professional, or 'yuppie'. The yuppie characteristically had a substantial disposable income and was focused on lifestyle and leisure activities. Many were finding well-paid employment in new technology industries and finance.

The Black Monday share market crash was the largest one-day decline in global share market history. Most markets around the world fell by 30–60 per cent over just a few days. In Australia, by the end of October, share markets had fallen by 41.8 per cent. Some investors were badly caught out and forced to sell their homes, businesses, boats—anything to pay back debts, but the consequent damage was nowhere near as bad as it had been in 1929.

Unlike the collapse of 1929, an economic depression did not follow. The markets gradually rebounded. Two further episodes, the 'dotcom crash' of March 2000, which corrected the trend of companies seeing their share prices soar if they put a '.com' at the end of their names, and the Global Financial Crisis of 2008 saw less panic and a greater faith in market recovery.

OVER
The front page of The Sydney Morning Herald *for 21 October 1987 headlined that the 'world panicked'. The paper was quick to suggest what readers should do in the face of the crash. For most Australians the impact of the collapse was still to be felt.*

The Sydney Morning Herald

No. 46,743 First Published 1831 Telephone: Editorial 282 2822; General 282 2833; Classifieds 282 1122 45 cents* 72 pages Wednesday, October 21, 1987

SPECIAL EDITION

THE STOCK MARKET MASSACRE

The end of the world is NOT nigh
Ross Gittins

1929: the way it was
Robert Haupt

FEATURES

Death of the bull market
Paul Erdman

PAGE 4

WHAT YOU SHOULD DO

MONEY TODAY

How the world panicked

Now comes the really worrying part

The stock market crashes around the globe do not necessarily mean that the world is going to be tipped into a rerun of the Great Depression.

However, the risk that we are on the brink of the worst recession since that catastrophe is now very real.

The free fall in share prices around the globe reflected both the global nature of financial markets and the inherently volatile – hysterical, would be a more accurate word – nature of financial markets that lack an exchange-rate anchor in a world of declining growth.

What pulled the rug out from under the stock markets can be summed up in the simple phrase: *I'm not going to be the last out.*

Just as there was no isolated and specific reason for the crash of Wall Street on Tuesday, October 29, 1929 the collapse of share prices this week does not have a causal relationship with any specific development.

Rather it is, as was the case in 1929, a symptom – one of many – of an international economic situation which had become dangerously unbalanced.

Even though it is only a symptom of a wider malaise, this week's crash may trigger off other developments which could lead the world into a nasty recession.

The institutions to watch are the securities houses and the banks. The individuals to watch are the high-flying individual entrepreneurs who have built huge personal empires based on funds borrowed against their equity holdings. The place to watch is Tokyo.

If we see cracks developing in any of these areas, then the odds on international recession shorten sharply.

While there will be no shortage of soothing words, especially from the politicians, that there is no risk of a replay of 1929 and what followed, there can be no guarantee that this will be the case.

With the advantage of hindsight, it is possible to look back to 1929 and the Great Depression, to what was done and what was not done.

A recent study which concentrated on the experiences of Germany reached the conclusion that the authorities there had acted in precisely the way in which a government handling a depression should have acted. The problem was that the population had simply lost confidence in the system and refused to respond to fiscal or monetary stimuli.

To say – as will be said – that "it could not happen again" is to ignore the many parallels that exist and have existed for some time between now and the pre-1929 years.

The most important of these are:

- **Collapses in commodity prices that threaten to produce major debt defaults in commodity-producing countries.**
- **A shift in the financial hegemony unaccompanied by the required shift in global responsibility on the part of the newly dominant power. The United States became the strongest economic power in the world after World War 2, displacing Britain.**

But it continued to run protectionist policies. In the last few years, Japan has become the largest capital-exporting nation, displacing the United States. However, it has refused to open up its agricultural markets to imports and persisted with land and tax policies which impede domestic expansion.

- **The lack of policy co-ordination between the major economies. This is perhaps the most threatening parallel. It is not a new development.Rather it represents but the latest stage in**

Continued Page 5

By SUE LECKY

A worldwide wave of panic swept stockmarkets yesterday, with an unprecedented 25 per cent slashed from prices on the Australian market.

Amid extraordinary scenes, investors crushed into public galleries around the country watched in horror as the key market indicator, the All Ordinaries index, crashed 515 points to 1549, wiping a massive $55 billion from the total value of all shares traded.

But in Canberra, the Treasurer firmly rejected any change in the Government's economic policy, playing down the impact of the share collapse on the Australian economy.

In Washington, a spokesman for President Reagan insisted there was no cause for alarm. "The underlying economy remains sound," the spokesman said.

The local rout came in the wake of a record 23 per cent plunge in New York, which far outstripped the great Wall Street crash of October 29, 1929.

- On Wall Street, the Dow Jones index collapsed a whopping 508 points, sending shock waves through world stockmarkets, which toppled like dominos.
- In Hong Kong, officials suspended trading until next Monday fearing an unsustainable wipeout after the Wall Street debacle. There were unconfirmed reports of a stockbroker being shot by a disgruntled investor.
- In Wellington, stock exchange officials also suspended trading, but not before the stock index had dived a record 504 points to 2,925.
- In Tokyo, share prices slumped 15 per cent – the index's worst ever one-day decline – as panic shot through the markets.
- London saw its most spectacular collapse of stock prices, with a further £60 billion ($A140 billion) wiped off share values last night.

At home, the country's biggest investor, the AMP Society, saw $3 billion wiped off the value of its investments. **(Full report: Page 41).**

Before this week's market crash, the AMP's various funds had about $12 billion of their total portfolio of $24 billion invested in the Australian stockmarket. The rest is in property and fixed interest investments.

Today, that equity investment is worth a little over $9 billion, according to the AMP's manager, portfolio investments, Mr Ray Greenshields, last night.

"The AMP became a little smaller overnight," he said.

While Mr Greenshields admitted the institution would not be entering the market as an aggressive buyer, he stressed they would "ride out the storm".

Leading Sydney stockbroker Mr Rene Rivkin described yesterday's events as "nothing short of a disaster".

"It makes race five at Randwick look like a good bet," he said.

"All rises go to excess and all falls go to excess. Whether this is *the* excess today, I really don't know."

One seasoned broker on the trading floor said: "We'll never recover from today, mate. This is the end of trading as we know it in Australia."

According to one senior institutional dealer, yesterday's sell-off was "a total bloody panic."

Another dealer, Bruce Bell of AC Goode & Co, said: "It was quite a day. I think anybody who bought today was quite heroic, and probably ought to be given a medal by a Governor."

He believed the shakeout from the small investor would be significant.

"I'm sure there are going to be some bad debts out of this, because the fall is beyond what anyone could imagine.

"People tend to gear up to do things, and it will be beyond their ability to honour the commitments. It was an interesting day to have lived through."

Banks, whose lending has fuelled Australia's great takeover boom, in turn boosting the market to new highs over the past year, were worried last night.

The Bank of New Zealand's general manager, Mr Graham Brown, confirmed that the bank had contacted several major corporate clients who had borrowed on the strength of their share prices, asking them to increase security on their loans.

He said the danger of individuals defaulting, having borrowed money to buy shares, was now more pronounced.

"The way we view it, it will be a little time before the credit impact of the stock market crash hits the people who have been imprudent, people who have done stupid things like borrowed more than they should have on stocks that had no intrinsic value, or no real asset backing."

INSIDE
PAGE 4: It's goodbye to property boom, Plunge is not a rerun of 1929. PAGE 5: Keating reassures a nervous Caucus. PAGE 18: Editorial. PAGE 41: Profits still in takeover stock.

HOW IT AFFECTS YOU...

SUPERANNUATION: Many people about to retire will see their lump sum payouts slashed. Others could take years to recoup yesterday's fall, which has wiped 25 per cent off the value of many super funds.

PROPERTY PRICES: Sydney's boom has suffered a major setback. Housing prices are likely to steady and may even fall. If losses due to the sharemarket crash are heavy some people may be forced to sell their homes.

RATES: Short-term interest rates jumped 2 per-cent yesterday. A short-term rise is likely to be quickly reversed. There is some hope of a drop in home loan rates, although Federal Government defence of the dollar would prevent rates falling.

OTHER INVESTMENTS: People with insurance bonds and retirement investments have been hit. Advisers warn against panic selling, saying it could prove costly. Equity trusts and market-linked Approved Deposit Funds have also been hit.

THE DOLLAR: The Australian dollar fell almost one cent, easing to US71.45c from US72.4c on Monday. Currency traders said the fall was much milder than expected. The yield on 90-day bank bills rose to 14.3 per cent from Monday's 12.1 per cent.

JOBS: Some areas of the financial sector will suffer job losses. The risk is that the market slump both here and overseas will undermine consumer confidence, depress demand and so trigger a overall lift in unemployment.

BANKS: Bank accounts are unaffected at this stage, as are savings with building societies and credit unions. The soundness of Australia's financial system should ensure that such investments remain highly secure.

AND THEM...

Rupert Murdoch
loses $1bn

Holmes à Court
loses $300m

Alan Bond
loses $200m

Larry Adler
loses $275m

It's not just the brokers: it's you

By PETER FREEMAN

The shockwaves from the stockmarket crash will spread much further than people with shares. Everybody will be affected.

House prices will fall, superannuation payouts will drop dramatically, and the value of investment funds will come under heavy pressure. On the bright side, there is the possibility of lower home loan rates.

For many people, the biggest consequence of Black Tuesday will be its downward pressure on housing prices. For others, the most important change will be falling interest rates – bad for depositors, good for those with outstanding loans.

Perhaps the most immediate, as well as the harshest, toll will be inflicted on people about to retire, whose lump sum superannuation payout is determined by the value of their fund's investments.

As a result of yesterday's bloodbath, the value of many of these funds will have fallen by a massive 25 per cent in one day, slashing the size of the benefits that can be paid out.

Also affected are people paying into private superannuation schemes which invest heavily in the sharemarket. Yesterday's fall has sharply cut the value of their accumulated earnings.

The only people to escape unharmed from the plunging value of superannuation funds will be those in schemes where the benefit is determined by a set multiple of their final average salary. In such cases, it will be the employer who has to pick up the tab for any shortfall.

The huge loss of purchasing power due to the crash can be expected to take much of the heat out of the real estate market.

Even those investors who got out before the fall are likely to stay cashed up for the time being, and wait to pick up bargains when people come under pressure to sell in order to reduce their debt.

While professional interest rates rose on the money market yesterday, this was largely a panic response to the sharemarket collapse, combined with a shortage of funds as investors scrambled to retrieve their cash.

Investors in managed funds – equity trusts, insurance bonds, Approved Deposit Funds and deferred annuities – are definite losers as a result of the crash.

Even conservatively managed investments, such as capital guaranteed funds and insurance bonds, could feel the impact if their existing portfolio of bonds has to be restocked with securities paying lower rates.

But the real blow will be felt by those managed funds which have a large sharemarket exposure, such as equity trusts and market-linked insurance bonds.

Oh no, not the Porsche: it's the yuppies' Armageddon

By DEIRDRE MACKEN

A Sydney stockbroker: "I've just heard of a guy who has lost a six-figure amount overnight. He's about 40 years old. He has two kids, and he's going to lose his home."

A lending institution: "I rang a client to ask him to cover the losses on his shares that he had borrowed on, and he said, 'I'm ruined'."

Another Sydney broker: "There's going to be the biggest second-hand market in Porsches and Ferraris that you've ever seen."

A fellow Sydney broker: "They're crying. They're crying on the phone to me. They've lost their cars, and probably their homes."

And another broker: "The only price that has gone up is the price of high diving boards."

In the wash-up of the great sharemarket crash, there are going to be Eastern Suburbs mansions under forced sale, scores of Porsches on the second-hand market, and dozens of young operators paying off debts for share purchases for many years.

The impact of the crash on the lives of the young hotshots who have plunged into the market over the last five years will be such that the whole market for luxury goods – from homes to cars to boats to champagne – is bracing for a downturn.

Every broker contacted in Sydney yesterday had a story about a client, colleague or competitor who had built up a lifestyle based around a booming market, and was seeing it dismantled in a day.

While many of the leading sharebrokers and professional investors will be protected from the effects of the crash, the junior staff of broking houses, merchant banks and lending institutions will be receiving calls from their lenders for money they do not have.

"It's the 25-year-old yuppies who have been burnt," said a leading broker. "There are several young dealers on the floor who are going to lose their Porsches. They're the people who put $20,000 of their own money into the market, borrowed $80,000, and now find their $100,000 investment is worth $50,000. Where are they going to get $30,000?"

Hardest hit will be those playing the futures market. Anyone who bought a futures contract yesterday on the basis that the market would rise would have lost $68,000 by yesterday afternoon.

It is estimated that $300 million is on loan to small investors in shares, and yesterday almost everyone who borrowed to buy stock received a call from a lending institution asking for the money to cover their losses.

A trader at Elders Finance, one of the biggest lenders for share purchases, said: "Some people have lost $100,000 today, and they're not rich people. They are ruined. One guy I spoke to was close to tears. Most of them are young jockeys. I only wish I

Continued Page 5

The day America lost its faith

By PAUL SHEEHAN, Staff Correspondent

NEW YORK, Tuesday: "This is as close to a market meltdown as I ever want to see," the chairman of the New York Stock Exchange, Mr John Phelan, told a press conference after the catastrophe on Wall Street yesterday.

So great was the panic, many US analysts speculated that it may signify a historic watershed – the day the world recognised that the United States was no longer capable of exercising the dominant economic role it has held for the past half-century.

America reacted with numbed disbelief to the stock market disaster. It was the worst in history, dwarfing even the great crash of October 28, 1929.

The obliteration of market confidence was devastating. Fuelled by last Friday's plunge and overnight panic on the London stock market, the floor of the New York Stock Exchange erupted in a frenzy of selling as soon as trading opened at 9 am. It continued unabated until trading closed, with a mighty roar, at 4 pm.

Throughout the city, crowds gathered at brokerage houses and watched the prices on the electronic tape sink relentlessly across the board.

Long lines stood outside the exchange building on Wall Street as hundreds waited to file through the public gallery. Inside, the trading floor was marked by fights, pushing, screaming and sweaty confusion.

At the midtown offices of Charles Schwab and Co, the US's biggest discount broker, dozens of worried upturned faces watched the green electronic tape slide by.

Exasperation was clear. "I've been trying to reach my broker all day." Humour was dark. "I've just lost my new car."

Share prices dropped an almost incomprehensible US$500 billion in seven hours as the Dow Jones Industrial Average plummeted 508 points to 1,738. The previous biggest drop was 108 points last Friday.

The 23 per cent slump in the value of the market yesterday was almost twice the size of the crash on "Black Tuesday" in 1929, when a market fall of 13 per cent ushered in the Great Depression.

In just one week, the market has wiped out all the gains of the last two years.

After trading closed, there was little respite for shocked investors and brokers. In the era of a global electronic stockmarket, it was only a few hours before the markets opened in Sydney, Tokyo and Hong Kong.

The first news came from Sydney, and it was disastrous. Then came reports of the closure of the Hong Kong exchange, and the crash on the Tokyo market.

The news exacerbated the tensions built up during the day here, and foreshadowed further selling today.

Consumer confidence has received a bodyblow. The property market, especially in New York, is expected to collapse.

President Reagan, in his only comment on the crash, defended America's improved trade performance.

"We reduced the deficit last

Continued Page 5

COLUMN 8

BOND Street, home of the Sydney Stock Exchange, was in a state of pandemonium yesterday as would-be capitalists and television crews ditched their vehicles anywhere in the street, and hurried into the building. Unaffected by the frenzy on the trading floor, three grey-suited parking police worked their way methodically along the line, booking all offenders.

IN the rain outside the Stock Exchange building, a man was selling umbrellas to hapless investors who had left theirs at home in the mad rush to get to town and sell before the market fell further.

A PADDINGTON reader received a quarterly investment newsletter yesterday from his brokers, one of Sydney's leading firms. Dated October 1987, it read: "It is unlikely the 'crash' predicted by some will occur during the next six months."

LARRY ADLER was asked by Jane Singleton on the ABC's *7.30 Report* what was the difference between a crash and a correction. "A crash is when I lose money," he replied. "A correction is when you lose money."

ONE city office close to the exchange set up a "Make Some Cash from the Crash" sweepstake, gambling on how far the All Ordinaries index, which closed at 2064 points on Monday, would fall by the end of trading yesterday. The range was set from 2000 down to 1670 points – but the index had fallen below that before lunch.

THE INFORMATION booth in the public gallery of the exchange has a chart mapping the peaks and troughs of the market over the past decade. Normally priced at $2.50, it was selling for $1 yesterday.

ON a lighter subject, daylight saving begins again this Sunday. But this year even the sun is a little muddled about the timetable – *The Sun* newspaper that is. The paper's early edition ran a full-page article yesterday telling readers how to spend the extra hour they would gain from turning their clocks back on Saturday night. Only problem is that you're supposed to turn the clocks forward.

EIGHT Bañdido bikies, who pleaded guilty to charges of affray at the Milperra Father's Day shootout, were led into the jury box when they came to the Supreme Court for sentencing yesterday. Seeing where they were, Justice Roden asked: "Who's to be the foreman?"

INSIDE

Agenda	21
Amusements	29
Arts	20
Business	41-49
Comics, Crosswords	68
Editorials	18
Law Notices	68
Lottery J'Pot No.3131	67
Lotto	66
Mails	68
Puzzles	68
Shipping	68
Sport	67-72
Stay in Touch	32
Television	32
Today's People	32

Personal Notices Page 27

Classified Index on Back Page

Classifieds: 282 1122

SMH 40 FR 60

*Recommended and maximum price only. Interstate by air extra

WEATHER

Metropolitan: Cloudy with showers easing. Temperature: City: 14-18, Liverpool: 14-19. Pollution: Low. Yesterday's temperature: City: 15-18, Liverpool 14-18. Pollution: Low.

NSW: Showers on the coast easing. Dry in the west. Fresh winds.

The sea: Rough seas on a moderate swell. TIDES: Low: 12.58am (0.3), High: 7.09am (1.5), Low: 1.15pm (0.4), High 7.18pm (1.5).

Sun: Rises 5.07 sets 6.13.

Moon: Rises 4.09am, sets 4.46pm.

Tomorrow: Mostly cool with a few showers.

Full weather details appear on Pages 32 and 68.

Our ultimate party 97

Bicentennial celebrations, 1988

AFTER THE TRIALS AND TRIBULATIONS OF THE 1987 SHARE MARKET COLLAPSE AND AN INTENSE, DECADE-LONG POLITICAL DEBATE ON AUSTRALIAN NATIONALISM, MULTICULTURALISM AND THE RECOGNITION OF THE BRITISH INVASION OF AUSTRALIA, THE 1988 BICENTENARY OF THE ARRIVAL OF THE FIRST FLEET WAS POTENTIALLY A HUGELY DIVISIVE MOMENT FOR AUSTRALIA.

The celebration of 26 January had never been so important to European Australians, who until as recently as the 1970s, had been more concerned with the arrival of Captain Cook in 1770 than Captain Phillip in 1788, with his eleven ships full of convicts. The 1980s had also seen a significant revision of how Australians saw their history, with descent from convicts becoming a prized mark of family and national history, rather than something to hide.

Despite this groundswell of interest in convict origins, the Bicentennial celebrations of 1988 were plagued with controversy. While Australians of Anglo-Celtic origin were discovering their convict ancestors, the proportion of the population who were migrants from non-British countries had grown significantly. The proportion coming from south-east Asian countries had increased to 20.6 per cent of all migrants in 1987–88. The need to consider the increasingly multicultural heritage of Australia was a prominent element that government and celebration organisers sought to deal with.

An increasingly vocal Indigenous population and their supporters were incensed that the moment of the beginning of the colonisation of Aboriginal Australia was being celebrated in such a fashion. A re-enactment of the voyage of the First Fleet was to be the high point of celebrations in Sydney Harbour and up to the last minute, appeared destined to cause more controversy than celebration.

The Bicentennial protests by Indigenous people and their supporters marked a significant moment in the wider recognition of what many regard as Invasion Day. Still, the following day's news reports of the Bicentennial celebrations in Sydney Harbour show an element of surprise in proceedings that were remarkably, and perhaps typically, Australian—more like a party than a history lesson.

The Sydney Morning Herald

Late Edition · No. 46,827 First Published 1831 · Telephone: Editorial 282 2822; General 282 2833; Classifieds 282 1122 · 45 cents* · 66 pages · Wednesday, January 27, 1988

8 PAGE LIFTOUT INSIDE

THE FIRST FLEET SAILS IN

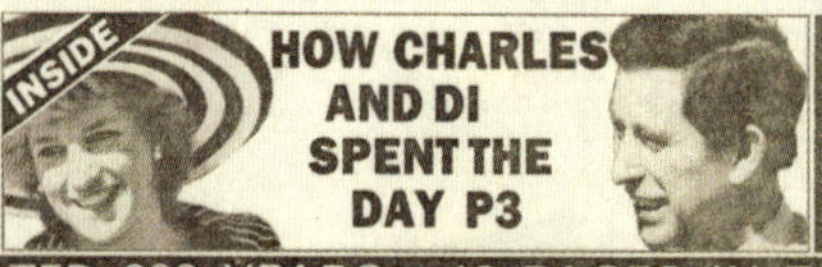

HOW CHARLES AND DI SPENT THE DAY P3

P15 ROBYN WILLIAMS THE NEXT 200 YEARS

HOW WE CELEBRATED 200 YEARS : 13 PAGES IN TODAY'S HERALD

OUR ULTIMATE PARTY

Millions revel into the night

By JANET HAWLEY

Prince Charles stood in Sydney Cove where, thanks to a decision of his British royal forebears, a new nation was founded on January 26, 1788, and said: "As history goes, 200 years is barely a heartbeat. Yet look around you and see what has happened in that time – a whole new free people and a whole new free country, Australia".

And come to look they did, by the million – in fact, an estimated 2.5 million, by far the biggest crowd to attend a single Australian event.

A few hung off the Sydney Harbour Bridge, but most watched from waterfront balconies, city skyscraper rooftops, and swarming along the Harbour foreshore, changing its colourscape to a thick, vivid confetti of humanity and its apparel. Others were in blimps, balloons and helicopters.

The Harbour was a glorious confusion of bow-to-bow boats, luxury yachts, ferries, battered motorboats, rowboats, inflatables, anything that could float. You could have leapt from boat to boat and many did, champagne bottles, beer cans and Australian flags in hand, ruddy grins on faces.

They had come since before dawn – on bicycles, skateboards, wheelchairs, strollers and on foot – to the traffic-free city.

English, Irish, Lebanese, Italian, Greek, Chinese, Russian, Vietnamese came, immigrants from the 130 nationalities that make up this country, wearing shorts, thongs and T-shirts, carrying Eskies, and now speaking in Australian accents, their children waving Australian flags.

And the First Fleeters' descendants came too, in period dress, stockings and breeches, long skirts, lace shawls and mop caps, looking strangely incongruous carrying video portapacks and bags of food and cold drinks.

Sydney has never seen anything like it. The look and the mood of the modern metropolitan city was transformed for the day. There was a spirit of happiness, of good fellowship with whomever you were squashed next to in the throng or spontaneously danced with, a bond of knowing everyone was out in the streets to celebrate what we've got.

And many moments of wet-eyed emotional pride and lumps in the throat as the day's spectacles overawed, from the grand beauty of the Tall Ships to the exuberant explosion of fireworks at night.

It took the Bicentenary to do it, berated, ballyhooed, argued about as an expensive irrelevance – yet it worked. It made us think about what it means to be Australian.

The day's official celebrations began at Customs House, Circular Quay, the spot where Governor Phillip raised the flag on January 26, 1788.

The chairman of the NSW Bicentennial Council, Mr Gerald Gleeson, stressed that Australia was celebrating the 200th birthday of European settlement, adding: "Today we recognise, clearer than before, the traditional owners were dispossessed, and 1988 offers the opportunity to alleviate those disadvantages of Aborigines and all other Australians who suffer disadvantages."

A small group of Aborigines cried "shame", and as the guard-of-honour fired three volleys, the Aborigines began wailing. The symbolism was moving and many of the official guests admitted they felt it.

The main official ceremony took place at the Opera House on Bennelong Point. It was an occasion heavy with ironies.

The point is named after the Aboriginal Bennelong, whom Governor Phillip captured in the white settlers' first ham-fisted attempt to get to know the natives.

Phillip then built a hut for Bennelong on the tip of the point.

The hut was replaced by the Opera House, the world-renown symbol of modern Sydney, designed by a Danish architect whom we hounded out of the country, yet he professes to still love the country and his daughter returned to live here, proving the lure of the spirit of Australia if nothing else will.

Prince Charles, in his speech, seemed to acknowledge the reality that Britain is no longer seen as the motherland, the monarch a ruler no longer but a figurehead.

While he was at school in Australia, he said, "I had the Pommie bits bashed off me", adding that he was delighted to come to help Australia celebrate "as if Aussies needed help in anything".

The band played *Britannia Rules The Waves* as a mighty flypast zoomed overhead, and one wondered if the aside Prince Charles muttered in Lady Diana's ear was: "Sadly dear, no longer."

There was an endearingly Australian moment when the band struck up *Waltzing Matilda*. Mr Gleeson stood up, then so did Prince Charles, the Prime Minister, Mr Hawke, everyone on the official dais and everyone gathered at the Opera House.

Then to round off the day a firework display that started with a 200-gun salute and ended with 200 Roman candles atop the Harbour Bridge.

After the ceremonies the VIPs boarded ferries to cruise the Harbour, and there were some memorable moments: the Foreign Minister, Mr Hayden, racing

Continued Page 2

Ambulances took more than 400 people from Circular Quay to hospital last night, following a big rush to get home.

Crush casualties following the display came in at almost one in every 30 seconds at one stage, said an ambulance spokesman.

The Deputy Chief Controller, Mr Colin Thistlewaite, said the service had barely enough vehicles to handle the situation.

People crammed up the escalators and on to the train platforms at the Quay and nearby Wynard station, creating a danger of people being pushed on to the tracks.

PAGE 3: Full report.

Picture by BRENDAN READ

The Japanese barque, Nippon Maru, moves slowly into the sunset, after the Parade of Sail.

The great land grab of 1988

By DEIRDRE MACKEN

It was a lesson in land rights when about two million people came to share a few square kilometres of Sydney Harbour foreshore to see the ships yesterday.

The spectators came on foot with tents, tarpaulins, rugs and blankets, Eskies, baskets of food and a reserve of goodwill that only birthdays and emergencies seem to generate – and this was to be both.

The people who arrived early – a day early – pitched tents and even when the hordes descended, those tents were treated with as much respect as the flag erected on the foreshore 200 years ago.

The later arrivals accepted their fate (to sit behind trees or in boggy grass) and marked their own territory with rugs, umbrellas, chairs, prams, little flags and discouraging stares.

The markers were as binding as a title deed when itinerants tiptoed over corners of rugs to scuttle down and claim a slippery rock or a flattened bush.

One young man with a broken leg built a tent from a towel and crutch and a man in a wheelchair was given right of way through all blankets.

Occasionally, people overstepped the boundaries. A group of yuppies living in waterfront apartments cordoned off parts of a reserve with a nylon fence and balefully told people who came within footfall that theirs was a private party.

At the house which ex-minister John Brown and publicist Jan Murray rent on Cremorne Point, offspring and friends were celebrating while John and Jan attended other events. The open garden was within easy reach of the young and brash but only one old lady gate-crashed and she was greeted with good cheer.

Even without authority, the common law principle that possession is nine points of the law was embraced by all. Not much separated the natives from the new arrivals – a few metres, an extra chill on the champagne, a few more airs and graces afforded by extra space. But the native residents of Cremorne Point had something that 50,000 new arrivals might have killed for that day – lavatories.

Of all the spots on Cremorne Point yesterday, the most sought after was the only toilet block. The queue for the Men's and Women's stretched around trees, bushes and picnics for an average of one hour and 10 minutes. The concept of separate toilets for sexes disappeared as people made a beeline to the shortest queue.

By midday, when people on the point asked for directions to the toilet they were directed to the pool or the harbour shore.

One woman who held up a blanket on the shore to screen her children found several mothers descending with children to queue up at the blanket. She held up the blanket for everyone, too kind to refuse.

With so many people with such a great need, one would have expected waterfront residents to be besieged by requests. Not so, said residents with relief. One woman at the top of the queue for the toilet block said she thought about asking a resident but decided she preferred the indignity of the wait to the indignity of asking. It was rumoured somebody was offering use of the home lavatory for $10 a visit.

Food and drink was lugged down to the foreshores in quantities that were to make mountains out of garbage bins. One groups of six campers from Canada brought 156 cans of beer, several chickens and boxes of packaged food for a two-day stay.

But for those less well prepared, local entrepreneurs pitched in. Up the road from Cremorne Point, residents in one flat made $150 from selling cans of drink for a dollar each.

Three boys on the point had invested in 500 cans of drink and had pocketed $86 by midday. Just after dawn a resident took an urn of coffee down for the campers to ease hangovers with, at one dollar a cup.

Of course, the natives were not always so friendly.

The owners of the reserve-fronting houses ands flats looked uneasily at the hordes gathering before their homes and wondered when they would all move on again. Owners stood back from their fences with their friends and clan, and sometimes had a few heavy men at their gate to reinforce the title deeds that lay buried in a file somewhere.

There were some salutary lessons in land rights yesterday.

COLUMN 8

MANY harbourside residents found their driveways blocked by parked cars yesterday. But not the one in McMahons Point which had a notice pinned up: "Park here for 4 flat tyres."

NSW Police Minister George Paciullo was so delighted by the peaceful nature of the Aboriginal rally yesterday that he rang the *Herald* himself to say there had been no arrests.

THE STEADY stream of pollies and Queen's representatives received a fairly lacklustre welcome from the public gallery as they arrived at the Opera House's Man o' War steps yesterday. The Master of Ceremonies felt obliged to chide the crowd: "That's not a Sydney welcome."

AT the other end of town, the Aboriginal marchers were marshalling in Belmore Park. As a group of elderly Aboriginal women made their way from the bus, slowly across the park, the crowd drew back, giving them an ovation like none received at Bennelong Point.

THE CROWD at Dover Heights got an extra kick out of the fly-over yesterday. The last of the aircraft had just roared overhead, provoking comment but no cheering, when three seagulls made an unscheduled appearance. They sailed quietly overhead, holding the fly-over course and in a rough arrowhead formation, and received a huge cheer from the throng.

TWO former Prime Ministers arrived in the Opera House forecourt for the official Australia Day ceremony almost simultaneously yesterday. The cars pulled up, the two men alighted, recognised each other and walked off in opposite directions without exchanging a word. But when Gough and Margaret were shown to their places, who should be seated next to them . . . Malcolm and Tammy.

THE BICENTENNIAL spirit was infective. Channel 9's cameras caught Sir Frank and Lady Susan Renouf soaking up the spectacle on the harbour from the terrace of their much contested abode, presently known as Paradise sur Mer.

HOW many missed out? The Bicentennial *Heralds*, all 280,000 copies, sold out so early yesterday that two extra print runs of 5,000 and 3,000 copies were produced during the morning.

ALONG the Rocks' golden restaurant strip near the overseas passenger terminal, one restaurant pinned a $5 surcharge on each guest yesterday. The menu listed the public holiday surcharge as $3. When a Brighton le Sands reader queried the price the manager said: "Oh, let them pay the $3."

HAWKERS selling luminous yo-yos, glowing necklaces and head bands did a roaring trade in Hyde Park. Beside them a woman selling plastic Australian flags hardly made a sale.

RAY Smith, of Concord West, watched the release of thousands of green and gold balloons from Fort Denison yesterday afternoon – on his television. About an hour later he went walking through the Bicentennial Park at Homebush and as he crossed the park one of the green balloons floated down in front of him.

INSIDE

Classifieds: 282 1122

SMH 36 FR 70

*Recommended and maximum price only. Interstate by air extra.

WEATHER

Metropolitan: Mild to warm and mostly sunny. Temperatures: City 17-25, Liverpool 15-28. Pollution: Low. Yesterday's temperature: City 17-25, Liverpool 15-25. Pollution: Low. **NSW:** Mild to warm on the coast. Warm to very warm inland and sunny with light winds.

The sea: Slight on a low swell. Tides: High 4.01am (1.4); Low 10.43am (0.6). High 4.32pm (1.1). Low 10.14pm (0.6). Temp: 21 deg.

Sun: Rises 6.11 sets 8.05.

Moon: Rises 2.48pm, sets 12.54am.

Full weather details appear on Pages 30 & 53.

Tomorrow: Very warm and humid with northerly winds. Chance of late showers.

The Sydney Morning Herald's *front page of 27 January 1988 headlined the partying and pictured the arrival in Sydney Harbour of the tall ships commemorating the arrival of the First Fleet on 26 January 1788.*

Soldier's sadistic 'music'

ARMY recruits were forced to kneel in a line with their backsides in the air then sing musical notes as they were hit by a Corporal wielding a baseball bat, a court martial was told today.

"They were in effect turned into a human xylophone," said an army prosecutor.

Brian Thomas, 29, now a sergeant in the Royal Regiment of Wales, is charged with hitting six recruits – including three whose heads were in rubbish bins.

He is also alleged to have forced a recruit to swallow shampoo and shaving foam, urinated on another, stoned one after forcing him into a river and exposed recruits to CS gas.

UNSWORTH TOLD: HAVE POLL NOW

PREMIER Barrie Unsworth is under strong pressure to announce a February 27 State election in the wake of yesterday's Bicentennial jubilation.

Senior ministers believe the Government's best chance of re-election is to launch straight into a strong, hard-hitting election campaign promoting Labor as being "positive".

But Mr Unsworth said today: "We're not cynical enough to think that the marvellous events of yesterday are enough to win an election.

By MURRAY TREMBATH

"There are more important issues to be considered, particularly the direction we are moving on priority areas such as law and order, health and education.

"Certainly, though, the Bicentenary celebrations reflected a positive approach to our country, and that's something we believe is very important."

Mr Unsworth said yesterday was "just a fantastic day".

"I think the people of Sydney and the many thousands of visitors should be congratulated for the way they conducted themselves.

"They enjoyed themselves thoroughly, without going too far.

"It was a day worthy of our 200th birthday.

"With so many people in the City, it was inevitable that there would be big delays in getting home, but it appears that on the whole people were patient and accepted the situation, many with good humour."

Mr Unsworth praised the organising team headed by the NSW Bicentennial Council chief, Mr Gerry Gleeson, who is also head of the Premier's Department.

"It must be remembered the planning for yesterday's events started five or six years ago," he said.

The official functions went off with clockwork precision, with the First Fleet ships entering Farm Cove "right on the dot" despite having to make their way through thousands of small craft.

Waves of aircraft flew overhead in precision with the music being played in the forecourt of the Opera House.

Government ministers revelled in a series of functions throughout the day.

"We've got to keep the momentum going," said one minister, summing up the feelings of several others.

They were tipping Mr Unsworth would announce the election soon after Prince Charles and Princess Diana leave Australia.

Some ministers thought it could be as early as February 27, or March at the latest.

'I am claiming this land'

● ONE MAN INVASION . . . Burnum Burnum lays claim to England

ABORIGINAL FLAG SIGN OF PROTEST

ABORIGINAL activist Burnum Burnum today took possession of England on behalf of his people.

He staked his claim – which is very unlikely to be recognised by the British – by planting the Aboriginal flag on the sands of Dover in Kent.

"In claiming this colonial outpost we wish no harm to you natives but assure you that we are here to bring you good manners and refinement," he said.

"Henceforth, an Aboriginal face will appear on your coins and stamps to signify our sovereignty over this domain."

Although Burnum said the Queen and her family were now his subjects, the Royal standard still flies above Buckingham Palace.

The ceremony on the Kentish coast was intended as a mockery of Captain Cook's claiming of Australia as a British possession in 1770.

But it also had its serious side as a mockery of Australia Day and the Bicentennial celebrations.

"My declaration here today was an absurdity, but it is only as absurd as Captain Cook's was 200 years ago," he said.

"Aboriginal people should again be allowed to walk tall as regal landlords in their own country.

"And it is my job as a regal lord of my country to regain the land stolen from the Aborigines."

The only witnesses were journalists and photographers.

Besides risking exposure in the icy sea air, Burnum found himself stranded after the ceremony and had to ask a journalist for a lift back to his hotel.

ELTON, ART TO PART

● Elton John

ELTON John is to sell a $7.5 million slice of the art collection he has built up over 20 years – because he is moving to a new country mansion.

The singer, who has failed to sell his $5 million stake in Watford Football Club, has instructed Sotheby's to go through the collection of paintings and furniture.

Sotheby's said today: "He seems to be quite a hoarder and has a massive collection.

Condoms for Royal

PRINCESS Anne was handed a pack of condoms at a conference on AIDS in London today.

As the Princess toured displays warning of the AIDS danger, Mexican Dr Gloria Ornelas rushed up and thrust the package into her hands.

"You cannot come to an AIDS conference without receiving one of those," joked the Princess's guide, Dr Hilary Pickles.

The startled Princess hurriedly passed the gift to an aide.

Earlier, Princess Anne had opened the world summit.

GUN HELD AT WOMAN COP'S HEAD IN BRAWL

A SYDNEY policewoman had her service pistol held to her head and was beaten with a baton during a violent clash outside a Redfern hotel last night.

The young policewoman was also punched in the face during the hour-long confrontation with more than 300 Aborigines.

Eight police officers were injured during the melee but no one was arrested.

Senior police said today investigations "were continuing".

Police were called to Regent Street just before 11pm after an argument between a group of Aborigines and a truck driver.

Twelve officers went to the scene where they arrested a 29-year-old man.

By SIMON BOUDA

As police tried to bundle him into a police truck they were surrounded by more than 300 Aborigines. Officers were threatened and abused.

As the young policewoman called for reinforcements, her pistol and baton were taken from her belt. She was beaten about the legs and body and the pistol was allegedly pointed at her head. Police said another officer recovered her pistol a short time later.

Today Sydney Police District Commander, Executive Chief Superintendent Ken Chapman, said he was investigating reports that the 12 officers at the scene were ordered to withdraw and make no arrests.

Mr Chapman said there had been a communications breakdown during the melee and the order was misinterpreted.

He said the inspector in charge concluded that the incident was "not sufficient" to require additional police.

Mr Chapman added there had been a long-standing arrangement in Redfern that police do not attend incidents in large numbers unless required.

LATE EDITION ● TV PROGRAMS: P29 ● MONEY: P54 ● PUZZLES: P40 ● JACKPOT 3197: P52

THE SUN, Wednesday, January 27, 1988 3

Sydney's Sun*, an afternoon newspaper, of 27 January 1988, recorded an Indigenous protester's action against the Bicentennial celebrations. In a reverse re-enactment, activist Burnum Burnum raised the Aboriginal flag at Dover in England, claiming the country for his people.*

98 *A new beginning*

The Mabo case and land rights for Indigenous Australians, 1992

THE TORRES STRAIT ISLANDS BETWEEN THE NORTHERN TIP OF QUEENSLAND AND PAPUA NEW GUINEA HAD LONG BEEN AT THE CROSSROADS OF AUSTRALIA'S ENGAGEMENT WITH NEIGHBOURING COUNTRIES. THE ISLANDS WERE TOUTED AS THE 'GIBRALTAR OF THE NORTH' AMID LATE NINETEENTH AND EARLY TWENTIETH CENTURY FEARS OF INVASION. THEY HAVE ALWAYS BEEN AN IMPORTANT SITE IN AUSTRALIAN HISTORY, BUT IN THE 1990S THEY WERE TO BECOME A MAJOR FOCUS OF ATTENTION AS THE LAND OWNERSHIP TITLE OF THE ENTIRE CONTINENT CAME INTO QUESTION.

On 20 May 1982, Eddie Koiki Mabo (1936–1992) and others commenced a legal claim for ownership of their lands on the island of Mer in the Torres Strait. Meanwhile, the Queensland government passed an act that attempted to extinguish Indigenous peoples' claims to land ownership. However, the High Court found that the act conflicted with the *Racial Discrimination Act 1975* and was thus invalid.

The Mabo case was finally decided ten years later on 3 June 1992. By then, two of the original petitioners—Celuia Mapo Salee and Eddie Mabo—had died.

The judges held that British claims to possession of Australia in 1770 had not eliminated the ownership title of Indigenous peoples. Following this decision, federal Parliament passed the *Native Title Act 1993*, enabling Indigenous people throughout Australia to claim traditional rights to 'unalienated land'. At first, many pastoralist leaseholders believed the decision undermined their land title, in particular, and there was widespread misunderstanding and political statements that suggested even suburban backyards might be under threat.

However, support among non-Indigenous Australians for some redress of the effects of dispossession on Indigenous communities was growing. By the time of the Mabo decision in 1992, what was to become a widespread popular movement of reconciliation between the First and Second Australians, and eventually, in 2008, a formal apology from the government for past injustices, was well underway.

The Sydney Morning Herald

WEDNESDAY, DECEMBER 22, 1993 — NO. 48,767 FIRST PUBLISHED 1831 44 PAGES 70c*

EQUITY TRUSTS Best since the crash PAGE 27

Making the most of DUTY FREE PAGE 25

Invest in a RACEHORSE PAGE 26

MONEY

Found guilty of tax cheating, MP will devote his time to an appeal

'Dishonest' Smiles quits

By MARK COULTAN
State Political Correspondent

The Liberal MP Mr Phillip Smiles resigned yesterday after being convicted of civil tax charges, forcing a by-election in the seat of North Shore and a political crisis for the Fahey Government.

The by-election will be held within two months. The seat is vulnerable to a strong Independent challenge, and its loss would reduce the Government to 47 seats, the same as the ALP, which has already announced that it will not run a candidate in the seat.

This would mean that the Government would need the support of two of the non-aligned Independents for each piece of legislation.

Mr Smiles's resignation was unexpected, given that he was not convicted of a criminal charge.

But his career was brought to a halt by the combination of the damning words of the magistrate, Mr Derek Price, which accompanied his conviction, a legal opinion from the Solicitor-General, Mr Keith Mason, QC, and a conversation with the Premier, Mr Fahey.

Liberal sources said that it had been made clear to Mr Smiles that, following the judgment, he had no future in State politics.

A tearful Mr Smiles said he was interested in running for Federal politics at some time in the future.

He was resigning because the appeal against his conviction would take up much of his time and he would not be able to represent his constituents.

"There comes a time when you have to be realistic," he said. "Today I chose to be realistic and I have got to say it is not something I do with any glee."

The magistrate convicted Mr Smiles on eight tax charges and imposed a fine of almost $30,000. Mr Price said Mr Smiles's evidence "lacked credibility", was marked by "exaggeration and verbosity", and that the MP had been "dishonest".

A spokesman for Mr Fahey would not confirm the existence of the legal advice from the Solicitor-General, which would significantly widen the reasons under which MPs can be disqualified from Parliament.

Government sources said the Premier had been given the advice, which suggested that the civil tax charges alone might be considered an "infamous crime" under the Constitution Act, and would therefore be grounds for an automatic expulsion from office.

If this were the case, Mr Smiles's resignation would be of no consequence, as he would have ceased to be an MP upon the guilty verdict yesterday morning.

The issue would have ramifications for Mr Smiles's superannuation, believed to be worth about $330,000.

If Mr Smiles's resignation survived a challenge in the light of this advice, he could collect his super. If his convictions amount to an infamous crime, then he is not entitled to his parliamentary pension.

Mr Fahey talked to Mr Smiles yesterday afternoon and, Government sources say, made it clear to him that he did not want the issue to drag over Christmas.

It is believed that the the idea of recalling Parliament tomorrow to decide Mr Smiles's fate was canvassed at the meeting.

Despite Mr Fahey's words, Mr Smiles is believed to be unhappy at the lack of support from his own party. Privately he is bitter that he received more support from Labor parliamentarians than his own colleagues.

Mr Fahey said yesterday: "There have been a number of discussions with Phillip. I made it abundantly clear, as did a number of colleagues who were present, that if Phillip wishes to carry on he would have the support of his party.

"I accepted Phillip's decision with regret and want to place on record very firmly the appreciation of the Government, the Liberal Party, the Coalition, the contribution that Phillip has made over the past nearly 10 years.

"He has been a great supporter and a great team worker.

"I wish him well on behalf of all members of the Government, both in respect of the court case which he has indicated he intends to fight and also in respect of whatever future career he may take on."

Earlier, the ALP spokesman on legal matters, Mr Paul Whelan, called Mr Smiles a "tax cheat" and demanded that Mr Fahey sack Mr Smiles.

PAGE 4: Convictions cost $30,000; Independents eye "safe" Liberal seat; A crisis career.

Mr Smiles in his office after resigning. Picture by STEVEN SIEWERT

WHAT THE MAGISTRATE SAID

'You made claims in each of the relevant returns which you knew to be untrue.'

'Your high standards of integrity and honesty deserted you, unfortunately due to financial pressure.'

'I am satisfied beyond reasonable doubt that (Smiles) actually knew that the salaries paid had not been incurred in the carrying on of the business, that payments made had been claimed as deductions and he signed the tax forms with the knowledge that these claims were false and he knew they were false.'

'At times the defendant's evidence is marked by exaggeration and verbosity. In many respects, his evidence lacks credibility.'

Page 4: Court report

Advice with an infamous sting

By ELIZABETH JURMAN and MARK COULTAN

One of the nastiest surprises in a day of nasty surprises for Mr Smiles was a legal opinion given to the Premier by the NSW Solicitor-General, Mr Keith Mason, QC.

It is understood that the advice said that certain types of tax conviction might be considered an "infamous crime", which, under the NSW Constitution Act, means expulsion from Parliament.

It is generally acknowledged, even by Mr Smiles, that a conviction under the Crimes Act would have been an infamous crime, but the general opinion, and one shared until yesterday by the ALP and Independents, is that civil tax charges do not amount to a hanging offence for a parliamentarian.

If Mr Smiles has been convicted of an infamous crime, then so was Dr Terry Metherell, who pleaded guilty to tax charges in 1990. But no one at the time questioned his standing in Parliament, apparently content at his fall from ministry to backbench.

This may lead to a curious revision of history, since the Metherell Affair would never have happened, and, Mr Nick Greiner would still be Premier.

While "infamous crime" is difficult to define, the last person to be caught out by the provision cheated on his tax.

In 1940, Theodore Charles Trautwein lost his seat in the Legislative Council after being convicted of tax charges under the Commonwealth Crimes Act.

Mr Trautwein had falsely represented that a document had been signed by the parties whose signatures it bore in an attempt to avoid bankruptcy and gain time to raise money owed to the State and Commonwealth Taxation Commissioners.

The court said this was an infamous crime.

According to one legal opinion obtained by the *Herald* – not that of Mr Mason – in Mr Trautwein's case, this false representation to the Commonwealth was held to be analogous to forgery.

Whether or not a conviction for forgery might be obtained, such conduct amounted to an infamous crime under the common law because it was "contrary to the faith, credit and trust of mankind".

Yesterday, the magistrate found that Mr Smiles had made claims on his tax returns that he knew to

Continued Page 4

COLUMN 8

AND IT'S three days to Christmas. Greg Emerson, 43, of Guildford, has been a quadriplegic for 20 years. His widowed mother, Ada, 73, had a stroke this year – but she still has been able to drive him around in a maroon 1972 HQ Kingswood automatic, JEJ 641, fitted with a Flocon hoist to get him in and out. Last Wednesday, about 2.45 pm, Ada parked in a disabled zone in a car park in Memorial Drive, Merrylands, while she walked, with a stick, to the post office. In 10 minutes, some (thanks, PM) scumbag stole the 21-year-old car, obviously owned by handicapped people. It was insured for a mere $1,000 (or $700 when you take off the $300 excess), which is less than the hoist is worth. So now, the Emersons are grounded. Some Christmas.

THE ECONOMY is up on its toes. The Australian Ballet reports it's topped $1 million in advance subscriptions to its 1994 season, starting on March 18, the highest response for three years. And there's more than a week before bookings close.

AIN'T Love Grand (1): Linda Cameli was reading her local paper, the *Wellington Times*, on Monday when she came to a half-page ad: "Linda Cameli will you marry me? – Rob." Yes, yes, yes, she screamed. Robert Bucci, of Florida, met Linda on a flight within Australia three years ago. According to the *Dubbo Liberal*, which ran the story yesterday, Rob had proposed once before, on top of the Statue of Liberty, but she said no. Rob, visiting Linda for Christmas, booked the ad for Monday to coincide with his arrival. The wedding will be in October in Wellington.

AIN'T Love Grand (2): Lynsay Oxborrow, of Greystanes, was in George Street about 11 am yesterday when a teenage boy stopped her and asked: "Can you do me a favour?" She waited while, at a payphone, he dialled a number and told her to ask for a girl by name, saying: "Her dad won't let me speak to her." Being a true romantic, Lynsay obliged. "Who are you?" asked the father. "Are you from McDonald's?" Lynsay assured him she was but, unhappily, the girlfriend was off shopping – so the course of true love again failed to run smooth.

AIN'T Love Grand (3). Jenny, a Balmain grandmother, was wistfully watching a tender tableau in the park opposite her home office. Blue sky, shady tree, picnic lunch, a tender embrace, lingering kisses . . . suddenly, the woman pulls away, and grabs her handbag. Is she leaving? What has he said? Wait . . . out of the bag comes . . . a portable phone. He lolls while she chats, then back to business . . . tender embraces, lingering kisses. Times have changed.

AN EXTRACT from the *Twelve Days of Christmas* in the card sent by one of Dr Hewson's staff:

Seven Seattle sorrys,
Six Lodge staff a-staying,
F-i-v-e L-i-b-e-r-a-l S-t-a-t-e-s.
Four foreign frocks,
Three French clocks,
Two Thai teak tables,
And a Mabo grant up a gum tree.

Mabo a new beginning, says PM

By PAUL CHAMBERLIN
in Canberra

The Federal Mabo bill will be passed by Parliament today, 565 days after the historic High Court decision was handed down.

Amid celebrations by Aboriginal negotiators, the WA Greens senators announced yesterday that the Government had made enough changes to the bill to allow them to join the Democrats in supporting it.

The Prime Minister said the bill's passage would be a turning point for all Australians, while Aboriginal leaders said it was a vital first step towards reconciliation.

But the Opposition Leader, Dr Hewson, said the bill would be a disaster and it was "a day of shame for the Australian Parliament".

And support from the States and territories is either completely gone or only tenuously held.

After almost 70 hours before the Senate, the bill passed through the chamber on the stroke of midnight. It will move to the House of Representatives today, where Government numbers will ensure its passage.

Mr Keating said the legislation would end "the great lie of terra nullius and the beginning, we all hope, of a new deal, the basis of social justice and reconciliation".

"At the start of the debate I was told by a great many people that this could not be done, that the interests were too conflicting, that there was no sufficient goodwill.

"I was told that the scaremongers would prevail, we all heard them, the people who talked about Australians losing their backyards, and we should never forget who they were.

"The passage of this legislation will demonstrate that this generation of Australians will not buy that sort of bigotry, or that brand of politics."

In paying tribute to many Aborigines, politicians and industry leaders involved, Mr Keating also thanked the Greens for coming on board at the end.

"It was a very hard process, I think too hard, but nevertheless the bill will be there."

The core principles remained, he said, and the amendments wrought in the Senate affected only the "operability" of the bill. The first stages of the new native title system will begin operating from January 1.

After his press conference, to the applause of many Aboriginal representatives, Mr Keating kissed and threw his arm around Ms Lois O'Donoghue.

A key negotiator and the chairwoman of the Aboriginal and Torres Strait Islander Commission, Ms O'Donoghue said the important legislation now had to be put in practice.

The director of the Northern Land Council, Mr Noel Pearson, said it was a most important first step in the process of reconciliation.

It was a credit to the "steely nerves" of Mr Keating, the Democrats' leader, Senator Cheryl "Walk on Water" Kernot, and the "glorious greenies", he said. He also praised the performance of the Leader of the Government in the Senate, Senator Evans, in steering the bill through.

There was a need to educate miners that it was not 1958 any more and "the rules have absolutely changed, forever".

Members of the Aboriginal Provisional Government, who had pressed for changes to the original legislation with other Aborigines, said they were now satisfied.

But Dr Hewson said the bill was bad for Aborigines, the economy and the nation, and vowed that the Coalition would make it a major issue between now and the next election. It would divide the country, and millions of people opposed it for being inadequate and hastily cobbled together.

"This bill should never be used as a benchmark for measuring a commitment to justice, dignity and self-respect for Aborigines," Dr Hewson said.

He stood by the tactic of opposing all amendments to the bill, even those which were pro-industry. "This is disastrous legislation; it can't be improved."

He believed the Greens always planned to support the bill, and predicted that it would be significantly amended next year and

Continued Page 6
PAGE 6: PM deserves credit

Your present's under the tree

Mr Keating celebrates the Mabo victory with Ms Lois O'Donoghue and other Aboriginal representatives at Parliament yesterday . . . a turning point for all Australians. Picture by PALANI MOHAN

Johns wins ministry spot

By MICHAEL MILLETT and ANNE DAVIES

CANBERRA: Caucus ended the factional jockeying over the spoils of Mr Dawkins's departure from the Keating ministry by appointing the Centre Left's Mr Gary Johns to the front bench yesterday.

Mr Johns, who narrowly missed promotion in the post-election reshuffle, becomes the third Queenslander in the 32-person ministry.

The Caucus ballot went along factional lines with the dominant Right joining the Centre Left in supporting Mr Johns over the Left's candidate, Mr Warren Snowdon. The result was 59 to 49, with one informal.

The main interest now is the detail of the new frontbench, to be announced by Mr Keating, possibly today.

While the Prime Minister is giving little away, it appears he may be extending his reshuffle beyond the minimum required to simply accommodate the Finance Minister, Mr Willis, as the new Treasurer.

There was intense speculation last night that the Minister for Transport and Communications, Senator Collins, may be assigned to a new portfolio, probably Primary Industries.

Senator Collins's political ascent has been severely checked by the problems arising in the pay TV tender, and a move to the Primary Industries portfolio would be regarded as a sideways move at best. It has again fuelled speculation that the Prime Minister will split the Transport and Communications portfolio, which has long been regarded as too large and too complex for one senior minister.

The Resources Minister, Mr Lee, is tipped to take over the Transport side, retaining his Tourism responsibilities, although it is possible he will become the senior minister if it is not split.

Senator Collins's junior minister, Mr Beddall, who has responsibility for the Communications side of the department, was also tipped to move, after a lacklustre nine months in the job.

He is likely to be moved to a lower-profile portfolio, such as Veterans' Affairs.

Last night the Minister for Arts and Administrative Services, Senator McMullan, was putting in a strong bid to have communications policy brought within his portfolio to create a department of communications and culture.

The Minister for Employment, Education and Training, Mr Beazley, appears likely to move into Mr Willis's Finance job, with Mr Crean shifting from Primary Industries to Employment.

The Right declined to nominate a candidate for the ministerial vacancy, acknowledging the claim of the Centre Left for the position.

According to faction members, there was no explicit deal involved in the Right's decision to support the Centre.

But it is understood the "bargaining process" has increased the chances of another Queenslander, Mr Con Sciacca, gaining the next ministerial promotion.

Despite predictions of a big leakage of Right votes because of animosity in the Queensland Right to Mr Johns, the faction's vote was well disciplined.

Left sources said they estimated only about four or five defections in the final vote, well short of what was needed to get Mr Snowdon over the line.

Mr Johns, parliamentary secretary to the Treasurer, said after the ballot he was not concerned about which portfolio he would be offered by Mr Keating.

Mr Johns . . . elevated to the front bench.

Fairfax director resigns

Mr Gary Pemberton has resigned from the board of John Fairfax Holdings Ltd, citing his additional commitments as chairman of Qantas Airways and president of the Sydney Organising Committee for the 2000 Olympic Games. PAGE 35: Full report.

Light relief for the Blues

The Sheffield Shield clash at the SCG ended last night with NSW escaping defeat by Victoria when umpires agreed to an appeal against the light with one wicket left and 31 runs still needed. PAGE 44: Match report.

WEATHER TODAY Sydney: 19 to 26. Rain and thunderstorms. Liverpool: 18 to 28. NSW: Cloudy with rain and isolated storms contracting east. TOMORROW Sydney: An early shower and a maximum of 24. NSW: Showers in the south-east corner and on the coast. FULL DETAILS 39.

PHONE Editorial 282 2822, Classifieds 282 1122, General 282 2833, Fax 282 1640

In The Sydney Morning Herald *of 22 December 1993 Prime Minister Paul Keating's welcoming comment on the successful Mabo case is headlined. He is seen here with Lois O'Donoghue and other Indigenous representatives at Parliament House.*

99 Terrorism strikes home

The Bali bombing, 2002

AUSTRALIA HAD EXPERIENCED MINOR TERRORIST-STYLE ATTACKS ON HOME SOIL IN THE PAST, SUCH AS THE BATTLE OF BROKEN HILL IN 1915, WHERE TWO DISAFFECTED MUSLIM MEN SHOT AND KILLED SEVERAL PEOPLE ON A TRAIN CROWDED WITH PICNICKERS, BEFORE MAKING A NINETY-MINUTE LAST STAND IN A SHOOT-OUT WITH POLICE AND CIVILIANS. THE TWO CAMEL DRIVERS LEFT SUICIDE NOTES THAT SAID THEY WERE GIVING THEIR LIVES TO THE OTTOMAN (TURKISH) SULTAN WHO WAS AT WAR WITH THE BRITISH EMPIRE.

As a relatively isolated country, and well after violent conflicts with Aboriginal Australians had ceased, modern Australia had generally escaped serious political violence. However, after the devastating terrorist attacks on the United States on 11 September 2001 and a closer political alignment with the US, Australia had become increasingly connected with the tensions and conflict between Islamic extremists and Western nations around the world.

The island of Bali in Indonesia was a favourite tourist destination for Australians, but its serenity and party atmosphere were shattered when two crowded nightclubs in Kuta were bombed by terrorists, with the aim of killing as many foreigners as possible. The two explosions killed more than 200 people and wounded many more: 88 Australians were among the 162 foreign nationals killed; 38 Indonesian citizens (mostly Balinese) were also killed.

News of the attack and the initial death toll of eighty-seven Australians shocked the nation. The idea that Australians were relatively immune to the increasing terror attacks around the globe was bitterly shattered on the night of 12 October 2002.

The Sydney Morning Herald

Monday October 14, 2002 — **First published 1831** No. 51,511 **$1.20** (incl GST)

HORROR TOLL IN BALI

TERRORISM STRIKES HOME

"There was a massive explosion . . . from the front of the club. It was the biggest bang you can handle." The Sari Club, in the heart of Bali's Kuta tourist strip, ablaze in the early hours of yesterday morning. Photo: Per Wiklund

■ Act of barbarity: Howard ■ 182 dead ■ Emergency medical teams sent

Tales of horror
Walking wounded tell their survival stories.
Page 3

Bad news warning
Australians told to brace for casualties.
Page 3

Security alert
John Howard flags major security review.
Page 5

ISSN 0312-6315
9 770312 631018

Weather details – Page 2

Matthew Moore
in Kuta
and Mark Riley

The bomb blast that ripped apart Bali's entertainment precinct late on Saturday night has killed 182 people and injured more than 240, stamping terrorism's bloody fingerprint on Australia's door.

The devastating attack has also raised serious questions about the stability of Indonesia, Australia's nearest and most powerful neighbour.

Scores of Australians who were holidaying in the Indonesian tourism capital are believed to be among the dead and injured. Sixty-three of those listed as injured were said to be Australians, although large numbers of people are still missing as friends and families search hospitals and the morgues.

Indonesian authorities have confirmed that the blast which destroyed two nightclubs on Kuta's main street, the Sari Club and Paddy's Irish Bar, was caused by a car bomb. Witnesses reported two explosions in quick succession about 11.30pm, the second bigger than the first.

The clubs were filled with holiday revellers, many on end-of-season football trips from Australia. "It's nothing quite like anything I've ever seen – there was more blood, the smell of burnt skin and the pain that they were in, you can't really put that into words," said a tourist from Melbourne, Martin Lyons.

Damon Brinson, who was with teammates from the Kingsley Australian Rules club in Perth, said: "One minute we were partying – the next, the whole lot went up. We ran for our lives."

The Prime Minister, John Howard, labelled the attack a "wicked and cowardly" act.

"The indiscriminate, brutal and despicable way in which lives have been taken away on this occasion by an act of barbarity will, I know, deeply shock all Australians," he said.

"I can only say again that the war against terrorism must go on with unrelenting vigour and with an unconditional commitment."

There had been no specific warnings before the attack but that Australia had raised general concerns with Indonesia in recent months, he said.

Mr Howard called an urgent meeting of cabinet's National Security Committee for this morning to review Australia's security arrangements.

Shortly after the Kuta blast, another smaller bomb exploded near a United States consular office in the Balinese capital of Denpasar. There are also suspicions that a blast earlier in the day at the Philippines embassy in Manado, the capital of Sulawesi island, may be connected.

A team of Australian Federal Police and ASIO investigative, forensic and intelligence agents flew to Bali last night to join Indonesian police in the hunt for those responsible. The Balinese police chief, Brigadier-General Budi Setyawan, vowed to resign if he did not find those responsible within a month.

The Department of Foreign Affairs and Trade estimated about 20,000 Australians would normally be in Bali at this time of year.

An RAAF C130 Hercules aircraft flew a team of surgeons and specialist nurses to Bali yesterday amid concerns that the island's basic hospital services were being overwhelmed. The most seriously hurt of the Australian casualties were being airlifted back to Australia for treatment last night.

The biggest terrorist attack ever involving Australians comes after months of US criticism of Indonesia's efforts against terrorist groups, including al-Qaeda, operating within its borders.

Indonesia's Security Minister, Susilo Bambang Yudhoyono, yesterday issued his Government's first official admission that terrorists were operating within its borders, describing the bombing "as a warning to all of us that terrorism is in our backyard".

But he and President Megawati Soekarnoputri and the police declined to say who they believed was responsible.

A senior military source said indications pointed to a foreign group.

"The message is not for Indonesians, it's probably for the Australians given the fact many of the victims are Australian," he said.

"People understand Australian and Britain support the US plan to attack Iraq."

'People were burning, dying. It was an inferno'

Philip Cornford, Brigid Delaney, Elisabeth Sexton and agencies

Both nightclubs were bursting at the seams. Hot, sweaty, noisy, they pulsated with a frantic life force. Mostly, they were young, single Australians on the make, in beautiful and sensuous Bali for a blowout.

None of the patrons blasting Saturday night into oblivion at the Sari or Paddy's Irish Pub, the two most popular nightspots along the raunchy Jalan Legian, could have had a hint of the disaster about to befall them.

This was Kuta, playground of Denpasar, a place where the excesses were alcoholic and sexual and entirely permitted.

At Sari's, aka SCs, the most popular drink was the local Bintang beer, served in huge bongs. With a high thatched roof which let in the rain, it had an uneasy Balinese touch, out of step with the modern beat. It also had the distinction of refusing entry to locals.

Paddy's was directly across the JL Legian, the city's busiest entertainment strip, lined with bars and clubs and small shops catering to tourists. A two-storey structure described as a "cross between a *Gilligan's Island* hut and a Smurf village house", it showcased bottle-juggling bartenders, a classic rock band downstairs and techno groove in the huge upstairs room.

After 11 on Saturday night, both bars were full to bursting. Among drinkers at Sari Club were Australian Rules football teams from Melbourne, Geelong, Perth and Adelaide on season-end celebrations.

Twenty-five players from the Platypi Rugby Union club from Forbes in western NSW
Continued Page 7

The Sydney Morning Herald of 14 October 2002 records the horror of the Bali bombings. By now, colour images, which could be transmitted around the world in seconds, commonly accompanied headline stories.

100 *From bushfire to firestorm*

Black Saturday bushfires, 2009

AS NEWS DEVELOPED OF SERIOUS BUSHFIRES IN VICTORIA DURING EARLY FEBRUARY 2009, NO-ONE WAS PREPARED FOR THE TRAGEDY THAT WAS TO UNFOLD OVER BLACK SATURDAY.

In late January a heatwave continued over many days across Victoria, and dangerous fire conditions were anticipated. On 6 February, when strong winds were predicted, more than 3500 fire-fighters were deployed across Victoria. The next day Melbourne recorded its hottest day ever, the temperature reaching 46.4 degrees Celsius. By mid-morning on Saturday, 7 February, hot north-westerly winds blowing at more than 100 kilometres per hour, combined with extremely high temperatures and low humidity, made conditions incredibly dangerous.

A series of smaller fires that began in several areas across central Victoria merged into the most intense firestorm ever seen in Australian modern history. Several rural towns were completely destroyed. The townships of Kingslake and Marysville were two of the worst hit: in Marysville, all but fourteen of the town's four hundred buildings were destroyed, and thirty-four people died.

At first the scale of the tragedy could not be properly established until the fires were contained. Several fires continued to burn for days. By the following Tuesday, when police and then journalists could visit the devastated areas, the nation witnessed some of the most horrific images in its history.

The damage from the fires was unheard of. More than 3500 buildings were destroyed; thousands of head of livestock killed; and infrastructure and forests saw massive damage. The total number of deaths was eventually confirmed at 173. It was the worst fire disaster in Australian history. The subsequent scale of public response to appeals for victim assistance was unprecedented, and a royal commission into the state government's bushfire strategy began in 2009. Significant changes in the warning system were recommended, and ideas and policies on exactly when to 'stay or go' (evacuate or protect a home) came under particular scrutiny.

THE SUNDAY AGE
FEBRUARY 8, 2009
theage.com.au
$2
"It was only when the ash started to fall like black confetti and the sun above, obscured by smoke, turned the colour of a red-hot ball-bearing that the threat seemed real. As it burnt through the bush the fire was an alien force."
IN THE EYE OF THE FIRESTORM PAGE 3
• At least seven dead • Bushfires threaten Melbourne • More than 100 homes destroyed

DAY OF HORROR

MICHAEL BACHELARD
CAMERON HOUSTON
CARMEL EGAN, TOM REILLY,
STEVE HOLLAND
WINSTON TAN

AT LEAST seven people were dead last night, more than 100 homes razed and dozens of rural communities fighting to save houses and livestock as bushfires ravaged Victoria from east to west.

As temperatures soared to record highs yesterday, more than 3000 firefighters battled blazes across the state.

There were unconfirmed reports last night that 150 people were gathered in the CFA in station at Kinglake.

Police said another two badly injured CFA officers had been airlifted out of the town of Buxton, north of Marysville.

The town of Kinglake was under severe threat as the afternoon's cool change pushed one of the most ferocious fires, raging out of control north of Melbourne, towards the town.

It is believed at least one person was killed in a four-car collision on the Whittlesea-Kinglake Road.

Police said there were serious concerns for the welfare of Communities from Brandy Creek and Rokeby in the east, through Healesville to Flowerdale in the north were battling to save homes last night.

The squally cool change opened up new fire fronts on a number of fires, rendering them even more dangerous.

The fires were driven by temperature of 46.4, which topped the previous record, set on Black Friday in 1939, and a hot wind of up to 98km/h.

One farmer was in critical condition in hospital with burns to 50 per cent of his body, and another suffered facial burns. A spokesman for Ambulance Victoria said numerous firefighters for heat, stress and smoke inhalation.

Russell Rees, chief fire officer with the CFA, predicted more losses over the next day and a half.

Hot weather, high wind and fires also threw the state's transport into chaos with the Hume Freeway, the Princes Highway, Eastlink and three regional rail lines closed, and 200 Connex suburban services cancelled.

A fire burning at Ferntree Gully severely damaged the Belgrave train line, with trains between Belgrave and Ringwood out of service for at least a few days.

The mercury in the city topped 46.4 degrees at 3.04 pm.

Electricity was nearly cut to the city when fires at Kilmore knocked out two major transmission lines from NSW, and two of the four lines from the Latrobe Valley to Melbourne were also cut.

However, 60,000 customers were still suffering blackouts, mostly in the fire-effected east of the state, and north-east, from Kilmore, to Pakenham and Traralgon.

A spokesman for electricity market regulator NEMMCO said if one more Latrobe Valley line had gone down, the state would have been forced into widespread blackouts.

"The fact that stayed in place enabled us to resecure the network . . . we're in a much better position than we were two hours ago," said spokesman Paul Bird.

The most dangerous fires were at Horsham, where 5700 hectares were burned out before the cool change tamed it; Kilmore, which swept through the towns of Wandong, Hidden Valley, Heathcote Junction and almost to Whittlesea; and Bunyip and Churchill, where 2400 hectares were burned.

Last night other fires threatened Yarra Glenn, Marysville and Buxton, while Healesville residents were warned of ember attacks.

Melbourne's hospitals were on high alert in preparation for a deluge of cases, but the feared medical crisis largely failed to materialise.

Both the Royal Melbourne and St Vincent's admitted six people uffering from conditions linked to the sweltering temperatures but no case proved fatal, unlike last weekend when scores of deaths were linked to the heatwave.

Despite this, the triple-0 service experienced such a high volume of calls, most related to the firest, that other callers were struggling to get through.

"We have been trying to let people know through the ABC, not to call triple 0 unless it is an emergency," a police spokeswoman said.

There were at least 10 uncontrolled fires burning last night.

INSIDE
How we sweltered PAGE 2
Fires special PAGE 3

Happy 21st for soap

THE enduring popularity of *Home and Away* has been demonstrated by fans who snapped up a magazine to mark the Channel Seven soap's 21st anniversary. Seven has admitted being caught out and hurriedly commissioned a second print run of the magazine.

Home and Away forever PAGE 12

WEATHER

TODAY Shower or two, 24
TOMORROW Few showers, 21
TUESDAY Showers, windy, 20
WEDNESDAY Early shower, 20
THURSDAY Morning cloud, 25
FRIDAY Sunny, 28
DETAILS PAGE 25

ISSN 1034-1021
9 771034 102008

Top advisers warned against desal plant, north-south pipe

MELISSA FYFE
STATE POLITICS

ONE of the State Government's top strategic consultants advised cabinet against building the controversial desalination plant and the north-south pipeline in an alternative water plan that has since been suppressed.

The $295,000 cabinet-commissioned review of the city's water crisis was delivered to ministers in early June 2007. Two weeks later, the Government unveiled its $4.9 billion water package, featuring the Wonthaggi desalination plant and the pipeline, two of the state's most contentious projects.

The consultancy firm ACIL Tasman, which sits on a variety of strategic advice panels for the State Government, had told cabinet not to commission projects such as the desalination plant until it was absolutely necessary. Rather, it advised cabinet to ensure it was "ready" to proceed if required – by, for example, smoothing the way for planning approval and conducting feasibility studies.

The Sunday Age believes the report also recommended a significant investment in water-saving measures.

The report, *Review of Victorian Water Supply-Demand Options and Risks*, was described by the Department of Sustainability's media advisers as "highly sensitive" and suppressed by the Government, which cited cabinet confidentiality. Attempts by *The Sunday Age* to obtain it under freedom-of-information laws have twice been thwarted by the department.

In denying *The Sunday Age* access, department secretary Peter Harris said the document was "specifically commissioned and prepared for consideration by a Committee of Cabinet".

Critics of the Government's water plan say cabinet failed to consider and investigate other alternatives – such as reusing and recycling water, rain tanks and stormwater capture – before committing to the energy-intensive desalination plant and the pipe that channels water from the country to the city.

But Water Minister Tim Holding told *The Sunday Age* that if the Government had followed the report's advice "Melbourne would run out of water in the next couple of years". The advice was based on the inflows of water to the city's catchments between 2004 and 2006. These years saw an average of 354 billion litres of water flow into Melbourne's dams each year, but the annual average for 2006 to 2008 was 274 billion litres.

"The 'worst-case scenario' outlined in the report has since proven to be far too optimistic," he said. "The Government adopted a far more conservative and prudent approach through committing to build Australia's largest desalination plant and implementing a $2 billion project to save water lost through leaky old irrigation channels.

"The current state of our storages and the extreme weather pattern we are experiencing reinforce the importance of the Government acting immediately to invest in major projects to boost water supplies."

Opposition urban water spokeswoman Louise Asher said the Government's water strategy had been to pray for rain. "That hasn't worked and the existence of this report is evidence that the Government is . . . making decisions not based on proper advice."

ACIL Tasman is one of the 20 hand-picked contractors on the Department of Treasury and Finance's $8 million strategic research panel. According to the Government's contract website, it was initially contracted to "deliver a best practice urban water investment decision-making framework".

Victory knocks off Adelaide

MELBOURNE Victory defeated Adelaide 2-0 in its clash at Hindmarsh Stadium last night and now has the upper hand going in to next week's rematch at home against the Reds in the first stage of the A-League finals.

SPORT

Turnbull takes cash from market 'vulture'

JOSH GORDON
FEDERAL POLITICS

MALCOLM Turnbull has taken a large campaign donation from an American billionaire closely linked to the predatory lending practices that triggered the subprime lending crisis and global recession.

An investigation by *The Sunday Age* revealed that Peter Briger, chairman and director of controversial "vulture company" Fortress Investment Group, contributed $US50,000 ($A75,000) to the Liberal campaign fund for the Opposition leader's seat of Wentworth last year.

Mr Turnbull previously held shares in Fortress, but offloaded them in 2007, just after US presidential hopeful John Edwards was forced to distance himself from the firm following controversy over its practices and foreclosures on victims of hurricane Katrina in New Orleans.

Mr Briger made the campaign donation in March, but Mr Turnbull disclosed it to the Australian Electoral Commission in November.

A spokesman for Mr Turnbull confirmed the links, but stated "many global institutions, including many Australian ones, have had a direct or indirect connection to the subprime crisis". The Turnbull family had sold its Fortress shares for a profit of just over $1000, he said.

The spokesman refused to say why Mr Briger had contributed to Mr Turnbull's campaign coffers and if he was an appropriate source of political funding.

"Like the Rudd family, Mr Turnbull makes full disclosure of all his interests," he said, alluding to the pre-election controversy over Therese Rudd's businesses interests. "Like the Rudd family, Mr Turnbull does not discuss personal family finances."

The spokeman would not clarify how a donation to the Wentworth campaign fund could be considered personal family finances.

Fortress is referred to as a "vulture company" because it preys on vulnerable businesses and debtors, and picks over financial carcasses. Mr Briger was listed by *Forbes* magazine in 2007 as having a net worth of $US2.3 billion. He is also a former partner at Goldman Sachs, the same company where Mr Turnbull made his millions as a merchant banker.

Mr Turnbull altered his parliamentary register of interests in March 2007, stating he had sold his interest in Fortress after *The Washington Post* attacked Mr Edwards for working for, and investing in, the firm.

Revelations that Mr Turnbull held shares in the company and received a generous political donation from its director come at an awkward time for the Liberal leader.

Labor has spent much of the past week in Parliament trying to paint Mr Turnbull as an agent of unrestrained greed and wanton neo-liberalism.

EDITORIAL PAGE 22

Melbourne's Sunday Age *of 8 February 2009 headlined what became known as Black Saturday as a 'Day of Horror', recording some of the earliest news of the bushfires. It would be days before the full extent of the horror of the firestorm across central Victoria would be known.*

Newspapers

The Abo Call, Sydney, 1938.

Adelaide Advertiser, Adelaide, 1931—.

The Age, Melbourne, 1854—.

Argus (Melbourne Argus), Melbourne, 1848–1957.

The Australian, Sydney, 1964—.

The Bulletin, Sydney, 1880–2008.

Colonial Times, Hobart, 1828–1857.

Colonial Times and Tasmanian Advertiser, Hobart, 1825–1827.

The Courier–Mail, Brisbane, 1846—.

Daily Mirror, Sydney, 1941–1990.

The Daily Telegraph, Sydney, 1879–1990.

The Daily Telegraph–Mirror, Sydney, 1990–1996.

Geelong Advertiser and Intelligencer, Geelong, Victoria, 1840—.

The Herald, Melbourne, 1855–1990.

Hobart Town Gazette and Van Diemen's Land Advertiser, Hobart Town, 1821–1825.

London Evening Post, London, 1771.

Melbourne Morning Herald, Melbourne, 1840–1855.

The Perth Gazette and Western Australian Journal, Perth, 1833–1847.

Port Phillip Patriot and Melbourne Advertiser, Melbourne, 1839–1845.

The Referee, Sydney, 1886–1939.

South Australian Gazette and Colonial Register, Adelaide, 1836–1839.

The Sun, Sydney, 1910–1931.

The Sun News–Pictorial, Melbourne, 1922–1990.

Sunday Telegraph, Sydney, 1939—.

The Sydney Gazette, and New South Wales Advertiser, Sydney, 1803–1842.

The Sydney Herald, Sydney, 1831–1842.

The Sydney Mail, Sydney, 1912–1938.

The Sydney Monitor, Sydney, 1826–1840.

The Sydney Morning Herald, Sydney, 1842—.

The True Colonist. Van Diemen's Land Political Despatch, and Agricultural and Commercial Advertiser, Hobart Town, 1834–1844.

The Truth, Melbourne, 1902–1958.

The Truth, Sydney, 1890–1958.

The Voice of the Maltese in Australia and Farmers' Advocate Weekly, Sydney, 1931.

The West Australian, Perth, 1879—.

Journals

Dampier, William. *A New Voyage Round the World*, A. and C. Black Ltd., London, 1937 (1697). Retrieved 21 May 2010, from http://gutenberg.net.au/ebooks05/0500461h.html#ch16

Mitchell, Thomas. *Three Expeditions into the Interior of Eastern Australia: with Descriptions of the Recently Explored Region of Australia Felix, and of the Present Colony of New South Wales*, 2nd edn, T. & W. Boone, London, 1839.

Pelsaert, Francisco. *Ongeluckige voyagie van't schip Batavia* (The Unlucky Voyage of the Ship *Batavia*), Jan Jansz, Amsterdam, 1647. Retrieved 21 May 2010, from http://www.slwa.wa.gov.au/treasures/pelsaert/index.htm

Price, John. 'Journey into the interior of the country New South Wales, 24 January–2 February 1798'. Retrieved 21 May 2010, from http://www.sl.nsw.gov.au/discover_collections/history_nation/exploration/early/interior/price.html

Tench, Watkin. *A Narrative of the Expedition to Botany Bay: With an Account of New South Wales, Its Productions, Inhabitants etc.* Printed for J. Debrett, London, 1789.

Books

Abbott, G. J. and Nairn, N. B. (eds). *Economic Growth in Australia 1788–1821*, Melbourne University Press, Carlton, Victoria 1979.

Albany Advertiser. *Albany Advertiser 1888–2003: 115 years of news*, Albany Advertiser, Albany, Western Australia, 2003.

Alpin, Graeme (ed.). *A Difficult Infant: Sydney Before Macquarie*, University of New South Wales Press, Kensington, NSW, 1988.

Atkinson Alan, *The Europeans in Australia: A History*, Volume 1, Oxford University Press, Melbourne, 1997.

Australian Dictionary of Biography, Australian National University, Canberra, 2006. Retrieved 21 May 2010, from http://adbonline.anu.edu.au/adbonline.htm

Australian Newspaper History Group. *Australian Newspaper History: A Bibliography* Australian Newspaper History Group, Middle Park, Queensland, 2004.

Baker, D. W. A. *The Civilised Surveyor: Thomas Mitchell and the Australian Aborigines*, Melbourne University Press, Carlton, Victoria 1997.

Bird, Wal. *Me no go Mally Bulla: Recruiting and Blackbirding in the Queensland Labour Trade 1863–1906*, Ginninderra Press, Charnwood, ACT, 2005.

Blaikie, George. *Remember Smith's Weekly? A Biography of an Uninhibited National Australian Newspaper, Born 1 March 1919, Died 28 October 1950*, Rigby, Adelaide, 1975.

Bramble, Thomas. *Trade Unionism in Australia: A History from Flood to Ebb Tide*, Cambridge University Press, Melbourne, 2008.

Brett, Judith. *Robert Menzies' Forgotten People*, Melbourne University Press, Carlton, Victoria, 2007.

Butlin, Noel. *Forming a Colonial Economy: Australia 1810–1850*, Cambridge University Press, Melbourne, 1994.

Camm, J. C. R., and McQuilton, John (eds). *Australia: A Historical Atlas*, Fairfax, Syme & Weldon Associates, Sydney, 1987.

Campbell, Judy. *Invisible Invaders: Smallpox and Other Diseases in Aboriginal Australia 1780–1880*, Melbourne University Press, Carlton, Victoria, 2002.

Cannon, Michael. *Famous News Pages in Modern Australian History*, Heritage Publications, Melbourne, 1973.

Chronicle of Australia: The Complete Story of Our Nation, Viking-Penguin, Ringwood, Victoria, 2000.

Coad, David. *A History of Tasmania Volume 1*. David Coad, Kingston, Tasmania, 2009.

Connor, John. *The Australian Frontier Wars 1788–1838*, University of New South Wales Press, Coogee, NSW, 2000.

Connor, Michael (ed.). *Pig Bites Baby*. Duffy and Snellgrove, Potts Point, NSW, 2004.

Docherty, James C. *Historical Dictionary of Australia*, Scarecrow Press, Plymouth, UK, 2007.

Dunn, Frank Penrose. *A Century of Sundays*. Sunday Times, Darlington, Western Australia, 1997.

Dutton, Geoffrey. *The Squatters: An Illustrated History of Australia's Pastoral Pioneers*, Viking O'Neill, Ringwood, Victoria, 1989.

Evans, Neil, and Cannon, Mary (eds.). *Eureka Stockade: As Reported in the Pages of the* Argus *Newspaper*, State Library Victoria, Melbourne, 1998.

Ewer, Peter. *Forgotten ANZACS: The Campaign in Greece 1941*, Scribe, Carlton North, Victoria, 2008.

Famous News Pages in Modern Australian History, Heritage Publications, Melbourne, 1973.

Fitzgerald, Shirley. *Red Tape Gold Scissors: The Story of Sydney's Chinese*, Halstead, Sydney, 2008.

Fraser, Bryce (ed.). *The Macquarie Encyclopedia of Australian Events*, Macquarie Library, North Ryde, NSW, 1997.

Gammage, Bill. *The Broken Years: Australian Soldiers in the Great War*, Melbourne University Press, Carlton, Victoria, 2010.

Gapps, Stephen. *Cabrogal to Fairfield: A History of a Multicultural City*, Fairfield City Council, Fairfield, NSW, 2010.

Gibbs, R. M. *A History of South Australia: From Colonial Days to the Present*, Southern Heritage, Mitcham, South Australia, 1999.

Goodall, Heather. *Invasion to Embassy: Land and Aboriginal Politics in New South Wales, 1770–1972*, Allen & Unwin, St Leonards, 1996.

Gregory, Jenny, and Gothard, Jan. *Historical Encyclopedia of Western Australia*, University of Western Australia Press, Claremont, Perth, 2009.

Hocking, Geoff. *Mr Burke and Mr Wills: Epic Journey to a Lonely Death*, Five Mile Press, Waverton, NSW, 2005.

Hocking, Geoff. *Gold: A Pictorial History of the Australian Goldrush*, Five Mile Press, Rowville, Victoria, 2006.

Hoskins, Ian. *Sydney Harbour: A History*, University of New South Wales Press, Coogee, NSW, 2009.

Inglis, Ken. *Australian Colonists: An Exploration of Social History 1788–1870*, Melbourne University Press, Carlton, Victoria, 1993.

Irving, Helen (ed.). *The Centenary Companion to Australian Federation*, Cambridge University Press, Melbourne, 1999.

Irving, Helen. *To Constitute a Nation: A Cultural History of Australia's Constitution*, Cambridge University Press, Melbourne, 1999.

Isaacs, Victor. *Looking Good: The Changing Appearance of Australian Newspapers*. Australian Newspaper History Group, Middle Park, Queensland, 2007.

Isaacs, Victor, and Kirkpatrick, Rod. *Two Hundred Years of Sydney Newspapers: A Short History*, Rural Press, North Richmond, NSW, 2003.

Isaacs, Victor, and Kirkpatrick, Rod (eds). *The Australian Press — A Bicentennial Retrospect.* Australian Newspaper History Group, Middle Park, Queensland, 2003.

Isaacs, Victor, Kirkpatrick, Rod, and Russell, John (eds). *Australian Newspaper History: A Bibliography.* Australian Newspaper History Group, Middle Park, Queensland, 2004.

Johnston, Gary, and Simmelhaig, Helen. *Frontpage History*, CCH Australia Ltd, Sydney, 1980.

Jones, Howard C. *The Border Mail: A Century Together*, Border Morning Mail, Wodonga, Victoria, 2003.

Jones, Ian. *Ned Kelly: A Short Life*, Hachette Livre, Sydney, 2008.

Jupp, James. *From White Australia to Woomera: The Story of Australian Immigration*, Cambridge University Press, New York, 2003.

Karskens, Grace. *The Colony: A History of Early Sydney*, Allen & Unwin, St Leonards, NSW, 2009.

Kepert, Lou V. (ed.). *History as it Happened*, Nelson, Melbourne, 1981.

Kirkpatrick, Rod. *Country Conscience: A History of the New South Wales Provincial Press 1841–1995*, Infinite Harvest Publishing, Canberra, 2000.

Kirkpatrick, Rod. *Press Timeline: Select Chronology of Significant Australian Press Events 1802–2005*, Australian Newspaper History Group, Middle Park, Queensland, 2006.

Levell, David. *Tour to Hell: Convict Australia's Great Escape Myths*, University of Queensland Press, St Lucia, Queensland, 2008.

Lord, Peter. *125 years of the* Advertiser, Advertiser Newspapers, Adelaide, 1983.

Milliss, Roger. *Waterloo Creek: The Australia Day Massacre of 1838, George Gipps and the British Conquest of New South Wales*, McPhee Gribble, Ringwood, Victoria, 1992.

Nairn, Bede. *The Big Fella: Jack Lang and the Australian Labor Party 1891–1949*, Melbourne University Press, Carlton, Victoria, 1995.

Reynolds, Henry, *The Law of the Land*, Penguin, Camberwell, Victoria, 2nd edn, 1992.

Rose, Michael (ed.). *For the Record: 160 Years of Aboriginal Print Journalism*, Allen & Unwin, St Leonards, NSW, 1996.

Rutland, Suzanne D. *Pages of History: A Century of the Australian Jewish Press*, Australian Jewish Press, Darlinghurst, NSW, 1995.

Savvas, Adrian, and Gaylard, Geoff. *Over a Century of News from the Archives of Truth*, Adrian Savvas, College Park, SA, 1993.

Stanley, Peter. *Invading Australia: Japan and the Battle for Australia 1942*, Viking, Camberwell, Victoria, 2008.

Stephenson, M. A., and Ratnapala, Suri, *Mabo: A Judicial Revolution*, University of Queensland Press, St Lucia, Queensland, 1993.

Sydney Morning Herald. *Picture Perfect: 100 years of* Herald *Photography*, Sydney Morning Herald, Sydney, 2008.

The Australian: A Pictorial Record of a Great Newspaper, News Limited, Canberra, 1964.

Willey, Keith (ed.). *News News News: 100 Years of Australian Newspapers*, Sunshine Books, Sydney, 1982.

Usher, Jim. (ed) *The Argus: Life and Death of a Newspaper*, Australian Scholarly Publishing, North Melbourne, Victoria, 2007.

Young, James. *News News News: Momentous Events and Daily Life as Reported in the Australian Press*, Newtown, Woollahra, 2004.

Picture credits

Courtesy of *Canberra Times*: page 275

Courtesy of Fairfax: pages 277, 279, 289, 299, 300, 315, 318, 324, 326, 328, 329, 331, 333, 335

Courtesy of Mark Day: page 321

Courtesy of News Ltd: pages 280, 281, 282, 291, 293, 295, 297, 298, 303, 305, 313, 316, 319, 323

Getty Images: pages 172, 263, 309

National Library of Australia, Manuscripts Collection: pages 28, 123

National Library of Australia, Maps Collection: pages12, 21

National Library of Australia, Newspapers & Printed Books Collections: pages 19, 20 (bottom), 23, 24, 25, 31, 41, 54, 69, 70, 81, 82, 91, 115, 125, 129, 132, 135, 138, 140, 146, 149, 151, 155, 162, 163, 165, 167, 175, 177, 179, 183, 184, 186, 193, 195, 197, 199, 205, 206, 210, 214, 215, 219, 224, 229, 233, 234, 245, 247, 249, 250, 252, 254, 256, 257, 259, 265, 266, 268, 270, 272, 274

National Library of Australia, Pictures Collection: pages 47, 67, 97, 133

Newspix: page 351

Photolibrary.com: page 103

State Library of New South Wales: pages 27, 36, 40, 49, 51, 57, 73, 84, 87, 92, 96, 105, 127, 157, 158, 181, 208, 212, 226, 231, 236, 341

State Library of Victoria, Manuscripts Collection: pages 101, 102

State Library of Victoria, Newspapers Collection: pages 119, 188, 189, 191, 217, 221, 222, 227, 238, 239

State Library of Victoria, Pictures Collection: page 109

State Library of Victoria, Rare Books Collection: pages 32, 33, 59, 63, 64, 75, 99

State Library of Western Australia, The Battye Library: page 20 (top)

Tasmanian Archive and Heritage Office: pages 94, 167 (right)

Author biography

STEPHEN GAPPS is a Sydney based public historian and museum curator, currently at the Australian National Maritime Museum. He has worked extensively as a professional historian on a variety of oral and written history projects ranging from histories of pastoral sheep and cattle stations, to Sydney pubs, to deserted gold mining towns.

Stephen has published widely on his particular research interest; historical re-enactments and commemorations of national history. He was Visiting Fellow in Re-enactment at the Australian National University in 2007 and his 2003 doctoral thesis was a history of historical re-enactments. In the course of his research, Stephen has been known to dress as both a British redcoat soldier and an Irish convict rebel.

OPPOSITE
A full page of the Sun newspaper of 26 April 1935 dedicated to Sydney Anzac Day commemorations. *(See page 230 for the full story relating to this image.)*

The Spirit of Anzac Lives Again... THE SUN *...Immense Crowd Throngs Domain*

THURSDAY, APRIL 25, 1935.

Above: THE greatest Anzac gathering ever witnessed in Sydney congregated to-day in the Domain, where thousands of Diggers, their friends and relatives, converged to take part in the main service.

At right: THEY passed through these gates—and never returned; so those who will always remember, placed wreaths on the closed Gates of Remembrance at Woolloomooloo.

Below: Uncle must have his rosemary so Shirley Watson sees that he has some. Charles Pakes, of the 55th Batt., is proud that his niece, too, recognises Anzac Day.

Above: AN outstanding figure in the display was Sir Charles Kingsford Smith, who marched at the head of the Air Force members taking part in the procession.

Above: "WHERE did you get that one?" The old-timer is proud of his medals, while his younger companion displays a natural interest. Digger L. Woods and Lieutenant J. Wasson, D.C.M., M.M., have a friendly chat.

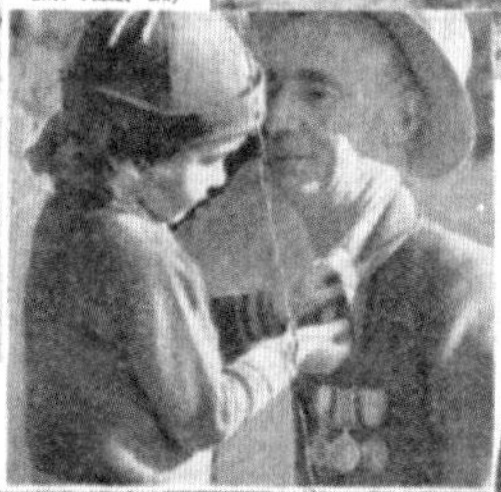

Circle: DEVOUT remembrance of Australia's history-making day. This touching picture was taken in St. Mary's Basilica during the service there. Behind the woman whose hands are clasped, while her heart remembers, is another who is fondling her rosary beads.

At left: THE GREAT ARMY of Diggers march past the Cenotaph in silent reverence, while the large crowd stands behind the sturdy police barriers in respectful silence. The sun shone brightly on this greatest of Anzac commemoration days.

Above: Smothered with floral tributes from friends, relatives and sweethearts of the men who paid the supreme sacrifice, the Cenotaph presented an impressive spectacle as the first blue streaks of dawn appeared in the heavens. The Custodian (Col. Murphy) is seen in the foreground, in charge of the proceedings.

At left: Bearing tokens of the remembrance of their fellow-members, representatives of the various legions were among the first to arrive at Martin-place. The beautiful colo[illegible] tribute sent by the Gallipoli Legion was surmounted by a big crown.

A

ABC 218
Age, The Melbourne 276, 289, 300–1
expedition 150–3
air flights 204–6
Alexander, Joe 211–2
Alfred Edward, Prince 131–3
animals 35–8
anti-apartheid demonstrations 299–301
anti-transportation movement 93–4
anti-war demonstrations 312
Anzac Day (1935) 230–1
ANZACs 178–9, 244–5
apartheid 299–301
Archer 161
Argus, The 122–3, 161–3, 250, 259
Armstrong, Louis 198
art 304–5
Arthur, George 62, 66–7, 68, 93
Asian refugees 308, 317–9
atom bombs see nuclear weapons
Australasian Chronicle 62
Australasian Sketcher, The 139, 140–1
Australia
  Vietnam War 296
Australia Felix 90–2
Australian, The 62, 80, 83–5, 295, 313, 319
Australian Abo Call, The 235–6
Australian Broadcasting Commission 218
Australian Colonies Act 1850 108–9
Australian Constitution 294–5, 296
Australian Cricket Board 226
Australian Defence Forces
  Australian Army 264, 281–3
  Australian Army Reserve 291
  Australian First Corps 244–5
  Australian Imperial Force 178–9, 180–1, 246–7
  navy 176
Australian Labor Party 164, 170
  dismissal of Jack Lang's government 223–4
  dismissal of Whitlam government 314–6
  fall of Scullin government 211–2
  New Guard and 216–7
  Whitlam election 302–3
Australian National Gallery 304–5

B

Bali bombing 333–4
Ballarat 118–21, 209
bank crashes 164–5
Banks, Joseph 26, 29, 39
Barnard, Lance 302
Batavia, wreck of 15, 18–21
Bathurst 114
Bathurst Plains 59
Batman, John 100
The Beatles 286, 288–9
Bennelong 278
Bent, Andrew 62–5, 68
Bent's News and New South Wales Advertiser 62
bicentennial celebrations (1988) 327–9
Bjelke-Petersen, Joh 299
Black Friday bushfires 237–9
Black Saturday bushfires 334–5
blackbirding 134–6
Blackett, Reverend 161
Blaxland, Gregory 58, 60–1
Bligh, William 56–7
Blue Mountains crossing 58–61
Blue Poles (Pollock) 304–5
boat people see refugees
Bondi Beach mass surf rescues 232–4
Bonegilla riots 281–3
Botany Bay (1789) 30–4
Bourke, Richard 85, 95–6, 100
Bradfield, John 172
Bradman, Don 206, 207–8, 225
Brahe, William 122–3

Brisbane, Thomas 62
Britain
  Australian citizenship 174–5
  Australian Colonies Act 108–9
  Australian independence from 145
  British migrants 112, 209, 282
  claimed by Indigenous Australians 329
  Colonial Office 72–3, 95
  Empire Service Club 230–1
  first newspapers 15
  German invasion of Greece 244–5
  Industrial Revolution 16
  New Guinea 150–3
  New Zealand Wars 128–30
  Royal Navy 246–7
  Sudan Wars 154–5
  tests nuclear weapons in Australia 264–6
Broken Hill, Battle of 332
Bryan, Robert 93–4
Buckley, William 100
Bulletin, The 148–9
Bullwinkel, Vivian 253
Bunuba War 192
Burchett, Wilfred 253
Burke and Wills expedition 122–3
Burke, Robert O'Hara 122–3
Burnum Burnum 329
bushfires 237–9, 334–5
bushrangers 74–5, 137–41, 166

C

Callam, James 30
Calwell, Arthur 251
Canberra Times, The 270, 275
cannibalism 93
Carbine 161–3
Carl (blackbirding ship) 134–6
Carrington, T. 139, 140–1
cartography 21
censorship 166
Chamberlain, Azaria 322–4
Chamberlain, Lindy 322–4
Chifley, Ben 258
China
  becomes People's Republic of 258
  Boxer Rebellion 150
  Chinese migrants 170
  Lambing Flat race riots 113, 124–7
  Opium Wars 154
citizenship 174–5
Clay, Sonny 198–9
Cold War 256, 258, 271–2, 291
Collier, Thomas 41
Collins, David 100
Colonial Times and Tasmanian Advertiser 62–3, 93–4
Commercial Bank of Australia 165
Commonwealth of Australia 209
communism 202, 271, 291
Communist Party of Australia 213–5, 258
Coniston massacre 192
Conroy, Daniel 41
conscription 182–4, 290–1, 312
consumerism 262
convicts
  anti-transportation movement 93–4
  bushrangers 74–5
  centennial celebrations 156, 327
  First Fleet 34
  hanging of 50–2
  Irish 38, 50, 53–5
  musters 39
  Myall Creek massacre 104–7
  non-English 50
Coogee Beach shark attack 185–6
Cook, James 22, 26–9, 72, 95, 156
Corneliszoon, Jeronimus 18
Coughlan, Milton 185–6
Country Party 223, 258
Courier-Mail 247, 255–7, 255–7
Cowra prisoners of war camp 253
Cox, William 58
Crete, battle for 244–5
cricket 207–8

bodyline series 225–7
Cruse, William 88–9
Cunningham, Phillip 53
Curtin, John 255
Cuthbert, Betty 276–7

D

Daily Mirror 251–2, 280, 291, 304–5
Daily Telegraph, The 181, 183–4, 224, 323
Dampier, William 15, 22–5
Dardanelles 178–9, 230–1
Darling, Ralph 83–5
Darling River 90
Darwin, bombing of 246
Darwin, Charles 66
De Groot, Francis 216–7
Deakin, Alfred 190
Democratic Labor Party 302–3
demonstrations against Whitlam dismissal 314–6
demonstrations at Springbok tour 299–301
Department of Information 251
depressions, economic 144, 164–5, 202–3, 206, 211–2, 213–5
Deutsche Post, Die 209
Dharawal 104
Die Deutsche Post 209
Donohoe, Bold Jack 74–5
dotcom crash (2000) 325
Doyle, J. T. 127
Dutch East Indies 246–7
Dutch exploration 14–5

E

Edison, Thomas 166–7
Elizabeth II, Queen 269–70
Emu Field nuclear tests 264
Endeavour 26–9
English and Chinese Advertiser 209
Eureka Stockade 118–21
evangelism 161
Evans, George William 58–61
Exmouth Gulf oil discoveries 267–8
exploration 78–9, 90–2
exports 170

F

facism 202
Fairfax, John 80
fascism 216–7
fashions 172, 292–3
fauna 35–8
Fawkner, John Pascoe 100–3
Federal Bank of Australia 164
Federation Day 174–5
Fenton, James 211–2
financial crashes 325–6
Finn, Edmund 108–9
firestorms 334
First Fleet 30–4, 95, 156–60, 235–6, 327–9
First World War 148, 174, 185
  Dardanelles 178–9, 230–1
  enlistment 182
  Western Front 180–1, 182
foreign policy 171, 190, 242, 333
  see political alliances
Forrest River massacre 192–5
Frankland, George 66
Fraser, Malcolm 314–6, 320
frontier violence 192–5

G

Gallipoli 178–9, 230–1
Game, Phillip 223
Geelong Advertiser and Intelligencer 119–21
German migrants 209
Gerritsz, Hessel 21
Gill, S. T. 127
Glenrowan 137–41
Global Financial Crisis (2008) 325
gold rushes 112–3, 114–21, 124–7, 209, 228–9
Goossens, Eugene 278
Gordon, Charles 154

governors recalled 83–5
grazing 78–9, 90–2, 192
Great White Fleet 176–7, 190
Greece, invasion of 244–5
Greycliffe ferry disaster 196–7
guerrilla war 39–41
Guthega Power Station 272, 275

H

Hall, Edward Smith 83, 104–7
Hamilton, Ian 230–1
Hargraves, Edward 114–7
Hartog, Dirk 18
Hasleham, Frank 119
Hawke, Bob 319
Hawkesworth, John 26–7
Heath, George 135
Heegan 88
Herald see Melbourne's *Herald*
Hertz, Carl 166–7
High Court of Australia 251–2, 330–1
Hiroshima 253, 264
Hobart Town Gazette 62–5
Holt, Dame Zara 296
Holt, Harold 273, 296–8
hooligans 187–9
Horler, Ken 196
horse racing 161–3, 220–3
Howard, John 320
Howe, George 44–5, 48, 50
Hughes, Billy 182
Hughes, Davis 278
Hungary at Melbourne Olympics 276
Hunter, John 16, 35–8, 58

I

Illustrated Australian News 133
immigrants *see also* refugees
  Bonegilla riots 281–3
  foreign-language newspapers 209–10
  gold rushes 118
  Kalgoorlie race riots 228–9
  Lambing Flat race riots 124–7
  population policy 255, 258, 273
  Snow Mountains Hydro-Electric Scheme 258
independence from Britain 145
Indigenous Australians
  1967 referendum 294–5, 296
  apology for Stolen Generations 309
  bicentennial celebrations (1988) 327
  black trackers 139, 194
  Black Wars in Van Diemen's Land 66–7, 68–71
  Burke and Wills expedition 122–3
  Cook's journal 29
  Dampier's journal 24–5
  Darug 35
  first newspaper 235–6
  forms of communication 14–5
  Forrest River massacre 192–5
  freedom rides 294
  as guides 90
  Invasion Day 327
  Kulin 100
  land rights 330–1
  Mabo case 330–1
  Maralinga nuclear tests 264
  Myall Creek massacre 104–7
  National Day of Mourning 235–6
  Pemulwuy 39–41
  reconciliation 330
  Yagan 86–9
Indonesia 246–7, 333–4
Institute of Anatomy 220
International Olympic Committee 276
Irish
  convicts 38, 50, 53–5
  Fenians 131–3
Irwin, Sam 119

J

Jacobsz, Ariaen 18
Jandamarra 192
Japan 176
  atomic bombing of 253, 264

Cowra prisoners of war camp 253
fall of Singapore 242, 246–7
midget subs attack Sydney 248–50
seppuku 253
wartime atrocities 253–4
Jewish refugees 233, 255–7
Johnson, Amy 204–6
Johnson, William 53
Johnston, George 53, 56–7
Jones, Richard 89

K

Kalgoorlie race riots 228–9
Keates, James 88
Keating, Paul 331
Keats, William 88–9
Kelly, Ned 137–41, 166
Kerr, John 314–6
King, John 123
King, Philip Gidley 39–41, 45, 53
Kingslake 334
Kuttabul (naval depot ship) 248

L

La Perouse 202
Lambing Flat race riots 124–7
land rushes 90–2
landings 270
landowners 83–5
Lang, Jack 213–5, 216–7, 218, 223–4
language 35
English language test 229
foreign-language newspapers 209–10
Lansdowne Bridge, opening of 95–7
larrikins 148–9
Lawson, Harry 187
Lawson, William 58, 60–1
Leichhardt, Ludwig 122
Lennox, David 95–6
Liberal Party 258–9
Liberal–Country Party Coalition 302–3
Luddit, Simon 41
Lyon, Robert 86
Lyons, Joseph 211–2, 223

M

Mabo, Eddie Koiki 330–1
Macarthur, John 56
McDermott, Lloyd 299
McGarvie, William 80
Macleay, Alexander 48
Macquarie, Lachlan 58, 62
Maltese migrants 209–10
manufacturing industry 262
Maori 128–30, 299
Maralinga nuclear tests 264
Martens, Conrad 97
Marysville 334
Mathews, Marlene 276
Melbourne 103, 161–3, 187–9
Melbourne Advertiser 100–3
Melbourne Morning Herald, The 108–9
Melbourne's Herald 188–9, 220, 239, 282–3, 316
Melville, Henry 93–4
Menzies, Robert 258–9, 271, 291
Millers Point Push 148
Mitchell, Thomas 90–2
Montebello Islands nuclear tests 264
Morrin, Berryl 185
Morris, William Charles 136
Morrison, George Ernest 150–3
Mount, Henry Clark 136
moving pictures 166–7
Muggleston, Michael 74
multicultural policy 273–5
Murray River 90, 92
My Lai massacre 312
Myall Creek massacre 104–7

N

Nagasaki 253, 264
National Day of Mourning 235–6
National Gallery of Australia 304–5
National Party 258
nationalisation 258

nationalism 144–5
natural science 22
New Guard 216–7
New South Wales 95–7, 190
assassination attempt on Prince Alfred 131–3
Battle of Vinegar Hill 53–5
centenary of settlement 156–60
dismissal of Jack Lang's government 223–4
early communication 16–7
gold rushes 114–7
Great White Fleet 176–7, 190
Sudan Wars 154–5
New South Wales Corps 44, 53–5, 56–7
New South Wales Government 278–80
New York stock market crash (1929) 202
New Zealand
ANZACs 178–9, 244–5
New Zealand Wars 128–30
South Africa 299
Newcastle 248
news media
advice from 326
birth of free press 62–5
books 26–7, 30–1
breaking news 217
broadsheets 147
censorship 242, 244, 251–2
colour images 333
commemorative images 221, 222
convict musters 39
cover girls 303
earliest headline news 18–20
early communication 14
erroneous headlines 244–5, 272
expeditions by 150–3
film reviews 167
first book published 40–1, 48
first issues 98–9
first newspaper photographs 158
first newspapers 15, 44–5, 48–9, 80–2, 83, 145–7
foreign-language newspapers 209–10
freedom of speech 251–2
freedom of the press 93
government standing orders 40, 48
growth of 192
hand-drawn maps 163
handbills 39, 108–9
headline style 137–9
illustrated 133, 140–1, 147
industry journals 210
international scoops 264, 265
investigative reporting 282–3
journals 22–5, 28–9, 36–8, 90–2
leading with front page news 150–3
manuscript newspapers 100–3
news stands 221
newsreel films 182
as organs of grievance 83–5
photographs, eyewitness 234
photographs, use of 184, 186
photojournalism 190–1, 197, 215, 218–9, 264
political use of 314
posters 167
press sheets 122–3
printing press 14
publication of private telegrams 211–2
radio 218–9
readership 16
regional newspapers 147
sensationalism 198–9, 214
souvenir issues 280
special editions 175, 189
special supplements 134–6, 157
sport in 207–8, 225–7
suppression of news 246
tabloids 198–9, 304–5
technological changes 146, 227
telegraphic despatches 132
television 276
war correspondents 128–30
world's first feature film 166
News, The 298

Nicholls, Douglas 235–6
Nixon, Richard 312
Northern Territory Coniston massacre 192
nuclear weapons 253
  atomic bombing of Hiroshima 253, 264
  testing by British in Australia 264–6

O

O'Donoghue, Lois 331
O'Farrell, Henry 131–3
oil discoveries 267–8
Olympic Games (1956 Melbourne) 276–7

P

Pacific Islanders 134–6, 170
Parkes, Henry 131
Paterson, Colonel 54–5
Pearce, Matthew 93
Pelsaert, Francisco 18
Pemulwuy 39–41
Penton, Brian 251
Perth Gazette, The 86–9
Petrov Affair 271–2
Phar Lap 161, 220–3
Phillip, Arthur 30, 72, 156–60
Phillips, Commodore 34
plantation owners 134–6
police
  Eureka Stockade 118–21
  Queensland as a police state 299
  seizure of newspapers 251–2
  strike and Melbourne riots 187–9
political alliances 171, 190, 242, 333
political parties 164
Pollock, Jackson 304–5
population increases 112, 144
population policy 255, 258, 273
Port Phillip 108–9
Portland, Victoria 90
power generation 273–5
Price, John 35–7
prisoners of war 246, 253
public holidays 230
public housing 281–3

Q

Queensland 134–6, 144, 150–3, 164, 209

R

race riots 124–7, 228–9
racial policy *see* White Australia Policy
radio 218–9
reconciliation 330
Rede, Robert 118
referenda
  Aboriginal rights 294–5, 296
  conscription 182–4
refugees
  Asian 308, 317–9
  Jewish 233, 255–7
Returned Soldiers Leagues 229
Rickards, Harry 166
riots
  at arrival of The Beatles 288–9
  at Bonegilla 281–3
  in Melbourne 187–9
  race riots at Kalgoorlie 228–9
  race riots at Lambing Flat 124–7
Robertson, Gilbert 93
Robinson, George August 68
Roosevelt, Theodore 176
Rose, Murray 276
Ross, James 70
Royal Commissions 195, 264, 334
Royal Prince Alfred Hospital 131
royal tour 269–70
Royal Veteran Company 61
Rudd, Kevin 309
Rum Rebellion 56–7
Russia 176, 256, 258, 271–2, 276

S

Salee, Celuia Mapo 330
Samuells, Joseph 50–2
Save Our Sons 291

Scullin, James 211–2, 223
Second World War
  battle for Crete 244–5
  fall of Singapore 246–7
  Jewish refugees 233, 255–7
  news censorship 251–2
share market crash (1987) 325–6
shark attacks 185–6
Shrimpton, Jean 292–3
Singapore, fall of 242, 246–7
slavery 223
Snedden, Billy 320–1
Snow Mountains Hydro-Electric Scheme 258, 273–5
soldier settlement schemes 202
Sonny Clay and the Coloured Idea 198–9
South Africa 299–301
South Australia 98–9, 209
  Maralinga nuclear tests 264
South Australian Company 98–9
South Australian Gazette and Colonial Register 98–9
Springbok tour demonstrations 299–301
Springbok tours 299–301
squatters (landed) 78–9, 112
Stalin, Joseph 271
Standard Oil 268
Stephens, Alfred Ward 80
Stevens, Bertram 223
Stevenson, George 98
Stirling, James 72
stockmen 104–7
Stokes, Frederick 80
Stolen Generations 309
Story of the Kelly Gang, The (movie) 166
Strickland, Shirley 276
Sturt, Charles 90
subcultures 288–9, 290
Sudan Wars 154–5
sugar-cane 170
Sun see Sydney's *Sun*
Sun News-Pictorial, The 187, 191, 217, 222, 227, 238, 293
Sunday Age 335
Sunday Mirror 303
Sunday Telegraphy 251, 254
surf lifesaving 232–4
surveying 58–61
Suttor, George 39
Swan River Colony 86–9
Sydney 160
  Cumberland Plain 209
  early history 44–7
  Federation celebrations 174–5
  Greycliffe ferry disaster 196–7
  Japanese midget subs attack 248–50
  Union Street battle 213–5
Sydney Gazette, and New South Wales Advertiser, The 44–5, 48–9, 50–2, 60–1
Sydney Harbour Bridge 172, 196, 216–7, 248
Sydney Herald, The 80–2
Sydney Mail, The 155, 157, 165, 175, 186, 205
Sydney Monitor, The 80, 83, 104–7
Sydney Morning Herald, The 80–2, 178–9, 195, 197, 206, 214–5, 249, 272, 274, 279, 318, 324, 326, 328, 331, 333
Sydney Opera House 278–80
Sydney's *Sun* 208, 212, 226, 231, 233, 245, 314, 315

T

Tahiti (passenger ship) 196–7
Tasmania see Van Diemen's Land
technology 145, 218–9, 227
tenants' rights 213–5
Tench, Watkin 30–1
terra nullius 100
terrorism 333–4
Thomas, Robert 98
Torres Strait Islands 330–1
trade unions 144, 164, 170, 258
treason 131–3
trials
  Carl (blackbirding ship) 134–6

of Lindy Chamberlain 322
Myall Creek massacre 104–7
True Colonist 93
Trugernanner 68
Truth 198–9, 320–1
Turkey 178–9, 230–1

U

Unemployed Workers Movement 213–5
Union Street battle 213–5
United Australia Party 211–2, 223, 258
United States
American Civil War 190
atomic bombing of Japan 253, 264
battle fleet visits Australia 190–1
Cold War 256, 258, 271–2
death of Phar Lap 220–3
dismissal of Whitlam government 314
Great White Fleet 176–7, 190
Vietnam War 290–1, 312
urban development 144
Utzon, Jørn 278–9

V

Van Diemen's Land 61
anti-transportation movement 93–4
birth of free press 62–5
Black Wars in 66–7
Victoria 108–9
bank crashes 164
Black Friday bushfires 237–9
Black Saturday bushfires 334–5
Bonegilla riots 281–3
Eureka Stockade 118–21
Melbourne Cup 161–3
Melbourne riots 187–9
Melbourne Spring Racing Carnival 292–3
Olympic Games (1956 Melbourne) 276–7
visit of US battle fleet 190–1
Victoria, Queen 170
Vietnam Moratoriums 312
Vietnam War 290–1, 296, 312–3
Vinegar Hill, Battle of 53–5
Voice of the Maltese in Australia and Farmers' Advocate Weekly, The 209–10

W

war casualties 180–1, 182, 185, 312
war correspondents 128–30
Wardell, Robert 62, 83–5
Weeip 88, 89
Wentworth, D'arcy 83
Wentworth, William Charles 58, 60–1, 62, 83–5
West Australian Petroleum Pty Ltd 267–8
West Australian, The 192–4, 229, 264–6, 268
Western Australia
Forrest River massacre 192–5
Kalgoorlie race riots 228–9
Montebello Islands 264
oil discoveries 267–8
Swan River Colony 72–3
Western Front 180–1, 182
White Australia Policy 124, 198–9, 209–10, 229, 255, 296
Whitlam, Gough 302–3, 304–5, 314–6
Whittle, Thomas 56
Willoughby, Howard 128–30
Wills, William 122–3
Wilson, John 35, 58
Wirrayaraay 104–7
women
feminism 173
first solo flights 204–6
Melbourne riots 148–9
voting rights for 170
Wood, G. T. 194
Woodfull, Bill 225

Y

Yagan 86–9
Yallowgonga 89
Yandruwandha 122–3
youth culture 148–9, 286, 288–9

Paperboy selling the Melbourne Herald *in August 1952. The number of paperboys has dramatically decreased since the '50s, mainly due to the disappearance of afternoon newspapers and the advent of the Internet, where most newspapers can be read online.*

Published in 2010 by Pier 9, an imprint of Murdoch Books Pty Limited

Murdoch Books Australia
Pier 8/9
23 Hickson Road
Millers Point NSW 2000
Phone: +61 (0) 2 8220 2000
Fax: +61 (0) 2 8220 2558
www.murdochbooks.com.au

Murdoch Books UK Limited
Erico House, 6th Floor
93–99 Upper Richmond Road
Putney, London SW15 2TG
Phone: +44 (0) 20 8785 5995
Fax: +44 (0) 20 8785 5985
www.murdochbooks.co.uk

Publisher: Diana Hill
Editor: Meryl Potter
Project Editor: Paul O'Beirne
Designer: Katy Wall

National Library of Australia Cataloguing-in-Publication Data

Author:	Gapps, Stephen.
Title:	Front Pages that Shaped Australia / Stephen Gapps.
ISBN:	978-1-74196-466-0 (hbk.)
Subjects:	Australian newspapers—Sections, columns, etc.—Front pages.
	Australian newspapers—History.
	Australia—History—Sources.
	Australia—History.
Dewey Number:	994

A catalogue record for this book is available from the British Library.

Printed by 1010 Printing International Limited, China.